DRAGONS

TEN ENTREPRENEURS
WHO BUILT BRITAIN

LIAM BYRNE

HEAD
ZEUS

First published in the UK in 2016 by Head of Zeus Ltd

This paperback edition first published in the UK in 2017
by Head of Zeus Ltd

1 3 5 7 9 8 6 4 2

A catalogue record for this book is available from the British Library.

ISBN (PB) 9781781857496
ISBN (E) 9781781857465

Designed and typeset by e-type, Aintree, Liverpool

Printed and bound by CPI Group (UK) Ltd, Croydon, CR0 4YY

Head of Zeus Ltd
First Floor East
5–8 Hardwick Street
London EC1R 4RG

WWW.HEADOFZEUS.COM

DRAGONS

Rt Hon Liam Byrne is a Member of Parliament, a writer, reformer and campaigner. A former Cabinet minister and technology entrepreneur, he was a Fulbright Scholar at the Harvard Business School.

To Alex, John and Lizzie

The propensity to truck, barter and exchange one thing for another...
is common to all men, and to be found in no other race of animals

Adam Smith, *The Wealth of Nations* (1776)

CONTENTS

A Note on Modern Monetary Equivalents

Attempting to translate historic sums of money, or amounts of wealth, into modern equivalents is a notoriously difficult exercise, full of variables, and the result is then open to interpretation. What do those amounts *mean* in the relative contexts of then and now?

Nevertheless, in a book like this, it is desirable to suggest *something* of the scale of a transaction, or an individual's fortune, or a company's market value.

Unless otherwise noted, the modern equivalents given – which invariably offer a range, and typically appear in phrases such as 'between £2 billion and £5 billion in today's money' – use estimates constructed by using multipliers for both 'average earnings' (generally the lower end of the range given) and 'per capita GDP'. These are sourced from the respected website measuringworth.com, whose goal is to offer data 'rigorously refereed by the most distinguished researchers in the field'. I am grateful to this valuable resource.

PREFACE

Entrepreneurs change history. Yet 'History' rarely does them justice.

Entrepreneurs are the flesh and blood, the bones and brains, connecting 'great men' and 'great forces'.* And yet they are typically missing from the roll-calls of change-makers that shaped the past, left out of a cast-list dominated by kings and queens and, dare I say it, rather too many politicians.

The balance is beginning, happily, to change. David S. Landes, Joel Mokyr and William J. Baumol's remarkable book *The Invention of Enterprise*, published in 2011, is a wonderful example of the new honour paid to the argument that without entrepreneurs 'we would have basically nothing of the unprecedented growth miracle of the recent centuries'.[1] *Dragons* is one more push along a trend that I hope will grow. It is an effort to better emplace business change-makers more squarely centre-stage in our national story.

As a history student in Manchester, the spiritual home of free trade, I became well versed in the debate about whether the nation's entrepreneurs had 'failed'.[2] But in my own years as a tech entrepreneur, I came to see first-hand that entrepreneurs respond to, and reshape, the opportunities around them. And so I became fascinated by the idea of an economic history that offered a better balance between biography and 'big forces'. This book is an attempt to get the balance right.

Dragons tells the stories of the outstanding British entrepreneurs who helped to shape our national story from the beginning of the

---

* See E. H. Carr, *What is History?* (CUP, 1961).

thirteenth century when England's wealth could be measured in wool, and when the first early masters of trade and finance – men like William de la Pole, Dick Whittington and Thomas Gresham – created for themselves new power behind the thrones of kings and queens. Their heirs helped build what is today the world's fifth-biggest economy.

Here are entrepreneurs who created the first colonies and companies in America, winning along the way rights and freedoms not just to trade but to keep their profits safe from despotic sovereigns. They were the commercial adventurers who campaigned for a great navy to help fight their wars abroad; they built great trading empires amid the giant old economies of the East, creating at home the world's largest consumer market and the world's greatest capital market; they pioneered steam engines that revolutionized power for the business of digging fuel and driving forges and factories; they built the world's first railway system; they brought mass production to new consumer products, from chocolate to soap; they humbled old empires by trading opium and built new ones digging diamonds and gold, copper and coal; they created the world's first brand-based multinationals, and found ways of bringing the produce of the world to every corner of Britain. Along the way, they laid the foundations of the nation's wonderful cities and welfare state, as they not only created wealth, but invented new ways to share it.

Together, these portraits reveal the best and worst of human endeavour, for here are explorers, inventors and moral leaders, along with fraudsters, warmongers and unembarrassed imperialists. All were risk-takers. Some made fortunes. Some lost them. But together, entrepreneurs such as Robert Rich, Thomas Pitt, Matthew Boulton, Nathan Rothschild, William Jardine, George Hudson, George Cadbury, Cecil Rhodes, William Lever and John Spedan Lewis helped build not only Britain, but the modern world.

*

Picking the figures for the book was, of course, devilishly difficult. If my omissions and choices provoke debate, then I will have succeeded. We *should* debate far more the 'new cast' of characters who formed today's Britain and today's world. In that spirit, let me explain how the line-up here was selected.

I wanted stories that were perhaps under-told and unfamiliar; stories that helped me illustrate a particular chapter of capitalism through the prism of a life lived; stories that helped me relay the history of places special to our economic advance. I wanted, too, individuals whose impact stretched beyond their business lives to the public realm and the world beyond, to help me make this point: entrepreneurs *shape* history.

The obvious omission here is women. And that in itself makes a point. The power structures of history left women with little room to flourish – and yet, even in the stories I tell here, it is clear that women, often wives, played a critical role as capital-suppliers and counsel in the business worlds of their husbands. I very much hope this will prove a field of business history studied in far more depth that I have been able to offer here.

In every phase of British capitalism tackled, there were choices to make. Why illustrate Britain's push into India with Thomas Pitt and not Josiah Child? Why pick Matthew Boulton and not Richard Arkwright as an exemplar of the early Industrial Revolution? The choices get only harder as the Victorian era unfolds. Why the free-trading opium baron William Jardine and not a domestic manufacturer? Why the railway magnate George Hudson and not Isambard Kingdom Brunel? Why none of the great nineteenth-century retailers? Or, in the modern era, why the retailer John Spedan Lewis and not the industrialist Arnold Weinstock? These questions are the stuff of the discussion I want to provoke. In every phase of history, I tried to choose the best illustrator of the dominant trend of the time *and* someone who remoulded not only business, but Britain itself. My judgement will be imperfect. And I look forward to hearing why.

There is no hero-worship here. Some of the leaders here do extraordinary things. But others were corrupt and dangerous. This is a picture, warts and all.

My final hope – as a lover of economic history, a former entrepreneur and a politician keenly interested in the future – is that we continue to change, adapt and improve the way we teach economic and business history. The economic history I was taught in Britain – admittedly many years ago now – was still recovering from that fashion to lump together many aspects of the 'British disease' with entrepreneurial failure. The history taught in my schooldays began with endless chapters on the Agricultural and Industrial Revolutions, the dynasties of Tudors and Hapsburgs, wars of religion and eras of exploration. Much of it seemed impossibly remote. None of it taught me how small Cotswold communities found the resources to build such spectacular, exquisite, Perpendicular churches. In short, the way I was taught history *explained* too little of the wonder of the Britain built by its people.

What struck me when studying economic history at Harvard was a different tradition – a far better use of biography as a window on to history and a far greater recognition of entrepreneurs as prime-movers. I came home determined one day to make a contribution to the 'Dick Whittington' school of study, and in a way this book simply reflects my own journey of discovery, seeking to understand how, as a country, Britain has arrived where it now stands. I am convinced that enriching ourselves with the stories of entrepreneurs helps us connect the dots between the 'grand forces' of which we're all such a small part and the achievements we see in the world around us – from wool churches to production lines to iPhones.

Historical biography, of course, has its weaknesses. Endlessly I found myself frustrated by the most fine-grained of detail in the stories I read, recorded without much reference to the forces shaping the stage on which the actors played their parts. Entrepreneurs provide a good corrective. Entrepreneurs spot and exploit trends. They can advance their times – but they rarely create the balance of forces they find. So we cannot study entrepreneurs without spending some time explaining the world they faced.

My last point is this. Today I work as a reformer in politics. For over a decade, I have come to see the truth that the economist Sir Andrew Dilnot once gave me: that we all make better decisions when blessed with a keener sense of the tides on which we ride. Hence the importance of appreciating how one thing led to another. So this is the story of

British capitalism's evolution. It's the book that I wish I'd had, perhaps not as a young teenager but certainly as a young man. It's been an amazing story to write. And I hope it is a pleasure to read.

Liam Byrne

THE NATION'S FOUNDATIONS

*Pioneers of fleece and finance: William de la Pole,
Dick Whittington and Thomas Gresham*

S omewhere beneath the church of St Michael Paternoster Royal
on College Hill in the City of London, lie the bones of England's
most famous entrepreneur. There is no statue to Dick
Whittington in his final resting place. The English merchant –
immortalized in plays and poems, whose name and story inspire
pantomimes every Christmas – is remembered there with a simple
Modernist stained-glass window, in green, red and blue. High in the
church's south wall, it portrays a handsome, clean-jawed young man in
an overcoat and flat cap, his worldly goods bundled in a red handkerchief
tied to a stick across his shoulders, and beside him, of course, his cat.

The legend goes that Whittington, a poor Gloucestershire lad,
walked to London, where he had heard the streets were paved with
gold. Lodged in the home of a rich merchant, he fell in love with Alice,
the daughter of the house, and bought a cat to eat the mice in his attic
room. When the merchant invited his servants to invest in a voyage
abroad, Whittington had only his cat to offer. Down on his luck, he
resolved to quit the city, but on Highgate Hill he paused to hear the
bells of St Mary-le-Bow ringing, 'Turn again, Whittington, three times
Lord Mayor of London.' Inspired, young Dick turned back to learn that
his master's ship had not only reached a foreign land, but in the rat-
infested court of a foreign king his cat had rendered so great a service
that it was bought for great sums of gold. Suddenly a very wealthy man,
Whittington married Alice, invested wisely, and, as predicted by the
bells, became Lord Mayor of London.

It is a marvellous story, probably inspired not by the perfect truth but by a Persian folk-tale. Yet when archaeologists searched for Whittington's bones after the Second World War in the ruins of a bombed-out St Michael's Church, they found no body – it was perhaps plundered by grave robbers – but there *was* a mummified cat.

In truth, Richard Whittington was born in 1350, not long after England's great poet Geoffrey Chaucer, and was the youngest son of Sir William Whittington. Standing to inherit nothing, he turned his hand to trade, settled in London and made a fortune. He became the capital's leading mercer, with a huge business selling fine cloth to king and court. Whittington and his generation were immortalized by Chaucer in *The Canterbury Tales*, but in fact, they stood on the shoulders of the giants who had come before them: the pioneering English merchants who had wrestled control of the nation's great trade in fleeces and royal finance from the Flemings and Florentines who dominated the commerce of medieval Europe.

Their marketplace was the Continent where in the millennia since the Mesolithic era intricate social networks had taken shape, providing the pathways along which were swapped commodities, money and ideas. As far back as 3000 BC, roads, rivers and coastal sea lanes connected farming communities and market-centres, where traders could exchange food, metal, stones and furs. At Europe's centre, Alpine passes connected the lands of the later Holy Roman Emperors, while the 'amber route' from the Adriatic around the East Alps led to the Danube, Oder and Baltic. To the east, river routes linked the Baltic to the Black Sea, and Byzantium to Baghdad via the Caspian Sea and Caravan routes along the Silk Road. This network allowed merchants to show up in unusual places. Thus the Viking prayer, 'I wish that you would send me many merchants with many dinars and dirhems who will buy from me whatever I wish and will not dispute anything I say.'[1]

As the population of Europe doubled between AD 950 and 1200, the number of urban areas quadrupled, and as heath, forest and marsh were rolled back across the Continent, towns multiplied.[2] In 1200, perhaps forty-five European towns were founded; in 1300 it was two hundred and fifty. Often as small as 200 or 300 souls, these towns were set apart from the surrounding countryside. But behind their walls citizens enjoyed rights their rural neighbours did not. They flourished from trading the surplus of surrounding manors, becoming centres of skills and monopolies of the production of goods and services. Out of the so-called Dark Ages a 'new West' emerged – the progenitor of the first *world* economy – wider and more impressive than the Roman Empire, its ambit stretched not just to the Mediterranean but to the Baltic too, and the lands beyond Rome's old northern Rhine border.

Despite the great division of Dark Age Europe, between a Frankish-west, a Greek-dominated east (better known as the Byzantine Empire), and the Islamic south, major transcontinental corridors connected the communities that lived between the Mediterranean and the Baltic to two great northern and southern hubs of trade.* In the south, the great marketplace was the end of the Silk Road – first, Byzantium's capital, Constantinople, and then Venice and its islands of the Rialto. In the north, the great trading hub comprised the towns and fairs of Champagne and Flanders. Here, an English merchant could buy a dizzying array of goods: Bordeaux and Gascon wine; salt from Biscay or the Bay of Bourgneuf; Spanish iron; candles; fishing furs; silks and spices from the Orient; dyed plants from Picardy and Toulouse; wood ash from Polish forests, alum from Genoa and Gascony, and wool oil from Spain; dyes such as woad, orchil and brasil from Castile and Portugal; iron from Biscay, timber and flax from Ireland, and fish from Iceland; hundreds of thousands of furs – squirrel, ermine, sable, marten and beaver – from Russia and the Baltic lands, along with potash; and, from Italy, spices, medicinal plants, silk, satin, velvet, cloth of gold, oriental carpets, pottery, glass, tapestries, jewellery, monkeys, marmosets, ostrich, linens, felt hats, and leather.

In return, the English produced and sold wool, for in the long centuries of peace, cloth production boomed in Italy and the Low Countries. But Europe's spinners lacked sheep. So wool had to come from Burgundy, from the Spanish hills – and from England, where it

---

* Development in the north in particular began to accelerate when the Carolingian seat of power was moved to Aix-la-Chappelle, after which the Hanseatic League began to flourish.

was bought and sold at the fairs of Champagne and, in time, Bruges.[3] Indeed, by the late thirteenth century, Flemish cloth-makers were so dependent on English wool that if supplies were stopped Flemish weavers starved. A giant opportunity so emerged. And of the English medieval entrepreneurs who built their fortunes in 'fleece and finance', none was greater than William de la Pole, the Hull-born commoner who became known, within a generation of his death, as 'second to no English merchant'.[4]

*

William de la Pole was born in about 1290, 170 miles south of the frontier with Scotland. He lived his childhood amid the ferocious – and ferociously expensive – border wars of the last years of King Edward I's rule. His early life is shrouded in mystery. According to his son, most of the family's business records – 'their charters and muniments' – were 'burnt by the insurgents' in 'the late insurrection', the Peasants' Revolt of 1381. But we know that Pole was one of at least three children, along with elder brother Richard and younger brother John. And like Chaucer, they were the sons of a reasonably successful wine merchant.[5]

William's hometown was Hull. Once a tiny port on England's Holderness peninsula, sheltering a few Viking ships huddled in the mouth of the Humber, it grew as a 'new town', developed by entrepreneurial monks of the nearby Abbey of Meaux, who were keen to cash in on the continental wool trade.[6] They were so successful that Edward I bought the town, developed the port, and rechristened the place Kingston upon Hull. It became so prosperous that in the tax of 1203, Hull was the Crown's sixth biggest money-maker.[*] By the time Pole was born it was a busy harbour, and in 1275 it is recorded as shipping some sixty-seven cargoes. In came a wide variety of goods: stockfish, eels, sturgeon and white herrings; timber, oil, iron, litmus, pitch tar and ashes; corn and beer; wax and candlewick; furs, purses and thread; copper, gunpowder and grindstones; boards, bowls and

---

[*] In 1203, only London, Boston, Southampton, Lincoln and Kings Lynn paid more tax than Kingston upon Hull.

barrels; weaponry in the shape of lances, bow-staves and arrow-shafts, but most important of all, wine, imported from the Crown's lands in Gascony to supply the nearby Archbishop of York and the royal armies stationed nearby, standing ready for war with Scotland.

Wine was an enormous business.[7] Nothing else was as important to the medieval diet other than grain and fish, and while it was not a drink for all classes, men above the lowest stations were drinking plenty of it by the fourteenth century. Indeed, by 1415, Britain was importing 4 million gallons of wine a year largely from Bordeaux.[8]

Hull enjoyed a huge share of the business, and as Gascon wine came in, wool went out. Indeed, by the time Pole was born, Hull's wool shipments were second only to those of Boston, in Lincolnshire, and London. As Pole grew up, the wealth of his town multiplied. Watermills, brickyards, markets, quays, a mint, an exchange, a gaol and a gallows were built, as the borough became the king's chief supply port in the interminable border wars with Scotland.

According to the chronicler Thomas Burton, the Cistercian abbot at Meaux, Pole served his apprenticeship locally. 'Sir William de la Pole was first a merchant,' he wrote, 'and was instructed in the knowledge of trade at Ravensrodd.'[9] His apprentice master was probably John Rottenherring, a wealthy and well-connected man who made his money in shipping and later became the first merchant appointed as the King's Warden.*

William de la Pole appears in public records while he was still in his twenties, along with his elder brother, Richard. Already a burgess, Richard was dealing in corn, victuals, and – from 1317 – buying wine for Edward II as a deputy of the king's butler. By the age of thirty, William was already sharing property in Hull Street with some of the most substantial men in town, holding the sort of civic and royal posts filled by senior men, lending money† – and buying large quantities of wine, occasionally it seems with a bit of sharp practice, delaying payments on wine bought for the king, and, worse, buying more than was needed for the king and re-selling the product for profit.

---

* John was possibly the son, or brother, of Robert Rottenherring, who in 1295 was one of Ravensrodd's seven most highly taxed citizens.

† An example is a loan of £20 made to one Ralph de Grene, a merchant of Pontefract.

Ensconced in the royal bureaucracy, the two Pole brothers were soon rich enough to acquire John Rottenherring's house for the sizeable rent of £4 a year, and on 18 January 1321 Richard was rewarded with the key role of Collector of Customs at Hull, assessing cargoes, handling import-and-export payments and delivering cash to the Exchequer, a position that brought with it the privilege of deciding when to pay his own dues. With the cash-flow that came with it, it seems the brothers moved fast to enlarge their money-lending enterprises – and took aim at breaking into England's pre-eminent industry.

*

By the 1320s, the English wool business was centuries old. The Romans had known England primarily as a great mine of minerals such as tin, lead and silver – and a market of slaves. But in the centuries after the Roman evacuation of Britannia, the cloth trade grew. From the eighth century, the most active traders with England were probably the Frisians of the northern Germanic coast, who bought and sold wine, timber, grain and fish from towns like London and York and, from at least the late seventh century, traded a certain amount of English cloth, known, appropriately, as Frisian. A famous late eighth-century letter from Charlemagne to King Offa of Mercia complains about the short length and quality of cloaks supplied: 'What's the use of these little bits of cloth?' wrote the irritated Emperor, 'I can't cover myself up with them when I'm in bed. When I'm riding, I can't protect myself against wind and rain. When I have to go and answer a call of nature, I suffer because my legs are frozen!'[10]

By the time of the Norman Conquest in 1066, England's sheep flocks already numbered 3 or 4 million, and they multiplied exponentially in the centuries that followed.* By early 1200, England boasted at least 6 million sheep,[11] and the chronicler Henry of Huntingdon could describe 'most precious wool' as foremost among the nation's treasures. By the middle of the thirteenth century, flocks may have tripled to as much as

---

* These estimates are based on the Domesday survey of the sheep population in eight counties.

18 million, and by 1297 England's barons declared wool, 'the sovereign merchandise and jewel of this England'. It made up perhaps half of the nation's wealth. [12]

In the years before William de la Pole was born, perhaps one-third of the wool trade was in the hands of just 450 English merchants – men such as Nicholas of Ludlow, reputedly the richest merchant of his day, or William Grevel, described as 'the flower of all merchants of all England'. Wander through the graveyards of England's exquisite Cotswold churches and you get a sense of just how much was made by so many of the country's medieval wool-men, now memorialized in their stone and brass effigies, their feet resting on little carved sheep in the naves and churchyards of Oxfordshire. A motto for many is inscribed on one memorial window: 'I praise God and ever shall, it is the sheep hath paid for all.'

In the early fourteenth century, a young Italian banker, Francisco Balducci Pegolotti, left us a guide as to how the business worked.[*] In his handbook, the *Pratica della mercatora*, Pegolotti set down everything he knew about sheep, now bred out of history. In all, the nation's sheep produced some fifty-one grades of wool. The sheep of the Welsh and Scottish borders, Yorkshire moors and chalk downs produced short wool used to make a heavier cloth, the most famous of which was the Ryland, named after the land between the Severn and the Welsh Marches. Larger sheep produced a longer wool, prepared by combing, and used for serges. Happily for the English, they could demand a very high monopoly price on the international market. The country could sustain only so many sheep, and with no alternative sources of high-quality wool available, merchants could make profits of up to £2 per sack on an investment ranging between £8 and £10.

There were no greater growers than the monks, lodged in some 650 abbeys and monasteries all over the country, and the business of the biggest was gigantic. By 1259, the Bishop of Winchester owned 30,000 sheep on a giant ranch-like estate,[†] while the three great

---

[*] The Florentine Pegolotti worked for the house of Bardi.

[†] Monastic flocks had been large for many years; some abbeys boasted owning over 13,000 sheep at the time of Domesday.

monastic houses at Tintern Abbey, Abeydoray and Stanfield in Lindsey, could boast wool that sold for 28 marks a sack: four times the value of the worst.*

In total numbers, however, the flocks of peasant farmers may have been even greater – the 1 million small tenants and leaseholders who often paid their rent partly or entirely in wool. In the late 1200s, for instance, the residents of one small Oxfordshire hamlet owned 500 sheep, while near Merton, south-west of London, a body of 200 villages managed a flock of over 3,700 sheep. The sheep were so ubiquitous that in 1297, the country's barons could complain that 'the whole community feels itself burdened by the tax on wools'.†

Nurturing the burgeoning flocks was the great English shepherd, equipped with candles to light the sheep house through the night in the lambing season, with pails of milk warmed in great earthenware pots for the new-born, frenetically rounding up, washing and clipping his flock in the annual sheep-shearing festivals immortalized by Shakespeare in *The Winter's Tale*. Once collected, the wool was packed in the county of origin, checked by the king's agents and dispatched in great bails, on packhorses, for the ports, where it was checked and customs were paid – along with tips to the officials, wine for the clerks, and money for the porters – before shipping to Calais. Often, the merchant sailed with the goods and lodged in Calais, which meant more bills from innkeepers, before meeting and selling the wool to the dealers of Flanders, Genoa and Venice, or riding on to the great fairs of Antwerp, Bruges and elsewhere. The trip might take several months – assuming piracy, bad weather, or the vicissitudes of local politics did not intervene.

In the extraordinary papers of the Cely family, the daily reality of wool-men's lives is laid out. Here are the prices, deals and the challenges of changing currency. 'By your letter you advise me for to buy wool in Cotswold', writes Richard Cely in one typical letter to his son, 'for which I shall have of John Cely his gathering 30 sack, and of Will Midwinter of Northleach 40 sack. And I am avised to buy no more; wool in Cotswold

---

* A mark was worth about two-thirds of a pound sterling.

† They were referring to the tax imposed three years before, in 1294.

is at great price, 13s. 4d. a tod, and great riding for wool in Cotswold as was any year this seven year.' Another letter complains of difficult customers – an attorney who is 'a wrangling fellow' who will accept 'no other money' but 'Nimueguen groats'. Yet another describes the counting houses that contend with eighteen different currencies, from the Andrew Guilder of Scotland to the Florin Rhenau of the Bishopric of Cologne.[13] For good reason, the merchants' quarters in Calais included a mint to which all foreign coinage had to be submitted and reminted in English coin to pay customs duties and the garrison guards.[*]

*

It would seem the fortune for the Pole brothers' 'fleece and finance' business owed much to their extraordinary position as suppliers to Edward's border conflicts, the most expensive wars in the country's history. Edward's last six campaigns against Scotland, over eight years, cost nearly £1 million, requiring taxes on the English like never before.[14] In 1322, when the Scots launched a deep attack as far as Yorkshire, Richard de la Pole was elected one of Hull's two MPs, appointed as Commissioner of Array, and required to help raise soldiers. In October, as Edward took flight from the Scottish onslaught and lodged in Burstwick, in Holderness, the brothers raised gifts and supplies for him and his leading men, whom the Poles were keen to cultivate. Wine worth £52 5s was despatched to the king's treasurer, to his chief justice and to the Keeper of the Privy Seal; when the king opened a second front in Gascony, in 1324, it was Richard who helped marshal war supplies for the expedition.

The Poles' royal and civic offices now multiplied. Both brothers were appointed chamberlains of the town of Hull, and so responsible for its finances. They levied taxes to fortify the town, repaired the old harbour, had the town moat dug, fitted out a ship (the *Trinity*) for the king, and bought land for the town's brickyard. With their burgeoning power and wealth, the brothers began slowly, but surely, to expand

---

[*] In August 1478, the Cely family paid twenty-one different masters for shipping their wool that summer. See Power, *Medieval People*, p. 136.

their 'fleece and finance' business. They shipped twenty sacks of wool in 1321, twenty-eight the following year, and fifty-six in 1325. With the proceeds, William bought property nationwide, including acquiring half the manor of Linby in Nottingham. When, in 1325, France and England agreed on territorial divisions in Aquitaine, William de la Pole was among those selling the Crown £1,000 in gold florins to help finance Prince Edward's voyage of homage to French King Charles IV, half as much as the loan from the mighty Bardi bankers.

However, it was events in England not adventures abroad that would bring to an end Edward II's reign and life. His power rested on the powerful but hated Despenser family. In 1326, Edward's Queen Isabella, in cahoots with her lover Roger Mortimer and the French – Charles IV of France was her brother – invaded and destroyed the Despensers and deposed the king, who was infamously murdered in Berkeley Castle in January 1327. Edward's fifteen-year-old son took the throne as Edward III. But it was Isabella and Mortimer who controlled the kingdom – and the new regime was to prove very profitable for the Pole brothers. Their good fortune was to be trusted by a ruling couple blessed with an extraordinary ability to burn through money just as fresh war threatened in Scotland and the House of Bardi faced a credit crunch. Within days of Edward III's accession, the Scots mounted a new assault, the first in what would become a two-decade-long conflict. The Poles seized their chance, lending, over the next three years, some £13,500 – worth somewhere between £176 million and £522 million in today's money – almost the size of the entire loan book of the House of Bardi.

It was an extraordinary, and risky, bet for two provincial merchants. But Pole had a clear plan for profit. His brother Richard was quickly ensconced in the new royal bureaucracy, being appointed within months of Edward II's death, as the new king's chief butler and wine gauger, with his own department at the Exchequer, a fee of 20 marks a year, two robes, rations when at court, a deputy, two clerks, and the right to collect 'butlerage' of 2 shillings a tun on wine imported by foreign merchants. Crucially, the Poles acquired control of customs revenue along the entire eastern seaboard of England, including London, as a means to secure their loan repayments; those repayments detailed in 1327 as a 'royal gift' suggest an interest rate of 22 per cent.

By 1328, the brothers' business was big enough for Richard to move south, acquiring the former Bardi headquarters on Lombard Street.* But politics was soon shifting the ground beneath them. In late 1330, the young Edward III effectively staged a royal coup, forcing his mother into genteel retirement and dispatching Mortimer to death. Now, for unknown reasons – but possibly sparked by the birth of William's heir Michael by 1330 – William and his brother decided to go their separate ways. On 12 July 1331, they ended their partnership, solemnly renounced past quarrels, promised fraternal amity for the future, and divided an enormous wealth of £11,200 – equivalent to some £2.8 billion today (as a share of GDP) or a third of the entire royal taxes imposed on the laity in 1332.

Yet regime change simply brought new business. The newly empowered monarch now began the long campaigns that would define his kingship, settling old feuds in Scotland and commencing the Hundred Years' War with France. Conflict would prove, for the entrepreneurially inclined, a gigantic business.

After the king made Hull its own borough in 1331, William was elected its first lord mayor, and the following year Edward III moved both his court and Chancery to York, putting potential new allies for Pole within easy reach. In the spring of 1333, the king began the first of his four giant Scottish campaigns. Scotland's Robert the Bruce had died in 1329, the new king, David II, was only five years old, and the country had slipped into civil conflict. Edward spied his chance to intervene, backing the regal contender Edward Balliol. Supplying Edward's marauding forces was a vast enterprise, and Pole was perfectly poised to profit. He could lay out great sums for supplies (amounting to nearly £5,500 between 1333 and 1335); he knew the wine business; he knew how to procure a ship; he had assembled powerful allies in John Stratford, then Bishop of Winchester, the king's chancellor and a key adviser; and Richard Bury, Archbishop of Durham. Pole spent the campaign filling Hull's granaries with wheat; hiring local ships to freight

---

* He also received a royal gift of 1,000 marks for his service at Christmas in 1328.

flour, hay, Gascon wine, salt and siege engines; and lending cash – some £3,700 between July 1331 and June 1335. When Flemish pirates began attacking the English supply lines, he even travelled to Flanders to negotiate the release of English hostages.

But when Edward III resolved to fight not on one front but two, the king required finance – and financial ingenuity – on a completely new scale. When his uncle Charles IV died in 1328, he left no heir, and Edward saw his chance to enlarge his continental possessions to match the empire once enjoyed by his Angevin ancestors. It would cost some £413,000 – twice the annual budget of Elizabeth I's administration two centuries later – financed between 1337 and 1340 by a variety of loans and taxes, totalling over £500,000: the biggest tax take for forty years. Marshalling the money would prove the making of William de la Pole and require every ounce of his mastery of the intricacies of the 'fleece and finance' business.

*

Until the early fourteenth century, much of the wool export business had been controlled not by the English but by the Flemish and Italians, who used their commercial strength in wool to dominate the business of royal lending. Mustering money was intimately connected with selling fleeces. Wool-sellers were paid just a third of the price upfront in cash.[15] The remaining two-thirds were paid in bills, or IOUs, redeemable at a later date. Small Cotswold wool dealers, for example, bought on credit from sheep farms. Big traders, such as the Celys, bought on credit from the small dealers, and Dutch and Flemish customers in Calais bought on credit from the Celys. The Celys would then present their bills and collect their money some six months later – perhaps at one of the great fairs in the Low Countries – before money was remitted back along the chain, arriving eventually with the sheep dealer. The bills carried interest, which was often hidden in the rate of exchange or in discounts. The ability to manage credit was thus crucial to financing the wool trade, and over the years the famous Italian banking houses used their positions in the wool business to build great balance sheets, which they then redeployed in loans to needy monarchs.

The Flemish knew the English wool trade well* but the Italians were bigger players, controlling perhaps a third of the wool trade at the end of the thirteenth century. In Lincolnshire, for instance, seven different Italian companies† traded with thirty-eight monastic houses, shipping English wool to Florence for the two great guilds, the Arte di Calimala and Arte della Lama, which deployed 30,000 people to finish cloth. The Italians could organize vast block contracts with monasteries, which sold *future* supplies of wool – for between two and twenty years ahead – in exchange for big down-payments in cash. Indeed, in 1262 the citizens of Lincoln were complaining to the king that the county's monasteries 'caused wool and other things to be bought in small quantities by their lead brethren and diverse places in the said county and afterwards caused these to be sold to merchants from beyond the sea'.

The Italians traded from Florence, then Europe's greatest commercial centre and home in the 1330s to hundreds of companies, including the banking houses of Bardi and Peruzzi.[16] Along with Frescobaldi, Bonsignori of Siena and Raidi of Lucca, they dominated lending to commerce and kings alike. Edward I had initially borrowed a fortune from the Ricciardi to fund his crusade of 1272, repaying his debts by turning over to the Italians a customs duty of 6s 8d on the precious wool exports. Their successors were the Frescobaldi, Antonio Pessagno of Genoa and, most importantly, the giant House of Bardi, which was at least 50 per cent bigger than its nearest competitor.[17] Far and away Europe's greatest super-company, the Bardi had a huge stake in southern Europe's grain trade and boasted some 346 factors. This was the competition that William de la Pole set out to dislodge in order to bring the 'fleece and finance' business home. And along the way he

---

* The first grant of privileges to a Flemish city was to Ghent in 1081, and in 1173, when the Earl of Leicester led an army of Flemish soldiers into battle in eastern England, the soldiers sang: 'We have not come into this land to sojourn / But to destroy King Henry the old warrior / And have his wool, which we long for'. See T. H. Lloyd, *The English Wool Trade in the Middle Ages* (Cambridge University Press, 2005), p. 7.

† The seven companies were: Bardi, Cerchi, Frescobaldi, Motzie, Pulci, Ricciardi and Spini.

also helped create one of the first great corporations of England: the English Wool Company.

We do not know precisely where, and when, the blueprint for the English Wool Company was finalized; but it was very elegant. From August 1336, a complete embargo was imposed on all English wool exports, driving up the price and starving the weavers of Brabant (whose prince had allied himself to the new French king, Philip VI) of raw materials. To cover the gap in customs duties, huge stop-gap loans of £103,000 were negotiated for the English Crown – £10,000 of which William de la Pole offered himself. A select group of merchants was then empowered to compulsorily purchase wool from suppliers big and small, and to ship the cargo to the Continent for sale to Edward III's new allies. The profit was split fifty–fifty between the merchants and the king, but with the agreement that out of their share the merchants would advance a loan of £200,000 to Edward. This debt would then be repaid by a new, higher rate of tax on every sack of wool – a tax effectively passed on to buyers through higher prices – to stay in place until the loan was reimbursed.

In June 1337, a small circle of twenty-four merchants, headed by William de la Pole, met at Stamford, Lincolnshire, to finalize the plan. They set out to begin buying wool. Pole had been stockpiling fleeces since May, ready for the embargo to fall. It was a good year to buy, as 'there was a great abundance of wool in the kingdom and it was a very good season for purveying wool', while in Ghent the weavers were starving and demanding of their leaders 'to find the necessary remedies for the re-establishment of industry'.[18]

Yet, for all it's elegance, the Wool Company's design proved in practice a disaster. Merchants smuggled wool wholesale so the promised 30,000 sacks of wool to be compulsorily purchased could not be assembled. At a heated meeting at Geertruidenberg, in Brabant, royal envoys demanded from the merchants £276,000 between Christmas and mid-Lent or else 'the Kingdom of England and all the other lands of the king were in danger of being lost'.[19] When the merchants refused, the envoys confiscated all the wool they could find and sold it, in return issuing bonds (the so-called 'Dordrecht bonds') to the merchants, which they might redeem against future customs duties, and asked the

Bardi and the Peruzzi to make good the gap. By February 1338, King Edward was forced to ask Parliament for a forced loan paid in wool, which was handed over to the Bardi and Peruzzi to sell.*

Somehow, William de la Pole managed to avoid the blame for the king needed him, and when Edward sailed for Antwerp on 22 July 1338, William de la Pole went along in tow. The credit lines of both the Bardi and the Peruzzi were now almost exhausted – and this was Pole's moment. While on duty with the king, William de la Pole earned a salary of 8 shillings per day and spent his days negotiating loans, paying allies, financing spies and managing his own retinue of 1 knight, 34 men at arms, 200 archers and 2 ships with over 200 sailors. From November 1338, he became Edward III's most important banker, ramming through agreements with merchants to increase duties, skilfully securing for himself customs-collection powers with which to repay his loans, and acquiring leases on valuable royal estates near Hull, including the hugely profitable estate of Burstwick, along with Gringley and Wheatley in north-east Nottinghamshire. To round out his portfolio, he acquired in September 1339 the mansion on Lombard Street that was once the London headquarters of the Bardi, and which now served as the base for the King's Great Wardrobe, from where much of the court's procurement was organized.† William was now the conduit not only for loans of his own, but for money lent by those who feared lending directly to the Crown. Between June 1338 and October 1339, he advanced the king a staggering £111,000 – about 29 per cent of the total funds that Edward raised, and almost as much as the Italians offered.[20]

Pole's genius – and the reason why so many merchants trusted him with money of their own – was his ability to get the money back through his control of English wool sales. In August 1338, a new fixed market, or Staple, was established at Antwerp, and this was now where all English exporters were required to retail. Pole was appointed its mayor, and all exporters were required to pay their duties through

---

* Eventually, £113,595 was raised in this manner – much less than the English Wool Company had promised. See Fryde, *William de la Pole*, op. cit., p. 85.
† Lombard Street was secured on 27 September 1339. See Fryde, *William de la Pole*, p. 114.

Pole's account. When, in January 1339, 'free export' was restored, Pole was assigned control of customs revenues through all English ports. Along with the income derived from the royal estates that he now controlled, Pole managed, by December 1340, to recover an enormous 80 per cent of what the Crown owed him. For his service, he was raised to the nobility with the rank of 'banneret'. Yet the strains of his assiduous efforts were obviously great enough to warrant exemption from further service in royal office unless he chose to 'in consideration of his being wearied with labour and diverse vexations under the burden of the king's service'.[21]

The tide of events, however, was now turning against him. Edward III had begun his continental campaign in Flanders, gathering allies, but the failures of the Dordrecht bond scheme meant he could not pay them. His subjects were restless at the war's financial burdens, and in October 1339, Pole was sent home as a royal commissioner representing Edward in Parliament, with the title of Second Baron of Exchequer. There, he faced fury from merchants outraged at the sharp practices of the English Wool Company and led by a devoted enemy, the veteran Baron of Exchequer, Robert de Sadington. As the tax yield faltered in the summer of 1340, Edward, in his second continental campaign, faced defeat. His siege of Tournai miscarried, and a bad truce was signed in September 1340. Enraged, the twenty-eight-year-old king arrived unannounced at the Tower of London's Watergate on 1 December 1340 and set upon the servants he judged to have failed him, including his Chancellor, Treasurer, judges, financiers – and William de la Pole.

Pole was arrested and sent to Devizes Castle and when his trial opened on 23 April 1341,[22] he was charged with abuses perpetrated as head of the English Wool Company. He spent the months between December 1340 and May 1342 detained at the king's pleasure; he was also fined £56,083 – a sum that looked likely to ruin him – and his lands, including Burstwick, were sequestered. And yet his sovereign soon found he could not fight without Pole's counsel and financial cunning.

On 16 May 1342, a discharge was ordered, the fines were (eventually) written off and William de la Pole bounced back with a new plan, launched in April 1343, for a new English Company to fund Edward's campaigns. Pole was not mentioned in the new company's documents, but he was the initiator of the whole venture, agreed between the king and thirty-three merchants on 29 April 1343. The plan, in essence, was that the king would hand over control of the nation's customs to the company, which would collect new duties on wool of 40 shillings per sack – as secured by Edward from the Parliament of 1343 – in return for an annual rent paid to the Crown of £50,000. On this security, the merchants could then raise loans that they would relend to the king. The English Company was, in theory, led by Thomas Melchebourn of Lynn, the new mayor of the Staple now established at Bruges, where all exporters were required to sell 'so that all those who pass wool are of one condition and agreement to keep the wool at a high price'.[23]

On the back of this scheme, Pole constructed an ingenious way of turning a profit, while reducing royal debt. The company's cash would be used to buy up Dordrecht bonds – effectively, the king's old debt – at discounts of up to 60 per cent from lesser merchants who needed the cash, which the company then redeemed at face value, from customs revenues. There was wide opportunity for fraud, and Pole clearly sold bonds back to the English Wool Company at nearly par even though many bonds had already been half redeemed. The new model he created for such 'customs farming' lasted until the Black Death of 1348, and the idea of discounting and reselling royal debt became part and parcel of royal financing for the next eleven years. As new syndicates took on the job of customs farming, they were required to redeem fixed portions of outstanding royal debt, and so the practice grew of buying up debt from small lenders and reselling it to the customs syndicates.

By 1344, Pole had regained much of the property he had lost, secured cancellation of the court judgment against him, and abroad his new model of royal finance underpinned Edward III's extraordinary advance. Despite renewed war with Scotland in 1341, Edward's provincial strategy in France – of battles on multiple fronts – reached its climax at Crécy on 26 August 1346. The French forces collapsed. Within two months, Edward's northern lords led a devastating assault on the Scots at Neville's Cross, near Durham, taking King David II prisoner. Sustaining his momentum, Edward III collected together 32,000 men, the largest English force ever to be marshalled during the Hundred Years' War, and laid siege to Calais. It fell in the summer of 1347, and would remain in English hands for over 200 years.

Over the next twenty years, Pole both prospered and proved a great survivor. He survived the first outbreak of the Black Death, in 1348–49, and, in autumn 1353, a second trial with the king. As relations between England and Flanders collapsed, Edward III – now in a more comfortable financial position owing to some years of relative peace – spied an opportunity to check the English wool merchants' power. He banned them from export, turned over the wool trade to foreign merchants and singled out William de la Pole for a renewed and concerted legal attack, despite the fact that the entrepreneur was 'said to be impotent and of great age'.[24] Pole's final trial opened on 26 November 1353. He was forced to surrender all claims over the profitable royal manor of Burstwick, but eventually secured a pardon for a fine of £16,728. He lived thereafter in peace until 1366, bequeathing to his son, Michael, enough wealth to make him one of the leading magnates of England. As one of the closest associates of Edward III's son, the Black Prince, Michael rose in time to become Lord Chancellor, was created Earl of Suffolk and married the only daughter and heiress of the Black Prince's chief councillor and business manager, Sir John Wingfield. In one of the great possibilities of English history, a descendant of William de la Pole even came within reach of the throne itself. Not long before the Battle of Bosworth (1485), King Richard III named John de la Pole as his heir. He might have been a King of England.

*

Thanks to the success of men like William de la Pole, the country was familiar with a good 'rags to riches' story by the time Dick Whittington stepped on to the stage, in the next century. In Chaucer's *Canterbury Tales*, published when Whittington was in his thirties, we catch a glimpse of the generation of which Whittington was the leading light. Here, Chaucer describes the merchant, 'Beneath a Flemish beaver hat', who has much to say of his work:

He told of his opinions and pursuits
In solemn tones, he harped on his increase
Of capital; there should be sea-police
(He thought) upon the Harwich–Holland ranges;
He was an expert at dabbling in exchanges.
He was so stately in administration,
In loans and bargains and negotiation. [25]

As a mercer, Whittington dealt not in wool but in silks, fine textiles and dress accessories, in a trade that was centuries old.[26] The mercers came together early on to win privileges to protect and ease their trade. In 1133, for instance, Henry I allowed them to face trial exclusively in London, with exemption from trial by battle and freedom from tolls on the roads and in the ports. Being travellers, mercers found advantage in banding together, not least to keep the records that proved their hometown was London and testified as to their freedoms and privileges. By 1304, the mercers had the rudiments of a guild in place; by 1348, we can find their ordinances and accounts, and in 1394 their company – the *premier* city livery company – was founded as an association of traders involved in buying and selling cloth.

A century after the Norman Conquest, the poet Thomas of Britain was writing of merchants spreading silks on the quays of London so that the sovereign might have first pick. London, as the largest and wealthiest town of the Norman, and then Angevin, empires, boasted plenty of demand for luxuries, and trading regulations from 1130 and 1180 suggest a steady flow of traders from Tiel, Cologne, Bremen and Lorraine with silk cloth of Constantinople and Regensburg, fustian, and fine white and unbleached linen for transformation into laces, loops, tassels, girdles, braids, shirts, sheets, underwear, headwear and kerchiefs. By the end of the 1100s, all kinds of mercers – from the lowly pedlar at a fair with a tray around his neck and a pack on his back, to the richest of bulk dealers – were a familiar sight. The centre of their trade was London's Cheapside, where today the Mercers' Hall, where mercers held their festivities, can still be found a minute or two from St Lawrence Jewry and the Guildhall. Hereabouts, mercers had houses, churches, their shops – which, in the 1300s, might boast some large chests, a couple of stalls and 200 items of inventory. Most business, though, was still done at the country's great fairs, such as those at Stamford, Boston, Winchester and Northampton, and from London a trading network of towns stretched out across the country.* In 1377, Salisbury was the country's most important cloth-making town, where the trade employed a quarter of its residents; but slowly, other centres grew up in Yorkshire, Essex, Suffolk, Oxfordshire, Warwickshire, Wiltshire and Somerset, each specializing in its own particular weave, such as Colchester's russets and greys, or Suffolk's kerseys, Coventry's blues, or the rays of Salisbury. From here, cloth was collected for finishing before exporting to Flanders and the trade nexus of northern Europe. [27]

In his day, Dick Whittington was a great master of this world. Between 1392 and 1394, he sold nearly £3,500 worth of cloth to King Richard II, and with the proceeds, carved out a role as a royal moneylender like William de la Pole's, supplying nearly sixty separate loans between 23 August 1388 and July 1422. Clearly a favourite of the king, Whittington was elected London's lord mayor in 1397 and was the principal royal lender in the final two years of the monarch's life – the years dramatized in Shakespeare's *Richard II*, before the sovereign was finally 'unking'd by Bolingbroke.' As lord mayor, Whittington ensured London's law and order during Richard II's last, turbulent parliaments; according to the medieval chronicle *Brut*, he 'ordained at every gate and in every ward strong watch of men of arms and of archers, and principally at every gate of London during this same Parliament'.[28]

Although a member of King Richard's Council in 1399, Whittington smoothly transferred his loyalties to the new regime when the king fell, and while he added little to his fortune after 1407, Whittington was prominent as a royal adviser, creditor – and above all, benefactor. Among his many bequests, he made provision for the support of 'young women that had done amiss' at St Thomas's Hospital, Southwark, and in all left over £5,000 in ready money, jewels and plate, along with his

---

* For instance, trading towns included Coggeshall, Hadleigh and Lavenham around Colchester; Devizes, Trowbridge and Warminster around Salisbury; and Wells, Taunton and Bridgwater in Somerset.

London home and country estates. Thirteen years after his death, the author of the political versification in *The Libel of English Policy*, provided a epitaph: 'penne and papere may not me suffice, Him to describe so high he was of prise, Above marchaundis to sett him on the beste, I can no more, but God have hym in reste.'

For generations, Whittington provided the English with the mould of the model merchant; and, as the country moved into the Age of Exploration, many sought to live by, and live up to, his example, but on a commercial stage that was suddenly much bigger. For within a few decades of Whittington's death, England ceased to be a European backwater and instead found itself seven hours' sailing time from the greatest emporium on earth: Antwerp. In this new world, few were greater heirs to Whittington than 'the greatest merchant in London', Sir Thomas Gresham (c.1518–79); a mercer who made a fortune dealing cloth and capital in England and Antwerp; who became a mission-critical servant of the Crown; and who brought home the lessons he learned abroad to help found London's capital market and the Stock Exchange.

*

The Gresham family hailed from the country's great cloth factory that was East Anglia. The family's roots were probably as prominent farmers in Norfolk, then one of the richest corners of the kingdom. The name 'Gresham' derives from the Anglo-Saxon for 'grass-farm', and indeed a village of similar name – Gressam, meaning 'grass homestead, or enclosure' – is recorded in Domesday Book. Their roots inspired the Gresham clan's grasshopper symbol, and in Holt, Thomas Gresham's great-grandfather, James Gresham, founded the family fortune in the mid-1400s, building the manor house that is today part of Gresham School.

Here, Gresham's father grew up, 20 miles north of Norwich, where 150 years earlier Flemish weavers had settled. Invited by Edward III, they made the city of Norwich their home. At times they numbered a

---

* 'Libel' in this context means 'a little book'.

third of the local population. Their symbol, the yellow canary, was adopted by the borough and their skill helped make the town the second-richest in England, with a wealth built on wool, cloth and continental trade – which paid for more churches than in any other town west of the Alps. The county around it bred around one-third of England's mercers, with the greatest number it seems from Eynsford, the manor bordering the Greshams' family seat, in Holt.

Thomas Gresham's grandfather, John Gresham, married well and was blessed with four extraordinary sons, at least two of whom, Thomas's father Richard and uncle John, sought their future, fame and fortune in London as apprentices to the greatest mercer of the day, John Middleton. He tutored them in trade, royal finance and the government of the City of London. In time, both Gresham sons would sit as lord mayor and, like Dick Whittington, Thomas's father built a career of great wealth based on good judgement and gigantic generosity, for he was no ordinary trader and no ordinary lord mayor. He joined the Mercers' Company aged just thirteen and made a successful living, trading with Antwerp, Prussia and Bordeaux, exporting textiles and importing grain and wine. In 1531, aged thirty-seven, he was elected Sheriff of the City of London, and six years later was lord mayor. His tenure was exemplary. He laid the new foundations for both the city's hospitals, the Mercers' Company's great livery hall – the birthplace, incidentally, of Thomas Beckett – Bedlam Hospital, and its stock market. Cardinal Wolsey, who often relied on Richard Gresham for intelligence advice, called him his 'fast friend', and in 1530 it was Gresham who financed the cardinal's funeral in Leicester Abbey, before transferring his loyalties seamlessly to Wolsey's successor, Thomas Cromwell, who went on to inherit the mantle of Henry VIII's chief minister. One Victorian historian was moved to write of Richard Gresham: 'the City of London had perhaps never before known a greater benefactor'. When he died in 1548, the streets along the route to his tomb in St Lawrence Jewry, the beautiful church next to the Guildhall, were hung with black cloth.

*

Thomas Gresham was the youngest of Richard Gresham's children, born in 1519, possibly in Milk Street, London – or possibly in Norfolk. He was dispatched, aged fourteen, to Gonville College in Cambridge, then a filthy, dark and dirty place, scarred across by the open sewer of King's Ditch, where natives and visitors alike complained of the seeping cold of long winters. Here, among some of the future stars of England's Protestant Reformation, Thomas Gresham acquired a lifelong love of learning. He left in around 1535 and began life as an apprentice mercer with his uncle, John, a trader in Ottoman silks and spices. 'I myself was bound prentice 8 years, to come by the experience and knowledge that I have,' wrote Gresham later in life, adding that 'my father Sir Richard Gresham being a wise man knew although I was free by his copy... I were bound prentice... whereby to come by the experience and knowledge of all kinds of merchandise.'[29]

Following his graduation, in 1543, the twenty-four-year-old Thomas was admitted to the Mercers' Company, and by June of that year he appears in royal records at work on the Continent, sourcing military supplies including gunpowder and saltpetre, which were ordered to be 'delivered to young Thomas Gresham, solicitor of the same'. Around this time, Gresham married Anne, the daughter of a well-to-do Suffolk family and the widow of a certain William Read, a fellow mercer who must have known the family well, for Richard Gresham was his executor. History has left us a magnificent painting of Thomas Gresham aged twenty-six, painted on the occasion of his wedding. It is the first known full-length portrait of a non-royal Briton. Tall, lean with an intelligent face, he is dressed in the expensive but sombre black robes of the Tudor elite, and the painting is inscribed with his merchant's mark and a simple inscription: 'AG – love, serve and obey TG'.

For nearly the next decade, Gresham prospered as he rose to pre-eminence in the family's commercial enterprises, buying fine fabrics, wool and kerseys but also armour and weaponry for shipping to England. He even exported, at one stage, Cornish tin, to relieve the stranglehold of a German cartel on Europe's tin supplies. But his greatest strength was his growing mastery of what had become the world's most important marketplace, now but a short journey from his native Norfolk: the city of Antwerp.

*

Antwerp's rise to become the first centre of a new global economy was somewhat sudden. It was settled in the second and third centuries AD by the Frisians; Charlemagne built a fort there and when the river connecting neighbouring Bruges to the sea began to silt up, northern Europe's traders began to come to Antwerp, followed by the Spanish and Portuguese, who brought with them the fruits of the New World.

In spring 1498, six years after Columbus's history-making expedition to America had commenced, the Portuguese Vasco da Gama spent twenty-three days crossing 2,800 miles of ocean to land in India. Ill-equipped for trade talks, da Gama had weighed anchor in Calicut with just '12 pieces of stirred cloth, four scarlet hoods, six hats, four strings of coral, a case containing 6 handwash basins, a case of sugar, two casks of oil and two of honey' with which to trade.[30] The Zamarin of Calicut was unimpressed yet when da Gama left, three months later, he packed enough cinnamon and cloves into his hulls to pay for this expedition sixty times over. Just four years after he arrived home, it was on the quaysides of Antwerp that Portuguese ships were unloading cargoes of peppers, cinnamon and saffron. Within a few decades, the exchange of corn, wheat, coffee, tea, gold, slaves and crops had become the life-blood of this new trading system – and Antwerp had begun to supplant Venice as the greatest hub of the new global market.

For the Portuguese, there was no better place than Antwerp to raise the money for voyages and to sell the cargoes brought home. In 1460, near the great market in Antwerp's Wolstraat (Wool Street), the city had created the world's first modern bourse, or stock exchange, where traders could do business all the year round. It was a revolution in the way medieval business was done. Traditionally, merchants had come together at the major fairs, such as at Champagne, to exchange goods and then settle up weeks later. When goods were swapped, notes promising the requisite cash were written and handed over. Before long, there was a trade in swapping these notes, just as we buy and sell debt today. The first bankers served the traders by buying these bills and promising to pay out cash in a distant part of the Continent.

The bourse was soon the hub of finance for New World trade. By 1560, Europe was consuming as much as 7 million pounds of pepper. Sugar soon followed the trade stream, along with New World silver, after discoveries of huge deposits in Mexico and Peru transformed the world's money supply. While the ships plied the waves, in the money markets merchants discounted and swapped bills of exchange, advanced credit and traded the cargoes of goods still far out to sea in the Indian Ocean or elsewhere.

Typically, the King of Portugal would sell a commodity – say, pepper – to syndicates as a cargo of East Indies' ships. The syndicates would then be granted a monopoly to sell the goods on landing. These syndicates might buy the cargo while it was still at sea, advancing the money and then reselling the goods in advance. These practices created huge opportunities for speculation, which grew to an art form and drew merchants and nobles alike. In 1567, the Florentine Lodovico Guicciardini noted: 'Nowadays... A part of the nobles and merchants employ all their available capital in dealing in money, the large and sure profits of which are a great bait.'[31] The King of Portugal's returning ships would now dock briefly in Lisbon and then head for Antwerp, where up to 3,000 vessels might be seen, anchored in the River Scheldt – four times the shipping of London. Soon the Flanders city was the centre of trade in Portuguese spices, south German copper and silver, and cloth, some 200,000 pieces of it, worth perhaps £2 million.

By Gresham's day, Antwerp was enormous. It was a polyglot, cosmopolitan place. On the Antwerp bourse, you could hear 'a confused sound of all languages... and one saw a parti-coloured medley of all possible styles of dress; in short the Antwerp bourse seemed a small world wherein all parts of the great worlds were united'.[32] Absolute freedom was granted to foreign merchants, with no restrictions in bills, money or precious metals. In 1567, Guicciardini observed that 'it is a wonderful thing to see such a great coming together of so many people and nations. It is even stranger to hear the many different languages: as a result, without the need to travel, one can discover, or even follow the nature, habits, and customs of many nations.'[33] The 1568 census recorded 89,996 residents, of whom over 10,000 were 'foreign merchants daily coming and going' along with 3,822 soldiers with their wives, children, and servants. The Spanish had acquired control of the city through a series of clever Hapsburg dynastic alliances and when the future Philip II of Spain entered Antwerp* for the first time, on 11 September 1549, his courtiers gasped at the opulence of a city 'which could with good reason be called the marketplace of the world'. Indeed, such was the attraction of trade, Guicciardini lamented, that 'the soil remains untilled, trade in commodities is neglected, the poor are fleeced by the rich, and finally even the rich go bankrupt'.[34]

By the reign of Elizabeth I, among this international throng were a hundred Englishmen living permanently, along with some five hundred compatriots who regularly worked in the city. In theory, all traders were equal. But the English were more equal than others. Indeed, such were their privileges that they had their *own* bourse, as Guicciardini could testify: 'The merchants go morning and evening at a certain time to the Bourse of the English. There they do business with the help of brokers of every language who are there in great numbers.'[35] Few were as intimate with Antwerp's ways as Thomas Gresham, and he now offered all the fruits of his experience to help save his king.

*

King Henry VIII had breathed his last in 1547. He bequeathed to his nine-year-old son, Edward VI, a divided kingdom and an empty treasury. By 1550, royal debt, largely lent by foreigners, had reached £100,000, and it rose to £150,000 in 1552. Interest rates were 16 per cent a year, and interest payments topped £40,000. The new king's first financial agent, Sir William Dansell, was so bad that Edward's Council sacked him, noting that 'You have done His Highness marvellous ill service.'[†] In his place, the king's men sent for the thirty-four-year-old

---

* Philip had at one time debated ceding Antwerp from his territories. In the first debate in his Council of State in 1544, his councillors argued about whether it would be better to give the city of Milan or the Netherlands as a dowry in a marriage alliance with France. Philip's father, Charles V, concluded that the Netherlands was vital to Spain's economic interests and could never be relinquished.

† It is alleged that Dansell's mismanagement cost the Crown some £40,000.

Thomas Gresham. His father and uncle had, over the years, performed many services for the Crown, and, given Thomas's intimate knowledge of trade and currency exchange, the Council in 1551 was keen to hear about his most ingenious scheme to clear the royal debts.*

Owing something in inspiration to the methods of William de la Pole, Gresham suggested, first, manipulating the exchange rate by drip-feeding £1,300 each week to carefully buy up small quantities of sterling on the Antwerp exchange, so that 'it shall not be perceived nor shall be occasion to make the exchange fall.'[36] When the exchange rate rose as a consequence, there should be, Gresham proposed, a last-minute halt on the Merchant Adventurers' bi-annual cloth fleet, lifted only when the merchants agreed to make a loan in foreign currency from the proceeds of their cloths sales, to be paid in Antwerp and to be repaid in London at a new fixed exchange rate, more favourable to the Crown.† The Council was sold on the idea. It created a new supply of short-term loans, and allowed Gresham to control availability of sterling in Antwerp, thereby forcing up the price of sterling on the international market.[37] Gresham was appointed royal agent to the Low Countries, and he promptly departed with his wife to Antwerp on a journey he would repeat some forty times in the next two years.

Gresham quickly got to work. He was extremely well-connected in Antwerp, where he had set up home with a family friend, Jasper Schetz, a poet, connoisseur of coins and later Treasurer General of the Low Countries. Gresham's first instructions from the Council were to resolve a £10,000 loan from the German financier and speculator Lazarus Tucher and then to return home quickly 'to the intent we might more certainly confer with you'. There followed instructions to renegotiate loans with the German Fuggers, then the biggest bank in Europe, a task he executed with plenty of entertaining. His receipts included notes such as 'paid for a supper and a banquet that I made to the Fugger and to the Chet [another banker] – £26', a very large sum. He navigated skilfully both the shoals of the Antwerp exchanges and

* Gresham set out the detail of these schemes in a letter dated 21 August 1552.
† Gresham went one step further and proposed that the king use his royal prerogative to create a lead monopoly.

the unreasonable instructions of his masters, protesting against one command to stop loan payments with the warning: 'I say to you the end thereof shall neither be honourable nor profitable to His Highness'.*' By mid-1552, Gresham was handling more than £106,000 and rarely had he needed to borrow at more than 14 per cent interest – some 2 per cent cheaper than the terms offered to Holy Roman Emperor Charles V. By 1553, the pound's value had improved nearly 40 per cent[†] – and at that moment Gresham proposed clearing the king's debts.

The young king was delighted. 'You shall know', declared the monarch, 'that you have served the king.' In 1553 he conferred on his royal agent property and estates around Norfolk worth some £100 a year. But for Gresham, it was a temporary triumph. He was about to learn there is little gratitude in court politics. Edward, still only fifteen years old, was ailing, and on his death on 6 July 1553 Gresham's opponents moved against him.

In a wonderful memorandum, Gresham explained his achievements: how he counselled against clearing Edward's debts of £260,000 Flemish pounds with a debasement of the coinage, which would have, he explained, prompted the 'transport [of] the treasure out of the realm'.[38] Instead, he, Gresham, had managed to pay all debts except 100,000 marks by manipulating the exchange rate, underpinned by trading on his account, and halted the expensive purchase of jewels. But the power-players of Mary I's new court, not least the powerful and conservative Bishop of Winchester, Stephen Gardiner, were hostile. It was Gardiner, said Gresham, who 'sought to undo me, and whatsoever I said in these financial matters'.[39] At first, the hapless Christopher Dauntsey was reappointed royal agent, whereupon he promptly ruined the queen's credit by accepting loans from Lazarus Tucher at 2 per cent *above* the rate Charles V was able to enjoy (which was then 12 per cent) and broadcasting his terms throughout the market. Nor did Dauntsey keep the Council well briefed. By November, the ill-starred emissary had so undone Gresham's work that the Privy Council quickly

---

* At the end of August 1552, some eight months after his appointment, he was asked to arrange deferral of a £56,000 loan repayment. See Burgon, *The Life and Times of Sir Thomas Gresham*, op. cit., p. 91.

† The pound now bought twenty-two gilders, instead of sixteen.

resummoned Gresham to royal service. He was not entirely without friends, in particular the mysterious Sir John Leye, who, Gresham noted later, 'preserved me when Queen Mary came to the throne; for which I do account myself bound to him during my life'.[40]*

Thomas Gresham resumed his work on behalf of the Crown in November 1553. His first task was to clear up his forebear's failures. But he minuted the Council with the assurance that 'I do not doubt but to bring all things (to pass) according to your heart's desire.'[41] Over the next two-and-a-half years, as Queen Mary saw off rebellion at home and negotiated marriage with Philip II of Spain, Gresham embarked on a run of missions: raising loans of £50,000, smuggling home bullion and arms to replenish the Tower of London's arsenals, amassing vast quantities of bills of exchange, and supervising the import of 320,000 ducats to England from Philip's Spanish court, escorted into harbour by Her Majesty's warships.†

By March 1556, his principal work for the queen was complete. He was now of sufficient rank that the queen wrote to him direct. He remained an assiduous gift-giver,‡ and whenever he was on the Continent he made sure to write to Mary with news of her husband. 'I have been at Brussels,' ran one letter, 'where as I saw the King's Majesty in right good health thanks be to God – in his robes and the Duke of Savoy with him; which feast was very honourable and solemnly kept by his majesty in all his nobles and gentlemen around him.'[42]

Gresham's private business now burgeoned. One year he shipped some 4,500 kerseys,§ and in 1555 he was probably involved in helping his uncle found the Muscovy Company. In 1556 he was awarded manors worth £200 per year, and in 1558, when Mary joined her husband's war on the French (much to the chagrin of her Council),

---

* History has not left us much information about Sir John Leye, but we know that he was a well-travelled man who was related to the Duke of Norfolk and close to the new queen.
† Gresham even had to bribe the chief searcher at Antwerp dock. Military supplies included gunpowder and armour.
‡ For example, he gave her a bolt of fine Holland cloth for Christmas in 1555.
§ Kersey was the fine cloth much regarded by the Italians, and for which Gresham's family was well-known as shippers.

Gresham was dispatched for a final mission negotiating loans for £100,000, buying military stores and delivering a ring to Philip II. Seven thousand English troops left for the Continent, delivering, with the Spanish, some early victories. But in January 1558 they were undone. Under attack from the French, Calais – the last English foothold on the Continent – was lost. Mary did not have time to recover from the shock. Weeks later, she was dead.

*

Around Mary's half-sister Elizabeth, now queen, a new court quickly gathered at Hatfield House, where she had her household, to take stock of an exhausted country. 'The queen is poor,' wrote one former councillor, 'the realm exhausted, [the] nobility poor and decayed. The people are out of order. Justice is not executed. All things are dear... There is steadfast enmity but no steady friendship abroad.'[43] At her right hand, however, was one of the greatest public servants in England's history, her thirty-eight-year-old secretary, William Cecil.

Born in Stamford, a little after Gresham, Cecil went on to serve Elizabeth for another forty years.* His grandfather had fought for Henry VII, and while at Cambridge William Cecil had acquired a reputation as a great scholar. He trained as a lawyer at Lincolns Inn and served as private secretary to the Duke of Somerset – England's Lord Protector in the first years of Edward VI's reign – becoming one of the administration's rising stars. Cecil was frozen out of office under Mary I, but he remained on excellent terms with her key adviser, Cardinal Reginald Pole.

Obsessive, passionate and driven, Cecil developed a unique relationship with Elizabeth. At Hatfield, she formally appointed him her secretary, three days after her accession, requiring of him: 'you will be faithful to the state and that without respect of my private will you will give me that council that you think best'.[44] Thereafter, among all the

---

* His biographer Stephen Alford described him as 'the most powerful and capable politician of the Tudor century' in *Burghley: William Cecil at the Court of Elizabeth I* (Yale, 2011), p. 13.

queen's servants he was able to speak truth to power; and he proved ruthless in Elizabeth's service. This was a man Thomas Gresham knew well, and with whom he would work for the next twenty years to help build the Elizabethan Age.

We do not know precisely when Gresham and Cecil met. They were born within three years of each other, and while both studied at Cambridge they may have just missed each other there. Both were heavily influenced by the Protestant reformers then ascendant in the university faculty. As young successful men at court and in the city, their paths must have frequently crossed in 1540s London. During Mary's reign, when neither of them was in frontline royal service, they may have met during Cecil's tour of the Low Countries in 1554. They certainly did business together, since Cecil wiled away his time working on his fortunes, investing in the Muscovy Company founded by Gresham's uncle. Thomas Gresham would become a key financial adviser to Cecil, one of the most important of Elizabeth's intelligence agents on the Continent, as well as a supplier of foreign luxuries, from clockwork timepieces to silk stockings to Dutch stone for Cecil's country houses, and a mentor to Cecil's slightly wayward son, Thomas, during his first years studying on the Continent.

Gresham arrived at Hatfield House on Sunday 19 November 1558. His interview went well. 'Her Highness', wrote Gresham later, 'promised me by the faith of a queen that she would not only keep one ear shut to hear me; but also if I did none other service than I had done to King Edward, her late brother and Queen Mary her late sister, she would give me as much land as ever they both did; which two promises made me a young man again.'[45]

Immediately, Gresham took steps to put himself at Master Secretary Cecil's service: 'I have commanded my factor', Gresham wrote to Cecil in 1558, 'give his attendance upon you every morning to know your pleasure whether you will have anything said to me... sir I have commanded him to be with you by 6 of the clock in the morning every morning.'[46]

Like Edward VI, Elizabeth confronted a world full of enemies and an Exchequer empty of money.[47] On the night that Gresham arrived at Hatfield, Cecil received an extraordinary handover note from

Mary's former secretary, Boxhall, explaining that 'you shall receive also herewith Gresham's doings touching borrowing of money to the use of this realm'. He apologized for two bonds being missing: 'the two bonds were of I spoke unto you of cannot be found; they were left in the bedchamber of the late queen's highness to be signed with her hand'.

Gresham's first task, therefore, was to assure creditors in Antwerp and arrange cash for the coronation. Before his departure he set out a full account of the queen's credit, a history dating back to the days of her father and a fiscal strategy for the future. His story starts with 'the great fall in England's exchange rate from 26s 8d to 13s 4d', following the debasement of the coinage which 'was the occasion that all your fine gold was conveyed out of this your realm'.[48] King Henry 'by reason of his wars fell into great debt in Flanders,' he continued 'and for the payment thereof they had no other device but pay it by exchange'. Privileges granted to the German merchants of the Hanseatic League, in their London fastness of the Steelyard, meant that wool and other commodities could escape the kingdom. As such, they represented the 'chief point of the undoing of this your realm and the merchants of the same'. Gresham then explained how he had restored the exchange rate and cleared Edward's debts, only for things to come unstuck under Mary. His advice was simple: 'keep foreign debt low and keep up your credit and especially with your own merchants'.[49] He concluded by underlining that a restoration of the exchange rate to 22 Flemish shillings to the pound sterling would mean in a few years that the queen would have 'a wealthy realm'.

Gresham's account is an extraordinary document. Throughout her reign, Elizabeth was to stick remarkably closely to its principles, as Cecil now crafted a plan to deal with Elizabeth's debts of £226,910 – more than her annual income of £200,000 – and to fund a new national defence at a cost of some £300,000.* For while England's Hapsburg alliance had died with Mary, and war with France was ended, a new Franco-Scottish threat took shape through the course of 1559.

---

* By ruthless economy alone, Cecil aimed to achieve a surplus of £65,000 a year, earmarked for the next two years.

Elizabeth's young cousin, Mary Stuart, Queen of Scots, had married the French dauphin in 1558, and his sister, Mary of Guise, governed Scotland as regent. In July 1559, the dauphin became King Francis II – and the new leader of Catholic antipathy towards the Protestant queen, edged with Mary Stuart's claim to the English throne itself. England was on the defensive, and Cecil needed some £187,000 to pay for war preparations and to satisfy imminent creditors. New customs rates were introduced, dramatically raising the Crown's taxes on trade and increasing the returns on cloth exports from £30,000 to £110,000 a year – as much for the entire Parliamentary subsidy of 1559.[50]

Thomas Gresham was dispatched back to Antwerp, where he set about juggling and smuggling loans, arms and intelligence. On 5 March 1559, Gresham was sent to Antwerp to delay loans and seek 200 barrels of saltpetre. By 3 April he was advising the Council to ready 'three or four of best ships of war... for the sure waifting [sic] of this munitions and armour'.[51] In Zeeland, in the Low Countries, he placed his man, 'Waddington', to report and 'to visit all Havens and courts for the quantity of ships and what preparations of ships of war they do prepare'.[52] Richard Payne was placed in Guelderland, Henry Gerbrand in Dunkirk, John Gerbridge in Toledos, and John Waddington in Amsterdam; all fed in reports. There were nuggets too from Gresham's old partner, Jasper Schetz, now 'factor and counsellor' to Philip II of Spain, lubricated with a constant flow of gifts – 600 crowns here, a 500-crown gold necklace there – to keep his friendship strong. In the summer of 1559, Gresham was in Antwerp again, delaying old loans and installing new spies. In December, he was appointed the queen's ambassador to Brussels, capital of the Spanish Low Countries, and was made a knight of the realm.

When Elizabeth decided to back a rebellion of Scottish Protestant nobility against Mary of Guise to try and forestall the arrival of French forces in Scotland, a new surge of arms and loans was required.* New

---

* In February 1560, the Duke of Norfolk agreed with Scotland's Protestant nobility to take Scotland under Elizabeth's protection for as long as Mary Stuart, Scotland's rightful queen, stayed in France. Elizabeth's ships subsequently blockaded the Firth of Forth, but in a disastrous confrontation at Leith, the English were driven back.

credit of £200,000 was needed, along with armour and 500 shirts of mail. Much of what Gresham ordered, he smuggled, often by bribing the 'chief searcher' in Antwerp. He had to operate in a covert fashion. For example, in February 1561 he warned the queen of the need for total secrecy and that Dutch spies in Europe and London were watching for the unloading of prohibited cargoes. The arrival of bullion, Gresham warned, 'must be kept as secretly as Your Majesty can devise: for if it be known or perceived... it were as much as my life and goods were worth'.[53]

Peace came to Scotland when Mary of Guise died of dropsy in June 1560. After weeks of torturous negotiation, Cecil struck the Treaty of Edinburgh in July. By its terms, the French agreed to recognize Elizabeth as Queen of England and drop all pretence to the English throne.

With peace in place, Gresham saw a window for some vital reform: an overhaul of England's coinage and credit. Since his first letter to Elizabeth, he had effectively argued for recalling all the kingdom's currency and reissuing it with a higher and more consistent gold and silver content. In his view, Henry VIII's original decision to reduce the coinage's value in 1544, by diluting it with alloy, had simply led to foreign merchants demanding payment in 'good' coins rather than bad, and so good coins were exported while bad coins stayed in England. It was the clearest statement of a behaviour well-known to traders but now immortalized as 'Gresham's law': that bad money drives out good.

Gresham argued for a bold plan and urged the queen to start work. 'The enterprise is of great importance and the sooner it is put in hand that more honour and profit it will be to the Queen's Majesty', not least for the positive effect it would have on the exchange rate. By November 1559, the queen was content, and in September 1560 a proclamation was issued to recall coins for melting down and reissue. Gresham advised that one Daniel Wolstat, 'an honest man to whom I am much beholden', be appointed to refine the coins, when the process got underway in late 1560.* Gresham now followed up with a plan to

---

* Wolstat's name sometimes appears as 'Wolfstadt' or 'Ullstat'.

exploit the nation's new currency strength and repeat a forced loan from the Merchant Adventurers, first paid in Antwerp in March 1559.[54]

It was in essence a similar plan to that presented to Mary's Council: first, to improve the exchange rate, then to delay, at the last minute, a licence to the Merchant Adventurers for cloth shipments until a forced loan (payable in Antwerp) was agreed, paid with cash from cloth sales – and to be repaid in London at a rather more favourable exchange rate for the Crown. The prize, advised Gresham, was large: 'you shall advance the queen's homeward credit in such sort as you shall astonish Prince Philip and the French king'.[55]

By August 1561, the scheme was ready. But a last-minute hitch allowed the ships to sail before the £60,000 Flemish loan was agreed. The Council had lost its advantage. Gresham was forced to descend on the City of London with threats of a huge tax if the merchants did not agree to the royal loan. By 15 October 1561, he could report a deal: £30,000 was paid between 15 and 30 November, in return for Gresham's help in ensuring that all the cloth was sold.

The immediate threats to Elizabeth had now been confronted. There was peace on the island of Britain. The urgent financial crisis had been contained. Dependence on foreign creditors had been reduced. London merchants lent more, in return for greater trading privileges, which strengthened their position against the Germans, Italians and Flemings.

But, while Gresham's life returned to order, the Catholic powers of Europe descended into chaos.

In the summer of 1562, civil war commenced in France, as the long Wars of Religion pitted Catholics against Huguenots. In October, Elizabeth ordered 6,000 troops to Newhaven and Dieppe, under the command of the Earl of Warwick, to aid the French Protestant cause. Gresham had spent the summer on the Continent laying preparations and advising on the acquiring of £400,000 worth of saltpetre. But the effect on the queen's credit was awful: 'these money men be afraid to deal any further with the Queen's Majesty,' minuted Gresham, 'they cast so many doubts of this troublesome world... glad is the man who may be quit of an Englishman's bill!' By March 1563, the French Protestants, under duress, struck peace – for now – and while Elizabeth insisted that her besieged troops maintain their occupation of Le Havre, plague decimated their ranks until they surrendered. The plan had been to trade Le Havre for Calais. It was not to be. Peace with France was concluded in 1564.

A mere two years later, the rising Calvinist tide in the Low Countries spilled over into war against Spanish imperial control. Iconoclasts began destroying religious images. Gresham's agent, Richard Cloth, described in his weekly bulletins an Antwerp in chaos: 'I with 10,000 more went into the churches to see what stir was there; coming into our lady it looked hell; where were 1,000 torches burning and such a noise! As if heaven and earth had gone together with falling of images and beaten down of costly works; in such sort that the spoil was so great that a man could not well pass through the church.'[56] There were, minuted Gresham, '40,000 Protestants in this town [Antwerp] which would die rather than the word of God should be put to silence'.[57]

In the summer of 1567, Philip II imposed his enforcer, the Duke of Alba, on the hostile and volatile provinces. It was to prove the beginning of eighty years of intermittent fighting in the Dutch War of Independence, and the beginning of Antwerp's decline. As Alba's uncompromising retribution began, thousands of Antwerp's merchants upped sticks and headed for London; indeed, in 1567 the Bishop of London's census recorded that 3,838 of the 4,851 strangers in the city were Dutch.

*

Antwerp's loss was London's gain. The migration of merchants across the Channel was a wonderful boon to Gresham's creation of a bourse – the London Royal Exchange. Three decades earlier, in 1537, Gresham's father had lobbied Henry VIII with the idea to create a home for the merchants who tended to meet near Lombard Street. 'Their meetings', recorded the chronicler Stow, 'were unpleasant and troublesome by reason of walking and talking in an open narrow street... being there constrained to endure all extremities of weather.'[58] Richard Gresham had proposed a plan on the lines of the bourse that he had seen in Antwerp. He had written to Thomas Cromwell in 1538 to say: 'The last year I showed your good lordship a plate that was drawn out for to make a goodly burse in Lombard St for merchants to repair to... I do suppose it would cost £2,000 or more which shall be very beautiful to the city and also to the honour, of our sovereign lord the king.'[59]

On 4 January 1565, his son Thomas finally persuaded the City's alderman to build an exchange at his own expense, if a site could be found. A subscription to buy land was quickly met,* and in June 1567, near Cornhill, Gresham laid 'the first stone of the foundation being brick accompanied with some alderman every of them laid a piece of gold'.[60] In common with his father, Gresham wanted an exchange that was similar in style to Antwerp's Beurs, built in 1531 near Lange Nieuwe Straat, where Gresham lived while in the city: a quadrangle of arched, covered walkways, around which were situated shops to help pay back the costs. Sir Thomas Gresham sent his agents across the Low Countries in search of materials; he supervised the building, provided stone and wood from his own estates, and immodestly mounted his symbol, a huge grasshopper, over every corner of the building.

By 1568, merchants were gathering outside its walls. It was finished in late 1569. On 23 January 1571 Queen Elizabeth progressed in state into the City from Somerset House on the Strand, down Fleet Street and Cheapside, to Gresham's house on Bishopsgate, where she dined. 'After dinner Her Majesty returning through Cornhill entered the Burse on the Southside: and after she had viewed every part thereof above the ground, especially the pawn which was richly furnished with all sorts of finest wares in the city she caused the same... by a herald and a trumpet to be proclaimed the Royal Exchange.'[61]

The timing was perfect. Mounting foreign threats to the Elizabethan regime meant mounting bills. Mary, Queen of Scots, under house arrest in England, remained a focus of discontent: in 1569, leading Catholic nobles in the north rose in revolt. Although it failed, in 1570 Pope Pius V excommunicated Elizabeth, encouraging both her subjects and foreign princes to dethrone the heretical queen. Thousands

---

* Seven hundred and fifty citizens paid up to the subscription, and in 1566 houses from Cornhill's Swan Alley to St Christopher's Alley were bought for £3,532.

of Spanish troops were massing in the Low Countries, with one eye on the rebellious Dutch provinces and the other on a possible invasion of England to support Mary Stuart and Catholic factions. Anglo-Spanish relations were at a low, after a Spanish ship loaded with gold was pillaged upon landing in Southampton during a storm. A tit-for-tat trade embargo was now in place, freezing England's continental cloth sales. The catalogue of threats required new defences for Elizabeth's England – and new money to pay for them.

Long ambitious to mobilize English lenders, Thomas Gresham now set out to rejuvenate the London gilts market – through the sale of government bonds. Gresham wrote to Cecil in 1570, opining that 'I would wish that the Queen's Majesty in this time should not use any strangers but her own subjects whereby the Duke of Alva and all other princes may see what a prince of power she is'. The Merchant Adventurers were less sure: they initially voted down the idea of a loan, but after a rebuke organized by Gresham, £21,000 was raised from fourteen merchants at an interest rate of 12 per cent.[62] It was not long before Gresham was forced to intervene to insist that Elizabeth's Council honour its debts. Six months after the loan was raised in March 1571, Gresham told Cecil – now Lord Burghley – 'I am daily called upon amongst the alderman and others that they may not fail of their money due in May next.'

*

We know little about Gresham's last decade. His letters became less frequent. There are no diaries to read. But his service had proved extraordinary. He once, in 1563, set out a summary for the queen when she dared propose cutting his expenses. A furious defence of his record followed: he had secured, Gresham argued, £830,000 of credit for Elizabeth – somewhere between £3 billion and £7.5 billion in today's values, and £70,000 more than for Edward and Mary combined – on some twenty-four journeys, often 'in great danger of my life with drowning… and beside this my leg was broken in Her Majesties service whereby I am become lame'. One has to admire his record-keeping: three versions of this letter are lodged in the State Papers, including a personal note to the queen.

In his final years, Gresham feted and financed Elizabeth's Protestant allies during their sojourns in London. He built great houses fit to entertain the queen. Intwood House in Norfolk remained in the family, although a family legend suggested that Lady Gresham found it very dull. He ran his great house on Bishopsgate in the City of London along with Mayfield in Sussex and Osterley Park in Kent, where, on her progress in 1576, Queen Elizabeth came to stay. Finding fault in one quarter of the building, which she judged would appear 'more handsome' with a wall in the middle, the queen woke up the next day to find Gresham's workmen had completed the job. He provided for Gresham College, which was founded posthumously in 1597 in his Bishopsgate mansion. In short order it became London's greatest place of study and later the meeting place for the foundation of the Royal Society.

Sir Thomas Gresham breathed his last on Saturday, 21 November 1579. Somewhere between six and seven o'clock in the evening, he had returned home to Bishopsgate from the Royal Exchange, just round the corner. Suddenly, in his kitchen, he fell down and 'being taken up, was found speechless, and presently dead'. The richest man in Elizabethan England had died of a heart attack.

Eighteen days later he was buried in St Helen's Church, 200 yards from his home. Two hundred of the City's poorest walked in black gowns in procession, in an affair so grand it cost twice as much as burying an earl. There today, Sir Thomas lies in the tomb he built, surrounded by the friends with whom he lived and worked, under the stained-glass window that bears the Gresham coat of arms, complete with the family grasshopper.

*

Between the birth of William de la Pole and the death of Thomas Gresham, England's entrepreneurs carved their foundations into the country. Over those 300 years, the population had fallen by more than half a million people, to a little over 4 million souls.[63] The economy, growing slowly, had expanded by perhaps a half. By Gresham's day, power in the land remained indisputably in the hands of the sovereign along with perhaps as few as sixty great noble families, the new leaders of what had been an armigerous class of some 3,000 in the days of Pole.[64] But within these limits, the entrepreneurial classes had now multiplied to become a powerful group, several hundred strong.

The greatest of them, such as Pole, Whittington and Gresham, mastered the greatest trade – textiles – served the greatest customer, the monarch, and supplied the greatest enterprise: war. But around them was a new class of trader: wealthy enough to juggle credit, including credit to the Crown; well-organized enough to join companies that were powerful enough to venture to the known corners of the earth; and well enough connected in Parliament and the court to argue their case for privileges. They were now masters of their nation's trade – perhaps just 5 per cent of the nation's cloth exports were in the hands of foreigners by 1600 – and some of them were now very wealthy men; in 1606, just 219 Merchant Adventurers divided cloth exports worth £800,000 between them, equivalent to between £2 billion and £5 billion in today's money.[65] Over the generations to come, the ambition, wealth and ingenuity of this new enterprise class would help make history by creating new futures; and they would start by building companies to encircle the world.

2

ROBERT RICH

Atlanticist, colonialist, pirate

I n the stormy weather of Thursday, 3 July 1642, in a patch of sea off the coast of Kent, between Deal and the Goodwin Sands, four of the king's battleships were surrounded. It was the eve of the English Civil War, and trapped aboard the *Rainbow*, an 800-tonne middling warship, the 'honest, stout, generous and religious' Rear Admiral John Mennes was weighing a dilemma. For nearly twenty years, dissension between king and Parliament had doubled and redoubled. And the tension was about to snap.

The previous day had proved a day of chaos. King Charles I had issued royal orders sacking his Lord High Admiral, the Earl of Northumberland, and commanding Robert Rich, 2nd Earl of Warwick, to 'relinquish the command you have, or pretend to have, in any of Our ships of our fleet, and forthwith to leave our ship the *James*'. But, catching wind of the king's orders, Parliament had boldly countermanded them and authorized Warwick 'to do all other acts in as ample manner as any Admiral hath formerly done'.[1]

Famous as a Puritan with the most 'unpuritanical' of manners, Warwick had immediately convened a council of war – and proposed to follow Parliament, 'the great council by whose authority the Kings of England have ever spoken to their subjects'. His captains had all 'unanimously and cheerfully' agreed – except for Mennes and five of his followers. Fast losing patience, Warwick summoned Mennes, who once more refused to yield. 'I have this day received a warrant from His Majesty,' Mennes pleaded, adding that 'His Majesty expressly commands me... not to obey your commands... How destructive this may prove to me, I leave the world to judge.'[2]

Over the night that followed, Mennes' comrade-in-arms, Captain Burley – commander of the *Antelope* – threw in his hand, and as dawn broke on Thursday, 3 July, Warwick acted: he ordered his ships to weigh anchor and surround the four skippers still holding out. Mennes could stand it no more. Along with Captain Fogg, he surrendered. Only captains Slingsby and Wake now remained defiant. But Warwick knew precisely what to do. I 'let fly a gun over them', he wrote, 'and sent them word that I had turned up the glass upon them; if in that space they came not in, they must look for me to aboard them'.[3] The boarding boats were readied, whereupon 'my masters and sailors grew so impatient', said Warwick, 'that although they had no arms in their boats at all… as in a moment they entered them… seized upon the captains being armed with their pistols and swords and struck their yards and topmasts and brought them both to me. The like courage and resolution was never seen amongst unarmed men.'[4]

In the name of Parliament, the Earl of Warwick, England's greatest pirate and colonial entrepreneur, had seized control of the king's navy. For years, his ships had harassed the Spanish foe; within a decade, he would help steer England's strategy in war with the Dutch in a battle to help build the world's pre-eminent enterprise power.

*

Robert Rich was heir to an income of £15,000 a year and great estates. Possessed of good looks, jollity, wit and blood ties to a great deal of aristocratic England, his family had won wealth from some notorious royal service, and with that wealth had gained some illustrious relations.

The family fortunes were laid by Rich's great-grandfather, the first Lord Rich. Born into a mercer's family in the City of London, Richard Rich was a dicer and gamester and, sent to train as a lawyer, proved quick-witted enough to win royal office with Henry VIII, first as Attorney General of Wales and then England's Solicitor General. His evidence proved decisive in convicting Sir Thomas Moore, who had refused to swear loyalty to Henry VIII as head of the English Church.

At the trial, it was Rich's evidence of a private conversation that proved the turning point; Moore did not spare Rich in his valedictory. And yet Rich's rise seemed unstoppable.

As the 'lesser hammer', he was a loyal partner to Henry's chief minister, Thomas Cromwell. Elevated to the position of Speaker of the House of Commons in 1536, he helped steer through the enabling laws of the English Reformation. He became lord chancellor under Henry's son, Edward VI, until, with perfect timing, he retired to spend sixteen peaceful years at Leez Priory, a beautiful Augustan priory lying in ancient undulating parkland in northern Essex, seven miles due north of Chelmsford. He died in 1567 and was buried in Felsted church, 'where the recumbent figure of the chancellor is most characteristic. The small head and keen features mark the skill of the lawyer and the wariness of the statesman.'[5]

Richard's son did little to advance the family's fortunes, though he was employed by Queen Elizabeth on diplomatic missions; but Richard's grandson Robert (1559–1619) was quite a different man, famous for his wealth and his wife. He was, said a contemporary, 'rough and uncourtly in manners and conversation, dull and uneducated, proper in nothing but his wealth',[6] which would extend beyond Leez Priory to nearly a hundred Essex manors. He acquired in 1618, from King James I, the Earldom of Warwick (a county to which he lacked any connection), but, equipped with an illustrious title once worn by the Beauchamps, Nevilles, Plantagenets and Dudleys, he cemented an alliance with the House of Essex through marriage to the Earl of Essex's daughter, Lady Penelope Devereux.

Penelope was one of the most beautiful women in England. She was, wrote the Duke of Manchester, a woman liked and admired by everyone, 'witty and satirical, high in spirits as in blood, a good hater and an ardent friend. In the midst of her errors she was never heartless.'[7] Lady Penelope was in love with the poet Philip Sidney, who immortalized her as 'Stella' and who wrote passionately of her for the rest of his life; but her guardians decided that 'the rich Lord Rich' was the better husband. It was not a marriage blessed with happiness, but it was blessed with children, including their eldest son, also named Robert, born in 1587.

Young Robert grew up in the shadow of Elizabeth's wars with Catholic Spain, in a rebellious, Puritan family in the most exquisite of surroundings. Leez Priory was one of the finest homes in England, a 'fragment of Hampton Court palace married to an old grey farm'.[8] Its park was both ancient and admired. Morant, the historian of Essex, wrote that 'here was a park even from the ancientest times first licensed by King John for the prior of Leez and extending to 1,300 acres stocked with both woods and deer'. A huge rich red-brick gatehouse greeted visitors, etched with the Rich arms and the motto 'Garder Tafoy', beyond which lay the mansion formed in the ruins of the priory. Robert Rich junior, said a family friend, 'had good reason to make sure of heaven; he would be a great loser in changing so charming a place for hell'.[9] It was, wrote his daughter-in-law in the 1640s, 'a secular Elysium… a worldly paradise, a heaven upon earth'.[10] Yet it was also a stage for a turbulent childhood.

When Robert was eight years old, his mother left to take up with the 8th Baron Mountjoy, Charles Blount, a man renowned for his looks, his scholarship, his oratory and his courage.[*] When Robert was fourteen, his uncle – Robert Devereux, 2nd Earl of Essex and self-appointed champion of 'strong Protestantism' – failed in his coup against the queen's 'basely born evil councillors' and became the last person beheaded at the Tower of London. Robert was superbly educated. At Rochford Hall, bought from the Boleyn family in 1550, Robert would listen on the long winter nights to radical local preachers such as Samuel Purchas, who had become one of the country's pre-eminent promoters of England's colonial expansion.[11] After a schooling at Eton College, Robert was dispatched around June 1603, aged sixteen, to complete his education at Emmanuel College in Cambridge, a place already well established as the closest thing to a finishing school for Puritan ministers destined for the Anglican Church. After a tour of Europe, where he acquired a good command of French, he was betrothed in secret, on 26 February 1605, to the fourteen-year-old heiress Frances Hatton. She was sole heiress to Sir Francis Gawdy and

---

* Philip Sidney died in August 1589. Penelope would bear a total of ten children by both Rich and Blount.

the immense Norfolk estates amassed by the late lord chancellor, Sir Christopher Hatton, worth some £2,200 a year. Shortly thereafter, Robert Rich was admitted to the Inner Temple to study law.

Wealthy, winsome, well-married and with wide horizons, Robert Rich was soon an adornment to the new court of King James. The young man's brownness, wrote Arthur Wilson, was 'accounted a lovely sweetness and transcending most men the other features and pleasant aspect equal the most beautiful women'. His manners were as fine as his looks. He was 'a man of a pleasant and companionable wit and conversation', noted the Duke of Clarendon, 'of an universal jollity'.[12] By the age of twenty-one, Rich and his brother Henry (b. 1590) were recorded taking part in tilting, festivities and theatricals, performing Ben Jonson's *Masque of Beauty* in 1608–09.

Rich's beauty and manners, however, masked a mettle and drive to make the very best of his inheritance. For Robert's father was not only a great landlord, but owner of the largest privateering fleet in England, complete with commercial partnerships in Middleburg and Amsterdam for the disposal of captured Spanish prizes.[13] With recourse to both sea-craft and cash, the young Robert Rich would never prove content with a mere life at court. He was soon taking aim at a fortune from 'sin-goods' and stealing as the country's greatest tobacco king and pirate captain. And he started by taking a stake in one of the most fashionable new corporations of Stuart England: the Virginia Company.

*

By the time King James took the throne in 1603, his subjects could be found on the waves of the Indian Ocean and the South China Seas and scattered across 3,000 miles of America's eastern seaboard, from the frozen harbours of Newfoundland to the flooded mouth of the Amazon. Their instinct for expansion was captured best by one extraordinary book: Hakluyt's *Principal Navigations, Voyages and Discoveries of the English Nation*. Inspired by his uncle's stories of foreign lands – of 'sea gulfs, bays, empires and territories of each part of the earth, their special commodities and particular wants'

– Hakluyt published three volumes of his handbook for sailors. It became a manual for adventurers and a manifesto for England's imperial ambition.

The English were, in fact, not early expansionists. The Spanish heirs to Colombus, the conquistadors de Soto and Cortés, had by the early sixteenth century already annihilated the ancient empires of Peru and Mexico, triggering the deaths of 18 million people from a toxic combination of what Jared Diamond has famously summarized as 'guns, germs and steel'.* The greatest business of the day, the mighty merchant guild, the Casa de la Contración, was already organizing an extraordinary river of silver. It travelled from the jungle mines to the port of Nombre de Dios, on the coast of modern Panama, across the Atlantic in the annual convoy, the *flota*, to the quaysides of Seville. In Brazil, the Portuguese had succeeded in transplanting the system of slave-based plantations first pioneered off the coast of Africa, to spread sugar-growing across the Cape Verde and Biafran islands.

So, while Hakluyt might have *boasted* that the English 'in compassing the vast globe of the earth more than once, have excelled all the nations and people of the earth', the truth was rather different.[14] Despite the intrepid voyages of exploration – John Cabot to North America in 1497, Sir Hugh Willoughby's quest for the north-east passage to the Orient in 1553, and Frobisher's search for a north-west passage in 1576 – English *colony building* had proved impossible.[†] And so England's merchants had embarked on founding companies instead, not to finance settlements and colonies but to bankroll cargoes and ships – and piracy.

The greatest English company of all remained the Merchant Adventurers. The £500,000 generated by the Adventurers in 1553, for instance (worth anywhere between £2 billion and £6 billion today), was many times larger than the £6,000 raised to finance Willoughby's voyage that year. But over the course of Elizabeth I's reign, companies devoted to finding direct new routes and new trade, both to the east

---

* This was also the title of Diamond's book, *Guns, Germs and Steel*, published by Vintage in 1998.

† John Cabot was in fact Italian, named Giovanni Cabotto, but had sailed under English royal commission.

and the west, began to multiply, grow and profit. For instance, when Portugal's hegemony in North Africa collapsed, English traders quickly organized their first voyage to Morocco (in 1551), followed two years later by the creation of the Company of Merchant Adventurers to New Lands to finance the search for a north-east passage to China. This in turn inspired the creation of the Muscovy Company in 1555, which forged an overland link to Persia, via Russia, in search of silks and spices. Twenty-two of these merchants together forged a core of the forty-four shareholders who founded the Guinea Company.

The Spanish Company followed in 1573, the East Land Company in 1579, and seven years later the Spanish Company joined the Muscovy Company to create the Turkey Company aimed at revolutionizing Mediterranean trade with a direct route to Constantinople, the ancient nexus at the end of the Silk Road. The Venice Company followed in 1583, dominated by Spanish Company merchants, and a decade later, in 1592, the Venice and Turkey companies joined forces to create the Levant Company. This, in turn, was to lay the foundations, in 1600, for the greatest English company of all: the East India Company.

It was a company-building revolution, which helped transform the size of England's economy after the centuries of decline that had followed the Black Death in 1348–50. Between the 1550s and the 1600s, the economy's output surged by almost half, to £38.5 million, finally outstripping the level of output last seen in the 1300s.[15] It was a rate of annual growth not seen again until the 1760s.[16] The average person finally began to grow richer, as wealth per head started to rise, almost imperceptibly by (0.2 per cent) a year, again after centuries of decline.[17] Industry, too, was growing – to now over a third of the economy.

The company-builders were closely connected in a small web of family links. Commercial connections, credit and intellectual capital tended to stay in the family. Indeed, nearly half of all active Levant Company traders had fathers or fathers-in-law or brothers already engaged in the trade, and even by the 1630s the great core of the Levant Company could trace their family connections back to the company's founders.[18] By 1604, while as many as 6,000 people were 'free' to trade as members of the great trading companies, real control lay in the hands of just 200 of the wealthiest.* Among these, the young Robert Rich was about to take his place as one of the 500 investors in the Virginia Company.

*

The Virginia Company was different. Indeed, it was practically unique in corporate England, because it *was* a company created to build a colony across the Atlantic, as it happened, a colony christened in calamity.

It had taken England some four decades to found. In 1561, Elizabeth's chief minister, Sir William Cecil, concluded that Spain and Portugal's self-interested division of the world, sealed in the Treaty of Tordesillas, was baseless,† and so English explorers were sanctioned to sail forth. It took another sevente₁n years, however, before Sir Humphrey Gilbert secured letters patent authorizing him to 'discover and occupy' American lands 'not possessed by any Christian prince'. He eventually made it to Newfoundland, which he claimed for the Crown, only to subsequently sink with his ship, the *Squirrel*. He was last seen reading Thomas More's *Utopia* on deck as the vessel plunged beneath the waves.

Gilbert's half-brother, Walter Raleigh, proved luckier. A Devon man who 'spake broad Devonshire until his dying day', Raleigh was tall, handsome, bold, 'damnably proud' and penniless. He had seen war in France and Ireland and the inside of prison for 'affrays' at least twice. He secured Gilbert's patents, and invested in a voyage to cross the Atlantic. Raleigh drew into Roanoke Island, near the Carolina Banks, on 13 July 1584, to claim it for Queen Elizabeth. For six weeks his crew admired 'the sweet and aromatic air', hunted, and met and traded with the Indians, enticing two of them – named Manteo and Wanchese – back to England. By December 1584, Raleigh was home again, elected to Parliament and calling, from the floor of the House of

---

* This was the conclusion of a 1604 House of Commons committee considering a bill for free trade.

† The treaty divided the known (and unknown) New World between Spain and Portugal along the meridian 370 leagues west of the Cape Verde islands.

Commons, for a colony to be established. Knighted by a delighted queen on 6 January 1585, Raleigh was permitted to name his lands 'Virginia' in her honour – whereafter it was all downhill. His first settlement at Roanoke – of soldiers and adventurers – was distracted in attacking passing Spanish treasure ships. Reinforcements dispatched in 1587, under John White, were attacked by Indians, and a relief fleet was fatally delayed to preserve English strength against the Spanish Armada. When White eventually arrived at Roanoke on 17 August 1590, he found a lifeless ruin. 'We let fall our grapnel near the shore,' wrote White in his journal, 'and sounded with a trumpet and call, and afterward many familiar English tunes and songs, and called to them friendly. But we had no answer.'[19]

With James I's accession to the throne and a new peace with Spain, came a fresh attempt at a colony. Backed by a great slice of the court and corporate London – including the lord chief justice, the Lieutenant of the Tower, the solicitor general and the Recorder of the City of London – two companies of Virginia adventurers, in London and Plymouth, were chartered in 1606 with a gigantic ambit: nothing less than the 'coast of Virginia or America', from the mouth of the Cape Fear river in North Carolina to a point halfway up the coast of Maine. The Plymouth Company failed to survive the winter. But the 105 settlers of the London venture – the Virginia Company – pushed into Chesapeake Bay, a little south of today's Washington, DC, on 6 May 1607, and 40 miles up the Powhatan river they founded Jamestown. The town's survival through the tough winter made the settlement and its leader, Captain John Smith, famous throughout London.

By 1609, the capital's broadsheets and clerics were trumpeting the opportunities for emigrants. In February, a wider charter of land arrived and a new joint stock fund opened at £12 10s a share. Fifty London companies and 500 'adventurers' signed up to the reorganized Virginia Company, including the Earl of Southampton, the Lord Mayor of London – and the young Robert Rich, listed on 23 May as one of the shareholders. The following year he was, at the behest of his father, elected to Parliament as the Member for Maldon; but it would prove his adventures abroad that would mark him out as one of the country's greatest colonial entrepreneurs. And they rested on a turn of fate.

*

On 2 June 1609, the eight ships of the 'Third Supply' relief sailed out from Plymouth to relieve the Virginia colony led by Sir George Somers, packed with livestock and 600 new settlers. It ran headlong into a terrible hurricane. 'All that I had ever suffered gathered together,' wrote one passenger, William Strachey, 'might not hold comparison with' the storm.[20] But, driven ashore in Bermuda, the voyagers discovered that an island once considered 'the most dangerous, unfortunate, and more forlorn place in the world' was 'in truth the richest, healthfullest, and pleasing land... as ever man set foot upon.'[21] It would soon inspire Shakespeare's *The Tempest*; indeed, it proved so pleasant that it was hard to persuade Somers' sailors to leave for Virginia which was felt to be, by contrast, cold, chancy and hard to cultivate.

Inspired by Somers' reports, a group of Virginia Company shareholders – including Rich – decided in 1611 to invest £2,000 to plant a Bermudan colony, and the following year, the colony's first governor, Richard Moore, sailed with sixty souls to establish the first base in what were christened the Somers Isles. They were the first of 600 settlers to land between 1612 and 1615[22] encompassing 'all sorts of artisans and their wives', 'gentlemen and men of fashion', as well as Robert Rich's cousin, also christened Robert Rich (brother to Nathaniel Rich), who would take the lead in building the family's first colonial business – as tobacco barons.

Governor Moore worked hard to build up the island's infrastructure, experimenting with potatoes, corn, wheat and sugar cane. But Spanish tobacco, or 'pudding' tobacco, which was first sent to England in a 170-pound cargo in January 1614, would prove the real moneymaker. Although smoking was definitely an acquired taste – James I went to the length of penning a book attacking the habit, which he excoriated as 'loathsome to the eye, hateful to the nose, harmful to the brain [and] dangerous to the lungs'[23] – tobacco was soon lucrative. Indeed, at the height of the tobacco rush in 1617, tobacco sold for 3 shillings a pound. A 25-acre plot might yield £75 (roughly between £188,000 and £416,000 in today's money), which even after levies and customs was three times what a labourer might earn in England.[24]

Over the next decade, Bermuda became far and away the biggest tobacco exporter, sending 615,000 pounds of the stuff – some 25 per cent more than the Virginia colony[25] and valued at £62,000, twice the price of Virginian exports.* The Rich family was soon among the biggest of the Bermuda tobacco barons. In 1614, the Somers Isles shareholders bought out the Virginia Company's interest, and two years later the island was divided in eight areas or 'tribes' of 1,250 acres, of which Rich and his cousin, Nathaniel, took the biggest share, controlling between them 900 acres (36 shares)[26] in four 'tribes'.[27]

Tobacco growing was, however, not easy. 'So fickle and dangerous a nature is this tobacco', wrote one settler 'that one hour's neglect or the least want of help may spoil a whole year's crop.'[28] Rich therefore took a healthy interest in supplying the things his tenants needed to prosper, as one tenant, Lewis Hughes, explained in 1617. After thanking Rich for the barrels of biscuit and cheese and remarking on the prospects for catching whales, Hughes wrote: 'Your men have been upon uncertainties till now, so as they had no heart to build or plant… There are other hopes of profits to be raised in time, if the rest of the Adventurers would follow your good example in supplying the poor people with necessaries.'[29]

Rich was clearly involved in supplying not only goods and provisions to the colony, but also slaves shipped from Africa, for which there was some competition among tenants; as one tenant wrote to Rich in 1620, 'Your Lordship's people are much discontented because they have not, as others, servants sent them; 3 or 2 apprentices at the least to every master of a family would give them great encouragement.'[30] In 1618, both Rich and his father were among the thirty-eight shareholders who founded the African Company, a business with the exclusive

---

* The good times were not to last. By the 1620s, the tobacco depression hit the island hard, and by the 1630s soil exhaustion had dramatically cut yields and forced diversification into a range of new crops. And, in time, Bermudians could never hope to match the size of the estates – and fortunes – of the Virginians, who by the 1630s were exporting 1 million pounds in weight of the stuff.

rights to Guinea and Benin – which at the time constituted the whole of the then explored West African coast importing ivory, spices and hides. Although the company failed within three years, it probably helped source slaves for the Rich plantations.

Yet, Rich's interest in Bermuda was not confined to slaves and tobacco. For, as heir to one of the greatest privateering fleets in England, Rich had quickly spotted that the island was a perfect base not only for a pastoral business – but also for a piracy business, stealing from the Spanish and the Portuguese in a tradition now well established by generations of England's corporate elite. Rich was about to prove himself a master of both the broadside and the balance sheet.

*

England's 'corporate pirates' boasted a long history and a long tradition of royal support. Perhaps inspired by the French Huguenots and the Scots, who began attacking the Spanish in the West Indies in the 1520s, Henry VIII had issued a proclamation in December 1544, authorizing his subjects to wage unrestricted naval warfare without legal safeguards. Prizes soon followed. On 1 March 1545, a wealthy Southampton merchant, Robert Reneger, took the Spanish *San Salvador* together with its treasure of 20,000 ducats. Under Edward VI, sailors such as Thomas Winderman and William Hawkins plundered freely from the eastern Atlantic to West Africa; but it was Elizabeth I who proved the pirate's greatest royal friend, licensing attacks with 'letters of reprisal', or 'letters of marque', and issuing a general promulgation permitting privateering in 1563.

Elizabeth's finest pirates were soon among her most senior servants. Sir Walter Raleigh, Vice-Admiral of Devon, was a very active pirate, while the Captain of the Isle of Wight turned the island into an important base for pirates in the English Channel. None, however, was

---

* Technically, these were licences that authorized those who had suffered from foreign piracy, and who had failed to secure any kind of redress in a foreign court, to attack back. In principle, a claimant was supposed to limit their score-settling to the actual value of their losses. In practice, the distinction was impossible to enforce.

greater than Sir Francis Drake, whose extraordinary adventures 'inflamed the whole country with the desire to adventure unto the seas'.[31]

In 1573, Drake captured a Spanish mule train in Panama, which was transporting silver. He arrived home in Plymouth on Sunday, 9 August, in time for the Sunday sermon, and acquired instant fame. When he sailed again, four years later, aboard the *Pelican*, England's leaders – such as Secretary Sir Francis Walsingham, the future lord chancellor, Sir Christopher Hatton, and the earls of Leicester and of Lincoln – were among his backers. In an extraordinary voyage, Drake became just the second European to pass through the Magellan Straits and into the Pacific, where, sailing north, he 'found by the seaside,' as he wrote, 'a Spaniard lying asleep who had lying by him 13 bars of silver which weighed 4,000 duckets Spanish; we took the silver and left the man'.[32] Up the coast of Ecuador, Drake hit the jackpot; Spanish ships loaded with twenty-six tonnes of silver. Drake stole the lot, and eluding all pursuit he crossed the Pacific, stopping in the Moluccas to pick up a cargo of spices. In September 1580, Drake sailed back into Plymouth, having completed the second-ever circumnavigation of the world. Officially, his cargo was valued at £307,000. In reality it was worth nearly twice that. The queen's share alone was worth £300,000 – more than her entire annual income. She was able to repay her entire foreign debt and still have £42,000 left over to invest in the Levant Company.

Inspired, the nation's merchants began buying into piracy, transforming English naval power. In 1582, England boasted twenty merchant ships above 200 tonnes. Over the following fifteen years, more than another seventy were built. By 1600, the merchant fleet was twenty times bigger than the queen's navy.[33] During the years of war with Spain, an estimated 150 English privateering voyages were launched, and soon the prizes landed were worth between £100,000 and £200,000 a year – the equivalent of 10–15 per cent of the nation's imports.* Occasionally, individual prizes were extraordinary. In 1592,

---

* English captains and merchants – such as John Watts, Captain Christopher Newport, Sir Anthony Shirley and William Parker – could all boast major victories and profits.

Raleigh and Charles Howard – Earl of Nottingham and Elizabeth's Lord High Admiral – captured a huge Portuguese carrack with a cargo worth nearly £250,000.[34] This earned the queen £80,000 from just selling the pepper alone.

By the time King James struck peace with Spain, English piracy was irresistible and unstoppable. Despite James's Piracy Commission of 1608, the years between 1608 and 1614 proved to be the heyday of English (and Dutch) piracy across the North Atlantic, from Iceland to the Canary Islands, from the Newfoundland banks to the English Channel.

*

For many men, privateering fortunes became their equity in business building. In the late 1580s and 1590s, for instance, Levant Company leaders made fortunes stealing sugar from Portuguese ships sailing home from Brazil. The voyage of the *Amity* to the Barbary Coast in 1592 is a good example. The *Amity* was a powerful ship, capable of firing a devastating broadside, according to Hakluyt. In a fierce engagement with two Spanish ships, she returned with prizes totalling 1,400 chests of quicksilver and 100 tonnes of excellent wine, all worth more than £20,000. The voyage's backers were four members of the Guild of Grocers – Henry Calthurst, Simon Lawrence, Oliver Style and Nicholas Style – and both of the Styles went on to become active members of the East India Company. Those at the top led by example; thus James Watts, described by the Spanish ambassador, Pedro de Zuniga, as 'the greatest pirate that there has been in this kingdom', was a member of the Spanish, Levant, Virginia and East India companies – and in 1607 Lord Mayor of London to boot. But of all Elizabeth's pirates, few were greater than the Riches and their relations. Robert's father and the Earl of Essex, for example, financed the ships that attacked Cadiz in 1596, bringing home two new Spanish warships, 1,200 pieces of ordnance, booty worth 20 million ducats, and the Bishop of Faeroe's library, which was donated to form the Bodleian in Oxford.

With his investments in Bermuda beginning to flourish, the younger Robert Rich now set out to master the business that had served the family so well. At the age of twenty-five, Rich was prominent enough at court to be asked to join Sir Henry Wotton's elaborate embassy to Turin to negotiate a royal marriage treaty with the Duke of Savoy. He would prove something of a star. The Venetian ambassador was moved to commend both Robert's wealth and manners. After a fortnight of entertainment in great style, with feasts, hunts and dances, Rich was the personal guest at dinner with the duke, after which followed a long private conference and – upon Rich's departure – a present valued at 1,000 crowns. Rich's visit to the Duke of Savoy was, however, more than just diplomacy. It was business. The duke wanted allies on the seas, while England's peace with Spain meant the Rich family needed legal cover for their privateering, and a port in which to sell their prizes. In 1616, Rich's father dispatched three ships, unknown to James I, with a commission from Savoy to attack the Spanish, including two ships sent to the West Indies on a two-year plundering spree.*

With his burgeoning business experience, Robert Rich was soon ready for a mission of his own. In 1618, together with a London-based Genoese merchant, Philip Barnadi, and equipped with more privateering commissions from the Duke of Savoy and the Duke of Florence, Rich's little fleet set sail for the Red Sea – and a diplomatic disaster. Intercepting a cargo worth £100,000, destined for the queen mother of India's Great Mogul, Rich's ships prepared to attack – only to be halted by the chance arrival of the transport's East India Company escorts. The company's shareholders were furious: 'I praise God with all my heart that we lighted so on them,' wrote the fleet's commander, Captain Pring, to his superiors, 'for if they had taken the junk and known to be English… all your goods in this country (of India) could not have made satisfaction.'[35] Sir Thomas Roe, ambassador at the Mogul's court, declared 'I know Sir Robert Rich well' and ordered the seizure of his prizes and goods.[36] Both the Turkey and East India companies presented petitions to the Privy Council arguing that Rich had sought the foreign protection of Savoy, 'to the dishonour of His Majesty's prejudice of their country and great danger of both these companies'.

---

* Relations between Savoy and Spain had broken down in 1614 over the disputed succession to Montferrat, in northern Italy.

Rich, however, was not about to take this lying down. He quickly filed suit in the Admiralty Court for the recovery of damages, and a decade-long court case now ensued. It was to prove, however, merely the warm-up for his combat with the colossus of trading London, Sir Thomas Smythe, in the first great corporate battle of Stuart England.

*

Sir Thomas Smythe was the leading light in a new generation of City entrepreneurs, who made their fortunes, not from the old City companies or the Merchant Adventurers, but from the new exploring companies. The eldest of the thirteen children born to Thomas 'Customer' Smythe, a Kent trader who built a fortune farming the customs revenue for Queen Elizabeth, Smythe became governor of the East India Company, a post he held for twenty years, and chairman of the Virginia Company.

Smythe's leadership of the Virginia Company, however, was under pressure. While Bermuda was flourishing, the Virginian colonies were not. John Rolfe had perfected a sweeter strain of Virginian tobacco in 1613, which he had brought back to London, together with his new wife, Pocahontas – who proved the greater sensation – but the crop was hard to commercialize. Facing cash shortages, the Virginia Company had been forced to invent the 'headright' system, granting fifty acres to anyone who sailed for the colony and who met his own costs. Soon, pamphleteers waxed lyrical of a land offering the 'abundance of mulberries, minerals, rubies, pearls, gems, grapes, deer, fowls, drugs for physic, herbs for food, roots for colours, ashes for soap, timber for building, pastures for feeding, rivers for fishing and whatsoever commodity England wanteth'.[37]

The company's investors, giving up on early profits, decided to build a monopoly – the 'Magazine' – dominated by Smythe's East India Company associates. It was to supply the colonists, while exporting their tobacco, but it neglected the colony's wider development. Many Virginia shareholders were unclear how much of the proceeds from the Magazine's sales was going into the company's coffers and how much was going into Smythe's pockets; worse, the company was now £8,000 in the red. The Magazine's directors appeared reluctant to invest in anything other than the Magazine, and as one shareholder, Robert Cushman, put it, 'The main hindrance of our proceedings... is the dissentions and factions as they term it among the Council and Company of Virginia; which are such as that ever since we came up no business could by them be dispatched.'[38]

Three unhappy investors – Sir Edwin Sandys, the Earl of Southampton and Sir John Danvers – promptly decided to appoint auditors to see what was going on, with disturbing results. 'It was found that many and great sums of money collected and brought in... were so expended and lost as a very small growth and improvement of that colony could there be any way discerned.'[39] It was a sentiment with which Rich agreed. 'The merchants', he said, 'who then swayed the courts affected nothing but their immediate gain, though with the poor planters extreme oppression as appeared by their Magazine'.[40]

Smythe was furious, and throughout 1617 and 1618 the argument intensified until Rich's piratical adventures took it to combustion point. Smythe's enmity with the Rich family ran deep. When Elizabeth I had issued warrants for the arrest of Rich's uncle, the Earl of Essex, it was the forty-year-old Smythe who had delivered the orders. In 1617, Smythe's ally Tucker, Governor of Bermuda, had the Rich family's agent – the younger cousin, Robert Rich – imprisoned. And just to round things off, Rich's sister Isabella secretly married Smythe's son, without Smythe's permission and in a match he strongly opposed. In 1618, another Smythe ally, the Governor of Virginia, refused Rich's ship, the *Treasurer*, permission to dock. It was full of Spanish booty and 'so weather-beaten and torn, as never like to put to sea again'.[41]

Rich was now determined to act, combining with Sir Edwin Sandys at the annual meeting of the Virginia Company's shareholders to outvote the old chairman. Seeing the votes stacked against him, Smythe declared he was 'repining at his many offices and troubles wished the Company of Virginia to ease him of his office'.[42] Sandys was elected treasurer and in May, Rich's candidate, Nathaniel Butler, was selected for the governorship of Bermuda. Rich may have felt the Virginia Company and its Atlantic ports were now open to him. He certainly needed them. On the death of his father that year, the thirty-two-year-old Robert Rich, as eldest son, inherited not only the title of (2nd) Earl of Warwick and over a hundred Essex manors, but also his father's privateering fleets.

The new earl's alliance with Sandys was, though, about to become unstuck. Sandys quickly installed William Yeardley as the Virginia Company's governor who promptly began reporting Warwick's privateering, warning that the *Treasurer* 'had gone to rob the King of Spain's subjects by seeking pillage in the West Indies and that this was done by direction from my Lord of Warwick'.[43] Fearing poor relations with Spain, Sandys minuted the news not only to the Privy Council, which was his duty, but to the Spanish ambassador as well. Warwick was furious. Three years earlier, Sir Walter Raleigh had been executed for attacking Spanish ships. Now, as Warwick's cousin Nathaniel warned, Sandys's action would put the earl 'in the mercy of our own king' and 'under the clutches of the King of Spain which perhaps would not have been removed till he had crushed him to pieces'.[44]

Warwick realized that his only hope now lay in a new alliance with his old enemy Thomas Smythe. The uneasy pairing came together to persuade King James to bar Sandys's re-election and for the next two years, the factions fought for votes among the shareholders. Rich and his allies at first gained the upper hand – but when Sandys won election to the House of Commons, he began arguing for a new Crown monopoly, importing tobacco in exchange for fixed payments to the king, which would destroy the Rich plantations in Bermuda.* But, as the factional struggle grew bitter throughout 1623, fought out in the company's court and the House of Commons, news reached London of the terrible massacre of 350 Virginia colonists. The company had sent insufficient aid and a further 500 would perish before the year-end. King James was now petitioned for a full investigation into the Virginia Company's affairs. The Privy Council summoned the parties amid 'much heat and bitterness', and a special investigation was launched 'to examine the carriage of the whole business'.[45] 'The factions in these

---

* New taxes of one shilling per pound had been introduced on tobacco in early 1620, when the Virginia Company's seven-year exemption from import duties expired. They were a heavy burden on a product selling at between two shillings and five shillings a pound. See Craven, *The Virginia Company of London*, (Virginia 350th Anniversary Celebration Corporation, 1964), p. 53.

two Companies are grown so great,' noted one observer, 'as Guelfs and Gebellines, were not more animated one against another; and they seldom meet upon the Exchange, or in the streets, but they brabble and quarrel.'[46] On 20 May 1623, James decided to intervene directly in what was ostensibly a private company, issuing an order expressing his 'understanding of the great differences and distractions that have happened by means of divers turbulent persons', and making it clear, 'out of our special care to the good and the welfare of that Plantation', that Sandys and his faction were not to be re-elected.

*

Amid the chaos of the company's affairs, Warwick had one final gift to give: a North American home for the radical religionists known to history as the Pilgrim Fathers. After failing to secure a religious settlement with the Anglican Church, the Pilgrims had fled England in 1608 in search of freedom of worship. They headed to the Protestant Dutch province of Holland, settling first in Amsterdam and then Leiden. But, hungry for a home of their own, they set their sights on the Atlantic seaboard. Negotiations had begun with the Virginia Company in 1619, only to suffer continual delays. Almost uniquely among England's statesmen, Warwick (and his circle) had kept in touch with the group and were ambitious to find a solution.

Warwick had, at first, proposed a settlement in Guinea, around the mouth of the Amazon, where he and his father had invested in a tobacco colony (led by Warwick's cousin, Captain Roger North).[47] Amid a degree of confusion, the Pilgrims' ship, the *Mayflower*, finally sailed from Plymouth for Virginia, on 6 September 1620, landing wide of its mark up the coast in today's Massachusetts, on territory left 'as desperate and [our] business as abandoned' since the failure of the original Plymouth branch of the Virginia Company.[48] As it happened Sir Fernando Gorges, a descendant of an old Somerset family who originally fought alongside the 2nd Earl of Essex, was at the time seeking a new Crown patent for the land that he hoped would become a great feudal empire. Gorges' ambitions for various monopolies had provoked enough objections to require a Crown enquiry, and it was this 'powers gap' that required the new settlers to write some new terms of conduct, the Mayflower Compact, which was to become an early predecessor of the American constitution.

On 30 November, King James finally set his seal on the Charter for New England, to empower official efforts to colony-build between the 40th and 48th parallels* from the Delaware river to St Lawrence Bay. Thus was created 'for the better Plantation, ruling, and governing of the aforesaid New-England' a council of forty notables, prominent among whom was Warwick, who now lobbied for the Pilgrims' home.[49]

*

The old Virginia Company was now in its final days, and events would now crystallize Warwick's interests further north, in Massachusetts. In June 1623, the Council of New England, which had become a board of proprietors rather than a joint-stock company, with the power to issue patents and land grants of its own, agreed to divide up its land into twenty shares, distributed by lottery to the shareholders. On 29 June, in the presence of King James, Warwick was allocated share Number 7, the area around Massachusetts Bay. The same year, the Council issued patents to land to the puritans of the Dorchester Company,† who would in due course go on to found the Massachusetts Bay Company and help build modern Boston.[50]

It was good timing, for in the following month the Virginia Company entered its terminal stage. In July 1623, a furious row exploded at a board meeting of the Somers' Island Company. Sandys, it was said, 'fell foul of the Earl of Warwick'. Warwick openly accused Sandys of lying, and Sandys's ally, Lord Cavendish, responded in equally strong terms. A challenge to a duel was issued, and, barred

---

* The northern limit of the London branch of the Virginia Company had historically been set at the 41st parallel. The original Plymouth branch was patented to settle between 34 and 45 degrees north latitude.

† Created in 1623, the Dorchester company was not a puritan company, but a 'company of puritans'; its effort to build a fishing business off the New England coast largely failed, hence the migration of its shareholders to the new opportunities of Massachusetts.

from fighting on English soil, both Warwick and Cavendish departed London for Holland on 17 July. Hearing the news, the Privy Council promptly ordered a search of the ports. Cavendish was arrested by the Chichester sheriff, but Warwick escaped, crossing the Channel disguised as a fisherman, only to be discovered a month later by the English ambassador in Brussels, whereupon he was ordered home. In London, noted one observer, 'their ladies forget not their old familiarity, but meet daily to lament their misfortune'.

King James's investigation of the Virginia Company proved fatal. Sandys admitted that just 2,500 colonists remained. The company was bankrupt. In autumn 1623, it was invited to surrender its charter. When Sandys refused, *quo warranto* proceedings began in the Court of the King's Bench, and on 24 May 1624 the court recalled the charter. And so ended the Virginia Company.

A new commission for Virginia, packed with Warwick's and Smythe's supporters, was tasked with drawing together plans for another arrangement. But it would never finish its work. On 23 March 1625, at Theobalds House, James I breathed his last and his son Charles was proclaimed King of England.

*

The 2nd Earl of Warwick, now well established in his empire, was nearly forty when Charles I ascended the throne, and at first it appeared that the two might form a common cause in their shared enmity for Spain. Warwick had by now married again, having been widowed in 1623. His new wife, Susan Halliday, was a widow, too, and daughter of a one-time Lord Mayor of London. Charles, by contrast, was contemplating a failed alliance with the Spanish infanta, Maria; but the ignominious collapse in 1624 had left both Prince Charles and Parliament bitterly hostile to Spain and Hapsburg interests. When Charles became king, therefore, battle plans were well advanced, inspired by the tried and tested strategy of striking at Spanish strength by cutting off Spain's finance from the West Indies.

Charles quickly drew together a network of European alliances, arranged to buttress an Anglo-Dutch naval offensive against the

Spanish Caribbean fleet. They included an agreement with France, fastened tight with Charles's marriage to Henrietta Maria, the younger sister of French King Louis XIII. Optimism was high. As the old king's favourite George Villiers, Duke of Buckingham – blamed by many for inept diplomacy over Charles's marriage negotiations – explained to Parliament: 'If the king and the Low Countries joined they shall be the master of the sea, and Spain's monarchy will have to stop.'[51] But the first fights were a fiasco. Buckingham had been Lord High Admiral since 1619, and his attempt, in October 1625, to emulate the Earl of Essex's 1597 attack on Cadiz failed, amid complete disorder.* Parliament demanded Buckingham's impeachment, and Nathaniel Rich was among the MPs demanding the duke's head. To make matters worse, Charles's foreign policy and the *entente* with France soon required deployment of English ships in Cardinal Richelieu's efforts to subdue the Huguenot stronghold of La Rochelle – provoking great grief in English Protestant opinion.

The relationship between the king and Warwick was, at first, complicated. Charles needed both Warwick's pirate fleet and his defence of Essex. Warwick was appointed Lord Lieutenant of Essex (whereupon he fortified Harwich), and in 1626 was issued three letters of marque modelled on the licence Elizabeth I had issued to the Earl of Cumberland – in effect, *carte blanche* to prosecute a private war on the Iberian coast, which allowed Warwick to attack assets of the King of Spain or his allies, to press and levy as many men for sea and land as he needed, and to administer martial law. Unusually, Warwick was allowed to enjoy all and any plunder he captured – although this was later amended to provide at least a tenth for the Crown.

It was not long, however, before the division emerged between King Charles and Warwick that would help shape England's history. Warwick's friends, family and faction proposed a bold new attempt to take on Spain. Sir Dudley Digges and Sir Nathaniel Rich advanced a

---

* At Cadiz, English ships had lacked orders and the troops had landed without food, but soon found plenty to drink, whereupon some promptly started shooting each other. The English army was evacuated, but on the voyage home the fleet was scattered. Several ships almost sank, including the *Anne Royal*, which returned home with six feet of water in its hold.

fresh plan to create a private company – 'the most famous company in Christendom' – costing £200,000 per year, for four years, to pursue war in the Spanish Caribbean, using Bermuda as its privateering base. The king, though, had other designs. He wanted a royal war not a privateers' war. But, having suspended Parliament in July 1626, to scupper the impeachment moves against Buckingham, Charles lacked taxes. He was forced therefore to attempt a forced loan from his richer subjects, and it now fell to Warwick and his friends to lead the opposition in the nation's courtrooms and the nation's churches.

Charles's unpopular 'new churchmanship' – with its new physical layout of churches, new ceremonialism, and a repudiation of Calvinist belief in predestination – had already unsettled the puritans. Now, Charles was using sympathetic clergy to make the case for his great loan. And Warwick was determined to fight back.

Using his power of direct appointment to nineteen livings within his gift, Warwick had already begun to offer a safe haven to Calvinist ministers, who now found themselves falling foul of the king's reforms. His appointments in Essex included the great puritan Thomas Hooker, who became a lecturer in Chelmsford from 'where the light of his ministry shone through the whole country of Essex'. Warwick also protected Hugh Peter (sometimes called Peters), curate at Rayleigh in 1623–26, who then became a notable militant preacher in London of sermons opposing the forced loan and the Catholic queen. Soon, Warwick was known as 'the great patron and Maecenas to the pious and religious ministry', and his home at Leez became 'the common rendezvous of all schismatical preachers'.[52] Edmund Calamy, Jeremiah Burroughes, John Gauden (Warwick's chaplain), Obadiah Sedgwick and Calybute Downinge, all of whom became famous in the 1640s, found jobs in the pulpits of Rich's parishes.

In 1627, as military failures multiplied under Buckingham, who was now attempting to *relieve* the Huguenots in La Rochelle, political pressure grew. Buckingham was assassinated in 1628. Charles was forced to accept the Petition of Right, constraining arbitrary royal powers. In 1629 he was forced to call his second Parliament, but as arguments about religion and tax grew hot, the king's patience evaporated. When he attempted to suspend the sitting, MPs furiously voted for a motion branding anyone who introduced popery or paid illegal taxes as a traitor to the Commonwealth. The king promptly had the leaders of the debate incarcerated in the Tower of London, and the nation stepped decisively down the road to civil war.

*

Many now thought to flee – and it was Warwick who helped create for them a safe haven. A number of shareholders active in what was the failing Dorchester Company had formed, on 19 March 1628, the New England Company to create plantations in the Massachusetts Bay, around today's Boston.[53] The company's patent for land between the Charles and Merrimack rivers was granted by Warwick, in his role as President of the Council of New England – it was probably carved from land of his own in somewhat dubious circumstances, but nevertheless later confirmed by a royal charter issued on 4 March 1629,* which Warwick helped facilitate.

To these lands, Warwick now began aiding East Anglia's puritans to seek an escape. In 1630, John Winthrop (who as a boy had joined Warwick listening to tales of foreign adventure at Rochford Hall), Matthew Cradock and a hundred-strong group of London citizens and East Anglian puritan gentry were equipped with £2,000 from Warwick and his friends to set sail in one of the earl's ships, the *Warwick*, for lands controlled by the newly chartered Massachusetts Bay Company (created from the New England Company). Six ships and 350 people sailed in the first expedition, the first wave of the 20,000 English men and women who would follow them to this new puritan home. Settling first in Salem and then Charlestown, before moving to a commanding position where the Charles river meets the Massachusetts Bay, it was here they built modern Boston.

Warwick pondered joining the exodus himself – but not to New England; rather, to a new island that appeared perfect for both puritan settlement and piracy. Over a thousand miles to the south of New

---

* The charter was granted to the Governor and Company of the Massachusetts Bay in New England, in 1629.

England, three of Rich's ships – the *Earl of Warwick*, the *Somers Islands* and the *Robert* – had discovered, in 1628, Catalina, or Providence Island. Now called Providencia, and lying about 120 miles east of the Nicaraguan coast, its islands lay in a wide lagoon, surrounded by a massive coral reef, on the flanks of the Spanish galleon route from Central America to Cuba.

Praising both its 'pleasantness and rich fertility of the soil' and the islands' fortification, Rich's captain had recommended securing, in all possible secrecy, the patent to the islands 'before they be discovered which will be easily obtained and will take away all the claim and opposition of my lord of Carlisle or any other'.[54] Dispatching a rapid expedition to the islands, Rich quickly divided up the land, planted tobacco, built a fort and drummed up colonists in Bermuda and London.

In November 1629, Rich gathered an alliance of the leading puritan nobility, MPs and traders at Brook House, in London's Holborn, to found the Providence Company – more fully, the 'Company of Adventurers of the City of Westminster and the Plantation of the Islands of Providence or Catalina, Henrietta or Andrea and the Adjacent Islands Lying upon the Coast of America'. Its patent of December 1630 gave the company a reach over some 720,000 square miles, from the northern shore of Haiti to the isthmus of Darien, on the coast of today's Panama.

Quickly, £4,000 was raised from England's puritan elite.[*] John Pym, later to lead Parliament's rebellion against the king, was company treasurer. Rich's younger brother Henry, the Earl of Holland, became the company's governor, and in February 1631 ninety colonists set sail in the *Sea Flower*, armed with twenty pieces of ordnance. The voyage was terrible. The passengers were fed mouldy bread and sour beer, and the master, John Tanner – who owned a share in the ship – held back the rations for private sale when he reached the island.

Before the colonists even landed, the Providence Company's

---

* These included Sir Thomas Barington, Viscount Saye and Sele, Lord Brooke, Sir Benjamin Rudyerd, Sir Gilbert Gerard, Sir Edward Harwood, Richard Knightly, Sir Anthony Rouse, John Roo Bartais and a large number of East Anglian gentry.

shareholders back in London had annexed the neighbouring island of Association (modern-day Tortuga), just two miles from Haiti and a few miles from the opening of the Windward Passage. Known to the French as the Isle des Porceaux, on account of the free-roaming wild hogs, it was the perfect base from which to attack the Spanish *flota*.[55] The island had been offered to the company shareholders by an entrepreneurial captain, Anthony Hilton; by the end of May 1631, the company's leaders agreed to absorb it, and company subscribers stumped up the money for a first magazine of supplies, six pieces of ordnance and a supply of ammunitions. A second ship, the *Charity*, soon sailed for Providence loaded with 150 passengers from Essex, Devon, Warwickshire and Oxfordshire, and in July, settlers bound for Association sailed on the ship *Little Hopewell*.

Within two years, the Providence Company was expanding again. In spring 1633, the *Golden Falcon* was acquired, refitted under Warwick's personal direction and dispatched under his relation Captain Sussex Camock.* After disembarking a fresh batch of puritan emigrants on Providence and picking up some cannons, Camock made for the natural harbour near the mouth of the Cape river on Central America's Mosquito Coast, close to some villages of Mosquito Indians, where amid stiff attempts to control the private trade of the sailors – including fines for trading parrots and monkeys – he founded a successful trading post dealing largely in flax. Indeed, it did so well that Warwick spun the venture into a new company, the 'Company of Adventurers of the City of London for Trade upon the Coast and Islands of Diverse Parts of America' in March 1635, with a flax-trading monopoly.

By contrast, the Providence Company itself proved hard work. In 1634, puritan settlers were difficult to find. The *Long Robert* sailed from England in September 1634, with orders to round up Caribbean colonists for Providence, only to return from the islands the following June with a meagre cargo of tobacco and cotton, returning planters, and a ton of complaints. By 1635 investors had sunk in £120,000

---

* Sussex was brother to Captain Thomas Camock, who married Frances Rich, daughter of the second Lord Rich, and aunt to Warwick. See Newton, *Colonising Activities*, p. 141.

(between £285 million and £700 million in today's money) for little return, and the shareholders were reluctant to spend more.[56] And – as events would prove – the exposed Providence and Association islands, with a busy trade in piracy, invited Spanish attention. Frustrated, Rich now switched attention back north to New England and the lands south of Massachusetts.

*

In the years after the demise of the Virginia Company, Virginia itself had grown richer – and Massachusetts had begun to boom. The West Indies was still the biggest colonial base, boasting some 25,000 settlers in 1640; but the lands further north were now developing fast. In Virginia, the 'headright' system allowed settlers to pool their holdings and set up a business of 100,000 acres for just £6,000 down. In 1634, 175 men were trading tobacco; by 1640, there were more than 300 of them, tobacco exports to England topped a million pounds a year and 8,000 colonists had put down roots.[57] But Massachusetts was even bigger, home to some 20,000 people, now spreading out from the Massachusetts Bay to found Connecticut and Rhode Island.

With Caribbean settlement proving increasingly tough, Warwick and some of his closest associates began to explore how the verdant Connecticut river valley, 80 miles east of Boston, could now supplant Providence Island as the best base for a puritan community. In March 1632, Rich had transferred a large tract of land to a group led by Viscount Saye and Sele and Lord Brooke, and which included Rich's son,[58] and over the months that followed the 'Saybrook Company' developed its plans for a new colony and new government. On 7 July 1635, it commissioned John Winthrop junior to lead an expedition, equipped with £2,000, to sail from England to found the Saybrook colony, Connecticut, where the river flows into the Long Island Sound.

Warwick was quickly ensnared in fighting a ferocious rear-guard action with Sir Fernando Gorges, the man who had once fought along-side Warwick's uncle, the 2nd Earl of Essex, only to give evidence against him after the rebellion of 1601. Gorges' goal was to become the king's Governor General of New England; he challenged the grant issued by Warwick to the Massachusetts Bay Company in 1632, whipping up a campaign for a Privy Council investigation, which, in the event, found in favour of the Company. But Gorges had the case reopened, and, in a battle of wills, Warwick was required to surrender the Council of New England's great seal on 29 June 1635 and the company's meeting place was moved from Warwick House to Captain Mason's house in Fenchurch Street.

Warwick dragged his feet – two further requests for the seal were made over the next five months – but Gorges eventually took his place as Council president.* It mattered not. The puritan colonies of New England had now reached critical mass. Between 1630 and 1643, 200 ships ferried 20,000 men, women and children to New England alone. Over the 1640s, 100,000 more would emigrate from the country where the stage was now set for the greatest drama, in which Warwick and his friends set out to fight the kings of both Spain and England, to defend their colonies abroad and their property rights at home. Remarkably, they would win.

*

Like Warwick, Charles I knew that a secure defence against Spain and France required a bigger navy. Indeed, he had been fascinated by naval affairs since his father had encouraged his interest in reform of the fleet in the late 1610s. In 1631, Charles had demanded a full navy audit, undertaking personal inspections of dockyards, and clambering aboard ships to ask questions. Conscious of Spain's growing Baltic fleet and escalating French expenditure, Charles determined to restore the fortunes of his navy, rebuilding, reorganizing and reasserting a claim to a right of salute from any ship sailing in English seas.

Initiative, however, needed money, and lots of it. Determined to avoid summoning Parliament, Charles was soon short of cash and so began the enforcement of ancient rights, long in abeyance. In June

---

* The dispute eventually went to the court of King's Bench, and the Massachusetts Bay Company was required to surrender its charter in May 1637. See Bremer, *John Winthrop*, op. cit., p. 240.

1634, Charles ordered a wide-ranging review of sources of supply for the navy. Among the ideas presented was the 'ship money' scheme. Assessed on the maritime counties, it was notionally a levy in the form of ships, but it was designed so that rich citizens would contribute the cash instead. The first levy was published in October 1634, and the full force of the Privy Council was employed in securing the money. Local sheriffs were badgered for returns. Disputes over complicated ratings were tackled expeditiously. The king himself instituted regular Sunday-morning sessions of his Council, examining accounts, reviewing progress, interviewing officials in person.

The first of the vessels paid for with ship money set sail in a nineteen-strong fleet in 1635, by which point the Venetian ambassador was warning of rising tension in Charles's realm: 'the situation daily becomes worse and more embittered... unless it ends in some honourable composition there is manifest danger of it resulting in a troublesome rising'.[59] He was right. Other revenue-earning measures were coming into force. In early October 1634, Warwick was among those presented with huge new 'forest taxes', as the king renewed defunct forest laws, which threatened to hit wealthy landowners such as Warwick hard. Furious, Warwick insisted on his prerogative to 'enjoy with quietness the possessions of our ancestors, which had been out of the forest for three hundred and fifty years' and ordered a search of precedents in the archives in the Tower of London, at a personal cost of some £2,000.[60]

Warwick, however, was soon fighting on two fronts. In the Caribbean, the Spanish were using a respite in the war with France to evict the raiders on their West Indies' traffic.* In January 1635, Don Ruiz Fernandez de Fuenmayor launched a devastating surprise attack on the island of Association, murdering captives and razing the colony to the ground. Providence was next. On 2 July 1635, Spanish soldiers attempted landing only to meet a huge bombardment from Warwick fort. Under seven days' heavy musket fire the Spanish vessels slipped their cables and retreated.

---

* Spain and France had been at loggerheads in northern Italy over disputing claimants in the War of the Mantuan Succession (1628–31).

The battle changed everything for the Providence Company and its puritan shareholders. News of the victory reached England in the ship *Expectation*, in December 1635. Sir John Coke warned Charles over Christmas that 60,000 of his subjects were now scattered across the Caribbean, that the costs of running the island were £8,000 a year, and that 'this charge cannot be raised otherwise than by war or reprisal'. Charles, as it happened, was sympathetic. Charles's Council was considering alliance with France. And so verbal permission for reprisals against Spanish ships was given by the king,* who blessed the Providence shareholders – who had raised £10,000 to fight the Spanish – with licence to seize Spanish treasure as compensation for the losses sustained on Association island.

Three ships, the *Blessing*, the *Expectation* and the *Hopewell*, set sail from England in May 1636 and, after exchanging fire with Spanish frigates, launched their first attack in October 1636. Providence was reinforced in August 1636, and now became the most famous pirate base in the West Indies. Reporting from the Mosquito Coast in 1637, Sir Thomas Gage declared that 'the greatest fear that possessed Spaniards... was about the island Providence... whence they feared some English ships should come against them with great strengths. They cursed the English in it and called the island the den of thieves and pirates, wishing the King of Spain would take some course with it.'⁶¹ The prizes were now significant. In 1638, when Warwick's ship the *Providence* was itself attacked by pirates, its crew told the Admiralty Court that their cargo had been worth £30,000 (between £67 million and £150 million today), made up of 'great quantities of gold plates, monies, diamonds, pearls, jewels and other goods and commodities'.⁶²

Victory in the Caribbean was for Warwick perhaps a little consolation for his setbacks at home, for in his battle of wills with the king, he was losing. Charles had raised so much money from the ship money tax – it yielded £79,586 out of the predicted £80,069 – that he decided to extend it to inland counties in 1635. Warwick and his allies decided to fight the tax in court. Their defeat at the hands of the Crown's

---

* In the presence of Sir Henry Martin, a judge of the Admiralty Court. Martin is sometimes referred to as 'Marten'.

lawyers and judges, on St Valentine's Day 1637, now crystallized their opposition to their sovereign.

In January 1637, Warwick had stood before the king to argue passionately for the recall of Parliament, the repeal of ship money and for war with Spain. He was, noted Anzolo Correr, the Venetian ambassador, speaking 'practically [as] the chief' of his followers. The King, 'smiling and composed', politely refused the requests. Meeting at Lord Saye and Sele's house in the country, at Broughton, the shareholders of the Providence Company were now no longer acting as a commercial company – but as a political force. 'The malcontents used to meet,' wrote Anthony Awood, 'and what embryos were conceived in the country were shaped in Grays Inn Lane, near London where the undertakers for the Isle of Providence did meet.'[63]

'The malcontents' at first contemplated exit. On 31 January 1638, Lord Saye and Sele announced that he would emigrate. A fortnight later, Warwick, together with Lord Brooke and Henry Darley, announced they too would follow, and on 9 April 1638 Warwick acquired from the Earl of Pembroke all rights to the islands of Tobago, St Bernard and Barbados, collectively known as the province of Montgomery. It was now that events in Scotland suddenly changed everything.

Rebellion, sparked by a long-running religious battle between the Crown and the Church of Scotland, now opened the door to a new Parliament and new privileges. In July 1637, King Charles and Archbishop Laud had attempted to impose a new Scottish Prayer Book, in the Anglican mould, on the Church of Scotland, seeing a measure of uniformity in religious affairs as integral to Charles's design of an 'Imperial Crown'. For the Scottish Church, influenced so heavily by the Calvinist John Knox, it smacked of 'popery'. Riots ensued, fuelled by the accumulated grievances of the Scottish nobility, who for over a decade had grown more and more offended at reforms that undermined their land ownership, and appointments that undermined their influence. By February 1638, the rebellion's leaders had a rallying cry, along with a National Covenant, replete with the oath to purge the Scottish Kirk of bishops and other 'novations'. The Covenanter rebels had established a new aristocratic government in Edinburgh, which

Charles believed reduced his powers in Scotland to the level of a 'Duke of Venice'.

By October 1638, the king, in an effort to win allies, had widened Warwick's licence to attack the Spanish, granting his pinnaces the *Warwick* and the *Robert*, bound for the West Indies, rights to 'assail, attempt, encounter, surprise, take, vanquish and possess or otherwise to sink, burn or destroy' any hostile ship found on the West Indian or American seas.[64] In May 1639, Charles joined his army – which included Warwick's brother Henry, Earl of Holland – gathered at the border. But the king's force failed, and after skirmishes between Covenanter forces and Scottish royalists, the king moved quickly to agree a truce in June 1639.

Warwick and his allies now saw their chance. Suspending plans to leave the country, they set about, instead, organizing the recall of Parliament.* Charles's resistance quickly failed. As the Scottish Church and General Assembly rejected the authority of both bishops and the king, in spring 1640 Charles agreed to summon not just one Parliament, but two.[†]

Equipped with powerful electioneering preachers, Warwick and his allies soon succeeded in getting their candidates elected in puritan strongholds nationwide. On election morning, great crowds thronged about Warwick's home threatening the pro-royalist candidate that if he won 'they would tear the gentleman to pieces, for which words was apprehended, but bail was accepted by the Earl of Warwick... to his great popular glory'.[65] When the results were in, Warwick's faction was satisfied. 'The game', wrote Warwick to a friend, 'was well begun.'

*

---

* The Scots' hope, it seemed, was not for a second front, but a diplomatic push for moderation among Charles's councils; 'fair terms for intercession with our prince' as a later letter put it. See Adamson, *The Noble Plot: The Overthrow of Charles I* (Phoenix, 2007), pp. 37–9.

† The Irish parliament was convoked to meet in Dublin on March 1640; under the control of Strafford, it voted through £180,000 and an army of 9,000 men – one-third of the troops needed in Scotland.

Quickly, Warwick and his friends – men such as John Pym and Oliver St John in the Commons, and the other two great southern earls in the Lords: the urbane and courtly Francis Russell, Earl of Bedford, and Warwick's cousin Robert Devereux, 3rd Earl of Essex and one of the most experienced soldiers in the kingdom[66] – had formed a 'knot' and were colluding secretly with the Scottish Covenanters through their London agent, code-named 'Mr Bartlett'.

When the new Parliament assembled in the cramped medieval chapel of St Stephen's, next to Westminster Hall, on 13 April 1640, Sir John Finch – Speaker in the 1629 Parliament, and now Charles's Lord Keeper of the Great Seal – was deputed to make the opening speech. Finance for the war, he said, was now pressing. There was clear evidence, he asserted, of the Covenanters treasonably disputing with the French, and while MPs would no doubt want to air their grievances, that would have to wait until taxes were agreed. Immediately, MPs began their assaults, on the king's policies and agents. The assembly 'fell into almost as great a heat as ever you saw. I perceive our House [of Lords],' wrote the Earl of Northumberland, 'apt to take fire at the least sparkle.'[67]

Within days, Charles had dissolved this 'Short Parliament' on account of the 'malicious cunning of some few seditiously affected men',[68] and his ally, the Earl of Strafford, had swept the Committee of War – the Privy Council's war cabinet – into a strategy of decisive attack in Scotland. Only Sir Henry Vane's scribbled notes of that meeting remain: 'Go vigorously on... Go on with a vigorous war... loosed and absolved from all rules of government... [I am] confident as anything under Heaven Scotland shall not hold out five months. One summer well employed will do it.'[69]

Warwick was now under suspicion. Agents of the Privy Council were dispatched to search the homes, and even the persons, of the earl and his allies. Warwick was even forced to turn out his own pockets. The king now sought to finance his ambitions with a large Spanish loan, while Warwick, together with the earls of Essex and Bedford, Viscount Mandeville, and lords Saye and Sele, Savile and Brooke agreed with the Scottish rebels an audacious plan. It was to secure 'a free Parliament to try all offenders and to settle religion and liberty', using an ancient custom, last used in 1298, whereby twelve peers of the realm might summon a parliament in their own name, where the king had failed to do so. Within a fortnight of a pre-emptive Scottish invasion, on 17 August 1640 – described as 'the greatest [danger] that had threatened this state since the [Norman] Conquest'[70] – the group met together to finalize their Petition of Twelve and to bring the king's advisers to 'legal trial and condign punishment'.* The petition was soon signed by a quarter of the English nobility.[71]

The king's general, the Earl of Strafford, was so enraged that he proposed that the petition's messengers be shot in front of the army.[72] Meanwhile, the Scots were advancing: they had knocked out an English army and progressed as far as Newcastle. The Privy Council, still in London, grew close to panic. Whitehall and the Tower were fortified. All peers in the capital were ordered home to attend to their duties as lord lieutenants of the counties. But the temperature simply rose.

On Sunday, 6 September 1640, both Bedford and his brother-in-law were summoned to the Privy Council's Committee of War and warned to 'wash their hands from the mischiefs that would happen if the Lords [of the Council] do not join with them'.[73] By Monday, the petition was circulating widely in the City of London. John Pym had travelled to Leez the previous Thursday to consult Warwick on the timing of the petition's release, and to leave a copy with Warwick's secretary to make copies for circulation.

Forewarned of the petition's publication, Charles summoned the first Great Council of Peers since the death of Elizabeth I. 'I desire nothing more than to be rightly understood of my people,' he intoned, 'and to that end I have of myself resolved to call a Parliament.'[74] The country was about to commence a twenty-month descent into civil war. It would prove the final fight of English merchants to enjoy the fruits of their trade unmolested by an arbitrary king.

*

In the period that followed, Warwick emerged as one of the key figures around the group of contemporaries called 'the Junto' – 'the great

---

* In legal terminology, 'condign' means 'appropriate'.

contrivers and designers' at the sharp end of the struggles, that would see the triumph of the traders over their king. While men like St John, John Hampden and Pym were at the centre, in the House of Lords none could match, in the words of the Venetian ambassador, Warwick's 'courage for the greatest enterprises'.[75]

The new Parliament was the cue for an avalanche of petitions from around the country – a 'bulging portmanteau of complaint'[76] on everything from arbitrary rule to 'innovations' in Church services, imprisonment of clerics who had fallen foul of Laud's reform to the poor organization of local militias, the unfair raising of military charges to monopolists unfairly pursuing their rights, and the corruption of local officials to the illegality of ship money and the prohibition on sermons in the afternoon. The 'knot', who dominated the Lords Committee for Petitions, set about not only establishing a comprehensive audit of Charles's misdemeanours, but also took to itself the legal authority for prescribing remedies. In the Commons, a sweeping attack on the king's prerogative powers was driven through, with a bill to automatically call parliaments and to route all funds for the army fighting the Scots through the English Lords Commissioners, a private treasury, backed by new taxes of around £240,000 and headquartered in Warwick House on Holborn, through which soon poured almost £500,00.[77] Indeed, such was Warwick's status in the land that, despite his views and positions, in April 1641 he was admitted to the Privy Council.

As the year unfolded, the king's key ally and general, Strafford, was impeached and executed. Slowly, a policy emerged not only for regular parliaments, but for Parliamentary control of money and military force. In struggle after struggle, Charles fought and lost. His control of London, the Tower and then the appointment of 'good lord lieutenants and deputy lieutenants' was lost to Parliament's nominees, along with control of navy finance.[78*] His plot to arrest the Covenanters' noble leadership was botched. War broke out in Ireland, as Irish Catholics rebelled, fearful of the growing Protestant tide. His attempt to

---

* Indeed, on 6 September 1641, Warwick, Pym and Sir Henry Mildmay assumed control of paying the navy.

personally arrest Parliament's leaders provoked MPs and peers to retreat to the Guildhall, defended by huge crowds.

Warwick was in the thick of it all: presenting the bill of Strafford's attainder; bringing forward measures for London's defence; taking control of the Committee on Irish Affairs; developing plans for the war in Ireland and for its finance (Rich himself would provide the ships for the troops); and, stationing in the Thames, at the height of the tensions, a 400-tonne ship armed with up to thirty cannon.

By spring 1642, as civil war in England loomed, the king and Parliament were scrambling to take control of arsenals, magazines – and the navy, which Parliament ordered to surrender to Warwick on that fateful day off Goodwin Sands. On 31 March 1642, Charles was insisting in a blistering letter that 'we believe that it is the first time that the Houses of Parliament have taken upon them the nomination… of the chief sea commander'.[79] But by lunchtime on 3 July 1642, Charles was left 'without one ship of his own in his three kingdoms at his devotion'.[80] By the summer of 1642, king and Parliament were gathering armies. On 22 August, Charles raised his royal standard in York, and England's civil war began in earnest.

*

Parliament appointed the Earl of Warwick as Lord High Admiral in December 1643. Amid the factional squabbles of the Parliamentary cause, it was a position he lost, and then regained. His effective mastery of the navy proved critical, interrupting and intercepting efforts to supply and reinforce Charles from the Continent or Ireland, and supporting the Parliamentary military effort on land. He returned to the Admiralship in 1648, as hostilities between royalists and Parliamentarians were renewed and a large part of the navy 'revolted' against the Prince of Wales (the future Charles II). Warwick's personal popularity with the seamen was such that he was able to win back a critical portion of the fleet, which he used to blockade the prince's vessels in Dutch harbours.

Warwick's obligations stretched well beyond the navy, and his influence ran deep. He was one of those attempting an accommodation settlement with Charles – indeed, he trod a fine line, regarded by some on the Parliamentary side as too ready to settle.

In one respect, Warwick was pre-eminent. As the man with more interests than any other in the New World, he was appointed by Parliament, on 2 November 1643, as 'Governor in Chief and Lord High Admiral' of all islands and plantations of British subjects in America, assisted by a seventeen-member commission from the Lords and Commons, overwhelmingly composed of his friends and allies. Enforcing the territories' loyalty to Parliament was not straightforward, given that the independence of the colonies was already growing. Puritan New England bent to the Parliamentary cause, but its leaders argued that their charters exempted them from England's laws; others simply refused to recognize the commission's mandate. But Warwick was not without influence. He recognized, for instance, the 'Incorporation of Providence Plantations in the Narragansett Bay', founded by emigrés from Massachusetts, and which in due course became the state of Rhode Island. Warwick would later order the Massachusetts colonists to respect their new neighbours, and in 1648, in gratitude the Rhode Islanders renamed their plantation, 52 miles south-west of Boston, 'Warwick'.

Warwick generally chose the course of pragmatism. He delivered freedom of trade, which was vital to London's customs revenues required for Parliament's war effort. But politically he gave ground. 'We have resolved it to be most commodious', he told the Virginians, if they elected their own governor, ideally Captain Matthews, to regulate their affairs. In 1645, Warwick told New England's leaders that 'in causes personal, criminal or capital', cases no longer needed to be referred across the Atlantic. The colonies were now their own judge and jury.

In the Caribbean, though, Warwick was stricter. As governor of the Somers Isles Company, he issued a long proclamation in 1644, declaring that company policy was to behave as Parliament saw fit, including a ban on 'tippling houses, idleness and ill company'.[81] He urged the West Indian colonists, especially the leaders of Barbados, to follow a similar line; but in the absence of strong government, much colonial trade was lost to interlopers, especially the Dutch. This was not the only loss, for by now Providence island itself was gone. The island had successfully repulsed another Spanish assault in 1640, but in May 1641 it finally fell to a renewed onslaught.

In January 1649, following two eventful years of escape, renewed war, and recapture, the trial of Charles I began. It had been opposed by the House of Lords, but pushed through by a House of Commons in this 'Rump Parliament', already purged by the military of its more conciliatory MPs. Charles was indicted as a 'tyrant, traitor, murderer, and a public and implacable enemy of the Commonwealth of England', and his death sentence was quick to arrive. [82] On the afternoon of 30 January he stepped out, in the icy cold, on to the scaffolding erected outside Whitehall's Banqueting House before an enormous silent crowd. 'I go', he declared, 'from a corruptible crown to an incorruptible crown'. The whole thing, recorded the French ambassador, was over in fifteen minutes.

*

Warwick now faced trials of his own. His younger brother, Henry, Earl of Holland, who had once been a favourite of James I (and lover of the famous French aristocrat and intriguer, Marie de Rohan), had defected to the royalists during their victory at the Battle of Chalgrove in June 1643. Captured after the Battle of St Neots, in July 1648, he was imprisoned in Warwick Castle and brought to trial in February 1649. He was condemned as a traitor and sentenced to death, but he claimed that he had surrendered and spared St Neots in return for his life. Warwick, along with many others, petitioned Parliament to commute the sentence. The votes were evenly divided. But the Speaker broke the tie with a casting vote for death, and on 9 March 1649 Henry was beheaded.

Warwick, by contrast, now took his place among the men of power – men who, with Oliver Cromwell, put commercial and colonial expansion centre-stage politically, creating in the House of Commons a co-ordinated radical party of MPs who worked together intimately with the leaders of the Rump Parliament. [83] The end of the monarchy brought with it the disbandment of the House of Lords and, in February

1639, an end to Warwick's tenure on the Admiralship. But Warwick remained an integral part of the alliance cemented between government and merchants, with a shared ambition to both build a navy and use it.

From 1649, the Commons Committee of the Navy was dominated by the radical Parliamentarians, and it encouraged the creation of a permanent navy funded by higher customs rates.[84] 'The government of the Commonwealth and that of its trade', wrote the Venetian ambassador to Cromwell's court, '[is] being exercised by the same individuals.'[85] He added in June 1651 that 'owing to the care of Parliament, [the English] have 80 men of war, which are certainly the finest fleet now afloat... they can increase their numbers with incredible facility to 150, 200 or more sail'.[86] It was not long before this powerful new navy was taking aim at a new enemy.

Proposals for a political confederation between England and the seafaring Dutch United Provinces collapsed in mid-1651. The Dutch had won their independence from Spain, after eight decades of war, at the Peace of Munster (1648), but now, instead of co-operation with their neighbours across the North Sea, competitive maritime and commercial interests created a wedge, and soon war. When peace came between the Dutch and the Hapsburgs, English traders found themselves hopelessly outclassed in the Mediterranean, in the East and West Indies, and even in Virginia. A decade previously, in 1641, Sir Thomas Roe had noted that 'our great trade depends upon the trouble of our neighbours but if a peace happen between France, Spain and the United Provinces, all these will now share what we possess alone'.

The Commons Council of Trade began to propose action. In October 1651, the Navigation Bill was passed, requiring that all imports should arrive in English vessels only, and that goods should be shipped directly from the place of origin – cutting out the Dutch middlemen. The policy's architects were two Providence Island shareholders and Warwick allies, Maurice Thompson, a highly successful Virginian tobacco grower who also chaired the Committee of the Navy, and William Jessop, who, guided by Warwick, led the Council of State committee tasked with overseeing the subjugation of the last royal loyalists in the American colonies.[87]

Skirmishes with Dutch shipping, between privateers and convoy escorts, now escalated. In the first six months of 1652, 106 Dutch vessels were captured, and by July fighting in this First Anglo-Dutch War had broken out; it lasted until the Westminster Treaty of April 1654.[88] In the peace that followed, the Dutch had no option but to accept the Navigation Act, and Cromwell's idea of a renewed political union with the Dutch, or at least an anti-Spanish alliance, came to nothing.

By contrast, England was now courted by both France and Spain, as the Catholic powers fought one another in the Spanish Netherlands. But most on Cromwell's Council saw Spain as the greater threat. Cromwell, who became Lord Protector on 16 December 1653, was now blessed with a navy that boasted 160 ships, boosted by spending between 1649 and 1654 that totalled £1 in every £5 of the government's budget.[89] And so evolved a plan known as the 'Western Design', to take advantage of England's maritime strength, and 'gain an interest' in the Spanish Indies.[90]

*

The continued challenges of colonizing Virginia created a sense that settlers might move south. Many ascribed the failure of Providence Island to its small size rather than its location. And there were plenty like Thomas Gage, who argued in 1648 that Providence, 'though but little, might have been of a great, nay greater advantage to our kingdom, than any other of our plantations in America'.[91]

Central to the debate of the 'Western Design' was an analysis of whether England could beat the Spanish in the Caribbean. Here again, the experience earned settling Providence Island was key to the plan's dimensions. Between 1642 and 1645, Warwick's privateering fleet, financed by Maurice Thompson, had temporarily captured Jamaica, fuelling a sense that the foundations of the Spanish West Indies were weak. 'The veil is now drawn aside, & their weakness detected by a handful of men,' wrote Warwick's captain.[92] That message, along with report of the island's beauty and fecundity, was relayed to Cromwell.

Providence Island veterans now urged Cromwell on, not least to seek revenge for the loss of Providence, and soon the Lord Protector had concluded he would indeed follow the puritans' policy of the last thirty years, and 'strive with the Spaniard for the mastery of all those seas'.[93] Summoning the Spanish ambassador, Cromwell told him that the price of peace was freedom of worship and trade for the English throughout the West Indies. The ambassador replied that 'to ask for these concessions was to demand of his master his two eyes'.[94] And so the English fleet was dispatched in December 1654.

The English crewmen were not the finest; according to one contemporary, they comprised 'hectors, and knights of the blade, with common cheats, thieves, cutpurses, and such like lewd persons, who had long time lived by sleight of hand, and dexterity of wit'.[95] The campaign itself started badly. An attack on Hispaniola (today's Haiti and Dominican Republic) was a disaster, resulting in the loss of 1,000 men. So grave was the loss, that an apology for the policy was issued, and in its pages, probably drafted by John Milton, is revealed the full influence of Warwick's Providence Island experience. The Spanish crimes of the capture of Tortuga and Providence are set out in detail, along with the logic for their possession, as raiding bases for attacks on the Spanish fleet.[96]

Frustrated in Hispaniola, the fleet's commanders fell back in April 1655, turning their fire, in May, on thinly defended Jamaica, 100 miles west. Ten times the size of England's Caribbean possessions, the island was as poorly developed as it was defended, and after a rapid landing and march to St Jago (Santiago) de la Vega, at two o'clock in the afternoon of 11 May 1655, the expedition's leader General Venables greeted the Spanish outside the town to declare that 'he came not to pillage, but to plant' – and took control of the island. Spanish attempts to wrest control back were defeated in 1657–58.[97] The English won a magnificent new Caribbean base, and from it English privateers harassed Spanish ships long after the Anglo-Spanish War officially ended, in 1659.

*

Throughout Cromwell's rule, the Earl of Warwick remained a close supporter. In 1657, their families were even enjoined when, on 11 November, Warwick's grandson (yet another Robert Rich) married

Cromwell's daughter Frances. The event was celebrated with a spectacular wedding feast, replete with forty-eight violins, fifty trumpets, Barbary wine, and 'mixt dancing' until five o'clock in the morning. Old royalists such as the Earl of Newport were invited, and the Countess of Devonshire blessed the couple with £2,000 of gold plate. The party stretched on at Warwick's home for seven days.[98]

Warwick was, however, not long to enjoy his family's union with the house of Cromwell. In February 1658, he died of consumption. Like a prince, he was mourned in purple for three days as he lay in state at Warwick House. Cromwell mourned the loss of 'an old friend for thirty years'. On 1 May 1658, Warwick was buried at Felsted, Essex, the centre of his world.

It was a world he had helped to remake, a country where traders, merchants and entrepreneurs now wrote the laws in Parliament, used courts to shield themselves from rapacious rulers, and raised taxes to fund a navy that protected and advanced their trade throughout sea lanes and colonies worldwide. In the years that followed, the colonies that Warwick did so much to found, prospered. By 1684, Jamaica boasted some 246 sugar plantations worked by over 10,000 slaves. By 1699, the Americas supplied 20 per cent of England's imports – worth over £1 million, and took over 10 per cent – £0.5 million – of exports.[99]

Within two generations of Warwick's death, England's enterprise power was well-founded, and England's entrepreneurs were on their way to founding a global empire.

3

SIR THOMAS 'DIAMOND' PITT

East India entrepreneur

Sparkling in the Louvre's Galerie d'Apollon is what many consider the finest diamond in the world. Weighing in at over 140 carats, the Regent diamond is not the world's largest, but its perfect white brilliance 'of the first water' and its unparalleled cut, mark it out as truly unique.

Like so many great gems, its story is confused with myth and packed with tragedy. Some said it was plucked from the eye of a temple idol. Others told of a slave who discovered the huge jewel deep in a diamond mine and, thinking quickly, jammed the gemstone into a bandaged wound cut into his calf to smuggle it out. Desperate to cash in on his luck, the slave sold the stone to an English sea captain in return for safe passage to a free country. But the captain betrayed the slave, throwing the hapless soul into the sea before selling the diamond for himself, only to fall prey to drink and, racked with guilt, to hang himself.

The truth was probably more prosaic. The Regent was very likely discovered in the greatest diamond mine on earth – the Kollur, in Andhra Pradesh, dug on the right bank of the mighty Krishna river, the finest of the thirty-eight mines of the diamond fields on India's Deccan plateau.[1] Here, 60,000 men, women and children dug for their fortunes and sometimes found it in the shape of great stones such as the Koh-i-noor discovered in the thirteenth century, and the Great Mogul (discovered in 1650). Here, wrote the great French traveller and diamond expert Jean-Baptiste Tavernier in 1676, great merchants came to buy: 'every morning from 10 to 11 o' clock the masters of the mines, after they have dined... take their diamonds to show them [the merchants]. If the parcels are large, and contain many stones of the value from 2,000 up to 15,000 or 16,000 écus (£450–£3,600), they entrust them to the foreign merchant for seven or eight days or more in order that he might examine them with care.'[2]

The Regent, discovered in 1698, was a monster. Weighing in uncut at 426 carats, it soon wound up in the hands of Jamchund, India's greatest diamond dealer. For a stone this large, Jamchund knew there was only one market: the merchants of the East India Company, the traders buying and selling Eastern wares who wrestled with a particular problem: how to ship their fortunes safely home. Over the years, diamonds had become the perfect answer. Small, easy to stow and cheap to buy in India, they made a tidy profit in Europe.

None was a bigger buyer than Sir Thomas Pitt, the greatest India trader of his day and Governor of the East India Company's Madras headquarters, Fort St George. And so in December 1701, Jamchund and Pitt sat down to talk. Jamchund opened the bidding at 200,000 pagodas (£74,440).[*] 'As I best remember,' wrote Pitt later, 'I did not bid him more than 30,000, and had little thoughts of buying it for that. I considered there were many and great risks to be run, not only in cutting it, but whether it would prove foul or clean, or the water good.'

For two months they haggled until, in February 1702, Pitt had his price. 'I brought him down to 55,000 padagoes [sic] and [I] advanced to 45,000,' wrote Pitt. 'So, believing it must be a pennyworth if it proved good, I offered to part the 5,000 padagoes [sic] that were between us.' They settled on 48,000 (around £17,836 or between £35.6–£49 million in today's money), and Sir Thomas Pitt took ownership of one of the largest diamonds in the world.

The gem would take him another decade and a half to sell. Smuggled home on the *Bedford*, hidden in the heel of Pitt's son's shoe, it was entrusted to one of Europe's most prominent jewellers, Sir Stephen Evans, for the cutting. Working with crystal models, today carefully stored in the British Museum, the stone was sliced down by two-thirds to 137 carats, at a cost of some £5,000. The off-cuts were sold to Peter

---

* The (gold) pagoda was replaced by the Rupee in 1818, and worth £0.372. See M. Edney, Mapping An Empire, (University of Chicago Press, 2009).

the Great of Russia, and the diamond dust and shavings alone made somewhere between £7,000 and £8,000.

Not until 1717 did a customer arrive, in the shape of Philippe Duc d'Orléans and the French Regency Council, who sought the stone on behalf of the future French King Louis XV. Pitt presented the treasure to the court jeweller, Rondet, in Calais for inspection: taking it to the window to assess it in the best light, he concluded that it was 'in all respects perfect'.[3] The bargain was struck. The Regent diamond passed to its royal French owners, later adorning the French crown, and Sir Thomas 'Diamond' Pitt – grandfather to the future prime minister William Pitt the Elder – became one of the richest men in England.

*

The town of Blandford – now Blandford Forum – has been a fording point on the River Stour since the Iron Age. Here, a settlement and then a market grew in a natural cut in the Dorset chalk, through which the waterway pours into the English Channel just north of Poole's harbour. It was known as 'Blaneford' in the Domesday Book, and generations of Blackmore Vale farmers came here to buy and sell their livestock.[*] After fire swept through Blandford in 1731, the borough was rebuilt as one of the most beautiful and complete Georgian towns in England, home in Pitt's day to nearly 2,500 people.

Here, Pitt's family had lived for at least six generations, the first probably one Nicholas Pitt in the days of Henry VIII. His grandson, John Pitt, founded the family fortunes, becoming Clerk of the Exchequer under Elizabeth I. John's eldest son was knighted as Sir William Pitt, whose three grandchildren became respectively a physician, a Mayor of Dorchester and the rector of the neighbouring village of Blandford St Mary. It was the last of these, John Pitt, who became the proud father of Thomas Pitt, on 5 July 1653, in the last days of the English republic and the first days of England's empire.

Thomas was just five years old when, towards the end of summer 1658, Oliver Cromwell breathed his last. Sickening of 'a bastard tertian

---

* 'Blaneford' meant a ford of the river of blay or bleak.

ague' (a form of malaria), the Lord Protector expired on 3 September 1558. Even in death, Cromwell was irrepressible: he burst from his lead-lined coffin, 'from whence came such filth, [raising] a deadly and noisome stink'.[4] He was quickly buried, and before long, so too was his dynasty. Despite his competence, Cromwell's son Richard never won the army's full backing. Factions fractured his support, and when Parliament was recalled, there arrived a majority content to invite the king across the water to come and take up his throne. Amid euphoric scenes, Charles II was welcomed home by, among others, the young diarist Samuel Pepys, who recorded for posterity how, after a breakfast of pease, pork, and boiled beef, Charles landed at Dover around noon on Friday, 25 May 1660. 'Infinite [was] the crowd of people and the horsemen, citizens, and noblemen of all sorts... The shouting and joy expressed by all is past imagination.' Charles processed from the coast to his capital through jubilant crowds – 'as if the whole kingdom had been gathered' – and entered London on his thirtieth birthday, 29 May, 'with a triumph of above 20,000 horse and foot, brandishing their swords and shouting with unexpressable joy: The ways straw'd with flowers, the bells ringing, the streets hung with tapissry, fountains running with wine.'[5] Charles was crowned in Westminster Abbey as monarch of a nation now enriched by Cromwell's alliance of government and merchant, and by the burgeoning trade they had built in the great Caribbean empire, in the East Indies – and in India.

*

Thomas Pitt's family was not poor – his father's income was £100 a year – but it was large. Five siblings survived childhood, and Pitt's elder brother stood to inherit what the family had. As such, when Pitt's father passed away in 1672, Pitt had little choice but to seek his fortune elsewhere. Within the year, he had signed up for the East India Company and by 1673, aged twenty, he was bound for India aboard the *Lancaster*.

In a sense, young Pitt was following in the footsteps of Sir Francis Drake, the great adventurer who had electrified and enriched England with his explorations and profits of his piracy. On the final leg of his circumnavigation of the world in 1580, Drake had stopped at Ternate, in the Spice Islands of the Moluccas and Java. Nestling in the Moluccan triangle in the Indonesian archipelago, 500 miles north of Australia, the isles lay at the centre of Indonesia's volcanic ring of fire where, on average, eruptions every five years deposited on the surrounding hills and mountains a volcanic ash that was excellent for nurturing spice groves. Drake loaded his hull with cloves, which were sold at a huge profit once home.

Inspired, the Levant Company promptly dispatched Captain James Lancaster in Drake's wake, on an ill-starred adventure to the Malay Peninsula. Lancaster may well have served with Drake and, leaving Plymouth in 1591, he eventually reached Penang. It took him another three years to struggle home via the West Indies. His voyage was hit by scurvy, shipwrecks and slaughter at the hands of Comoro Island natives. Two ships were lost, just 25 of his 198 men remained, and the prizes he had stolen from the Portuguese in the West Indies were sunk. But the intelligence Lancaster brought home was priceless. On the small Moluccan Banda Islands of Run, Ai, Lonthor and Neira for instance, ten pounds of nutmeg could be had for a halfpenny but sold in Europe for the equivalent of £1 12s. Ten pounds of mace cost less than 5d, but could be resold for £10 – a 32,000 per cent profit.

The Levant Company's directors soon saw a specialized business was needed. The business logic was simple. England was small, while the East was great. For all its progress, the England of the 1600s accounted for perhaps 2 per cent of global output. China, on the other hand, accounted for 30 per cent and India another 20 per cent. A sea lane to these great markets would avoid the long and dangerous overland Silk Roads that ended miles away, in Venice or Constantinople. And so, six years after his arrival home, Captain James Lancaster was among the 218 petitioners celebrating, on New Year's Eve 1600, the creation of the 'Company of Merchants of London Trading into the East Indies' – the East India Company (EIC).

Dominated by Levant Company merchants, the EIC was organized in a very new way. Unlike the administration of the Levant Company, the EIC's twenty-four directors or committees were in complete control of day-to-day business. Over the course of the subsequent decade, five major voyages proved the viability of high-value trade in nutmeg, mace, cloves and pepper, establishing along the way England's first colony in the East on the nutmeg island of (Pulo) Run.* Business in India began with David Keeling's voyage; departing in 1607, he reached Table Bay on the South African Cape in time for Christmas, before stopping at Madagascar – where one of his men was 'shrewdly bitten with an alligator'. After collecting a cargo of aloes at Socotra, the trading archipelago off the coast of Yemen, Keeling's ships docked at Surat, the principal port of the Mughal Empire, on 28 August 1608. Keeling had become the first EIC commander to set foot in India. And it was not a warm welcome.

The Portuguese had been trading throughout the Arabian Sea for over a century and were well established at the court of the Mughal emperor. Surat's Portuguese commander immediately challenged the new arrivals to leave, telling Keeling's second-in-command, William Hawkins, that his king was a 'king of fishermen, his island of no import, and offering a fart for his commission'. Hawkins immediately challenged the man to a duel – at which point the latter beat a tactical retreat. Despite two attempts on his life, Hawkins, who spoke Turkish, soon secured an audience with the emperor in Agra, quickly becoming a favourite at court, winning not only trading rights but an annual salary of £3,200 and the rank of 'khan'. Not to be outdone, the Portuguese managed to manoeuvre Hawkins into a state of disfavour, and he was dismissed in November 1611. When the second English fleet, commanded by Sir Henry Middleton, arrived that month, it found no factors and no trading agreements. Evicted in February 1612 by Emperor Jahangir's local commander, Mukurat Khan, Middleton promptly set about attacking Indian shipping in the Red Sea.

Unaware of the debacle, the EIC in London had dispatched two more ships, under the command of Thomas Best. Arriving six months after Middleton had left, Best's crew was just settling down to 'drinking drunk (*sic*) with whores ashore' when the arrival of four Portuguese galleons and twenty-five inshore frigates, carrying orders to disperse the English by force, sobered them up. In two days of skirmishes, Best scored a major victory. His second assault was watched by the whole

---

* The first two voyages produced a return of 95 per cent, but the third, fourth and fifth brought back a return of 234 per cent.

Mughal army lining the shores, and his victory unlocked the commercial privileges the EIC had been seeking. He sailed home with his holds full of Indian cottons, thrilling English tastes.

When the Portuguese and Jahangir fell out in 1614, the EIC saw the chance to advance from its early beachheads. A fortune was raised in England to build the business. Although it remained much smaller than the Levant Company – which even by 1638 was 'for its height and eminency… now second to none other of this land'⁶ – the first issue of EIC stock in 1613–16 raised £418,000, and the second issue in 1617–22 raised an enormous £1.6 million (worth between £3 billion and £7.2 billion in today's money). While the company was still compact enough in 1620 to be run from the grand home of its governor, Sir Thomas Smythe, in Filpot Lane, off London's Fenchurch Street (with a Bishopsgate warehouse around the corner), the Company soon controlled one of the greatest enterprises in the land, the mighty East India Dock at Blackwall, where its ships were built; it was a sight that drew strangers and ambassadors alike to admire the wet and dry docks, timber yards, foundry, cordage works, bakery, saltings – and its 200 craftsmen. Between 1611 and 1620, fifty-five ships set sail under the company colours. Embassies to India were dispatched under Sir Thomas Roe and Sir Robert Shirley, and even when spice prices fell during the 1620s and 1630s, and the EIC's returns and subscriptions both suffered,* the company nevertheless expanded its toehold in India. It was eventually violence not diplomacy that made the difference. In a joint operation organized by Sir Robert Shirley with the Shah of Persia, on 23 January 1622 'it was resolved to invite our enemy's (*sic*) to a banquet of fire flying bullets', and the Portuguese garrison at Hormuz was defeated on St George's Day (23 April).† A settled peace

---

* On the first joint stock, investors had harvested an 87 per cent return. However, on the second joint stock, the return had fallen to just 12 per cent – on an annual basis, an appreciation of under 1 per cent. When the third joint stock was launched in 1631, only £420,000 was raised.

† It was a disaster for the Portuguese. The commander of the Hormuz garrison was tried in his absence and hanged in effigy. Fleets from Goa attempted to strike back, blockading an English trading post near Jask, and in 1625 a final reckoning was fought over three days. The Portuguese lost up to 500 men.

took another thirteen years to arrive, but the English had now firmly won a position in the ancient trade of the Indian Ocean.

*

In 1672, someone, somewhere in Thomas Pitt's family must have had a connection to someone, somewhere, in the East India Company. A patron was generally a prerequisite for such a job. Half a century later, Lord Egmont in desiring that 'my cousin Percival, at Fort St George might enter the company's service' was told by the company's director that 'there are so many nobleman's relations already in service that it could not be... he said he would do what he could'.[7] Pitt appears to have started at the bottom, as a ship's mate on a company ship.[8] But, few careers offered such promise, for over the course of Pitt's childhood, from 1666 to 1675, the EIC's receipts had multiplied more than five-fold to an extraordinary £2.7 million (somewhere between £5million and £12 billion in today's money).[9] Indeed, such were the profits of private trade that 'interlopers' – traders seeking to dodge the EIC's monopoly – were beginning to flourish, and it seems that sometime between leaving England and arriving at Balasore, in the Bay of Bengal, Thomas Pitt had decided to join them. On landing in India, he promptly absconded in cahoots with a renegade EIC commander. Pitt's company career had lasted as long as his journey.

When the EIC's directors discovered Pitt's disappearance, they were furious. On 24 December 1675, the Court of the Company blasted its chief officer: 'We understand that Capt Goodland of the *Lancaster* left there one... Pytts [*sic*], and that he is entertained by our Chief there... whether he had a hand in it or not, we do require you to take care to send them to the Fort to remain there till next year's shipping and then to be sent to England.'[10] The director's instructions, of course, took months to arrive, and so it was another year before the EIC's agent, Streynsham Master, reported that Pitt had been summoned. 'The council sent for Thomas Pitts,' minuted Master, 'and read the hon'ble company's order to send him to England by the first ships, and required his observance thereto, who promised to comply accordingly.'[11]

Pitt did anything *but* comply. He bolted once again, and for the next two years the EIC dispatched fruitless orders for his return. Yet, while Pitt's exit was rapid, he fast made a fortune working for the company's renegade 'chief', Matthias Vincent. Quite how Pitt connected with him remains a mystery. Vincent hailed from a family of troubled clerics in a parish 10 miles from Exmoor's Jamaica Inn and over 120 miles from Blandford. He was appointed an EIC factor in 1661, partly on account of his languages and partly for his wife, 'a Portugal merchant's daughter and heir', who brought 'a great quantity of riches, goods and chattels'.[12] Perhaps there was a family connection between Vincent and Pitt. But what is certain is that young Pitt had landed on his feet.

Pitt was quickly employed helping Vincent run his own private trade between India and Persia, organized together with the company's factor in Balasore, Richard Edwards. Not that business always ran smoothly. On 21 February 1678, Vincent noted to Edwards that the twenty-five-year-old Pitt appeared to be buying and selling Persian horses – possibly with Vincent's money – which Vincent wanted for sale. 'Pray let me have an accompt what Mr Pitt has sold his horses for,' noted Vincent, adding: 'I hear that he has agreed to go to Persia upon Naroola Cawn's ship. Pray when he comes thence hitherward let somebody come with him that may give me timely notice... he being between 4,000 and 5,000 rupees in my debt. Pray take what care you can that he escapes me not.'[13]

Thomas Pitt was clearly using his freedom to trade on his own account. Three months later, on 11 May 1678, he was pleading for permission to sell horses in Persia to make good some serious losses: 'Sir, I am certain you are sensible what a loss I have,' he wrote to Vincent, 'and am like to sustain... with what I lost in your ship and that Mr Budgen gave away of mine, as he said it was for the company's interest, and also my being put by (as I was) my employ, which was promised me and I depended on it; not only that but other inconveniences attended it certainly no one can think but that this must be a vast loss to a young beginner as I am'.[14]

His apprenticeship with Vincent, it seemed, had not been without its issues, as the letter explained: 'Sir, I have been formally advised and since have perceived it that you are much my enemy, but for what I know not... .' The letter goes on to suggest that Pitt may have been care-less with some of Vincent's money, but Pitt goes on to accuse 'two persons' for smearing his name.[15] Whatever the cause of the dispute, Pitt had within a year transformed his position, possibly by making money, but more certainly by offering marriage to Vincent's niece, Jane Innes. By October 1679 they were wed, and ever after, Pitt never seemed short of capital and his 'country' trade around the Indian Ocean pros-pered in partnership with another interloper, William Alley.

By the age of twenty-eight, Pitt had made enough money to come home. He sailed on the *William and John*, with both an infant son and a well-selected cargo for sale on behalf of himself and Vincent, His cargo quickly sold at a huge profit, winning him instant fame as an interloper, while his son, Robert, would in time become the father of the future Earl of Chatham, the prime minister, Pitt the Elder.

*

By the time Pitt arrived back in England, in 1681, there was such a healthy market of brokers, agents, administrators and investors famil-iar with handling Eastern traffic that it was now possible, and profitable, to make a fortune working not *with* the East India Company but *against* it. Although the EIC was technically a monopoly, its strat-egy and its organization allowed scope for much private trade alongside the 'official' merchandise. The company did not own its own ships – it leased them – and paid its officers and agents a pittance, allowing them instead cargo space to freight their own goods to sell as they could. With capital, a captain[*] might fit out on his own account some 56 tonnes available on the outward journey – and around half that on the return. But, EIC employees often lacked the funds to fill the space, and so they would rent out the cargo space and take a healthy commission – or, if enterprising, raise a loan.[†]

---

[*] An apprentice might earn £5 a year; a 'writer' £10; a factor £15, and a governor or president, £300 (just three times the income of Pitt's father as Rector of Blandford St Mary). Mentz, *The English Gentleman Merchant*, op. cit., p. 129.
[†] Indeed, a healthy market supplying loans grew up in London and Cadiz, where a captain could raise cash he did not want his masters to see.

In London, a network of people developed to supply the capital and receive the goods. Traders would typically use a 'commissioner' – an agent – to organize the London end of the business. They would gather silver to send eastwards, often thousands of pounds at a time, organize insurance and receive and sell on the goods when they arrived in England, according to the merchant's instructions, and administer the money (for example by buying and selling shares in the EIC or lending out to others). A good year might entail £20,000 worth of goods such as raw silk, musk, tea and quicksilver. The best estimates suggest that these forms of private trade might have accounted for a little in excess of 10 per cent of the EIC's Indian business.

Crucially, there was plenty of demand for what India had to sell. By the time Charles II took the throne, fashionable England was in love with Eastern textiles such as Bengal silks, silk-cloth taffeta and plain white cotton muslins. The EIC had transformed England's taste with its first imports of muslins and calico.[16] Pepys recorded, in 1663, that he gave a gift of 'a very noble parti-coloured Indian gown' to his wife. By 1664, over a quarter of a million pieces of calico had been imported into England,[17] and over the course of 1675–83 a river of English silver ran east.[18] As much as £4.5 million worth of bullion was shipped from London – up to a million pounds in private shipments – to purchase luxury goods for import, such as musk or bezoar stones, silk, tea, but above all the cotton goods of muslin, daris, chintz and salempore.* Bigger traders staked out bigger business, buying and selling bills of exchange, whereby money would be paid into Indian 'factories' in return for a bill of exchange, which could then be cashed at the EIC offices in London.[19] And nothing the private traders shipped quite matched the scale and profits of the diamond trade.[20]

*

In 1681, Pitt the interloper had clearly chosen his cargo well. The EIC's directors, furious at the commercial damage, dispatched a note of his

---

* 'Bezoar stones' were stones found in the intestines of goats, which were highly valued because they were thought to remove toxins from the body.

ship's contents back to India to chastise its own agents, so 'that you may see what kind of new goods she brought and how they sold here'. The directors blasted: 'they [Pitt and Vincent] come to the Bay but for a short time... and yet they bring home more in proportion of those new desirable goods by far than our ships, which is such an unanswerable reproach to those that managed our affairs formerly'.[21]

Pitt's sojourn in England was just long enough to organize his next audacious attack on the EIC's business, chartering a new ship for India to bring back goods, his patron Vincent and the remainder of his fortune.

The EIC's directors, however, had other ideas. Pitt's marriage to Vincent's niece afforded the company sufficient proof that Vincent was acting largely for himself and not for his employers. And so the directors resolved to reorganize their affairs abroad and bring Vincent home under force of arms to answer for his misdemeanours. The directors chose as their instrument one William Hedges. The son of a Wiltshire family, which had relocated to County Cork, Hedges was a former Levant Company treasurer in Constantinople, who spoke colloquial Turkish and Arabic. His wife was a sister to the wife of Sir Jeremy Sambrooke, the scion of a wealthy family of merchants long connected with the East India Company and Madras. Although well-qualified, Hedges would prove one of the company's unluckiest servants.

The company wanted an enquiry into allegations that Vincent was skimming 2.5 per cent of the company's bullion, taking a cut of the prices paid for goods, and using EIC resources to buy and sell on his own account. Hedges' orders were simple: 'with all possible speed... to seize upon the person of Mr Matthew Vincent, our late chief in the Bay, and send him forthwith a prisoner on board the ship *Defence*, Capt Heath, Commander, where let him remain under safeguard'.[22] A new agency was then to be established at Hugli (Hooghly), in Bengal, with Hedges as the new governor policing all Bengal trade.

When, however, the company caught wind of Pitt's new adventure, the directors saw that their plans were in jeopardy. They immediately applied to the Court of Chancery to stop Pitt; but the wheels of justice were too slow. On 15 February 1682, the court heard that Pitt had already left, aboard the *Crowne*. Orders were issued to stop him, and an EIC ship, the *Welfare*, with Hedges aboard, was urgently dispatched to the Bay of Balasore. Orders were dispatched for Fort St George to supply a corporal and twenty soldiers to help arrest Pitt, this 'fellow of a haughty, huffing, daring temper'.[23]

But Pitt was too fast. In April, Hedges, who had sailed aboard the *Defence* in January, spied Pitt's ship ahead. They saluted each other before the *Crowne* sped away, and on 19 July 1682 when Hedges drew into the Balasore Roads, he found not only that the *Crowne* had arrived eleven days earlier, but that it was accompanied by two other interloping ships. Once on shore, Hedges discovered the gigantic dimensions of Pitt's plan.

Pitt had arrived in Bengal with enormous fanfare, including guards and trumpets, had taken a huge house to which had been carried great chests of money, and promptly set up shop as the EIC's great rival. He 'lands in great state with 4 or 5 files of soldiers in red coats,' reported Hedges, 'well armed, and [with] great attendance of native soldiers and trumpeters, and takes up his quarters with the Dutch by the name of the new company's agent, bespattering the old company [EIC]'. It seemed that Pitt was busy buying up goods and spreading rumours that the EIC was in such a poor state that it could only afford to send two ships that year with fewer than twenty chests of treasure. Worse, declared Hedges, Pitt and Vincent were now working openly together, with 'Vincent joining him[,] builds warehouses, the Dutch everywhere assisting them and the company's black merchants by Vincent's influence'.[24]

Hedges' plan to arrest Pitt and Vincent quickly went awry. Proceeding up-river in one of the company's sloops, Hedges became detached from his guards only to be greeted by Vincent near the Dutch Garden, a few miles from the company's factory at Hugli, armed to the teeth. Alerted by Pitt, Vincent had not only surrounded himself with a huge guard, but put himself under Dutch protection. When Hedges found him, Vincent was 'attended by several boats and budgerows, guarded by 35 Firelocks and about 50 Rashpoots and Peons well armed'.[25] So confronted, Vincent invited the poor Hedges to join him at the Dutch Garden, 'where he had provided an entertainment for me and made preparations for my reception'.

Perhaps most seriously of all, Pitt, it seemed, was circulating the idea 'that there was a new company erected, and he, the said Pitts, was their agent'.[26] Pitt was claiming legitimacy. 'He treats with the governor as agent, obtains a *perwanna* order [i.e. a warrant], under the title of the New English Company, to trade, and also liberty to build a factory to continue forever and defames the company's servants.'

As part of Pitt's strategy, he had encouraged local Indian rulers to suspend the EIC's 'Phirmaund', an order exempting the EIC from paying customs to local rulers on its trade; this was a twist that took Hedges months of negotiation to resolve. 'If God gives me life to get this Phirmaund,' Hedges wrote in his diary, 'the Hoble Compy [Honourable Company] shall never more be troubled with interlopers. I bless God for this great success I have had beyond all men's expectations.'[27] Eventually, Hedges won a new agreement – at the cost of a 20,000-rupee commission and a promise to pay the customs bills seven months hence. He left for Dacca (now capital of Bangladesh) on 15 December 1682 to supervise the loading of the EIC ships before the monsoon set in. But Pitt and Vincent were both still free and on 2 February 1683, Hedges was treated to the sight of Pitt floating past in his sloop, *en route* home. The East India Company directors were furious. Having looked forward to the 'wreck of the interlopers', they were treated instead to the spectacle of Pitt's return to London, his ship loaded with valuable cargo.

For Hedges, it was a career-ending moment. He was dismissed from EIC service and eventually fled India – in an interloping ship – to Persia, from where he slowly wandered home with the bones of both his wife and his infant child. He ran unsuccessfully for the Lord Mayoralty of London in 1700 and died the following year.

As for interlopers such as Pitt, the EIC was not giving up. What the company failed to achieve with its agents abroad, it now sought with its lawyers at home. It would find English judges better servants than its Indian factors.

*

For many years the precise privileges of the East India Company had been disputed, because they had never been confirmed by the House of

Commons; indeed in 1680, the Levant Company had embarked on a major challenge to its monopoly. But Pitt's attack on its interests was so flagrant that the company had to act,* and it began by dragging the interlopers through the courts. The directors chose as their test case not Thomas Pitt, but an East India trader called Thomas Sandys, who had loaded up a ship bound for the East Indies. The company approached its case with optimism. The EIC had for long been supportive of the Stuart Crown. In the days leading up to the civil war, its board had been overwhelmingly royalist in sympathies, and it elected a prominent royalist, Sir Henry Garway, as its governor, refusing to let Parliament use its ordnance, and offering loans to the king.[28] Now, it was payback time, and its new governor, Sir Josiah Child, was playing to win.

Sir Josiah was the trading titan of Restoration London, worth some £50,000 (between £95 million and £173 million today).[29] He made a fortune selling wine to the king's navy before clambering up the EIC's ranks to the board. He was, said the diarist John Evelyn, 'sordidly avaricious' and an example of the new class of 'overgrown and suddenly monied men', who 'from an ordinary merchant's apprentice & management of the East India Company's common stock' had 'arrived to an estate ('tis said) of £200,000 and lately married his daughter to the eldest son of the Duke of Beaufort, late Marquis of Worcester, with £30,000 (some versions £50,000) portion at present, & various expectations'.[30]

Child was a passionate advocate of the EIC's monopoly. In 1681, he helped defeat an idea promoted by the company's deputy governor, Sir Thomas Papillon, to cancel the company's old shares and issue new shares so that a much wider range of traders could buy into the company.[31] Rather, Child fought to restrict control of the company to a narrow band of friends, growing rich along the way by trading the company's shares on the basis of inside information, for example by spreading rumours of lost ships and buying up stock when the share price fell.

---

* Its options were simple: to place orders in the Court of Admiralty prohibiting voyages; file action for damages in the Court of King's Bench, or informations in the Crown office in the king's name.

To shore up the EIC's position, Child had recommended in 1681 that the company begin offering 'presents' to the Crown of 10,000 guineas, and a grateful Charles II was quite content to support the board. He ordered his advocate in the Admiralty Court to insist that Sandys promise to honour the company's charter. Sandys's ship was stopped from sailing just when Pitt had arrived home with Vincent and their small fortune in cargo. They were promptly arrested and only released on giving security worth £40,000. The EIC had no legal basis for seizing goods that were, according to contemporaries, sold 'to great advantage'; but twenty-five further interloping ships were now stopped on the 'Sandys principle', and with the wind in its sails, the EIC pressed its luck, asking the court to confirm the company's privileges with a case in the Court of King's Bench. [32]

'The Great Case of Monopolies Between the East India Company... and Thomas Sandys', launched in 1683, enthralled commercial London. The EIC's argument was calculated to enlist the sympathy of royalists everywhere, and chairing the Law Lords in Westminster Hall was the greatest royalist seneschal of them all, Judge Jeffreys. The king, argued the EIC's lawyers, had power to control trade with foreigners, especially with 'infidels', and as the inhabitants of India were infidels, it was correct for the king to exercise enormous care in selecting who could trade with them. Reporting in the last days of Charles II's life, Jeffreys and his fellow judges found for the EIC. Arguing that 'it would be very strange if the king might prohibit foreigners from coming here... and not prohibit his own subjects from going into foreign countries', the EIC's charter was, concluded Jeffreys, 'a good grant in law'. [33]

With the EIC victory in Westminster Hall, interloping on a serious scale was, at least temporarily, suspended. In 1684, some forty-eight interlopers were restrained, among them Thomas Pitt.[34] He was, for now, beached. And so he furled his sails and settled down to invest his fortune in Restoration London.

*

In the fifty years before Pitt's birth, London's population had doubled to 400,000, to become the biggest town in Europe.[35] Now home to one in nine Englishmen, it was ravaged by plague and fire in the 1660s, when Pitt was a teenager, and was subsequently transformed by Sir Christopher Wren, whose metamorphic designs replaced an architecture that was – said the diarist, John Evelyn – all 'turrets and pinnacles, thickset with monkeys and chimeras' with 'more majesty and solemn greatness', better fitting its rank as one of the greatest ports on earth and a hub of the new global trading system of the transatlantic 'triangular trade'. [36] Above the roofs rose the magnificent new dome of St Paul's, and above the people, rose an extraordinary new class of long-distance traders.

In the thirty years after the Restoration, national wealth had risen by a quarter – and savings had doubled.[37] When the City's first business directory was published in 1677, it listed some 1,786 merchants, men worth anything from £1,000 in value to giants like Josiah Child, worth £50,000. But within their ranks, an important shift was underway. As the cloth trade to Europe stagnated between 1660 and 1700, the long-distance traders rose to take their station as the new elite. Between 1660 and 1670, the East India trade grew by 80 per cent, while the value of imports from the West Indies and North America doubled.[38]

Dominating trade was a small elite. Perhaps 600–1,000 of them were merchants, who, in their counting houses (wrote Daniel Defoe) 'at once converses with all parts of the known world… this, and travel, makes a true-bred merchant the most intelligent man in the world'.[39] They dominated the city's rich list: between ten and twenty at the very top were the merchant princes who commanded the great overseas trading houses of the EIC and the Royal African Company, along with the Levant Company, the Eastland Company in the Baltic and the Merchant Adventurers in Hamburg. None of these individuals was richer than Peter Vansittart, a Danzig immigrant worth £120,000. Most of them were worth between £5,000 and £15,000, and alongside the English were Huguenots, Jews, Dutchmen, Germans and Baltic traders, all now calling London home. Many were beginning to diversify, too, from – say – importing sugar and tobacco and exporting 'sortable cargo' into slaving or continental re-exports to the Baltic.

The ships on which the cargoes sailed crowded the River Thames, which resembled 'a floating forest from Blackwell to London Bridge'.

Nearly 7,000 ships docked in London in 1700, landing 70 per cent of the country's imports,* and by 1720 John Strype could write with confidence in his *Survey of the Cities of London and Westminster* that it was trade 'which makes London to be London', a city where 'the shipping lying at anchor in the River Thames resemble a Wood, or Forest'.[40] The goods were landed in the heart of the rebuilt city on twenty-one 'legal quays', a mile long, 40 feet deep, stretching on the north side of the Thames from London Bridge to the Tower.[41] Here arrived sugar, rum, cocoa from the West, tea and porcelain from the East, elephants' teeth and palm oil from Africa, whale oil from Greenland, tobacco, cotton and corn from America, timber and wool from Russia, and wine, oil and fruit from Turkey. Domestically, coal and herring were landed from Newcastle, ferried by lighters and barges to shore, and carried up to Thames Street and the warehouses beyond. Down-river, the Savoy and Rotherhithe docks could handle another 120 ships. The Greenland Dock handled whaling, while at Blackwall stood the imposing East India Dock.

Financing it all were the scriveners, the writers of bonds – the intermediaries who connected borrowers and lenders, for a small commission; the forty-four goldsmiths listed in 1677, who kept 'running cashes' to draw and cash cheques; the money-lenders and pawnbrokers, who flourished; and, more importantly, the merchants who came together at the Royal Exchange, rebuilt after the Great Fire of 1666. Here, as *Mr Spectator* noted, one could observe 'disputes adjusted between an inhabitant of Japan and an alderman of London' or 'a subject of the Great Mogul entering into a league with one of the Czar of Muscovy'.

Around the docks were the coffee houses – some 124 within the City walls alone, home to the auctions where goods were 'sold by the candle', company offices, reading rooms and listening posts.

Amid this huge metropolis was emerging a middle class. There were between 3,000 and 5,000 families of the 'West End gentry', the

---

* By 1795, this number had increased to 14,800 ships, as tonnage quadrupled and value tripled to £31.4 million. See Jerry White, *A Great and Monstrous Thing: History of London* (Bodley Head, 2012).

upper middle class, below which were the 20,000–25,000 households where a comfortable lower-middle-class life could be secured with a wealth of a few hundred pounds and an income of £50 a year.[42] Perhaps one-third were lawyers. The grandeur of the city was increasingly matched by the grandeur of its citizens. In place of the puritan plainness came a flamboyance; in 1661, Evelyn noted a man strolling through Westminster Hall, with 'as much ribbon about him as would have plundered six shops and set up twenty country pedlars; all his body was dres't like a Maypole'.

The king and his former court in exile had done much to make French style fashionable; but even Charles complained to Parliament that 'the whole nation seemed to him a little corrupted in their excess of living. All men spend more in their clothes, in their diet, in all their expenses than they need to'.[43]

To find their fashions, Londoners invented modern shopping. Connecting the City with Westminster, the major roads – the Strand, Fleet Street, Cheapside and Cornhill – were lined with shops in such profusion that they stunned visitors to the capital; in the eyes of one observer they were 'so great, and indeed so far beyond any foreign city, that it is to strangers a just matter of amazement'.[44] And through the streets rang the calls of the street-sellers hawking pies, milk, muffins, fish, offal, 'sweet China oranges', oysters, fruit and breads.

*

In this extraordinary city, Thomas Pitt was, at the age of thirty-one, one of its richest men. 'I had a house in London,' he wrote in later life, 'kept coaches and horses, servants... always three or four dishes of meat at my table, as good wine as the world afforded and plenty, and made my friends and relations very welcome.'[45] He reckoned his income at £1,000 a year (between £2 million and £3.5 million a year in today's money); indeed, he was richer than a baronet, and almost as rich as a bishop.

Confined to England, Pitt decided to gild his cage. And so, he began investing wholesale in country places, politics and piracy. In 1686, he leased Mawarden Court, neighbouring Old Sarum outside

Salisbury. He made his peace with the East India Company the following year, which cancelled the majority of his court fine, and in 1688 he was admitted to the Freedom of the Company, acquiring in the same year the manor of Stratford-sub-Castle, now a northern suburb of Salisbury, from the Earl of Salisbury, where he acquired a love of planting trees.

It was to prove fortunate timing, for Sir Josiah Child, operating from the EIC's headquarters on Leadenhall Street, was about to overplay his hand, with disastrous consequences.

When Charles II died of 'apoplexy' on 6 February 1685, the EIC was blessed with a sympathetic successor. Charles's Catholic brother James II had been an EIC shareholder since April 1684, and once enthroned he confirmed and extended the EIC's privileges to include the power to arrest and try interlopers and to deploy troops and ships against Indian princes.[46] In his battle for riches, Child now took the opportunity to take arms and militarize his trade war against the Indians, the interlopers – and the Dutch.

Historically, the EIC had resisted the philosophy of armed trading. In 1677, for instance, the Committee of Correspondence had noted that 'our business is Trade not War', and two years later had condemned armed trading. But the EIC was now embattled by the greatest trading force on earth, in what was the latest chapter of a long trading saga.

By 1650, the Dutch East India Company (Vereenigde Oostindische Compagnie, known as the VOC) was quite simply the world's biggest transnational corporation, sending east, in the record years of 1657 and 1658, some 2 million florins in gold, silver and ingots. Hundreds of millions of florins were raised to build a fleet and trading posts, bringing the Dutch total dominance over the Portuguese in the East Indies. Over four decades, the Portuguese and Spanish were successively turfed out of Melaka, Ternate, the Moluccas, Banda, Jakarta and Malacca as the Dutch established great bases in Formosa (Thailand), Japan and, in India, Broach (Bharuch), Cambay (Khambhat), Admidabad (Ahmedabad), Agra and Burhampa (Berhamper).

Across this incredible Eastern trade zone, the Dutch shipped Chinese gold, silver from Spanish mines, Japanese copper, the silk of both China and Bengal, and the fine spices of mace, nutmeg, cloves and cinnamon, bringing home to Europe cowry shells, sugar and silk. By the end of the 1690s, some 160 vessels with 30–60 cannons apiece were moving the Dutch company's goods, employing some 8,000 sailors. In its ports in Batavia (Jakarta), one could not only see fine spices from Indonesia, gold, copper and silver from Japan, tea, porcelain and silk from China, Indian fabric, the finest silks, gold porcelain and precious jewels, but also up to 200 ships and 30,000 men sailing under the VOC's colours, throughout the Indies.

The Dutch had not proven much minded to let the English in on their trading networks, and over the years a terrible record of commercial conflict had grown between the EIC and VOC, backed by their respective governments. A bone of contention was, in 1623, the notorious episode on the island of Amboyna, where English traders were accused of treason, imprisoned and tortured in a Dutch fort: 'They kept twelve of us in a dungeon where they pissed and shat upon our heads and in this manner we lay until we were broken out from top to toe like lepers having nothing to eat but dirty rice and stinking rain water.' Eventually, ten of them were executed. The Dutch authorities, pressured by England to investigate the case, eventually acquitted their compatriots of any wrongdoing in 1632 – but a war of words continued.

By 1680, the VOC and EIC had evolved a balance of power; the VOC predominated in the Indonesian archipelago, Ceylon and the southern tip of India, while the EIC controlled the rest of the subcontinent and the Persian Gulf. In the 1680s, however, Dutch pressure resumed. Child feared Dutch plans for a fort at the mouth of the Ganges, leaving the Dutch 'masters... in effect of all the trade of India'.[47] Fearing wipeout on the Malabar coast, and following the sack of an English factory in 1686, Child now turned to arms.

Adopting the widest possible interpretation of new powers from the king, he now sought to establish 'such a polity of civil and military power, [as would] create and secure such a large revenue to maintain... the foundation of a large, well grounded, sure English dominion in India for all time to come'.[48] In 1686, the company's secret war committee decided to fortify its Bengal base to resist both the Dutch and

Mughal officials; 'we have no remedy left,' minuted the directors, 'but either to desert our trade or we must draw that sword His Majesty hath intrusted us with to vindicate the rights and honour of the English nation in India'.

Child's war, however, soon aimed beyond the VOC. At sea, a naval vessel, *Phoenix* – a forty-two-gun, fifth-rate ship – was dispatched east of the Cape of Good Hope to tackle pirates, foreign and domestic, if necessary with violence. In 1687, an interloping captain intercepted in the Red Sea was killed in his cabin, 'because he would not surrender his ship voluntarily'.[49] In September 1688, the EIC deployed the largest naval force it had ever assembled to blockade ports, arrest the Mughal emperor's ships and seize the town of Chittagong.

The results were disastrous. The emperor naturally resisted. The EIC was forced to evacuate Surat, factories in Bengal were seized, and the factory at Hugli was besieged: indeed, Job Charnock found Hugli so hard to defend that he proposed another site, which in time became the foundation of Calcutta. By 1691 the company's trade was so damaged that its imports had collapsed by 90 per cent.* Trade at Surat and Bengal was almost banned and a huge indemnity demanded.

Yet, worse was come for Child and his faction, for a new English revolution was about to offer the EIC a military peace abroad – but a political war at home. A new deal with the Dutch would create new riches – but Child would never get to pick the fruits.

*

The mounting opposition to James II's policy of Catholic toleration exploded into rebellion when his son, James Stuart, was born in June 1688, and the nation's Protestant leaders suddenly faced a Catholic heir to the throne. Many in Parliament had, before Charles's death, spent a decade trying to exclude the Duke of York from the succession. Now that he had an heir, a full-scale constitutional revolution was in progress as the group of English leaders known as the 'Immortal Seven' invited James's Dutch son-in-law (and nephew) William of Orange to

---

* Their value had fallen from £800,000 in 1684, to just £80,000 in 1691.

intervene to restore England's 'ancient laws and liberties'.* William landed at Brixham on 5 November 1688, with a fleet four times the size of the Spanish Armada, James's cause melted away, and the old king fled abroad.

A 'Convention Parliament' deemed James to have abdicated, and William was crowned in April 1689. The 'Glorious Revolution' was complete; it marked a new relationship between sovereign and subjects. Rather than taking the oath to uphold 'the laws and customs... granted by the Kings of England', William swore to govern according to 'the statutes in Parliament agreed on', namely a new Bill of Rights, ratified in December 1689, which limited royal power and established the supremacy of Parliament. Of greater significance to the EIC, the political developments affecting the two major Protestant mercantile and maritime powers of northern Europe also opened the possibility of the greatest commercial 'merger' of the age.

Strategically, the arrival of a Dutch king transformed English trade in India, by bringing the prospect of a division of the East's trading zones between the EIC (in India) and the VOC.

There may never have been a formal 'deal with the Dutch'. But the settlement was just as good. The VOC ceased its warlike aggression, and harassment of English trade on the Malabar coast. The English were free to fortify their positions. Hostile propaganda ceased. Inter-company correspondence in November 1689 noted: the 'friendliness' between 'two nations so closely bound to one another and allies in so good a cause'.[50] The VOC all but abandoned its markets on the Coromandel coast to the English, and turned its attention to prosecuting the Nine Years' War (1688–98) with France, a conflict in which the English were now allies.

King William had been quick to throw his new kingdom on to the Dutch side (as part of the Grand Alliance) in the conflict – and in the finest traditions of English warfare at sea, England's private citizens with ships were encouraged to fight. Together with a number of

---

* Born in The Hague in 1650, William was the only child of Stadtholder William II, Prince of Orange, and Charles I's eldest daughter Mary, the Princess Royal. In 1677 William married his first cousin and James II's daughter, Mary, who, despite her father's faith, was a Protestant.

merchants, Pitt secured one of the 490 letters of marque issued during the conflict, authorizing pirate attacks on the French.[51] It would, though, deliver a major setback. On 10 July 1690, the French defeated the combined English and Dutch fleets in the Battle of Beachy Head, gaining temporary control of the English Channel.[52] Pitt, it seems, was one of the casualties. Writing nearly a century later, his great-grandson Lord Camelford recorded an old family tradition, alluded to in Latin on Pitt's memorial. 'I have heard', wrote Lord Camelford, 'that having accomplished such a sum as he thought would enable him to pass the remainder of his days in peace, he [Pitt] was taken prisoner together with the greatest part of his effect on his return to England, and released at the intercession of the Duchess of Portsmouth, who was then in France.'[53] His fortune fractured, Pitt now faced a stark choice: to live out his years poor, or to return once more to India.

The political revolution in London would soon offer a way back to riches. On William's accession, Sir Josiah Child and the EIC faced an immediate problem. Child had lost James II, his patron-in-chief, and the new king was far more ambivalent about the EIC's privileges. Pitt, spotting his moment, threw himself into support for the new regime. Determined to sit in the Convention Parliament, he acquired the Old Sarum borough from the Earl of Salisbury in 1688.* 'Mr Pitt, interloper, has the making: the baily returns the writ,' reported the king's agents of the borough, and although his initial election to the Commons was subsequently annulled, he was quickly re-elected for Salisbury, taking a seat in Parliament and on the committees considering trade with France. Pitt hastily assembled petitions attacking the East India Company, which a turn of fortune now gave him a strategic interest in destroying.

For many years, campaigners and pamphleteers had railed against the EIC's monopoly. Under the Stuarts, a mere fourteen shareholders controlled about one-third of the company's stock and were a bastion for royalist loans and a bulwark of royalist power. Child's disastrous

---

* Old Sarum had few, if any, resident voters and yet was represented by two MPs in the House of Commons. It became one of the most notorious examples of a 'rotten borough' before the 1832 Reform Act.

Indian policy, however, set the stage for change. And in the Williamite House of Commons, the EIC's opponents now skilfully seized on news of the company's abuses in its supply base of St Helena. For years, the island had been used as a supply station, but local smallholders had been effectively enslaved, and in 1683 violent punishments – including ear-clipping and branding – had been meted out to two apprentices accused of stealing. In the ensuing riots, seventeen protestors were killed or wounded, and another nineteen sentenced to death. The widow of one of those killed accused the perpetrators of murder and was promptly given twenty-one lashes and thrown in prison. In 1689, a petition from the widow's companions found its way to the House of Commons, and the EIC's opponents saw their chance. In the Commons, on 6 November 1689, a number of Privy Councillors along with 'Captain Pitts' were ordered to study the company's imposition of martial law in St Helena. They issued a damning report and quickly established a new enquiry into the whole business of Eastern trade, which at first recommended radical plans to create a new company, established by Parliament rather than the Crown, and subsequently suggested constraining the old company and creating limits of £10,000 on any single shareholder – effectively evicting the great Sir Josiah.[54]

The New East India Company, known as the 'Dowgate Adventurers', based in the rebuilt Skinners' Hall, was quickly launched and raised £180,000. On 6 February 1692, the new company asked the king to dissolve the East India Company and transfer its charter. But the EIC was not about to give up. King William, smelling trouble, was ingenious. Rather, he suggested, why not double the capital of the old company, issuing the new shares to new subscribers. In March 1693, the company's officials consequently 'forgot' to pay the required tax on its shares, triggering cancellation of the EIC's rights. Sir Josiah Child now channelled £80,000 in EIC bribes to secure a regrant of the EIC monopoly in November, which was issued on condition that the company's stock was enlarged, allowing new subscribers to join the firm.[55]

It was amid this confusion that Pitt spied his chance to sail east once more. On 1 April 1693, King William convened his Council at Kensington, for a 'great hearing' between the EIC and Captains Gifford and Pitts [sic]. 'The company', said reports of the Council, 'pressed to have the interlopers hindered from going to sea, alleging it would be detrimental to the company by informing the Indian of the state of their concerns.'[56] The king, however, was reluctant to help, and Pitt set sail forthwith in his ship, the *Seymore*, with the EIC once more determined to stop him. Orders were issued by the directors to their chief in India, Job Charnock; 'We are very much disposed to frustrate her [the *Seymore*'s] voyage, whatever its cost,' wrote the directors on 28 April 1693, 'not that we would have blood shed.' On 1 October 1693, as Pitt's ship drew into Balasore, the company's agent, Goldsborough, tried to have him arrested as a pirate,* warning that any entertainment by Indian merchants of Pitt 'would bring about another war'. But the EIC's position was weak, and Pitt's skill as a trader indomitable.

On 16 April 1694, the Hugli Agency's new chief, Mr (later Sir) Charles Eyre, was admitting defeat. Thanks to a large bribe of 4,000 rupees to the Governor of Hugli, the interlopers were thriving, he reported, buying and selling for ready money. 'Notwithstanding all our endeavours… to frustrate and oppose the interlopers in their designs, they are rather countenanced and encouraged by the whole country in general.'[57] A crisis in London now forced the company to fold its hand and strike a deal. Its agents minuted Fort St George on 2 February 1694 that because 'the concern in the two ships sent out by the interlopers, being now by bargain with most of the interessed become so our own', what was left of the cargo was to be 'befriended and sent home into the joint interest'.[58] Pitt set sail for home in early 1695, with a new fortune to his name. The EIC had failed to foil him once more. Indeed, events in London now prompted the company's directors to conclude that if they could not beat Thomas Pitt, they needed to hire him. Fast.

The crisis propelling the EIC's change of strategy in 1694 dwarfed the ructions of the previous year. When the Commons met in January 1694, there was fury at Child's corruption. A new enquiry was ordered into the company's monopoly, concluding once again that it should be

---

* He declared: 'These strangers that steal out of their own country in this nature are general those people that rob and plunder on the seas'; see Dalton, *Thomas Pitt*, op. cit., p. 93.

removed. As the year unfolded, £80,000 in EIC bribes was discovered. When Child's kinsman Sir William Cook refused to name the lucky recipients, he was thrown into the Tower of London. Eventually, he squeaked, and the king's chief minister, the Duke of Leeds, was impeached for receiving bribes.

Searching for a way through the crisis, the company's new leader, Sir Thomas Cook, turned to Thomas Pitt with an offer of the governorship of Fort St George. This was the chance of a lifetime for Pitt to mollify the old EIC and to organize his own private trade between Madras and London. On 24 November 1697, Pitt was elected unanimously as president of the company's affairs on India's eastern seaboard, on the Coromandel and Orissa coast, and governor of the forts of St George and St David. He sailed out with '52 chests of wine, 4 chests of Nottingham ale, 21 hampers, 5 cases of pickles', a princely wage of £200 a year, and a lifetime's experience.

*

Pitt's new dominions were not enormous; but they were profitable. The EIC's headquarters at Fort St George were home to as many as 120 merchants, 34 women and perhaps 200 soldiers.[59] In smaller stations, such as Masulipatam, the population perhaps numbered thirty.[60] Trade was not frenzied; in Madras, for example, a busy year like 1695 might see thirty-nine ships arrive and thirty-one depart. A quiet year, such as 1691, could see less than half that traffic.[61]

In England, Indian textiles remained highly popular. An anonymous catalogue from 1696 describes cloths 'checkered with a variety of colours, as red, yellow, blue and green… wears very well in anything you shall think fit to use it for'. By 1699, John Cary recorded that 'now few think themselves well dressed till they are made up in calicoes'.[62] Between 1670 and 1760, the EIC was importing three yards of cloth per person, per year, and Indian cotton-makers were working to European designs. Indeed, Jean-Baptiste Tavernier noted that in India 'the workers print their calicoes according to the design given by foreign merchants'. Within a year of his arrival Pitt was cashing in, dispatching nearly £7,000 of dorras, mulmul, chintz, salempore, brampore, raw silk, and long cloth* aboard the *Tavestock*, the *Anne*, the *Martha*, the *Nethune*, the *Sidney*, the *East India Merchant* and the *Benjamin*. Indeed, he bought and sold anything he thought could turn a profit. In 1701, for example, he dispatched forty kandies of Chinese tea, dragon's blood and mace, along with Chinese silk, six pots of tea and three fine lengths of beteela, a fine cotton fabric. Musk, quicksilver, China ware, Madras paintings and neckcloths all followed.

Alongside his merchandise, Pitt made a fortune from financial transactions, sending home bills of exchange, dealing in *respondentia* – loans secured against the cargoes of vessels – and taking cash in India in exchange for diamonds shipped home and sold in London for a commission. The financial instruments were popular with big traders. For instance, when Governor Sir Charles Eyre, who was also a great Bengal trader, decided to retire, he confronted the problem of how best to ship his fortune home safely – some 23,000 pagodas. The capital was placed with Pitt in India. In return, Pitt issued Eyre with a bill of exchange that Eyre could cash with Pitt's commissioners in London, at an agreed exchange rate of 12 shillings per pagoda. Pitt then used the money to buy diamonds which Eyre would hand over to the commissioners. The commissioners would issue the cash – £13,800 (about £1.7 million) – immediately and then try and profit on the sale of the diamonds. Sometimes, Pitt together with Sir Stephen Evans made a turn raising money in England and sending it to India, from where it was returned as a bill of exchange struck at a better exchange rate[†] compared to the company's official rate of 9s/pagoda.[‡]

In the British Library sits an impressive set of continuous accounts, which Pitt kept with his wife, across which are scattered the secrets of Pitt's extraordinary life as an East India entrepreneur.[63] His salary appears to have been under 10 per cent of the value of the goods he

---

* This cargo would amount to about £800,000 in today's money.

† This better rate was 13 shillings per pagoda.

‡ As Pitt wrote to Evans in 1705, 'I thank you for your advice in buying of diamonds, which I believe may be much better than paying my money here at 9 shillings per pagoda but I can get 13 shillings 6 pence, I shall think it the best way of remitting what little I have.' Mentz, *The English Gentleman Merchant*, op. cit., p. 149.

shipped; silk and quicksilver were another 10 per cent of his income, and bills of exchange were 20 per cent. But diamonds were 55 per cent.[64]

In January 1687, the Mughal Emperor Aurangzeb had conquered the greatest diamond fields in the world, around the ancient Golconda fort, near modern Hyderabad, and Pitt was quick to assemble a fortune for the purpose of buying diamonds for a syndicate of traders, including his commissioner Evans, Francis Child and his son Robert. Some £5,246 was shipped out to India aboard the *Anna*, *Thordon*, *Fame* and *Martha*, in chests, ingots and coins.[65] By 1699, Pitt's diamond shipments totalled £9,652 and over the next three years, the value tripled. Sometimes Pitt traded on his own account, and sometimes he acted as buyer for others, simply taking a cut. In the same year, for instance, he sent home a bulse of 116 diamonds, weighing in at anywhere between 10 and 41 carats.* They were sold at the company's official auction to buyers who got a discount of 2 per cent for paying in cash, and the sale raised £5,011. The company got 3 per cent in duty; the auctioneers got a little commission, and four partners in the sale – William Wallis, John Evans, Captain Browne and Sir Stephen Evance – got their cut. Pitt's final take was £797 – about 15 per cent of the sale.[66] 'In the decade from 1698 to 1708, Pitt's diamond investments were rarely less than £13,000 and, at their peak in 1700, over £26,000.

Pitt's trade within the East and Middle East might even have outstripped the value of his diamond business with England. His strength allowed him to take huge positions on trade with Manila, Persia and China. In 1704, for instance, Pitt shipped 3,720 pagodas on the *Queen the China*, asking the captain to return with gold, porcelain, copper and tin; he then resold the goods through his own networks, all over India. There were, of course, good years and bad years. Sometimes a ship to China made a 20 per cent profit; sometimes a voyage to Persia made a 40 per cent loss.

The bigger challenge to Pitt's profits, however, was no longer the vicissitudes of Eastern trade, but the poverty of King William. Peace with France had arrived in 1697, just as Pitt had departed England.

---

* 'Bulse' is a term for a purse containing diamonds.

With an empty Exchequer to fill, William began exploring how his Eastern traders could fill the hole.

*

William had sought the English throne, in part to secure English resources for the generational Dutch struggle against the French. The English did not let him down. Before the Glorious Revolution, royal spending was perhaps £2 million per annum. Between 1689 and 1702, it spiralled to £72 million,[67] as the Nine Years' War – the first of seven major Anglo-French wars between 1689 and 1815 – gathered pace.[68] The king needed credit, and lots of it.

What now ensued was a financial revolution that entailed the wholesale import of the tried-and-tested techniques of Dutch high finance. Short-term loans gave way to long-term debt, backed by the statutory pledge of the king, the Lords and the Commons to honour it, alongside a tax system capable of collecting taxes with certainty in order to pay interest. Happily for William, James II had transformed tax collection, now making it possible for *reliable* tax receipts. These could service a much larger stock of debt, which would come to finance around one-third of war spending. The new system would give the decisive edge in defeating France over the century to come.* Revenue doubled between 1688 and 1697,† as the Treasury abolished tax farming and professionalized itself, drawing on the expertise of families that would serve for generations. As the author Jonathan Swift wrote, 'Few of this generation can remember anything but war and taxes… 'tis certain we are the most undone people in Europe.' The Excise man and the Customs official became ubiquitous up and down the country, enforcing an extraordinary multiplicity of money-raising duties. 'Let any gentleman but look into the statute books lying upon our table,' railed William Pulteney,

---

* Paul Kennedy is among those who point out that during the eighteenth-century conflicts, three-quarters of extra finance used to support war came from loans. See Kennedy, *The Rise and Fall of the Great Powers*, op. cit., p. 81.

† The main reason for this was the land tax, charged at 4 shillings in the pound, but Customs and Excise revenue made up half of state revenues.

pointing, '[and] he will there see to what a vast bulk, to what a number of volumes, our statutes relating to taxes have swelled since the Revolution.'[69]

The problem was that it was not enough. William needed more, and so turned to extract money from the City of London, which had now become a hubbub of financial innovation, a world of 'projectors', of men 'joining their heads to understand the useful things in life'.[70] In 1692, there were perhaps twenty companies. Between 1692 and 1695, 150 companies were created, covering everything from banking to fisheries, aqueducts to insurance companies, and the manufacturing of paper, linen, lead, plate glass and bottle glass. England was a place where people, ideas and money collided, greasing the wheels of the nascent Industrial Revolution. By 1695, more than a hundred joint stocks boasted a combined nominal capital of £4 million – one-ninth of the whole value of personal property in England.

Into this great market, the new king sought cash from 'schemes'. The Million Adventure lottery was launched in 1694. It offered a guaranteed return on £10 tickets, with a first prize of £1,000 a year for sixteen years, in a dramatic draw often organized outside the Banqueting House. 'Lottery loans' were raised in 1694, 1697, 1711 and 1712.

The Bank of England was a different sort of scheme. This new creation could buy government debt with a guaranteed return, and then sell shares to the public. It was, in effect, a debt for equity swap. The idea had been discussed for a good forty years, before Charles Montagu invited proposals for a 'Perpetual Fund of Interest' in 1692.* In 1694 the Bank was founded as a great 'Conveniency', drawing income from the state in return for a loan. Crucially, it was allowed to issue notes. Proposed by William Paterson as 'a bank to exchange such current bills the better to give credit thereto and make the said bills the better to circulate', the Bank of England offered at first £1 million to the state, raised at cost of £65,000 in perpetuity.[71] In the event, it raised £1.2 million in just twelve days, and it immediately generated £1.2 million

---

* This would produce first the 'tontine loan', paying interest on annuities for 99 years.

in notes, lent to the government, which paid within days £112,000 to the Exchequer. The Bank went on to contribute some £6.9 million out of the £72 million spent by the government between 1688 and 1702. It was the first step in a popular shareholder democracy. By 1709, there were some ten thousand public creditors; by the outbreak of the Seven Years' War, in 1754, there were sixty thousand.

Loans, too, were sought from the great chartered companies,* which too lent to the government, received a guaranteed rate to return, and sold shares in the company to the public – and none proved as great as the East India Company's challengers, the Dowgate Adventurers, who would spell the end for Josiah Child.

The pressure on Sir Josiah Child had only grown in the wake of Parliamentary enquiries into the grant of its monopoly in 1695. In 1697, a London mob had stormed the company headquarters on Leadenhall Street, and the situation was only rescued by the militia. To confirm the company's privileges, the directors offered up loans to the Crown of £700,000, declaring 'our joints are too stiff to yield to our juniors'.[72] But they were trumped by the Dowgate Adventurers, with an extraordinary offer of £2 million at 8 per cent interest to buy the monopoly on Eastern trade and displace the old East India Company.[73] In July 1698, the Governor of the EIC minuted that Parliament had passed the 'Act raising a sum not exceeding two million, upon a fund for payment of Annuities, at the rate of £8 per annum, and for settling Trade to the East Indies'.[74] The old company's rights would expire in 1701.

The New East India Company's bill received royal assent on 5 July 1698, days before Pitt landed at Fort St George. Subscription books opened in the Hall of the Mercers' Company on 14 July 1698, and the whole amount was subscribed within a day. The New Company's Act of Parliament provided the East India Company with a three-year grace period – until September 1701– in which to wind down its business. It was part of a new pattern as in the years after 1688, Parliament acquired control of regulating companies.†

---

* Loans such as these were raised in 1694, 1688, 1709 and 1711.
† For example, Parliament deprived the Hudson Bay Company of its trading monopoly in 1687, destroyed the Royal Africa Company monopoly in 1698, and ended the Russia Company's control over Muscovy tobacco re-exports in 1699.

*

In reality, the EIC owned £315,000 of the New Company's stock, and while the latter initially lacked money for ships, £178,000 was eventually scrabbled together, the title of 'king's consul' was secured for its captains, and an embassy agreed to be led by the king's new ambassador, Sir William Norris. The second son of Thomas Norris of Speke Hall, Norris was heir to an old Lancashire family that had sat in Parliament since the 1500s. He arrived in India in the summer of 1699 with his two new consuls, Nicholas Waite and Pitt's distant cousin, John Pitt, and immediately began disturbing the peace; issuing orders, demanding salutes, summoning audiences and insisting on exclusive rights to fly the New Company's flags.

In tense exchanges with his relative, Thomas Pitt, as poacher turned gamekeeper, acted instantly to assert his employer's rights. 'Sugar Candy how-do-you-do letters... will not do,' stormed Pitt. 'You may lock up your consul's commission till my master's time is expired... for here shall be but one governor whilst I am here.'[75] Thomas promptly issued a proclamation, signed by his council on 23 August 1699, stating that in order to 'prevent the great mischiefs... we require all English in our company's service as also all that live and trade under their protection not to obey or regard any summons or order that they shall receive from Mr John Pitt or anyone else under the pretence of being a president for the new company'.[76]

The following month, Norris arrived in Masulipatam in impossible grandeur in a warship with a three-frigate escort. He was determined that his style would be such that 'the machinations of the Old Company's servants will vanish like clouds before the sun when I come to make my appearance'.[77] Instructing John Pitt to prepare to receive him 'with great grandeur and all imaginable demonstrations of friendship', Norris insisted that no representative of the old EIC should negotiate with the Mughal emperor without clearing it with him first.[78]

Thomas Pitt was having none of it. He warned Norris on 16 January 1700 that 'we think your proceedings not only destructive to our masters at present but will also prove fatal hereafter if not entail a perpetual ruin on the trade'.[79] Pitt was quite correct, for Norris's associate, Sir Nicholas Waite, had fatally compromised the mission. On arriving on India's west coast, amid a large row between the emperor and foreign traders about the suppression of piracy, Waite had offered an impossible guarantee of safe navigation for the entire coastal trade. Undermined from the start, Norris promptly compounded the problem by falling out with his Persian translator, the vastly experienced Italian Niccolao Manucci, before setting off with almost no preparations for a 470-mile journey to meet Emperor Aurangzeb, who was busily laying siege to Panhala Fort, 'the home of serpents', which guarded a strategic Deccan trade route on the western side of the country.

When Norris arrived in the emperor's camp, matters quickly went awry. His procession was headed by his commander of artillery, followed by twelve cartloads of brass cannon. Five hackeries* loaded with broadcloth followed on, along with glassware and looking glasses; then four Arabian horses, more soldiers, the Union Flag, red, white and blue flags, and then the ambassador's and king's crests and coats of arms. King William's coat of arms was so large that it took sixteen men to carry it. There were musicians, troopers and a splendid palanquin (litter) to bear the ambassador, in front of which was the ambassador's master of horse and the great sword of state. A coach with more officials brought up the rear.[80] Gifts were welcomed. Phirmaunds were granted.[81] But the emperor expected Norris to make good both Waite's offer to suppress the pirates and Indian losses.

After an elegant stand-off and an ultimatum or two, Norris was forced to flee. He struck his tents without a further audience. Aurangzeb was furious. He ordered his forces to chase down the hapless emissary and detain him. Norris only escaped six months later, only to die of dysentery before his ship reached St Helena. His embassy had cost the New Company £80,000.

The chaos provoked both contempt and conflict. Infuriated, the emperor condemned the Englishman's broken promise 'to defend our subjects from piracies committed on the seas' and ordered 'all manner

---

* A hackery was a two-wheeled cart commonly used in Asia.

of trade be interdicted with those nations throughout our dominions, and that you seize on all their effects whatsoever, wherever they can be found'.[82] Thomas Pitt, still Governor of Fort St George, was now fighting for the EIC's life – and his own. Up and down India's coasts, Aurangzeb's armies closed in on the company's factories, and on 29 January 1702 the imperial subedar Daud Khan – who became Nawab of the Carnatic in 1703 – appeared outside Fort St George with a great force of cavalry and foot.*

Pitt knew him well. Indeed, the governor had entertained this lieutenant of Aurangzeb on an earlier, sly reconnaissance of the fort. Khan had claimed that he was coming to see the sea and to wash in it, but during his visit, clearly formed a good impression of Pitt's cellar, for in 1700 he wrote to Pitt asking to buy some liqueurs.

Pitt promptly levied the surrounding town and erected defensive walls. Catching wind of Daud Khan's approach, Pitt requisitioned all the horses he could, raised the trainbands (the local militia), posted his Portuguese militia to outposts, hired 300 rajputs and 60–70 lascars, and put the company's soldiers under arms. On Thursday, 12 February 1702, Daud Khan demanded possession of the mint and a survey of the town, or else he would 'fall in on us and make us surrender by force of arms'. And so Pitt settled down to negotiate. Dispatching forty-eight China oranges to the besieging commander, he politely asked Khan's intercession with the emperor for peace, and promised investment as well as to keep the local seas clear of pirates.[83] When Khan then demanded money, Pitt's response was that 'we owed them nothing, their king nor their country nor would we give them anything' – but four days later he sent another 200 oranges.

His cool-headed stubbornness paid off. By March, the EIC agreed to pay for two lost ships, and when Khan demanded another 30,000 rupees, Pitt simply sent more oranges – though they proved too much. The oranges were sent back, and in May orders were issued to liberate trade. The nawab was squared with 20,000 rupees and a huge gift of liquors, and on 25 May the governor and his council splendidly

---

* The Carnatic was India's southern region, including Madras, so the nawab was effectively a regional ruler under the authority of the emperor.

entertained the officers and trainbands with a supper in the company's garden.[84]

Yet Pitt's challenges were not over as Aurangzeb's commanders were to prove less of a headache than the company's chiefs, haphazardly piloting England's first great merger deal.

The EIC had attempted one last time to displace its upstart rival in 1701, with an orchestrated run on its bankers, the Bank of England, and with a fresh loan offer to the government. When it was rejected, the EIC company directors were left with no choice but to propose the country's greatest merger, to create a United East India Company. The idea was first intimated by Sir Thomas Papillon on behalf of the New Company in November 1699. In the event, a highly complex deal was eventually steered through by Sir Basil Firebrance in 1702. The EIC would now transfer to the combined company its forts and factories, its warehouses in Leadenhall Street and its islands of St Helena and Bombay, no separate trading would be permitted for seven years, and a consolidated loan would be offered to the Crown of £3.2 million (worth somewhere between £6 billion and £9 billion in today's money) with a similar sum raised from the public in short-term loans to finance day-to-day trading.

Effecting the merger in India would, though, prove a different task entirely. Pitt was confirmed as Governor of St George, and his expertise in winding up the old company's affairs was such that the directors entrusted him with clearing up in both Bengal and Madras. However, he quickly discovered that the New Company's men had been trading on very little capital. A fortune had been wasted on Norris's embassy, and worse, a New Company ship, ironically called the *Norris*, had exploded when a cask of brandy caught fire, sending 130 chests of treasure to the bottom of the sea. Desperately hunting for it, Pitt's cousin John had had an apoplectic fit and died.

The traders could not now pay their creditors. And so they ran away, arriving in the governor's garden at five o'clock in the afternoon of 14 October 1703, after a perilous overland journey. Pitt had no choice. To protect the company's credit, he raided 39,000 pagodas from his own private fortune and rounded up a syndicate to pay the remaining 28,500 pagodas to make good the company's debts, praying that

London would redeem him. He dispatched bills of exchange to London on 5 February 1704, whereupon the company promptly began quibbling about both the exchange rate and the interest rate. The row was still rumbling on two years later, by which time Pitt insisted that 'I have received the protests and enough of them to have roasted a Bartholomew Fair pig' and threatened to sue them. In 1706, the company relented a little; but Pitt was forced to retort: 'The proprietors here are greatly dissatisfied and think they have unparalleled injustice done them.'[85] The company threw in the towel in 1707, and left settlement of any outstanding debt in Masulipatam entirely in Pitt's hands.

The United Company's policies were, however, antagonizing not only creditors in Masulipatam but also citizens in Madras. Around the trading post of Fort St George had grown a huge settlement of 300,000 people, known as Black Town. Its residents were divided into two castes, known to the company as the 'left-hand caste' and 'the right-hand caste'. Traditionally, the company had placed its orders on credit with networks of merchants predominantly from the right-hand caste, and some, such as the great 'Casa Verona' (Kasi Veranna, d. 1680), had grown very rich indeed. Many were suspected of bribing EIC brokers for exclusive supply contracts.

In search of lower prices, the United Company now decided to replace exclusive supply contracts with big merchants in an open market at Fort St George's Sea Gate, and when the first new orders were placed with left-hand-caste merchants in June 1707, rioting ensued: '2–300 men of the right hand cast rose at midnight upon the left hand who were making a wedding in their own street, and untiled some of their houses,' recorded the governor.[86]

The trouble was quelled only when Pitt sent soldiers to arrest caste leaders and shut them in the fort until they came to terms and agreed a division of the city. But Pitt's task was complicated by an enemy within. The new United Company had brought together plenty of people determined to check Pitt's power. At the centre of the conspiracy was William Fraser and his accomplice, Roger Braddyl, a man who had joined the company in 1682 and proceeded to run up huge debts to the company, trading haphazardly throughout Bengal. 'I must say this much,' recorded Pitt, 'I never met with so knotty a villainy in my life nor ever with anything that gave me so much trouble and perplexity as this has done.'[87]

Ordered to Fort St George, Braddyl had married the widow of a company worthy and was admitted to the governor's council until his behaviour, 'full freighted with malice and inventions of his own', provoked his suspension.[88] Pitt sent him home in 1701, whereupon he began circulating rumours of Pitt's corruption – namely, that he had used 60,000 pagodas of the company's money for his own private trade – and conspired with Pitt's enemies to win appointment as general supervisor of the United Company's affairs in 1702, as part of a wider scheme to check the governor's power. ''Tis generally reported', wrote Pitt to friends in 1704, 'that 'twas urged there was a necessity of adding two to the council, for spies and checks upon the president.'[89]

Meanwhile, William Fraser – Deputy Governor of the Fort of St David and a man that Pitt regarded as without 'a grain of sense nor manners' – was also appointed to the council of Fort St George, from where it appeared he acted in collusion with the right-hand caste during the riots of 1707.[90] At one stage, a mob in the San Thome area, advancing on the fort, openly avowed that they would not return home except on terms agreed by Fraser. Acting in concert with his council, Pitt promptly locked him up. 'We were merciful', Pitt later wrote to his son, 'in not hanging of him.'[91]

With his enemies multiplying, Pitt was exhausting both his own patience and his political capital; yet his last act was perhaps his greatest gift to the company he had fought against for so long. He would save it in its hour of need.

In March 1707, India's great Emperor Aurangzeb died. In life, he had been one of the world's greatest rulers. In death, he divided his empire among three sons, who instantly commenced a murderous battle to gain pre-eminence and reunify the lands. Within months, the elder son, Prince Shah Alum, had defeated and slaughtered his step-siblings to succeed as Bahadur Shah I. Pitt knew the new emperor's chief advisers well; indeed, he had offered service to the wife of the new Lord High Steward of the Imperial Household, Zoodee Khan (Zainudin Khan). In the summer of 1708, Pitt was told that he 'may depend upon His Majesty's royal favour'.[92] The United Company's privileges were confirmed, at which point Pitt promptly pressed his luck.

Dispatching to Zoodee's wife a generous gift of rose-water, Persian fruit and cloth of gold, and a loan of 500 pagodas, Pitt gently enquired what presents the court might find most acceptable. He also hinted subtly at the virtues of customs-free trade inland to the fort of Golconda and Bijapur, of salvage rights for shipwrecks and of United Company control of Millipore (Mylapore, containing San Thome) and Trivatore, outside Fort St George, on the grounds that 'it would make us easy and increase the riches of the king's country'. When Daud Khan joined the shah's forces, he too promptly received gifts and money.

Rarely had the company spent its money better. Within weeks, a *perwanna* was received for Trivatore and four neighbouring townships, together valued at 1,500 pagodas, which Pitt promptly relet the following month for an annual rent of 1,200 pagodas. 'The favours from the present great mogul', Pitt wrote to his son, 'are without precedent'. There was little left for Pitt to achieve, as well he knew: 'I delivered it [Madras] up in the most flourishing state that ever any place in the world was in… in May or June last there was at some time 50 sail of ships in the road besides small craft of at least 200, the revenue of last year amounting between 70 and 800,000 pagodas of which above 10,000 arises out of the mint.'[93] He was ready for home. And the company was ready to see him gone.

Pitt's life as governor ended on Sunday, 17 September 1709. He knew it was coming. In November 1708, his son Robert warned of machinations at the company's court of directors, whereby 'the grounds on which they pretend to lay you aside are the unhappy troubles between the castes and your treatment of Fraser… whose party they espouse in the most violent manner'.[94] In August 1709, Pitt had been forced to confront Seaton, a man circulating rumours that Pitt had sold the office of Chief Dubash – his intermediary with the local populace – and spirited the immense diamond that would become the Regent out of the country 'to the company's prejudice'. On the very day that Pitt's dismissal arrived, he penned a letter home expressing his wish for relief.

That afternoon, the *Heathcote* drew into the bay. After dark, its commander, Captain Tolson, arrived with orders to relieve the governor. Pitt refused to open them. Rather, he summoned a council for the morning, whereupon the blunt, cold message was read out: 'Sir,' ran the letter, 'you having for some time past intimated to us your desire to return to England, we have granted your request.'' Pitt immediately took stock of the company's cash position and demanded the board to 'charge him with an unjust action during the whole time of his government or that he had ever refused a kindness to any one that asked it'. With that, he rose out of the chair, placed the new governor in it and prepared to leave for England.

*

Thomas Pitt had lived away from England for over a decade. Upon his return in 1704, his money, his mettle in the Commons and the marriages of his children would put him at the very centre of events. His homecoming was anything but straightforward. War raged still with France, so Pitt sailed in a Danish ship of the United Company to Amsterdam, ending up in Bergen, Norway, from where he issued instructions to his son to prepare for his arrival. He ordered his great diamond to be moved to the care of his cousin George Pitt and made other vital preparations. 'If there be any vacancy for a Parliament man, set me chose if you can do so honourably... Have your eye on some good and reputable lodgings for me in the city and provide me with two footmen, and a valet, trusty... pray get me a neat campagne perwigg not too bushy nor too long... Be sure to send the prices current of all diamonds.'[95]

Pitt was back in England in time for re-election to the Commons in the election of October–November 1710 – again as Member for Old Sarum – and promptly settled down to life in London's Pall Mall, equipped with an exceptionally good cellar and servants to liberally entertain his old friends in the City and his new friends in Parliament. He made his peace with the United Company, threw himself into Parliamentary life and set about organizing matches for his children.[†]

---

* Mr Gulston Addison was appointed president and Governor of Fort St George in his place. Dalton, *Thomas Pitt*, op. cit., p. 371.

† The directors had deposed Fraser and installed an old protégé of Pitt, Captain Harrison. The directors and Pitt soon patched up any dispute about the diamond's

But he found his family's fortunes distinctly mixed. Robert, his son and heir, was a constant source of grief. Dispatched home from India with the diamond in 1703, he had been implored by Pitt to stay on good terms with his mother, join the Inns of Court, become an expert in civil law and master fortification and gunnery. He promptly ignored his father's instructions, neglected to provide updates on the diamond's progress, violently fell out with his sisters and his mother, married, and took a hugely expensive house in Westminster's Golden Square. He entered Parliament, in 1705, also for Old Sarum, where both his politics and his profligacy were calculated to infuriate his father. He fell in with the Tories, forsook Parliament, and spent wildly. 'All your actions', railed his furious father in 1705, 'seem to be the produce of a hot head and giddy brain'.[96]

Pitt's wife, meanwhile, having fallen out with Pitt's cousin, moved at vast cost to a pleasant estate in Bath. His third son, the Eton-educated John, was on the other hand a great pride, while his second son, Thomas, was bought a captaincy in the Duke of Ormond's troop of Guards, a post that occasionally required attendance on the queen.

Pitt's focus, however, was his daughters. In January 1709, he wrote that 'My daughters are my greatest concern, and heartily wish they were well disposed of.'[97] In 1712, Lucy, perhaps his favourite and graced with a reputation for gentleness, was married to one of the greatest statesmen of the early eighteenth century, General James Stanhope, a popular military hero, distinguished in battle, and a joint leader of the Whig opposition to Walpole's Tories.* Stanhope was appointed second secretary of state when, following the childless Queen Anne's death, the Elector of Hanover arrived to take the throne as George I, on 18 September 1714.†

Within weeks, Pitt was presented to the new Hanoverian king, with his immense diamond in tow. 'I was this day above an hour with the

---

ownership, and in honour of Queen Anne's birthday, the great diamond was put on display.

* He had distinguished himself in the Spanish campaigns, especially at the battles of Almenar and Zaragoza, for which a medal had been struck.

† Pitt was appointed to the committee tasked with drawing up the Commons' address and to the Committee of Privileges and Elections.

king and prince,' Pitt wrote to Robert on 2 October 1714, and 'certainly their aspects promises prosperity to the country. I showed them the great diamond, which they admired and seemed desirous of it, but I believe, hope the nation will give it.'[98] In the elections that followed in 1715, no fewer than four Pitts were elected to the Commons – the former governor and all three of his sons. Moreover, through Stanhope's good offices, Robert Pitt was offered a position at the court of the Prince of Wales.

George I's first months were not smooth. He had come to the throne as a result of the 1701 Act of Settlement, which attempted to fix a Protestant succession by settling it on Sophie of Hanover – grand-daughter of James I – and her heirs. Within the year, the Catholic Pretender James Stuart, son of James II, had raised his standard in Scotland in his bid to take the throne. As rebellion loomed, Pitt and his family leapt to Protestant England's defence. Stanhope acted quickly to disable the revolt in England's west. Pitt personally set out for Dorset to raise a regiment of men at his own cost. Over the course of October 1715 his letters were packed with news of the rebels' manoeuvres; in November he took pride in reporting his participation in the final fight in Preston.

With peace at home and with France, Pitt, now sixty-four, was presented with what would be his last chance to serve – and profit. On 19 June 1716, he was appointed Governor of Jamaica by the king. Still the pearl of Britain's empire, Jamaica had fallen, in Pitt's words, into 'great disorder and confusion'. He immediately set about a study of the island's problems, recommending that firm governorship, with new powers, was required to set things straight, not least in raising the revenue to properly garrison the island. But after months of delays, as Pitt tied up his business affairs and accounts, as King George continued to be distracted by the threat of fresh rebellion, and as royal officials scoured the law books and precedents to examine the possibilities of changing the island's governance, Pitt lost patience with the slow pace of events. Before getting sight of Jamaica, he tendered his resignation, on 21 June 1717, in time to return to Parliament (for Thirsk, in a by-election) and to prosecute the sale, at last, of his diamond to the Regent of France.

The eventual sale of this most precious stone made Pitt one of the richest men in England. It had taken fifteen anxious years, and now Pitt was determined to put the proceeds to good use. Fifty-three thousand pounds was laid out for the Boconnoc estate, the finest in Cornwall, bought from the Mohun family, along with Swallowfield Park acquired soon after, which lay 6 miles south-east of Reading and which included the house that would become his favourite.

*

It was at Swallowfield where Pitt spent many of his final years, and where his happiness provided relief from the pain he felt at his son-in-law's ruin in the first great crash of the new global economy. Stanhope – now Earl Stanhope – had triumphed in brokering a peace among England's neighbours that denied safe haven to the fleeing Pretender. Appointed Chancellor of the Exchequer on 15 April 1717, he accompanied George I on his visit home to Hanover, whereupon the monarch declared his hope that Stanhope's new South Sea Act would happily help liquidate the national debt. Public debt had vastly increased – owing to the costs of, first, the Nine Years' War and then the War of the Spanish Succession (1701–14) – and in the years after 1707 nearly a third of state income was required each year just to keep up the repayments. Between 1711 and 1714, short-term debts were funded with new taxes.* More annuities were sold, too, but a comprehensive solution was needed.

The Sword Blade Company had tried unsuccessfully to seize the Bank of England's monopoly when its charter was renewed in 1707. In 1711, it proposed instead the South Sea Company, to consolidate £9 million of short-term government debt, financed by selling company shares. Nine years later, it proposed something far more audacious: to privatize the entire public debt. In essence, the company would issue £31 million in stock at a market price in a complex scheme that would, over seven years, knock £400,000 (around one-sixth) off the annual

---

* Duties were placed on coffee, tea, books, playing cards, calicoes, candles, coal, hackney coaches, linens, leather, paper, parchment, soap, silks and Irish salt.

debt bill.[99] The company's enabling bill allowed the shareholders to offer either cash or shares to subscribers. When the shares were issued, a bubble began to grow. Between January and July 1720, the share price rose from £128 to £950, and some 85 per cent of the government's irredeemable debt was swapped for company shares. But after months of a speculative boom, the stock collapsed and hundreds were ruined. Pitt himself lost a small fortune. Stanhope, intimately associated with the disaster, defended himself in the Lords on 4 February 1721, only to collapse and die the following day.

Thomas Pitt was Stanhope's executor, and made a home for the earl's children and Lucy at Swallowfield. But when she died three months later, Pitt was devastated. For the rest of the year, he reported ill-health, complaining to son Robert in March 1723 that 'for my part, I grow weaker and weaker, and think cannot hold it long'.[100]

By his final days, Sir Thomas 'Diamond' Pitt had seen the great East India Company help set the stage for a revolution abroad and at home. In London, the company – once a capital-starved trading venture – had become the biggest corporation in private hands, aside from the Exchequer and the Bank of England. It was a vital part of the new bedrock of the capital's burgeoning capital market. Up and down the country, the company's trade had transformed English tastes, flooding the land with the goods of India, South-East Asia and China, triggering vast new demand for cotton, for porcelain, for Chinese tea and Arabian coffee, and creating the market for the cotton-spinners, pottery-makers and foreign traders of the coming Industrial Revolution. And in India, as the Mughal empire slipped towards decline and the Dutch VOC began to wane, the company's armed ships and fortified bases became the foundation of Britain's eastern empire, which in time would lead to war in China and dominion in Africa.

Pitt held on until, on 2 May 1726, when Robert announced his father's death after two days of illness. 'His distemper', he reported, 'was a mixture of apoplexy and palsy.' Sir Thomas 'Diamond' Pitt was buried at Blandford St Mary on 21 May 1726 – whereupon his children promptly set about contesting their inheritance.

4

MATTHEW BOULTON

Wedgwood, Watt and the Steam Revolution

From the moment it opened in April 1786, the Albion Mill was famous. Five storeys high, on the 'Surrey-side of Blackfriars', London's first great factory towered over Southwark. 'There has not been any public edifice perhaps ever erected in the country', wrote one observer, 'with a more patriotic view than the Albion flour mills.'[1] Its great grinding machines could pulverize so much grain, so fast the mill slashed the capital's bread bill, knocking 2 shillings off the price of a bag of flour – and knocking Lambeth's windmills out of business.[2]

More spectacular than its size was its power, for the 'arduous and laudable undertaking' was driven entirely by steam. At its core revolved nine pairs of millstones – which soon multiplied to twenty-seven – all driven on by steam engines. Engine-powered hoists lifted corn from barges on the Thames. Machine-powered fans filtered out the impurities. The Albion Mill was a revolution. It 'calls our attention', wrote the *Scots Magazine*, 'to the great changes it is probable this agent [steam] may hereafter produce in the appearance of the civilized world… Every lover of science and every friend to mankind will receive pleasure from the inspection of this immense machine.'[3]

But William Blake was not so sure. The twenty-nine-year-old radical poet and engraver ran a print shop not far away. From his window, in Lambeth's Hercules Buildings, he could see the mill and what he saw he thought was evil. It seems his neighbours shared the sentiment.

Late on the evening of Wednesday, 2 March 1791, fire was spotted in the factory. Within minutes, the flames burnt with such a ferocity that the buildings all around were scorched. With the river low, water-pumpers could not get near the conflagration.[4] When the roof collapsed, a column of fire spiked into the London skies, 'so awfully grand as to illuminate for a while the whole horizon', sending parched wheat on the wind miles away to Westminster, where it 'lay in great abundance' on the parade ground of St James's Park. Within hours, the mill was lost.[5] Miraculously, the company's pigs, fattening in the yard next door, survived. But 2,000 sacks of corn and flour had burned, along with the wheat barges.

Yet despite the apparent catastrophe, in the fire-light could be seen groups of millers, dancing. As the factory burned, observers could not help but notice 'a very curious scene... instead of the usual sentiments of compassion and instead of rendering active assistance, [the crowd] stood idly by with folded arms and testified only satisfaction at the overthrow of a work which they considered as pernicious in its tendency'. Placards mysteriously appeared with slogans such as 'Success to the mills of ALBION but no Albion Mills'. By the morning, celebratory poems and songs were circulating on Southwark Bridge. Within a week a ballad was doing the rounds including the lines 'but very few did sorrow show, / That the Albion Mills were burned so low.' The workers had burned down the mill.

For twenty years, Albion Mills' burnt-out hulk haunted the London skyline, an inauspicious augury of a new era fast taking shape. In his poem 'Jerusalem', later put to music as the hymn, Blake immortalized the 'dark, satanic mill'. The Industrial Revolution, with all its force and tension, was well underway – and one man – the industrial revolutionary behind Albion Mills – was determined to make a fortune in the process: Birmingham's Matthew Boulton.

*

Matthew Boulton was born at home in Whitehall's Lane, two years after the death of Sir Thomas Pitt, on Birmingham's northern border, on Tuesday, 3 September 1728.* He had the very good fortune to arrive as the third child into an old established family in a young, exciting city.

---

* Whitehall's Lane is now called Steelhouse Lane.

It was the era described for us in glorious richness by the author of *Robinson Crusoe*, Daniel Defoe, who left London six years before Boulton was born on a tour of the new nation of Great Britain, formed by the union of the English and Scottish parliaments in 1707. Commissioned by his mysterious employer Robert Harley, Defoe spent each day travelling, before finding an inn in which to compose his reports. The bulletins made up an extraordinary book: *A Plan of the English Commerce, being a Complete Prospect of the Trade of This Nation*. Here, we find the sights of 'the most flourishing and opulent country in the world'. 'Every new view of Great Britain', wrote Defoe, 'would require a new description: the improvements that increase, the new buildings erected, the old buildings taken down: new discoveries in metals, mines, minerals; new undertakings in trade; inventions, engines, manufactures, in a nation pushing and improving as we are: these things open new scenes every day.'

This was a country where more than a quarter of the population were now making things and where nearly one in five were engaged in 'industry', a figure some 50 per cent higher than the European average.[6] Since around 1700, Britain's regional industrial specialisms had begun to settle, and everywhere on his travels, Defoe found hives of industry: the Exeter serge-makers, the Norfolk weavers, the Essex bay-makers, Wiltshire's fine clothiers, the hardware and cutlery makers across the Midlands, and the cottonware, ironware, Yorkshire cloths and kerseys made across the northern manufacturing districts of Manchester, Sheffield, Leeds and Halifax. In general, 'industry' meant 'cottage industry', organized by middlemen who farmed great networks of activity that would predominate for another century. In the 1730s, one Lancashire merchant estimated that he put work out to 600 looms; in the Black Country, another guessed he supplied work to small forges and 'little masters' in 1,000 homes.[7] But, amid the commotion, the first signs of a revolution in factories, forges and fuel could now be seen.

The country's greatest business was probably still the Royal Dockyards in Chatham, Kent, where Defoe found that: 'The building yards, docks, timber-yard, deal-yard, mast-yard, gun-yard, rope-walks... are like a well-ordered city; and tho' you see the whole place as it were in the utmost hurry, yet you see no confusion, every man knows his business.'[8] But entrepreneurs were assembling new ways of doing business, and in Derby, Defoe found a harbinger of things to come. Crossing 'that fury of a river called the Derwent', he remarked on a 'fine, beautiful and pleasant' town – and the country's first factory: Thomas Lombe's £30,000 silk mill, built for 300 workers to designs smuggled out of Italy by his half-brother John in covert sketches hidden in bales of raw silk. 'Here is a curiosity in trade worth observing,' wrote Defoe, 'as being the only one of its kind in England, namely a throwing or throwster's mill, which performs by a wheel turn'd by water' and which 'performs the labour of many hands'. The Italians, in their fury, dispatched 'an artful woman [who] came over in the character of a friend' and slowly poisoned the twenty-nine-year-old John Lombe 'who lingered two or three years in agonies, and departed'.[9] He was given the most superb funeral ever seen in Derby. Thomas's mill, protected by patent, was luckier: it made a fortune.

As factories began to spread, so the nation's forges began to multiply. In the Midlands, Defoe saw the hearths fuelled by Shropshire coal, shipped in abundance along the Severn, at half the price charged in London. 'Every farm has one forge or more,' he noted, and 'we cannot travel far in any direction out of the sound of the hammer'.[10] He did not, of course, spot everything on his journey. Defoe missed the new iron trade's great entrepreneur, Abraham Darby, busy with his break-through mastering the art of smelting iron from abundant coal instead of limited, expensive charcoal.[11]

Darby had served his apprenticeship in Birmingham and set up shop in Bristol, with fellow Quakers, as brassmaker. He eventually leased the old Vale Royal furnace on the deep gorge-like valley of Coalbrookdale next to the Severn, an old established iron-making centre, where coal lay exposed along the margins. Here, he started a business worth an estimated £2,804, imitating Dutch techniques for casting brass pots. But, soon frustrated with the business of ferrying in wood for charcoal, he began to experiment. In 1709, according to his daughter-in-law Hannah Rose, 'sometime after he suggested the thought that it might be practicable to smelt the iron from the ore in the blast furnace with pit coal; upon this he first tried with raw coal… but it did not answer. He not discouraged, had the coal coked into cinder, as is done for drying malt, and it then succeeded to his satisfaction.'[12] It was a breakthrough that would transform the British iron industry, and it was not too long before men such as Ambrose Crowley, who began as an apprentice to an ironmonger, opened his first nail manufactory in 1684. By 1728 he had built a business of slitting mills, steel furnaces, foundries, forges, warehouses and ships worth some £250,000.[13]

Nor did Defoe have much to say about the 'coal rush', which was already prompting gentlemen to scour their estates for tell-tale signs of seams. If, like Lord Paget, they found it under their flower-beds or parklands, no matter. Mining began at once. By the beginning of the eighteenth century, the north-east of England was already shipping 1.3 million tonnes of coal; 450,000 tonnes more came from Scotland, and the West Midlands was not far behind.[14]

Lombe's mill, Darby's forge, the mines of Newcastle, Shropshire and Cornwall – here was the cutting edge of a revolution that would soon transform the new Great Britain and create, in the process, important new hubs, such as Matthew Boulton's Birmingham.

*

Situated close to iron ore, coal and running water, Birmingham was a town of smiths, scythesmiths, bladesmiths, nailers, ironmongers and wheelers (making arms and weaponry). Its industry dated back to at least the 1500s.[15] In 1538, John Leland found 'many smiths in the town that use to make knives and all manner of cutting tools, and many lorimers that make bits and a great many nailors, so that a great part of the town is maintained by smiths who have their iron and sea-coal out of Staffordshire'.[16] By the time William Camden arrived in 1610, the antiquarian-topographer found a town 'echoing with forges, most of the inhabitants being iron-manufacturers'; and around the same time, William Smith recorded 'Bromicham' as a place where 'great store of knives are made; for almost all the town's men are cutlers, or smiths'.[17]

By the early 1700s, Birmingham boasted an extraordinary range of trades: braziers, founders, casters, bell-founders, gearmakers, locksmiths, nailers – and, like Matthew Boulton's father, toymakers. The town's lack of guilds offered freedom to new arrivals, and it became a haven for religious Non-conformists. Ambitious newcomers were drawn by its diversity of craftsmen and wealthy families prepared to back new ventures – some of which, by the 1650s, were making fortunes in the ironmongery business and building great homes like Erdington Hall. The town made a fortune from the Civil War; in one deal, for instance, Robert Porter sold the Parliamentary army 15,000 swords, and by the Restoration of Charles II, the town boasted 178 smiths' hearths, and many owners had diversified into gunmaking.

By the time Matthew Boulton was born, Birmingham was a town of 15,000 people, packed into nearly 4,000 houses spread over 100 streets, including the old thoroughfares leading to the medieval Bull Ring.* Matthew lived in the upper half of town, on the sandstone ridge where Birmingham's new merchant classes were building their homes around classical squares. Nearby was the new St Philip's Church, with its elegant dome modelled on St Paul's Cathedral, beyond which fields and orchards stretched back into the Warwickshire countryside.

In Low Town, 'filled with workshops and ware-houses of the manufacturers', were the old timber buildings densely packed with forges. Steel-houses sat along Steelhouse Lane and Cole's Hill Street, while the markets – for meat, flowers, cattle, pigs, sheep, horses, and corn and garden produce – were laid out around the Bull Ring, around which the cock-fighting, bowling green and theatres offered a little respite from the noise of the metal-bashers. William Hutton, the town's first historian, described the scene in 1740, when Boulton would have been twelve: 'I was, each morning by three o'clock, saluted with a circle of hammers…I had been among dreamers but now saw men awake. Their very step shewed alacrity. Every man seemed to know what he was about. The town was large, and full of inhabitants and those inhabitants full of industry.'[18]

The air was full of new ideas, whether offered in the public lectures on electricity or on offer in exhibitions of 'mechanical marvels'.

---

* Local builder William Wesley produced the first-known plan of the city in 1731.

Through this bustling town, Matthew walked to school in Deritend, a few miles south across the River Rea, to Reverend Ansted's private academy, where he studied mathematics and drawing and acquired – in the words of Samuel Smiles – 'the rudiments of a good ordinary English education'.[19]

Some time before the age of seventeen, Matthew started work for his father, who by all accounts was a man in the right place at the right time. The elder Boulton, also named Matthew, had started as an apprentice. He was descended from an old, landed Staffordshire county family: his grandmother's line boasted a Chancellor of Lichfield Cathedral (the Reverend Zachary Babington) and his great-grandfather, Richard Dyott, was a Staffordshire knight. After marrying in 1723, in St Martin's Church in Birmingham's Bull Ring, the elder Boulton had set up shop as a toymaker, a trade that encompassed the manufacture of an infinite variety of small metal goods in gold, silver, tortoiseshell, steel and iron: buckles, trinkets, watch-chains, hooks, cork-screws, seals, tweezers, buttons, snuffers, candlesticks and clocks. It was a booming business. Indeed, Edmund Burke would later christen the city 'The Toyshop of Europe', a rather more charitable description than Thomas Telford's denunciation of the place as 'famous for its buttons and its locks, its ignorance and its barbarism'.[20]

It was not long before the Boulton family was moving up in the world, to Snow Hill, where the houses – set back from the road – had great chimneys for hearths big enough for metalwork. Of the toymaking trade's two most important branches – buckles and buttons – the elder Boulton was a specialist in the former, buying steel on credit from the big ironmongers who dominated the industry and crafting it for market as fashionable goods for export to France, from where they might be reimported to England as the latest French 'novelties'.[21]

As a teenager, the younger Boulton was quick to introduce improvements into methods of manufacture, inventing inlaid steel buckles, with enamel,[22] and having mastered his craft, the young Boulton, was soon a master of commerce, for he had the fortune to work among one of the most brilliant generations of English entrepreneurs. Into Birmingham in the 1720s had come an extraordinary constellation of innovators. John Baskerville (1706–75) arrived from Worcestershire, trading in *papier-mâché* and japanned goods, before he became a printer and inventor of the Baskerville typeface. Samuel Garbett (1717–1803) was an influential button- and hardware-manufacturer, and later co-founder of the important Carron Ironworks in Scotland, one of the greatest in Europe and worth some £150,000 by 1773. His business partner, John Roebuck (1718–94), was a pioneering industrial chemist, whose experiments with smelting and acid inspired Birmingham's first refinery of precious metals. All helped teach Boulton the arts of finance and patronage, the appliance of science, and the importance of art. Along with these men, Boulton would one day join some 209 Birmingham citizens each worth more than £5,000 – as much as £9 million today – who, according to William Hutton, 'began [in] the world with nothing but their own prudence'.[23]

In little over a decade after starting work, Matthew Boulton's energy and enterprise took him from apprenticeship to leadership of the family firm. Having mastered his trade by the age of twenty-one, he settled, marrying his distant cousin, Mary Robinson, on 9 February 1749, at St Mary's Church in Lichfield. With marriage came money – a small fortune in fact, for Mary was the daughter of Luke Robinson, a wealthy mercer, and had inherited a substantial estate from her god-mother. When Mary's father died, within a year of her marriage to Matthew, Mary inherited another £3,000.

Boulton's father soon made his son a partner, and as Matthew's twenties progressed, the Boulton business powered forward. Such was the demand for its products that in 1755 Matthew's father took out a lease on a rolling mill – Sarehole Mill – to ensure supplies of more sheet metal.* Two years later it was clear that although Matthew was signing letters 'Father and self', it was in fact he who was now driving the business.[24] Theirs was an industry that was now expanding fast, and buckles were worth a fortune; indeed, by 1760 some 8,000 people in England were making buckles in an industry worth around £300,000.[25]

Matthew's letter-books for the period are packed with orders. He was clearly a man who sought the best; in one letter to Sheffield's

---

* Sarehole Mill was later immortalized as The Shire by J. R. R. Tolkien in his book *The Hobbit*.

pioneering steelmaker, Benjamin Huntsman, in 1757, he sent 'a parcel of goods of the newest patterns' in return for a request for the best steel Huntsman could muster.[26] And when Boulton joined his fellow trades-man to testify to Parliament on the state of the toy trade, he offered a wide knowledge of business in the Netherlands, Spain and Portugal.[27]

Success at work, however, was marked by tragedy at home. Before 1753, Matthew and Mary lost three children – Dorothea, Anne and Maria all died in infancy – and now Mary herself was unwell. Among Matthew's early papers are notes on 'Hystericks'; on one sheet, he wrote out the symptoms – creeping coldness, headaches and spasms, adding that 'hence it is that hysterickal women feel constriction in the throte as if strangled'.[28] Another paper lists a host of anti-epileptic remedies. In August 1759 calamity came. Mary died, and a month later Boulton's father, too, was dead. Matthew buried his wife in the Robinson family crypt in Whittington, near Lichfield, with a eulogy:

> If bearing many children, & enduring many pains & illnesses,
> With patience under his Eye
> If preserving fair Virtue around her unpolluted Bed,
> If passing through Life without one Black Spot upon her Fame,
> If these things can endear a Wife to a Husband
> Thou wert dear to me

At the age of thirty-one, Matthew Boulton had lost his wife, his children and his father. And so he proceeded to fling himself into his future.

*

Within months of his loss, Boulton was back on the road to London, pushing sales hard among the capital's elite and presenting a sword hilt to Prince Edward, the Duke of York, which so impressed George, Prince of Wales, that a royal order followed. His second front in Birmingham would bring even more. Boulton had decided to woo his now very rich sister-in-law, Anne, who had inherited her sister's share of the Robinson family estate, worth some £28,000 (between £45 million and £65 million today). By the spring of 1760, he was address-ing Anne as 'My dear Heart', 'My dear charmer' and 'My dear Angel'. Under ecclesiastical law, a marriage to his sister-in-law was not strictly legal and Anne's friends were not keen.* But, inspired by a pamphlet he had found which bolstered his case, Boulton pressed on.† When Anne's mother died in May 1760, the pair stole away to London, and on 25 June 1760 they were married in St Mary's Church, in Rotherhithe.

The new Boulton family, now very wealthy, settled down in Birmingham's Snow Hill. Over the five years that followed, with his old confidence and his new resources, Boulton set about building the factory and friendships that would help define the Industrial Revolution: the Soho Manufactory and the Lunar Society.

Boulton was probably inspired in his methods by the city's greatest toymaker, John Taylor (1704–75), who, instead of 'putting out goods' to networks of artisans, had created a 'factory' of specialized workshops employing 500 people.‡ Boulton now began plotting a factory of his own. Backed by his new wife's wealth, in 1761 he took the lease on Soho House and its estate – 13 acres of windy Handsworth Heath, replete with a rolling mill, 2 miles north of Birmingham, where the owners had dammed Hockley Brook to create a wide millpond for a new mill.

Having bought the lease and all the buildings for £1,000, Boulton set about rebuilding the house, replacing the mill, and creating ware-houses, workshops and somewhere for his workmen to live. The market around him was now booming – in 1759, Birmingham's manufacturers explained to Parliament that 20,000 people now worked in the city's toy trade, manufacturing £600,000 worth of goods. But, despite the family fortune, Boulton needed a dizzying array of loans. He soon found himself over-stretched. He needed a partner, and on a business trip to London in January 1762, he found one.

John Fothergill had trained as an apprentice in Königsberg, Prussia,

---

* Smiles also notes that Anne's friends offered some opposition on account of Boulton's trade in Smiles, *Lives of Boulton and Watt*, op. cit., p. 166.

† The pamphlet was John Fry's 'The Case of Marriage Between Near Kindred', published in 1756.

‡ John Taylor later founded the Birmingham Bank, which would become Lloyds Bank.

and had wide sales experience on the Continent – in one year travelling through Hamburg, Lübeck, Königsberg, Denmark, Sweden, St Petersburg, and returning via Narva (Estonia), Riga (Latvia) and Königsberg.[29] He liked Boulton and offered to invest alongside him, adding £5,000 to the £6,000 Boulton was sinking into the Soho site.* More was to come two years later, when Boulton's brother-in-law died and the entire Robinson estate passed to the Boulton family. Boulton now seized the chance to begin building on a truly magnificent scale, creating, as he so modestly put it, 'the largest hardware manufactory in the world'.[30]

Completed fully around 1766, the new Soho Manufactory 'engaged the attention of all ranks of people'.[31] Built at an alleged cost of £20,000, it was five times over budget and big enough for 1,000 workmen.[32] Clerks, managers and their families lived on the upper floors; a rolling mill was on site; and the factory was packed with the latest tools. Within two years, Boulton had mastered the art of making the silver-and-copper 'Sheffield plate', the only such factory in the West Midlands.

Boulton and Fothergill had set out to build not simply a factory but also a *brand*. The partners took the exceptional step of employing the architect William Wyatt to design an industrial building beautiful enough to express the proprietors' grasp of classical taste, and exquisite enough to adorn their continental publicity.[33] Boulton understood something crucial. Success required him to conquer the terrible reputation of 'Brummagem wares' – the term that stuck to Birmingham's mass-market trinkets and cheap reproductions. As Boulton noted to a friend, 'The prejudice that Birmingham hath so justly established against itself makes every fault conspicuous in all articles that have the least pretension to taste.'[34]

It was not a cheap strategy. In 1764, the Boulton & Fothergill partnership lost £3,000, and so slowly over the course of 1764 and 1765 Boulton centralized the production that had hitherto been scattered across the city, and evicted Fothergill so that he could move in and personally supervise the factory floor. Fothergill, Boulton discovered,

---

* Fothergill moved into the manor house on the hill above the rolling mill in 1762.

had not been the best of factory managers, as he noted: 'As Fothergill is not of the least use in the Manufactory, if he will not live near a warehouse in Town[,] Query[:] of what use will [he] be?'[35]

The fame of Soho and its Manufactory continued to outperform its finances. Despite Boulton's supervision, manufacturing was still run in a 'spectacularly disorganised way', with a very poor grip on the workforce, stock control, pricing or the basics of collecting money.[36] Yet, by the summer of 1767 Boulton was writing of the foreign and other visitors that arrived every day, 'who are all much delighted by the extension and regularity of our manufactory'.[37] In August 1767, he had to apologize to one frustrated customer for a delayed order on account of the fact that 'I had lords and ladies to wait on yesterday; I have French and Spaniards to-day; and tomorrow I shall have Germans, Russians and Norwegians'.[38]

Boulton could now boast the best of customers. In 1767, he was presented to George III and Queen Charlotte, who acquired from him 'a pair of cassolets, a Titus, a Venus clock, and some other things'. Writing to his wife, Boulton noted that 'I was with them, the queen and all the children, between two and three hours... Never was a man so much complimented as I have been.'[39]

*

Boulton's influence owed as much to his enquiring mind as to his expanding wealth. As a young man, he was fascinated by science. In his late twenties, he was studying electricity and planning a scientific library of his own, and jotting down experiments on everything from precipitation, boiling points and the freezing points of mercury, to the human pulses, the movements of the planets and the manufacture of phosphorus.[40]

When the future framer of the US Constitution, Benjamin Franklin, settled in England in 1757, he met Boulton in Birmingham. Together they attempted to seal Leyden jars to prevent leakage of 'electrical fluid' in 1760. Boulton occasionally supplied Franklin with new glass for his instruments. He soon owned two electrical machines and met experimenters from across the country. But it was a different friendship that was to prove the more significant: Boulton met the doctor, poet and inventor Erasmus Darwin in the late 1750s, and together the pair soon formed the kernel of Britain's leading provincial philosophical society.*

The Lunar Society, so named because the members met on the night of a full moon to light the ride home – was not unique to Birmingham. Indeed, such clubs existed all over Britain; but only in Birmingham did the members mix pioneers of experimental chemistry, physics and medicine with leaders of manufacturing and commerce. Their science prompted their innovation. And their innovation soon transformed their industry.

The Lunar Society's empirical methods were born through a century of scientific endeavour, which had been revolutionised by the foundation of the Royal Society. The country's greatest scientist – Isaac Newton – had died the year before Boulton was born. 'On the 28th past,' ran the *London Gazette* on 4 April 1727, 'the Corpse of Sir Isaac Newton lay in State in the Jerusalem Chamber, and was buried thence in Westminster-Abbey near the Entry in the Choir.' 'What a nation', wrote a French observer, 'that buries its scientists with its kings.'[41] His pall bearers included the lord chancellor, the dukes of Montrose and Roxburgh, and the earls of Pembroke, Sussex and Macclesfield, all 'being Fellows of the Royal Society'.

Boulton's generation would not make breakthroughs of the magnitude of Newton and his peers. But in the thousands of little inventions and innovations, and in the hundreds of amateur laboratories, workshops, lectures and discussion clubs, it was Boulton and his contemporaries that allied science to invention and invention to industry.

Boulton's blessing lay in his ability to draw on traditions and techniques that were now well-established around him. England was not a land of pure free-thinkers. Both culture and the constitution supplied plenty of constraints on anyone not judged a proper Anglican, for example. But it was a land where reason also flourished. In the first

---

* Erasmus was the grandfather of Charles Darwin. He moved to Lichfield to open a medical practice in 1756.

decades of the eighteenth century, the stage, the newspapers, the parks, the markets, the Royal Exchange, the bustling wharves of the Thames, and above all the coffee houses, all became new arenas for news, gossip, scandal, but also ideas – and energy.* They provided the space and place for ideas to be weighed, surveyed and applied.

Here was the formation of society that would remain recognizable to the Victorians. Informing day-to-day conversation was a new industry of newspapers. In 1695, the press Licensing Act fell, and newspapers began to proliferate, first in London and then around the country. In 1718 Ambrose Phillips launched the *Free-thinker* magazine with its motto adapted from Horace, 'dare to know'. 'All Englishmen', wrote the Swiss visitor Cesar de Saussure, 'are great newsmongers. Workmen habitually begin the day by going to coffee-rooms in order to read the latest news.'42

No longer was the royal court the prime mover in the sponsorship of ideas. Indeed, the very concept of the monarch's divine right to rule was slowly being dismantled and supplanted with a theory of social contract, set out with eloquence by John Locke in his *Two Treatises of Government* (1689). In this new atmosphere, rich and poor mingled freely at hustings, races, spas, parks, on stagecoaches and, of course, in coffee houses. The country was, Defoe noted, a land where lords played bowls with tradesmen, where peasants rode on horseback, where the status of gentleman was open to anyone who looked and behaved the part. By 1726, Voltaire – having spent three years in English exile – could write: 'The English are the only people upon earth... who, by a series of struggles, have at last established that wise government, where the prince is all powerful to do good, and at the same time is restrained from committing evil.'43

---

* In 1739, there some 551 coffee houses in London – ten times more than in Vienna. It was in these coffee houses and clubs that great men held court: John Dryden and Alexander Pope at Will's, in Covent Garden; thespians at the Bedford; artists at Old Slaughter's; Tories at Smyrna in Pall Mall, all part of a scene that boasted more than 2,000 clubs and societies, from the Sublime Society of Beefsteaks, to the Kit-Cat, or Dr Johnson's Literary Club, the Spitalfields Mathematical Society and the burgeoning lodges of Freemasons, which boomed in the years after 1717.

In this atmosphere of diffusion – an Age of Reflection – there was one arena of especial importance: the Royal Society, a meeting of minds that would prove as important to the Industrial Revolution as the Royal Exchange or the Royal Navy.

The Society first met on Wednesday, 28 November 1660, when, after a lecture by Sir Christopher Wren, a dozen men came together for the purpose of the 'promoting of experimental philosophy'. At first steered by Robert Hooke, the author of the first popular-science book, *Micrographia*, which Samuel Pepys described as 'the most ingenious book that ever I read in my life', the Society was soon meeting once a week.[44] By 1665, over a hundred Fellows were actively engaged in the Society's work, with weekly attendance of anywhere between a dozen and twenty. Under Sir Isaac Newton, however, the Society became the driving force in the evolution of British science. Taking office as president in 1703, Newton helped establish careful rules of experimentation and over the next twenty years he missed just three meetings, transforming a society of scholars into a truly scientific movement.[45]

Inspired by the model, the Birmingham Lunar Society, which was never more than fourteen in number, drew together not only Boulton and Darwin, but James Watt, the perfecter of the steam engine, Josiah Wedgwood, the pottery pioneer, Joseph Priestley, the discoverer of oxygen, William Murdoch, the inventor of gas lighting and creator of the first steam locomotive to run on roads, and Dr William Small, tutor to Thomas Jefferson, the future President of the United States.[46]

By 1766, the circle was meeting as often as it could, dining at two o'clock until eight in the evening. Wine flowed. Tables were full. And when the eating was done, out came the instruments, plans, models, minerals or machines. The 'philosophical feast' often lasted into the next day, or longer, and the gathered friends were able to share news and feed back ideas to London, the Royal Society, the Society of Arts, and the coffee houses like Slaughter's in St Martin's Lane to where Boulton (and various 'philosophers and artists') would repair when he was in the capital and at a loose end.

Enthused with the Lunar Society's inventive spirit, Boulton would put it to good use in two extraordinary partnerships that would help him establish his claim on history: the first with Josiah Wedgwood, and the second with Mr James Watt.

*

Josiah Wedgwood (1730–95) was one of the greatest entrepreneurs of the Industrial Revolution. He was born into an old family of Staffordshire potters, in Burslem, surrounded by the Midlands' soft yellow and brown clays that his forebears had shaped, baked and glazed into 'butterpots, pitchers and patterned plates'. He had the good fortune to work just as the East India Company's china imports were fuelling demand for distinctive blue-and-white fine Chinese porcelain. In 1708, Europeans had cracked the long-concealed secrets of its manufacture, and in 1745, soft-paste porcelain was made for the first time in Chelsea.

Wedgwood, who lost his father young, was apprenticed to his older brother. Aged twenty-four, Josiah joined Thomas Whieldon, a pioneer of new production methods, who gave Wedgwood the freedom to begin the first of 5,000 carefully recorded trials with new glazes and manufacturing techniques.[47] Like Boulton, Wedgwood had married well and used his wife's dowry to pioneer a successful line of brilliantly glazed earthenware aimed at the squire's table, before winning his first orders from Queen Charlotte, for a tea-set. The title of 'Potter to Her Majesty' followed, and then a brand, 'Queen's Ware'. Soon, members of the aristocracy were beating a path to his door at Burslem to place their orders.

It was, however, not ceramics but canals that first united Boulton and Wedgwood. Moving the raw materials needed for manufacturing into their factories, and the finished goods out of them, at acceptable speed and cost, were significant problems for entrepreneurs such as Wedgwood and Boulton. Together they would transform the region in which they worked, creating connections to England's cities, its ports and its markets around the world.

By the time of their collaboration, some 15,000 miles of road connected up the country. With an absence of local taxes, the country represented a single marketplace, which, said the Venetian ambassador in 1706, explained why 'industry was further advanced in England than in any other part of the world'.[48] But bulkier and heavier goods, such as coal, needed to travel by water, and so throughout Boulton's lifetime, in additional to the coastal traffic, rivers were deepened and canalized, and waterflows controlled with new locks and sluices. The Thames, all the way from Oxford, along with the Wey, the Lea and the Medway were crowded with food and timber coming down to London, while Tyne coals were dragged up.

When the opportunity for riverine improvements reached their limits, the country's entrepreneurs began digging canals. Inspired by the Canal du Midi in France, the Duke of Bridgewater had, in 1759, won a Parliamentary battle to develop a 41-mile route from deep within his coal mines in England's north-west to the docks and wharves of Manchester's Deansgate. When the Bridgewater Canal, designed by James Brindley, opened in 1761, the price of coal in Manchester halved. In the ensuring canal mania, discussed in coffee houses and councils all over Britain, it was Josiah Wedgwood who emerged as campaigner in chief for a new 'Grand Trunk', a 93-mile canal to link Staffordshire's Potteries to the River Trent, the Humber Estuary and then the North Sea, and to Liverpool, the Mersey Estuary and out into the Atlantic.

In 1763, a petition for a local turnpike noted that the 150 potteries around Burslem employed 7,000 people and exported huge quantities to America, the West Indies and Europe. Inspired by Bridgewater's example, Wedgwood set about building a consortium of Midlands entrepreneurs and landowners with persuasive arguments about the profits to be had by lowering everyone's cost of transport. By 1765, he was discussing the idea of a Staffordshire project with fellow potters, winning the backing of Lord Gower, a major local owner of land and mines (and the Duke of Bridgewater's brother-in-law), publishing pamphlets, lobbying Parliament and countering competing petitions.

In May 1766, Wedgwood's scheme won its royal assent and the following month he was appointed its treasurer. On 26 July 1766, every pottery in Burslem was closed as the town dressed in its best and poured on to the fields beneath the town as Josiah Wedgwood cut the first sod of the Trent and Mersey Canal. It would take another five years to finish, but when it opened, transport costs fell by almost 90 per cent.

Matthew Boulton and Wedgwood had collaborated on the project – Boulton was among the canal's shareholders. When Wedgwood first visited the Soho site in May 1767, he concluded that Boulton was 'the first – or most complete manufacturer in England, in metal. He is very ingenious, Philosophical and Agreeable.'[49] Within a year, Wedgwood spotted the opportunity to work further together.

Since the late 1750s, the architectural work of the Adam brothers, fresh home from Rome, had begun to shape a penchant among Britain's elite for the antique and neoclassical. In the years after peace with France in 1763, and with fresh discoveries at Herculaneum and Pompeii, a craze for antiques swept fashionable society. When England's ambassador to Naples, William Hamilton, arrived home in 1771 with the first collection of Etruscan vases (now in the British Museum), Britain's elite began demanding classical vases of their own, offering hundreds of pounds for just the right design. It was, said Wedgwood, 'vase madness' – 'an epidemical madness reigns for vases, which must be gratified'.[50] At his London showroom, ran one report, 'vases, vases was all the cry'. In spring 1768, therefore, Wedgwood proposed a partnership to bring together Boulton's metalwork and Wedgwood's ceramics in a new line of ormolu-mounted ceramics, of the type that Boulton had seen in Paris in 1765.*

As the wealth of the country increased, the two entrepreneurs could envisage a huge new market opening up before them. By 1750, Birmingham, Manchester and Liverpool had grown from almost nothing to become three of the largest six provincial towns. Indeed, by the time Boulton died, one in six of the population were big-town dwellers, nearly twice the rate on the Continent.[51] Although the vast majority of towns remained small, between 1700 and 1800 the number of towns with a population of more than 2,500 people trebled to almost two hundred. Their inhabitants had larger incomes and were more cheaply fed. These new towns also supported an ever-growing middle class, who created a seemingly insatiable demand for food and goods.

---

* Ormolu derives from the French *or moulu*, meaning 'ground gold'. Gold was ground to a powder to allow amalgamation with mercury, for use in fire-gilding metals.

No town was greater than London, where what Defoe had called 'the middling sort' were perhaps a quarter of the population.[52] Defoe was struck how 'this whole kingdom, as well the people, as the land, and even the sea, in every part of it, are employed to furnish something and I may add, the best of every thing, to supply the City of London with provisions'. The sheer size and power of the capital was now driving the expansion of agriculture and industry across provincial England – and the evolution of taste, which Boulton and Wedgwood sought together to satisfy.[53]

Boulton now expanded Soho, raising £3,000 on his wife's estate, borrowing another £5,000 from his friend Baumgarten, and selling property inherited from his father.[54] Over a weekend at Soho, wrote Wedgwood, 'We settled many important matters & laid the foundation for improving our manufacture, & extending the sale of it to every corner of Europe.'[55] Together, Wedgwood and Boulton now hunted out works of art from clients, friends, rivals, the British Museum, Oxford colleges and Blenheim Palace to inspire designs created by modellers, craftsman and painters. By 1769, Boulton was taking orders for ormulu from the Earl of Shelburne and the banker Henry Hoare, and receiving compliments – if not cheques – from the king.[56] In 1763, the firm's takings had been some £7,000; by 1767, they had more than quadrupled to £30,000, worth between £45 and £62 million today.[57]

But Boulton and Wedgwood's partnership stretched beyond products, to production. On the Soho site, Boulton had become among the first to use a mill to power grinding tools. A steel-house had been built for converting iron to steel, with a shakebox for polishing it. 'I have almost every machine that is applicable to those arts,' noted Boulton to a friend in 1770 '[along with]... two water-mills employed in rolling, polishing, grinding, and turning various sorts of lathes'.[58]

Wedgwood, too, had created his own revolutionary factory at Etruria, opened on 13 June 1769, spread over seven acres of land and bounded by the new canal. Unlike Boulton, Wedgwood experimented personally, including for the first time with proper cost accounting. Indeed, Wedgwood's pioneering study of business costs in 1771 exposed the huge sums that were tied up in working capital and unsold stock, which the pricing of goods failed to reflect. His work inspired a careful 'price book of workmanship', costing everything from clay to sales staff, and he started to increase production runs over which to amortize the costs. It was an approach emulated by Boulton's foreman, John Scale, in 1773.

Both Wedgwood and Boulton also experimented with company care. Factory walls were whitewashed. Ventilation was installed. Schools, health schemes and homes were provided for workers. Good weekly wages were paid, on a par with those for skilled craftsmen – up to £1 for a skilled man; and in the early 1770s, the first insurance scheme for workers, the Soho scheme, was established.

The Boulton and Wedgwood partnership remained strong until around 1772, by which point fashion was moving on – and Boulton's cash-flow was severely stretched. The great and good now had their vases and ormolu, and Boulton was left with great stocks of the products, which he was forced to ship off to the court of Catherine the Great in St Petersburg. When one of his key lenders, one Mr Tonson of London, from whom he borrowed £10,000, died in 1772, Boulton struggled to raise new credit.[59] But he was determined to keep his show on the road. 'We have a thousand mouths at Soho to feed and it has taken so much labour and pains to get so valuable and well-organised a staff of workmen together, that the operations of the manufactory must be carried on at whatever risk.'[60]

*

Another market – and another product – was needed. With Wedgwood's help, Boulton had moved from toys to ormulu; now, he moved from ormulu to silverware, using the skills of the craftsmen he had assembled at Soho to create exquisite – and exquisitely expensive – candlesticks, plate, jugs and tableware.[61] His designers were world-leading, and Boulton's products were widely exported – but, Birmingham lacked the power to certify the authenticity of its silverware, gravely limiting Boulton's ability to expand.

His connections to market were now excellent: 'Our navigation goes on prosperously', wrote Boulton to the Earl of Warwick in 1772, 'we already sail from Birmingham to Bristol and to Hull.'[62]

But the lack of a local assay office was proving problematic. Since 1300, silver goods had to be checked before sale and hallmarked in one of the 'assay' offices; Boulton used those at London and Chester. To add to the problem, the roads were so bad that Boulton was beginning to lose a fortune in damaged goods. Therefore, he fixed his mind on a plan.

As early as 1766, the Earl of Shelburne had noted that 'it is very hard on a manufacturer to be obliged to send every piece of plate to Chester to be marked'.[63] Boulton had long mooted the idea of a Birmingham assay office and in 1771, furious at the near ruin of some expensive candlesticks for Shelburne, he decided to turn ideas into action. Writing to Shelburne, he declared that 'I am very desirous of becoming a great silversmith, yet I am now determined never to take up that branch in the large way I intended, unless powers can be obtained to have a marking hall at Birmingham.'[64]

Boulton quickly joined forces with his parliamentary lobbyist-in-chief Samuel Garbett and began raising a petition. By January 1773, his diary recorded a list of more than forty dukes and earls along with three bishops whose arms he had gone to twist. Petitions to halt Birmingham's efforts circulated from Sheffield and London. But in a *coup de grâce*, Garbett's committee, dominated by Midlands MPs, rounded up twenty-two pieces of London silver and found all but one to be well below standard. Boulton won his vote, and royal assent was granted on 28 May 1773. On 31 August, the Birmingham Assay Office opened for business in two rooms above the King's Head Inn on New Street. The company of Boulton & Fothergill was its first customer, submitting 104 items.* It was decidedly a step forward. And yet within a month, a twist of events would conspire to offer Matthew Boulton a prize that was even greater: a partnership with an unlucky Scottish engineer called James Watt. Together, they would change the course of the Industrial Revolution.

---

* Today the office stands in the heart of Birmingham's Jewellery Quarter and is the last Assay Office in Britain.

*

James Watt was born in Greenock, on 19 January 1736, into a practical and prosperous trading family. His grandfather was a 'teacher of navigation', and his uncle a lecturer in mathematics, astronomy and surveying. His father was a merchant, shipwright, carpenter, vessel-owner and instrument repairer to the captains, who brought to him their navigational equipment at a journey's end. The years after Isaac Newton's death had witnessed a burgeoning market for all manner of instruments – telescopes, microscopes, barometers, thermometers, chemical balances, orreries and armillary spheres – and all needed making, fixing, repairing.

A sickly child, James Watt nevertheless found he thrived on mathematics at school; at home, he spent time making things in a little workshop equipped for him by his father. At the age of seventeen, however, disaster struck: James's mother died, and his father lost a ship along with a lot of money. Watt needed work, and so he moved in briefly with his uncle, a don at Glasgow University. But, despairing at the lack of tuition available for his chosen craft of instrument making, he persuaded his father to find two guineas to send him to London. Two years later, he opened his own shop in Glasgow's Saltmarket, where, inspired by his physicist friend John Robison, he began to tinker with the principles of the steam engine, studying and experimenting with the weight that could be lifted by steam escaping from a kettle.

Steam engines, or 'fire engines', had been evolving for nearly five decades by the time Watt began his experiments. Indeed, in 1698, William III had left his apartments at Hampton Court and crossed his baroque gardens to watch a fire engine designed and demonstrated by a military engineer, Thomas Savery. It was neither beautiful nor efficient. It consisted of a low brick shed between two chimneys of brick and pipe, into which an assistant threw shovels of coal in the direction of two great iron eggs, while another caught a trickle of water, the condensed steam, in a bucket.[65] It would take Savery another fourteen years before, in 1712, he and his partner Thomas Newcomen, a Dartmouth ironmonger and blacksmith, perfected the first successful steam engine. Installed near Dudley Castle, west of Birmingham, it was capable of pumping water from Lord Dudley's coal mine at a rate of 10 gallons per stroke from a depth of 150 feet.

In 1760, Glasgow University asked Watt to repair a model Newcomen steam engine which had come their way. Frustrated at its inefficiencies, he began a series of experiments to puzzle out how to perfect the engine – in particular how to reduce the huge quantity of coal that the engine needed to consume to create steam. The Newcomen engine relied on heating water to create the steam that raised a great piston linked to a large rocker beam, to which in turn was attached the pump. But because cold water was then deployed to condense the steam back into water, and allow the piston to fall in a downstroke, huge amounts of coal were needed to heat up the water again to repeat the whole cycle.

For years, Watt puzzled over the problem, until, in spring 1765, on his Sunday walk, he realized the solution. 'The idea came into my mind, that as steam was an elastic body it would rush into a vacuum, and if a communication was made between the cylinder and an exhausted vessel, it would rush into it, and might be there condensed without cooling the cylinder... I had not walked further than the golf-house when the whole thing was arranged in my mind.'[66]

The following day, Watt built himself a model and was delighted to see his theory worked. His calculations showed that his own designs were nearly 40 per cent more powerful than the Newcomen design, and by the summer of 1765 he had perfected a design 'that shall not waste a particle of steam'.[67] In September, Watt joined forces with John Roebuck, a serial entrepreneur who had started a medical practice in Birmingham before co-founding the Carron Ironworks, in Scotland, with Lunar Society member Samuel Garbett before branching into coal-mining. Roebuck also knew Boulton well – indeed, he invited Boulton to take a 10 per cent share in the mine.[68] Looking for a better engine to drain his fast-flooding mines, Roebuck asked for Watt's help.

Watt, however, faced a problem. Hard as he tried, he could not get his engine design to work at scale. Over the summer of 1766, as his money troubles multiplied, Watt sold his instrument-making shop and turned his hand to surveying. In his spare time, his experiments continued, until in April 1768, he finally cracked the problem of keeping cylinders air-tight and built an engine capable of 20 strokes a minute.

Roebuck was now interested enough to step in with serious money. In return for clearing Watt's debts, he took a two-thirds share of the invention. And at this point, Watt's path and Boulton's – who was fascinated by the potential of steam power to drive his Soho machinery – began to cross.*

In April 1767, Watt set off to London to file his patent. Curious to see the famous Soho House and Manufactory for himself, he stopped off in Birmingham. Boulton being absent, Watt was escorted round by Dr Small, who now encouraged Watt to relocate to Birmingham: he wrote to him the following year, to urge Watt to 'get your patent and come to Birmingham, with as much time to spend as you can'.[69]

On hearing of Watt's breakthrough, Boulton had immediately made him an offer. But despite spending a fortnight in the mechanic's paradise at Soho, all Watt would offer was a franchise to sell the engine in three Midland counties. Boulton wanted much more. 'I was excited by two motives to offer you my assistance which were love of you and love of a money getting, ingenious project,' Boulton explained: 'To... produce the most profit, my idea was to settle a manufactory near to my own, by the side of our canal, where I would erect all the conveniences necessary for the completion of engines, and from which manufactory we would serve all the world with engines of all sizes.'[70]

Watt's patent was granted on 5 January 1769 (and on Small's advice, it was filed with general principles rather than a specific design). He returned to Roebuck's mine to start building. It proved a nightmare. Dogged with practical problems and short of money, Watt was forced to resume surveying work for canals to pay the bills. Progress with the engine ground to a halt. And then, just for good measure, in the

---

* Boulton had begun studying fire engines in 1766, writing to Benjamin Franklin (who was then in London) that: 'My engagements since Christmas have not permitted me to make any further progress with my fire-engine; but, as the thirsty season is approaching apace, necessity will oblige me to set about it in good earnest.' Smiles, *Boulton and Watt*, op. cit., p. 183.

summer of 1772, the Scottish economy froze. Crops failed. Trade stalled. Banks collapsed.

Boulton was among those who lost thousands in the downturn; but Watt's partner Roebuck lost everything. He was declared bankrupt in March 1773. His misfortune was to prove Boulton's gain. As luck would have it, Boulton was among his creditors, owed £1,200. At the end of March, Boulton proposed he cancel the debt in return for Roebuck's share of Watt's steam engine. Within two months, Roebuck accepted. The engine constructed at Roebuck's Kinneil House was dismantled and shipped to Soho.

For Watt there was one more tragic twist of fate to come. While out surveying for the Great Glen Canal in the Highlands in September, a letter arrived pronouncing his wife to be dangerously ill. Setting off home through the beating rain, Watt arrived in Dumbarton two days later on 29 September 1773. But he was too late. He was greeted with the news that his wife had died five days before. Devastated, Watt could not bring himself to return to his house. It was now that Dr Small begged him to throw himself into work and, better, to move to Soho. With debts mounting, Watt settled his affairs, placed his children with relations in Glasgow, and set off for Birmingham. He arrived on 31 May 1774 and set up shop with Matthew Boulton.

*

There was perhaps no better time for James Watt to arrive at Soho. The Industrial Revolution was gathering speed, in no small part fuelled by England's booming markets overseas. Britain's new manufacturers were now well connected to America, the West Indies and the markets beyond. Exports were driving perhaps a fifth of Britain's growth, and a gigantic 40 per cent of the country's manufacturing. By the 1750s, over 100,000 people were already employed in the textile business, largely in woollens and the first cotton linen and silks mills. By 1760, the nation was importing 1.2 million pounds of cotton. In 1771, Jedediah Strutt and the great Richard Arkwright opened their huge new water-powered Cromford Mill, just 20 miles north of John Lombe's old mill in Derby, and soon it employed 1,000 people, living and working in the country's first industrial village.[71] Strutt was a silk manufacturer, familiar with Lombe's mill, who had met Arkwright in Nottingham. In partnership together, they decided to build their factory on a stream flowing from the lead mines, which reputedly never froze. By 1800, 1,000 mills similar to Arkwright's were sucking in from abroad 52 million pounds of cotton.[72]

Meanwhile near Coalbrookdale, where the iron revolution had begun, a great new symbol of Britain's iron power was taking shape. Soon hailed as a wonder of the world, the first pure iron bridge was opened by Abraham Darby's son in 1781.* It was assembled like a giant jigsaw puzzle from huge pieces cast in a forge that now employed over 1,000 people, described by the traveller, Arthur Young. Young marvelled at the 'furnaces, forges, &c. with the vast bellows that give those roaring blasts, which make the whole edifice horridly sublime. These works are supposed to be the greatest in England.' Within weeks, the *Shrewsbury Chronicle* could report 'great numbers of carriages, besides horses and foot passengers have daily passed' across the new arch.[73] Yet Coalbrookdale and Ironbridge were simply the most spectacular symbols of an industry that now boasted many giant firms, which by 1780 together produced some 62,000 tonnes of iron.† The country's mines too had multiplied; many gave work to over 1,000 workers and, by 1800, England's north-east, Scotland and the West Midlands were producing 10 million tonnes of fuel.[74] In all, the last eighteen years of the 1700s witnessed half of the total century's growth in coal shipments and copper mining; three-quarters of the increase in broadcloth manufacture; four-fifths of the increase in printed cloths; 90 per cent of the growth in exports of cotton goods; and half of the century's patents.

As such, the country had become an extraordinary potential market for steam engines. And so with Watt's arrival, Matthew Boulton wasted no time in getting down to business. New perfections and new patents

---

* Darby won the Royal Society of Arts Gold Medal in 1788.

† Asa Briggs, *A Social History of England* (Penguin, 1991), p. 186. Other large iron firms included the Carron Iron Company, which was founded in 1759 and boasted a capital of £12,000; by 1773, it was worth £150,000. William Reynolds and Co. was worth £138,000 by 1793. Walkers of Masboro', which started as a smithy in 1741, was worth £235,000 in 1801.

were needed, and neither took long to arrive. Over the summer of 1774, Boulton offered James Watt his old house in Newhall Walk. With Soho's engineers on hand to help, by November 1774 Watt's 'fire engine' was working better than any before it.[75]

Boulton, however, now spotted an enormous problem. With just eight years left on Watt's patent, there was not enough time to build an engine plant and make a decent return. He now turned to Parliament with a petition for a private bill extending the patent for twenty-five years. It was a lot to ask – and the timing was terrible. Across the Atlantic, on 19 April 1775, an exchange of fire in Lexington, Massachusetts, confirmed that the crisis that had raged since the Boston Tea Party in 1773 was now a full-blown war of independence. Parliament was understandably distracted. Yet, for three intense months, Boulton and friends rounded up votes, and on 22 May 1775 secured a new Act, including an extension of the patent to Scotland. Protected by the legislation, Boulton and Watt now began the search for profit in mines, mills – and a mint.

By the summer of 1775, Boulton brought in his first two big orders, including a commission for a huge 50-inch cylinder to power the pump at the Bloomfield Colliery in nearby Tipton. By March 1776, the engine was assembled, and at a special ceremony the pump was started. Moving at 15 strokes a minute, it proved a spectacular success, draining a 60-foot pit of water in under an hour, 'after which', according to *Aris's Birmingham Gazette*, 'a name was given to the machine, viz, the Parliament Engine, amidst acclamations of a number of joyous and ingenious workmen'.[76]

Boulton was completely seized with the potential of the market before him. 'If we had a hundred wheels ready made, and a hundred small engines like Bow engine, and twenty large ones executed, we could readily dispose of them all. Therefore, let us make hay while the sun shines,' he wrote to Watt. That summer, James Boswell, whose *Life* (1791) of Samuel Johnson would cement his fame, came to Soho and wrote up his encounter with its 'iron-chieftain': 'The vastness and the contrivance of some of the machinery would have "matched his mighty mind". I shall never forget Mr Bo[u]lton's expression to me. "I sell here, sir, what all the world desires to have – POWER".'[77]

Boulton's appetite for steam was whetted. In a letter to Watt in February 1776, he averred: 'I have fixed my mind upon making from twelve to fifteen reciprocating and fifty rotative engines per annum. I assure you that of all the toys and trinkets which we manufacture at Soho, none shall take the place of fire-engines in respect of my attention.'[78] For the next decade, Boulton & Watt took orders for ten engines a year[79] – the vast majority from Cornwall, where the boom in brass had triggered a search for the deep-lying Cornish copper.* Far from coal, and with their mines constantly flooding, the Cornish mine-captains had been early customers of the haphazard Newcomen engine, of which sixty were installed across the county. Boulton and Watt knew how important the Cornish market would prove, and when the first order for an engine arrived from the Tingtang mine, near Redruth, Watt moved south to set up shop among the obstreperous, hard-drinking, hard-bargaining miners to deliver his engine personally. It was tough work. 'Certainly,' Watt wrote to Boulton, 'they [the mine-captains] have the most ungracious manners of any people I have ever yet been amongst.'[80]

Constantly vexed by wrong parts and shoddy work, Watt took until September 1777 to get the engine running. Soon, though, the orders began to quicken from other mines – Tregurtha Downs, Chacewater, Hallamanning, Poldice, Wheal Chance and United.[81] The Chacewater engine in particular proved spectacular. 'All the world are agape to see what it can do,' wrote Watt to Boulton in 1777; 'we have had many spectators and several have already become converts'. The new converts included foreigners, for in the following year the first engines for export were sold, to France.

Orders did not, however, mean financial comfort. Boulton's cash-flow became seriously stretched, such that by the summer of 1778 the business was in crisis. A fire had wrecked his Soho workshops, and creditors were multiplying. Fothergill was going so far as to urge his partner to declare the Boulton & Watt venture bankrupt. With his

---

* The mines of the county were divided between two loose competing federations, eastern and western, owing allegiance to the bitter rival landlords Sir Francis Basset and Lord Falmouth.

back against the wall, Boulton fought like never before. Some 550 of his 700 staff were laid off; huge new loans of £17,000 were secured on the back of his engine patent, and new fixed-price deals were agreed with the Cornish mine-owners to secure some certain cash. Boulton's engine-pricing policy had proved unwise for an undercapitalized business: the owners paid for the components, and then Boulton & Watt assembled them, taking payment as an annual royalty calculated on the savings to the mine-owners' coal bill.

As stability returned, Boulton made a breakthrough. Not with a new machine, but rather with two new men. A former glass manufacturer, James Keir, also a Lunar Society member, was enticed to Soho in 1777, and slowly he brought order to Boulton & Watt's appalling accounting.*[82] Two years later, William Murdoch, the son of an Ayrshire millwright and a hugely talented engineer, arrived bringing both machine skills and people skills.† He was dispatched to Cornwall in 1779 – and stayed for another twenty-one years.

Together, the new team steered the business through the rapids. By the summer of 1780, Boulton and Watt had sold forty engines – half of them in Cornwall.[83] But Boulton had to become a partner in four mines, to help keep the business going, while in 1781 Boulton & Watt had to borrow from Boulton & Fothergill to pay the Christmas balances and the workmen's wages. Over the years, relations between Boulton and Fothergill had been getting worse. In November 1781, Boulton had to sack Fothergill, claiming that he had been cheated.‡

*

It was not until the early 1780s that Boulton & Watt was at last turning a profit.[84] By now, it was clear to Boulton that the bigger market would not be engines for mines, but for mills, and this would require harnessing the steam engine not to a pump but to a wheel. On Midsummer

---

* Keir's incentive was an offer to run the factory for a quarter of the Boulton and Fothergill profits.

† Looking for work at the age of twenty-three, Murdoch had impressed Boulton with an oval wooden hat he had turned himself on a homemade lathe.

‡ Fothergill died a bankrupt the following year.

Day 1781, Boulton wrote to Watt in Cornwall: 'I do think in the course of a month or two, we should determine to take out a patent for certain methods of producing rotative motions from the vibrating or recipro-cating motion of the fire engine.'[85]

Watt was not keen. But slowly, innovation came. Murdoch devised a clever 'sun and planets' movement. Watt added a double-acting design, in which steam was manipulated into both pushing and pulling a piston. By the spring of 1783, the first rotary engine was grinding corn in Ketley, Northamptonshire, and orders soon followed from the great brewers Goodwyn and Whitbread in London. George III himself visited their installation and pronounced himself much impressed. In 1784, both Boulton and Watt were elected to the Royal Society.

Boulton's instinct was right: rotary motion was exactly what mill owners wanted, and with the Albion Mill, Soho won the chance to build the greatest factory in London and the largest mill in Europe. Begun in 1783, it was the capital's first engine-powered mill, using the first rotary engine with a parallel motion. Rounding up enough share-holders, Boulton applied for a charter for it in 1784 – but such was the novelty and potential power of this monster mill, that it was refused, and instead the mill was constituted as a partnership. Undeterred, Boulton was determined not to undersell the new venture, even orga-nizing a masked ball in the mill to celebrate its opening in spring 1786, much to Watt's irritation: 'What have dukes, lords and ladies to do with masquerading in a flour-mill?'[86] Supervised by the great engineer John Rennie, the Albion Mill shattered the price of flour across the capital. By the end of 1786, Boulton & Watt was finally in profit.

And yet this was to be no *annus mirabilis*. The summer was scorch-ing. Never had a month been hotter than July. On 11 July, a maid carrying beer to haymakers in the meadow at Soho noticed Ann Boulton walking by the pool. Ten minutes later, as the maid strolled back, she spied Ann 'upon her face on the water in a shallow part of it'.[87] Anne had often complained of giddiness. She may have had a massive stroke. Boulton, who had been on business in Coventry, was greeted in Soho's garden with the news upon his return. 'The scene', he later wrote, 'is not describable by pen or tongue.'[88] She was buried in the family vault in Whittington, near Lichfield. Boulton's health collapsed, and in August he attempted to combat the gloom by disappearing to Dublin, Edinburgh, London and Cornwall. 'I think if we could but keep our spirits up and be active we might vanquish all the host,' he wrote.[89]

The health of his business, by contrast, was much improved. Now in profit, Boulton & Watt was poised on the threshold of its greatest era – booming into the business of powering mills, and, literally, minting money.

*

Boulton's experience as a coin maker and medallist dated back many years. In 1772, he was commissioned by the Admiralty to produce 2,000 medals for Captain Cook to take on his second voyage, to the Pacific. Boulton's engineers had acquired a legendary speed and flexibility. When George III ordered 200 silver medals to celebrate his wife's birthday, Boulton was given just days' notice; but the king had been told it could not be done except by Boulton, 'as nothing was impossible with him'.[90]

Boulton had acquired something of a copper mountain from his Cornish mine customers in the early 1780s, and now, in search of a use for it, saw an obvious opportunity: to create the world's first steam-powered mint. It was housed 100 yards from the Soho Manufactory to keep it secret. A new watermill, built in 1785, allowed a new rolling mill to roll out sheets of copper. New steam engines were designed to power the presses, and a warehouse was built in 1787, in Birmingham's Livery Street. Boulton constantly experimented with novel configurations of machines, new methods for hardening dies, and different techniques for rolling copper and burnishing blanks. Alongside raw materials and machines, Boulton assembled artists and engineers. Expert engravers, including some of the best in the world, were employed to produce beautiful designs. Some of the craftsmen had trained at Soho but others, such as Jean-Pierre Droz, hailed from Paris, and his successor Conrad Heinrich Küchler (who produced the dies for the regal coinage), Rambert Dumarest and Noel-Alexandre Ponthon were all recruited abroad by Boulton. By 1789, Boulton's new venture had cost him some £8,000.[91]

Boulton's first order was to strike 100 tonnes of copper coins for the East India Company, for its trading posts in Sumatra, complete with inscriptions stamped around the rim, drawing on techniques he had seen in Paris. More requests for trade tokens followed for companies nationwide, along with further medals and commemorative medallions, including one to mark the recovery of George III's health in 1789. Soon, the new mills were rolling copper ingots into sheets for new machines to cut out blanks, before six presses thumped out copper coins for the American colonies, pennies for Bermuda, silver for Sierra Leone, and *faluces* for Madras.

Orders from His Majesty's Government were, however, harder to secure. For years, the shortage of small change vexed the business community of Britain which had to pay the wages of a burgeoning working class, and the problem of organizing his own weekly wage bill kept the matter before Boulton. Very few low-value copper coins had been issued since 1754, and as far back as 1771 industrialists were complaining that 'the scarcity of cash in this part and for many miles round us has been for some time past greater than I ever remember'.[92] In 1788, the government finally started talking. Boulton reported to his son that he 'was sent for to Town by Mr Pitt [the Younger] and the Privy Council about a new copper coinage which I have agreed for, but at a very low price... I am building a mint and new manufacture for it in my farm yard behind the menagerie at Soho.'[93] But it took another ten years for the order to arrive.

In the meantime, Boulton had other problems to solve. His interests in Cornish copper mines initially provided him with plenty of raw materials, but as coin production boomed, securing adequate supplies at steady cost proved a huge headache. Much of it came up from Cornwall via Bristol, and then on barges along the River Severn to Stourport, before arriving in Birmingham on the local canals. But by the end of the 1790s, Boulton was tracking copper prices as far away as Calcutta and Basra, and the business had to juggle the challenge of delivering casks, containing tonnes of coins, by road or canal to Liverpool or Hull, or down the Severn to Bristol, or to Oxford and along the Thames for the East India Company docks at St Botolph's, in London. The enterprise meant managing an array of costs and challenges: exchange rates, the credit-worthiness of foreign factors, insurance, customs, wharfage and the constant threat of French privateers.

Luckily for Boulton, the market for steam engines, slowly growing for twenty years, was now about to blossom. As France began to descend into political revolution, a very different kind of revolution was about to transform Birmingham's northerly neighbour, Manchester. The cotton revolution was gathering pace, and among the revolutionaries would be more than a few new customers for Boulton & Watt.

Boulton had foreseen that Manchester would one day offer rich pickings: 'The Manchester folk will now erect cotton mills enough but want engines to work them.'[94] It was not long before the partners had some helpful advocates on the ground. Much to his father's frustration, Watt's son, also called James Watt, had – after much agonizing – decided not to join his father and Boulton in the engine business. Breaking the news to his father in August 1788, the younger Watt wrote: 'My education has been general and not such as to fit me for any particular business... You made your way in the world without fortune! Why should not I?'[95] And so it was agreed that he would take an apprenticeship with a fustian maker, printer and dyer in Manchester – where, as fate would have it, he would help deliver Boulton & Watt's breakthrough technology into the booming Manchester cotton business.

For some years, Boulton and his friends had been trying to persuade the magnate Richard Arkwright to take a steam engine to power his textile mills, but to no avail. In correspondence with Boulton, Erasmus Darwin had reported Arkwright's view that 'Mr B's engine was so subject to disorder and so complex'.[96] But the conversations continued. In the view of Gilbert Hamilton, reporting from the Glasgow cotton-spinning boom, Arkwright seemed admiring of Watt but somewhat uninformed of the potential for savings.[97] The breakthrough came instead in 1785, in some unusual circumstances. The Robinson family's mills at Papplewick, Northamptonshire, were contending with a temperamental river flow to drive their factory wheels: up-river, Lord Byron was building ornamental ponds on which to stage naval battles with his servants. Starved of the river's flow, the Robinsons became, therefore, the first mill owners to order an engine to help pump water for their wheel.'[98] More orders followed, and by November 1788 Boulton & Watt had supplied some eight engines for textile mills, and had a rough idea of how many spindles an engine could drive. A year later came the Manchester breakthrough.

In the extraordinary archives atop the magnificent Library of Birmingham, in the city's Centenary Square, is housed the vast collection of papers, technical diagrams and thousands upon thousands of letters from the Boulton & Watt business. It is an incredible vat of information and data, describing how one of the first industrial businesses in the world ran day-to-day. And deep in the archives are the letters between Watt, his son, Boulton and the first merchant to buy a steam engine for a Manchester cotton factory.

Peter Drinkwater hailed from a family of fustian makers.[99] The pioneering Robert Owen, who worked for him in Manchester, described him as a 'a good fustian manufacturer and a first-rate foreign merchant', who shifted during the 1780s from his position as a textile middleman into manufacturing, creating his own cotton factory in Northwich. He now wanted an engine for his four-storeyed Bank Top Mill, in Manchester's Piccadilly, 'for finer spinning'.[100]

A steam engine from Boulton & Watt was not cheap.[†] Indeed, cost – and the temptation of securing a semi-legal alternative engine, or an old-style and far less efficient Newcomen engine – limited Boulton & Watt's sales. Moreover, the shortage of engineers capable of designing and installing the magnificent machines meant that lead-times were long.[101] As the younger Watt noted to his father, the 'gross sum which your engines cost at first startles all the lesser manufacturers here (Manchester), and it is scarcely possible to make them comprehend the advantage'.[102] For many, water power would prove cheaper for some years to come.

---

* As it happened, the firm won its lawsuit against Byron, and the engine was never used much.

† The 16 h.p. engine proposed for McConnel and Kennedy in 1797, for example, came in at £927s 5d, plus the cost of stalling the factory for six months while the engine was assembled. One horsepower could drive 350 spindles and there were few cotton factories with more than 4,000 spindles at work.

Nevertheless, on 3 April 1789, in his spidery copper-plate, Drinkwater declared to Boulton and Watt his ambition 'respecting a fire (or steam) engine which I wish you to furnish me to use in the cotton manufactory'. Apologizing for his ignorance of the mechanics, he went on: 'The engine it would set out with – is one with a power equal to six horses.'[103]

In the nine letters that followed over the course of 1789 – including the enormous and magnificent contract signed and sealed by Drinkwater, Watt and Boulton, and scribbled all over with corrections to various terms – we get a flavour of the complexity of assembling the engines and getting them running.

On 4 April 1789, the younger Watt reported that 'Mr Drinkwater… is now come to a full determination to have one of your engines, he has called upon me twice to enquire about sundry matters… where I could I have answered him'.[104] Crucially, he advised his father that a successful engine at Drinkwater's would do wonders for Manchester sales, as it was 'universally known that he [Drinkwater] is a man of judgement'.[105] In fact, Watt's son, it seems, was a highly effective Manchester-based sales agent, able to provide his father and Boulton with news of Drinkwater's trials and tribulations. Drinkwater's obstacles included his neighbours, for 'the public yet are not all inclin'd to believe otherwise than that a steam engine of any sort must be highly offensive' – and he was forced to move his proposed factory several hundred yards further out of town.

In May, Boulton & Watt dispatched twenty-six carefully annotated cartridge-paper plans for 'one of the earliest sun and planet engines with wooden beam and wooden connecting rod, the air pump being worked from the valve operating plug rod'.[106] Exquisitely coloured, the plans laid out details and measurements for the engine, its framing, its firehouse, its ashpit and condenser, its pump, its cranks and mechanisms, each marked carefully on the back: 'This drawing (the property of Boulton and Watt) to be kept clean and returned as the engine is finished'.

Over the course of the year, detailed discussions and letters followed, tweaking the specifications – including raising the factory floor, refining the regulators and adjusting the pump – as well as providing assurances (for the engine proposed was very different to the one Drinkwater had seen in Warrington and which had so impressed him) and agreeing the pricing.

Follow-on success was far from instantaneous. Indeed, in 1791, a neighbouring merchant, Benjamin Lees, was advising Boulton and Watt that 'a great number of factories are now erecting in this town, the greatest part of which are intended for fire engines of the old construction[;] it is quite evident to me yours are very much preferable to them, but I think they are not generally known here'. He suggested advertising in the newspapers, 'and if you was to refer the public to look at that of Mr Drinkwaters... it might bring them to be generally used in the cotton & woollen branches.... I have taken several good mechanics to look at Mr D's engine who all agree that one of them is worth all the rest put together on the old principle.'[107]

Slowly but surely, from the breakthrough in Piccadilly, Boulton & Watt's business grew. Between 1785 and 1800, perhaps ninety-two Boulton & Watt engines were sold to cotton factories, with a combined 1,513 horsepower: indeed they made up nearly half of all the engines sold in Lancashire.[108] By 1789, Boulton & Watt had sold 162 steam engines – more than double the installed base of five years previously.[109]

Rotary engines had hitherto been only a third of sales. By contrast, in the years after the sale to Drinkwater, and despite the new difficulties of war with France, rotary engines began to power the partners' business.* From 1790, order books expanded. But as the firm hired more workers, manufacturing losses grew.[110] Production needed new methods. Bills needed calling in. The fire at Albion Mills in 1791 had cost a fortune – a loss estimated at £10,000, of which Boulton was on the hook for £6,000.[111] By the mid-1790s Boulton knew he needed to modernize both his firm and his factory.[112]

In October 1794, Boulton's son, another Matthew, along with the younger James Watt and the nineteen-year-old Gregory Watt were

---

* For many, the costs of an atmospheric engine, used to pump water to drive a wheel, remained as economical as a rotary engine, which directly drove machinery.

admitted to the partnership, and the firm's name changed to Boulton, Watt and Sons. William Murdoch was recalled from Cornwall to help. The mill-owners' demand for steam called for different pre-built engines, and in big numbers. So Boulton now embarked on creating the world's first steam-engine factory.

On 30 January 1796, the Soho Foundry was opened, a mile from Soho House and the Manufactory, on the banks of the Birmingham Canal, replete with smithy, forge, boring mill and turning shops, and capable of producing its own engine cylinders and fitting them to engines. On the occasion, 'When the dinner was over,' reported *Aris's Birmingham Gazette*, 'the founder of Soho entered, and consecrated this new branch of it by sprinkling the walls with wine, and then in the name of Vulcan, all the Gods and Goddesses of Fire and Water, pronounced the name of SOHO FOUNDRY, and all the people cried amen'.[113]

The bill for the foundry was £20,000, and the money would not be recouped for another fifteen years.[114] To fill the hole, Boulton and Watt now embarked on a host of court battles led by the younger partners to sue patent infringers (cashing in on the burgeoning demand for power) and poor-paying mine owners. Often the threat of court was enough to prompt a cheque. But the Cornish fought hard, and in 1795 a challenge to Boulton and Watt's patent went all the way to the High Court. In January 1799, the Court of the King's Bench unanimously decided for Boulton &Watt: a colossal estimated £162,052 (between £180 million and £228 million today) in royalties were now owing to the company.[115]

*

Over the course of the 1790s, Boulton's mint continued to churn out millions of coins for Sumatra and the presidencies of Bombay and Madras, silver coins for Sierra Leone, pennies for the Isle of Man, and trade tokens for industrialists, along with endless medals, before, finally, in 1797 came the great government order for coinage.

The French Revolution had divided the members of Birmingham's old Lunar Society, but for Boulton the trouble was good for business.

He offered the French National Assembly a deal to mint the country's new coinage; when that failed, he did a healthy trade supplying private coinage, until it was outlawed in 1793. When France and Britain fell to war once more, pressure grew on Britain's finances, and the Bank of England's gold reserves began to fall. The Privy Council suspended the convertibility of bank notes into gold to ensure that no gold left the kingdom, and with extraordinary speed the Bank was ordered to start issuing new £5 notes, restamp Spanish gold coins – and commission from Matthew Boulton 46 million halfpennies and farthings. Boulton was summoned to see the prime minister, Lord Liverpool, on 3 March 1797. He also attended the Privy Council on 7 March. By the end of the month, the order was his and, by the end of August 1797, the first coins to be embossed with Britannia holding a trident (rather than a spear) rolled off the production line.

As his final years approached, Boulton was rich in fame and fortune but poor in health. A kidney problem grew worse. And yet, his failing constitution could not stifle his curiosity or his civic flair. His fascination with science never flagged; in January 1801, his daughter was pleading with him not to spend quite so much time gazing through his telescope in the cold. The steam-engine business was in good health, employing in 1802 some fifty-four men, and from the 1790s customers could pay an upfront bill rather than an annual licence. The mint remained his great love – in 1800, he personally foiled a robbery there, lying in wait with an armed band of workers, following a tip-off. In his later years, he loved nothing more than to be carried down the hill in his chair to sit and watch the presses. 'Of all the mechanical subjects I ever entered upon,' he later wrote, 'there is none in which I ever engaged with so much ardour as that of bringing to perfection the art of coining.'[116] Between 1797 and 1807, over 20 million blanks were stamped for the new cents and half-cents of the young United States of America. 'Had Mr B done nothing more in the world than what he has done in improving coinage,' wrote his partner James Watt, 'his fame would have deserved to be immortalised.'[117]

The most illustrious leaders of the day beat a path to Boulton's door. He entertained with style. In 1794, after careful analysis, he bought the freehold of the Soho land, and in 1796 he commissioned James Wyatt to comprehensively remodel the house, with no care for expense. He led the campaign to uphold the quality standards of buttons, culminating in the Button Act of 1796. And his great Soho Manufactory continued to pioneer breathtaking new technology. In 1802, William Murdoch succeeded in lighting the entire works in a blaze of gas-light, a 'grand illumination' to mark the short-lived Peace of Amiens with France. That same year, Horatio Nelson arrived in person at Soho House, greeting the sick Boulton in his bed; three years later, the Soho mint struck a special Trafalgar medal to be awarded to every man who fought at the battle. In 1807, Boulton helped enliven his city by leading, and winning, the fight to open Birmingham's first theatre, in the teeth of much opposition from the city's Non-conformists.

Matthew Boulton's final days were spent at home. On 11 March 1809, in his last letter, he wrote in a shaking hand to his daughter Anne, who was in Bath: 'If you wish to see me living pray come soon for I am very ill.' He died not long before his eighty-first birthday, on 17 August 1809.[118]

The city Boulton helped to build laid down its tools to honour him. An old friend of Watt, then in Glasgow, relayed the scene of that August morning when 10,000 people lined the roads to watch ten coaches escort the great entrepreneur on his final journey to St Mary's Church, in Handsworth. 'The entrance to Soho & the road thence to Handsworth Church was lined with spectators on foot, on horseback & in carriages... Although the church was crowded in every part & multitudes remained without... the utmost stillness and solemnity prevailed.' Five hundred and thirty memorial tokens were struck for the 'Attendants and Workmen', with silver medals for the coffin-bearers, who were Soho's oldest, longest-serving workers. The men retired to public houses, where food and drink had been arranged. And there, in the words of the younger James Watt, after 'drinking the memory of their departed benefactor standing & in silence, they all repaired to their respective homes, and not a Soho man was to be seen upon the road for the remainder of the day'.[119]

Drawn Etch'd Pub' by R. Dighton. Oct' 1817.

A View from the Royal Exchange.

5

NATHAN ROTHSCHILD

From Cottonopolis to the City of London

I t was, said the Duke of Wellington 'the nearest run thing you ever saw in your life'.[1] The night of Saturday, 17 June 1815 had been wet, and on Sunday morning, eight miles south of Waterloo, Napoleon Bonaparte took the fateful decision to delay his attack on Wellington's forces so the battlefield might dry.

For more than two decades, war had dragged on, hot and cold, between Revolutionary France and Britain, the nation christened by the French emperor as 'the most powerful, the most constant and the most generous of my enemies'.[2] Months earlier, Bonaparte had been defeated, only to escape from his island exile on Elba, return in triumph to Paris, retake his throne, and raise fresh forces, which were now aimed at the armies of Europe's Seventh Coalition. On Friday, 16 June, Napoleon had struck in a pre-emptive assault to divide his enemies, and at the Battle of Ligny, he forced the Prussians into a tactical retreat. Only the Duke of Wellington now stood in his way, and some time between ten o'clock and 11.30 on the morning of 18 June, Napoleon's onslaught began.

Throughout the long day, the fighting raged. By early evening Napoleon had the upper hand. '[The] attacks were repeated', Wellington later recalled, 'till about seven in the evening when the enemy made a desperate effort with the cavalry and infantry supported by the fire of artillery to force our left centre.' Thousands of Napoleon's Imperial Guards now prepared to attack the ridge at the point where Wellington's hard-pressed forces were most vulnerable. But Wellington had a surprise: a detachment of troops hidden aside in the corn-fields. Having been ordered to retire at five o'clock to shelter from the French artillery fire, they now lay in wait. 'After they had pounded away at us for about half an hour,' wrote one soldier, Captain R. H. Gronow, '[the French] deployed... up came the whole mass of the Imperial infantry of the Guard, led on by the Emperor in person... we saw the bearskin caps rising higher and higher as they ascended the ridge of ground which separated us, and advanced nearer and nearer to our lines.' [3]

Wellington now gave the order: 'Guards, get up and charge!' 'After firing a volley as soon as the enemy were within shot,' wrote Gronow, 'we rushed on with fixed bayonets and that hearty hurrah peculiar to British soldiers.'[4] As the French troops pulled back in disorder, the Prussians rejoined the field, and Wellington ordered the counter-attack. The French fled, pursued through the dark.

When word of victory arrived in London, there was hysteria. 'Great and glorious news,' screamed the *Morning Post*, 'Annihilation of Bonaparte's whole army. And his own narrow personal escape.' The battle, reported Wellington, had been brutal – 'sanguinary' – but decisive; the loss of allied troops was 'immense', but 'the army, never, upon any occasion conducted itself better'. The prize of victory, added the *Morning Post*, was gigantic, and now 'Britain... may indeed be now truly considered as at the summit of glory.'

One man, though, was worried. Nathan Mayer Rothschild, the thirty-eight-year-old financier, had for the last year become as vital to Wellington's armoury as the artillery. His trade was not arms. It was money. Two decades of war with France had cost the British government a fortune.* Ferrying that fortune from bond sales in London to the baggage trains of the battlefield had become critical to Wellington's success, and since January 1814 the task had been Rothschild's to perform. Assuming that the war would be long, he had stockpiled a fortune in gold. But now victory brought the prospect of a crash.

Facing huge losses, Rothschild had one vital asset: early warning of victory. Forty-eight hours before Wellington's aide de camp, Major Henry Percy, arrived in London to tell of his general's triumph, Rothschild's own couriers had raced the news to him. He reacted immediately. On Tuesday 20 July, he fast began buying government

---

* Niall Ferguson wrote, 'Never had so many bonds been issued to finance a military conflict', in *The Ascent of Money* (Penguin, 2008), p. 81.

bonds, turning his stockpiles of gold into government gilts (consolidated annuities known as 'consols'). As the prices of consols began to rise, he kept buying and buying – for a year. In 1817, with prices up 40 per cent, he sold. His profits, in today's money, were £600 million.

It was the trade of the century, and with his profit Nathan Rothschild would prove as vital to saving the City of London as he had proved to the Duke of Wellington.

*

Nathan Rothschild was born, on 16 September 1777, in the tightly packed and persecuted Jewish ghetto in Frankfurt. A Jewish community, 100–200 souls strong, had lived there since the mid-twelfth century, and the pogroms had quickly followed:[5] three-quarters of the community were wiped out in the first *Judenschlacht* ('Jewish Slaughter') of 1214, and a second pogrom, in 1349, was followed by tight laws that circumscribed Jews' daily life. In 1458, the Holy Roman Emperor Frederick III finally ordered the Jews' confinement to the ghetto. It consisted of a single, narrow, gated street – the Judengasse (Jews' Lane) – a quarter-mile-long narrow road, curving from the Bornheimer Gate in the north to the Jewish cemetery in the south. No more than 12 feet wide, by 1610 the street was jammed with some 1,400 people. Capped at just 500 families, the ghetto was rationed to twelve weddings a year. Farming was banned. So was dealing in spices, wine or grain. A quarter of families were sustained by charity, and even when rules relaxed elsewhere in the empire, Frankfurt held out. Special taxes were levied on Jews, while the city's parks, inns, coffee houses and cathedral area were all off limits.

This 'dirty, damp street' was described by an observer three decades before Rothschild was born:

> Picture to yourself a long street, more than half a quarter of an hour long (to walk), shut in by houses at least five or six stories high. Think of these houses as having houses back of them with scarcely enough yard space to admit daylight, every nook up to the roof full of rooms and chambers in which are crowded together 10,000 human beings.[6]

For Nathan, this was home. Yet it was home with opportunity. At Europe's crossroads, the Imperial Free City of Frankfurt was, like all crossroads, a place of truck, trade and barter – but also crucially the financial centre for the princes, dukes and electors of the Holy Roman Empire. Here, they traded taxes and raised loans for their courts, for their wars, their *grands projets* and pipe-dreams, and here amid the trade winds that blew across the continent, Rothschild's ancestors made a respectable living for two centuries.

The Rothschilds' roots date back to the 1560s, when Isak, son of Elchanan, built a home designated as *zum roten Schild*, literally 'at the red shield': for the next six generations, the family used the name 'Rothschild' after their old address. At first, the family was very pious and moderately prosperous, dealing in, among other things, cloth. Before his death, Isak had a taxable income of some 2,700 Gulden (the gold coins standardized throughout the Holy Roman Empire) and a century later, his great-grandson, a money-changer who dealt in silk and wool, had merely doubled it. No one made enough money to move from the cramped house with its ground-floor office, first-floor kitchen and squeezed bedrooms, where Nathan's father, Mayer Amschel, was born in either 1743 or 1744.

Educated at a rabbinical school in Fürth, Bavaria, it was there that Mayer learned – at the age of twelve – of his parents' tragic death in the epidemic of 1755. But, rather than return home, he was apprenticed to Wolf Jakob Oppenheim to learn the trade that changed his life: court finance.

Oppenheim's grandfather had been the court agent to the Austrian emperor, and his uncle was agent to the Bishop of Cologne. Within a decade, Mayer had learned enough to return to Frankfurt and begin dealing in rare coins and medals, selling enough within five years to William, ruler of Hesse-Kassel, that he earned the title of 'court agent' for himself. With a wise marriage the following year, to the daughter of Wolf Salomon Schnapper, court agent to the Prince of Saxe-Meiningen,* Mayer Amschel was soon Frankfurt's leading dealer of coins, medals and antiquities, and by the mid-1780s he was worth

---

* This marriage came with the blessing of a dowry of 2,400 Gulden.

150,000 Gulden – about £15,000. It was enough to finance a move in 1787 to the middle of the Judengasse, opposite its western gate, to a home with a little courtyard, two cellars, three storeys and conceivably enough room for the nineteen children born to the couple between 1771 and 1792 – including, in 1777, Nathan Rothschild.

Ironically, it was Napoleon's progress that now transformed the family's prospects. Two years after the French Revolution of 1789, the new French National Assembly ordered the emancipation of French Jewry. Seven years later, when Napoleon's troops destroyed half the homes in the Judengasse in the siege of Frankfurt, the local Senate was forced to allow Jews temporary residence outside the ghetto.

Together with two partners,* Mayer Amschel now landed the supply contract for the Austrian Army. As his banking business multiplied, he was, by 1797, one of the richest Jews in Frankfurt. Mayer's balance sheet, dated that summer, revealed assets of some 843,000 Gulden[†] spread across state bonds, personal loans and credits from customers trading from Frankfurt, Bremen, Regensburg, Augsburg, Leipzig, Berlin, Vienna, and beyond the empire in Amsterdam, Paris and London. By 1800, Mayer Amschel was head of one of the Judengasse's eleven richest families, which together controlled half of the community's estimated 6 million Gulden in assets.[7] 'The House of Rothschild', remembered a contemporary from the ghetto, 'had already at that time entered upon its fabulous prosperity.'[8]

And yet, as prosperous as banking proved, Mayer Amschel could see a second revolution unfolding, not political but economic, and with even greater power: England's cotton revolution was already fast transforming the markets of Germany.

*

Impossible to grow in Europe's cold climate, cotton was long known in England as one of the wonders of the Orient. In the 1320s, Sir John

---

* Mayer Amschel's two partners were Wolf Loeb Schott and Beer Nehm Rindskopf.

† The balance sheet can be found in the Moscow 'trophy' archive and shows liabilities totalling 735,000 Gulden.

Mandeville had described how it grew on 'a wonderful tree which bore tiny lambs on the ends of its branches... so pliable that they bent down to allow the lambs to feed when they are hungry'. The first cotton reached England, from the Levant, in the 1520s, after which the East India Company transformed England's taste with its first imports of muslins and calico.[9] Cheap, plentiful and washable, cotton was soon in everything from ballgowns to navvies' trousers, provoking outcry from English weavers, whose campaign – 'the weavers' triumph' – succeeded in raising cotton duties in the 1690s, and prohibiting imports altogether in 1721.[10] As the Georgian eighteenth century unfolded, the demand for cotton increased as it grew in fashionability. From the 1780s, French designs such as the *chemise à la reine* – an unstructured white muslin, gathered at neck, sleeves and waist – were popularized in aristocratic London. By 1787, the *Lady* magazine could record that 'all the sex now, from 15 to 50 and upwards... appear in their white muslin frocks with broad sashes'.[11]

The demand was a huge fillip for British ingenuity, which raced to feed the frenzy. Since John Lombe had opened his pioneering Derby silk factory in the early 1700s, fifty years of invention had transformed the efficiency of spinning. In 1733, the Bury-born John Kay introduced the 'flying shuttle', revolutionizing the speed of cotton-weaving. Around 1765, Blackburn-born James Hargreaves pioneered the spinning jenny. But it was the Preston-born Richard Arkwright who delivered the great breakthrough.[12] Born on 23 December 1732, he moved to Bolton, aged eighteen, and quickly established himself in business with the 'most indefatigable industry and with some success'. Quite how Arkwright perfected his revolutionary new way of spinning cotton over rollers has never quite been discovered, but he was deploying his invention at scale in his first cotton mill in 1767, relocating to Cromford in 1768. Eleven years later, Samuel Crompton combined Arkwright's technology with the spinning jenny to create his 'spinning mule', which produced yarn faster than ever. Arkwright was, said Thomas Carlyle, 'an historical phenomenon' who gave England 'the power of cotton'.[13] Indeed, prime minister Sir Robert Peel later described him as 'a man who has done more honour to the country than any man I know, not excepting our great military characters'.[14]

A tidal wave of innovation followed, as anyone with a mechanical mind began tinkering with, and improving, the machines. Between 1700 and 1850, an extraordinary 2,330 textile patents were filed, and as Arkwright's patents fell, his technology was re-engineered by scores of would-be competitors, transforming the efficiency of production. In 1760, 100 pounds of cotton took some 2,000 man-hours to process; by 1825 it took just 5 per cent of that time, 135 hours.[15] In 1770, the cotton business contributed just over half a per cent of Britain's growth; by 1831, it was over 25 per cent, as the value of cotton output soared from £0.6 million in 1760 to £30 million by 1815.[16] British imports of raw cotton naturally boomed too, rising from 14 million pounds in the 1720s to 1,664 million pounds in the 1820s.

By the early 1790s, Germany's great markets – especially Frankfurt – had become the largest European customer for the British cotton of Lancashire and Lanarkshire, consuming between one-third and 45 per cent of all British cotton exports.[17] But, the Revolutionary War with France, which erupted in 1793, was a commercial disaster, as the turmoil of conflict, blockades and restrictions (notably Napoleon's 'Continental System') brought severe disruption. The trade of the old Dutch ports – governed by Napoleon's brother, King Louis I of Holland – ground to a halt, and trade began to shift to the old German markets of the Rhine, which remained beyond Bonaparte's control.[18] It did not take Mayer Amschel long to see a chance to connect his hometown of Frankfurt – and his son Nathan – with the centre of the British cotton revolution: Manchester.

Manchester had been the heart of the English cotton business for centuries. In the 1550s, the Tudor antiquary William Leland noted that the cotton trade had helped make Manchester 'the fairest, best builded, quickest and most populous town of all Lancashire', an achievement aided in no small part by the Flemish weavers who settled thereabouts in the days of Edward III.[19] Manchester and the surrounding towns, being unincorporated as boroughs, lacked guilds and the rules that went with them, and crucially were exempt from the 1558 Weavers Act, which limited apprentice numbers. By 1565, an Act of Parliament was referring to the town's trade in fustian[20] – a mix of cotton and linen – and from the late sixteenth, Lancashire was producing 40,000 pieces each year. 'The town of Manchester buys cotton wool from London, that comes from Cyprus and Smyrna,' noted the merchant Lewis Roberts in the *Treasure of Traffic* (1641), 'and works the same into fustians, vermilions, and dimities, which they return to London, where they are sold, and from thence, not seldom, are sent back into such foreign parts.'[21]

'Manchester men' became well-known, driving their packhorses for miles and offering credit to retailers in country towns. A merchant with a warehouse could now organize production with over 100 fustian manufacturers along with networks of spinners and weavers. When Daniel Defoe rode through the region in 1727, he noted that throughout Manchester and the Lancashire villages had grown a huge domestic industry: 'almost at every house there was a tenter, and almost on every tenter a piece of cloth, or kersey or shalloon'.[22] By the 1740s, half of adult males in parts of south-east Lancashire drew most of their income from textiles. Lancashire was exempted, too, from the Calico Act of 1721, which restricted cotton wares domestic and foreign in order to boost the wool trade,* and from the 1770s, industry intensified through the Pennine valleys to Bolton, Oldham and Manchester through the old and well established networks of middlemen; the linen drapers who put out yarn and cotton wool for spinning, winding, warping and weaving.

In this new world, Manchester was the centre. The town's directories of 1772–73 list around thirty traders describing themselves as merchants, importing cotton from India and Turkey and managing production in the towns around Manchester. With the end of the American War of Independence came the advent of huge new supplies from the United States, which entrepreneurs could suddenly now ship through Liverpool. The first bags arrived as early as 1784.

But Lancashire was blessed too with an old tradition of engineering and a vocational culture of thought and education in the region, underpinned by great institutions like the Warrington Academy (a polytechnic) or the Manchester Literary and Philosophical Society, all born of the Non-conformist tradition. Throughout the region, small

---

* The Calico Act was repealed in 1774.

shops made brass and pewter ware, watches, clocks and locks; indeed, a Lancashire watch could fetch three times the price of one made in London.

By the 1780s, entrepreneurs such as Peter Drinkwater were connecting new supply lines with old expertise, machines and steam, to create in Manchester, and with astonishing speed, the world's first factory city. By 1787, forty-three of the country's one hundred and forty-five Arkwright-type mills were in Lancashire; seven years later, Manchester directories were listing sixty firms that combined the mercantile with manufacturing. By 1811, the town's 50 mills boasted over 4 million steam mule spindles and there were more than 650 cotton mills within 60 miles of Bolton.[23] These were the mills that helped power a new British economy; soon the textile business had ballooned to over a quarter of the nation's economy, and nearly a quarter of a million people were turning factory yarn into cloth, 100,000 of them working in factories.[24] Little wonder that nineteenth-century Manchester was dubbed 'Cottonopolis'.

The city was the 'phenomenon of the age'.[25] In little over twenty years, Manchester's population nearly doubled.* You could, wrote Thomas Carlyle, hear 'the awakening of a [sic] Manchester on Monday morning, at half past five... the rushing-off of its thousand mills, like the boom of an Atlantic tide, ten thousand times ten-thousand spools and spindles all set humming'.[26] The people went to work in the 'the hundreds of factories in Manchester which tower up to six stories in height. The huge chimneys at the side of these buildings belch forth black coal vapours... The houses are blackened by it.'[27]

Contemporaries noted how 'trade has been kept open to strangers of every description who contribute to its improvement by their ingenuity'; yet even by the 1780s, observers could sense that it was a city of distinct classes, living not in harmony but in contention.[28] Its motive power was not the great upper classes, but a new breed of middle-class entrepreneurs.† Many were Non-conformists – Dissenters – still barred

---

* Manchester's population increased from 40,000 to 70,000 between 1780 and 1801.

† In 1787, nearly two-thirds of factory owners were from 'social class two'. Hall, *Cities and Civilizations*, op. cit., p. 334.

by the law from public office. Such 'new men' rose by effort and ingenuity. They represented a tough new, energetic order, engaged with
world trade but ruling, as Friedrich Engels later observed, with an
influence 'that went further than that of the Norman baron'. They
lived alongside a city of filth, as a visitor from Rotherham described in
1808: 'the town is abominably filthy, the steam engine is pestiferous,
the dyehouses noisesome and offensive and the water of the river as
black as ink or the Stygian Lake'.[29] Indeed, the River Irwell was
described as a 'flood of liquid manure'.[30] It would be Nathan's home for
over a decade.

*

History does not record the precise spark for Nathan Rothschild's
departure for England, although he was fond of telling a story in later
life:

> There was not room enough for all of us in that city [of Frankfurt].
> I dealt in English goods. One great trader came there who had the
> market to himself: he was quite the great man, and did us a favour
> if he sold us goods. Somehow I offended him, and he refused to
> show me his patterns. This was on a Tuesday; I said to my father,
> 'I will go to England.' I could speak nothing but German. On the
> Thursday I started...*

Whether the story was true or not, Hansa merchants had certainly
sent their children to England for generations, and many had spied the
opportunity to set up shop in Manchester.† Between 1799 and 1803, at
least eight German merchants opened for business, and in 1799 one
German, Karl Friedrich Brandt, was even nominated borough reeve.[31]
In Frankfurt, by 1800, some 15 Jewish firms were importing English
textiles – and some of them would have worked with the firms of L. B.

---

* This was related to the MP Thomas Fowell Buxton, in 1834.

† In 1795, Dr Aikin observed that 'the vast increase in foreign trade... caused...
foreigners to reside in Manchester'.

Cohen and Levi Salomons, with whom Nathan settled for a few months, before heading north to set up shop in Manchester.

'As soon as I got to Manchester,' Nathan once wrote, 'I laid out all my money, things were so cheap.'

In later life, he became fond of the maxim that 'money makes money', and on his arrival in Manchester he had plenty to invest on behalf of his father for the family and their partners on the Continent. He promptly put to work £20,000. His orders arrived from his father by post; he then placed them with manufacturers all over the north, often with small subcontractors producing cloth that was then finished by dyers and printers in and around the city. Rothschild quickly found that he could maximize profits by supplying manufacturers with material and dye, as well as buying their stock and reselling it, so he 'got three profits instead of one and I could sell goods cheaper than anybody. In a short time I made my £20,000 into £60,000.'[32]

To drive down the prices he paid – by as much as 15 or 20 per cent – Rothschild often paid upfront, which meant borrowing from his bankers in London. Keeping prices low let him undercut his competitors and boost his customer base. 'You cannot find any person in Manchester who will serve you with so small a profit as myself,' he assured one new customer, while also assuring his father in 1802 that 'No House in Manchester purchases the goods cheaper.'

Nevertheless, Nathan's father was often unhappy at his son's slipshod style. Mayer Amschel often had to intervene with disgruntled customers and creditors who complained about everything from incorrectly marked crates to late invoices and unsettled accounts:

Sometimes you write that you have sent, for example, the chest with this number, then later [it arrives with] another number. If you send a chest today, you only let Esriel Reiss know six months after. One of his clerks said to me that you are very disorganised. My dear friend, if you don't write down all the numbers of the chests when you send them off, if you don't write them down until you receive acknowledgement that they have arrived, if you don't pay attention, if you [don't] ask where the chest has gone when you don't receive an answer from your correspondent if you are so disorganised and don't have someone or a friend with you, then you will be swindled. What is the good of that[?] Everyone can be a millionaire if they get the [right] opportunity. I already complained in Frankfurt about your extraordinary expenditures and disorganisation, dear Nathan; I don't like it.[33]

Nor did this paternal lecture end there. Mayer Amschel went on to berate Nathan for failing to calculate his profits net (as opposed to gross); for doing business in precious stones ('But you are no jeweller'); and for failing to discount bad debts. In sum, he wanted to encourage his son 'to be more organised... You really have a good brain but you haven't learnt order.'[34]

And yet, organized or not, Nathan was beginning to show the mixture of speed, charm and aggression that would become the hallmark of his business career. 'My success', he once said, 'all turned on one maxim. I said: I can do what another man can... Another advantage I had. I was an off-hand man. I made a bargain at once.'[35]

In 1801, Nathan Rothschild diversified into manufacturing. He purchased a machine from Boulton & Watt and travelled constantly from Manchester to Scotland and London to build up his network of suppliers, often crossing the Channel to visit customers. In 1802, his continental trip saw links established with firms in Paris, Nancy, Lyon, Liège, Metz, Brussels, Maastricht, Antwerp and Amsterdam – and before going home he visited Germany and Switzerland. He even had a customer in Moscow. By 1804, Rothschild could boast a fine house in Ardwick – a prosperous part of Manchester – and a warehouse in Brown Street.

In the magnificent oak-shelved Rothschild archives at New Court, on St Swithin's Lane, London, is the expansive Rothschild collection, replete with files upon files of translations of the letters written in Yiddish (Judendeutsch) through which the Rothschilds, their friends, family and partners corresponded incessantly over the course of their careers. Here, we can read the excerpts from letters of 1804 between Hamburg and Manchester, detailing Nathan's business with textiles such as the blue 'Thicksets', cambrics and 'pressed Jaconets' and the constant struggle with quality: 'My Hamburg House', writes

Mr Hertz, the clerk at L. B. Cohen, 'mentions that the enclosed pattern is one of the best pieces[;] now you can form an idea how bad the others are.'[36] And here, too, in Hertz's letters of 1805, we can read how the circumstances of war meant trade was getting sticky: 'the present time is the most critical and the most unhappy for the Continentland', he wrote on 11 December 1805, 'the market over-stocked with goods, no trade coming in, where shall the merchant take the money to pay?'[37]

Times were changing. And it would now prove not cotton, but love and war that would be the making of Nathan's career.

*

In October 1806, Nathan Rothschild married Hannah, the third daughter of Levi Barent Cohen, a leading London merchant and Amsterdam-born international diamond dealer.[38] He was the founder of L. B. Cohen, where Nathan had started work in October 1804, on his arrival in England. Marriage now brought him a dowry of £3,248 along with a serious *entrée* into the business of smuggling to the war-torn Continent, now stuck behind Napoleon's new punitive trade barrier: the Continental System.

As Britain's conflict with Napoleon moved into a sharp war of commerce, trading conditions quickly began to deteriorate. In May 1806, capitalizing on the control of the seas that followed Nelson's victory at Trafalgar, Britain blockaded an 800-mile slice of 'hostile' coastline, from Germany to Brittany. Napoleon quickly retaliated. The 'Berlin Decree' of 21 November 1806 forced French allies into agreeing an embargo on trade with Britain. At least three of Nathan's European customers collapsed, putting his business under real strain. Bankers complained to his father that he was overdrawn, and it got harder to sell on his IOUs.

Together with his father-in-law, Cohen, Nathan Rothschild was determined to seek opportunity from others' adversity. He began smuggling goods on a grand scale, shipping cargoes – via the Baltic, Königsberg (then a Russian port), Gothenburg (Sweden) and Christiansand (Kristiansand, Norway), and above all the North Sea islands of Heligoland (where he placed his own agent, John Fox) – in foreign-registered ships with fake documents, in combination with a web of continental trading houses and new continental allies.

It was a fraught business. One of Nathan's partners, John Parish, was arrested when the French entered Hamburg; at least one large cargo was lost in Riga, seized, and only released with a heavy tax; another was taken in Königsberg. In October 1810, Mayer Amschel was raided (along with more than 200 other firms) and caught with 60,000 Gulden-worth of indigo. The result was a heavy fine, and the textiles were seized and publicly burned. Yet, Nathan Rothschild was a risk-taker, and much of his cargo still got through. By 1808, he was well embedded in his father-in-law's trading network, with a reputation for getting his goods to the Continent, and was now branching out into colonial goods, and credit.

The Cohen family were old hands trading in dyes, coffee and sugar, and Nathan's letters from 1808 to 1810 are full of talk of 'East India goods', African cargoes, 'madder roots', logwood, Canova soap, barrels of currants, Reggio silk, olive oil, Smyrna cotton, indigo, hemp, tallow, and iron.

By the time his father-in-law died, in 1808, Rothschild was rich. He owned a 'large and commodious' warehouse next to his substantial townhouse at No. 25 Mosley Street, 'the most elegant street in Manchester',[39] as well as a property in London.* Between 1800 and 1811, Niall Ferguson has estimated, Nathan's business probably turned over £800,000; assuming profits of 5 per cent, he made some £40,000 – worth somewhere between £30 million and £44 million in today's money. But disguised in his slipshod accounting were huge debts to his father-in-law's family, totalling, by the end of August 1808, some £27,000.[40] Indeed, his brother-in-law was forced to upbraid him weeks before Cohen's death: 'am sorry to observe that the Acct Court. can be of no use to me... you over throw every thing & begin anew, you will excuse Sir my refusal to submit to it'.[41]

Crucially, Nathan was relying on using Cohen's bills of exchange, which, unlike his own, were widely accepted, to underpin a banking

---

* The London property was at 12 Great St Helen's.

business that was now large enough to become a full-time occupation. In May 1809, Nathan took possession of No. 2 New Court, St Swithin's Lane, London, and that same month, briefed a friend on a 'new alteration arrangement in our business, and an alteration in the firm'.[42]

Having made a fortune with his father-in-law, Nathan Rothschild was now poised to build the world's greatest banking business as the London financial agent of an exiled ruler and an invading general. And it was a breakthrough by his father that made it possible.

*

Mayer Amschel's most important customer was William IX, the hereditary Landgrave of Hesse-Kassel, who in 1803 became the principality's Elector (as William I). He was one of the richest men in Europe, worth at his coronation some 30–40 million Gulden. The prince had made a fortune fighting Napoleon. And Napoleon did not forget it. The services of the prince's troops were generally available to the highest bidder – at £7 for a soldier and another £7 for any man killed – with the money paid in bills to the prince's bank account with Van Noten & Sons in London. But in 1806, when the powerful German state of Prussia was defeated by Napoleon at Jena, William fled and, according to legend, entrusted part of his fortune to Mayer Amschel for safe-keeping, just as the French troops were entering Frankfurt.

Mayer Amschel had broken into the banking syndicate through a friend at the court of Hesse, Karl Friedrich Buderus, a civil servant involved with the principality's war financing. From 1796, Mayer Amschel had sold the prince's English debts. Slowly, he widened his range of services to supply eleven major loans between 1801 and 1806, acquiring in the process promotion to 'senior court agent' (from 1803) along with appointments to five other courts, including that of the Austrian emperor. As William fled into exile, Mayer Amschel was tasked with helping manage William's assets in one of the greatest sovereign wealth funds in Europe – worth some 27 million Gulden.[43] There was nowhere better to invest than London.

Quite how Nathan now made his fortune handling the family's

London operation for the prince is a matter of some dispute.* From 1809, at Buderus's prompting, Mayer Amschel instructed Nathan to start buying British government gilts† – and Nathan later boasted the orders were worth a fortune: 'The Prince of Hesse-Cassel… gave my father his money [in fact his English portfolio]; there was no time to be lost; he sent it to me. I had £600,000 arrive unexpectedly by the post; and I put it to such good use that the prince made me a present of all his wine and his linen.'[44]

Some allege Nathan made a fortune with a 'double speculation', whereby William did not put up all the cash upfront, so that Nathan bought consols on the prince's account with borrowed money, putting down a fraction of the total cost, allowing speculation both on the final price of consols and on the exchange rate between Gulden and sterling.

Others, however, argue Nathan owed his fortune to a breakthrough in the gold bullion business, where the ongoing war was causing prices to spiral.[45] Nathan's gold dealing dated back at least to 1808, when he bought 38,959 Spanish dollars from Jamaica.[46] The following year he was buying heavily on his father's account, with bills sent through the Amsterdam bankers Braunsberg & Co.: 'You would I believe do well', wrote Nathan's father in November 1809, 'to continue with remitt[ance] of gold and silver to Ms Braunsberg & Co and I have recommended you very heartily to them.' By the end of 1809, Nathan, together with his father and brother James, had created a bullion-dealing partnership, smuggling gold to the Continent and using the proceeds to buy bills of exchange in London at the lowest possible exchange rate. James ran the business in Paris and Amsterdam, managing a network of buyers, while Nathan began buying gold wherever he could find it – including from English ports and even Brazil – and dispatching the metal on the Continent through a dozen trusted couriers and smugglers. They were relied on to assure him, like the Braunsbergs, that 'you may depend on us keeping secret any thing

---

* Kaplan, for example, somewhat disputes Egon Corti's assertion in his *The Reign of the House of Rothschild*, later reinforced by Ferguson, that Nathan Rothschild profited by handling the entirety of the £450,000–£500,000 (as Ferguson has it) earmarked by the Elector for investment in 1809–11.

† 3 per cent of these were consols, which were government gilts in the form of perpetual bonds, redeemable at the option of the government.

relating to this or any Similar transaction which may take place between us… you may depend on our managing your interests as our own'.[47]

By 1809, Nathan had received some £160,000 to buy bullion and purchase consols at 3 per cent interest; in 1810, the Braunsbergs remitted some £260,000, and the following year new partners, Faber & Co., remitted a similar figure. By 1811, when in London,[48] gold rose to 28 per cent above the official benchmark price – known as the English mint price – Nathan was trading tens of thousands of Spanish dollars, and doubloons, Portuguese gold, and hundreds of thousands of various coins. His business was now big enough to demand a move to London. In July 1811, a notice appeared in the newspapers that 'the business heretofore carried on by the undersigned Nathan Mayer Rothschild at Manchester… will cease to be carried on from this day and any persons having dealings with that firm are required to send their demands to pay their accounts to NM Rothschilds at his Counting House, in No 2 New Court, St-Swithins-lane, London'.

By 1812, as the gold shortage bit and the gold price hit 37 per cent above the English mint price, some £2.5 million in bills of exchange were remitted to Rothschild from France and the Netherlands alone. Nathan's letters from these years (in the Rothschild archives) are full of news of gold dealing, not just from Amsterdam and Paris but from across the Continent. In February 1812, for instance, his agents in Malta were writing to him about the price of 'dubloons', while in May 1813 agents in St Petersburg informed him that 'the eight bars of gold having got safe into our possession, as they can't be otherwise advantageously disposed of, will be delivered into the mint tomorrow… under the superintendence of a trusty person'.[49]

But having made a fortune, the thirty-seven-year-old Nathan was not about to retire from the field. Instead, he used his position of wealth to help finance an invading army, harnessing the extraordinary power of his new home: the City of London.

*

The French Revolutionary and Napoleonic Wars – and the challenge of paying for them – revolutionized the City. Financing two decades of war and seven grand European coalitions against Napoleon's empire cost the British government an extraordinary £1.7 billion, three times the cost of all the other wars fought since the Glorious Revolution and six times the pre-war national income.[50] The money had to come from somewhere – and by and large it came from borrowing, via a home army of investors mobilized through a revolution in methods and institutions – from token coins to savings banks, discount houses, the London Stock Exchange, a wave of foreign listings, and new powers for the Bank of England.

By the time Nathan Rothschild arrived in England, the wheels of the nation's commerce were oiled by three ways of paying for things. First, the integrity of the nation's ancient coinage had been restored by Sir Isaac Newton, who, as Warden (1696–99) and then Master of the Mint (1699–1727) put England on the 'bi-metallic standard', fixing the value of gold and silver coins in 1696. Second, merchants since the 1300s had been using bills of exchange – those private IOUs issued among them. Third, under Oliver Cromwell banks had been allowed to take deposits and issue bank notes – a promise to pay the bearer of the note the promised amount. This was a privilege subsequently limited to partnerships (of fewer than six members) and, from its founding in 1694, the Bank of England, with its royal charter and sub-scription list headed by the king and queen, where customers could settle debts by transferring money between accounts on a ledger.

In the late 1700s, banks were growing fast. Basic commercial banking was fairly simple: the banks took money from customers and either recorded the deposit in their ledgers, or issued a bank note. Notes were useful for both security, but also as a way of paying for things. Individuals and businesses asked little, or nothing, of the banks in return, while the banks used the cash to lend to, say, a merchant, who wrote the bank a bill of exchange – a promise to pay the bank a fixed sum on a specified day in the future. The bank typically paid out less cash than the face value of the bill. Hence, the bank 'discounted' bills of exchange.

The demands of war created an enormous new demand for equip-ment and supplies, and to finance Britain's home front, provincial banks multiplied, from about a dozen in 1750 to an astonishing 783 between 1797 and 1810. The number of London banks over the period doubled, as provincial banks set up in London. For those that lacked a London base, City banks created a clearing house to process offsets to balance-sheet ledgers. Provincial banks and City banks were now linked in a way that allowed individuals to move money to the City and overseas. Underlying it all was the Bank of England, serving as the bedrock of the system and home to a third of country's gold.

Just as important as the banks for money-raising was the bond market. Its foundations were laid, of course, by the early work of royal financiers like William de la Pole, and Sir Thomas Gresham, who helped create the Royal Exchange. And, in the later days of Sir Thomas Pitt, it was the new king, William, who imported the Dutch techniques and institutions that helped the bond market grow dramatically.

Bonds were invented by Venice in the twelfth century as a means of extracting loans for mercenaries from its richer citizens, and the subsequent five centuries of continental warfare had given Europeans plenty of time to finesse some basic bond finance techniques. The guaranteed nature of the deal, whereby the state guaranteed an IOU redeemable at a fixed interest rate, circumvented church prohibitions on usury, and bonds could pay up to 5 per cent, paid twice yearly from excise tax. Crucially, bonds once issued were transferable – they could be bought and sold, swapped and bartered in the marketplace. By 1427, the city of Florence had used the technique to support its public debts – the *prestanze* – of 5 million florins; and, as the Dutch displaced the Italians as Europe's pre-eminent commercial power, the scale of bond finance surged to unprecedented levels. By the 1630s, some 65,000 Dutch bond-holders subscribed to 250 million guilders.[51]

Thomas Gresham's creation of the Royal Exchange created a London base for methods pioneered in Antwerp, and Gresham had worked hard to organize the City's merchants as lenders to the Crown, freeing Elizabeth I from dependence on foreign debtors. But it was William III's accession as King of England that truly brought to London the Dutch system of finance. In the final triumph of the traders, William was offered a deal: in exchange for taxes to support the Nine Years' War, Parliament would control taxation. This development allowed England to commit tax revenues for servicing the debt that Parliament had authorized. 'Funded debt' now became possible for the first time. Issued from the 1690s, it created in England a new government bond (though common for years in the Dutch Republic): the annuity.

By the time George I inherited the throne in 1714, the royal debt was so large that interest charges paid on annuities made up a sum equivalent to half of government revenue. Generally, each new annuity issued was backed by a specific new tax. But this was complicated to administer, and so between 1749 and 1752, Lord Treasurer Pelham consolidated the funds into one perpetual annuity fund, paying 3 per cent interest a year. Thus the 'three per-cent consol' was born. An ordinary citizen could now acquire a £100 'consol', which came with a government promise to pay 3 per cent par value a year in perpetuity, or until the government exercised its right to buy back the bond at face value. Managing most of the business day to day was the Bank of England. Indeed, by 1764, the Bank was handling 70 per cent of government debt, with a further 25 per cent managed at South Sea House.[52] The nation's public-finance system had become, in the words of Thomas Mortimer, 'a national good... a masterpiece of human policy'.[53] It was not perfect. The duties levied to fund the interest payments, for instance, were becoming ever more complex. Indeed, by 1784 the Customs regulations were described by a contemporary as 'a cloud of complicated materials, and abstruse science'.[54]

But, crucially, the citizen could sell on their bonds in the marketplace. Indeed, by the mid-eighteenth century, the London bond market was booming with investors drawn from all over Europe: at the outbreak of the Seven Years' War in 1754, there were some 60,000 public creditors. Henry St John, Viscount Bolingbroke, described the scene well: 'A new interest has been created out of their fortunes, & a sort of property which was not known twenty years ago is now increased to almost equal to the *terra firma* of our island.'[55]

The epicentre of this evolving financial world was to be found amid the fifty steeples of the City of London. Here was the market for marine underwriting, and for the government and chartered company securities, centred on Garraway's and Jonathan's coffee houses in the narrow Exchange Alley, opposite the Royal Exchange at the intersection of Cornhill and Lombard streets. It took, perhaps, a minute and a half to walk through it, but there you could see in its infancy the buying of stocks and shares – in the Bank of England, the East India Company, the new Sword Blade Company. Here, it was said, 'you will see fellows, in shabby clothes selling ten or twelve thousands pounds in stock, though perhaps he mayn't be worth at the same time ten shillings, and with as much zeal as if he were a director'.[56] As demand grew to buy and sell shares, a Stock Exchange was opened on Sweetings Ally, in 1773, where for the first time a common set of rules and regulations emerged for traders. There were the 'jobbers', who took positions on deals on their own accounts, and the 'brokers' who matched buyers and sellers, with a cut for themselves. London's Square Mile was taking shape, and before long Nathan Rothschild would prove its master.

*

Nathan's great break came with Wellington's war. As early as 1809, some six years after war with France had resumed, the great general had written to the government complaining about cash shortages. In March 1811, he warned the prime minister, Lord Liverpool, that these were threatening his campaign in the Iberian Peninsula to push back the French, and two years later, in February 1813, he was encountering severe cash-flow problems. Hitherto, bullion had been shipped to Portugal or Spain and exchanged for local currency, or bills issued in London were sold to local merchants for cash. But by 1812, the Iberian market was so full of English bills they could only be sold at a prohibitive discount.

As Rothschild's luck would have it, Wellington's crisis coincided with a tumble for the greatest bank in England – Baring Brothers. Founded by John Baring, a young German who (like Nathan) had been dispatched to England in 1717 to learn the textile business, the bank had been built up by John's son, Francis, who had proved one of the most remarkable men of his generation, creating a huge banking business by first supplying the British forces fighting the American rebels and then floating debt for the wars against the French. Known as 'the first merchant in Europe; first in knowledge and talents and first in character and opulence',[57] Francis Baring was the man to whom the government turned when it needed to raise money and supplies.*

When the French wars broke out, Barings had effectively merged with Hope & Co., an Amsterdam-based bank (founded by an expatriate Scottish family) that had become the financial giant of its day. The merger created a partnership with huge expertise in public finance, and from 1800, Barings made a fortune as the leading dealer in government debt in twelve out of the subsequent fifteen years.[58] However, in 1810 Francis Baring died, just as the firm was handling a £22.3 million loan amid a small market crash: Barings lost £43,000 – and its appetite for new government work.

By 1814, and despite the fact that Napoleon had been forced back within his borders by armies of the Sixth Coalition, Wellington faced a cash crunch: writing to London, he warned 'there is not in the military chest a shilling to pay for any thing that the country could afford, and our credit is already gone in this country… It is obvious that an immediate and large supply of money from England is necessary.'[59] It was now that John Charles Herries, Commissary-in-Chief, turned to Nathan Rothschild. A Germanophile, he suspected Nathan could help because of the position he had carved out in the gold market. As Nathan later explained:

> When I settled in London, the East India Company had £800,000 worth of gold to sell. I went to the sale and bought it all. I knew the Duke of Wellington must have it. I had bought a great many of his bills at a discount. The government sent for me and said they must have it. When they got it, they did not know how to get it to Portugal. I undertook all that and I sent it to France: and that was the best business I ever did.[60]

---

* As his wealth increased, Francis Baring became Chairman of the East India Company (1793), and his work with the prime minister, Pitt the Younger, was rewarded with a baronetcy. Between 1794 and 1806, he sat in the House of Commons.

On 14 January 1814, Herries invited Nathan 'to favour him with a short conversation', which soon led to several tactical discussions – 'the various suggestions of Mr Rothschild' – and then a recommendation to the prime minister 'to employ that gentleman [Rothschild] in the most secret and confidential manner to collect in Germany, France and Holland the largest quantity of French gold and silver coins... not exceeding in value £600,000 for the use of the army under Lord Wellington, in France'. [61]

The venture proved an extraordinary success. For a 2 per cent commission, Rothschild eventually shipped 1,085,800 coins worth some £552,335. [62] By May 1814, helped by his brothers – Amschel in Frankfurt, James in Paris, Carl in Amsterdam and Salomon, based in Vienna – Nathan had supplied some £1.2 million. And this was only part of the operation. Herries calculated in June 1814 that the brothers had effected payments of some 12.6 million francs with such skill that he was able to report the war chest was supplied 'so rapidly & completely that the Commissary General was abundantly supplied of all his wants, without having occasion to negotiate a bill'. [*]

In the peace that followed Napoleon's first defeat and exile to Elba, in 1814, the Rothschild brothers had set about buying British and Austrian bonds in the hope of a bull market. When news of Napoleon's escape from Elba had became known, Nathan quickly changed tack, buying as much gold as he could lay hands on in London, Amsterdam and Hamburg. He rounded up gold coins worth some £2 million for shipment to Wellington and offered to route some £9.8 million in fresh subsidies to Britain's allies with a commission alone of £390,000. [63] Helpfully, the business of transferring Britain's subsidies to its allies allowed the Rothschild brothers to forge crucial relationships with courts from Vienna to Moscow, and in Russia, the brothers scooped a major loan deal with a huge commission and a new relationship with Gervais, the key Russian finance official.

The brothers' commission, paid for moving money around the Continent, was only part of the profit. For instance, a fortune was

---

* This was Herries' final Memorandum in 1816, quoted in Kaplan, *Nathan Mayer Rothschild*, op. cit., p. 89.

made handling a loan of £2.61 million in Treasury bills contracted in July 1815, and in handling huge inter-government payments between Britain's allies, where the Rothschilds could exploit important differences in European exchange rates. With permanent bases in Frankfurt and London, offices in Amsterdam and Paris, and crucially the relationship with Herries, the Rothschilds had together an unrivalled grasp of prices in different markets and forewarning of the timing of major money movements between Britain and its allies, which they communicated to one another by means of every method, from special couriers to pigeon-post. In the first half of 1814, for example, the brothers were able to exploit a gap in gold quotations between Paris and London, buy undervalued sterling in Frankfurt, make the most of the premium on ducats over *Louis d'or* in Berlin, and buy ducats cheap in Amsterdam before delivery to Russia in the autumn.*

The brothers' letters to and fro are rich in the detail of prices and trades proposed, brokered and completed. 'I hope to be able to forward you in the course of next week about 300,000 Spanish dollars and 100,000 dollars in bar silver and from 80–100,000 more Louis d'Or,' wrote Nathan to his brother James on 15 July 1814.[64] A month later he added: 'I have made some considerable purchases in bullion about £100,000 for account government… and hope to be able to dispatch the most part of it as I am only waiting for the vessel which I am enduced to do.'[65] On 7 October 1814 came the instructions 'from Mr Herries ordering the sum of £250,000 to be laid out in dollars[,] doublons and government bills on Lisbon, Madrid, Cadiz or Oporto, the sum of £100,000 to be disposed of in Paris, the remaining £150,000 in Amsterdam'.[66]

The Rothschilds had a very good war. Indeed, between March 1815 and July 1816, the brothers managed to double their capital to around £1 million. The Rothschilds were now bigger than Barings. They had won the war; the challenge now was to win the peace.

*

---

* A *Louis d'or* was a traditional gold coin, named after French kings, which began being minted again on Napoleon's fall.

The peace that settled on Europe after the defeat of Napoleon was unprecedented.* Despite domestic revolutions and the Ottoman Empire's disintegration, there was, with the exception of Crimea (1854–6), no war between two or more major powers for a century. London was now the capital of a country that was indisputably the world's leading nation, emerging from the peace talks at the Congress of Vienna in 1815 as the world's unchallenged super-power, on the threshold of its imperial century.

But it was, at first, a time of major frustration for the Rothschilds. Having financed Britain's war, they hoped to finance the European peace, managing the huge reparations payments between defeated France and the victors. With a strong economy and affordable indemnities, France emerged from the war in decent shape but in need of loans for £12 million, of which £2 million would need to be raised in London. But the Rothschilds were beaten to the business by Barings, which yet remained, in the minds of statesmen, the world's pre-eminent bank. ('There are six great powers in Europe,' the Duc de Richelieu remarked, 'England, France, Prussia, Austria, Russia and Baring Brothers.') From under the Rothschilds' noses, Barings snatched the business of raising some 315 million francs in three tranches and earning them so much money that one partner was moved to comment on their 'unheard of profit of £720,000... forming as I conceive the most profitable undertaking in which any mercantile house ever engaged'.[67]

With Herries' departure from office in 1816, the Rothschilds had little choice but to look east and south, to seek a role as bankers to the 'concert' of old Europe, and west, across the Atlantic, to the new opportunities of South America. In these forays, the brothers would prove highly successful, organizing, over the next decade, sixteen loans as far afield as Prussia, Naples, Russia, Portugal, Austria and Brazil.

---

* The great historian Eric Hobsbawn remarked: 'It was evident to all intelligent statesmen that no major European war was henceforth tolerable; for such a war would almost certainly mean a new revolution, and consequently the destruction of the old regimes.' Eric Hobsbawm, *The Age of Revolutions, 1789–1848* (Abacus, 1962), p. 127; 'Great battles are not always turning points in history,' wrote the historian Linda Colley, 'but Waterloo emphatically was.' Colley, *Britons*, op. cit., p. 338.

Nathan was not without some useful connections. Indeed, his brother James was moved to write that 'Nathan's relation with these gentleman [of the British Treasury] is such as between brothers... Our new court gives me the impression of being like a Freemason's lodge.'* With connections, came profits. At the end of 1816, for example, Nathan held £1.6 million-worth of British consols – equivalent to the entire capital of the firm – despite his brother's entreaties to sell; the price of consols kept rising into 1817, and when, in July, Nathan did sell, five months ahead of the market peak, he made a profit of some £250,000. Benefiting from inside information from the Chancellor of the Exchequer, Nicholas Vansittart, Nathan had timed his sale to perfection.[†]

But Nathan and his brothers knew that the key to future profits lay in breaking into the huge market for government bonds required to repay war debt, to found new companies and to build new railways and roads. Their breakthrough came in Prussia, with a deal that helped revolutionize international finance with a first step towards the creation of an international bond market.

The idea of a Prussian loan raised in London had first been floated by a merchant at a Prussian bank in London, in 1817; but intense work by Carl and Salomon Rothschild in Koblenz and Berlin had landed the deal for the brothers. With vast debts, the Prussian government was paying, at times, interest rates of 24 per cent.[68] In January 1818, Prussia's ambassador to London, the intellectual Wilhelm von Humboldt, was advising his finance minister: 'If the bond is to be a success here [in London], then, to my mind only if Rothschilds handles it... Rothschild is simply the most enterprising businessman here. Through his brothers he is closely acquainted with the situation of the Prussian state... [He] is also a reliable man with whom the government here does much business.'[69]

It was a revolutionary proposal. The loan was not in thalen, the Prussian currency, but sterling, with interest payable half yearly in London rather than in Berlin. A British-style 'sinking fund' – a pot into

---

* Salomon commented: 'Vansittart is a very fine man insofar as he gave you a hint of a forthcoming funding operation. He well knows that you were the only one who drove up the stocks.' Ferguson, *The House of Rothschild*, op. cit., p. 120.
† Nathan had probably heard about a government funding operation that would have depressed the price, and so got out first.

which regular taxes were desposited – was created to pay off the loan over time, and the loan was sold to investors in London, Frankfurt, Berlin, Hamburg, Amsterdam and Vienna. Nathan had to cut the price of the loan at the last minute to keep the business, but, as James noted, everyone had reason to be pleased: 'Prussia must be very satisfied, because… you gave them very good prices and it is (satisfactory) to us too.'[70]

The model transformed demand for foreign loans among London investors, and between 1817 and 1829 a stream of fifteen further loans followed. Many were for members of the new German Confederation, led by Austria, which superseded the old, defunct Holy Roman Empire.[71] As Carl Rothschild's relationship with Austrian Chancellor Metternich blossomed, so the brothers' business prospered, raising war loans for the Austrian intervention in Naples, designed to stop the slide there towards revolution.

By the early 1820s, Nathan Rothschild's position in London was such that one German banker could reflect: 'NM Rothschild, who is equipped with a vulgar talent, audacity and vanity, constitutes the centrifugal point around which the stock exchange revolves. He alone determines the exchange, buying and selling £100,000 each day.'[72] Key to the Rothschilds' strength was the brothers' ability to co-ordinate across the field of Europe access to the huge liquid market of London, where Nathan was now the family's 'general in chief'. By 1825, he was so powerful that when crisis came, he was strong enough even to save the Bank of England itself.

*

As with all major financial crises, the 'Panic of 1825' had deep roots. Deregulation in March 1797 had allowed an ever greater number of provincial banks to issue small-denomination notes, sparking a huge increase in liquidity, and during the Napoleonic Wars, the Bank of England had vastly expanded its issue of notes to merchants. In the first months of peace, income tax had been abolished (in 1816), thereby losing the Treasury 20 per cent of its gross income and the key source for repaying back debt and interest – and so the government desperately needed to reduce the costs of its huge war debts.

From 1821, using its contractual rights, the government therefore embarked on a major programme of swapping high-interest debt for bonds paying a lower rate of interest, swapping out of £150 million in 1823 and another £80 million in 1824. Investors therefore began looking for rather more than the 2 per cent interest now available on British gilts.

As early as 1819, Alexander Baring was noting the vast sums cashed in at home and invested abroad, including a speculative rush into Latin American securities, where newly founded republics from the old Spanish Empire were raising funds – and soon a bubble was inflating fast.[73] Speculators even punted a loan of £200,000 to the 'Republic of Poyais', allegedly in the Honduras, which could be found on no map. Between 1824 and 1825, 624 new companies were listed, including more than 200 new joint-stock companies, from railway companies to a Cemetery Company, were approved by Parliament. As a correspondent to *The Times* noted, 'bubble schemes came out in shoals like herring from the Polar seas'.[74]

A combination of Britain's return to the Gold Standard and a new policy of slashing import duties now brought the crisis to a boil: just as the Bank of England was to exchange on demand notes for gold, gold was flooding out of the country to pay for imports that were suddenly cheaper, because duties were lower.* Nathan Rothschild had spent much of 1824 helping create the Alliance British & Foreign Life and Fire Assurance Company, backed by a £5 million issue of stock and run from his offices in St Swithin's Lane. But, by April 1825, he was warning the Chancellor of the Exchequer that the 'consequence of admitting foreign goods… was, that all the gold was going out the country'. He added that he had, himself, 'sent two millions within the last few weeks', much of it borrowed from the Bank of England.[75]

With a ballooning asset bubble and a gold shortage impending, crisis was imminent. When the Bank of England began withdrawing bank notes from circulation in early 1825, the market began to slide, and panic fast set in. In September 1825, provincial banks in Devon and Cornwall were failing. By 8 December, the Bank of England's

---

* Britain returned to the Gold Standard with the Resumption Act of 1819, with full convertibility targeted for May 1821.

governor was forced to bail out a leading financier, Sir Peter Pole.* But when two major London banks failed, dozens of correspondent banks froze payments – and a general run on the country's 770 provincial banks began, 73 of which collapsed. In desperation, the banks turned to the Bank of England for cash – but its bullion reserves were beginning to run dry. Within days, a run on the Bank of England itself was underway. As six further London banks failed, the governor warned the government that cash payments might have to be suspended to avert a general financial collapse. A regiment of Guards was ordered to the City – and Nathan Rothschild stepped in.

On 17 December, Rothschild advised the government to buy Exchequer bills, redeeming Government IOUs held by the banks, thereby furnishing bank coffers with cash rather than paper, and increasing liquidity in the market. Nathan then rapidly began buying gold: £300,000 of sovereigns was delivered in December. His brother James dispatched another £500,000-worth in the first week of January 1826. By March 1826, £1 million in gold was pledged, and a total of £10 million by September. 'There was a good deal [of gold] supplied from the whole world,' explained Nathan later, 'I imported it and it was imported almost from every country; we got it from Russia; from Turkey; from Austria, from almost every quarter in the world.'[76] The crisis was averted. But, wrote the Duke of Wellington, 'had it not been for the most extraordinary exertions – above all on the part of old Rothschilds – the Bank must have stopped payment'.[77]

When the 'Panic of 1825' had settled, Nathan and his brothers gathered, both to renew their alliance and take stock of their wealth. Worth £4,082,000,† they now boasted the greatest private fortune if not in Europe, then certainly in England; it was massively greater than Barings Brothers' £452,654 of capital.[78] For the next five years, as Europe tumbled towards the political turmoil of 1830, the Rothschilds now built a dominance of the new European bond market through a burgeoning relationship with Europe's ruling classes, and through

---

* On the previous Saturday, they had both counted out £400,000 in bills to the Bank's partners, without any clerks present.

† This was the combined capital of the London and Frankfurt businesses.

their unique relationship with one another they forged a fortune from merchant banking.

Rothschilds' balance sheet from 1828 reveals that between a quarter and a third of the firm's capital was tied up in government bonds.* Nathan, between 1818 and 1832, accounted for just seven out of the twenty-six loans contracted by foreign governments in London but an incredible 38 per cent of their value; that was twice the value of his nearest rivals, B. A. Goldschmidt, a total of perhaps £86 million.†

Underpinning the Rothschilds' extraordinary success was a web of penetrating influence with politicians and royalty across Britain, France, Austria and the German states. Ambassadors and Treasury officials alike had bank accounts, overdrafts and help with speculating in stocks and securities. The Duke of Wellington was a long-standing customer. Loans to the future George IV had started in 1805, fifteen years before he came to the throne; within a year of his accession, he negotiated another £175,000. The Duke of York borrowed £10,000, and the Rothschilds were early in offering services, life insurance and stays at the Rothschilds' villas to the Saxe-Coburgs, the royal house that spawned Queen Victoria, to whom they would go on to lend 3.5 million Gulden between 1837 and 1842.[79] In Austria, Metternich enjoyed over two decades of gifts, loans of hundreds of thousands of Gulden to pay his expenses and buy estates, plus a discrete diplomatic channel and use of the Rothschilds' pan-European messenger service.

By 1828, Nathan Rothschild was a major business celebrity, as the year's newspapers reveal. On New Year's Day, he was reported at Downing Street, 'transacting business at the Foreign Office'; in June, the *Evening Standard* covered the knighthood conferred on him by the Emperor of Brazil, 'accompanied with a present of a superb diamond cross as a proof of the high esteem he entertains for that gentleman who is agent for the Brazilian government'.[80] Nathan's fabulous property empire,‡ including No. 107 Piccadilly acquired from a member of

---

* This number would rise to 37 per cent if Danish bonds are included. In France, 35% of assets were *rentes*.

† Compared to £2.5 million issued by Frankfurt, and the £60 million issued in France in 1823–47, as James acquired a near monopoly over French finance.

‡ In 1816, Nathan bought an eight-acre property between Newington and

the Coutts family in 1825, was now the hub of some serious entertainment. In July 1828, the *Morning Post* brought news of Nathan's spectacular 'grand entertainment' there, where guests included the dukes of Sussex and Gloucester, the Duke of Wellington, Prince de Polignac of France and Princess Esterházy of Hungary. Dinner was served on a magnificent service of gold plate, 'the exquisite workmanship of which was greatly admired', after which the concert and ball kept guests dancing until three o'clock in the morning.

It was not only Nathan who could live in style. In October 1828, the *Western Times* offered a glimpse of Nathan's brother James, travelling back home to Paris, in a suite of six travelling coaches each drawn by four horses, emblazoned with 'several royal crowns connected together in the middle of which were the words, "Alliance with the Powers"'.[81] On 5 December 1828, the *Standard* was captivated by the brothers' German and Austrian influence. 'The Funds at Vienna continue to rise,' ran the reports, 'which according to a letter from Frankfurt is attributable to the operations of M de Rothschild, who it says "exercises so great a power over all the exchange of Germany, as to be almost aristocratic".'

The public attacks did not take long to follow. In January 1828, after Herries was appointed Chancellor of the Exchequer,* the Whig MP Thomas Duncombe launched an attack on Nathan as 'a secret influence behind the throne... a new and formidable power till these days unknown in Europe; master of unbounded wealth, he boasts he is the arbiter of peace and war'.[82] Winding up his speech, Duncombe said that he 'trusted that the Duke of Wellington... would not allow the finances of this great country to be controlled any longer by a Jew'.[83]

*

Stamford Hill, a country estate where he was still annoyed by the squealing of his neighbour's pigs. The following year, in June 1817, Nathan offered James Cazenove £19,000 in cash for Grosvenor House, to make a home for Hannah, and five children; but the deal fell through.

* After the prime minister, Lord Liverpool, was found paralysed on the floor, Canning had taken over the role in February 1827, only to die in August. In the game of musical chairs that followed, the Duke of Wellington became prime minister in January 1828, at which point came Herries' appointment.

Just as important to the Rothschilds' success as relationship with the establishment was their relationship with one another, which became the foundation for an old-fashioned merchant banking business; buying and selling at a discount bills promising payment – IOUs – before they became due. These 'bills receivable' were a quarter of Nathan's assets in 1828. He made his money not from the commission charged for accepting them, but by reselling them on the Continent, where he made a decent return on exchange-rate movements.* When there was a gap in the volume of bills one way or the other, or trade deficits or surpluses that arose and which required settling in bullion, here the Rothschilds continued to undertake plenty of business with the Bank of England and the Banque de France, carefully calculating the 'gold points' at which it made sense to pay for the transportation, insurance and sometimes melting down of gold to shift it from one country to the next.

Key to success was the constant day-to-day exchange of information on prices, trafficked through the Rothschilds' communications network – Europe's most sophisticated. In 1814, Amschel had proposed a system of coloured envelopes to alert correspondents to whether the exchange rate was up or down. The risks of the public post had forced the brothers to build a private courier network so reliable and fast that, from 1814, it regularly carried diplomatic news between European capitals. As early as 1815, Nathan was also paying premiums to captains of ships to hasten the mail between his agents in Dover and Calais. His early notice of the Allied victory at Waterloo was perhaps the most famous example of how speed could help make a financial killing. In England, the service was often faster than that of the Foreign Office; as France's colourful ambassador, Talleyrand, noted in 1830, 'The English Cabinet always obtain their information by [Rothschild] ten or twelve hours before the arrival of… [their ambassador's] dispatches.'[84]

---

* As Nathan explained to the Bank Committee in 1832: 'I buy on the Exchange bills drawn from Liverpool, Manchester, Newcastle and other places and which come to every banker and merchant in London. I purchase 6,000 or 7,000 and sometimes 10,000 of those bills in a week and I send them to the Continent to my houses: my houses purchase against them bills upon this country which are purchases for wine, wool and other commodities.' Ferguson, *The House of Rothschild*, op. cit., p. 274.

Connecting the brothers was an alliance, agreed on paper but sealed with marriage. Their financial federation was originally drawn up in 1810, updated in 1815 (giving Nathan 27 per cent of the notional capital and an agreement to defray the expenses of London and distribute the profits at the end of each year) and in 1818, when Nathan's London profits were so great that the brothers agreed he should take half. Three businesses were then formed – in London, Frankfurt and Paris – with 4 per cent of their share capital as income to cover expenses, agreed charges and a weekly report to each other. In 1825, although Nathan's share of the joint capital was some £4 million, it was agreed to share profits equally.[85]

It was a relationship that the brothers ensured would continue down the generations. Before 1824, the Rothschilds had married into other leading Jewish families. From 1824, they tended to marry each other. Of twenty-one marriages between Mayer Amschel's descendants, fifteen were between his direct descendants. In July 1824, James married his own niece; in 1826, Nathan's eldest daughter married Salomon's son Anselm. It was an alliance that stood them in good stead as Europe descended into the chaos of the 1830s.

The European revolutions of 1830 onwards were a long time in coming. After years of war, the continental peace brought a slow and steady prosperity, as nations cleared away the internal barriers to trade, extending canals and roads, and abolishing tolls and taxes. Europe and America now stood on the brink of the railway age. Towns were burgeoning, and the new manufacturing classes, such as those Nathan knew in Manchester, were growing numerous and rich. And they wanted a political voice.

The great events began, of course, in France. Over the spring and summer of 1830, liberal opposition to the restored House of Bourbon grew. When the Prince de Polignac's government dissolved the Chamber of Deputies, slashed the electorate by three-quarters and suspended the free press, the barricades went up and soon the king, Charles X, was gone. It was not a 'European spring' but a European summer. Popular demonstrations across the Netherlands' southern provinces triggered votes for separation, which the Dutch could not suppress: and from which Belgium was born. In Portugal, constitutional marches came under attack from reactionary forces led by pretenders to the throne. Only a combined Franco-British intervention in 1833 drove them out, preserving the constitutional settlement while in Switzerland, popular movements broke out across the country demanding more liberal constitutions in the cantons.

Change did not always win out. In Poland, a provisional government was briefly established in November 1830 only to be crushed by Russian invasion in 1831, bringing harsh reprisals. Revolts broke out in Italy, where rulers were evicted by the co-ordinated action of secret societies, only to provoke Austrian invasion to restore the status quo. Across the German Confederation, some new constitutions were negotiated and liberal oppositions strengthened in local votes, provoking repressive reactions, from Prussia and Austria.

When the dust settled, Europe was broadly divided into two. West of the Rhine, liberalism of various shades had triumphed or made significant inroads; east of the Rhine, it had largely failed, and people continued to live in states that were either too small (as in the German or Italian statelets) – or too big (the multinational, polyglot empires of Austria, Russia or Turkey).

As a family at the centre of power, Nathan Rothschild and his brothers found themselves at the centre of the storm. They survived through a practical ability to support one another, a pragmatic ability to change sides, and the eternal truth that even revolutionaries need credit.

When the price of French debt collapsed, James Rothschild in Paris lost a fortune. Total disaster was averted only when Nathan shipped £779,000-worth of gold to the French capital to stabilize his brother's position. James had, though, taken care to keep good links with all sides. When Nathan's daughter Charlotte visited Paris in 1829, she found James giving dinner for leading liberal ministers, as 'it is best to keep friends with all parties'.[86] But from May 1830, the market began to slide, and James's losses began to mount.

Fresh French elections were but a prelude to new extreme measures, and James sensed financial disaster loomed. 'Believe me my dear Nathan,' he wrote, 'I am... losing my courage.'[87] Twelve days later he reported that 'the whole world is selling *rentes* [French government bonds]... My dear Nathan, you are an old warrior. Tell me truthfully, do you also fear what might happen in the end?'[88] In the chaos of the days that followed, the French throne was declared vacant, the Duc d'Orléans was installed as King Louis-Philippe in August 1830 and the constitution revised to create a more liberal, more democratic and constitutional, monarchy. The stream of letters from Nathan's son Lionel to his parents captured a flavour of the turbulence. 'It is difficult for an English mind to grasp [the] state of affairs here,' wrote Lionel on 27 July,[89] for it 'vacillates between eve of a revolution and tranquillity'. A few weeks later, he reported in August that 'Uncle J[ames] has been with most of the ambassadors today... Question as to when the Exchange ought to be opened,'[90] and on 16 August, 'Things very flat. So many reports, so cannot make up one's mind what to believe.'[91] It took until January 1831 before Lionel could report that 'Uncle James has seen most of the ministers, who are as much for peace as possible.'[92]

James took the precaution of burying his bonds in the garden. But James's relations with the new ministers were decent, and Talleyrand, now Louis-Philippe's man in London, opened a Rothschild account. James survived, but at a price. He was forced to sell at the bottom of the market in March 1831, at a 40 per cent loss. His competitors soon displaced him, and it became harder to win business floating government loans. 'I fear we may lose our fortune here,' he wrote to Nathan in 1831. But Nathan's help proved critical. He had been able to sell his own *rentes* before revolution broke out. And, as James's confidence – and business – recovered in 1832, Nathan's access to the London market remained his great trump card. But by now, the revolutionary fervour had spread to Britain. And despite his affinity and alliance with the anti-reformist Wellington, it did not take Nathan long to join the reformers' cause.

For thirty years, the argument for political reform in Britain had grown louder and louder. A new urban working class – and a new urbane, middle class – frustrated with the country's ills, were no longer prepared to tolerate a political system dominated by a narrow franchise that elected corrupt MPs to half-empty 'rotten boroughs' and 'pocket boroughs', which were no better than the personal fiefdoms of self-interested power-brokers. In 1791, Thomas Paine's *Rights of Man* had helped inspire radical organizations such as the London Corresponding

Society, but during the war years with France, reformers and revolutionaries alike were suppressed. In the long economic depression that followed the initial post-war boom, the argument returned. Campaigners such as Major John Cartwright travelled the country organizing petitions of Parliament and calling for a wider British electoral franchise. Soon, sky-high unemployment in towns like Manchester prompted marches on London, strikes and mass rallies. In 1819, thousands gathered on Manchester's St Peter's Field to hear orator Henry Hunt champion the cause, but while the brass bands played 'Rule Britannia' and 'God Save the King', the magistrates sent in the Dragoons to apprehend him. The cavalry charge killed 11 people and wounded 400 more and the 'Peterloo Massacre', as it became known, became a rallying call for reformers nationwide. By 1830, the demand for reform was irresistible – though resistance was still attempted.

In the election following George IV's death, on 26 June 1830, the Whigs made Parliamentary reform the issue of the moment. The Tories, with a reliable stock of rotten boroughs, scraped a narrow victory, and the decidedly anti-reform Wellington became prime minister. But his power base was so thin that he ceded office within a fortnight to Earl Grey, the first Whig prime minister for years. Up and down the country, mass meetings, music, emotive banners, campaigns and a liberal press provoked 3,000 petitions, between October 1830 and April 1831, demanding reform. The City of London watched aghast, as between January 1830 and March 1831 the price of consols plummeted 20 per cent,[93] and liquidity shrank as the Bank of England's reserves fell.

On 22 March 1831, Lord John Russell's Reform Bill was passed by a single vote, only to be shredded by amendments in the Lords. Fresh elections were called, which returned a large Whig majority, and in July 1831 riots broke out across the country, in which Nathan's windows were smashed. When Parliament was prorogued in December, Nathan Rothschild could see the inevitable. By February 1832 Nathan too was advocating reform. 'Rothschild… came to tell me', Charles Arbuthnot told Wellington, 'that if you let it be known as soon as you meet Parliament that… you are resolved not to disappoint expectations… you will surmount all your difficulties. He says that among the monied men there is an alarm lest there should be such an opposition to all reform as would cause commotions.'[94]

When the Third Reform Bill was passed in March 1832, only to be wrecked once more in the Lords, Grey resigned and Wellington was recalled. In the 'Days of May' that followed, Britain seemed close to revolution. But fear focused minds. Earl Grey was reinstalled as King William IV threatened to flood the Lords with pliant Whig peers. It was the final straw for the anti-reformists. On 7 June 1832, the Reform bill finally won royal assent.*

Throughout it all, the Rothschilds' business survived. Leaders and systems might change, but fiscal realities did not. Britain's national debt stood at £800 million in 1815, and by 1830 it was not much lower. Nathan's business was now highly diversified. His interest in bullion dealing never flagged, as he shipped silver and gold between London and Paris. Aside from the £15 million loan he helped organize for the government, to compensate the slave owners for the 1834 abolition of slavery, Rothschilds' new debt business was now primarily European rather than British. He floated, for example, a big new loan for the new Belgian government in 1831. But from 1830, Nathan's interest in commodities grew – cotton, tobacco, sugar, copper and mercury. Above all, his dominance of Thomas Gresham's old Royal Exchange remained absolute: there, he was widely seen as Thackeray described him in 1833 – 'the pillar of "Change"' and the master of Europe's bourses.

In 1834, a famous newspaper profile conveyed the power[95] 'of the great money-monger', 'a man of a fine port – about 5 feet 8 inches high with a claret coat, light waistcoat and blue coloured trousers'. This was 'the great capitalist worth fifteen millions of money', whose 'coming on

---

* It did not, of course, create democracy in a modern sense, since 80 per cent of men and 100 per cent of women were left without the vote, and there was no secret ballot. But it was the first major reconstruction of British Parliamentary representation since the Civil War, and the new electorate, at 656,000, was very large in European terms. Only in Scandinavia was suffrage wider. In the years that followed the 1832 Reform Act, popular discontent continued: the Chartist movement mobilized hundreds of thousands of working people in a campaign to broaden the electorate; and when six trade unionists in Tolpuddle were convicted of administering unlawful oaths and transported to Australia, huge demonstrations turned out in London and provincial cities.

"Change" [the Exchange] amongst the assembly of little men resembles the whale coming in amongst the little fishes and making the sea swell'.

'He has a new hat every month,' ran the report, 'and his practice is always as he gets into his carriage to throw his hat first on the seat; and if his mind is at all disturbed and in commotion, he sits upon and spoils it. In his counting house he has generally 20 pens lying by him which he frequently bites and pulls to pieces.'

*

In June 1836, it was again time for the Rothschild family to gather, in the old family home in Frankfurt for a big wedding and a big conversation about the future: about management, the markets and yet more marriage. Nathan's son Lionel, aged twenty-seven, was now old and experienced enough to be admitted to the firm as a full partner. Battle-hardened by his work for Nathan in Spain, this solemn and serious young man was about to be betrothed to his Uncle Carl's beautiful seventeen-year-old daughter Charlotte, a woman later cast by Disraeli in his novel *Tancred* as 'the perfection of oriental beauty'.[96] The family had seven more children between them of marriageable age, and over lengthy dinners and other, longer social events, the task was to determine who might best be suited to whom.

Decoding the markets was just as big a task. Three of the brothers had begun sizeable operations in the burgeoning market for railway shares – for which they needed Nathan's access to London's capital markets. Greece, Naples ('The Kingdom of the Two Sicilies'), Belgium and Spain were all 'hot' markets. In America, the economy was gathering pace, with many new opportunities for financing trade and infrastructure. Shut away in a room on their own, the brothers talked on, with none of the acrimony the younger children had expected. But they were not to make much progress.

En route to Frankfurt, Nathan had been revisited by an old medical complaint – a terrible eruption, probably an ischio-rectal abscess, made worse by the jolts along the road. By the time that he arrived, he was in an agony only exacerbated by his German surgeon, a celebrated professor from Heidelberg, who repeatedly lanced and cut the boil to draw and drain the poison.

It succeeded only in deepening the crisis. At six o'clock in the morning on 15 June 1836, Nathan steeled himself to walk to Charlotte's house and then to the celebration. He feigned good spirits, with jokes and efforts to shorten the rabbi's speech, but after all was done he collapsed and required more surgery. He sent for his doctors from London. For six weeks the family waited. Towards the end of July, it seemed clear that the end was imminent as a violent fever caught him. On 24 July, Nathan gave Lionel orders to sell across the board. Four days later, the family gathered around his deathbed.

Three days before he died, Nathan dictated new terms for his will. He revised his thoughts on the brothers' partnership, and gave guidance for his children to 'carry on in harmony and peace' his banking house, in consultation with his widow and brothers. He asked that the contract between his brothers and son be renewed for five years, and charged them 'always to apply all their efforts to keep the business property intact and not to participate in any risky ventures'. Minutes before he died, Nathan Rothschild received the condolences of his religion. His final words, it was said, were 'good night forever'.[97]

Few men or women of the nineteenth century shook the financial world with their departure. But Nathan Rothschild did. The prop of the market was gone. The price of consols fell steadily from £91 to £87. Bank rates were raised another half-point in September. The Rothschilds' London House suffered its first loss since 1830. *The Times* recorded his death as 'one of the most important events for the City, and perhaps for Europe, which has occurred for a very long time' and celebrated his transformation of European finance – 'the first introducer of foreign loans into this country'.[98]

The city that Nathan had helped create as the world's financial centre turned out to bury him. Seventy-five coaches conveyed, along Cornhill, the lord mayor and aldermen, ambassadors and noblemen. Nathan Rothschild was buried in the north-west corner of the Jewish burial ground in Whitechapel Road.

No man would die richer for another twenty years.[99]

6

WILLIAM JARDINE

Free trader and first Taipan of China

On Monday, 26 January 1841, Queen Victoria took breakfast as usual with her beloved husband Albert and settled down to sing a few of the prince's new songs. After a charming morning, the devoted couple took lunch in the new dining room at Buckingham Palace, overlooking the troops and cheering crowds, before setting off in the state coach to open Parliament.

At two o'clock in the afternoon, dressed in gold-embroidered white satin, beneath a crimson velvet robe, the queen, looking slightly pale, paused in the library of the House of Lords before taking her place to speak to her assembled Parliamentarians. She was, she confided to her diary, 'much less nervous in reading my speech, than usual'. From her gilded throne, she spoke of peace. 'Having deemed it necessary to send to the coast of China a naval and military force, to demand reparation and redress for injuries inflicted upon some of my subjects,' she declared, 'it will be a source of much gratification to me, if that government shall be induced by its own sense of justice to bring these matters to a speedy settlement by an amicable arrangement.'[1]

Fourteen hours earlier, and 6,000 miles way, Captain Sir Edward Belcher, commander of the survey ship HMS *Sulphur*, landed on some desolate rocks off the vast Pearl river estuary on the south coast of China. 'We landed on Monday 26th at fifteen minutes past eight,' he recorded, 'and being *bona fide* first possessors, Her Majesty's health was drunk with three cheers on Possession Mount... the squadron arrived; the Marines were landed, the union [flag] hoisted on our post and formal possession taken of the island.'[2] The Marines fired a *feu de joie*. The ships of war blasted a royal salute. The barren islands, bargained away by the emperor's mandarins in exchange for an end to the Royal Navy's vicious bombardment of coastal China, were now secured. The formal taking of Hong Kong, proposed by the emissaries of the British queen and the Chinese emperor to seal the truce, was complete.

Yet, despite the queen's best hopes, the island's acquisition was to prove a prelude not to new peace, but to more war. When the Chinese emperor, the British prime minister, the City of London and the English papers found out just what had been agreed, they were furious, as one old China-hand had suspected they would be. William Jardine heard the news from his old business partner James Matheson, who reported from a ring-side seat. 'The report in the community is that the… negotiations are not favourable to an immediate re-opening of the trade… there may be room for suspecting that we are not quite as near a final settlement as had been supposed.' Matheson added a 'ps': 'I witnessed the hoisting of the British flag at Hong Kong on this 26th. Afterward circumnavigated the Island.'[3]

As William Jardine read the letter, he probably suspected this was merely the opening gambit to hostilities. As 'first Taipan' – the leading entrepreneur – of the British community in China for decades, he had been, after all, advocate-in-chief of the conflict to come: the First Opium War between Great Britain and the Celestial Empire of China.

*

William Jardine was born on a small farm at Broadholm, near Lochmaben in Dumfriesshire, on 24 February 1784. Fatherless from a young age, his brains and his brother's benevolence catapulted him from Edinburgh to the Far East by the time he was just nineteen years old.

We know little of his childhood. William was the sixth child, and third son, of Andrew Jardine, who farmed a small slice of Lowland country, where the soft hills decline towards the estuary of River Nith at Dumfries and the Solway Firth beyond. For generations, the borderland of Scotland, home to royal Bruces, had been a market for the trade between England, Scotland and Ireland, and a cockpit of the interminable border wars that stretched back centuries. Three times since the union of Scotland and England in 1707, Scottish armies supporting Jacobite pretenders to the new British throne had crossed the border. In 1745, 'Bonnie' Prince Charlie had penetrated as far south as Derby, before his armies were brutally beaten at Culloden that year, a prelude to the terrible taming and clearing of the Highlands.

By contrast, Lowland towns such as Dumfries, just 9 miles from the Jardine farm at Lochmaben, had prospered. Not to say that Lowland farming was easy, as the Jardines' most famous neighbour, poet Robbie Burns, discovered, tending land nearby at Ellisland. Here, old farming habits like sowing the fields by hand had long persisted and like so many others, Burns found soil exhausted, and crops that failed. There was little, therefore, to keep a son like William Jardine on the land, especially after his father died when William was just nine. Fortunately for Jardine, he was clever. And so his brother paid his way, at the age of sixteen, to take the road 75 miles north-east to the intellectual headquarters of the Scottish Enlightenment: Edinburgh and its university.

Arguably, no other town of Edinburgh's size has had such an impact on the course of Western ideas since Socratic Athens. In the seventeenth century, Daniel Defoe found there 'a large, populous, noble, rich, and even still a royal city', blessed with a 'main street… the most spacious, the longest, and best inhabited street in Europe' and 'buildings… surprising both for strength, for beauty, and for height; all, or the greatest part of free-stone'.[4] He was being polite. The town was known colloquially as 'Auld Reekie', for good reason. But in the decade that followed Defoe, Edinburgh was a city transformed.

By the time that Jardine arrived, Edinburgh's population had reached 100,000 residents. Its famous New Town was taking shape, built to James Craig's beautiful 'Plan of the New Streets and Squares intended for the Capital of North Britain', boasting the neoclassical proportions so expressive of reason and rationality. The very stones of the city's ordered, elegant thoroughfares and façades sang of Edinburgh's leading place in both the scientific revolution and the self-confident rejuvenation of Scottish arts. By 1800, a generation of Scottish thinkers had revolutionized discipline after discipline in a flowering that was striking not simply for its excellence, but its sheer breadth.* 'We look to Scotland', said Voltaire, 'for all our ideas of civilization.'

Vitally for the young Jardine, Edinburgh's specialisms encompassed medicine; indeed, in the century after 1750 Scotland's universities trained some 10,000 medical doctors – twenty times more than Oxford and Cambridge. Here, Jardine settled down to learn, and he must have studied hard, for at the age of eighteen he received, on 2 March 1802, the full diploma of the Royal College of Surgeons. Within a fortnight, he was heading to London to meet Thomas Newte, one of the East India Company's most experienced managing owners, who needed a surgeon's mate for his ship the *Brunswick*. Jardine took the £5 advance for two months' wages, and on 30 March 1802 – less than a month after he had left Edinburgh – he set sail for China, on a smooth first voyage.

Stopping for brief repairs in Brazil and in Java for supplies, the *Brunswick* caught the July and August monsoon winds, driving the sleek ship forward at a hundred miles a day to reach, on 4 September, the Praya Grande promenade in the Portuguese colony of Macao (Macau), glistening with its white-washed baroque buildings.[5] From there, it was just three days' sailing inland into the Pearl river delta to Whampoa (Huangpu), where Jardine and China first met in a city as salubrious as any cosmopolitan nineteenth-century trading port. The brightly painted junks and cutters, stretching 3 miles out to sea, were home to some 3,000 sailors from all points on the planet: blue-jacketed British, white-robed Indian lascars, scarlet-clothed Malays. In the Chinese village of Bamboo Town, the brothels, hard liquor, arsenic, tobacco and opium dealers offered plenty of entertainment, while, for the more restrained, a ship's band might offer an hour's music every sunrise and sunset. Thirteen miles up the estuary lay Canton (Guangzhou), a huge walled city, where, carved out on the north bank,

---

* David Hume, who attended Edinburgh University at the age of twelve, published his revolutionary *Treatise on Human Nature* in 1739, beginning a tradition of empirical, 'common sense' philosophy that would prove highly influential in America. In 1784, Adam Smith began delivering public lectures on political economy. By 1800, Scotland was recognized as a leader in agricultural science, and from James Watt to Thomas Telford, Scottish engineers were pioneers of Britain's industrialization, and were widely celebrated.

was a corner, some 300 yards by 200 yards, where the foreign merchants lived.

Along the estuary-edge ran Respondentia Walk, 'which swarmed with pedlars, beggars and importuners of every description'.[6] From the bank, three narrow alleys ran north to Thirteen Factories Street, where could be found the foreign 'factories': long, thin frontages, behind which were courtyards separating warehouses, offices, safe-rooms, dining and reception rooms, and upstairs a bedroom or two. At the street's eastern end ran Hog Lane, packed with seedy drinking shops amid which was the grandest factory of all, the New English. Nestled behind a great outer gate, and adorned with a chapel and spire bearing the only clock in Canton, this was home to the East India Company (EIC), trading in Canton since 1715. Here, remembered an old American sailor, the English 'entertained with unbounded hospitality and in a princely style' in a 'dining-room… of vast dimensions, opening upon the terrace overlooking the river', later endowed with a life-size portrait of George IV. 'From the ceiling depended a row of huge chandeliers, with wax lights' and 'the table bore candelabra, reflecting a choice service amidst quantities of silver plate'.[7]

It was here where William Jardine learned the lessons that would last a lifetime.

*

Jardine's good fortune was to join the East India Company fifty years after it had conquered India, cracked open the Chinese market for tea, and created in the process an impressive ladder of opportunity for Jardine's fellow countrymen. The authority of India's old Mughal Empire had begun to collapse in the 1740s. Delhi had been weakened by the Persian shah's assault in 1739, and the following year India itself became a theatre of battle for the British and the French, fighting the War of the Austrian Succession (1740–48).* It was the stage on to which marched

---

* The War of the Austrian Succession, which involved all of Europe's major powers, resulted from disputes over the legitimacy of Maria Theresa of Austria to inherit the Hapsburg throne.

an audacious young soldier called Robert Clive, who spotted the chance
to transform the EIC.

Born into an impecunious but old, landed family in Shropshire,
Clive (1725–74) was a rebellious boy who earned an early reputation for
mischief. The politician-historian Macaulay labelled him a 'dunce, if
not a reprobate';[8] but one of Clive's many schoolmasters was kinder,
opining that 'if opportunity enabled him to exert his talents, few names
would be greater than his'.[9] Employed as an EIC 'writer', in essence a
junior clerk, Clive arrived in India, aged eighteen, and soon distinguished himself in battle, in the First (1746–48) and then Second
(1749–54) Carnatic wars, fought between the British, the French and
their respective Indian allies.

In 1756–57, Siraj ud-Daulah, the new ruler of Bengal (India's
'garden of Eden'), had captured the English factory at Cossimbazar,
near his capital of Murshidabad,[10] and attacked the EIC's Fort
William. Here, he incarcerated dozens of the company's men in a
tiny, dark room together, where, struggling for life in the hot,
cramped conditions, many died in what became known to history as
the 'black hole' of Calcutta.* When the news of Calcutta's fall reached
Madras, Clive was summoned from Fort St David and chosen to lead
a campaign of vengeance to bring Siraj ud-Daulah to talks. In the
fight that followed, and despite being hopelessly outnumbered, Clive
comprehensively defeated his opponents' armies at Plassey – and
proceeded to negotiate a near monopoly on all internal trade, including salt.

By the mid-eighteenth century, the EIC was making profits of
£600,000 on revenues of £2 million a year (between £3.5 billion and
£5 billion today), and paying a dividend of 7–8 per cent. But corruption thrived and, after several years in Britain, Clive was recalled to
India in May 1765 to introduce sweeping reforms, eventually securing
the 'grant of Divani' in 1765. This awarded to the EIC the right to
collect and distribute revenue for the vast princely states of Bengal,

---

* The British commander put the number imprisoned at 146, with just
23 survivors; some later historians believe the numbers incarcerated were
considerably lower. See http://www.historytoday.com/richard-cavendish/black-
hole-calcutta

Orissa and Behar that spread across the Indus-Gangetic plain. The East India Company's income soared – and yet there was now a business further east that looked set to be bigger still: bringing home the tea of China.

The first recorded request for a pot of tea appears to be from a Mr R. Wickham, an agent of the East India Company, who wrote to a colleague in Macao in June 1615 to ask for 'the best sort of chaw'. The first advertisements for tea circulated in London around 1658,[11] and two years later Samuel Pepys's diary – on Tuesday, 25 September 1660 – recorded a morning in the office, talking over the virtues of peace with Spain and war with Holland before sending 'for a cup of tee (a China drink) of which I never had drank before'. It was Charles II's Portuguese wife, Catherine of Braganza, who really brought the taste to the English elite. The revolution in England's West Indies sugar business triggered a revolution in demand. Sugar became England's largest import in 1750* and in the coffee houses of London, Englishmen could mix a cheaper tea with the sugar of the West Indies and the tobacco of the New World. By the 1740s, tea consumption had leapt to 2.5 million pounds a year.[12] By the 1770s the EIC's China trade in tea was bigger than the Company's trade in India. When duties were cut in the Commutation Act from 119 per cent to 12.5 per cent, imports went through the roof; tea sales increased from 6 million pounds to 19 million pounds, generating profits for the EIC in 1793–1810 of £17 million.

*

This was the commercial frontline on which Jardine found himself in 1802, and happily for him he was in the company of an extraordinary number of his compatriots. Since Thomas Pitt's day, the EIC, beginning with the leadership of Warren Hastings, had hired an extraordinary number of Scots. Indeed, Hastings' elite diplomatic corps were known as his 'Scotch guardians'. It was part of a plan. As Scotland's Highland

---

* This remained the case until the 1820s, when it was overtaken by raw cotton.

clan chieftains were emasculated* after 1745, the new 'United Kingdom' made a concerted effort to recruit Scots into the service of the state. 'I am all for having always in our army as many Scottish soldiers as possible,' said Secretary of War Lord Barrington to Parliament in 1751.[13] By mid-century, one in every four regimental officers – and a quarter of the EIC's army officers – were Scottish, and in the decade after 1775, Scots made up nearly *half* of the 249 'writers' appointed in Bengal and 60 per cent of the 371 free merchants trading with the EIC.[14]

As a surgeon's mate, Jardine would not have slept on land at first, but rather aboard his ship, where he was entitled to two tonnes of 'privilege cargo' to fill on his own account. The EIC's surgeons were a well-organized lot, with their own mess in the Company's headquarters in Canton, and over the years to come Jardine steadily gained expertise in buying and selling – cassia, cochineal and musk. We do not know much about his years with the EIC, which would last until 1817; but during his first six-week stay in Canton, it seems he met two of the men who would prove critical to his fortunes in later life: Thomas Weeding, one of the Company's senior surgeons, and Charles Magniac, recently made a partner in Canton's first independently trading 'agency house'. A near disaster would bring Jardine together with a third, Jamsetsee Jeejeebhoy, an Indian Farsee (Parsi), with whom Jardine would work for the rest of his life.

Jardine sailed home in summer 1802 during a moment of peace in the Napoleonic Wars. After a ten-month respite in London, he was promoted to ship's surgeon† in autumn 1803, dispatched once more on the *Brunswick* to escort the 66th Regiment of the King's Troops to Ceylon, and afterwards spent a few months shipping cotton and tea

---

* Linda Colley, among others, argues that the efforts of the EIC coincided with a decisive shift in British policy during the years after Culloden. Trade and the Protestant religion both provided spiritual and financial networks in which English and Scots might mix and there was a broadening of effort. After the '45, new laws banned the wearing of tartan and destroyed the old jurisdiction of the clan chieftains and the king's justice now ran to every part of the kingdom. But from the confiscated Jacobean estates, money was recycled into subsidies for Highland industry – tanning, whaling, paper-making.

† This promotion came with privileges, including a canvas cabin, a servant, and the right to walk on the weather side of the quarter-deck – and crucially tonnes of 'privilege cargo'.

between India and China. By now, Britain and France were again at war, yet, hoping to beat the competition, the *Brunswick*'s captain, James Grant, set off ahead of his armed escort – and ran straight into two French warships. Jardine was taken as a prisoner-of-war, along with the rest of the crew, and the *Brunswick* was forced to sail for the Cape of Good Hope under the guns of the French warship *Marengo*. During the voyage disaster struck – Jardine's ship was wrecked by a terrible storm. All cargo was lost, but all hands were saved, and Jardine and Jeejeebhoy found themselves together ashore.

Over the next decade, Jardine undertook five more voyages for the EIC, before, in 1817, at the age of thirty-three, he concluded that he had the experience, the networks and the money to combine with Weeding and Jeejeebhoy and build a business of his own, exploiting a freedom that Parliament in its campaign for free trade, had accidently thrown open: opium-dealing.

*

Of the 280 species of poppy that flourish in the temperate and subtropical zones of the northern hemisphere, just two – *P somniferum* and the more easily grown *P Bacteatum* – produce opium in significant quantities. Growing in just 120 days, they appreciate ample direct sunlight, do not need much irrigation and are not much bothered by pests. The drug produced was well known to the Sumerians back in 4500 BC (who knew the plant as *hul gil*, 'plant of joy'), as it was to the Persians, Egyptians, Athenians and Romans and Arab traders. In England, the drug was perfectly legal, popular with Romantic poets and familiar to many when mixed with alcohol to produce the painkiller laudanum.[15] William Wilberforce, the great anti-slavery campaigner, took the stuff every day for forty-five years, and commercial variations were sold, such as Godfrey's Cordial, Batley's Sedative Solution, Mother Bailey's Quieting Syrup to soothe babies and relieve everything from indigestion to toothache to hangovers, alcoholism and gout.[16]

The drug probably first arrived in China from the 'Western regions' – Greece, Rome, Turkey, Syria, Iraq, Persia and Afghanistan

– in the first half of the eighth century, when it begins to appear in medical texts and its recreational uses were well appreciated by the eleventh century.[17] In Ming Dynasty China, opium acquired a reputation as an aphrodisiac, stir-fried by cooks and combined with a bewildering array of ingredients but the boom years arrived when tobacco spread throughout China after its introduction in 1627.[18] Despite the occasional attempt to ban it, fields of tobacco were growing outside the capital's walls by the early 1700s, when Chinese sailors returned from Java with a new taste for smoking tobacco soaked in opium syrup. Smoking became chic. Equipped with ceremonial jade, ivory or tortoiseshell pipes and silver lamps for heating the opium, aficionados could be found on splendid couches in salubrious opium houses, the best of which employed opium chefs to prepare the family's pipes. It was an upper-class pleasure – demanding time and money – but one indulged in by some four-fifths of the local government officials (the 'yamen clerks') and a fifth of central government mandarins.[19]

It was not an indulgence that received official approval. Emperor Yongzheng prohibited the drug in 1729, railing that 'shameless rascals lure the sons of good families into (smoking)… youngsters become corrupted until their lives collapse, their families' livelihood vanishes, and nothing is left but trouble'.[20] The ban was reaffirmed in 1796, and between 1811 and 1813 punitive new measures were introduced, varying from a hundred blows with heavy bamboo to slavery for life.

Nothing, however, stopped the poppy's advance. Harvesting its dark brown, sticky gum was not hard, and few places on earth were as propitious for the poppy's cultivation as India, where poppies had been grown for centuries.* From the 1600s, cultivation in the rich Ganges delta, in north-east India, had been supervised by the Mahratta Opium Council;† but following Clive's victories, the

---

* It must be said they had been harvested largely for family consumption, with a little for the local market or local ruler.

† This council was composed of representatives of the five semi-independent states of the Mahratta Confederacy and meetings were convened every so often to give formal permission for the growing to start, to check that the produce was not adulterated, and to set the prices of different grades.

increasingly powerful East India Company – seeing a huge business opportunity – stepped in, determined to fix the 'shocking inefficiency and haphazardness' of production,[21] which either lost up to a third of the harvest or adulterated the product with cow dung. Warren Hastings originally took a dim view of the trade when he arrived as governor-general in 1773: 'the drug is not a necessity of life but a pernicious article of luxury which ought not to be permitted... I shall stamp it out,' he told the EIC's directors.[22] But within a year, the economic necessity of the crop became clear to Hastings who, far from banning it, now set about revolutionizing its production on an industrial scale.

Henceforth, Indian poppy growing was confined to Patna and Bihar, where the gum was collected, stirred and thrown into huge vats, where it was kneaded ready for moulding in the great sheds of Patna by old men and young children (as young as seven) employed to sit behind the broad tin pans ('tagars') of opium. Gently, they assembled cannonball-sized spheres, carefully wrapped in poppy petals, ready for resting on the vast shelves of the drying sheds, where boys turned them twice a day for weeks. From there, they were packed twenty to a box – known as 'catties' – and shipped off to Calcutta for auction sometime after Christmas. A little more than 4 acres of poppies might yield enough opium for a chest that, in a good year, traders like Jardine could sell for up to $3,000 (around £650). It took up to two years after the poppies were sown, in October, for opium to reach the market.[23] By the 1780s, 250,000 acres of poppies were under cultivation – enough for 60,000 chests of opium; and the principal flow of the drug was no longer west, but east, to China.

*

The growth of the Chinese opium business reflected the East India Company's attempt to solve a simple problem: how to pay for all the tea it needed to buy. The EIC, preferring not to upset the Chinese by selling opium into the country directly, sold stocks to 'agency houses', which then shipped the drug to China, depositing the proceeds in the EIC's bills of exchange, which could be cashed in London. The EIC then used the cash to buy tea, which it shipped to London and sold, using the proceeds to reimburse bills of exchange.

Agency houses had evolved from an array of (technically interloping) private traders, which sought to make a business outside the EIC's monopolies. Amongst the first was the pioneering John Cox, who in 1782 had first set up shop in Canton selling mechanical 'sing-songs', and bought two ships to carry cotton and opium. He realized that the East India Company could not regulate foreign diplomats, so he acquired the role of Prussian Consul. The idea caught on, and soon the EIC had given up trying to evict the largely Scottish traders working under the protection of the Swedish, Sicilian, Genoese, Hanoverian or Polish kingdoms.

As the tea trade with China boomed, country-traders began freighting a bigger and bigger slice of eastern cargo between India and China. By the 1780s, three-quarters of all British and Indian goods reaching Canton were shipped by country-traders, and by 1790 fifteen of the Calcutta-based partnerships were involved in trade to the east.[25]

By 1800, these private traders were being replaced by the new agency houses, which built their own ships or bought out the 'privilege tonnage' on EIC ships, and by 1803 twenty-nine East India agency houses were at work. They offered a range of services that allowed a speculator in London to send sterling bills from London to Bombay or Calcutta, where the agent bought opium at auction, sold it in Canton, and reinvested the proceeds in silk or EIC bills that were sent to London and sold for great profit.

This commercial progress made the EIC's notional monopoly less and less tenable. The political campaign against it had been waged in theory and in practice for decades, before Adam Smith helped make the fatal arguments.* The commercial breakthrough came with the Charter Act of 1813, which, while renewing the EIC's charter and authority in India, ended its commercial monopoly – with the exception of the tea

---

* Four years before the *Wealth of Nations* was published, Adam Smith had been a member of the Committee of Inquiry into the EIC's affairs. 'Perpetual monopolies', he concluded, 'were harmful to the long-term trading interests of any nation. They raised prices artificially, encouraged waste, fraud and abuse and, in India, had interfered with the sovereign interests of the British government.'

trade and the trade with China. It was a gift to men like Jardine. By 1815, there were eighteen British commercial houses in Calcutta. By 1820, it was thirty-two.

*

William Jardine quickly became part of the boom. In August 1818, Thomas Weeding applied for Jardine's licence to trade as his free agent in Bombay, where the partners planned to set up shop with Jeejeebhoy, buying a ship of their own, the *Sarah*, to run goods to China. But the new proliferation of traders was soon shipping a glut of cotton, and as prices and profits fell, the traders turned to opium on an ever greater scale. Between 1809 and 1824, opium shipments to Canton doubled to 9,000 chests – and by 1823, opium outstripped cotton as India's premier export to China.

Jardine was no exception to the trend. By autumn 1818, he was in India, with a cargo of $813,000-worth of opium from Malwa (approximately £176,149, or somewhere between £100 million and £200 million in today's money).* Business was so good that four years later Jardine relocated to Canton, and over the years that followed both the cotton and opium businesses did well, at one point turning over $2 million each year (some £430,000). By 1825, a year after he had settled in Canton for good, Jardine was making a personal profit of around $14,225 (more than £3,000), and opium – though by no means the only

---

* These figures are illustrative, but based on historic exchange-rate information set out in John Robert Morrison's *A Chinese Commercial Guide, Consisting of a Collection of Details Respecting Foreign Trade in China* (3rd edition, 1848). The exchange rate seems to have depended on the price paid for silver in London, since a Spanish dollar was essentially a given weight of silver. This price, of course, fluctuated. In Table VII of Morrison's book (p. 275) there is a table of 'Average rates of Exchange in China' between 1832/33 and April 1844 which gives the rates of sterling per dollar at six months' sight on London, quarterly. The value varies from 4s 1d per dollar to 5s per dollar, with the trend upwards. There is also a ready-reckoner table (pp. 270–1) 'For converting Spanish Dollars into Sterling Money, at various rates of Exchange'. For the purposes of these calculations, I have assumed an exchange rate of 4s 4d for the years 1808–32, and 4s 9d for years 1837–40.

goods he traded – had become the key product, his trade growing from 1,000 chests a year to 6,000 chests.

By the time of his fortieth birthday, Jardine had acquired a formidable reputation in Canton. He needed little sleep. He hated idleness. He detested humbug, and he had a tough constitution. His office famously boasted just the one chair for himself, to encourage visitors to stand and be quick. One day Jardine found himself presenting a petition at Petition Gate in Canton, when he was struck on the head by a bamboo pole. He did not even turn round, and ever after he was known to the Chinese as the 'Iron-headed Old Rat'.

When the leader of Canton's oldest agency house decided to retire, Jardine was the obvious choice to take over. The firm of Magniac & Co. had existed in one shape or another for around forty-five years; indeed, it could trace its origins back to John Cox. Early in the 1800s, three partners – Thomas Beale, Alexander Shanks and Charles Magniac – had established a business trading bills, Indian cotton and Bengal opium, and by 1808 they had made $96,000 profit (£21,000) on $1.2 million (£260,000) in sales, largely on commission. After deaths and bankruptcies, Magniac & Co. had soldiered on until 1824, when Charles Magniac died and his brother Hollingsworth stepped in. But, keen to retire, Hollingsworth offered Jardine the partnership in 1825, leaving $611,000 of his own for the firm to manage. It was simply too good an offer to turn down. Jardine took the helm – and within three years he joined forces with a younger man with an extraordinary reputation and energy: James Matheson.

*

Matheson was twelve years younger than Jardine. Born 270 miles north of Lochmaben, in Lairg, Sutherland, he was descended from a junior branch of a family with old connections to the East India Company. Like Jardine, Matheson had been educated at Edinburgh University, and on graduating had, aged just nineteen, secured 'Free Merchant Indentures' (a contract permitting trade) from the East India Company. Joining his uncle's firm, Mackintosh & Co., in Calcutta, he failed to thrive, and in June 1818 was persuaded by Robert

Taylor, another old Company man, to start the Canton office of an insurance business.

Quickly, the two men had begun trading in opium. But Taylor proved both chaotic and short-lived; when he died in August 1820, he left young Matheson with huge debts from which he was saved only by a sudden surge in the opium price. It took Matheson until 1821 to turn around his business, at which point he acquired the Danish consulship – giving him freedom from the EIC's controls in Canton – and a new trading partner, Xavier Yrisarri, a Spaniard with links to Larruleta & Co. His new partner brought new disaster: in 1822, Yrisarri & Co. tried to corner the market for Patna opium, but when the price collapsed, Matheson found himself with huge stocks and no buyers. His escape from the predicament taught him a lesson that he would never forget. Sailing under Spanish colours with his cousin William McKay at the helm, Matheson left the safe haven of Canton and headed north to Chinchew (Quanzhou), in Fujian. There, Matheson managed to offload $80,000- (over £17,000)- worth of the drug – enough to persuade him to return in the autumn – when storms forced his ship to take shelter 30 miles short of Chinchew in what turned out to be the region's principal opium port. Matheson successfully sold $132,000- (nearly £30,000)- worth of his addictive stock.

As prominent Canton men, Jardine and Matheson worked closely together in a shared ambition to finally finish off the EIC's dominion. In the years after the Company's charter renewal in 1813, the campaign against the firm's last shreds of monopoly rights continued. In 1820, the City of London presented a large petition to Parliament, describing 'the evils inflicted upon the country, by the unnecessary restrictions imposed upon their industry and pursuits'. In 1821, the Political Economy Club brought together in its twenty founding members such luminaries as Thomas Tooke, David Ricardo and J. S. Mill, 'for the purpose of discussing questions connected with Economical Science' and to lobby for change. They found a sympathetic Tory government; indeed, when Lord Liverpool received Thomas Tooke, the author of the 1820 petition, the prime minister told him that 'there was not a principle, not a sentiment in which he did not entirely and most cordially concur'.[26]

In China, Jardine and Matheson were soon among the driving forces of the free-trade campaign. In one of Matheson's first letters home, in 1821, he was denouncing 'that destructive monopoly which has so long existed';[27] five years later, Jardine was attacking the EIC's 'unbusinesslike' financial methods, and by 1828, Matheson's new newspaper, the *Canton Register*, was regularly attacking the EIC and contrasting the monopoly trade of Britain with the free trade enjoyed by Americans, observing that it 'seems impossible from the fettered state of all mercantile operations here, that intercourse can be increased substantially'.[28]

This contrast with American practice now became the pivot of the argument advanced by the campaign's British leaders, the Manchester Chamber of Commerce, which was packed with cotton merchants hungry for new markets.[*] On 27 April 1829, a public meeting was summoned at Manchester Town Hall to demand free trade with China and an end to the tea monopoly. Pointing to the boom in trade with India, Mr G. W. Wood ridiculed the EIC's justifications of 'the peculiar character of the (Chinese) people'. 'To this argument,' he declared, 'an answer would be found in the single word "America".' Both then and now the Americans carried on a very extensive traffic with China... if they could trade with the Chinese, surely private English merchants could trade with them also.'[29] Copies of the Manchester declaration were circulated nationwide. On 15 May 1829, deputies from Manchester, Liverpool, Glasgow, Bristol, Birmingham, Leeds and Calcutta met at Fenton's Hotel, in London's St James's Street, to lobby Parliament. Quickly, Sir Robert Peel's motion for an investigative Select Committee was agreed.

Jardine and Matheson now saw their chance. Working together with John McVicar, a man closely connected with the free-trade associations in Manchester and Glasgow, and who in 1830 was living in Canton, Matheson helped organize a remarkable petition that year, signed by forty-seven merchants. It demanded a muscular trade policy in China,

---

[*] A survey of 1811 showed Lancashire's 650 mills boasted over 310,000 water frames and 155,880 spinning jennies. A quarter of the mules were in Manchester. By 1835, there were 1,245 cotton factories and by 1841, 70 per cent of 1,105 cotton firms in Lancashire.

including permanent HM representatives in Peking and a British base 'near the coast of China'.[30] The petition was circulated by Matheson to friends in Glasgow, and submitted to Parliament 'from British subjects in China' on Christmas Eve 1830.[31]

*

In truth, the contortions of trade in China had long vexed the British. For almost all of Britain's history, the empire of China was a civilization not only far away but far ahead, and in their first adventures England's traders had not fared well. Unimpressed by 'barbarian merchants', the Chinese had promptly built a wall of regulation to keep them in their place.[32] From the Confucian perspective, it was assumed that the uncultured barbarian would recognize the superiority of Chinese civilization and 'come and be transformed' once in contact with the empire. In return, the emperor would be compassionate in his 'tender cherishing of men from far away'. The Chinese saw traders as no different to any other neighbour seeking relations, and so expected the humble submission required by court ritual, formalized in the Collected Statutes, which set out where a 'tribute envoy' could enter China, when they could trade, and with whom they could trade.

Confining foreign trade to Canton was the imperial court's way of keeping the tribute envoys as far away from Beijing as possible. Traders had to leave in the winter. No venturing into China was permitted. No books on Chinese history were to be sold, or the language learned. Worse, all trade was channelled through a licensed group of local merchants, the 'Co-Hong' (or Hong merchants), normally twelve individuals, which dramatically restricted trade, regulated by the *hoppo*, a fairly corrupt local official.[33] It was through this bottleneck that England's traders began organizing supplies for the nation's booming demand for tea.

Trade was, unsurprisingly, bedevilled by tension, as Chinese emperors endeavoured to keep the country aloof from the world, behind this great wall of protocol to the east and south, a barrier sometimes as impenetrable as the Great Wall to the north. In 1793, after years of frustration, the EIC had dispatched the best man they could find, Viscount George Macartney, at a cost of some £50,000, with an embassy of ninety-five people – including a painter, a metallurgist, a watch-maker, a mathematical-instrument maker, a botanist and fifty-three soldiers – to seek 'the benefits which must result from an unreserved and friendly intercourse between that country and his (the king's) own'.[34]

It was an absolute disaster. From the start, it was fraught with negotiations about whether the noble lord would *kow-tow* – the ceremonial approach entailing three separate bouts of kneeling, each followed by a full prostration with the forehead knocking the ground three times, to the shrill commands of an usher shouting 'kneel, fall prostrate, rise to your knees', a ritual designed to put beyond doubt one's place in the emperor's world.[35]

Macartney was entertained for months on end, before eventually he was summoned to the Forbidden Palace, led up a staircase to 'a fine yellow silk arm-chair representing the Majesty of China and containing the emperor's letter to the king', which was then conveyed by sixteen mandarins and their attendants.[36] It was a blunt dismissal. Requests for trading rights were declined as 'contrary to all usage of my dynasty and cannot possibly be entertained'. The very case for trade was spurned. 'Strange and costly objects do not interest me… as your ambassador can see for himself, we possess all things.' The idea of a permanent embassy was poo-pooed as a complete waste of time. China had nothing to gain from links with Britain. England, said the Emperor was a place trapped: 'the lonely remoteness of your island, cut off from the world by intervening wastes of sea' was nothing more than a poor relation to China, by contrast was the capital of which was 'the hub and centre about which all quarters of the globe revolve'.

By the 1830s, enterprising traders were finding ways around both Chinese imperial intransigence and the East India Company's almost expired monopoly. By now, around half of Britain's existing trade with China was now in private hands.[37] It was probably Jardine who penned a blunt call to arms in the *Canton Register*, which included a demand for a new British trade commissioner based in China. 'The basis of the new Commissioner's demand should be open trade with China… the scrupulous deportment of past embassies should be wholly laid aside.'

Jardine and Matheson now had a significant interest in finding a new way of doing business as together with their great rivals Dent & Co., the partners controlled two-thirds of the private trade with China, and about a third of 'the business of the port', which on 30 June 1832, Jardine and Matheson now brought together formally.[38] With the affairs of the Magniac family finally wound up, Magniac & Co. closed its doors – and the next day the business opened with a new name: Jardine Matheson.

Merely a year later, the debate on the East India charter bill opened on the floor of the House of Commons and on Thursday, 11 July 1833, Thomas Babington Macaulay, now Secretary of the Board of Control, stepped up to the Dispatch Box to speak. It was an open-and-shut case; 'there was not a man in the country', he declared, 'who would venture to raise his voice against [the] expediency and necessity' of opening the China trade to all comers.[39] 'No voice', he told the Commons, 'has yet been raised in Parliament to support the monopoly. On that subject all public men of all parties seem to be agreed.'

The East India Company's monopoly was over. It would make Jardine and Matheson a fortune – and within five months, spark war.

*

Jardine and Matheson had worked hard to keep themselves ahead of the Parliamentary debate. In particular, they needed to know precisely how the new rules would work. They hired Horatio Hardy, the manager of the Jerusalem Coffee House, in Cornhill – the centre of London's East India trade – to provide regular intelligence, and Hardy was able to report on 26 June 1833 (a month ahead of Macaulay's speech) that 'The Court of Directors and Proprietors [of the EIC] abandoned the China trade without any appeal or resistance', but that crucially the EIC would have a grace period so that 'no teas can be imported [by others] into Great Britain before that year [1836]'.[40]

The tea trade was now a huge scramble; indeed in the first season after the EIC's monopoly ended, 40 per cent more tea was sold in London. But Jardine was faced with building a tea business almost from scratch complete with tea-tasters, quality control, pricing policy, transports, warehousing and insurance. Nevertheless, on 22 March 1834 Jardine was able to dispatch the first 'free ship' to sail to England, the *Sarah*. Unfortunately, there was no tea on board: Weeding had failed to provide clear enough legal advice, much to Jardine's annoyance 'at not having been provided with your opinion as to the time when a ship now in China… may *legally* leave this port for England direct with a tea cargo'.[41]

On 24 April 1834, though, four ships crammed with tea sailed into Hull, London, Glasgow and Falmouth, and quickly Jardine became the biggest tea-buyer in Canton – mainly on account for friends. The EIC had not entirely withdrawn, and rows about unfair competition continued. Jardine wrote furiously on 23 April 1834 to Smith, his Parliamentary agent, that 'if the prayer of our petition to Parliament is listened to, the old ladies will drink good tea at about 3 shillings per pound'. It was a speculative business; 'really it seems quite a lottery', wrote Jardine, 'what estimation the most carefully selected teas may meet with in the English market'.[42]

Simultaneously, the floodgates to opium supply were unlocked – with the consequent effect of driving prices down to a level last seen a decade earlier. Where once there was just Bengal opium controlled through the two factories of Benares and Patna, now there was a stream of what was known as 'Malwa' from the princely states of India.* Opium supply to China doubled between 1830 and 1840.

Jardine had foreseen the problem. Sketching out a new strategy in 1831, he had written: 'it can hardly be worth our while pursuing on the old plane unless by operating on a large scale and on the secure footing of always being beforehand with one's neighbours in point of intelligence'.[43] He and Matheson knew that the only way to survive this brave new world was to reel in more customers and step up speed, with new ships hitting new markets on a completely new scale. And that meant breaking out of the so-called 'Lintin system' – and heading up the coast.

---

* Back in July 1819, Patna opium could be had for $1,170 a chest. In February 1820, prices hit $2,500 as Magniac & Co. cornered the market. Two years later, prices were below $2,000 but by the autumn opium had climbed to $3,000. By the following year it was down to $1,420.

Traditionally, opium traders alighted on the island of Nei Lingding, then known as Lintin Island – a 2,000-foot-high island in the Pearl river delta, 25 miles south-east of the Bogue strait (Bocca Tigris) at Canton – and stored their drugs in three or four of the old armed hulks anchored in the water. From there, opium cargoes were unloaded and trans-shipped by 'centipedes', 'scrambling dragons' or 'fast crabs' – the 40–50-oared boats rowed hard by Tankas, the Chinese rivermen, who forced their way up-river to the land distribution points run by the Triads. The drug then seeped through the empire in the packs of pedlars and on the backs of camels, into the remote corners of Xinjiang and to the capital, Beijing. Everyone took their cut – the brokers, the couriers, the Tankas, the Cantonese middlemen, the opium-shop owners, the restaurateurs, the tea-houses and the brothels. And everyone made money.

Matheson, however, had learned about the alternative possibility – the risky coastal trade – back in his voyages of 1823. In the autumn of 1832, with competitive pressure looming, the partners decided on a major coastal expedition up to Tientsin (Tianjin), chartering the clipper *Sylph* and a sales team led by one of the most extraordinary foreigners in China. The Reverend Karl Gützlaff was a Prussian missionary with a yen for English wives, who spoke not only Chinese but several dialects, including Fujianese. Jardine managed to overcome Gützlaff's Christian qualms about opium-dealing with the persuasive argument that no other trade could pay for the voyages to open up coastal China and so clear paths along which Christianity might spread. Eventually convinced, Gützlaff set sail on 20 October 1832.

The voyage was terrible. Bitter winds covered the ship with ice, inside and out, literally freezing to death one of the lascars. The vessel hit uncharted sandbanks and dared not anchor for fear of the northerly gales. Eventually, the *Sylph* put into Shanghai, Chapu (Zhapu), Chusan Island (Zhoushan), returning via the Fujian coast. The voyage was not a financial success. But the market intelligence acquired was invaluable, and so in November 1832, the 382-ton brig the *Jamesina* was dispatched north to Chinchew (Quanzhou) and Foochow (Fuzhou) on the Fujian coast, where opium prices were up to $100 higher than in Lintin. The *John Biggar* quickly followed, netting the partnership

$59,000 (nearly £13,000 or £10–£20 million in today's money) in Amoy (Xiamen), and on a return trip later in the year a further $214,000 (around £46,000 or £35–70 million). 'The trade at Chinchew', reported the *John Biggar*'s Captain McKay, 'may now be considered to be placed on a firm footing, although the mandarins may occasionally make difficulties such as we had to contend with at Lintin ten years ago.'[44]

Convinced of their new market, Jardine and Matheson invested heavily, including in steamships. In 1832, the partners acquired a half share in the *Red Rover*, a ship built to a revolutionary design copied from the *Prince de Neufchatel*, an American Atlantic raider captured by the Royal Navy in the later stages of the War of 1812. An old East India officer, William Clifton, had realized the potential of the ship's design in beating the monsoon winds, and he persuaded the Governor-General of India to commission a 254-ton copy. It could manage the round-trip, from Calcutta to Canton, in just eighty-six days. On 20 June 1833, the *Fairy* joined their fleet, and by November she too was anchored at Lintin as a supply ship servicing Dr Gützlaff's business in Chinchew Bay from where the firm's traders were soon bringing home hundreds of thousands of dollars in coins.*

The wider sales network thus created was key to Jardine Matheson's success. As Matheson explained:

> All our neighbours dispose of their import consignments in the same way (by barter with Hong merchants) but their extent is far short of ours and the less money they have the more disadvantageous are the terms they obtain. Thus, it is (that) command of money, which we derive from our large Opium dealings and which can hardly be derived from any other source gives us an important advantage.[45]

With the flood of new traders, it was perhaps only a question of time before the old constraints of the Co-Hong would fall apart. Now, Jardine

---

* The *Fairy* would continue in service until she was stolen, with $70,000 on board, by six Manila sailors, who murdered the captain along with the first and second mates.

and Matheson were determined to force the pace. Britain's Canton traders tended to divide into two schools of thought. The old Select Committee of the East India Company – known ironically in Canton as 'The Select' – had generally sought a compliant relationship with the Co-Hong, and Jardine's great rival, Lancelot Dent of Dent & Co., tended to agree. Jardine, however, saw things very differently. 'We must have a code with these Celestial Barbarians, before we can extend advantageously our now limited commercial operations,' he wrote, attacking arrangements in Canton in February 1832; 'We have a right to demand an equitable commercial treaty, so say we residents.'

The arrival of Lord Napier of Merchiston presented the partners with their chance. Following the end of the EIC's monopoly, Foreign Secretary Lord Palmerston decided that a new supervisory system was needed for Chinese trade, and so appointed Napier as 'Chief Superintendent of Trade'. Napier knew a lot about the Royal Navy but nothing about China, and – being neither a colonial governor nor a grand merchant – he presented the Chinese with a protocol nightmare. Palmerston managed to exacerbate the problem with impossible instructions to Napier to extend trade to other parts of China while not doing anything that might 'awaken the fears or offend the prejudices of the Chinese government and thus put to hazard even the existing opportunities of intercourse'.

Palmerston had told Napier that 'Your lordship will announce your arrival at Canton by letter to the [Chinese] viceroy,'[46] and so when Napier arrived in Macao on 15 July 1834, he put in at the Jardine Matheson house, appointed his team, and eight days later set sail in the frigate HMS *Andromache*, arriving in Canton at two o'clock on the morning of 25 July. Escorted from the quayside by William Jardine, he spent the night at the New English factory. Within weeks formalities had descended into farce, and farce into fighting. At Petition Gate, a succession of ever grander officials materialized at lengthy intervals to inspect Napier's letter – and then refuse to take it. As crowds grew and the Co-Hong merchants endeavoured to negotiate the letter's safe passage, the Canton viceroy lost patience. Translating 'Napier' as 'Laboriously Vile', he issued edicts demanding that the merchants eject the chief superintendent.

Jardine was clearly counselling aggression. Before Napier's arrival, he had written to Thomas Weeding in June 1834, anticipating the stand-off. Jardine now expressed the hope that Napier would retaliate, taking his frigate to Beijing to demand redress from the emperor; 'if this is done in good manly style I will answer for the consequences. It may do good but cannot do harm.'[47] Napier was of the same mind. He pressed the Foreign Office for an ultimatum to an 'imbecile govern-ment', along with reinforcements: 'three or four frigates or brigs with a few steady troops', he felt, 'would settle the thing in a time incon-ceivably short'.[48]

As tension mounted, an audience with the Chinese prefect was eventually conceded; but after an almost disastrous argument about the seating arrangements, and who should face the royal portrait, the meeting was eventually amicable, but without answers. Napier, now ill with a fever, discarded Palmerston's instructions to avoid offence and posted notices at street corners attacking the 'ignorance and obstinacy' of the Chinese. A furious viceroy retaliated, ordering a halt to all trade until Napier was gone – at which point Napier boarded his frigate and retreated, exchanging fire with the guns along the Bogue just to make a point. When the viceroy then blocked the channel, Napier was forced to leave on a Chinese boat, with Chinese escorts. The exhausted peer even-tually sailed into Macao on 26 September 1834 – and a fortnight later he died.

The rising tension did little to dent the Jardine Matheson business. But ambitious for more, the partners were keen to exploit the front-page news of what was christened the 'Napier fizzle'. Matheson quickly brought together his peers to found the Canton Chamber of Commerce to lobby for a remedy to the 'Napier insults'. He accompanied home Napier's widow and daughters, before embarking on a national tour to drum up support from politicians and cotton traders for the muscular China policy that he and Jardine had so long desired. He brought together his arguments in a pamphlet, *The Present Position and Prospects of the British Trade with China*, which underlined what he described as the wholly unreasonable attitude of the Chinese towards foreign trade. It was at this moment, when the future seemed freighted full of tension, that crisis in China reset the stage for not merely friction, but fighting.

*

It was clear to China's rulers that all was not well in the empire. On the country's borders and within, there were unavoidable signs of over-stretch and breakdown. Some half-dozen major revolts scarred the north-west frontier. Civil Service corruption was costing a fortune, and in 1832, when thousands of Qing Dynasty troops were defeated by rebels in Canton province (Guangdong), the Emperor Tao-kuang (Daoguang) discovered that many of his troops were 'opium smokers and it was difficult to get any vigorous response from them'.[49] The wide-spread opium use had made a mockery of official prohibitions – but the backlash was about to get more serious, as a vociferous anti-opium lobby emerged in the 1830s at the imperial court. Working parties were convened. Evidence in the shape of 'memorials' was sought from across the empire. And when a royal prince was found smoking opium in one of the Forbidden City's temples, and the largest ever opium cargo was seized in Tientsin, the emperor determined to act.

Few had been as prominent or practical in the arguments against opium as the Fujian-born official and intellectual Lin Zexu, known as 'Lin Clear-as-the-Heavens' for his diligent incorruptibility. In the opium debates he had been forthright, and so he was summoned to Beijing for no fewer than nineteen audiences with the emperor, before, in January 1839, he was dispatched to Canton to turn his arguments into action.

China's new war on drugs commenced just as William Jardine was preparing to sail for home. He had long been planning his retirement. By 1837 he had made a fortune estimated at some £300,000 (around £200–400 million today) a success built on a strategy that was highly opportunistic, varying as profits and prices moved around.* But by 1839,

---

* Sales of cotton goods, for instance, rose as high as $230,000 but were barely a third of that by 1839. Raw silk sales rose to $526,000 (£114,000) in 1830 and to $2.3 million (£546,250) in 1837 – but then collapsed during the First Opium War. Remitting bills of exchange to England was a huge business worth $1 million (£237,500) by 1840–41. Bullion shipments rose to $1 million in 1830 (£216,000), and increased six-fold a few years later. The tea account was worth $3 million by 1837 (£712,500), while opium sales also rose relentlessly to $7 million (£1.6 million) by 1838.

Jardine was fifty-five years old, and he had lived and worked in China for fifteen years. In the very month that Lin was dispatched to Canton, the British community gathered in the dining room of Canton's English factory for 'Mr Jardine's Going Away', to give its first Taipan a magnificent send-off with a grand dinner and a splendid gift of plate. The Chinese crackdown followed immediately.

Lin quickly organized the residents of Canton province into 'security groups' of five individuals, each required to monitor each other. Within two months, 1,600 people were arrested, and fourteen tonnes of opium were seized along with 43,000 opium pipes. Lin told the Hong merchants: 'I burn with shame for you', and on 17 March 1839 he ordered them to have the foreigners surrender their opium and pledge to import no more, on pain of execution.[50]

The task of fighting Britain's corner now fell to Her Majesty's new Chief Superintendant of Trade, Captain Elliot, a man, as it happened, who held contempt for the opium business. The grandson of an earl and son of a soldier-diplomat, Elliot joined the Royal Navy aged fourteen, graduated to the Foreign Office in 1830, and was sent to China in 1834, where, in 1836, he took over Lord Napier's old role. Opium was 'a trade', he said, 'which every friend to humanity must deplore';[51] but he knew his duty, and so when Lin's instructions were heard, he pulled on his naval uniform, sailed to the New English factory, raised the Union Flag to resounding cheers and took stock.

James Matheson was quite unfazed; the seizure of the opium was, he commented, 'the most complete exhibition of humbug ever witnessed in China'.[52] But others noted the terror now gripping Canton's richest merchant, Howqua, a man reputedly ten times richer than Nathan Mayer Rothschild. When Lin issued an arrest warrant for Lancelot Dent, Elliot took him under his protection. A Chinese blockade of the 350 foreigners in their factories was promptly ordered, and worse was to follow. Under acute pressure, at eleven o'clock on the morning of 27 March 1839, Elliot agreed to hand over 20,283 chests of opium – including 7,000 from the Jardine Matheson stores – and, without any authorization from his superiors, promised the merchants that the Crown would take responsibility for the £2 million of confiscated property (worth between £1.5 billion and £2.5 billion today). When Elliot was then presented by the

Chinese with a bond to sign, promising no further opium trafficking – on pain of death – he tore it up, dispatched the pieces into his fireplace, and on 23 May ordered all British ships to Macao.

Blissfully unaware of all this, William Jardine was, at the time, sailing home. *En route* back to England, he stopped off in Bombay to say farewell to Jeejeebhoy and his Farsee friends, before sailing to Suez and thence continuing overland to the Mediterranean and Europe. He had reached Naples when news arrived of the opium seizure – and he promptly leapt into action. Immediately acquiring a coach and horses, he pushed hard over the St Gotthard Pass to cross Europe, losing his passports along the way, and arrived in London in early September 1839 with $20,000 (£4,750; between £3.5 million and £6 million today). Swiftly, Jardine assembled his campaign – in the press, in the courts, and in the Foreign Office – to punish the Chinese and obtain restitution and trading rights for the merchants, even at the cost of war.

In London, however, he found Westminster in turmoil and a country in ignorance of Chinese affairs, despite the high value of China to the nation's finances. From the 1830s, opium made up one-seventh of the EIC's entire income, providing the revenue with which to purchase the tea that, once imported, provided 10 per cent of the British Exchequer's revenue. Yet, matters in China were subsumed by the chaos of the capital's politics. The Whig government had resigned in May 1839,[*] only to be recalled after the Tories quit in a dispute with Queen Victoria over her household.[†] Abroad, the world was more disordered still, with rebellions in Ireland, Jamaica and Lower Canada (Quebec), and trouble with the French in Egypt, while in Afghanistan a British army was embroiled in the First Anglo-Afghan War. Chinese events, wrote Jardine to Matheson, were 'very little understood here and many people are for doing nothing; they, very foolishly, mix up the insult and violence with the illicit trade and are for remaining quiet, pocketing the insult and refusing to pay for the opium'.[53]

---

[*] This was after the riots that followed the government's refusal to advance Chartist calls for reform.

[†] Queen Victoria had refused to alter the personnel of her bedchamber, which included the wives of many prominent Whig politicians, and so the new Tory prime minister, Robert Peel, resigned.

Undeterred, Jardine now put himself at the centre of one of the most remarkable episodes in British commercial history. Over the course of three weeks in September 1839, he and a group of fellow free-traders orchestrated a campaign for conflict with China, to be prosecuted on their behalf by the new might of the British government. Together with his friends, including the MP John Abel Smith and Thomas Weeding, Jardine began organizing merchants and petitions from members of the East India and China Association, collecting together over a hundred merchants with a common interest in Eastern trade. They were supported by some friends in the press, for Matheson had advised Jardine that he would 'find it expedient to secure the services of some leading newspaper to advocate the cause' and that it would be advantageous to have literary men to write 'the requisite memorials'.[54]

*

In the elegant 1930s Cambridge University Library, designed by Giles Gilbert Scott, are the tens of thousands of papers and letters of the Jardine Matheson archive. It is an absolute treasure trove. There is not a great deal in the way of correspondence with the British foreign secretary, Lord Palmerston, personally;[55] but in the letters and reports from Jardine and his friends to Matheson and others in the East, we can track the most extraordinary lobbying operation that took place in the last weeks of summer 1839.

John Abel Smith moved quickly to lobby the foreign secretary for action. In a letter from Palmerston to Abel Smith (14 September 1839), the author apologized that he had 'not… anything positive to tell you as yet, about the course which the government may deem proper to pursue with respect to China… we must wait to receive fuller accounts before we can finally make up our minds'.[56] Five days later, the association met to appoint a sub-committee to brief the foreign secretary. Palmerston was already armed with advice direct from Captain Elliot, received at the end of August 1839, in which Elliot opined that 'the response to all these unjust violences should be made in the form of a swift and heavy blow unprefaced by one word of written communication'.[57] In late September, Jardine reported that merchants were now readying petitions 'for protecting our commerce, and our merchants in China', that Abel Smith and Palmerston had met 'three days ago', and that while ministers had still not agreed their plan, Palmerston was now keen to see Jardine personally. 'His Lordship', recorded Jardine, 'said he was desirous of having an interview; as he has many questions to ask and added: "I suppose he can tell us what ought to be done".'58

On 28 September 1839, having kept Jardine and his colleagues waiting for two hours, Palmerston proceeded to interrogate him on his war plan for China. The meeting was vital, and while Palmerston revealed little, he asked much. Jardine recorded that the foreign secretary 'examined charts, maps, etc, etc. Many of his questions were to the point, but he did not appear to be aware of the want of power of their war junks.'59 A later letter (5 October 1839), circulated among a tight group, reveals a little more detail of the meeting. In it, Jardine explained that Palmerston's approach to the various delegations lobbying him was simple: 'my ears are open but my lips are sealed'. In their interview, 'the probability of a force was also alluded to, the extent of armaments, number of troops, necessary number of shipping, etc, were all described,'60 Palmerston had clearly asked not simply about Chinese vulnerabilities, but also about the economic risks to the tea business and the long-term aims of policy: many of his questions concerned where the tea was grown, its transport routes to Canton, as well as vulnerable points on the coast and the strength of Chinese war junks. Jardine added: 'On his asking me what I recommended to be done, [I] replied "make them apologise for the insult to HM representative, pay for the property extorted from him, get a commercial treaty signed as a security against a repetition of such conduct and open the northern ports to our shipping", adding a demonstration of force properly managed and under the orders of a cool, determined negotiator might probably accomplish the first two objects without a shot'.61

In Jardine's recollection, Palmerston 'carefully avoided committing himself to any line of conduct'. 'No direct avowal (was) made of a determination to coerce,' Jardine continued, all 'the conference ended in His Lordship retaining the charts and saying they were to hold Cabinet counsel Monday next'. Jardine's verdict was that 'All this is unsatisfactory enough but we must await silently,' for 'we cannot openly agitate the question of [the government] paying for the opium until the receipts reach us'. However, Jardine was now confident that the government could now be persuaded to act against the Chinese; 'general opinion appears to be becoming more favourable to our claim as the merits of the case become better known'. But his anxiety remained 'that there may be delay. Our govt should make themselves responsible at once, to prevent a loss of confidence and consequent mercantile distress in India and China.'

Jardine's meeting with the foreign secretary might have been the decisive moment, equipping Palmerston with vital intelligence ahead of the most important policy discussion for the new government. On 30 September 1839, the prime minister, Lord Melbourne, convened his ministers at Windsor Castle to survey the world's disorder. The conference was dominated by the 'Turkish question'. Only on the second day did the Cabinet finally get to China, on which opinion was divided. Macaulay, the secretary for war, was enthusiastic for military coercion, but many had their doubts.* John Hobhouse, President of the Board of Trade, kept a diary of the meeting, and he recorded Palmerston's plan: 'a small squadron of one line of battle ship, two frigates and some small armed vessels with three steamers might blockade the whole coast of China from the river of Pekin down to the Canton coast'.[62] The Chancellor of the Exchequer weighed in, wanting to know how the 'two millions of money' in recompense for the confiscated opium was to be found for the merchants. Melbourne was clear that the Exchequer would not pay for it. Backed by Macaulay, Palmerston suggested that the Chinese meet the bill, a view that met with support. And so, with a lukewarm Cabinet blessing, Palmerston prepared to act, albeit in secret, quietly instructing the Governor-General of India, Lord Auckland, to prepare forces for China, with a plan that closely followed Jardine's design.

By the beginning of October, Palmerston was striking a subtle change of tone. At a further meeting with a delegation of merchants to

---

* Those with doubts included Lord Melbourne, John Hobhouse and the Chancellor Baring.

discuss their petition for intervention, Palmerston once more kept tight (according to William Crawford), asking the assembled merchants simply to 'infer... the view of government'. But for Crawford, 'The impression left in my mind was that during the season 1839 the merchants at Canton must shift for themselves... until the armed force should arrive about the time of the South West monsoon, April or May 1840.'[63] Jardine was more optimistic, noting to Matheson on 14 October that 'Lord Palmerston has at last satisfied the public by stating that HM ministers have made up their minds to demand satisfaction for the insult and robbery but have not yet determined on the exact course to be pursued.'

As a precaution against official backtracking, Jardine and others engaged lawyers to – as he put it to Matheson in late October – 'look into the nature of our claims (against) HM government'. They also planned 'to engage the *Times* newspaper to write in favour' of their cause. But crucially, Jardine explained that he and others were now preparing a battle-plan: 'A paper containing a variety of hints mixed up with much useful information is now preparing for them.'

By 3 December 1839, from the snows of a Scottish winter, Jardine was writing to Matheson with more definitive news after a further meeting with Palmerston: 'HM Ministers intend to make the Chinese pay for the drug... They will succeed,' he added, 'if the force sent is sufficient.'[64] The plan Jardine had set out was probably the outline dispatched to Matheson on 19 December:

My advice is to send a naval force to blockade the coast of China from the Tartar wall [surrounding Beijing] to Tienpack [on the south China coast] or from 40 to 20 degrees north; the force to consist of two ships of the line, two frigates and two flat-bottomed steamers for river service, with a sufficient number of transports to carry... six or seven thousand men. The force to proceed to the vicinity of Pekin, and apply directly to the emperor for an apology for the insult... payment for the opium given up, an equitable commercial treaty, and liberty to trade with northern ports... say, Amoy, Foochow, Ningpo [Ningbo], Shanghai and also Kiaochow [Jiaozhou], if we can get it.

Jardine thought that:

The two first demands would readily be granted, but the third and fourth may be refused, and then we must proceed to take possession of three or four islands, say Formosa [Taiwan], Quemoy [Kinmen], and Amoy (or at least two... and intercept the trade from Formosa). We should also take the great Chusan island, which being near Peking would be source of great annoyance to the Emperor. Having these islands in our possession, the Chinese would most likely grant all our demands on condition of our giving them up.

Armed with a battle-plan, Palmerston was ready for war. But Parliament was now growing suspicious. In January 1840, MPs began demanding the blue books – the official records – of Elliot's correspondence, and on 11 March, a French newspaper blew Palmerston's cover, informing the world that a French frigate was off to witness the 'war'. Stonewalling, the foreign secretary insisted that the 40,000 tonnes of Royal Navy shipping and 16,000 men were merely 'communications'. The government survived a three-day confidence debate by just nine votes as Palmerston insisted he was simply protecting 'the honour of the British flag and the dignity of the British Crown',* a crown, Macaulay argued, that was 'unaccustomed to defeat, to submission or to shame'.

*

While Parliamentarians discussed the matter in London over the autumn and winter of 1839–40, in China the conflict had been running hot. On 4 September 1839, Elliot, in his fleet of three small ships, demanded access to Hong Kong to restock with water and supplies. When his ultimatum went unheeded, he opened fire. By 15 September, the British were permitted to drift back to Macao, and negotiations

---

* Palmerston basically argued that the Whigs' policy was no more than a continuation of the policy of the Duke of Wellington, that is maximizing trust in the officials on the ground. Lovell, *The Opium War*, op. cit., p. 107.

resumed. But the peace was short-lived. British ships arriving in port were asked again to sign Lin's bond. Elliot immediately sailed in to mediate. On 2 November, when Chinese officials refused to receive Elliot's communiqués, the *Volage* and the *Hyacinth* opened fire with such destructive force that what was left of the Chinese squadron retreated – only to counter-attack at the end of the month.*

In London, Jardine had fast become one of the war-party's pivots in the City and the House of Commons. On his arrival home, he had been feted by his peers: the East India merchants greeted him with a great public dinner in his honour.[65] He joined the Oriental Club, and with his huge wealth he acquired a London home on Upper Belgrave Street and the Lanrick estate on the edge of Loch Lomond,† where, as Sir Walter Scott once put it, 'the Highlands meets the Lowlands'. Jardine and John Abel Smith were especially close. They weekended together at Blendon Hall, and worked closely together in Westminster; in early March 1840, Jardine sealed the new alliance by joining his company, Magniac Smith & Co., as a partner in their offices at 3 Lombard Street (the headquarters of Jardine Matheson today). From here, Jardine stepped up the campaign for compensation for the opium surrendered by Elliot.

Before the House of Commons debate on war in April 1840, Smith, as a member of the Commons China Committee, had 'suggested a plan of their arranging [a] Committee in such a manner as they should advise the House to grant a loan in Exchequer bills for half the amount of the claim'. But the government was relying on victory against the Chinese emperor to settle the bill. In the summer of 1840, the British expedition arrived in China, pausing briefly in Macao before quickly proceeding north to attack. On 4 July 1840, the war fleet approached the Chusan islands with twenty-two warships and twenty-seven transports, loaded with 3,600 troops. Lord Jocelyn, Elliot's military secretary, demanded the islands' surrender. When nothing was heard, the Navy opened fire at 2.30 the following afternoon. By ten o'clock that evening, the British were in full control.

---

* The First Opium War is conventionally dated from this time.
† He initially sought the grand house of Castlemilk near his birthplace; the house was later acquired by his nephew Joseph.

A month later, the Royal Navy arrived just off the port of Tientsin, roughly 70 miles from Beijing, to demand talks. The Chinese governor, Qishan, with spectacular charm persuaded Elliot to withdraw and rendezvous with him in Canton. Qishan was the epitome of reassurance: 'the great emperor oversees the earth and seas – there is no place he does not regard with equal benevolence', he oiled; 'If foreigners should have the slightest grievance about their trade with us, we will immediately investigate and punish those at fault accordingly… the British admiral should return south and wait patiently for the matter to be dealt with.'[66]

The conflict proved not to be bad for business. The firm grew, trading on its own account as the commission trade faded. By 1840, with its fleet of twelve ships, Jardine Matheson was running profits of $1.6 million (£380,000 or £300–500 million today).[67] With Chinese forces distracted, and possessing control of large credit lines through their huge silver supplies, Jardine Matheson, operating from Macao, enjoyed a business in teas, sugar candy, rattans and opium, which oozed back and forth when the fighting was hot, but flowed freely in times of truce. The coastal trade in opium expanded – Jardine's superintendent, Jauncey, was at times supervising a dozen ships up and down the coast, and business could now be done in the middle of the Pearl river. 'For years to come,' wrote Alexander Matheson (James's nephew) to Smith, 'we shall not be in a better position, or trade to so much advantages, as during the continuance of the war, more especially if the opium trade is to be hampered.'[68]

When the Chinese and British emissaries reconvened in Canton, in November 1840, Elliot's patience was quickly tested. A month of exchanges – 'no-gotiating' the British merchants called it – produced little. Although Lin was dismissed, there was no movement from the Chinese on the British demands for $5 million of compensation, a base in Hong Kong and trading posts on China's eastern seaboard. But by this time, Elliot's reinforcements – including the *Nemesis* (which arrived in November) – were strengthening his hand. The *Nemesis* had revolutionized the term 'gun-boat'. Not technically a Navy or an EIC ship, she was a private armed steamer commanded by Royal Navy officers. Built in just three months by Forrester & Co., in Liverpool, she was launched for the Secret Committee of the EIC on the Mersey in 1839. Sailing east, the 184-feet-long ship became the first iron steamer to round the Cape of Good Hope. The *Nemesis* was specially designed for operations in coastal and river waters; she had a shallow draught, of just six feet when fully loaded, and a fearful armoury of two highly accurate pivot-mounted 32-pounder guns, five long brass 6-pounders, a rocket tube and a small howitzer. The Chinese christened her 'devil ship'.

Elliot now set a date of 28 December 1840 for progress in the nego-tiations. When nothing happened, he commanded his forces up the Pearl river on 7 January 1841 and ordered a devastating ninety-minute bombardment of the Chinese forts guarding Canton: within an hour and a half, they had fallen. In the face of such firepower, the Chinese sued for peace, offering the Convention of Chuenpee (Chuanbi), which entailed not just the handover of Hong Kong but an indemnity of $6 million. But the concessions remained on paper. The imperial prefect, Qishan, could never deliver the emperor's imprimatur to the agree-ment, and, losing patience, Elliot now ordered the invasion of Canton itself. In an operation lasting just three days, 3,500 troops subdued and occupied the ancient trading capital of over a million people, which had once been defended by 40,000 troops. In the city, 'when night fell, the fires burned as bright as day… neither officials nor soldiers dared come out to help – all you could hear was the noise of burning and death'.[69]

Flush with victory, Elliot now faced defeat in London, over the terms of the Chuenpee deal. When news of the agreement reached London on 8 April 1841, the reaction was furious. Queen Victoria stamped her foot. Lord Auckland declared: 'I am very mad with it all,' and on 20 April Palmerston set out Elliot's mistakes: there were no indemnities for British citizens, no 'reasonable tariffs or duties', no opening of northern Chinese ports, and no abolition of the Hong mer-chants' monopoly. 'You seem to have considered that my instructions were waste paper,' he wrote to Elliot, 'and that you were at full liberty to deal with the interest of your country according to your own fancy.'[70] It was for Elliot a career-ending moment.

Back in London, Jardine and Smith saw Palmerston in May 1841 to press their demands for compensation, and in the General Election of that year,* Jardine saw his chance to reinforce the China lobby in Parliament. Nominated as the Whig candidate for Ashburton, in Devon, he beat the Tory nominee of his great rivals, the Dents, who withdrew on the eve of poll. Jardine was thus elected unopposed. 'Thomas Dent laughed at the idea of my ever expecting to be returned,' he wrote to Matheson, adding with satisfaction that 'you will be glad to know that we have maintained our position here as well as in China'.[71]

To prosecute his plan for China, Palmerston now appointed Sir Henry Pottinger, a fifty-one-year-old veteran of the EIC and Britain's intelligence service, as Elliot's replacement. He arrived with a determination 'not to be humbugged' by the Chinese. Throughout Elliot's ill-starred campaign, Matheson had lent pilots for ships as well as interpreters and reconnaissance for coastal waters. Now, Matheson's nephew Alexander was by Pottinger's side as a military aide, when the new commander arrived and made for James Matheson's house. 'We gave him dinner to meet the commercial community,' wrote Matheson to Jardine, 'on all of who[m] he made a favourable impression.'[72]

The long war in the south now gave way to a brutal fifteen-month campaign north to Nanking (Nanjing). Amoy, Chusan, Chenhai (Zhenhai) and Ningpo were taken in quick succession before the winter. By August 1842, Pottinger was sailing down the Yangtze river to begin landing troops and howitzers outside Nanking. Under the threat of fire, the Treaty of Nanking was finally presented on 19 August and signed, finally, in the cabin of HMS *Cornwallis* on 29 August 1842. The war for Britain was over. And a century of humiliation for China was about to begin.

*

In the House of Commons, William Jardine MP was not a loquacious speaker; indeed, *Hansard* records just one contribution in the debate on prioritizing traders' compensation. On 17 March 1842, Hugh Lindsay,

---

* In the second election of Victoria's reign, Viscount Melbourne's Whigs lost heavily to Peel's Conservatives and Daniel O'Connell's Irish Repeal Party, campaigning for an end to the union between Great Britain and Ireland.

a former 'supercargo' (overseer of a ship's cargo) and secretary for the EIC in Canton, rose to propose a motion: that in the final settlement with the Chinese, the opium traders be compensated first before the bills of war were paid.[73] 'In his [Jardine's] opinion,' says *Hansard*, 'nothing was clearer than that the merchants ought to be compensated before the expenses of the expedition were taken into consideration.' Jardine was at a loss to see what claims the government had, except those that were founded on the claims of the merchants. If any similar cause arose in which the East India Company was concerned, there could be no doubt that the tribunals of the country would at once settle the dispute. It was the poverty, and not the will, of the late government that prevented their making compensation; now, argued Jardine, it was the cupidity of the Chancellor of the Exchequer that kept back the money. The motion was soundly defeated.

By 1842, as Pottinger was preparing his Yangtze campaign, Jardine developed a painful tumour. Yet he lived to see a victory of sorts in this long campaign for compensation. That year, sixty-five tonnes of Chinese silver reached Portsmouth, where it was carried away by railway wagons to the Mint. A year after the Treaty of Nanking, the traders finally got something – albeit far less than they expected.

In November 1842, in a letter to Smith, Lord Palmerston acknowledged the crucial role Jardine had played in events. 'To the assistance and information which you and Mr Jardine so handsomely afforded us, it was mainly owing that we were able to give our affairs, naval, military and diplomatic, in China, those detailed instructions which have led to those satisfactory results.'[74] He went on: 'It is indeed remarkable that the information we procured from yourself and various other persons... was so accurate and complete that it appears our successors have not found reason to make any alterations in them.'

By that autumn, Jardine was unable to write. When James Matheson arrived in London – himself ordered home on health grounds – he found his old partner very ill. Yet, in the last of the Jardine letters that survive, written to Jamsetjee Jeejeebhoy on 2 December 1842, Jardine noted (among news of his forthcoming tea sale) that 'my health is now greatly better'. He went on to speculate on 'the most unexpected news of peace with China' and to warn his old partner to be 'very timid and cautious in speculating in the drug at the high prices that will no doubt prevail with you'.[75]

In January 1843, John Abel Smith wrote to Jeejeebhoy with news about the progress of their opium claims, but he added that Jardine's 'bodily strength and physical powers are much reduced', though 'his resignation and fortitude are most extraordinary and really almost heroic'.[76] On 27 February 1843, Britain's first Taipan died at his home in Upper Belgrave Street. A few days later, Matheson broke the news to Jeejeebhoy, in his elegant copper-plate script. 'For the last few weeks,' he wrote, 'his sufferings had become considerably alleviated and his mind continued clear and composed to the last,' but, 'without suffering at 4 p.m. on the 27th ultimo from effusion of water in the chest', the great man had passed away.[77]

William Jardine's body was conveyed from London to the church-yard of Lochmaben, where, attended by his relatives 'and two or three country gentlemen (among them the Marquis of Queensberry)', he was buried.[78] There was no immediate family among the mourners, for he had never married. In the by-election that followed his death, James Matheson was elected to his old partner's seat of Ashburton, presenting himself, in his election address, as 'the friend and former partner of your late lamented Member, Mr Jardine'.[79]

In the ensuing years, the firm Jardine and Matheson founded went from strength to strength, under the leadership of many of their kin. James Matheson had made sure that the firm was among the first bidders at the Hong Kong land auctions, where they 'secured three adjoining lots and have built on the centre one, but contemplate estab-lishing our chief seat of business elsewhere, on a point jutting out into the sea'. Here, the firm stored bales of raw cotton sent over by Jeejeebhoy, and the Hong Kong anchorage became the key trans-shipment point for opium. By March 1844, the Hong Kong headquarters was big enough for the twenty HQ staff of Jardine Matheson & Co., now under the leadership of Alexander Matheson; and in the same year, Alexander Dallas, an Inverness-trained medal-list, opened the firm's office in the treaty port of Shanghai. By 1850, the port was of the first importance and Western merchants based on Shanghai's waterfront, the 'Bund', developed economic policy for the

Yangtze Valley. The firm's Shanghai Taipan was almost as important as the company's leader in Hong Kong.

Reflecting on William Jardine, his obituarist wrote that it 'was a source of satisfaction to him on his death-bed to learn that the ports opened to British trade, by the late treaty, were the identical ones which he had recommended at the beginning'.[80] By Victoria's middle years, the free-trade policy for which Jardine had worked so hard was transforming the country's fortunes, funding an ever expanding empire – while in China an imperial dynasty began its descent into dust.

7

GEORGE HUDSON

Britain's Railway King

Wednesday, 29 May 1839 was 'a gala day for the good people of York'.[1] The morning sun, wrote the correspondent for the *Yorkshire Gazette*, shone brilliantly in 'a cloudless sky of an azure more deep than is often seen above our misty atmosphere'.[2] A gentle breeze blew in from the north-east, floating the cheery flags. From York Minster the bells rang out, while on the river cannon boomed, as thousands of men and women lined the track, banks and bridges of the new York & North Midland Railway to wave off the town's first steam train. It was 'the day on which a new era was to begin'.[3]

At eleven o'clock, the railway's directors – handsomely decorated with white rosettes and escorted by officers of the 1st Dragoon Guards and 7th Hussars, the Mayor of Leeds, the minster's canons, the magistrates and members of the City Corporation – trooped into the Guildhall to breakfast with the two men who would help make Britain's railways: the chief engineer, George Stephenson, and the Lord Mayor of York and chairman of the company, Mr George Hudson.

After breakfast finished, the speeches began. Hudson congratulated his fellow citizens and expressed his certainty that the guests would take home stories of 'the antiquity of our venerable city and the beauty of our fair sex'.[4] 'Many bachelors would be induced to come from other towns by the railway,' he forecast, 'for which they would be richly repaid if it were only to see those fair ladies who had this morning honoured them with their company.'[5]

The guests then formed a line behind the marching band, which led the assembled dignitaries off to the station to take their seats in the nineteen carriages pulled by two engines. At 1.05pm, to the huzzahs of the crowd, the 'huge snake like body', with 'imperceptibly increasing speed', stole away, with a piercing whistle, under the broad arch of the Holdgate Lane bridge. The train arrived thirty-six minutes later, at Milford junction, to meet the train from Leeds. It paused for half an hour, the band played a few more overtures, and then the party puffed its way back to York for an enormous party at the Guildhall, where 'every delicacy of the season loaded the tables' and 'a very bountiful supply of champagne' flowed.

When Hudson rose to speak to the hundreds of guests, his most heartfelt thanks were for the man who had sat through dinner at his right hand, and without whom his venture would have failed. Without George Stephenson, said the lord mayor, 'there would have been no railway to drink success to':

> If ever there was a man who deserved to be held up to the public approbation of the whole world, that man was Mr Stephenson. His genius had conferred the greatest possible benefit on the poorer classes of society... He had brought the inhabitants of towns together and formed into one family; space and distance had been put an end to.[6]

The dancing continued until four o'clock in the morning, 'when everyone retired highly delighted with the day's festivities'.[7] A few hours later, the 27-mile line connecting Leeds and York, in a journey of an hour and a quarter, opened for business.[8]

It was the beginning of a journey that would take Hudson to his throne as Britain's 'Railway King', on to the House of Commons – and in time, to complete and utter ruin.

*

George Hudson was born on Monday, 10 March 1800 in the little village of Howsham on the east bank of the River Derwent, 12 miles north-east of York. The fifth son, and seventh child, of tenant farmer John Hudson and his wife Susannah, George was born into a family that was poor, respectable and unlucky. Like his father before him, John Hudson was not only a farmer but also High Constable of the Wapentake of Buckrose.[9] When George was just six, he lost his mother to consumption, and two years later his father was dead too. At the age of eight, George, together with his eight brothers and sisters, was left an orphan.[10]

Hudson's early years and education are a mystery. When their father died, George's eldest brother John, then aged twenty, took over the farm and position of High Constable. He failed to cope with both, resigning the constableship and surrendering the farm to his brother William.[11] At the age of fifteen, George Hudson lost both his elder sisters and made his first appearance in official records.[12] It, too, was inauspicious. The 1815–16 edition of the *Howsham Poor Book* coldly records: 'Received of George Hudson for bastardy, 12s 6d'.[13] The name of the mother is unrecorded, as was the fate of the child. But the offence was the trigger for George to up sticks, leave the poverty of his village, and travel the road to York, a small sleepy town in a rapidly industrializing county.

*

The year Hudson left for York was the year in which the Duke of Wellington secured his glorious victory at Waterloo against Napoleon. Yet for many, the sense of victory did not last long. 'All triumphant sensations of national glory seem almost obliterated by general depression,' wrote one observer.[14] A national economy geared to battle slumped with the new peace. A third of a million men poured out of the army and back home to their villages, farms and towns. Food prices spiralled, as a Parliament filled with those of landed interest ushered through the new Corn Laws, which prohibited the entry of foreign corn until the home price of corn sailed high. Worse still was the deflation, as a House of Commons committee chaired by Robert Peel secured a return to the Gold Standard in 1821, and convertability of sterling to a fixed quantum of gold. The move triggered a sharp fall in credit and cash, in which the circulation of £5 notes, which totalled £7.4 million in 1819, fell to just £900,000 in August 1822. 'Peel's Act' created, in the eyes of Birmingham banker and ironmaster Thomas Atwood, 'more misery, more poverty, more discord, more of everything that was calamitous to the nation, except death, than Attila caused in the Roman Empire'.[15]

The mannered, genteel world of regency rooms, balls, fast and cheap stagecoaches, and the pleasant coaching inns described by Jane Austen and a young Charles Dickens* felt an awfully long way from the damning surveys of one soldier-turned-social-campaigner. William Cobbett's hard-hitting five-year study of the national condition, *Rural Rides*, portrayed a starving country of 'walking skeletons', held to ransom by corrupt statesman and middlemen. 'There must be change', wrote Cobbett, 'a complete and radical change; or England must become a country of the basest slavery that ever disgraced the earth'. Yet, amid the national gloom the young George Hudson's luck was about to change for the better.

*

On the edge of York's Goodramgate and College Street, in the Tudor row on the little green outside the east end of York Minster, stood a simple draper's shop, Nicholson and Bell, run by one Rebecca Bell.[†] Rebecca had taken over the business in 1813, after her husband had died at the tender age of twenty-eight.[16] In need of help, Rebecca now took on the young Hudson as an apprentice – and by all accounts he was soon a model worker. In September 1817, she handed over the shop to her brother Richard, and gradually he was impressed enough by Hudson's diligence to offer him a partnership on 17 February 1821, just shy of Hudson's twenty-first birthday.[17] The business could boast £6,000-worth of new equity and even better, the partnership came with a promise: that upon Hudson's marriage to Richard's elder sister, Elizabeth, they would live above the shop for a rent of £35 per year. [18]

George and Elizabeth were married on 17 July 1821, at the beautiful Holy Trinity Church in Goodramgate, and by all accounts their first days were very happy. 'The happiest part of my life', said Hudson years

---

* Austen's *Sense and Sensibility* was published in 1815, while Dickens's *Pickwick Papers* was published over a decade later.

† This is now the National Trust shop.

later, 'was when I stood behind the counter and used the yard measure in my own shop.'[19] Here, Hudson acquired his knack with figures and the peculiar accounting techniques of the shopkeeper: 'The true chandler's shop system is to keep no books at all. A cross for a halfpenny, a down stroke for a penny, a little O for sixpence, and a larger for a shilling, all in chalk, on a board or cupboard door, constitute the accounts of many a money-getting shopkeeper.'[20]

Fate now blessed them, not immediately with children, but with a fortune. Almost nine months to the day after their wedding, their first child, James Richard, was born, only to die before he was one.[21] Two more children, Richard and Matthew, followed, and both died young.* But the Hudsons' luck was about to turn. A few minutes around the corner from the shop, through York's splendid old Monkgate, lived Hudson's great uncle Matthew Bottrill in a vast five-storey terrace mansion, which today lies opposite the Methodist church. Here, George and Elizabeth were often welcomed as guests, and by all accounts Bottrill enjoyed offering his great-nephew guidance and direction. When, in early 1827, Bottrill fell seriously ill, George was his constant companion at his bedside. By the end of May 1827, Matthew Bottrill was dead, and when his will was read out George Hudson's life changed forever. 'I give and devise', wrote Bottrill, 'all my said lands tenements hereditaments and real estate situate at Osbaldwick and Huntington as aforesaid unto my great nephew George Hudson... his heirs and assigns for ever' along with property 'not hereinfore specifically bequeathed'.[22]

It is hard to pin down the total value of this enormous legacy. A final page to the will, dated five months after Bottrill's death, records 'the whole of the goods, chattels and credits of the said deceased do not amount in value to the sum of ten thousand pounds' – worth between £7 million and £13 million in today's money – which was the amount recorded for probate. He left his gold pocket watch to 'Richard, son of George Hudson' and an annuity to his housekeeper, along with 'the clothes and wearing apparel of my late wife and the small silver

---

* In due course three sons – George, John and William – and a daughter, Anne, would survive into adulthood.

cup which she commonly used'.[23] But very little was left to anyone else.

Rumours abounded for decades. Thirteen people were mentioned in the will. All were closer by kinship to Matthew than George Hudson, and the will had been changed on 21 April, a little under a month before Matthew died – a month in which George was always in attendance. As late as 1850, a court heard evidence that 'Certain it is, that Mr Botterill [sic] altered his will on his death-bed, and that Mr Hudson was his constant companion during his latter hours.'[24] Whatever the truth, the farmer's son, orphaned at eight and expelled from his village at fifteen, was now one of the grandest men in York.

Yet, York itself was not grand. Within booming Yorkshire, the county town was becoming a backwater.

*

Once the prestigious capital of the north, York was falling behind the times – and the city fathers knew it. The place was a market centre, where the countryside came to the shop. The city's markets may have been doing well – new pens for the sheep and cattle were ordered in the 1820s, and the banking business began to grow in the 1830s; but shop-keeping, cattle-marketing and banking were not great job creators, and nor were there local factories. When the census of York's occupations was completed in 1831, manufacturing was so small than it was merely a footnote in the tables, and – apart from the 500 people working in retail distribution, of which Hudson was one – most workers in 1831 earned their keep in transport, leather, the building trades or domestic service.*

York's elders knew that the town was slipping. When, in 1825, a suggestion was made to create a university, it was welcomed as a plan to confer dignity on the old city and 'to raise it to its proper rank in the national account'. Yet still it was lamented that 'everything is going away from us and nothing is coming… the great advantages and benefits which York possessed have rapidly flown away from her lately, notwithstanding the increase of the population'.[25] 'We have no manufactures,'

---

* Out of a survey of 1,922 people, there were 88 coach drivers for instance, along with owners and grooms, and 182 hotel and inn keepers and beer sellers.

wrote one commentator in 1827, 'we have no complicated machinery in operation; we have no weavers, no dyers, no shipbuilders, no mines.'

Some blamed the high price of coal. Some blamed the city's division into 30 parishes. Some blamed the old restrictions imposed by the city's guilds. The population may have been rising fast – by some 71 per cent in the first four decades of the nineteenth century – but Leeds, by contrast, had nearly tripled in size, while Bradford more than quadrupled. The reality was that York's government – self-elective, recruited from freemen and Anglicans – lacked both cash and creativity.

The contrast with the county around the city was striking, for Georgian Yorkshire was thriving. When Domesday Book had been compiled, Yorkshire was a wasteland of forest, fen, moorland and mountain. But by 1164, weavers had founded York's first guild, and by the thirteenth century, York, Beverley, Hedon, Selby and Whitby were all marked as centres of weaving. Yorkshire's links with Flanders (easier to reach than London) multiplied,* and from the 1340s, the York Freeman's Roll vividly illustrates the huge influx of Flemish weavers, fulling, weaving, dying, tailoring, shearing, wool-packing and card-making. By 1379 Flemish weavers were at work across the county.[26]

Guilds however brought restrictions, and over the years new production oozed into the villages and the cottages of the West Riding, where, noted the Georgian merchant Josiah Tucker, 'journeymen… being so little removed from the degree and condition of their masters, and likely to set up for themselves by the industry and frugality of a few years… thus it is… the goods are made, and exceedingly cheap'.[27] Cheap proved popular. In 1797, one Georgian writer, John Smith, in his *Memoirs of Wool* (1747) estimated that across Britain some 800,000 people toiled away in the textile business, in the West Country, East Anglia but above all in the West Riding of Yorkshire,[28] where, 30 miles east of Hudson's York, the industry had its centre in Leeds. Here, in the great cloth halls, twice a week in the two hours after opening at 7am, many of the 3,500 broadcloth manufacturers could sell between £10,000 and £20,000 of broadcloths and kerseys to merchants buying from

---

* Beverley became home to Flemish merchants and weavers, celebrated in the naming of the town's Fleming Gate.

London, Holland, Germany and Austria. By 1772, 90 per cent of West Riding cloth was exported, and by the time George Hudson was born, Britain was churning out £14 million-worth of cloth a year, 60 per cent of which was made in the West Riding.*

The textile business was then still an industry dominated by hand-work and outwork – 'home working' and 'putting out' remained a huge part of the industry until well into the second half of the eighteenth century. But, in the space of twenty years, those traditions were transformed by the creation of 166 powered mills across Yorkshire, 54 of which were powered by the new steam engines (including Boulton & Watt's).

Just as important as its factories to the county's fortunes were Yorkshire's forges. Few towns could rival Sheffield, Rotherham and Doncaster – 60 miles south of Hudson's York – where iron had been smelted since before Roman times and which was now the greatest steel centre on the planet.[29] By Elizabeth I's day, there were many literary allusions to Sheffield's metalwork: at the foot of hills where five rivers meet, the town had plenty of power to drive the bellows and grinding, forging and rolling machines in 115 watermills. When Defoe saw the town, he recorded its 'houses dark and black, occasioned by the continued smoke of the forges, which are always at work: Here they make all sorts of cutlery-ware, but especially that of edged-tools, knives, razors, axes, etc and nails'.[†] In the early 1740s, in a nondescript stable-sized stone building in Abbeydale, Benjamin Huntsman poured Sheffield's first steel ingot. It was, said a French customer, 'without doubt the best of all the steels produced commercially; it is the hardest, the most uniform and the most compact'. Boulton and Watt were among the first in the queue for the new cast steel for tooling, mint dies, hammers and rolls.

---

* Fifty-one ships sailed from Hull in 1738, and soon towns like Oporto and Lisbon were as familiar, as were the buyers of Amsterdam, with the low-cost goods and aggressive marketing of the merchants from Leeds, Wakefield and Halifax. Over the course of the eighteenth century, this share of national industry rose from 20 to 60 per cent.

† The Company of Cutlers was authorized by Parliament in 1624, and boasted 2,000 members by 1679.

Although, for centuries, at least ten major parts of Britain could boast rural domestic industries, now the west and south of Yorkshire could be considered together, with south Lancashire and the west Midlands, the country's four great 'factory districts'.[30] And, in the days of Hudson's youth, these were the places turbo-charged by the years of war with Revolutionary and Napoleonic France, which saw hundreds of millions of pounds poured by the government into the economy. A quarter of all iron production went for armaments, ballast for the fleet or gun metal boosting cities like Birmingham, which produced an incredible 8 million weapons between 1804 and 1815.[31] The Royal Navy doubled in size, transforming demand for guns, uniforms, boots, sails for ships and balls for the cannon, and by 1810, the Merchant Navy boasted 12,198 vessels, sixteen times the size of the Royal Navy, flushing new business through the country's shipyards. Between 1796 and 1806, England's iron production went from 125,000 tonnes to 344,000 tonnes.[*]

The war against Napoleon – along with the export boom to America – was very good for Yorkshire. The county could now boast factories to rival Lancashire, producing not cotton, but woollens. Sheffield steel now cut the trees, swamps and prairies of the American frontier: up to a third of the town's output was sent west. Plenty of men could set up shop as a 'mester' with a worker or two; 'any man willing to risk a few hundred pounds might become a steel manufacturer', wrote one Sheffielder, and the town's ten steel producers in 1787 had tripled to thirty-four in 1817. Some of the forges were huge. Walkers of Rotherham had a steel and armaments plant worth £214,393 by 1797; Joseph Rodgers was employing 300 people by 1800, and in the early 1820s, the Great Sheaf Works and Globe Works opened for business. Soon the area was home to great firms like Vickers, John Brow, Cammell, Firth, Hadfields and Jessop.[†]

---

[*] The average blast furnace might produce 20 tonnes a week. See Birch, *The Economic History of the British Iron and Steel Industry, 1784–1879* (Frank Cass, 1967), pp. 46–8.

[†] Together on the road out to Rotherham, the steel firms created 'a long drawn horror of confluent damnation'; a street 'separated from Hell only by a sheet of tissue paper'. Tweedale, *Steel City*, op. cit., p. 5.

Within a decade of Cobbett's dark *Rural Rides*, a new story was taking shape, and it was set down by another old soldier, Sir George Head* in his tour of the 'Factory Districts'. In his pages, Sir George described a revolution reshaping the north of England: from the 'commodiousness and magnificence of the docks' in Liverpool to the packet steamers plying the canals, from the cavernous Marston pit with a chamber the size of Grosvenor Square, to the great cotton warehouses of Manchester steam-pressing thousand-pound bales of cotton yarn for Russia. He described the continuous dispatch of great coal wagons on the railways from St Helen's to the bustling Coloured Cloth Hall of Leeds and its steam-powered worsted manufactories, and the Gazelle coastal steamer from Hull to London and the sheet lead casting by the quayside of Greenock. In the great foundries of Wibsey Low Moor, 'massive piles of brickwork' with huge furnaces boiling 'a glowing lake of fire', churning out cannonballs, one of hundreds of new iron-works. Everywhere, the north was in motion.

Except, it seemed, in York itself. The City Corporation badly needed new blood, and with George Hudson they got plenty. He set out to change everything.

*

A man with money in the bank and time on his hands is often attracted to politics, and the newly enriched Hudson was no exception. Over the first three years enjoying his great-uncle's inheritance, he had begun to make some important political friends, not among those riding high, but among the Tories, then at their lowest ebb for a generation amid the national battles for reform of the franchise.

Hudson appeared at his first election campaign meeting in 1830, at the George Inn on York's Coney Street, and spoke as an opponent of electoral reform. He had clearly been involved in the campaign for some time. He had 'no objection to reform', he declared to 150 cheering supporters, 'but wished it to be carried and obtained in a constitutional way... It was the duty of every friend of this country to come forward at

---

* Head was a cavalry officer who had served in the American wars and had found fame with his book, *Forest Scenes and Incidents in the Wilds of North America*.

the present crisis in support of the king, who had been deserted by his ministers'.[32] Despite the Tories' subsequent defeat, Hudson's campaigning won him some useful connections, in particular the Parliamentary candidate John Henry Lowther, a well-heeled Tory and the son of a wealthy baronet whom Hudson backed with impressive energy, enthusiasm and cash.[33]

Hudson's first political breakthrough came two years later, in 1832, when a disaster, in the form of a cholera epidemic, struck the city, taking up 'its deadly stand on the vitals of the vitiated'.[34] In his capacity as a member of the York Board of Health since 1831, Hudson frequently visited the afflicted and provided a running stream of public reports.[35] Almost 200 people lost their lives from the disease,[36] and when the City Corporation quibbled about where to bury the dead, Hudson, to great cheers, lambasted its members for their insensitivity to the bereaved and their seeming disrespect to the dead, taking on the Whig leaders of the city, including one Joseph Rowntree. The corporation backed down within days, and Hudson became a city personality.[37] It was a fine political apprenticeship for a man who was now the treasurer of York's Tory Party, and in 1832 he carried the lion's share of election work, organizing the bribery and corruption of voters – and indeed became the object of a local campaign song:

Oh Geo Hudson, Geo Hudson, pray sir what do you trust on
For a seat in the House of the Nation;
Even poor Whistling Billy, the man what is silly
Has a far better qualification[38]

The Tories were defeated again, but it proved no setback to Hudson's rise. When, in 1833, Lowther's father, Sir John Lowther, helped start the York Union Bank, Hudson became one of his partners, buying a number of shares and taking office as a director.[39] The bank opened its doors to the public on 1 May 1833, with an impressive balance sheet of £500,000 – and an impressive chairman of the bank's London agency: George Glyn, who happened to be one of the leading promoters of the railway mania that was beginning to sweep the country. It was a craze that would make Hudson a fortune.[40]

*

After the first canal ventures of entrepreneurs, such as the Duke of Bridgewater and Josiah Wedgwood, great engineers like Thomas Telford had quickly built a national network of both waterways and turnpike trusts.[41] By 1830, 1,000 turnpike companies were running 20,000 miles of road, on which ran the stagecoaches, employing some 30,000 people, while 2,200 miles of canal meant that no place south of Durham lay more than 15 miles from a waterway.[42]

The challenge of moving bulky coal, however, sparked the search for something better, for the fuel powered the nation's vast expansion in forges and factories.[43] The coal could now be dug from ever deeper shafts below the water table, up to 1,000 feet beneath the earth, thanks to steam pumps such as Boulton & Watt's that could drain the flood-waters. Accordingly, between 1700 and 1830 output from the coalfields rose ten-fold to over 30 million tonnes.[44] Indeed, by 1800, Britain was already producing five times as much coal as the rest of Europe, and mines were the biggest enterprises in the country; by 1850, some 2,000 collieries employed 400,000 people digging £40 million-worth of coal – representing around 6 per cent of the economy.[45] But, cumbersome and therefore costly to move, even on the canal network, coal needed a cheaper mode of transport.

Thus, the nation's entrepreneurs had begun to explore the possibilities of modern railways. Railways *per se* were not new – they had been trialled by kings and colliery-owners alike since at least the seventeenth century.* By 1660 there were nine wagon-ways on Tyneside using simple railways to move coal trucks downhill, by force of gravity, from pits to the port-side.[46] The breakthrough came with steam, and after Boulton & Watt's innovations, engineers had quickly begun testing steam loco-motives – not always successfully. Nicholas-Joseph Cugnot's *Fardier* was declared a public menace when it ran amok in Paris in 1769. In 1800, however, the Cornishman Richard Trevithick created a model steam locomotive, followed by a 'steam carriage', and three years later a

---

* King Louis XIV's engine, the *Roulette*, with which he entertained his guests was built in the gardens of Marly near Versailles, and pushed by three valets.

locomotive mounted on rails hauled 9-ton wagons all the way from Coalbrookdale, Staffordshire, to Pen-y-Darren in Wales. Around the same time, the Surrey Iron Railway provided a 9-mile freight route between Wandsworth and Croydon. Horse-pulled railways soon began to proliferate, along with ideas for a 'general iron railway'.

It took until May 1818 for a rail plan of any scale to emerge. After the Earl of Strathmore had announced a canal from his colliery to the River Tees, a group of local businessmen were inspired to commission designs for a competing 37-mile railway line, open to anyone prepared to pay the access charge. An initial route was presented to Parliament; it was revised and passed in April 1821, and thanks to its far-sighted promoter, Edward Pease, an extraordinary young engineer was employed to make a reality of the bold blueprints: George Stephenson.

Stephenson had long been fascinated by the potential for steam to out-pull any other form of engine. Born in 1781, he was the son of the fireman at the Wylam Colliery, Northumberland, where his father stoked the mine's steam engines to pump water from the flooded pits. As a young man, George had won a reputation for straight-talking, incessant tinkering and constantly searching for ways to improve his engines. He was taken on as chief engineer at the Killingworth Colliery at the age of twenty-one, where he found a job and a patron prepared to invest in his experiments making steam-powered 'iron horses' to pull great trucks of coal to the quayside. Later, as engine-wright at the Killingworth Colliery, he had created the locomotive *Blücher* in 1814, to pull 30 tonnes up a gradient at 5 mph.

George Stephenson now persuaded Pease and his fellow shareholders to opt for a steam locomotive rather than a horse-pulled trolley. And so, on 27 September 1825, amid worldwide publicity, thousands gathered to watch Stephenson's *Locomotion* reach 15 miles per hour, hauling 700 people on its maiden voyage along the Stockton & Darlington Railway.[47] Within three months, the engine was outpacing local riders and had soon carried some 10,000 tonnes of coal, halving its price in Stockton. Within a year, seven passenger coaches were running, and within two years the shareholders were enjoying a 5 per cent dividend.

Copycat plans were soon everywhere. Indeed, between 1824 and 1825, £22 million-worth of lines (£1.32 billion in today's money)[48] were proposed, including the revolutionary Liverpool–Manchester line, designed to move not just coal but millions of pounds in weight of imported cotton to feed Manchester's 30,000 steam-powered looms.[49] Trade between the two cities then totalled some 1,000 tonnes a day, but the turnpike road offered an exhausting five-hour slog, while the canal journey, which took a couple of days, was subject to storms, freezes or low water in the summer. Lying, backed up, on Liverpool's dockside, the cotton was starting to take longer to get from Liverpool to Manchester than to cross the Atlantic. A Liverpool–Manchester wagon-way had first been proposed in 1797, but in the wake of his Stockton success, Stephenson was hired to design and build the rail line that, in September 1830, was ready to open.

The public thronged to the event. 'The town itself was never so full of strangers,' reported the *Liverpool Mercury*; 'all the inns in town were crowded to overflowing… never was there such an assemblage of rank, wealth, beauty and fashion in this neighbourhood'.[50] The carriages, decorated in silk flags, pulled out to military airs played by the 4th King's Own Regiment. To the sound of a cannon and 'See the Conquering Hero Comes', the Duke of Wellington and the Marquis and Marchioness of Salisbury stepped aboard. Amid the 'deafening plaudits' of half a million spectators, the trains set off. Seventeen miles from Liverpool, the trains stopped for water. And then disaster struck. Passengers began to disembark – straight into the path of the second ongoing train. 'An alarm being given, most of the gentleman sprang into the carriage,' but Mr Huskisson, the Liverpool MP and former President of the Board of Trade, stumbled and 'fell under the engine of the approaching carriages, the wheel of which shattered his leg'. 'Where is Mrs Huskisson?' he cried, 'I have met my death. God forgive me.' Then he passed out. Such was the anticipation of the crowds at Manchester that the party pushed on to the city, passing banners emblazoned with 'Vote by ballot' and 'No Corn Laws!', where it took refreshments in silence while the duke spent over an hour shaking hands. By the time they all arrived back in Liverpool at about seven o'clock, Huskisson was dead.

The tragedy could not, however, lessen the impact of the occasion. 'Thus ended a pageant', said the *Liverpool Mercury*, 'which for importance as to its object and grandeur in its details is admitted to have

exceeded anything ever witnessed.' And neither could it hinder the
revolution in trade that the line unleashed. Prices for moving goods
fell by nearly half. In 1830, the freight price on the canal was about
3d per ton per mile; by rail, it was just 1.67d. Within a year, the
railway was carrying 150 tonnes a day, of cotton, oil, spice, coffee,
tobacco, and thousands of pigs. By 1832, all but one of the twenty-six
Liverpool–Manchester stagecoaches had stopped. Where produce
went, passengers followed, as people hankered after the experience of
rail travel, as eulogized by the actress Fanny Kemble. She had jour-
neyed some weeks before the line had officially opened: 'you cannot
conceive what the sensation of cutting the air was; the motion is as
smooth as possible… when I closed my eyes, this sensation of flying
was quite delightful and strange beyond description'. Within three
years the line was moving 1,100 passengers a day – nearly twice as
many as the old stagecoaches conveyed. And the venture made for
some very happy shareholders; in under four months, the railway
paid a £2 dividend for every £100 share, returning nearly 10 per cent
in its first year.

Profit-seekers now surged to the railway business. Over the next six
years, entrepreneurs and engineers began haphazardly creating rail
companies to connect cities wherever they smelled a profit – encouraged by a new and crucial legal protection: the freedom to raise capital
from more than five people, protected by limited liability. Over the
course of the remaining century, railway building peaked in the three
great waves of 1837–40, 1846–50 and 1860–66. First, the main trunk
lines were built radiating from London, then came the secondary and
branch routes, fanning out like veins through the countryside.

As the railway boom gathered pace, York's leaders – and George
Hudson – began to consider their options. There was a wide sense that
the absence of factories in the city owed much to the high local price of
coal. And so in December 1833, city businessmen, lawyers and entrepreneurs came together to formulate a plan at Mrs Tomlinson's Hotel,
in Low Petergate, in a meeting chaired by James Meek, owner of York's
big glassworks (burning 1,000 tonnes of coal a year).[51] The prospectus
that emerged was very clear: coal was centre-stage: 'If Coal be supplied,
as undoubtedly it will, if the railway go forward, on very low terms,

there is nothing to prevent various manufactories being commenced at York which at present cannot exist for want of… cheap fuel.'[52]

Two alternative lines were proposed: a direct route from York to Leeds, and one to South Milford connecting with the Leeds–Selby line, and running close to local collieries and quarries. Profits, reported the prospectus, were likely to be high. Pointing to the 10, 12 or 15 per-cent dividends of other lines, it asked: 'When capital is so abundant that people know not where to place it – when the funds [consols] offer only 3½ per cent… would not such an undertaking… offer an investment, at once safe and permanent, and also yield a high rate of interest?'[53] The committee raised its capital within three weeks.

Now well connected with the city's civic leaders, and a partner in the town's new bank, George Hudson was nominated to the post of the railway's treasurer. He was soon the committee's largest investor. George Rennie was engaged to draw up a report to further the project; and yet the committee dithered, partly persuaded by both Hudson and Meek, who wanted to see how other schemes in the area fared.[54]

It was at this point that Robert Stephenson, the only son and protégé of the great engineer, stepped on stage. He was heavily involved in the North Midland Railway Company, formed in September 1835, to connect Leeds and Derby to the existing London line. Hudson may have caught wind of the concept when he met Stephenson by chance in the summer of 1834, out in Whitby where he was inspecting a property inherited from his Great Uncle Matthew.* The York committee was clearly seized by the chance to connect with the line, and thus to London. On 13 October 1835, at a Guildhall meeting, Hudson seconded the motion to build – rapidly – a 14-mile connection to the North Midland, with a capital of £200,000. Hudson was confirmed as treasurer, and Robert Stephenson was asked to prepare a report with the utmost speed.

The report, a Parliamentary bill, the raising of £370,000 capital and the formation of a new company all followed in quick succession over the first half of 1836.[55] Hudson doubled his own stake to £21,000 – 17 per cent of the new York & North Midland Railway Company – and was

---

* Peacock strongly refutes this well-established story in his book *George Hudson*, op. cit., p. 46.

elected its chairman in August 1836, at the inaugural meeting.[56] His career as a railway baron was about to begin in earnest. And so was his breakthrough in politics.

*

Hudson finally secured the election of his old associate John Lowther to Parliament in 1835, to their mutual delight. But Hudson's bribery for the cause – sending gold sovereigns in the post to reward Tory supporters[57] – was so extensive that he was summoned to a Select Committee in Westminster to answer charges. Ducking and diving through three days of questioning, he emerged unscathed only when it was revealed that the York Whig Party had behaved almost as badly. Hudson's case was dropped, and in December 1835 he confirmed his rise in prestige and power by winning election to the York Corporation.[58]

In Parliament, Lowther was able to help steer the Enabling Bill for the York & North Midland Railway through, with little opposition. It did not take Hudson long to use arguments and disagreements – for example over Sunday running – to provoke the resignation of his opponents from the board, which now was stacked with Hudson allies, including his brother-in-law, Richard Nicholson. Work began on the new line from York in April 1837; from its terminus at Tanner Row, within the city walls themselves, it would soon stretch to meet the North Midland line at Altofts.[59]

The Tory Party dominated the local York elections that year, and on 9 November 1837 they controversially elected their leader, George Hudson, as the city's lord mayor. While the *York Gazette* reported that Hudson was endorsed with 'the hearty concurrence of the citizens of York',[60] for the *Yorkshireman* it was a step too far: 'With Mr Hudson as a private individual, we have no fault to find. We have no objection that he should possess the civic honours of York; but that the Corporation and representation of this important city should be in his hand, is a thing most monstrous.'[61]

Hudson knew how to put on a good show, but he used his time in office to pursue a vindictive war of attrition against his political opponents. He was, said one opponent in 1839, a 'thorough party man', who could not help 'considering every political opponent a personal enemy', and who used 'his rank, influence and money' to crush them.[62] Yet, Hudson knew the sense of making more friends than enemies; he entertained on a lavish scale with banquets and feasts throughout the city; indeed, his popularity was such that despite the rules of the York Corporation, he was elected lord mayor again in 1838, in time to preside over the opening of the York & North Midland Railway on Wednesday, 29 May 1839, a day that 'was as favourable for the occasion as could have been possibly desired'.[63]

*

The York & North Midland line was, in truth, but a small piece in the gigantic British railway jigsaw now taking shape, as the four great skeleton lines that connected up the country began to open. The route of today's West Coast Mainline was laid with the 112-mile London–Birmingham line and the 78-mile Grand Junction connecting Birmingham to Manchester and Liverpool. The Great Western Railway, designed by Isambard Kingdom Brunel, connected London and Bristol, while the fourth, the London & Southampton, became the first line running south of London.

The Grand Junction was the first great piece of the puzzle – although the initial attempt at a Parliamentary bill went down with the government collapse over the Great Reform Bill. Once authorized, in 1833, its design was reshaped to circumnavigate James Watt's Birmingham estate. But it ran from the city 82 miles north-west to connect with the Stephensons' Liverpool & Manchester Railway.

The Great Western was also underway in 1833, when a group of Bristol businessmen in January appointed Brunel for the job – by just a single vote. Amid the usual objections to the line (John Keate, headmaster of Eton, warned that his scholars would be tempted to use it to go to London and fall into 'degrading dissipation'), Brunel produced a beautiful route of easy gradients, terminating in London at Paddington. It became the country's fastest railway.* Renowned for its high-design

---

* You could travel from London to Oxford in little over an hour.

specifications, its elegance and its engineering showmanship, the Great Western cost a fortune; the 1.75-mile box tunnel near Bath alone cost £1 million.

The London–Birmingham line was, however, quite simply the engineering feat of its age, with a price tag of £3.5 million. Its surveying was largely conducted at night to avoid landowners and their violent servants, and at its peak of construction, 20,000 workers toiled for five years on a line that included nine tunnels and three long cuttings.[64] When it opened in June 1838, the journey time between London and Birmingham was cut to just six hours. A little over a year later, the first section in the London & Southern opened with a line from London to Basingstoke; it finally reached Southampton in 1840.[*]

Amid this railway fever, Hudson was determined to profit. Within a year, Robert Stephenson's plan, as sketched out for the directors of the York & North Midland, was complete. On 30 June 1840, the simultaneous opening of the completed line and the Midland Counties Railway created a direct rail link from York to London, a journey that could be completed in one uninterrupted stretch of fewer than ten hours.[65] Four trains ran the route in each direction, daily.

Fresh from their success, Stephenson and Hudson, now lauded by the *York Herald* as 'the able and indefatigable Chairman of the Directors', immediately began plans to expand. [66] Both of them saw a big future business in moving not only goods but also people, and not simply for work but for leisure too. So they began work on a scheme for a railway from York to Scarborough, 43 miles away – which Hudson was confident could soon become the 'Brighton of the north' – and then onward to Whitby.[67]

Hudson announced his plans at the annual meeting of the York & North Midland in 1840, where the shareholders, delighted with their 6 per cent dividend, were more than happy to permit Hudson to pay a surveyor at the company's expense to assess the York–Whitby line.[68] But, Hudson had also spotted the threat now posed by his regional rival, the Leeds–Selby Railway Company, which threatened to corner an east–west route linking Liverpool, Manchester, Leeds and Hull. When

---

[*] 40 per cent of the capital for this line was raised from Manchester businessmen.

the Leeds–Selby Company refused to sell out to Hudson, he managed to negotiate a lease of their line instead for thirty-one years, with a later option to purchase, beginning on 9 November 1840.[69]

Already, early cracks in Hudson's methods were beginning to show. Within two days of his lease deal, misfortune arrived at the junction of the York and Leeds–Selby lines when a freight train and a passenger train collided, killing two passengers. Widespread condemnation of the company ensued, when it was revealed that one of the train drivers suffered from poor eyesight.[70] Hudson's financial management was to prove just as reckless. His strategy was simple: high dividends, paid by any means necessary. In 1840, Hudson was able to tell his shareholders that the York & North Midland Railway had delivered a 'first'. 'He believed', said the reports, that 'they had already accomplished more than any other company, as he was not aware of any other which, after a partial opening, had paid a dividend.'[71] A 21-shilling dividend had been declared six months before the line was fully open. Six months later, another 24 shillings was announced. Yet when asked where it came from, Hudson promptly replied: 'out of… capital'. In January 1841, more was declared, 'such a dividend that no company in the kingdom would excel it'.[72]

A few, though, began to express their doubts. One shareholder, Thomas Laycock, said the accounts were confused; they included, he said, 'a number of items jumbled together which men like himself could not understand'. But when another shareholder, Mr Coates, suggested appointing auditors, Hudson was provoked into a furious response: 'If Mr Coates doubted the competency of the directors,' Hudson stormed, 'he had better move a resolution to that effect.'[73] Rallying to his defence, fellow directors told the meeting that Hudson was 'the best railway manager in the kingdom'.[74]

Hudson's biggest challenge now, however, was neither suspicious shareholders nor scrupulous safety-inspectors. It was the shifting strategy of his competition. In 1841, the Board of Trade finally recommended a route from London to Edinburgh, which ran along the west of England rather than along the eastern side where Hudson's railways lay.[75] There was a caveat. If a line in the west between Lancaster and Carlisle were to be delayed and the line between Darlington and Edinburgh completed, then an eastern line would be preferred. The report was the starting gun for the race to build a line from London to Edinburgh. It was a race George Hudson intended to win.

*

During the 1830s, and backed by £1 million, the Great North of England Company had made a little progress in building the railways north of York, reaching Darlington, but had not managed the final link to Newcastle, and by August 1837 it had effectively run out of money.[76] It was, said the *Railway Times*, 'one of the worst-managed undertakings in the kingdom'.[77] Hudson knew he would have to move fast if he wanted to seize control of the route to Scotland. There was a competitor – the Northern Union – waiting in the wings to swoop on the exhausted Great North. Hudson quickly convened the directors of the six railway companies that had bits of line that could be connected into one through-route to Newcastle, and he proposed a final piece of the jigsaw: a new line from Darlington to South Durham, to cost between £120,000 and £130,000.[78] To raise the cash, he proposed, in September 1841, a 'simple but audacious' scheme, whereby a 'new company shall be formed', issuing shares in the new line to the shareholders of the eight companies involved in its construction, together with a guaranteed dividend of 6 per cent.

The potential profits of the venture were enormous. For Robert Stephenson, it had the added advantage of rescuing him from a disastrous investment in one of the companies. By December 1841, shareholders had agreed, and the Newcastle & Darlington Junction Railway was born. With a Parliamentary bill* in place for it in July 1842, Hudson moved swiftly to put his placemen into the new company's key positions.

In the archives of the National Railway Museum in York lies an intriguing petition, campaigning for the bill's approval. It affords a fascinating insight into how the skills Hudson acquired in politics as an

---

* The bill transferred to the N&DJ, the Great North of England's power to build a line to Darlington.

election fixer most likely equipped him for the business of organizing petitioners for his campaigns to build railway tracks and to take over railway companies. On a magnificent undated piece of vellum, from the 'Undersigned Inhabitants of the City of York and its Vicinity', the petition notes the proposed York and Newcastle Railway Company's goal as 'to improve their mainline of railway and to make certain branches in the County of Durham'. It adds that the City of York has not only enjoyed a population that 'has of late years increased considerably', but is 'a convenient town for travellers on account of the number of railways going from thence to different parts of the kingdom'. The line through York and along the east coast, linking London and Edinburgh, therefore deserves to be 'as perfect and as complete as possible'. It concludes with a plea that the 'bill may pass into law'.

By 1842–43, the first great phase of railway mania was coming to an end. After growth of 30 per cent a year, the country's rail network boasted 1,800 miles of line.[*] The lines that today make up the West Coast Mainline were broadly in place. But the east-coast line was not yet started, and here was the gap that Hudson now set out to fill with a further big, bold step: the consolidation of the principal Midlands railway companies.

In 1842, Hudson had been invited to lead an investigation into the disappointing profits of the North Midland line, running from Derby to Leeds. He promptly recommended slashing the company's operating budget, using cheaper materials, and cutting jobs and wages,[79] arguing that 'the most intelligent servants of the company' all agreed that the cuts were practical.[80] In some alarm, the directors disagreed. But the shareholders had spotted their chance to make a profit. A note issued in November 1842 observed that a company connection with Hudson would be good for the share price. On the promise that Hudson could deliver the same profit levels as for his own firm, the North Midland's directors were prevailed upon to resign, and George Hudson was moved in as its chairman.

By August 1843, Hudson had quickly pursued his advantage, and was soon persuading the North Midland's shareholders of the virtue of

---

[*] This had increased from 250 miles in 1838.

merger with two competing, but struggling, lines: the Midland Counties Railway and the Birmingham & Derby Junction Railway. He was not without opponents. The Midland Counties' chairman, Captain Dicey, led the counter-attack, arguing that the proposal for amalgamation was a 'blind bargain' and 'a parody on the old fable of the two foolish animals who quarrelled about the division of the oyster and appealed to the monkey which ate the whole oyster, and gravely returned to the disputants the shells'.[81] But Hudson, claiming that he could save the company £25,000 annually[82] plus a dividend of 5 per cent, and arguing his expertise as 'a great authority in matters of economy', won the day at an electrifying shareholders' meeting on 21 September 1843. George Hudson was voted in as chairman[83] of the new, merged Midland Railway – and the country began to talk of the new 'Railway Napoleon'.[84]

Parliament approved the amalgamation on 10 May 1844, and, without faltering for a moment, Hudson pressed on. He presented a plan to buy the Leeds–Selby companies along with the faltering Durham Junction Railway, and to build the new line to Scarborough, first proposed some years earlier. The plans were approved at the next shareholders' meeting.[85] But now Hudson's rapid roll-up of the east-coast lines confronted their stiffest challenge, from both public opinion and Parliament.

Within a year, Hudson's empire, run on the cheap, was suffering high-profile accidents. In 1843, a passenger had been killed when the inexperienced driver of one train crashed at full force into another. Elsewhere, Queen Victoria's cousin, Prince George of Cambridge, was mildly injured.[86] Hudson's network was developing a reputation for being the most dangerous in England and shareholders' unrest was quelled only with more high dividends.

Parliament's challenge was more serious. The government had finally become concerned about the random proliferation of private railways, many of which hurt the potential of important strategic connections. And so, in February 1844, a young up-and-coming politician called William Gladstone established a Select Committee to consider the question of government regulation or ownership of railway lines.[87] The resulting bill, proposing wide state control, was regarded by Hudson

as a looming disaster that needed to be resisted. In a high-profile cam-
paign, it was effectively neutered. In the end, the final draft of the 1844
Railway Act posed little threat to Hudson's empire or his ambitions.[88]
The Railway King was not about to be dethroned – not just yet.

*

On 18 June 1844, George Hudson experienced one of his finest hours:
the grand opening of the Newcastle & Darlington Junction Railway.
At five o'clock in the morning a special train left London's Euston
Station carrying the chairman of the London & Birmingham, and
drew into Gateshead at 2.25pm. The Thames and the Tyne were now
connected by rail, fulfilling George Stephenson's long-cherished ambition to see the day when 'the mails would be carried by steam power
from London to his native Newcastle'.[89] At a magnificent dinner that
evening, for 500 people in Newcastle's Assembly Rooms, guests marvelled at the sight of the morning newspapers, published in London
and carrying speeches delivered in the House of Commons not twelve
hours before.[90]

And yet, with every success came a challenge. Spying Hudson's
happy profits, his rivals once more conspired to create a challenger line.
In May 1844, the London & York Railway Company proposed a competing, and much more direct, route from London to York, which would
significantly cut journey times.[91] Hudson knew that he had to respond.
Alerting the directors of the Midland Railway to the danger, he outlined
a counter-plan to build a new line in the path of his rivals. Such were his
skills of persuasion that the directors immediately voted £2.5 million to
turn ideas into action.[92]

Over the course of 1843 to 1844, George Hudson had become a
national figure. And now he wanted more – more firepower than mere
money could provide to stop his rivals. So he set his sights on a seat in
Parliament. When the MP for Sunderland, Earl Grey, suddenly died in
July 1845, Hudson saw his chance. But there was a problem, for
Sunderland had not been a Tory seat since 1832, and when the ballots
opened on 14 August 1845, leading figures in the town were convinced
that Hudson could never win. The Whigs fought him with all the

vituperation of Victorian campaigns. Posters appeared adorned with
the ghost of 'old Botterill', referring to 'the tin thou so "adventitiously"
got'.[93] The press, at least, was on his side, eulogizing Hudson as 'the
author of his own fame', whose magic 'touch has revolutionised the
world', and concluding that 'such men are formed to rule and direct
the energies of others'.[94] Hudson had taken the precaution of position-
ing himself as the saviour of Sunderland industry, and in particular of
the Durham & Sunderland Railway and the Wearmouth Dock.[95] And
when the votes were counted, he had won.

*

George Hudson took his Parliamentary seat on 22 January 1846, and he
promptly established court in London.

He was already a very rich man by the time of his election success;
now, he quickly began spending to gild his glittering reputation,
buying the opulent Albert Gate East – then the largest private home
in London – along with a portfolio of country estates, including
Newby Park near the River Swale and Londesborough Park in east
Yorkshire. Soon, he began throwing lavish parties, to the delight and
somewhat morbid curiosity of London's social elite, who enjoyed a
good deal of entertainment from Hudson's wife, Elizabeth, who was
mocked endlessly for her affectations and vulgar sense of style.[96] Lady
Dorothy Nevill labelled her 'the Mrs Malaprop of her day', and
Elizabeth's pronouncements, such as 'People in Turkey should do as
Turkeys did', were widely circulated.[97]

In Parliament, by contrast, Hudson was in his element, finding a
ready home as a prominent member of the Tory Protectionists, opposed
to free trade. In Sunderland, he set to work transforming the town's
dock; in York, he was re-elected lord mayor for the third time; and in
the City of London, his ambitious plans to consolidate England's mish-
mash of railway companies found ready support as long as the dividends
stayed high. His London timetable was packed – he would rise in the
early hours of the morning, spend the day on Parliamentary or railway
work, and entertain until late into the night. But it took its toll. Hudson's
appreciation of fine wine and spirits soon became a dependency; the sly

jabs at his intoxication and his confused interjections in Parliament began to multiply, and were soon a running joke.[98]

Hard at work in London's social stratosphere, Hudson worked hardest of all at blocking his competition and the London to York Bill, which would give his railway rivals the power to build. But his power was limited. In an embarrassing, and extremely public, defeat, the bill for the competing line became law on 28 June 1846.[99] Hudson wasted no time in responding to the new challenger. He pushed through his buy-out of the Selby & Hull Railway, integrated links between Birmingham, Gloucester and Bristol into his Midland lines, and successfully propelled a Parliamentary bill to connect Newcastle and Berwick.[100] Crucially, Hudson had seen the chance to build his own faster line to London, by connecting his lines to the capital through a currently failing network, the Eastern Counties Railway.

The Eastern Counties was notoriously inefficient and dangerous, and from 1844 Hudson had been agitating among its shareholders to secure the chairmanship. There was an appetite for him. In early 1845, the directors had disappointed shareholders yet again with a 2 per cent dividend, prompting complaints that 'they were now assembled after nine years' operations, to receive less than any other company in existence'.[101] One of their number, James Scott, began to demand that Hudson be invited to join the board: 'Let them [the directors] look to what Mr Hudson has done... who had displayed so much energy in the North Midland Railway.'[102]

In the National Railway Museum's magnificent archives is some of the evidence of George Hudson's elaborate campaign. On a wonderful large piece of parchment is written the petition – a plea signed by J. Scott, 'Chairman of the Committee of Shareholders', for Mr Hudson to come to their rescue. Accompanying it are the signatures of hundreds of others from around the country, including Manchester merchants, Cambridge professors, bankers from London, cotton dealers from the Midlands and Southampton traders. 'Urgently desirous [that] the George Hudson Esquire MP should join the directors', the petitioners demanded a special general meeting, 'to invite most urgently Mr Hudson to undertake the Office of Director of this Company, so that the capabilities of the line may be fully developed and all just grounds of complaint on the part of the public removed'. A delegation was dispatched to Hudson to plead he take the chairmanship, which he accepted. On 13 October 1845, he came to the special shareholder meeting, above a tavern, like a conquering hero; upon his entrance, reported the *Railway Times*, 'the Hon. Gentleman was received with a loud and long-continued burst of cheering from one of the most densely crowded meetings we have attended'.[103]

Over the next two years, Hudson drove his plans forward. True, the number of accidents on the Eastern Counties Railway remained high: in the first half of 1846, fifteen incidents accounted for a quarter of all the country's railway casualties in the year. But elsewhere there were successes. By the summer of 1847, Hudson had consolidated control of the main lines from York to the Scottish Borders with the opening of his Newcastle–Berwick railway.[104] He created new Eastern Counties branch lines, from Ely to Peterborough, St Ives to Cambridge, and March to Wisbech, acquiring new locomotives and laying electric telegraph cables. Queen Victoria, who appeared 'greatly pleased with the evident care which had been taken to promote her comfort', was conveyed in some style on the Eastern Counties line from London to Cambridge. At the Eastern Counties shareholders' meeting, the *Railway Times* reported: 'As the Chairman entered the room, the entire body of proprietors rose to receive him – a complement we have never yet seen paid at any railway meeting.'[105] Soon, Hudson announced, the Leicester–Peterborough line would be open, and the Eastern Counties would be 'in communication with the whole of the north of England'.

By 1848, the Railway King was managing over a third of all rail lines in Britain, equivalent to more than 1,400 miles of track, up from a mere 174 miles in 1839.[106] And all the while, politics had continued to smile on him: in 1847, he won an easy re-election in Sunderland.[107] But the cracks in the crown were beginning to grow.

*

Over the years, questions about Hudson's book-keeping had begun to proliferate. In the summer of 1846, as he negotiated the purchase of the Leeds & Bradford Railway, Hudson had had to buy off shareholders with great dividends, as questions arose about the apparent conflict of interest arising from his chairmanship of multiple firms.[108] In York, he experienced a different sort of setback. He had championed a bridge for his own railway over the River Ouse at Lendal to help block a rival line; but when he suggested that the city – rather than the company – shoulder the cost, he was forced to back down by a campaign led by his local nemesis, George Leeman.

The stock-market crash of 1847 exacerbated the pressure. Half-finished railway tracks were soon abandoned, credit was becoming near impossible to secure, and a general collapse of business was destroying the railway's traffic – and profits.[109] George Stephenson, Hudson's greatest ally and friend in the industry, died in August 1848, and for most of that summer Hudson was confined to his bed as he battled through painful attacks of angina and gout.[110]

That year, Arthur Smith's devastating tirade, *The Bubble of the Age, or, The Fallacies of Railway Investment, Railway Accounts and Railway Dividends*, singled out two of Hudson's firms – the Eastern Counties and the York & North Midlands – as companies that appeared to be paying dividends out of capital rather than profits.[111] Hudson was forced to offer answers, and when he admitted to one Midland shareholder that he had inflated dividends on the back of confidence in the next year's profits, investors were outraged.[112] With plummeting profits, Hudson could no longer fall back on his tried-and-tested approach of higher dividends.

By 1848, Hudson accepted that his chairmanship of four great competing railway companies was unsustainable. And so, he abandoned the struggling Eastern Counties and the Midland, deciding instead to focus on creating his London–Scotland route through the York & North Midland, and the York, Newcastle & Berwick companies.[113] But four shareholder meetings in early 1849 signalled investors' ebbing confidence. When the shareholders of the York, Newcastle & Berwick Railway met in February 1849, Robert Prance, who was also a member of the Stock Exchange, announced that his inspection of the accounts revealed manipulation of the share price by someone within the company.[114] Off guard, Hudson was unable to explain. The enraged shareholders voted in a committee of inquiry, chaired by Prance, to investigate the charges.

It was the beginning of the end for the 'Railway Napoleon', as the shocking breadth of fraud was now exposed. From January 1845 onwards it seemed, no accounts had been sent to company directors that had not been altered in some way first, in order to inflate the level of dividends.[115] The Eastern Counties accounts had gone to an examining committee, but because both Hudson and his chief accountant, David Waddington, had both sat on the committee, the other directors had not bothered to assemble. When committees of enquiry were first proposed, Hudson had warned that any statements relating to railway companies were, in the current market conditions, bound to depress share prices still further.

Thus, the shareholders of the York, Newcastle & Berwick were the first to impugn Hudson's management. In March 1849, the newspapers carried stories of the rowdy shareholders' meeting the previous month, in which Hudson appeared to have admitted wrong-doing. 'The charge publicly made against Mr Hudson', ran the reports, 'is that he being chairman of the York Newcastle and Berwick Railway, had sold to the Company, 2,800 shares in the Great North of England line at prices averaging 5 pounds per share above what they might have been bought at in the market.'[116] The deal would have netted Hudson some £14,000. Worse, said the correspondents, 'he did not attempt to deny or palliate the charge'. *The Times* concluded: 'All things would seem to portend that this reign is over. The bladder shows symptoms of collapse… Mr Hudson however may yet save himself if his hands be clean and his conscience void of offence. We sincerely hope it is so.'

Further enquiries discovered that the company had subscribed to 3,000 shares in the Sunderland Dock project that Hudson had driven through, and in addition had taken 2,345 shares for Hudson, payment for which was kept hidden from the company. Even more seriously, the committee concluded that when the Newcastle & Berwick line was created, its initial issue of 42,000 shares was secretly inflated by 14,000 additional shares, which were sold netting Hudson a profit of as much as £145,704. A further 590 shares (worth £4,000) were taken in the line's extension, without any approvals, and the accounts presented since 1845 were out to the tune of £75,000. It was a fraud that 'the committee hope and believe to be without a parallel in the history of public companies'.[117]

Hudson's defence was weak. 'The risk was mine and I was entitled to the advantages which ultimately arose to myself and the other guaranteeing parties.'[118] At the end of February 1849, Hudson decided at the last minute to send to the shareholders' meeting, at the London Tavern, in his place his loyal deputy chairman, Waddington; but he was received with hoots of derision. Outraged, the York, Newcastle & Berwick shareholders appointed another committee of enquiry, which was stunned to hear the scale and negligence of Hudson's accounting. When asked if he had ever altered the accounts, after the company accountant had finalized them, Hudson admitted that he 'may have added a thousand or two to the next account'.[119] But when asked if he had ever added £10,000 or £40,000, he replied: 'I cannot exactly say what may have been the largest sum I carried to the following account.'[120]

It soon transpired that Hudson and Waddington were not only paying dividends out of capital, but doctoring the accounts so that the dividends looked legitimately earned. Waddington had received £2,000 for services rendered in unauthorized payments, and another £9,000 had disappeared in Parliamentary expenses in a fund under Waddington's personal control.[121] One local newspaper observed:

> For four years, thirteen millions of capital have been at the mercy of Mssrs Hudson and Waddington with which they actually did as they chose, making and unmaking dividends, traffic, capital and revenue... disbursing sums of which they refused to render any account, pocketing cheques for which there is no authority.[122]

It was now only a matter of time before Parliament intervened. On 17 May 1849, F. W. Charteris, a Whig MP with a keen interest in the Eastern Counties investigation, demanded an enquiry into Hudson's alleged bribery of MPs, presenting a petition on behalf of John Spark and others 'complaining of the conduct of George Hudson, esquire, a Member of the House, and Chairman of the Eastern Counties Railway Company, and praying for [an] inquiry, and that he may be expelled from being a Member of the House'.[123] When Hudson rose to defend himself, followed by David Waddington, he offered the House only a stunted, unconvincing performance. 'I have no other explanation to give,' he concluded. 'I repeat that I totally deny that the alterations of the figures which is mentioned in the report were in my handwriting, or that I altered them at all in any way whatever.'[124] Hudson was heard in silence. The very next day, his brother-in-law, Richard Nicholson, unable to cope with the allegations that he too had been involved in share fixing and profiteering, drank half a pint of port and threw himself into the River Ouse.[125]

When the Commons' committee reported, it revealed that Hudson had used York, Newcastle & Berwick company money to buy shares in his own name and had diverted money, intended to compensate land-owners, into his own bank accounts.*[126] Hudson's liabilities were now fast approaching £1 million. In desperation, he sold his beloved Londesborough Park estate, and without any admission of guilt agreed to pay £200,000 in compensation to the York, Berwick & Newcastle Railway.[127]

The once lionized Hudson was now widely mocked. Cartoon books appeared, such as Alfred Crowquill's *How He Reigned and How He Mizzled*, packed with sketches of the great railway baron who 'leaves his old 'ooman [sic] to look after the shop' in York, portraying the Railway King as a great spider in the centre of a web of lines. He was depicted as the owner of a great house in London, where all society comes to enjoy his *soirées*, but who keeps his accounts by pouring sacks of coins into a chest, while a flamboyant and large Mrs Hudson, in a grand pink ball dress and feathers, looks on.

Hudson could still, at least, count on his local, loyal voters to support him. In the National Railway Museum is a vellum petition from the 'Electors of the Borough of Sunderland' to Mr Hudson, sending a message 'deprecating the unjust attacks and unmeasured abuse to which you have been recently exposed' and declaring their 'unabated confidence' in their MP. 'We are fully persuaded', they went on, 'that the aspersions which have been so unsparingly cast upon your reputation are more to be ascribed to the disappointed feelings of too sanguine

---

* Ironically, it also revealed William Cash as one of the more prominent members of a highly dubious railway scheme promoted by Hudson. Beaumont, *The Railway King*, op. cit., p. 130.

speculators and the excitement consequent upon the temporarily depressed state of the important concerns over which you preside.' The list of signatures, hundreds of names long, was headed by the lord mayor, and followed by the Justices of the Peace. Hudson remained a political organizer to his fingertips. It was crucial for him now to remain a Member of Parliament, for while the House of Commons was in session he could not be arrested for debt. To his considerable relief, he was re-elected in 1852.

But the pressures of his creditors only grew. In a fit of bravado, when the York & North Midland Company offered him a settlement deal of just £50,000 pounds, Hudson rejected it, maintaining his innocence. The company promptly sued, bringing three cases to court, which concluded that Hudson's liabilities topped £70,000.[128] He had no choice but to sell Newby Park and lease out his London home. But the final act was now upon him. In a third case at the Court of Chancery, Hudson somehow managed to reveal that he had indeed bribed MPs to obtain favourable rulings for his companies. The ensuing public outcry was only diverted by the advent of the Crimean War. By the autumn of 1854, it was clear that Hudson was sinking fast. Only Parliamentary immunity was keeping him from bankruptcy and debtors' prison.

In a last throw of the dice, and looking to the safety of the Continent between Parliamentary sessions, he proposed a new railway line in north-eastern Spain.[129] Hudson sailed in the summer of 1855, but his gout enforced a three-month confinement to bed, and his absences from Sunderland, now extended, hurt his electoral appeal. In the 1857 General Election he only just survived by giving a promise to raise his game.[130]

Two years later, it was election time again. In his attempt to save his seat, Hudson tried to rescue the flagging Sunderland Dock Company – which had opened with a flourish in 1850 – with an appeal for subsidies from the River Wear Commissions. But his proposition was laughed out of the Commons by MPs who refused to countenance public funds for a private company to operate on rules already agreed. Shareholders grew angry at their meagre dividends, and Sunderland's support for Hudson began to evaporate. Despite his frantic promises now to embrace electoral reform and free trade, which he had once scorned, Hudson's luck had run out. He was trounced in the vote, polling third place with just 790 votes of the 4,000 cast.[131]

Out of Parliament, and facing the very real prospect of incarceration for his debts, the defeated candidate summoned all his remaining dignity, made a gracious speech in Sunderland – and fled to France.

*

At his peak, George Hudson was a commanding presence. 'Mr Hudson's personal appearance', wrote one observer:

> is calculated to strike if not absolutely to command. There is a massiveness in the proportions of his bodily frame, evidently hereditary in his stock, and inclining to symmetric development. His head is large and scantily supplied with gray hairs; his forehead broad and somewhat elevated. The features of his face… convey to a casual observer the impression of harshness of disposition.[132]

Now, he was, according to Charles Dickens, a 'shabby man', almost unrecognizable in his poverty.[133] For the five years after his electoral defeat, Hudson eked out a simple but modestly comfortable life in exile, shuttling around the lesser hotels and boarding houses of Calais, Boulogne, Paris and various parts of Germany.[134] Some speculated that he was living a life of continental leisure with compensation received for his failed Spanish railway venture. But whatever his current straitened circumstances, nothing could stop Hudson plotting a return to power, prestige – and Parliamentary immunity.

He now sought his brother's help to return to the Commons. Charles Hudson had become, over the years, a prominent and well-liked Member of Parliament for Whitby, and George now planned to stand for election there too. When Charles died, in December 1864, George Hudson appealed to Whitby's Conservatives for their support. To the surprise of many, he got it, and as the election of July 1865 approached, Hudson launched a vigorous campaign. On Monday, 19 June, he spoke to Whitby crowds, declaring to a sympathetic, cheering audience:

The fact is, gentlemen, I have been made a scapegoat for the sins of the people, but I have borne all the obloquy showered upon me with much courage and strength of mind and my innocence has been a great support to me in the persecutions I have undergone. I can tell all my enemies and my detractors that I can bear their malice, however intense, and however long continued, with the same *sang-froid* and with the same resignation as I have endured attacks from much abler men.[135]

Nevertheless, and despite the deep unpopularity of the Liberal incumbent, Harry Thomas, victory would elude Hudson once more. And the consequences were fast to follow. On Sunday, 9 July 1865, he was shaken from his bed by the knocking on the door of the sheriff's officer from York, who arrested him and carted him off by the first available train to the debtors' prison in York Castle.[136] Two days before polling day, Hudson was no longer looking forward to reacquiring Parliamentary immunity, but rather the disgrace and discomfort of a three-month prison sentence.

When he was released, in October 1865, after the sympathetic colliery-owner George Elliot paid the debts for which he had been held,[137] Hudson immediately fled back to France. It was a brief escape. He returned to England in 1866 to contest his court case with the North Eastern Railway – only to be arrested once again, outside the Carlton Club in Pall Mall.[138]

This time, it took Hudson three weeks to secure release, on the grounds that he had a right to consult a solicitor, and once again he headed for the Continent. In his absence, the court battle with the North Eastern Railway rumbled on. Hudson won a brief respite when the Master of Rolls ruled that his outstanding debts now totalled just £14,000, not the £40,000 the company wanted; but it was a short-lived victory. The company appealed to the House of Lords, which, three years later – in March 1869 – ruled that the North Eastern was owed not just the original debt but interest and legal costs too, making a staggering total of £107,000 (somewhere between £58 million and £93 million in today's money) – which Hudson could never hope to pay.[139]

His darkest hour was not, however, without respite. Elliot, the col-liery-owner who had stood by him in 1865, raised a subscription to alleviate the pains of his poverty. On receiving the bank notes, tears sprang to Hudson's eyes, and he reportedly told the messenger: 'I would have been a better man today if I had never left that shop in York.'[140] Ironically, Parliament too was about to help. On 1 January 1870, the Abolition of Imprisonment for Debt Act passed, finally allowing Hudson to return to England without the fear of prison. He was reunited with Elizabeth to begin a new life at Churton Street, in London's Pimlico.[141] In April he commenced a small tour of the north to thank the friends who had saved him. At the Sunderland Docks, he was greeted with banners, flags and cheering crowds.[142] In London, he finally reached a settlement with the North Eastern Railway, and on 17 July 1871 he and Elizabeth celebrated their golden wedding anniversary.

Hudson continued to make small trips around the country, but on Saturday, 9 December 1871 he was forced home to London by a terrible attack of angina. He briefly recovered, only to suffer a massive heart attack on Wednesday, 13 December.[143] George Hudson died the following morning, aged seventy-one, in the arms of his youngest son William.

Four days before Christmas 1871, Hudson's body was carried from London on the railway he had built to York, and from there on to the family vault at Scrayingham, where, in a modest but well-attended funeral, he was laid to rest.[144] His will, when it was opened, was not long. Once one of the wealthiest men in Britain, he left a meagre £100 to each of his surviving sons, George and William.[145]

Hudson's legacy to the country was, by contrast, immense. Together, the new rail networks he did so much to create contributed more for the British economy than the British Empire. Some estimate it was a boost to the national economy worth around 10 per cent of Gross National Product.* Crucially, the revolution equipped a generation of investors

---

* The net costs of Empire are of course much debated. Michael Edelstein estimates that the net benefits could be as high as 5.7–6.8 per cent of national income in 1913 – much less than the value of the technical breakthrough of the railways, which may have been worth as much as 10 per cent of GNP. Edelstein, *Overseas Investment in the Age of High Imperialism: The UK, 1830–1914* (Colombia University Press, 1982), p. 215.

and engineers with the expertise required to export the capital and know-how to build railway systems all over the planet. By the outbreak of the First World War, a quarter of the £4.2 billion of British capital invested abroad was tied up in foreign railways.[146]

8

GEORGE CADBURY

A revolutionary in ethical enterprise

On Wednesday, 21 May 1919, six months after the end of the First World War, King George V and Queen Mary arrived in Birmingham, to tour their kingdom's second city. The weather was glorious. Following a morning spent opening the new Children's Hospital and decorating war veterans at the Town Hall, the royal couple stepped into their carriages to be escorted to Birmingham's southern suburbs by the city's Chief Constable and the mounted police. They were off to meet one of the country's most remarkable entrepreneurs, and to see for themselves the extraordinary fruits of his life's work.

As they pulled into Bournville Lane, the three royal carriages were greeted by the deafening cheers of 3,000 people lined up in the stands, and the British Empire's greatest chocolate-maker, George Cadbury, welcomed his sovereign to his 'factory in the garden'. Awaiting the king and queen was a reception guarded by injured Bournville veterans. While the Bournville Band played the national anthem, the royal party crossed the wooden bridge into the Girls' Recreation Grounds to meet some of the 4,000 Bournville women, dressed in white, waving handkerchiefs and singing 'Now Pray We For Our Country'.

A short stop at the almshouses followed, before it was time for the factory's oldest foreman to present some gifts. 'The Queen's Box', explained the *Bournville Works Magazine*, was 'of silver brocade, containing a selection in a setting of mauve and silver', while the king received a selection of chocolates dressed in 'fawn coloured silk, containing an assortment the colour scheme of which was chocolate-brown and gold'.[1]

Although the coaches were now waiting impatiently to depart, 'the queen expressed a desire to inspect more closely the village in which she has been interested so long'. 'It is understood', explained the Cadbury's company correspondent, 'that for many years past the queen has preserved cuttings and views of Bournville… realising long before public opinion was aroused that the health and happiness of the people depended on their home surroundings.' Here, the king and queen could see at first hand that the 'lilacs, laburnums, and other flowering shrubs in the gardens were at their best, and the front gardens were gay with spring flowers… [not] excelled in any village in England'.

Earlier that morning, in his speech at the Town Hall, King George had explained why Bournville was so important:

> Do not forget that the experience of war has taught us that its sufferings and sorrows have developed many noble qualities, foremost amongst which are the sinking of class differences and the realisation of common brotherhood… May I express the hope that in making your plans you will not merely aim at securing bright and healthy homes, but also provide ample facilities for recreation… They provide air space for the city, beautify it, and make for the happiness and health of the children.

There were, perhaps, few places in the king's empire that better exemplified his words than Bournville. For George Cadbury had created not simply a 'factory in the garden' but a new, model community like no other. It was, as the *Melbourne Age* had put it nearly a decade before, 'as important to England as a dreadnought'.*

That afternoon, George Cadbury was modesty itself. He had removed his hat as he walked with his sovereign through his gardens, and when the queen asked the eighty-three-year-old businessman to put it back on, he again demurred. Even an order from the king could not persuade him; only his wife Elizabeth's command to 'Put your hat

---

* 'Dreadnoughts' were the powerful iron battleships being built for the Royal Navy during the arms race against Imperial Germany, and which caught the public's patriotic imagination in the decade before the First World War.

on, George!'[2] did the trick. Yet Cadbury's achievement was anything but
modest, as the newspapers confirmed, two days later, on Friday 23 May.
'Big Cocoa Combine' ran the headlines, beneath which ran the story
that Cadbury's would complete the take-over of its oldest competitor,
J. S. Fry.[3] George Cadbury was no longer simply the nation's leading
ethical entrepreneur; he was now indisputably the British Empire's
greatest chocolate-maker. And the key to his success was his roots in
England's Quaker tradition.

*

The Cadburys hailed from England's south-west, where the place-name
Cada's burgh can still be found across Devon and Somerset. George's
first recorded ancestor was probably William de Cadeberi, of Newmarch,
who held land under Henry II in 1166, and whose descendants included
rebels, pirates, at least five vicars, and two centuries'-worth of wool
merchants trading from Uffculme. It was there, in the reign of Charles
II, that a certain John Cadbury along with his brothers and his wife,
Hannah Tapper, first joined George Fox's Society of Friends.

Amid the maelstrom of religious experimenters in the years after the
English Civil War, George Fox (1624–91) stood out as a prodigious
preacher and accomplished organizer, his progress unimpeded by stints
in prison. The son of a Lincolnshire weaver, Fox left home in the 1640s
at the age of nineteen, in spiritual crisis, and began preaching four years
later. 'God has visibly clothed him,' wrote his later contemporary
William Penn, the founder of Pennslyvania, 'with a divine preference
and authority, and indeed his very presence expressed a religious
majesty.'[4]

Fox believed that in every man there is a seed of God and that
knowledge of God came through direct communication with His spirit.
What mattered most, in Fox's eyes, was nearness to God, not observance of form or conformity to doctrine. This disregard for the tradition
and authority of the established Church inspired Fox's belief that tithe
payments were illegitimate, and soon Fox and his followers were seen
almost as outlaws. Years of conflict, imprisonment and persecution followed, including a bar on Friends – or 'Quakers' as they became known,

in a reference to 'trembling' before God – from entering the universities, the military, politics and public service. Yet such was the Friends' appeal that by 1680 their ranks had swollen to 60,000, and crucial to their fortunes, the Quakers' organization bound families close together. Quakers met in a pattern of monthly, quarterly and annual meetings and barred marriage outside the Society. Soon, extensive, well-connected, like-minded family groups had taken shape, sewn together with high levels of trust, which eased the business of raising credit and sharing information for budding Quaker entrepreneurs.

The Quakers brought a particular approach to business, set out in the Society's *Christian and Brotherly Advices*, published in 1738, with a host of rules of the road. 'None [should] launch forth into trading and worldly business beyond what they can manage honourably and with reputation among the Sons of Men,' instructed the pamphlet, and, furthermore, it 'advised that all Friends that are entering into trade and have not stock sufficient of their own to answer the trade they aim at be very cautious of running themselves into debt'. At the Society's monthly meetings, Friends were urged to keep a watchful eye on one another – and indeed were charged with launching inspections should anyone be found 'Deficient in Discharging Their Contracts and Just Debts'.

It was advice that worked. Over the course of the Industrial Revolution, Quaker families became the business leaders who melted the iron, built the bridges and railways, created the banks, spun the cotton, and started three of the greatest chocolate firms in the world.[*] By the early eighteenth century, two-thirds of the nation's iron-works were run by Quakers, including Benjamin Huntsman, the pioneer of purer-cast steel in Sheffield and the founders of the Bristol Brass Foundry. Indeed, by the early nineteenth century, 4,000 Quaker families ran 200 companies and 74 banks, the latter including (James) Barclay's bank in London and (John and Henry) Gurney's bank in Norwich.[5] Edward Pease in Darlington, the leading pioneer behind the first Stockton & Darlington Railway, was a Quaker. Stoke's Josiah Wedgwood,

---

[*] The Frys had entertained George Fox at their home in Wiltshire, and one Zaphania Fry had been imprisoned as a recalcitrant Quaker in 1684, just like Cadbury's ancestor.

Plymouth's William Cookworthy (shoemakers), Kendal's John Somervell (founder of K Shoes) and James Clark (of Clark's Shoes) were all Friends, as were the Crosfield family (pioneers of the English soap business), the food pioneers Reckitts, Huntley and Palmer, and the pharmaceuticals leaders Allen and Hanbury.

George Cadbury's Quaker credentials stretched back to the very first days of the Friends. His ancestor, Hannah Tapper's father, had shared prison with George Fox,* and it was Hannah's grandson, Richard Tapper Cadbury, who eventually carried the family's faith to Birmingham, on a journey that began in 1782. Richard was just fourteen when his parents sent him away, on top of a stagecoach, to begin work as a draper's apprentice – much like George Hudson. 'My mother and father got up early to see me off by the stage,' remembered Richard Cadbury in later life, 'and I thought my heart would break.' His early life is largely a mystery. He worked in Kent, but his master went bankrupt. He travelled to Gloucester. He considered emigrating to America, before finding work as a linen draper in London's Gracechurch Street until 1794 – when, at the age of twenty-six, he heard of opportunities in Birmingham from a friend, Joseph Rutter. When the two set off to visit, they found a small, strong Society of Friends that boasted some of the city's most successful families; including Lloyds the bankers, Pembertons the ironmongers and Galtons the gunmakers. Here was the Quaker community that would be a home for Richard and his descendants for generations to come.

Before long, Cadbury and Rutter had rented out No. 92 Bull Street – on the city's premier shopping street – to serve as a silk shop, and soon, they were successful enough to open another outlet a few doors down, at No. 85. Cadbury practised what he preached. He took a prominent slot in the city's life; an overseer of the poor, he sat on the boards of the General Hospital, the Dispensary and the Eye Hospital; he actively promoted the new railway line to Derby and Bristol, and for nearly twenty years he chaired the Board of Commissioners, presiding over its final meeting at the age of eighty-three. He was a keen abolitionist in the anti-slavery cause, and began a Cadbury family tradition of hosting workers for a Scripture reading before work.[6] 'I do not remember

---

* They were in Exeter gaol together in 1693.

receiving 1s[hilling] from my father,' Tapper later wrote, 'and knowing that he was not opulent – having in the course of his life met with many losses and sustained many difficulties – it was delightful to me to reflect I had no need to press upon him.' He and his wife Elizabeth were blessed with ten children,* including their son John, born and brought up above the draper's shop.

Like his father, John started working life as an apprentice, first in Leeds and then in a bonded tea-house in London, where he watched the sale of teas and coffees in the final years of the East India Company's warehouses, before his father set him up in a tea shop at 93 Bull Street, where it was said: 'He must sink or swim.' But John was well qualified to succeed, as his advertisements explained:

> Having had the advantage of residing a considerable time in a wholesale tea warehouse of the first eminence in London, and of examining the teas in the East India Company's warehouses and attending the sales… he is enabled to procure these articles equal to any house in the trade, and consequently can offer them on the most advantagous terms.[7]

John's store was beautiful. It boasted glittering windows of small squares of plate glass in mahogany frames, which he polished each morning, while inside was a cornucopia of tea chests, caddies, sugar loaves and Chinese vases, bedecked with flowers and butterflies. An exotically clad effigy of a Chinese man held court over the long counter. John Cadbury's first customer, Samuel Galton, bought 3 pounds of Souchong teas for 8 shillings and 6 pounds of coffee for 3s 4d. The Boultons, Watts, Murdochs and Lloyds all followed, and as business boomed, John Cadbury began his experiments with a different sort of stimulant appropriate for the teetotal Quakers: cocoa.

*

---

* One son, Benjamin, would inherit the draper's business; another, Joel, would head to America.

We do not know quite when the first Englishman tasted chocolate; but as late as 1825, just 143 tonnes of cocoa beans landed at Britain's docks to supply the coffee houses of London and provincial England. The beans were the fruit of the farming pioneered centuries earlier, by the people of the Amazon, Orinoco and Aztec Empire, who had learned to harvest the strange green pods (and the thirty or forty white seeds or 'beans' within) from the trunk of the sensitive cacao tree (*Theobroma cacao*), which grows just 20 feet tall in the rich alluvial soil of the tropics. When the conquistador Hernán Cortés first met the Aztec Emperor Montezuma, in 1519, he was almost certainly offered the emperor's favourite drink, *xocolatl*, flavoured with vanilla and spices and reduced to a froth-like honey, served up cold in golden goblets. The emperor reputedly got through fifty jars of the stuff a day.

Cortés brought the beans back to Spain, along with the secret of their preparation, which the Spanish guarded for nearly another century. It proved a popular product. 'The chief use they make of this cocoa', wrote the Jesuit historian José Acosta in 1604, 'is in a drink which they call chocolate... The Spaniards, both men and women, are very greedy of this.'[8] From Spain, the taste was spread to France, Germany and England, possibly by monks who translated a Spanish treatise on the art of mixing cocoa with sugar. Louis XIV's wife, Maria Theresa, was certainly fond of a cup, and by 1650 an advertisement for the sale of chocolate appeared in Oxford. Seven years later, the *Public Advertiser* announced: 'In Bishopsgate Street, in Queen Head Alley at a Frenchman's House is an excellent West Indian drink, called chocolate, to be sold, where you may have it ready at any time, and also unmade at reasonable rate.'[9] Nearly a decade later, Samuel Pepys was recording in his diary (24 November 1664) that he was off 'to a coffee house to drink jocolatte, very good'. It was a fashion that spread, and by 1772, the best drinking chocolate in London could be found – according to John Macky, a continental traveller – around the king's palace: 'At twelve o'clock the beau monde assembles in several coffee and chocolate houses,' he wrote, 'the best of which are the Cocoa Tree, White's Chocolate House, St James, the Smyrna and the British Coffee House.'

The first British chocolate-maker, Walter Churchman, had set up shop in Bristol in 1728, with a warehouse in London's St Paul's

Churchyard, from where he probably supplied London's coffee houses. Churchman invested in a waterwheel to help grind his chocolate as finely as possible, and in 1729 he was awarded a patent by George II for 'his new invention of making chocolate without fire… by its immediate dissolving, full flavour, smoothness on the palate and intimate union with liquids'.[10] It was priced at 6 shillings a pound. Churchman's son, Charles, carried on the business in competition with another manufacturer, Joseph Fry, who arrived in Bristol aged twenty, became a freeman in 1735, and by 1738 was advertising 'the best sorts of chocolate, made and sold wholesale and retail by Joseph Fry, Apothecary, in Small Street, Bristol'.

Fry – well trained in the apothecratic arts* – proved as entrepreneurial as he was inventive. When Charles Churchman died in 1761, Fry bought his patents and dramatically increased production. He patented the roasting of cocoa beans using a new steam engine (bought from Boulton & Watt), and he piloted new distribution methods, dispatching small packets of chocolate by scheduled coaches or through the penny post. Over the next fifty years, and despite high tariffs – against which the Fry's company campaigned – Britain's taste for chocolate drinks grew, encouraged by Sir Hans Sloane's discovery of the virtues of mixing chocolate with milk. The biggest customer of all was the Royal Navy, which introduced cocoa to the fleet, first in the West Indies around 1780 (in lieu of butter and cheese), and by the early nineteenth century half of the imported cocoa was bound for Her Majesty's ships.

The first hint of John Cadbury's move into drinking chocolate came on 1 March 1824, with an advertisement: 'J.C. is desirous of introducing to particular notice Cocoa Nibs, prepared by himself, an article affording a most nutrious beverage for breakfast'.[11] John, it seemed, was roasting cocoa beans, grinding the shells into nibs, and over the next six years, his wares proved so popular that in 1831 he acquired a 70-foot, four-storey old malthouse in Birmingham's Crooked Lane, at the bottom of Bull Street, in which to build a manufacturing business. It was perfect timing. The government's huge reduction in cocoa duties

---

* Fry had been an apprentice to his father-in-law, Dr Henry Portsmouth.

delivered in the 1832 budget finally allowed the sale of chocolate and cocoa powders at popular prices. By 1842, Cadbury was offering sixteen different types of drinking chocolate – including 'Broma', 'Churchman's Chocolate', 'Spanish Chocolate' and 'Grenada Chocolate' – in the form of powder, flakes, paste and nibs. A claim to quality was at the heart of his appeal. 'J.C. rests his claim to the public support', boasted his advertising bill, 'on his determination to maintain a character for a thoroughly good and uniform quality'.[12]

The business was soon so successful that his partner and older brother, Benjamin, threw in his drapery business to join in. Within two years, Cadbury Brothers were making enough money to close their retail business altogether and in 1847, a newer, larger factory was needed, on Bridge Street in central Birmingham, near to the canal. By 1852, their enterprise was a little famous. It boasted, wrote the journalist Walter White that year, a storehouse crammed with Caribbean cocoa beans; the roasting room blazed with heat and noise as four vast rotating ovens, driven by a 20-horsepower steam engine, which roasted and removed the husks of cocoa beans with a 'ceaseless blast from a furious fan', before the pulp was pressed and pounded into the rich chocolate mixture that emerged 'leisurely like a stream of half frozen treacle' to form a cake, from which shavings could be turned into cocoa.[13]

Marketed as 'free from the useless fibrine, fatty, indigestible portion of the nut', Cadbury's 'Homoeopathic or Dietetic Cocoa' was even exhibited at the 'Exposition of Arts and Manufactures' at Bingley House, home of the Lloyds.[14]* On 4 February 1854, Cadbury's was honoured with a royal warrant as 'Manufacturers of Cocoa at Birmingham to Her Majesty', and in the same year, opened their first London office.[15]

*

John Cadbury was very much his father's son. A vigorous, alert young man, his beliefs shaped his life, his work, and his home in Birmingham's wealthy Edgbaston suburb, where his third son George was born on

---

* Today this is the International Conference Centre.

19 September 1839.[16] It was a home where 'religion was the constant atmosphere'. George grew up believing, said his friend A. G. Gardiner, 'that the fundamental principles of the Society of Friends were nearest to the teachings of Jesus Christ in their recognition of the spirituality of the Gospel dispensation, the non-necessity of outward ordinances, the guidance of the Holy Spirit, the freedom of the Gospel ministry and the inconsistency of war with the teaching of Christ'. There was laughter in the house, but no luxuries or literature. Only two novels, both American and morally instructive, were approved: Harriet Beecher Stowe's *Uncle Tom's Cabin* and Susan Bogert Warner's *The Wide, Wide World*.[17] John Cadbury had given up the flute to please his father, and in his home music was banned – though George's mother, Candia, was known to sing a Scottish air.[18]

George's lifelong intimacy with the Bible began when he carried it everywhere as a child, memorizing it as he walked. From the age of four or five he made the 6-mile hike to the Friends Meeting House twice every Sundays, where George remembered that the 'afternoon meetings were often dull and heavy times'. However, the 'happiest experience was after meeting, for my father made it a point to call at some of the dismal courts of Birmingham, and always took his little sons with him. In this way he gave us early sympathy with the poor.'[19]

It was, by all accounts, a happy home, of sobriety and stability.[20] 'Our father went for a walk each morning, starting about seven o'clock, taking his dogs with him, and we were often his companions,' George wrote in later life. 'We returned home to breakfast punctually at eight o'clock. The family Bible reading followed, and by nine o'clock our father was ready to start for business… full of health and vigour – his Quaker dress very neat with its clean white cravat… Our home was one of sunshine… Home was the centre of attraction to us all, and simple home pleasures our greatest joy.'[21]

Unlike his brothers, George was educated at the nearby William Lean's School for Friends,* a place renowned for its emphasis on the classics and its encouragement of the 'martial spirit'; the playground

---

* George's two older brothers, John and Richard, were dispatched to a Quaker boarding school.

was a place of large-scale battles played with sticks, or games such as 'hardening', which entailed throwing lads into prickly gorse bushes.

In 1855, at the age of sixteen, pain of a quite different kind arrived for George – the first of many family tragedies to come. His mother Candia, struggling in her protracted battle with consumption, was taken seriously ill with rheumatic fever. She died on 5 March. His father took the loss badly. His own health deteriorated, for he was soon bedevilled with debilitating arthritis. George was now pulled from school and dispatched into an apprenticeship with family friends, the Rowntrees of York. It was here, at Rowntree's shop at No. 28 The Pavement – a handsome eighteenth-century terrace at the bottom of the Shambles, in a maze of winding streets – that George Cadbury learnt the retail business and hard work.[22]

'The object of the Pavement establishment is business,' ran Rowntree's Rules, in which 'The young men who enter it as journeymen or apprentices are expected to contribute… in making it successful.' George did not think much of the human company, however: 'On the one side (of the business), which it has fallen to my lot to work on, there are some rather foolish young men who talk a good deal of nonsense, but I have told them I much prefer sensible conversation and I think I have been enabled pretty much to keep clear of nonsense.' Time to write was a rarity; as he apologized from the shop on 22 May 1857, 'you will see that my letters are rather patchwork begun on one day finished on another, which may be attributed to my having but little unbroken time'.[23] Yet George's time in York, though formative, was brief, and it was another family bereavement that brought him home.

In 1860, George's grandfather died.[24] Richard Tapper was buried in a 'quiet and unostentatious manner' on Wednesday, 21 March, in the small meeting house in Bull Street where he had arrived in the city over six decades earlier. Fourteen coaches brought family, fellow Quakers and the mayor, Thomas Lloyd. It was now, after a decade of meagre returns, that John Cadbury decided finally to retire. In April 1861, he asked his sons George (aged twenty-five) and Richard (aged twenty-one) to take over his business, and the brothers now made a pact. From their mother, they had each inherited £5,000 (worth between £3 million and £4.7 million today). They would now do everything in

their power to save their father's struggling business, without borrowing a single penny. And if they failed, they would close the Cadbury's
shop for ever.[25]

*

The timing of the brothers' inheritance was auspicious. Indeed, 1861
was perhaps the 'high-noon of Victorianism', the moment when Britain's
consumer revolution was beginning to gather pace as the power of the
state at home and free trade abroad began to bear fruit. These were to
be years when national wealth grew at over 2 per cent a year, the fastest
rate until the 1950s, and when Britain became the most productive
country on earth; a country where wealth per head (some £32.60) was
nearly 50 per cent higher than in France, and nearly three times greater
than that of Germany.*

The roots of this 'British miracle' were deep, and its water was free
trade, which for its supporters had become almost a religion since the
days of William Jardine. Free trade's great prophet, Richard Cobden,
called it the 'grand panacea', capable of 'drawing men together, thrusting
aside the antagonisms of race'.[26] Between 1833, when the East India
Company's monopoly was abolished, and 1846, when the Corn Laws
were abandoned, the doctrine had reshaped national politics. In 1842,
Prime Minister Robert Peel had swept away Britain's muddle of customs
duties, raised income tax and opened the 'classical phase' of Victorian
finance. Indeed, the cult of free trade was such that in 1857 Lord
Palmerston's Whigs won an election majority on the principle of war in
China – the second Opium War – with the ostensible object of enforcing free trade on the Chinese emperor. It was the great spur to growth,
the magic ingredient in the 'golden age' of Victorian commerce,[27] which
saw the value of international trade double between 1830 and 1850, and
exports continue to grow at over 3.5 per cent a year between 1856 and
1873.

The great advance abroad was a boon to wealth at home, which

---

* In Germany it was £13.30 per head and in France £21.10. G. Best, *Mid-
Victorian Britain 1851–1875* (Weidenfeld and Nicolson, 1971), p. 3.

grew, per head, at a rate of 1.3 per cent a year, helping create a country where demand surged for new consumer goods, such as chocolate. This was the Britain of the Great Exhibition (1849), that wonderful moment which proved – as Queen Victoria penned in her diary – that 'we are capable of doing anything'.[28] In the engineering marvel of Joseph Paxton's Crystal Palace, almost 14,000 exhibitors showed 19,000 exhibits to the 6 million visitors that flooded to this 'palace of nations' between May and October. 'Astonishing,' pronounced the novelist Dostoevsky, 'You gasp for breath… it is like a Biblical picture, something out of Babylon, a prophecy… coming to pass before your eyes.'

Yet for the Cadbury brothers, in 1861 business felt anything but easy. The truth was that, after a decade of low returns, their father's firm was on the brink of collapse. 'It would have been far easier', said George years later, 'to start a new business, than to pull up a decayed one which had a bad name. The prospect seemed a hopeless one, but we were young and full of energy.' Staff numbers had fallen from twenty to just eleven;[29] morale was at an all-time low, and so was pay. Indeed, some of the shop-girls were scraping by on just 2s 6d a week.[30] From the mid-1850s, their father's absences from the business had grown longer and longer, and while John Cadbury searched for a cure to his arthritis, his competition had been growing stronger. Joseph Terry had begun selling to seventy-five towns in the Midlands and northern England. Henry Rowntree had founded his business, in 1862, in York, while in Bristol Fry's boasted an eight-storey factory the size of a small town. Indeed, Fry's, under the leadership first of J. S. Fry's widow Anna, and then his son Joseph, had become the biggest chocolate business in Britain, employing 500 people by 1861 – and going on to achieve sales of around £250,000 by 1878. They sold a quarter of all the chocolate in Britain.

George Cadbury, however, was a man with large dreams. 'I never looked at the small people or the people who had failed. I fixed my eye on those who had won the greatest success. It was no use studying failure. I wanted to know how men succeeded and it was their methods I examined and, if I thought them good applied.'[31] And so, with a bit of old-fashioned financial management and a new ambition for sales, the brothers set to work. They wasted neither time nor money. Indeed,

George put their survival down to the fact that he was still a bachelor. 'I was spending at that time for travelling, clothing, charities, and everything else about £25 a year,' he wrote; 'My brother had married, and at the end of five years had only £150. If I had been married there would have been no Bournville today – it was just the money that I saved by living so sparsely that carried us over the crisis.'

George Cadbury quickly began a study of the competition, sometimes even accompanied by a competitor from Fry's: 'I suppose we had some energy,' reflected George, 'for Francis James Fry elected to go round with me to see the cocoa and chocolate manufacturers.'[32] Cadbury's sales were in the hands of Dixon Hadaway, an enormous and extremely punctual Scotsman in a tall top hat and a smart tweed coat he had worn since the Crimean War. He toured the country from Rugby to Scotland by train or pony and trap, and he was soon joined on the road by Richard and George. Immediately, the brothers began experimenting with new products and new ways of marketing, exploiting Richard's gift for design. 'Iceland Moss' was quickly introduced, a mixture of the fatty cocoa bean and lichen, fashioned into a bar of chocolate (to be drunk) and sold in bright yellow packaging, complete with a picture of a reindeer. But as sales faltered, other products, with new messages, were introduced: 'Chocolat du Mexique is delicious as a beverage or as a confection and is more wholesome than coffee for breakfast' and 'Cadbury's Chocolate Confectionary is guaranteed pure and wholesome.[33] It is convenient and sustaining for excursionists.'[34] Soon, the sheer range was a problem; 'So numerous are the sorts,' wrote The Grocer, that 'the purchaser is much puzzled in his choice.'[35]

George worked all the hours God sent. In the winter he rose no later than six o'clock, and after his daily exercise was at work for seven sharp.[36] He lunched with his father at one o'clock, and then continued working through the evening, sometimes until nine o'clock when he would eat a meagre dinner of bread, butter and water at the factory. In the summer, the starts were even earlier; lodging at an engineer's cottage by the Bittel Reservoir, to be closer to work, he would start his day at 5.15am.[37]

In the first year of their control of the company, 1861, Richard lost some £226 (between £138,000 and £205,000 in today's money) and George probably about the same. By Christmas 1862, the losses had increased to £304 each. By 1863, the business seemed to be on the edge of disaster, as well the workers knew. 'The firm was in low water and losing money,' remembered one employee; 'at one stage [we] expected any day to hear that the works were to be shut'. The capital inherited from their mother was now gone, and, having sworn never to ask either creditors or their father for money, George and Richard began to make new plans – Richard to become a land surveyor, and George to take up tea planting in the Himalayas.[38]

Yet, their Quaker values never left them, either at work or at home. Determined not to let their worries show, George abolished the old formalities of titles, becoming just 'Mr George', and he and his brother won the nickname the 'Cheeryble Brothers' after the kind-hearted employers of Dickens's *Nicholas Nickleby*.[39] The business day began with a non-denominational morning prayer, and as George's schemes of incentives to encourage good habits (such as punctuality and sobriety) began to take effect, wages slowly rose.[40] A Saturday half-holiday was offered, and when the weather was clement, George and Richard were known to lead a round of cricket.[41] The brothers mucked in with everything, one worker fondly remembering 'Mr George' crawling down on his hands and knees to make sure that the water pipes were hot enough, making 'a great impression on all of us'.[42]

Nor was the factory George's only arena. He was soon, like his father and grandfather, a devoted entrepreneur in the city's Quaker movement. 'The service of God is the service of man,' he once said. 'We can do nothing of any value to God, except in acts of genuine helpfulness done to our fellowman.' Throughout the 1860s, the Cadbury family was constantly in the Birmingham newspapers, chairing Temperance meetings, supporting bazaars for the Winson Green Industrial School with the 'elite of Edgbaston', campaigning to free slaves in America, taking the minutes of the Birmingham Infirmary Board, or helping host great meetings of the radical politician John Bright.

George was among the most powerful men in the city, a group that included William White, one of the fathers of the adult-school movement that had begun in Nottingham, in 1798, and it was here that George felt called to serve. He joined central Birmingham's Severn Street Adult School as a twenty-year-old teacher in 1859, and here, he would teach almost every Sunday for the next half a century, until shortly before his death.[43] Beginning with a small group of boys, before graduating to a classroom of his own (Class XIV), Cadbury taught men from slums, pubs and prisons.[44] On Sundays, he rose at 5.30am and made the 5-mile journey into town to teach basic numeracy, literacy and Scripture. George later wrote of a burglar he had taught: the man 'brought two or three other housebreakers into the class. I found them by no means entirely bad men, but they told me it was not only for the sake of gain but for the intense enjoyment of the risk that they found it most difficult to give up the occupation.'

*

By 1864, after three years' hard work, Cadbury Brothers was finally solvent. But the product was poor. Cadbury's was still the smallest of the thirty or so cocoa-makers in Britain, and unfortunately its wares were among the worst, as George Cadbury later admitted: 'We made a cocoa drink of which we were not very proud. Only one fifth of it was cocoa. 3/4 of trade was from tea and coffee.' But, no longer losing money, George now saw an opportunity to transform both his product and his fortunes. His long march to become the Number 1 in British chocolate began with a simple insight: he needed a better product.

At the time, cocoa beans, being so rich in fatty 'cocoa butter', were generally mixed with additives such as potato starch, sago, flour or treacle to make the drink more palatable.[45] But in the early 1860s, Dixon Hadaway had brought back to Birmingham reports of the runaway success of a Dutch competitor's refined chocolate, which was manufactured using a hydraulic press to squeeze out the excess cocoa fat, reducing its content to 30 per cent, and thus allowing the cocoa to be sold 'pure' without the additives. Sensing an opportunity, George Cadbury made for Holland in 1866 to visit Van Houtens. As he later described, 'I went off to Holland without knowing a word of Dutch, saw the manufacturer with whom I had to talk entirely by signs and a dictionary and bought the machine. It was by prompt action such as this that my brother and I made our business.'[46]

The 10-foot-high machine, with its huge hoppers, was shipped back to Bridge Street, arriving by canal. Over the summer and autumn of 1866, Cadbury Brothers reorganized their production line, designed new artwork for the packaging, and, weeks before Christmas, launched their breakthrough product on to the market, with all the fanfare of full-page advertisements in newspapers, posters in shop-fronts and billboards on buses: it was called 'Cocoa Essence'.

The message was simple, and medicinal: 'Absolutely Pure. Therefore Best.'[47] 'Cadbury's Cocoa Essence', ran the ads, 'is nearly four times the strength of the best homoeopathic cocoas... two thirds of this is extracted by producing cocoa essence leaving an article long desired by medical men.'[48] Over the next year, sales reps were dispatched to deliver samples to doctors, as Cadbury Brothers stepped up the campaign to celebrate their product's wholesome virtues. Soon, the brothers were winning glowing write-ups from the medical profession's own house journal, The Lancet, which declared: 'We have examined the samples brought under our notice and find that they are genuine and the Essence of the cocoa is just what it is declared to be by Messrs Cadbury Bros.'[49] The following year, Cadbury's went one better with endorsements from both the British Medical Journal and one Dr Lyon Playfair.[50] 'We strongly recommend Cadbury's Cocoa Essence as a diet for children,' ran Playfair's endorsement, 'and as a constituent in the diet roll of all public and private establishments.' The British Medical Journal declared that 'Cocoa treated thus will, we expect, prove to be one of the most nutritious, digestible and restorative of drinks.'[51]

Despite the accolades, sales were not, at first, easy. One Cadbury salesman, David Jones, remembered giving hundreds of shopkeepers their first taste of Cocoa Essence, 'only to watch their faces lose their customary shape as if they had taken vinegar or woodworm'.[52] George Cadbury agreed: 'It was an extremely hard struggle. We had ourselves to induce shopkeepers to stock our cocoa and induce the public to ask for it.' Slowly, but surely, sales grew. By the end of 1868, fifty staff were working at Bridge Street, and the firm began diversifying into chocolate for eating rather than drinking, creating a 'Fancy Box', offering a mixture of chocolates with exotic names, in an eye-pleasing package, designed by Richard Cadbury.

Richard was a pioneer in chocolate-box design in Britain,

introducing evocative images of children and flowers such as gentians and cyclamen, along with other Alpine scenes. Fancy Box was a wonderful example, adorned with a winning picture of Richard's daughter Jessie and her kitten. The designs won plaudits. 'Among the pictorial novelties introduced to the trade this season,' declared *Chemist and Druggist* magazine on 15 December 1870, 'few if any excel the illustration on Messrs Cadbury's four ounce box of chocolate cremes... It is chaste yet simple, and consists of a blue-eyed maiden some six summers old... nursing a cat.' It was, the magazine declared, 'The most exquisite chocolate ever to come under our notice.'[53]

The brothers' struggle at work was made no easier by ever more tragedy at home. In January 1866, Richard and George lost both their younger brother Edward and their older brother John, who died in Australia. In 1868, Richard's wife also passed away. The two remaining brothers threw themselves into work. One of their staff, T. J. O'Brien, who started in 1869, had never known 'men work harder than our masters'. To him, George and Richard 'were more like fathers to us. Sometimes they were working in the manufactory; then packing in the warehouse, then again all over the country getting orders'.[54] They were, however, about to get a helping hand from the government.

A good deal of Victorian food was, literally, dangerous. So dangerous, that in 1872 a wave of indignation swept the Adulteration of Food Act into law. The *Birmingham Daily Post*, of Friday, 23 August, brought the news that 'After many years of pertinacious effort, Mr Postgate has at length succeeded in getting his bill for the punishment of adulteration of food, drink, and drugs passed into law' after 'heroic determination'. The campaign was five decades long, sparked by the German chemist, Frederick Accum, whose 1820 *Treatise on Adulterations of Food and Culinary Poisons* first raised the alarm.* The first edition sold out in months. The popularity of tea had incentivized the dubiously entrepreneurial to boil up used tea-leaves with a host of chemicals,

---

* The title in full was: *A Treatise on Adulterations of Food and Culinary Poisons: Exhibiting the Fraudulent Sophistications of Bread, Beer, Wine, Spirituous Liquors, Tea, Coffee, Cream, Confectionery, Vinegar, Mustard, Pepper, Cheese, Olive Oil, Pickles, and Other Articles Employed in Domestic Economy, and Methods of Detecting Them.*

plus sheep's dung, before reselling it. Indeed, tea could be found containing both lead and copper salts. Accum's campaign was taken up by Arthur Hill Hassall and Thomas Wakley – a surgeon, editor of *The Lancet* and MP – who commissioned studies of 2,500 samples of food and drink between January 1851 and the end of 1854. They revealed that adulteration was the rule rather than the exception, not least in confectionery, which was found to contain lead, copper and mercury.

A first Act of Parliament was passed in 1860, but there was no systematic regime of inspection. The new Act brought a law with teeth; inspectors were ordered and additives had to be declared. Cadbury Brothers immediately stepped up their advertisements, replete with quotations from *The Lancet* that 'absolutely pure was therefore best' and full-page pictures of bearded gentlemen, surrounded by test tubes, gazing at beakers of Cocoa Essence. When grocers were prosecuted for selling adulterated cocoa, George Cadbury started a public argument that any cocoa with additives did not deserve the name of cocoa – much to the fury of Fry's, who wrote: 'Messrs Cadbury, in order to push a speciality of their own, have not hesitated to cast a stigma upon all cocoa manufacturers in the country.'[55] The row was extraordinarily good for business. By 1874, Cadbury's Pure Cocoa Essence was so successful that the brothers gave up selling tea and coffee, and opened their first overseas branch. It would be a prelude to a sales push in Chile, Canada, Australia and Paris.[*]

With the business now growing, George Cadbury finally felt free to relax a little. In 1872, he married Mary Tylor, the daughter of the writer Charles Tylor of London, and together they would enjoy years of companionship and raise three sons and two daughters. In time, some of them would assume responsibilities in the firm.[†]

Throughout the years of growth, the Cadbury brothers retained their passion for happy staff. In 1871, they declared one day in August a day off for workers, 'a general holiday', regarded as 'a great boon to all, especially to those employed in shops'. They created a Sick Club, a works fire brigade,

---

[*] A French office was opened under Jules Socquet, who had worked at Bridge Street.

[†] The children were Edward, George, Henry Tylor, Isabel and Eleanor. Gardiner, *The Life of George Cadbury*, op. cit., p. 70.

and began an annual party. It was no surprise, therefore, that Birmingham's leading lights now sought to entice George into civic office. Late-Victorian Birmingham had become a centre for political reformers. John Bright, the Quaker and Radical MP for Birmingham, who had been elected in 1858, used to declare that 'Birmingham is radical as the sea is salt'; but it took until 1873 and the election of another Radical, Joseph Chamberlain, to the office of mayor before the city itself became known as 'the best governed city in the world'. George Cadbury was part of the team. Writing much later, in 1921, he described how the absence of practically all civic institutions was 'absolutely changed in a very few years by a band of young men, of whom at that time I was one, who did individual work – canvassing, holding meetings, etc and securing a majority of votes in favour of progress. We were led by ministers of religion… and Joseph Chamberlain, a magnificent leader of young men.'[56]

Much of George Cadbury's work at the time was devoted to advancing the Temperance cause;* but on Saturday, 13 July 1878, the newspapers brought news of his selection to stand for Birmingham Council. At an enthusiastic meeting of his supporters at Clark Street Board School, he declared to applause that 'in entering the Council he should do his best to assist Mr Chamberlain'. The newspapers were behind him: 'in Mr George Cadbury we have a member of an old and honourable Birmingham family, and one who has devoted much time and labour to works of charity and of education, notably in connection with the great Severn Street School'.[57] It was a close fight. Cadbury's support for Temperance and tougher alcohol licensing set the brewers against him. Nearly every pub in the ward became a committee room for his opponent, where, said the *Birmingham Post*, 'beer could be had as freely as rain-water'. His opponent's supporters paraded down Steward Street with jugs of the stuff. It was not to defeat Cadbury though, and on the night of 22 July he polled 1,245 votes to Dr Burton's 918.[58]

It was to prove a short-lived career. Cadbury retired from Birmingham Council after just a year, for he could now see another way to serve the people of his hometown. At Cadbury Brothers, he and

---

* He was, for instance, part of a committee established to explore the creation of a network of cocoa houses, 'another phase of the great temperance question'.

Richard employed twenty-four office workers and salesmen ('travellers') and two hundred others. The company now needed to change in order to grow. It was now time for the brothers' huge civic and commercial experiment: a 'factory in a garden' called Bournville.

*

Cadbury Brothers was, by the mid-1870s, very squashed in its Bridge Street headquarters, jammed in by surrounding factories, workshops, railway lines, canals and the rising population of a booming Birmingham. And so, every Saturday afternoon, George Cadbury began walking around the city with a few of the firm's managers on the hunt for a better site, until one day he found his spot: 14.5 acres of sloping meadowland, in the middle of several farms, 4 miles west of Birmingham in the district of King's Norton.[59] The area was bordered by the old Worcester & Birmingham Canal. To its north was a little trout stream, the Bourn, and to its east lay the new Midland Railway (opened in 1876), with a stop nearby in Stirchley. On Tuesday, 18 June 1878, Cadbury's bought the site at auction, and just six months later, in a very wet year, the first of 2 million bricks was laid. Over the summer of 1879, staff worked furiously to build up product stocks, and on 27 September 1879 Richard wrote to his father to say: 'I have cleared out all my furniture from the old spot; table, books, and safe are all deposited in my new office. It is with some regret that we part with old associations bringing back past memories, but the world and time move on and we must move with them.'[60] Bournville was born.

Richard Cadbury bought the railway tickets for the first girls to start work and accompanied them on the journey to the enormous new plant, where, laid out neatly, were huge rooms for storage, roasting, grinding, moulding, essence making, sieving, dressing and packing, along with offices for support staff, saw mills, tin shops, workshops, engine houses, machinery rooms, stables, a coach house, a smithy, a sugar store – and a reading room.[61]

The brothers quickly settled into their division of labour. The head of the general office for many years, Mr H. E. Johnson, left a portrait: 'The partners were in and around the works and offices continually...

Mr Richard gave most of his time to the Sales side whilst Mr George did the same for the Buying and Manufacturing side, but they consulted one another so much that no definite line seems to have existed.'[62] 'One has a vision of Mr George, with a row of small tins on a counter in front of him, the tins filled with roasted "beans" just brought in from the factory, and Mr George with unerring skill, testing them and pronouncing judgement.'[63] Their regime was as relentless as ever, as Richard's daughter remembered: 'Both the brothers had been accustomed to deny themselves luxuries… and they continued their frugal habits almost unconsciously. The somewhat monotonous bill-of-fare consisted week by week of leg of mutton… the bones and any scrap ends that were left furnished the meal for Friday.'[64]

In the wonderful Cadbury archives, up above No. 1 Lodge on Bournville Lane, is a book capturing the memories of many of those who worked at Bournville in its earliest days.[65] In its pages, senior and junior staff recalled their first impressions. One, Mr J. H. Palmer, fondly remembered how on many occasions 'Mr Richard and Mr George used to walk into the Moulding Department at 10.45am and call for a halt… we were marched to the playing field and a football was thrown to us and I believe both the directors enjoyed that 15 minutes game just as much as those who took part.'[66] The brothers' religion, remembered William Cooper, very much set the tone: 'The atmosphere of the Bournville of early days was decidedly a religious atmosphere as had been that of Bridge Street, but with many means of expression. (The brothers) made no secret of their trust in God in business as in all else. They took the risks of their faith.'[67]

Their faith was now richly rewarded. The business was growing fast, as it caught the rising tide of a booming market. Back in the 1820s, Britain had devoured just over half a million pounds of cocoa. Between the 1820s and the 1860s, consumption grew around 6 per cent a year, to 4.6 million pounds of cocoa. But, in the 1870s and 1880s demand exploded – annual consumption grew ten times as fast, at nearly 70 per cent a year, slowing to 50 per cent a year in the later 1880s and 1890s. The size of the chocolate market quadrupled, from 10.5 million pounds of cocoa to over 40 million pounds.

Into this great market, the Cadbury brothers sold a bewildering array of products. George had hired an expert French chocolatier, Frederic Kinchelman – affectionately known as 'Frederick the Frenchman' – who began to train the staff to make 'Nougat-Dragées', 'Pâté Duchesse', 'Avelines' and exotic centres, all carefully packaged in Richard's beautifully designed chocolate boxes – the first chocolate-box art.[68] In 1880, the printed list of products was perhaps five small catalogue-pages long; by 1890, the range of products had doubled. Now, 200 different fancy boxes of chocolates were selling for as much as a guinea each, along with 19 different lines of Easter egg, peddled into shops all over the country by 'travellers' who, like Richard's oldest son Barrow Cadbury, hauled around heavy sample bags. As range and quality of product increased, the old adulterated and inferior cocoas were phased out. In June 1891, Cadbury Brothers deliberately gave up manufacture of 'Chocolate Powder', the last of the lines that resembled the starch-adulterated cocoa of the past.

Bournville had soon become 'one of the wonders of England', as one visitor described it. It nestled in 'a charming valley which might have served for Rip van Winkle's "sleepy hollow" but for the hive of industry; with [the] ever present odour of freshly-poured-out chocolate'. Here, hundreds of women were making the boxes for chocolates and creams, 'admirable examples of art workmanship', amid machines pressing and folding 24,000 cartons for cocoa essence each day, and the great sieving and roasting cylinders for the cocoa beans. With the power of Bournville behind it, Cadbury's was fast becoming the country's biggest chocolate firm. When the brothers moved into Bournville, their annual sales were £117,505 (worth some £50–80 million in today's money), less than half the size of Fry's.* Fry's growth was fast; it quintupled in size, to boast sales of £1.3 million in 1900. But Cadbury's had grown *twice* as quickly, an extraordinary ten-fold boom to within £100,000 of the market leader, with sales of £1.2 million.

The firm's foreign business, too, was expanding. In 1881, within three years of opening Bournville, Cadbury's received its first order from Australia when Thomas Edwards opened the firm's Melbourne office; an export department was set up in 1888 and, by 1892, depots were up and running in Melbourne, Sydney, Adelaide, Brisbane,

---

* They were roughly 44 per cent the size of Fry's.

Wellington, Montreal and at 90 Rue de Faubourg St Honoré in Paris. In 1893, a sales office opened in South Africa, and in 1895, one in India. Over this period too, George and Richard Cadbury began to bring in the next generation of the family. Barrow Cadbury joined in 1882, after graduating from the new Manchester University, and quickly helped set up the firm's US and Canadian agencies. George's eldest son Edward joined five years later to push ahead the firm's export business. Richard's second son, William, who had trained in Gloucester but spent time in the German confectioner Stollwerck's factory, helped to keep Cadbury's at the forefront of mechanization; and the younger George Cadbury joined in 1897, after graduating in chemistry from University College (London) and spending time in the Public Analyst's Office of the Society of Apothecaries. Soon, the younger George began work on standardizing recipes across the business.

Yet despite Bournville's scale, the Cadburys saw it as a base where the business might live as a family, and it was this idea that would help the brothers almost perfect one of the greatest innovations of Victorian enterprise: the company town.

*

As early as 1821, some 2.4 million citizens of Britain were working in manufacturing – compared with just 1.8 million in agriculture[69] – and in the years that followed, the revolution in the railways, driven forward by entrepreneurs such as George Hudson, triggered a huge relocation of industry to the great urban centres that now sucked in thousands from the countryside.* By 1850, an extraordinary 67.4 million railway journeys connected new companies in old market centres to the coalfields and workers nationwide, and, through the ports, to customers worldwide.[70] The 1851 census, conducted when George Cadbury was just twelve years old,† revealed that Britain had become the first nation on

---

* Indeed, in 1851 more than three-quarters of the population of Manchester, Bradford and Glasgow aged twenty and above were born outside the cities, as were more than half the people living in Birmingham. Joyce, 'Work', op. cit.
† The census of 1851 reported that 54 per cent of the country's population lived in towns and cities. Best, *Mid-Victorian Britain*, op. cit.

earth where the majority of citizens lived in cities rather than in the countryside, with over 40 per cent of the population labouring in manufacturing, mining and building.

Eleven cities were home to over 100,000 residents each, and London was the largest urban centre in the Western world, 'a dreadful, delightful city' as Henry James put it. By 1861, in fourteen major cities more than half of the working men earned their living in manufacturing; ten of these cities could boast that 60 per cent of their citizens were factory workers.[*] Some of these workers lived in highly specialized industrial towns, such as the steel towns of Ebbw Vale, Middlesbrough and Motherwell, the ship towns of Jarrow and Birkenhead, or in engineering towns such as Crewe, Coventry and Derby. In the textile districts, factories grew bigger and bigger – around a quarter of textile workers were in firms of more than 100 people. But all cities had one thing in common: they were filthy.

'You enter the town as you would a farmer's house, if you first passed through the pigsty into the kitchen,' commented one American in the 1860s.[71] Untold thousands of people lived in 'courts', rows of houses built back-to-back, one room deep, and three rooms high, stacked one above the other.[†] Flimsy and without ventilation, 2,000 of them existed in Birmingham; Liverpool, in 1842, had nearly as many, which were home to 55,000 people.[72] The overcrowding was intense. As late as 1871, 30 per cent of Glasgow's population lived in one-room dwellings, while in Manchester nearly 10 per cent of the population lived two to a room. In that city, Marx's collaborator Friedrich Engels described the 'irregular cramming together of dwellings in ways which defy all natural plan, of the tangle in which they are crowded literally one upon the other'.[73] Cities were, in the words of one report, a 'pestilential heaping of human beings',[74] the nightmares of Dickens's Coketown in *Hard Times*:

---

[*] Of the major centres, only Edinburgh and Liverpool had substantially lower proportions (at 39 per cent). See David Reeder and Richard Rodger, 'Industrialization and the City Economy' in M. J. Daunton (ed.), *Cambridge Urban History of Britain, Vol. 3* (Cambridge University Press), pp. 565–7.

[†] Manchester did not prohibit them until 1844, while it took the city of Liverpool until 1864. Not until 1866 did flats spring up, such as the Peabody estate in Shoreditch. 'Though there is nothing picturesque in these buildings,' wrote an observer, 'the architect has done wonders for the health and comfort of the residents'. Best, *Mid-Victorian Britain*, op. cit., p. 25.

... a town of machinery and tall chimneys, out of which interminable serpents of smoke trailed themselves for ever and ever... it had a black canal in it, and a river that ran purple with ill-smelling dye, and vast piles of building... where the piston of the steam engine worked monotonously up and down.

The first reformers had started work not long after Matthew Boulton's death. After the 'Evangelical' William Wilberforce, a determined leader in the 'reform of manners', had won his victory to abolish the transatlantic slave trade in 1807, the clamour for domestic reform of all kinds intensified. In the campaign that eventually produced the Great Reform Act of 1832, the new urban centres finally acquired representatives in Parliament to campaign for their cause. Radicals, Utilitarians – 'a party, almost a sect' – and Evangelicals, with a crusading zeal now arrow-tipped with statistics, propagating a reformist 'faith hardening into a code', even reformed the centuries-old poor law.

The chaotic, desperate state of the urban poor seemed inextricably linked to the unfettered growth of industry and commerce. In the House of Commons, men like Thomas Carlyle, in his hugely influential *Past and Present*, assaulted the doctrine of 'Laissez-faire, Supply-and-demand, Cash-payment the one nexus of man to man: Free-trade, Competition, and Devil take the hindmost'.[75] Arguing that 'England is full of wealth, of multi-farious produce, of supply for human want in every kind,' Carlyle attacked railway speculators and landowners.[76] Meanwhile, among working people, the instinct to civilize sparked a movement to organize in a counter-attack on the crushing new realities of industrialism. In Rochdale, pioneers created the first co-operative venture, devoted to 'the moral and intellectual advancement of its members' and to providing members with 'groceries, butcher's meat, drapery goods, clothes and clogs'. On to the national stage in the late 1830s and 1840s marched the Chartist movement, with hundreds of thousands brought together to present their demands for enfranchising the working class by extending the vote to 'all men' over the age of twenty-one, irrespective of income.

Although conflict between Radicals, Tories and Chartists impeded progress in Parliament in the years after the Great Reform Act, inquiries flourished, and bills were presented – if only to be defeated. But crucially for the lives of cities and working people alike, over the course of the 1830s there began to grow a small army of inspectors for factories, prisons, schools, railways and mines. In 1833 the Factory Act began to tackle the issue of child labour, with statutory limits on working hours per day (twelve hours for a child over thirteen). In 1847, a fifty-eight-hour working week was legally enshrined. In 1846–52 there were five public health Acts in quick succession, creating the Board of Health; and the Education Minute of 1846 consolidated the grass-roots system of education, and introduced state support via co-funding from the Treasury. A permissive legal regime* now allowed a 'mish-mash' of local bodies to grow up: poor law unions (1834); registration districts (1836); bath and wash-house boards (1846); public health boards (1848); followed by burial boards, highway boards, sewerage boards, and finally, school boards in 1871.

Alongside these multitudinous new authorities came the newly invigorated centres of local government. After the Municipal Reform Act of 1835, major cities seized powers to set up corporations, which began to control housing, sanitation and water supplies, fostering a new appetite to use private Acts of Parliament to rebuild the urban spaces. Among the fruits were great city halls such as Birmingham's (1832), Manchester's Athenaeum (the 'noblest civic edifice in the country'), Liverpool's St George's Hall (1839), and those in Leeds and Bradford. In the great cities, at least, civility began to flourish as new public spaces took shape, providing a home to the arts, literature and debate.[77] Liverpool could date its Wellington Assembly rooms back to 1814. Most big towns had theatres by 1840. City centres and suburbs alike began to change as 'Renaissance' architecture, symbolizing efficiency, economy, probity and confidence, began to rise around the country. When Edward Walters' Manchester Free Trade Hall opened in 1842, it offered a handsome symbol of progress, which

---

* As the Report of the Royal Sanitary Commission put it, 'the principle of local self-government has been generally recognised as of the essence of our national vigour. Local administration under central superintendence is the distinguishing feature of our government. The theory is that all that can, should be done by local authority.'

before long was hosting Carl Hallé's concerts – the centre of musical life in the north.

Outside the growing cities, similar instincts began to inspire the great textile barons of late eighteenth-century England – Richard Arkwright, Jedediah Strutt, Samuel Greg and Samuel Oldknow – who had begun building villages to house workers near their mills. Over the forty years between Robert Owen's New Lanark Mills, on the Clyde, in the early nineteenth century and Titus Salt's magnificent, Italianate Saltaire, arranged on a elegant grid-plan outside Bradford, 'industrial villages' became more beautiful and richly equipped. Here was an effort to create, as Prince Albert put it in 1851, in reference to Barrow Bridge outside Manchester, a 'community of interest between the employer and the employed'.[78]

Bournville was calculated to perfect the reformers' best intentions. It was designed with plenty of green space, for cricket, and for a garden and playground. Inside were dressing rooms for drying clothes and kitchens for warming dinners. A professional cook was on site to dispense cooking lessons, and in the factory's first days,* the Cadbury brothers had built temporarily furnished bedrooms and sitting rooms for girls who wanted to stay on site. George Cadbury, remembered one worker, was constantly popping 'into a room at breakfast time to see we had a good meal'.[79] Amid this new community, George Cadbury soon acquired a home and a hub of community life. In 1881, he acquired Woodbrooke, a grand manor home on the Bristol Road in Selly Oak, and in its large wooded grounds, with their lake and island, George began grand staff parties replete with gallons of tea, piles of cake and bread and butter, and pans of lemonade scooped up with mugs.† Some attendees played cricket, some bowls; others fished, while George took parties of women out in the rowing boat.

By 1892, Cadbury Brothers was so famous that William Gladstone

---

* There were plenty of teething problems. The first train did not arrive until 8.30am – and workers who started at 6am had a long walk from Birmingham. Bournville Lane was lampless, and so the girls walked arm in arm, in twos and threes, 'groping their way along'.

† In 1894, Cadbury moved to Northfield Manor, and Woodbrooke was donated to become a Quaker study centre, which it remains today.

himself began to lobby George to stand for Parliament, penning him a letter to say 'I hope you will not think I go beyond the lines of my public duty in expressing the strong hope... that you will consent to add to your other labours for the good of the public and of your fellow creatures the burden of becoming a candidate for a seat in Parliament'.[80] But George already had the next stage of his 'ethical enterprise' in mind: not simply a model village for his firm, but a model community for his city. Already at Bournville, there were sixteen semi-detached cottages beside the foreman's beautiful house. But from 1893, George began buying land on a serious scale to the north and west of the site; and in 1895, he acquired 120 acres near the factory.[81] This was not to be an estate for factory workers, but a fully fledged new suburb, inspired by his long work as a teacher. 'I have not been a teacher of a men's class for 50 years,' he said later, 'without learning that the best way to improve a man's circumstance is to raise his ideals. [But] how can he cultivate ideals when his home is a slum and his only place of recreation the public house?'[82]

Plans were laid for one of the great innovations of the late Victorian age. The Bournville Village Trust was a place designed for a purpose: 'the amelioration of the conditions of the working class and labouring population in and around Birmingham and elsewhere in Great Britain, by the provision of improved dwellings, with gardens, and open spaces'.[83] It was to be a 'home for workers of many types, employers and employed, managers and operatives, tradesmen and clerks'. Eventually, 2,000 homes would be built – and Bournville would become famous worldwide.

*

In the summer of 1899, Richard Cadbury rewarded himself for years of work with a holiday to the Holy Land. His health was not perfect when he left. Abroad he succumbed to an attack of diphtheria. Within days, he was dead.[84] George Cadbury had lost his brother and his business partner of thirty-eight years.

The brothers had always planned to keep the business within the family; but, in the weeks before Richard's death, both brothers agreed that in the event of either one of them dying, the survivor would re-form the firm as a limited company. Cadbury's was simply catching up with its competitors. Fry's had already converted to limited company status, with a nominal capital of £1 million. Rowntree's incorporated in 1897, reorganizing the firm into new departments, with directors responsible for Purchasing, Finance, Labour and Sales. And so, on 13 June 1899, a little more than two months after Richard's funeral, Cadbury Brothers was incorporated as a limited liability company and capitalized at £950,000. George took the chair to convene the first board meeting on 5 July; around the table were George's sons Edward and George, and Richard's sons Barrow and William, appointed managing directors of the firm. Meeting weekly, they would preside over a revolution in the management of the business.[85]

Perhaps because of Richard's death, George now accelerated his civic and philanthropic work, delivering his vision of a new model community in Bournville. In 1899 he acquired more land – the Hay Green estate, a mile from the works – and so controlled in all by 1900 about 330 acres. By December 1900, more than 300 houses had been built on land adjoining the factory to Cadbury's specifications.[86] The houses were rented out on long leases, with money at low interest to those without means. Each home was allowed 600 square feet for a deep back garden, in which tenants could cultivate produce valued at 2s 6d a week throughout the year – amounting to a third of their yearly rent.[87] The non-profit enterprise was protected by a trust, largely composed of Cadbury family members, to safeguard the village ethos of 'alleviating the evils which arise from the unsanitary and insufficient accommodation supplied to large numbers of the working classes, and of securing to the workers in factories some of the advantages of outdoor village life, with opportunities for the natural and healthful occupation of cultivating the soil'.[88]

George Cadbury hoped that by mixing together families of all backgrounds the barriers of class and creed could fall away.[89] Clusters of homes, therefore, were to house mixed-income families, with larger homes owned by managers scattered throughout the more modest abodes. Thirty-three almshouses were built 300 yards west of the cocoa works, and homes for £600 were built next to the homes worth £1,500. Only half of the houses went to Bournville wage-earners. Shops, school,

recreation grounds and social activities were run by the Village Council
to foster a sense of community.

But as the village took shape, Cadbury's horizons stretched even
further, and when the Second Anglo-Boer War broke out in South
Africa in 1899, George decided it was time to take to the national stage.
He became one of the country's most prominent and vocal critics of the
war. Writing earnestly to the like-minded Battersea MP John Burns,
Cadbury declared his view that 'This war seems the most diabolical that
was ever waged. It is so evidently a speculators' war, and no-one else can
derive any benefits from it.'* Quaker anti-war literature was issued to
Cadbury workers, and at first George refused to send Cadbury's chocolates to the troops, relenting only after an order from the queen.[90] Even
then, George ensured that the Cadbury's brand was nowhere to be seen
and that no profit was made on the orders.

When the *Daily News* – founded by Charles Dickens, and once a
great beacon of Liberal radicalism and pacifism – adopted a pro-war
stance, Cadbury was outraged. Persuaded by the Liberal leader Lloyd
George to acquire the newspaper,[91] Cadbury not only advanced £20,000
to lead a syndicate to buy it, but snapped up the *Morning Leader* and the
Star for good measure. Page after page was now devoted to exposing the
machinations of mine-owners and the evils of 'concentration' camps
built to corral the Boers. When the syndicate split, Cadbury decided to
go it alone. 'I shrank at my time of life from taking up so heavy a responsibility,' he wrote to another MP, T. E. Ellis, 'but I was led into it step by
step.'[92] Thomas Ritzema was installed as chief executive of the *Daily
News*; the paper expanded to sixteen pages, and in came new machinery, new management and a remodelled headquarters. Circulation
soared from 30,000 to 80,000 as the newspaper became a crusader for
social reform, advocating old-age pensions, the suppression of exploit-
ative 'sweated' industries – inspiring the Anti-Sweating League, of
which George Cadbury became president – and new minimum-wage
laws. By 1907, when George's third son Henry Tylor Cadbury took over,

---

* To one MP he wrote: 'I am as honestly convinced that the war has been carried
on behalf of the speculators at Jo'burg, and that they are responsible for it, as
you are convinced that the war was sought for by the Boers.' Gardiner, *George
Cadbury*, op. cit., p. 215.

the newspaper was publishing simultaneously in Manchester and London with a circulation of 400,000 a day.

Cadbury's new interest in national life and progressive causes soon became more entwined with the messy business of politics. He offered £50 per week to trade unions during the engineers' dispute of 1897, backed the new Labour Representation Committee – founded in 1900 to organize union backing for sympathetic MPs and candidates – and after 1900 supported Labour candidates in by-elections, especially Robert Waite, candidate in Preston and North-East Lanark, who acted as Cadbury's political adviser and agent.[*] In the Liberal Party, George Cadbury declared he had 'no interest except in so far as it promotes the welfare of the millions of my fellow countrymen who are on or below the poverty line'.[93] 'We want a hundred working men in Parliament. Then the condition of the people will become a living issue.'[94]

*

As the twentieth century dawned, George Cadbury was a prominent public figure; but he still had a business to run. And while he would prove himself one of Britain's leading pacifists, he excelled too as an extraordinary warrior in Britain's first chocolate war. His success would leave Cadbury's the greatest chocolate firm in the British Empire.

Despite the great growth in Cadbury's, Fry's and Rowntree's at the end of the nineteenth century, the truth was that the British cocoa, chocolate and confectionery market was still dominated by foreign companies and products: Van Houten's alkalized cocoa, Swiss milk chocolate and French sweets.[95] In 1900, the UK's big three, together, served less than one-fifth of the domestic market for cocoa, moulded chocolate and sugar sweets, and in 1904, the foreign giants pressed their advantage. The Swiss company Nestlé, which already had large UK interests, reached agreement to start heavily importing the Swiss chocolate Kohler and Cailler. Two years later, depression hit the UK

---

[*] It was through Waite that unofficial talks between Labour and the Liberals laid the foundation for the 1906 election, which ushered Campbell-Bannerman in as prime minister.

market hard. For the first time in years, sales began to fall, by nearly 1 per cent a year, and in these tougher market conditions, competition was about to get nasty. Rowntree, long the baby of the three home-grown producers, was about to start an advertising war in a bid to grow its market share.

Rowntree had long been an advertising sceptic. Sales had grown quickly in the 1870s, but profitability was very tight even as late as 1878. Joseph Rowntree had spent some time with Cadbury's and in Holland, and then reorganized his business to begin selling his hugely popular cheap imitation pastilles in 1881. With the profits, he bought his own Van Houten press and relaunched Rowntree's 'Elect Cocoa' in August 1887 – now with heavy advertising. He was rewarded throughout the second half of the chocolate boom in 1890s, with sales that grew even faster than Cadbury's. In 1897, backed with new money from incorporation, Arnold Rowntree revolutionized his advertising, hiring the promotional guru S. H. Benson, and between 1897 and 1917 Rowntree's outspent its rivals – then spending £250,000 a year. A 9-foot-high tin of Elect Cocoa was sent on the road in a new motor car. Elect Cocoa sponsored the Oxford and Cambridge Boat Race. Thousands of new accounts were open. The firm decorated London buses with their advertisements asking: 'Have you had your ride on a Rowntree bus? Every lady passenger gets a free tin of "Elect Cocoa".' It was so popular, and caused such a rush for the buses, that the police threatened to stop it. A pioneering *Daily Telegraph* scheme followed, offering a penny stamp and a sample of cocoa in exchange for a coupon from the paper.[96] Ambitious to fight back, Cadbury's prepared to launch its game-changer: 'Dairy Milk'.

The precise history of milk chocolate's origins is not an uncontroversial subject, and deep in the Cadbury archives in Bournville lies an extraordinary cache of papers, letters and lectures detailing Cadbury Brothers' view of the matter, including the recorded recollections of J. H. Palmer, one of the Dairy Milk production team.

The firm's 'official view' was captured for the record in the *Bournville Works Magazine* in April 1955, to mark the Jubilee of Cadbury's Dairy Milk or 'C.D.M.' The origins of *milk* chocolate, it argued, lay with Sir Hans Sloane, who popularized the idea of mixing milk and chocolate before handing the recipe to the White family, from whom Cadbury

Brothers bought it.[97] Sloane's recipe, however, was for drinking chocolate. The first man actually to pioneer solid milk chocolate itself,
certainly for industrial production, was Daniel Peter, a manufacturer
near Lausanne, Switzerland, who began serious production – and
export to Britain – in 1895. By the early part of the twentieth century,
the Swiss were exporting 30 tonnes of it a week. It was so popular that
Cadbury's started serious research from the late 1890s, but, as the
younger George Cadbury recalled in a speech (in the Cadbury archives),
'None of the English milk chocolates made at the time was of a very
high class.'[98]

The problem was that Cadbury's was attempting to manufacture
milk chocolate using dried milk powder, which, said the younger
George Cadbury, had an 'unpleasant oily taste and odour, rather what
one would term "strong butter" characteristics'. Undeterred, the firm
kept up the research, but advised caution to its 'travellers' in 1899: 'We
have already made considerable improvements in this line… We hope
to send fresh samples before long but think it best not to do so till
further experiments are complete.'

To perfect the techniques, the younger George travelled to
Switzerland to study production techniques for condensing milk; seeing
the need to mix in solids of fresh full-cream milk, Cadbury's built its
own milk-condensing plant at Bournville. Thereafter, it was down to
trial and error. Reminiscing, the younger George recalled: 'I still remember those early experiments and the difficulties we had in controlling
the boiling and frothing over of the milk… The product of course was
a sticky mess.'[99]

Over the months that followed, his team – the chief chemist, a confectioner, the chief engineer and the foreman – strove for a product with
a far higher milk content. By July 1904, they had perfected their samples
for what was planned to be Cadbury's 'Dairy Maid'. On 9 August 1904,
there was a slight change, as a board minute noted: 'Agreed if possible
to adopt the name "Dairy Milk Chocolate" with plain label, of say blue
and white.' It was a vital tweak, apparently inspired by advice from a
customer. In Plymouth, one Mrs E. M. Creacy, whose parents owned a
local confectionery business, heard of the new product from a visiting
Cadbury's salesman. 'We are bringing out a new chocolate that will

sweep the country – Cadbury's Dairy Maid,' he said. Her reply was: 'I wonder you don't call it Dairy Milk – it is a much daintier name.' A large slab of Dairy Milk chocolate was Mrs Creacy's reward – and a marketing revolution was set in train.[100]

The new brand was launched in June 1905. By 1907, Dairy Milk's wrapping reflected its creaminess: gold and black on a pale lavender background, with the words 'Cadbury's Dairy Milk Chocolate' encircling a pan of milk. Nationwide, outstanding posters, designed by Cecil Aldin, which boasted a 'glass and a half of milk in every half-pound bar', were plastered everywhere.[101] The younger George Cadbury had initially suggested a production run of 20 tonnes a week. The board proposed 5, but within a decade output was up ten-fold, and milk chocolate was going into everything from chocolate bars to Easter eggs, to the new brand of milk-chocolate assortments called 'Milk Tray', sold in a half-pound 'box for your pocket' or a larger one-pound box. It sparked a new, additional market for popular boxed chocolates.

Meanwhile, the price war continued unabated. In 1906, the big three 'A' companies met to talk. Cadbury's frequently met with Fry's and Rowntree's to agree price policy and to not poach staff – and very occasionally to agree approaches to advertising.* On this occasion, Fry's and Cadbury's attacked Rowntree's new discounting scheme and threatened to introduce something similar, unless the scheme were withdrawn. A new agreement was struck on marketing and prices, but in truth Cadbury's was simply preparing the ground for its follow-up product to Dairy Milk. Branded 'Bournville Essence', it was a flavoured, alkalized cocoa.† Cadbury's now quickly followed through, slashing prices of its cheap chocolate bars and, together with Fry's, refused a co-ordinated price rise as the price of cocoa imports rose. The campaign forced Rowntree's to withdraw its leading 'Mountain Milk Chocolate' brand.

Another hard-fought year went by, before George Cadbury could induce his rivals to agree a truce. The price war would continue, but

---

* However, amid the controversy over William Lever's attempt to create a soap trust, the firms were careful to be circumspect.

† The alkalization process, invented by van Houten, removes most of the fat (in the form of cocoa butter) from the cocoa solids. The resulting powder is darker and milder in flavour.

advertising spend would, the firms agreed, come down by 25 per cent.[*][102] George Cadbury was now on the final lap of the race that would make him Britain's chocolate king.

*

Cadbury Brothers' victory in Britain's chocolate war was no accident. Its foundation was a wide-ranging change that followed the firm's incorporation as a limited company.

After Richard Cadbury's death, formal management, departments and committees were created.[†] In 1901, new offices were built, and a second railway line was connected to the plant. A 'suggestion scheme' started in 1902, based on a model seen first hand in the United States, along with a new Visitors Department to help shepherd some 4,000 annual visitors at Bournville. A Cost Office followed in 1903, helping the firm establish 'the scientific regulation of the price of goods', in turn prompting a complete reorganization of requisitioning, receiving, stock control and checkweighing.[103] Now, Cadbury's could allocate overhead charges to different lines of product to help price them.

In 1905, George brought in-house the firm's advertising business, under his personal direction, and the same year a Men's and Women's Works Committee was started, chaired by the younger George Cadbury, to advise on everything from works' rules to social activities, from health & safety and holidays to education and athletics. The Sales and Experimental committees set up in 1906 helped the business to keep evolving on the basis of advice from its army of travelling salesmen. In 1908, a huge factory expansion, encompassing new stock rooms, warehousing, dispatch decks and a vast boxing block (Q Block), transformed

---

* The arrangement suited Cadbury well. Bournville Essence was 12 per cent cheaper than Fry's Elect Cocoa, and in 1909, Rowntree finally persuaded the rivals to agree a price freeze, while it organized a new and cheaper cocoa of its own, Dutch Essence, with a £35,000 advertising campaign in the newspapers and a new coupon savings book. More and more, the firm threw money at the advertising challenge; by 1913, advertising spend was running at a third of sales. R. Fitzgerald, *Rowntree and the Marketing Revolution 1862–1969* (CUP, 2007), p. 116.

† This included defining the managerial staff, divided into 'Staff A' and 'Staff B', for the first time.

the factory. New committees for Advertising and Buying followed in 1910 and 1911 when the first subsidiary factories were opened in Knighton, down the canal from Bournville, to process condensed milk for Cadbury's Dairy Milk. A third factory followed in 1915.

Cadbury's sales were now swelling worldwide. The first permanent company representative in India, J. E. Davis, was appointed in 1895.* The Australian business built Cadbury's first overseas depot, in Sydney, in 1898. The business in South Africa was expanded, and the firm's agent there took on the islands of Madagascar and Mauritius. A full-time 'traveller' was appointed to serve the Mediterranean in 1900. Five years later, Cadbury's divided its world into three: China and the Far East, South America, and Canada together with the West Indies. By 1913, the exports from Bournville, overseen by Edward Cadbury, had grown twenty-fold.[104]

True to its founders' instincts, throughout this period of extraordinary growth, the firm's care for its staff intensified. A non-contributory sickness fund was started in 1903. Three years later, Cadbury's began its own contributory pension fund, one of only seven in the country to provide a pension from the age of sixty, based on aggregate lifetime earnings. In the same year, Cadbury's opened its new education scheme under the supervision of the Bournville Works Education Committee. Anyone taken on between the ages of fourteen and sixteen had to attend evening classes twice a week,† and the Evening Continuation School – including a School of Art – offered vocational education across the factory. In 1911, the Bournville Women's Savings and Pension Fund was created,‡ and in the same year Ruskin Hall opened as home to Bournville School of Arts and Crafts, a few yards away from an elementary school built for £30,000 at George Cadbury's expense.

Ensuring the well-being of Cadbury's suppliers, however, was to

---

* By 1921, the business was so big that the country was divided into two territories.

† From 1913, the 'continuation scheme' was turned into classes for half a day a week.

‡ The company savings scheme, begun in 1897 to celebrate the Diamond Jubilee, continued until the war, when a branch of the Birmingham Municipal Bank was opened at the factory.

prove a rather harder task. The discovery that slave labour underpinned the growing of Cadbury's cocoa beans sparked the firm's greatest crisis before the First World War, lit up in the public glare with a celebrated court case.

Nearly half of Cadbury's cocoa hailed from the Portuguese West African islands of São Tomé and Príncipe,* where the Cadbury board believed crops were produced through contract labourers.[105] In 1901, the board had first been alerted to the possibility that some of the cocoa was slave-farmed.[106] When Cadbury's met with Fry's and Rowntree's, they concluded that more proof was needed, and so an investigation was ordered, to which Cadbury's contributed £1,000.[107] George Cadbury's nephew, William Adlington Cadbury, was asked to take a lead, together with an independent Quaker agent, Joseph Burtt, whose investigation took until April 1907.[108] His conclusions were devastating: the cocoa plantations were essentially slave plantations with little respect for the dignity of human life.

Outraged, George Cadbury demanded that the foreign secretary, Sir Edward Grey, dispatch a gun boat to find conclusive evidence. When Grey demurred, Cadbury's began systematically eliminating cocoa sourced from São Tomé, until by 1909 the firm bought no more. But just as William Cadbury was preparing his follow-up visit to the islands, the *Evening Standard* caught wind of the story and a devastating '*exposé*' followed. Contrasting 'the plentitude of the solicitude of Mr Cadbury for his fellow creatures at home' with his indifference to 'those same grimed African hands whose toil is so essential to the beneficent and lucrative operations of Bournville',[109] the newspaper accused Cadbury's of knowingly profiting from the 'monstrous trade in human flesh and blood against which the Quaker and Radical ancestors of Mr Cadbury thundered in the better days of England'.[110]

George Cadbury immediately sued for libel, and a vicious court battle began. The *Standard*'s lawyer, Sir Edward Carson, relentlessly attacked the firm for its decisions to delay the boycott and to wait on further evidence. When the jury retired to deliberate, Mr Justice Pickford advised them to focus on a simple question: 'Did Cadbury's

---

* Both islands were referred to collectively as São Tomé.

delay the issue of slavery on São Tomé becoming known to the public for the dual purpose of maintaining its reputation and profiting off of the cheaply imported cocoa beans?'[111] After fifty-five minutes, the verdict was in: the jury cleared George Cadbury, but, in a stinging rejoinder, proposed damages of just one farthing.[112]

Cadbury's now faced a daunting challenge – of ensuring that its traditions of ethical enterprise extended well beyond the borders of Bournville and Britain to the Gold Coast (Ghana), where the firm set about building a plantation of its own. It was tough work, not least maintaining the quality of beans from new suppliers. As William Cadbury described it, 'at present not more than one load out of five is of such quality that it is possible to purchase… to buy 100 bags of cocoa it is necessary to handle and carefully test a thousand head loads [each of 60lbs]'. But the firm was clear about its obligations, and while just over 1,000 tonnes of beans were imported to Bournville in 1910, a joint buying agency with Fry's, created in 1917, drove the volumes up to 17,000 tonnes by 1929.[*]

Cadbury's diversification from cocoa into chocolate, especially Dairy Milk, was now beginning to look very wise indeed. While cocoa sales began to fall after 1906, general sales of chocolate began to boom – by an incredible 18 per cent every year – and Cadbury's was the biggest winner. In 1910, George Cadbury could pause to celebrate. With sales of £1,670,221, he finally overhauled his great rivals, Fry's, for the first time, to become Britain's biggest chocolate-maker.[†] By 1913, Britain was buying almost as much chocolate as it did cocoa,[‡] and Dairy Milk was one of the best-selling bars in the country.

On 28 February 1912, Cadbury's went public. Long wary of selling shares, George Cadbury was adamant that the market's thirst for profits should not compromise the company's values: ethical production, fair treatment of all workers and selling quality products. And so, to

---

* To diversify the risk, a second agency was established, again with Fry's, in southern Nigeria. Williams, 'George Cadbury', op. cit., p. 149.

† Fry's had achieved sales of £1,642,715. Wagner, *The Chocolate Conscience*, op. cit., p. 24.

‡ The country bought £3.3 million-worth of chocolate, compared to £3.5 million of cocoa in that year.

guarantee continuity, he ensured that the family kept a controlling share, selling just 200,000 6-per-cent preference shares.[113]

*

The First World War marked the final chapter in George Cadbury's long career. More than 2,000 of his workers joined up. One of them was awarded the DSO; two won the Military Cross; 218 lost their lives, and today their names are remembered on the tablet erected on Bournville Lane by their friends.[114] And yet, like a lucky few, Cadbury Brothers emerged from the war years stronger than ever. During his final days, George Cadbury devoted himself to supporting those wounded in the war.

He still followed the firm's affairs closely. At the age of eighty-one, he attended eighty-one of the firm's ninety-two board meetings.[115]

In the final months of war, the industry's giants had agreed a 30 per cent cut in their advertising spend. Cadbury's was now generating enough profit to announce a union with its old competitor, J. S. Fry.[116] The 'Big Cocoa Combine', otherwise known as the British Cocoa and Chocolate Company Ltd, was created to bring together the privately held shares of the two firms.[117] By 1919, Cadbury's was generating a staggering £8.1 million profit – £1.2–£1.9 billion in today's money.

*

When the First World War ended, George Cadbury was entering his eighth decade. He was still cycling or walking 5 miles every Sunday to his Adult School – until in his final year, it became too much. Confined to one floor of Northfield Manor, his residence since 1894, he spent his days reading the company minutes and sitting on his balcony, gazing out over the lake and gardens.[118] On the evening of 20 October 1922, his lungs filled with fluid. He struggled to breathe. He lapsed into unconsciousness. When he came round, three days later, he spoke tenderly to his wife of his great love for her – and wished her farewell. The following day, an hour after the five o'clock bell sounded the end of the shift at Bournville, George Cadbury passed away.[119]

The next morning, at 11.00am, the workers of Bournville bowed their heads to remember the man who had done so much to create the world around them. At the memorial service, 16,000 people joined them on the village green.[120] Among the condolences was a message from Queen Mary for the man who was, to the very last, a pioneer of ethical enterprise, a man who insisted 'I have only done what is the duty of every employer and Christian citizen.'[121]

9

CECIL RHODES

Entrepreneur-imperialist

At around half past nine on Sunday, 29 December 1895, the magistrate of Mafeking was sitting peacefully on his *stoep* in the warmth of the dark evening having just enjoyed the evening church service with his wife and his mother. Around them was a town that was not much to speak of. A few homes, a station, a hospital, a prison, a convent, a library, a court-house and a branch of Standard Bank were all that made up the capital of Britain's Crown Colony of Bechuanaland, through which ran the road to the Boer-ruled South African Republic of the Transvaal – the world's greatest gold state and soon to be home to more direct British investment than anywhere else on earth.*

Suddenly, through the darkness, loud cheering echoed from the police camp round the corner. Men of the recently disbanded Bechuanaland Border Police were saddling up to march along the dusty road to Pitsani to rendezvous with one of the most remarkable men in the British Empire: Dr Leander Starr Jameson.† A Scot with a lightning-quick mind, Jameson was about to lead an adventure that would earn him immortality as the inspiration for Rudyard Kipling's poem 'If'.¹ After issuing his orders, and offering a toast,

---

* By 1910, South Africa enjoyed £227 million in FDI from the UK. See T. A. B. Corley, 'Britain's Overseas Investments in 1914 Revisited', *Business History*, Vol. 36, January 1994.
† The BBP was dissolved when a border strip of Bechuanaland was transferred to the British South Africa Company on 18 October 1895, and its men were freed to enlist in the BSAC police. See Elizabeth Longford, *Jameson's Raid: The Prelude to the Boer War* (Littlehampton, 1982), p. 60.

Jameson set off to lead his men to storm the Boer capital: Johannesburg.

The 'Jameson Raid' had been conceived over months of growing frustration. For years, the charismatic entrepreneur-imperialist Cecil Rhodes, the British Empire's richest man and now Prime Minister of Britain's Cape Colony, had dreamed of a united Federation of South Africa, a 'United States of South Africa'.[2] But one thing stood in his way. The seventy-six-year-old President of the South African Republic, Paul Kruger, resisted every effort Rhodes made to inch together the Cape Colony and the Boer republic. After four years of arguing, Rhodes's patience was running out. And so he prepared for violence.

Jameson had readied his men, armed with the latest Maxim machine guns, in utmost secrecy. A convenient strip of border land was secured from the London government, allegedly for a railway, on which to marshal them. A communications centre was created in Rhodes's Cape Town company offices. Plans were drawn up to smuggle 5,000 rifles and a million rounds of ammunition, hidden in oil barrels and coal trucks, to pro-British rebels in Johannesburg, where Rhodes's brother Frank was dispatched to foment rebellion. Finally, a pretext for invasion was prepared in the shape of a forged letter of invitation from the English leaders of Johannesburg's community of 'alien' British workers, calling on Jameson for armed help to protect 'thousands of unarmed men, women and children… at the mercy of well-armed Boers'.[3]

Yet, on that fateful Sunday evening, as his troops were mustered, Rhodes was unwinding in blissful ignorance in his sprawling Dutch-style farmhouse, 'Groote Schuur.' Suddenly alarmed that a key part of his plan – the armed British uprising in Johannesburg – was not quite primed and ready, Rhodes had that morning ordered Jameson to stand down. But Jameson's men had cut the telegraph wires. The message to them did not get through. And so, on that Sunday evening Jameson marched off into disaster.

It was a week before news of a catastrophe began to arrive in London. 'Trouble in the Transvaal' screamed the headlines, late on 6 January 1896, and beneath the headlines ran a sorry saga. Around 500 of the former Bechuanaland Border Police, along with mounted officers from

Matabeleland and Mashonaland,* had crossed the border with eight Maxims and three field guns on their march to Johannesburg, led by the Earl of Coventry's second son, Major Coventry. After two days, shots were exchanged with Boer commandos 20 miles from Krugersdorp. The Boers fell back, but only to lure Jameson into a trap at Doornkop, where 4,000 Boers equipped with ample supplies of ammunition lay in wait. In a six-and-a-half-hour pitched battle, Jameson's force fought 'from 5am to 11.30 though cold and rain, starved and thirsty, till the ammunition failed and the Maxims got jammed for want of water to keep them cool.'[4] Major Coventry was among those who lay dead on the battlefield.

With the day lost, Jameson ordered a torn white shirt be hoisted in surrender. In Johannesburg, his allies, the rebels of the 'reform committee', capitulated. In London, Rhodes's key political ally, Colonial Secretary Joseph Chamberlain, rapidly – if mendaciously – protested ignorance of the raid. In the Cape Colony, Rhodes could not pretend to offer the same excuse.

Cecil Rhodes – Prime Minister of the Cape Colony, Chairman of the British South Africa Company, founder of the De Beers diamond company and the single most powerful entrepreneur in the British Empire – had fallen. He was thirty-eight.

*

Cecil Rhodes was born in the vicarage on South Street, in the thriving Hertfordshire market town of Bishop's Stortford, to a devoted mother and a diffident father in the early evening of 5 July 1853, after a wet fortnight had soaked the hay harvest.[5] His mother, Louisa, was descended from a family of well-to-do Lincolnshire bankers.[6] His father, Francis, in appearance tall and spare, enjoyed an education at Harrow School and Trinity College, Cambridge, before departing from the family's trading traditions and joining the Church of England.† It was the Church that eventually dispatched him to the living at St

---

* The former BBP troops joined a combined force known to contemporaries as the Rhodesian Mounted Police. See Ash, *The If Man*, op. cit., p. 224.

† Francis Rhodes boasted descent from a long line of Midland and Cheshire business people; his great-grandfather had owned a great brick and tile works in Dalston.

Michael's, Bishop's Stortford, where he lived on top of the hill, above the Corn Exchange. The town was rich in public houses, but its school was very poor, and it was to this challenge that Reverend Rhodes applied himself.

By all accounts, it was a happy home. Cecil's mother, a pleasant, plump woman with a cheerful nature, set the tenor, and while Cecil's relations with Francis were cool, Louisa adored her son. She called no one else, in her letters at least, 'my darling'. 'She was never flustered,' Rhodes later wrote, 'and seemed always to have ample time to listen to all our many and, to us, vastly important affairs.'[7] She remained a close confidante to Cecil for the rest of her life. The Reverend Francis Rhodes, by contrast, aged forty-six when Cecil was born, offered his son more instruction than warmth.[8] Cecil Rhodes later recalled that his father 'frequently, and I am now sure wisely, demolished many of my dreams as fantastical, but when I had rebuilt them on more practical lines, he was ready to listen.'[9]

Unlike his older brothers, Cecil was sent (in 1861) not to Eton or Winchester but to the local grammar school, where he proved a tough, thoughtful, attractive child, but only an average student, with a propensity for manipulation and a fiercely competitive streak. One teacher well remembered a game of cricket when Cecil took a hard ball to the arm. 'I was struck', said the teacher, 'by the Spartan way, almost indifference with which the child bore pain.'[10]

At the age of thirteen, Rhodes chose himself a motto, 'to do or to die', and his habit of carefully weighing decisions earned him a nickname from his brother Frank, 'Long-headed Cecil'.[11] Academic prizes, however, never followed, and while he won a school silver medal for elocution, his Latin and Greek were poor, and a place at Oxford University eluded him.[12] Uninspired by the Church or the army, which employed all four of his brothers, Rhodes took aim at a career at the bar. 'I still above everything would like to be a barrister,' he wrote in an early letter to his Aunt Sophy, 'but I agree with you it is a very precarious profession. Next to that I think a clergyman's life is the nicest'.[13]

But Rhodes would never train either as a lawyer or a clergyman. Early in 1869, he began to suffer unexplained heart pains and a shortness of breath. His symptoms were diagnosed, incorrectly, as consumption, and his doctor recommended a long sea voyage and a change of climate. On this misdiagnosis his fortune turned. For not only had Rhodes's risk-loving eldest brother, Herbert, just departed – with impeccable timing – to southern Africa, but Aunt Sophy was a very rich woman; now she, worried for Cecil's health, offered her nephew £2,000 (between £1 million and £1.7 million in today's money) to follow his brother. Rhodes set off for the British Colony of Natal to join Herbert, who had set himself up in cotton farming.

Among the many ships that arrived at Gravesend on 25 March 1870, from all over the world, was the old wooden barque, the *Eudora*, which drew in from Natal for a quick turnaround. When she headed back out to sea, just a few days later, Cecil Rhodes was on board. Over the course of the next seventy-five days, he recovered his health, studied maps of his future home and began to dream. 'They will tell you that I came on account of my health or from a love of adventure,' said Rhodes later in life, 'and to some extent that may be true. But the real fact is that I could no longer stand cold mutton.'[14]

On 1 September 1870, the *Eudora* anchored in the roads off the Bluff, the promontory at Durban, and the tall, lanky, anaemic fair-headed seventeen-year-old was ferried across the sandbar to the harbour. Blinking in the bright afternoon sun, he scanned the quayside for his brother – but no brother could be seen.[15] Rather, there were just two letters. The first, from Herbert, explained his departure north to the diamond fields of Griqualand West, around Kimberley, and enclosed £20 to help Cecil get his start in cotton growing. The second was from Dr Sutherland, the Surveyor-General of Natal, who invited him round for tea. Rhodes took up Sutherland on his offer, and, after a tour of the surrounding countryside, was invited to stay, until Herbert's return.[16] When Herbert arrived, the two brothers set off for the Umkomanzi Valley, just south of Pietermaritzburg, there to commence what would turn out to be a disastrous foray into farming.

'Nothing can exceed the beauty of the valley we are in,' Rhodes wrote on 18 October 1870, in one of his first letters back to his mother, 'the hills are for hundreds of feet all round us, their sides covered both with bush and tropical vegetation.'[17] But it was not long before he had to admit that cotton was a difficult business; 'It really seems an ill-fated valley,' Rhodes wrote to his mother. 'You would be surprised if I told you what a sink it has been.'[18] Herbert had planted his cotton rows too close together. The crop failed, and Rhodes was left with nothing to show from an entire year's work. A second year of modest improvements followed, and Rhodes was now learning the vital business of managing labourers, rubbing along with officials and getting to know his fellow traders; but his cotton sold for a poor price, and once again he turned no profit for the year. And so, Cecil Rhodes began to survey the options opening up 400 miles away, across the Drakensberg Mountains, in the astonishing new diamond fields on the western edge of the Orange Free State.

Herbert Rhodes had already left in May 1871 to stake a claim. Cecil now decided to join him. And so, thirteen months after he set foot in southern Africa, Rhodes loaded up his ox-cart for the month-long trek past the Mooi river and across the Tugela, up through Van Reenan's Pass and on to the high *veldt*, through Boer villages, to Kimberley, the town which had become – in the words of Anthony Trollope – 'the most remarkable sight on the face of the earth'.[19]

*

Cecil Rhodes was not alone in his odyssey. Indeed, he and Herbert were but two of the extraordinary 4,250,000 people who left the British Isles in the last forty years of the nineteenth century, transforming Britain's global footprint – and trade balance. Between 1815 and 1874, Britain extended its formal imperial control worldwide – across western Australia, New Zealand, western Canada, India, the Colony of Natal, the Gold Coast and Lagos, and Fiji – and Britons quickly travelled to fill the new spaces.* Unlike most of the Irish and the Scots expatriates, who headed to America, 60 per cent of English colonialists –100,000 a year – headed to Canada, Australia, New Zealand and southern Africa.[20] In all, 8 million Britons left between 1853 and 1920.

Some travelled for high purpose. The China Inland Mission and

---

* Australia was annexed in 1824–29 and Western Canada in 1859–70. In India, imperial control was asserted over the Maratha territories, Assam, southern Burma, Mysore, Sind, Punjab, Jhansi and Oudh.

Church Missionary Society, along with other similar organizations, had recruited 8,500 missionaries. Others served the new machineries of state: by the 1890s, the Indian Civil Service and the Colonial Service employed 20,000 administrators and 146,000 soldiers. Most, however, such as Cecil and Herbert Rhodes, were simply looking for a new life in a new world that was suddenly smaller, thanks to the extraordinary advances in Britain's capital markets and communication methods: fast steamships, global telegraph links and new railway lines now allowed entrepreneurs to move people and money all over the world. When Isambard Kingdom Brunel's first transatlantic steamship, the SS *Great Western*, sailed from New York to Bristol in 1838, it slashed the crossing to just fourteen days and twelve hours. It was the first in a gallery of engineering masterpieces, culminating in the gigantic 700-foot SS *Great Eastern*, designed to carry 4,000 passengers and enough fuel for the journey to the Far East and back.*

A mobile, well-connected emigrant population was hugely good for British business. In the decades after 1860, multilateral trade increased ten-fold, for where the British went, exports followed.[21] In the words of Arnold White, 'The constant travelling of the Colonialists backwards and forwards to England makes it absurd to speak of the colonies as if they were a foreign land. They are simply pieces of Britain distributed about the world.'[22] Whereas, in 1815, the 'settlement empire' consumed just 20 per cent of Britain's 'visible' or physical exports, from the 1850s the figure rose to 50 per cent.[23] By the 1870s, a third of *all* exports – both physical goods and services such as insurance or banking – were bought by imperial markets, which became, by the end of the century, *the* key markets for Britain's staple commodities, such as pig iron and cotton. And, from foreign lands Britain brought back the fruits of the world: textiles from India, tea from China – and soon, the treasure that lay deep beneath the earth of southern Africa.

*

---

* James Watt of Birmingham supplied the engines for the steamer and Robert Stephenson advised on the launch. There was no bigger ship for another forty-nine years. When it proved too big for commercial success as a passenger liner, it was redeployed laying submarine cables.

Kimberley's first diamonds had been discovered some four years before Rhodes arrived. In 1867, one Schalk van Niekerk was visiting his neighbour Jacob, near Hopetown on the Orange river, when his eye was caught by one of the brilliant stones their children were using to play marbles. According to the legend, Jacob was generous: 'take it away with you, by all means, if you fancy it'. Dispatched by post to Grahamstown, and on to Cape Town, it was studied by the British Colonial Secretary Richard Southey, who immediately saw the significance of the solitary stone. 'Gentlemen,' he announced, 'this is the rock on which the future success of South Africa will be built.'[24] Two years later, van Niekerk came across another gem, owned by a local witch-doctor; he offered all he owned for it, and subsequently sold the 84-carat 'Star of Africa' for £11,000.

More diamonds were then found along the Orange and Vaal rivers, and out on the open *veldt* around Kimberley. Before long, speculators were arriving to buy the farms, snapping up claims on Du Toits Pan, Bultfontein and Vooruitzicht, the latter farm owned by the De Beer brothers. The rush of diggers was now immense. By the time Rhodes arrived, the great plateau of the Kimberley mining area had become a jam-packed British protectorate, after Lieutenant-Governor Keate of the Natal was summoned to adjudicate competing claims to the land – from the Griqua (a mixed-race group descended from early European Cape settlers), led by Nicholaas Waterboer, the indigenous southern Tswana (Tlhaping), and the local Boers.[25] In October 1871, Keate awarded the land to Waterboer, who promptly placed the territory – 'Griqualand West' – under the administration of Queen Victoria.

'I should like you to have a peep at the *kopje* from my tent door at the present moment,' wrote Rhodes to his mother; 'It is like an immense number of ant-heaps covered with black ants, as thick as can be.' Around him were 10,000 white settlers (a quarter from abroad) and 30,000 black labourers digging on 3,600 plots, each 30 x 30 square feet, spread across four great mines named after the original farms: Dutoitspan, Bultfontein, and – the two richest, on the Vooruitzicht land – De Beers and Colesberg Kopje. Along the fourteen parallel roadways lined with carts, the diggers dashed in and out of the pits, carrying dirt and diamonds with them.

'Fancy an immense plain with right in its centre a great mass of white tents and iron stores,' Rhodes went on, 'and on one side of it, all mixed up with the camp, mounds of lime like ant-hills; the country round is all flat with just thorn trees here and there; and you have some idea of Dutoitspan'.[26]

Kimberley's promise, however, was not enough to hold Rhodes's brother; Herbert – as Cecil wrote to his mother on 18 October 1870 – 'had not much luck' in the diamond fields.[27] He offered young Cecil a rapid introduction to the business, left his claims under Cecil's control, briefed his brother on Kimberley's social world – and promptly left for England.[28] The tall and fair Cecil, 'moody and deaf to the chatter around him', was left to cut a distinctive figure on his own; a fellow miner remembered him: 'wearing flannels of the school playing field… his tall figure crumpled up on an inverted bucket, as he sat scrapping his gravel surrounded by his plucky Zulus'.[29]

Rhodes worked every waking hour. On days when a digger failed to show up – usually because he had made enough money to return to his village – he would roll up his sleeves, climb down into the mines, and dig for himself.[30] His three claims proved lucky. 'On this *kopje*,' Rhodes wrote, 'I should think nearly every day they find a diamond over 50 carats.' Here were rough diamonds 'of all shapes, sizes and colours under the sun'. 'I find on average 30 carats a week and am working one of the few whole claims in the *kopje*; a claim in fact that will take me four years to work out at the present rate.'[31] Within just two months, Cecil was making £100 a week (worth somewhere between £50,000 and £70,000 a week in today's money), and striving just as hard above the ground as he did below it, making good friends among the wealthy claim-holders, administrators and professionals who had arrived from all over the world.[32]

When Herbert returned to Kimberley, he had in tow the third Rhodes brother, Frank, who was asked to mind the Kimberley claims while Cecil and Herbert set off to the Transvaal to test the emerging news of new gold finds. One look at the potential there was enough for Herbert to sell his Kimberley diamond claims to Cecil, who, with his rapid profits, was now worth some £10,000.[33] But it was no safeguard against the sudden strike of what appeared to be a minor 'heart attack'. Desperately needing to recuperate, Rhodes turned his mind from mining. It was, he decided, time to reapply to the University of Oxford. As luck would have it, the Provost of Oriel College, Dr Edward Hawkins, was the uncle of a Kimberley acquaintance, and, notwithstanding some uncertainty about Cecil's qualifications, he was quickly offered admission.[34]

Oxford, however, was to offer little respite. For on 1 November 1873, Rhodes received news that his beloved mother had died. Struggling to cope with the loss, he caught a chill while rowing on the Isis.[35] Weak and worried, Rhodes sought the advice of a London chest and throat specialist, Dr Morell Mackenzie, whose prescription was simple and urgent: he should return to the hot, dry climate of Kimberley immediately.

In no mood to quibble, Rhodes was back in Africa within weeks, only to discover Kimberley in chaos but British policy on the brink of break-through. A worldwide recession had sparked a sharp fall in diamond prices. Banks were foreclosing on struggling mine-owners. A year of drought, followed by flooding, had triggered the collapse of mines and a surge in prices for food and transport. The crisis would prove the making of Rhodes.

Together with an old friend, Charles Rudd – a man a decade older and a cool counterbalance to Rhodes's often impulsive nature – Rhodes bid aggressively for a De Beers mining board contract to drain the flooded mines.[36] It was now clear in Kimberley that the future of diamond mining lay with large-scale ventures big enough to drive shafts deeper underground, where the soft yellow dirt turned to the 'hard blue' clay that required mechanized digging.[37] But, as the mines went deeper, so they filled with water. Within a year, it was obvious that Rhodes's ramshackle machinery was failing. A temporary contract was awarded to a rival, only for their machinery mysteriously to break down on Boxing Day 1875. Furious allegations of sabotage were flung at Rhodes, who promptly threatened to sue for libel. Together, Rhodes and Rudd survived, and when prohibitions on stock companies were lifted in 1876, which had had the effect of protecting the smaller digging inter-ests, the partners put their Vooruitzicht mine claims together and looked to what they could roll up around them.

By spring 1876, Rhodes was secure enough to return to Oxford, where life would now prove rather more congenial than his first term.

He remained deeply engaged with business; indeed, among his letters in the Oxford University archives, are detailed orders for a pumping engine to be shipped to Rudd & Co., 'with all the latest improvements in the economy of fuel' and at 'the utmost speed possible'. But Rhodes worked harder socially than academically, and before long his social life was expensive enough to require a loan from Rudd's brother ('It is very unpleasant being under an obligation to any one... but I had not a six-pence and do not like to bother my father') and absorbing enough to provoke a battle or two with his professors.[38] 'My dons and I', he wrote to Rudd, 'have had some tremendous skirmishes.' He was elected to the Bullingdon Club in 1877, and later joined the Freemasons in the Apollo University Lodge.[39]

And while Rhodes was ascending socially in Oxford, Britain was about to surge ahead in southern Africa.

*

The British were relative latecomers in Africa, compared with, for example, the Portuguese or the Dutch. Britain's African trade dated back to the barbarities of slavery and although England entered the slave trade late in the day, its merchants soon dominated, as demand for slaves to work the Caribbean sugar plantations multiplied in the years after 1660. By the 1750s, around 28,000 slaves a year were shipped west by the Company of Royal Adventurers (formed in 1660).* Between 1662 and the abolition of the transatlantic trade in 1807, British ships orga-nized by the slave traders and ivory dealers who built cities such as Liverpool, carried 3.4 million people across the sea – some 50 per cent of all the slaves transported.[40] Indeed, in the final quarter-century of the trade, Liverpool merchants were financing 75 per cent of all the slave voyages, buying men and women for £25 on the Gold Coast and selling them for twice the price in the West Indies.

Perversely, it was the abolition of slavery that accounted for Britain's first territorial possessions on the African continent, as British forces

---

* The Royal Adventurers were reconstituted as the Royal African Company in 1672.

moved in to suppress the last outposts of the slavers in Sierra Leone, Gambia, the Gold Coast and Lagos. From this inauspicious start, it was British power in Africa which helped trigger the European 'Scramble for Africa' whereby within two decades of 1880, 10,000 African kingdoms were reduced to just forty states determined by the Europeans. A third were under British control.[41]

Britain flexed its imperial muscles everywhere. In Africa's west, George Goldie, a son of Manx smugglers, had carved out the Royal Niger Company. In the north-east, Egypt was invaded as a 'temporary expedient' on 31 July 1882, to preserve the safety of British and France ownership of the Suez Canal – acquired in 1875 from a bankrupt khedive, but now jeopardized by local nationalist demands.[42] In the south, the old Dutch Cape Colony, strategically so vital to Britain's communications with India, had fallen to Britain in the months after the Battle of Trafalgar in 1805. Neighbouring Natal became a British colony in 1843, and by the 1870s was home to 17,000 white settlers and 300,000 Africans, surrounded by the territories of the Zulu to the north, the Sotho to the west and Mpondo of the still independent 'Pondoland' to the south. Within just twenty years, a polyglot region of twenty southern African states and territories would be rolled up and a further 1 million square miles added to the British Empire.

Not long after Rhodes returned to the Cape Colony, Henry Herbert, the Lord Porchester and 4th Earl of Carnarvon, was appointed as Secretary of State for the Colonies in Benjamin Disraeli's Conservative government of 1874. Known as 'Twitters', on account of his nervous tics, he was responsible for the self-rule and confederation of Canada; but southern Africa worried him. He saw there 'the threat of a general and simultaneous rising of Kaffirdom against white civilisation'. South Africa, he concluded, needed the sort of self-government he had introduced to Canada.[43] Carnarvon had hoped initially that the Cape Colony would take a lead. Now home to 237,000 whites (representing about two-thirds of southern Africa's white population), its first self-governing administration had been elected in 1872. But, after two abortive attempts to call a conference on confederation in southern Africa, and then a failed London conference in August 1876, Carnarvon decided to force matters by exploiting a Boer defeat at the hands of the Pedi.

In January 1877, he instructed the local Natal secretary of 'Native Affairs', governor, Theophilus Shepstone, to march across the Orange River and annex the South African Republic as the Crown Colony of the Transvaal, with a nominated legislature. Three months later, Shepstone was joined by Sir Bartle Frere, appointed High Commissioner of Southern Africa and Governor of the Cape Colony in March 1877. The suppressor of the slave trade in Zanzibar, Frere was a devotee of Disraeli's 'new imperialism', and quickly embarked on a series of border wars with the African kingdoms along the coast between the Cape and Natal, intervening first to defeat the Xhosa in the Transkei in 1877.

For Rhodes in Oxford, the advance of imperialism no doubt influenced what was perhaps the most important piece of his written work, the 'Confession of Faith', set down on the day he was inducted into the Freemasons. It crystallized Rhodes's world-view: the duty of the Anglo-Saxon race to embark on imperial expansion in order to civilize other races through intensive colonialization.[44] To the document, Rhodes appended a will, drafted in September 1877 (and the first of many wills), to provide for a secret society to support the aims of his 'Confession' along with funds for the Secretary of State for the Colonies, who had so inspired him.[45]

Six months later, reports in the 'Ecclesiastical Intelligence' columns of Friday 8 March 1878 brought sad news. 'The death of the late Vicar of Bishop's Stortford (Mr Rhodes) is announced,' declared the *Essex Standard*.[46] His servant, reported the *Chelmsford Chronicle*, 'found him lying upon the floor dead, evidently having fallen while dressing'.[47] Both of his parents were now dead. There was nothing in England to hold him, and so Rhodes set sail for southern Africa once more, even more ambitious than when he left.

*

Over the decade that followed, while his personal life grew complicated, Rhodes's political career and his commercial powerhouse brought him a brief and brilliant domination of southern Africa.

Once back in South Africa, and against the backdrop of a newly assertive British policy, Rhodes quickly became the centre of an extraordinary knot of Kimberley men – the 'twelve apostles' who messed together on the diamond fields.[48] Dr Leander Starr was a brilliant Scottish doctor, Robert Graham was a lawyer, and Alfred Beit was a financial mastermind. When Rhodes and Beit first met, they discovered some similar ambitions. Beit supposedly announced: 'I'm going to control the whole diamond output before I'm much older'. Rhodes simply replied: 'That's funny. I've made up my mind to do the same. We'd better join hands.'[49]

One friend, however, was particularly special. Neville Pickering, the son of a Port Elizabeth clergyman, was a cheerful young man, a decade younger than Rhodes who took him on as a secretary. A deep companionship began that would last until Pickering's untimely death in 1888.[50] They were seldom apart. 'They shared the same office and the same dwelling-house, worked together, played together, shot together,' said a friend, while a contemporary described the relationship as 'an absolutely lover-like friendship'.[51] No letters, diaries, or notes exist to illuminate their relationship any further.

Together, Rhodes and the men around him now set about amassing a fortune by the tried and tested method of building a monopoly. Rhodes owned the largest share in the De Beers mine, but both he and Rudd knew that in order to set the price of diamonds, they needed to be the biggest diamond-sellers, and that meant becoming the biggest buyers of their competitors' mining claims, with enough financial muscle to finance the costs of digging the ever deeper mines. Between 1878 and 1880, therefore, Rhodes and Rudd began rolling up their rivals' shares of the De Beers mine.* The copies of letters between them, stored in the Oxford University archives, are a fascinating insight into the daily business of organizing everything from pumps to buy-outs, building a business capable of digging ever deeper as the ground began to collapse. 'I do not think the *kopje* will hold out until the 1st of December,' Rhodes penned in October 1879, noting the need to access pumping machines. He preferred to give shares rather than sign bills – 'I hate liabilities,' he noted in September 1882, discussing the buy-out of rival claims.

---

* These rivals included R. Graham, Dunsmure, Alderson, Stow and English, and other lesser-known De Beers claims-holders.

On 1 April 1880, the pair took a huge step forward, joining forces with a host of claim-owners to float the De Beers Mining Company with a share capital of £200,000[52] to create one of twelve joint stock companies worth a combined value of £2.5 million[53] (worth between £1 billion and £1.8 billion today) which together controlled seventy-one Kimberley claims and dug £4 million-worth of diamonds a year.

Rhodes's timing was fortunate. An economic depression struck again in 1882–84, and many small De Beers miners were happy to sell out,[54] not least because the political crisis on the Cape's eastern frontier in the Transvaal and Zululand was taking a turn for the worse. It was a crisis in which Rhodes now decided to deal himself a hand, with election to the Cape's Parliament.

Not long after Kimberley's traditional chief, Nicholas Waterboer, had placed his ancestral home under British protection, both the Griqua and Tlhaping were slowly evicted. When they rebelled, they were crushed, and Kimberley was incorporated into the Cape Colony, with the right to elect members to the Cape assembly. In April 1881, Rhodes won his place as the junior Member for Barkly West and wasted no time in advancing the mine-owners' cause.[55] He quickly became chair of the select committee investigating illegal diamond trafficking and ensured the stiffest possible penalties in the subsequent Diamond Trade Act of 1882.*

Rhodes now acquired a habit for which he became famous – of pulling out maps of southern Africa and declaring: 'All this to be painted red; that is my dream.'[56] He acquired a majority share of the *Cape Argus*, the largest newspaper in the Cape Colony, and while he promised never to interfere with the paper's opinions, his speeches, infrequent though they were, received plenty of attention.[57] There was certainly much news to cover, for the 'forward policy' of Lord Carnarvon, who had resigned in 1878, had begun to collapse as African tribes and the Boers (and their German allies) fought back against British power.

Sir Henry Bartle Frere had followed his annexation of the Transvaal

---

* The law now allowed entrapment of individuals suspected in trading in illicit diamonds, police searches without warrants, and assumed guilt until innocence was proven. Only a proposal for public flogging did not quite make it to the final draft.

and the Transkei by attempting to disarm the Sotho in Basutoland in 1878, before then provoking conflict with King Cetshwayo's Zulu nation, on the border of British southern Africa. His forces were at first disastrously defeated by the Zulus at the Battle of Isandhlwana, in January 1879, before eventual victory over Cetshwayo later that year. The subsequent division of Zululand into competing chiefdoms, sparked years of civil war. On another front, Boer resistance to the consolidation of British control in 1880 erupted into the First Anglo-Boer War and the British defeat at Majuba in the Transvaal prompted the new British prime minister, Gladstone, to withdraw from the annexed lands.

A new, delicate balance of power was not agreed until the London convention of 1884. The Boer republics, now independent once more, were emboldened and expanding into neighbouring lands where the British had destroyed the power of African kingdoms. To contain their ambitions, Britain now took a direct stake in the region, declaring a protectorate over Bechuanaland, the vast swathe of 276,000 square miles of south-central Africa up to the lands around the Limpopo and Zambezi. But the balance lasted merely months. In August 1884, the chancellor of the newly united Germany, Bismarck – long an admirer of the East India Company – was persuaded by a Bremen businessman, F. A. Luderitz, to extend German control of a tiny coastal enclave around Angra Pequeña further along the south-west African coast and inland, claiming for Germany territory that become its colony of South West Africa (Namibia). The risk was obvious: a German–Boer alliance could now forge a united territory, from the Boer republics in the east to Germany's new territory in the west, creating a northern barrier hemming in British southern Africa.

The reaction in London and the Cape was furious. 'In these circumstances,' declared Joseph Chamberlain in London, 'I do not think that we should allow him [Bismarck] to forestall us again in South Africa.' Sir Donald Currie, a well-known London financier, spoke for the Cape business community when he told Gladstone that 'since the political unrest and uncertainty east and west of Transvaal, the trade of South Africa has fallen off more than 15% and is rapidly diminishing.'[58] Under pressure, Gladstone's Cabinet agreed to annex the entire south-eastern African coastline up to St Lucia Bay, 150 miles north of Durban, instructing the HMS *Goshawk* to hoist a flag and have it 'saluted at more than one place'.[59]

As Rhodes predicted, the Boers reacted immediately. On 16 September 1884, President Paul Kruger of the Transvaal issued a 'Provisional Proclamation' absorbing the territory of Goshen in Bechuanaland, carved out by Boer mercenaries two years before. It was the first step to connecting the Transvaal across the great expanse of Bechuanaland with the new German south-western territories.[*] In London, on 19 November 1884, the Cabinet met to agree its response. An extra penny was put on income tax to finance, among other ventures, an expedition to keep Bechuanaland British, led by Major-General Sir Charles Warren, and in a final effort to forestall war, a small commission was established to negotiate a peaceful resolution, and Cecil Rhodes joined up to do his bit.

Rhodes approached the talks as a Boer sympathizer. Rhodes thought Kruger 'one of the most remarkable men in south Africa'. When, in a discussion on the 1880–81 war, the founder of Afrikaner nationalism, Jan Hofmeyr, expressed pity at fighting between British and Boers, Rhodes replied: 'No, it is not, I have quite changed my opinion. It is a good thing. It has made Englishmen respect Dutchmen.'[60] Crucially, Rhodes wanted a South African empire run from the Cape, not from London, and so he wanted a solution that minimized conflict with Afrikaners so that their representatives in the Cape Parliament – the Afrikaner Bond Party – would acquiesce in the Cape Colony's annexation of southern Bechuanaland.[61] As Rhodes saw it, control of southern Africa's interior was vital to Cape interests. 'I solemnly warn this House,' he once told the Cape Parliament, 'that if it departs from the control of the interior we shall fall from the position of the paramount state in South Africa which is our right.'

General Warren, on the other hand, wanted something very different; he saw Boer/Afrikaner ambitions as an impediment to Britain's relations with indigenous Africans, and so favoured an imperial

---

[*] Boer mercenaries had intervened in tribal conflicts in 1882, taking up arms on behalf of Tswana chiefs, and in the process declared the two small republics of Stellaland and Goshen. See Thomas, *Rhodes*, pp. 135–6.

protectorate run from London. 'If such a policy is pursued,' Rhodes declared later in Parliament, 'it will endanger the whole of our social relationships with colonists of Dutch descent.'[62] At odds with Warren, Rhodes resigned his commission post in February 1885 – but not before negotiating security of Boer mercenaries' land titles in the new little republic of Stellaland, under Cape protection.[63] Warren on the other hand saw his task as eviction of the white 'freebooters' and the creation of a protectorate under the security of the Crown, which he duly secured a month later, on 23 March 1885.

*

Rhodes may have been frustrated with his political progress; but business, on the other hand, was on the brink of a breakthrough. In 1882, there had been more than a hundred companies competing in the diamond fields of Kimberley. But the industry was fast consolidating. By 1885, just forty-two companies and fifty-six private claims held the ground – and it was Cecil Rhodes leading the charge.[64] Now worth £50,000 a year, Rhodes and his friends at De Beers were mining in richer grounds, and since 1883, they had paid far more attention to the nitty-gritty of comparative costs and yields. As the buy-outs of Rhodes's competitors continued, the value of De Beers quadrupled to £841,550.[65]

A study of De Beers' annual reports reveals how Rhodes's ambition was grounded in a big but simple strategy: control of an entire mine would let the firm shift from open-cast mining to digging tunnels underground, transforming the scale and profitability of the business. It was a shift becoming imperative, as the reef began to collapse. 'Your directors have realised more and more daily the absolute necessity for doing all in their power to promote amalgamation,' commented the annual report in 1883.[66] Over 1885, De Beers swallowed London & South African along with Independent Diamond Mining Co., Baxter's Gully, the Australian Gully Block and Eagle Diamond Mining Company, creating a compact block of 360 claims. It was a critical development, 'especially in view of the absolute necessity of adopting at once a system of working underground'.[67]

The following year, the mining firms United and Elma were added, along with more claims, as the directors pushed through a London share registry to ease capital-raising. In 1887, the directors reported that they had 'continued their policy of promoting, by every legitimate means in their power, the amalgamation of the several interests in the mine', wrapping up Gem D.M. Co., Oriental and the Victoria Company, largely through secret share buy-ups. The result was that Rhodes was now able to report: 'We are now relying entirely on the underground.'

Better still, Rhodes was surrounded by some of the best minds in the business, for both Frederic Stow and Alfred Beit had joined the De Beers board. Both would now prove vital in Rhodes's most important battle of all – the titanic struggle with Barney Barnato to control South Africa's diamonds.

The grandson of a rabbi, and son of a Whitechapel shop-keeper, Barney Barnato had invested his life-savings in sixty boxes of cigars, which he had ferried to Kimberley and sold at enormous profit.[68] With the proceeds, he set himself up as a '*kopje*-walloper', shuttling between the diamond diggers' tables and buying up diamonds as they tumbled from the gravel. Amassing £3,000, he sunk the lot into some of the best blocks of the Kimberley ground.[69]

By the end of 1886, Rhodes's De Beers had extracted diamonds worth just under £324,000 – more than a five-fold increase on the value of the output in 1881.[70] By 1887, De Beers and Barnato's firm, Kimberley Central, were the kings of the diamond fields; but Barnato remained the biggest. His firm was valued at £2.45 million, with an annual output of £1.41 million,[71] but he shared control of the Kimberley 'pipe', the deep, narrow cone of solidified, ancient magma rich in diamonds, with Compagnie Française, the biggest remaining independent firm.[72] De Beers, worth £2 million, was smaller with an output of £1.022 million – but it controlled its own field.[73]

With careful selection of engineers and good methods, Rhodes cut the cost of extracting a carat of diamonds, from 16s to 7s 2d, and cut the rate of theft by putting his workers in compounds. But, he calculated the market size for diamonds at around £4 million a year, and to keep the prices up he needed to reduce supply – under the control of just one firm. Barnato had precisely the same ambition. And so battle for the richest diamond monopoly in the world now commenced.

Rhodes's genius was to realize that the key to victory lay not in southern Africa, but in London, from where he could channel cash thirsty for foreign investment into his own designs for an African empire. He needed a London finance partner and found the perfect match in the House of Rothschild.

*

Since the days of Nathan Rothschild, Rothschild's had become a leader in the new British services industry that, in a world of fast steamships, global telegraph links, booming commodity prices and worldwide industrialization, now dominated banking, insurance and shipping.* From around 1780, Britain was already the world's service leader; a little more than a century later, the nation boasted more registered shipping tonnage than the rest of the world put together, underpinning London's place at the centre of the world's insurance and trade settlement business.[74] Wherever British merchants organized cargoes, they insured in London, discounted in London, and banked in branches of British banks flung around the world. Britain's new global banks built their business oiling the wheels of Britain's new multinationals, as firms built on the foundations of the old agency houses of the 1830s which organized the export, shipping, insurance and sales of Britain's cotton-makers. All over the world, similar patterns emerged as new multinationals took shape; perhaps with a headquarters in London or Glasgow or Liverpool, they grew blessed with a secure currency backed by the Gold Standard and a vast army of British investors were happy to invest abroad.

The Bank of England's promise to switch a pound, on demand, into gold was critical in giving the world the confidence to trade. Investors knew that when crises came – as they did in 1847 and 1866 (and later, in 1890 and 1907) – the Bank would always defend the pound. To spare the need to ship gold to settle debts, traders were fixing their deals in sterling from the 1870s, knowing that their own currencies were fixed

---

* In fact, more than 40 per cent of shipping tonnage was in the hands of just eight firms. See Stephen Broadberry, *Market Services and the Productivity Race, 1850–2000* (Cambridge University Press, 2006), p. 148.

to the pound, which in turn, was firmly pegged to gold. For industrialists, of course, the Gold Standard had its problems. Interest rates tended to move 'pro-cyclically' as the Bank tended to put up interest rates in an export boom to off-set any strain on reserves as the money supply (and hence possible calls on the Bank) went up. In part, this was because the Bank, still run privately, kept reserves as low as possible in order to maximize profits.* The result was interest rates that moved constantly: between 1851 and 1885, the bank rate changed on average every six weeks, and thereafter every two months.

The Gold Standard, however, suited British merchants well, and they diversified into extracting, financing, shipping, and trading the natural resources of the world, whetting the appetite of British investors for foreign assets. All over the world, old merchants moved into commodities, services and infrastructure. The Holts of Liverpool, for instance, started in cotton but soon diversified into shipping, creating the famous Blue Funnel Line, and worked closely with John Swire & Co. to expand throughout Asia. John Swire had started as a small textile import–export company, and began trading in Shanghai when the American Civil War disrupted the cotton trade in 1861. Within a few years, he founded the China Navigation Company, sending Mississippi-style paddle-steamers up the Yangtze river. James Wilson was another example. Born in 1805, the son of a wealthy textile mill owner, he was granted a royal charter by Queen Victoria to found the Chartered Bank, which boomed as the Suez Canal opened in 1869 and the telegraph reached China in 1871. The Hongkong and Shanghai Banking Corporation Limited was founded by another Scot, Thomas Sutherland, in 1865, who was working for P&O and realized that roaring trade in Hong Kong needed trade banks. Other firms, such as Jardine Matheson and Dent & Co., simply took over the trade of the old East India Company.

Together, these businesses delivered a flow of dividends and returns on Britain's overseas investments from 1870 that were bigger than capital exports. The companies tended to be highly profitable, building

---

* By 1881, the Bank's reserve was just 14 per cent of the combined British, French, German and US treasury totals.

great networks with very little capital, and generating huge returns of 10 or 11 per cent a year.* Together, between 1870 and 1913, incoming payments to Britain outstripped capital exports by around £1 billion, earning the nation some £200 million a year – about 10 per cent of national income – by the eve of the First World War.[75]

For the individual investor, the returns were excellent. Provincial industrialists tended to keep their fortunes at home, but investors in London and England's south-east were happy to spend abroad, earning a better return on what was on offer at home.† Indeed, London investors took half of the shares in businesses operating abroad.[76] A quarter of shareholders in foreign- and empire-based firms were 'peers and gentleman', and many big landowners, such as the 8th Duke of Devonshire, systematically moved money out of agriculture and into overseas railways and government stocks. This was a pattern emulated by the big institutional investors such as insurance companies, whose foreign stocks and bonds rose from 10 per cent of their portfolios in 1870 to a massive 40 per cent by 1913.[77] Naturally, they now had a vested interest in their foreign investments staying safe and secure; and in Her Majesty's government, they had a doughty defender of their interests.

Southern Africa was now poised to become one of the world's greatest foreign investment markets for UK investors. Britain's investment pattern had therefore begun to change around the time that Rhodes first arrived in Africa. Back in 1854, some £195–£230 million was invested overseas; but, following two great surges – the early 1880s to 1891 (when domestic interest rates fell to 3 or 3.5 per cent for most of the decade), and then the early 1900s to 1913 – foreign investment multiplied to total some £1.7 billion (by 1913).‡ The total nominal value of British overseas investment was now £4.2 billion, twice as much as

---

* This is an average observed by Geoffrey Jones on a sample of great firms between 1895 and 1914. Jones, *Merchants to Multinationals: British Trading Companies in the 19th and 20th Centuries* (OUP, 2000), p. 82.

† With the exception of Lancashire and southern Scotland, manufacturers were four times more likely to invest in a domestic business. However, between 1900 and 1910, government bonds earned under 4 per cent while a blue-chip foreign bond could make over 5 per cent.

‡ This represented some 4–5 per cent of GNP.

any other nation's investment, and up to one-half of *all* the world's foreign-owned assets.[78] A third of national wealth was now tied up abroad.[*]

Between 1850 and 1914, around 70 to 80 per cent of investment was 'portfolio investment', channelled into share issues of thousands of companies – for railways, docks, tramways, telegraphs, telephones, gas and electric companies, including the railroads connecting America's eastern seaboard with the Midwest (£650 million), the railways of the British dominions (£325 million) and India's rail network (£150 million).[*]

But the balance of investment was direct investment into thousands of traders around the world. It was overwhelmingly concentrated in mining (25 per cent), railways (27 per cent) and land (18 per cent).[80] From the 1890s, most of the investment was flowing to the British Empire, overwhelmingly to the 'white settlement' countries such as in southern Africa, to back entrepreneurs the likes of Rhodes.[81] [†] In the mid-1880s, Rhodes had plenty from Britain's investing classes.

*

To secure Rothschild's help, Rhodes first engaged Gardner Williams, a mining engineer once employed by Nathaniel Rothschild, to persuade the great banker to back a hugely expensive plan to buy out the Compagnie Française. 'If the French would sell,' declared Rothschild, he would 'see if they could raise' the £1 million required.

In Paris, Rhodes negotiated a price of £1.4 million. But Barnato was determined not to lose, countering with an offer of £1.7 million. Rhodes now threw in his hand, but cunningly exchanged the Compagnie Française shares he had accumulated for 20 per cent of Barnato's firm, Kimberley Central. With Rothschild's help, Rhodes

---

* 'Never before or since,' wrote the historian Michael Edelstein, 'has one nation committed so much of is national income and savings to capital formation abroad.' Edelstein, 'Foreign Investment, Accumulation and Empire', in Floyd and Johnson (eds), *Cambridge Economic History*, op. cit., pp. 194–5.

† With the exception of Lancashire and southern Scotland, manufacturers were four times more likely to invest in a domestic business. However, between 1900 and 1910, government bonds earned under 4 per cent while a blue-chip foreign bond could make over 5 per cent.

now raised £2.4 million of debenture stock* and began buying Kimberley Central shares until he was within inches of control. 'We saw', Rhodes explained later to De Beers shareholders, 'that you could never deal with obstinate people until you get the whiphand of them.'[82]

In March 1888, negotiating through the night, Barnato surrendered: 'when you have been with him half an hour', he later sighed 'you not only agree with him but come to believe you have always held that opinion'. He gave up control of Kimberley Central for a holding in a new, merged firm. On 13 March 1888, Rhodes formally registered De Beers Consolidated with a balance sheet of £3.1 million and appointed Barnato as governor for life. The pair appeared together in some triumph at De Beers' annual general meeting.

'Since we met last,' declared Rhodes to shareholders, 'we have completed the entire amalgamation of the De Beers mine and I might point out to you on what a profitable basis it was effected.'[83] The ability to tunnel deep under the ground of their old rivals, Gem and Victoria, had created enormous value: £1 million of share value for an acquisition price of £100,000. With the ability to extend deep tunnels throughout the whole De Beers mine, Rhodes now foresaw output worth £3–4 million, equal to the value of the entire Cape Colony. 'We have got an industry,' he boasted, 'which is almost like a government within a government'.

Crucially, the key risk faced by the diamond industry, announced Rhodes, was now no more. 'The risk of over-production is over. You possess the whole of De Beers, three-fourths of Kimberley and a controlling interest in Bultfontein and Dutoitspan. It is merely a question of a few months – well I will say a year – when you will have complete control of the diamond industry.' To his backer, Lord Rothschild, Rhodes was a little more circumspect, advising him on 29 October 1888 that 'I think we must expect to pass another two years before we have a complete monopoly, when I think we might fairly expect to make nearly £2 million per annum.' But there was no disguising the triumph: Cecil Rhodes had created a behemoth that controlled over 90 per cent of

---

* 'Debenture stock' was a bond – or loan – contract specifying to return borrowed funds, along with interest, secured on the company property.

South Africa's diamond output. Its profits were about to go through the roof. Profits on capital steadily increased, from around 7 per cent to 28 per cent a decade later.

Rhodes moved quickly to exploit his new control of the diamond fields. Production costs dropped to 10s/carat, and profits rose to 20s/carat, as half the black labour force and a quarter of the white workers were made redundant.[84] Compounds were established to house the remaining black workers, who were now subject to humiliating routine strip searches.[85] It was a welcome rush of revenue, for Rhodes was now about to require every ounce of his capital – and his connections – to profit in a southern Africa suddenly transformed by a new discovery.

*

On 5 June 1885, at 11am, a man named Harry Struben arrived on the tennis court behind the Union Club in the Transvaal's capital of Pretoria to brief President Kruger's advisers and assorted business associates with important news. There had been rumours of gold in southern Africa since the 1850s, and small deposits had been found in the Transvaal. But it now appeared, said Struben, who with his brother had been investigating their land in Transvaal's Witwatersrand area, that the gold reefs there were the richest ever found.

He was not wrong. The 40-mile-deep seam, along the ridge of mountains between Heidelberg and Potchefstroom, was soon producing a fifth of the world's gold. In September 1886, the 'Rand was declared a public digging, and within three years, the new city of Johannesburg, built beside it, had become one of the wonders of the world. 'Never in the history of the universe,' penned Lady Bellairs during her journey through town in 1889, 'was such an extraordinary city conceived or carried out as Johannesburg… Day after day comes the news of fresh discoveries… We are simply living in a sea of gold.'[86]

Fortunes were made. Soon, 130 of the principal companies working the mines were worth £103 million. By 1892, the first deep-level mines were in operation, and by the end of the century a myriad of firms had consolidated into just eight mining giants, with huge access to capital markets, and centralized research services. The country was now producing a quarter of the world's gold, worth some £16 million a year. By 1904, a million white settlers, most of them British, would call the place home, with Johannesburg becoming one of the biggest cities on earth. British investment rose from £34 million in 1884 to an incredible £351 million in 1911, the sharpest rise in the nation's foreign investment anywhere on earth.

Rhodes had been monitoring developments carefully, but in truth was late to the party. In a letter to Rudd, scribbled on 12 December 1886, he noted that 'E. Jones returned yesterday he has a high opinion of the Witwatersrand'. But Rhodes was already lamenting how the prices of claims had risen: 'It is very difficult to purchase anything worth having.' Two months later, Rhodes and his partners launched their prospectus for the Gold Fields Company of South Africa, 'with a capital of £250,000' as the media announced, 'for the purposes of acquiring and dealing with certain auriferous and other mineral properties, interests and rights... and also for carrying on general exploration'.[87]

However, as Rhodes admitted to Rothschild in October 1888, 'I have had bad luck, as though I have done well and hold a good deal, I missed the best part and... thus have returned too late to buy into the richer parts.' Eventually, by the end of the century, Rhodes's Consolidated Gold Fields would – along with Wernher, Beit & Eckstein, which mined half the gold on the 'Rand – dwarf its rivals.[88] More immediately, there was a silver lining too, for Rhodes's real opportunity lay not in the gold fields themselves, but in the change they provoked in the balance of power between Britain and the Boers.

Gold transformed the might of the Boers' South African Republic. By 1890, the republic boasted annual revenues of £4 million[89] – far more than the Cape Colony budget – and the new might of the Boers presented the new Conservative government in London with a dilemma: how to keep Bechuanaland secure, sandwiched as it was between German South West Africa and the Transvaal. It was too large and expensive a territory either for London or the Cape Colony to administer or defend.[90] General Warren had recommended a Crown Colony complete with a civil service and an army; but that would cost London some £250,000 a year 'as well as risk of future wars in the interior'. Nor was the Cape government keen to pick up the tab.

Flush with the profits of De Beers, Cecil Rhodes now offered a plan. A 'British South Africa Company' – paid for not by taxes, but by a new trading monopoly – could control the space between the Namib desert on the south-west coast and Portuguese East Africa (Mozambique), extending northwards to meet the missionary trading colonies founded by David Livingstone around the Great Lakes of Central Africa.

Quickly, Rhodes marshalled his friends to advance – and finance – his vision. An old Oxford friend and politically committed Cape colonist, Sidney Shippard, had been appointed Administrator of Bechuanaland on 1 September 1885, and with his deputy, the Reverend John Moffat, was sympathetic to Rhodes's idea. They soon persuaded Lobengula, the tribal king of the Ndebele (Matabele) lands, to agree a treaty – the so-called 'Moffat Treaty' – barring 'foreign interference' from his dominions.

Rhodes now quickly drew together his political and financial backers. Shippard liked the idea of a chartered company securing the space, and so Rhodes dispatched Charles Rudd 'to look at the country and see what he can do'. Writing in August 1888 to Shippard, Rhodes expressed his fear of losing Lobengula's territory to 'adventurers'; 'it is no use my stepping for my company to assist in the government of a shell', Rhodes wrote; 'If we get Matabelland (sic) we shall get the balance of Africa[.] I do not stop in my ideas at [the] Zambezi, and I am willing to work with you for it.'[91] Just as assiduously, Rhodes lined up the support of Rothschild. From the Kimberley Club on 20 January 1888, he wrote: 'My Lord… I also wish to have a talk with you over the Matabele concession as to which, when I have explained everything, I hope you will take a share.' It was, said Rhodes, a wealthy land. 'As to the gold all my reports only verify previous statements – the gold bearing reefs are simply endless.'*

By October 1888, Rudd, with the connivance of Shippard and

---

* So convinced was Rhodes that Rothschild would support him, that he changed his will in June 1888 to bequeath him his fortune.

Moffat at the court of Lobengula, had secured a famous concession, ceding 'full power to do all things necessary to win and procure minerals'. 'Our concession is so gigantic,' wrote Rudd, 'it is like giving a man the whole of Australia.' The Cape's High Commissioner, Sir Hercules Robinson, quickly gave his imprimatur; 'it appeared to me,' minuted Robinson, 'although a monopoly of the kind was not free from objections, it was, on the whole, in the interests of the Matabele'.[92]

When Lobengula discovered the Concession's true sweep, he was furious: he dispatched his *indunas* to London in cahoots with a rival syndicate, led by Lord Gifford and George Cawston, who were arguing for an alternative charter.* It was now that Robinson proved truly decisive. In January 1888, Rhodes had asked for Rothschild's help in keeping the high commissioner in place, because 'he has steadily fought out the expansion northwards and completely surrounded the republics... If we leave matters now quietly to work, with the development of the gold in the Transvaal, we shall have a united South Africa under the English flag.'[93] Sure enough, Robinson argued to London that any contender for a charter must boast Cape colonial support – support that only Rhodes could muster. It was the decisive argument.

Rhodes now squared his rivals, through the simple device of a merger of the rival syndicates. Fearful of German expansionism in what Germany called 'Mittelafrika', the British Cabinet agreed Rhodes's plan on 10 July 1889. 'I don't say it is an ideal solution,' commented Lord Milner, 'but it is better than letting the whole thing out of our fingers.'[94] Lord Rothschild would take a major stake, and among the shareholders – as was later revealed – was to be Robinson himself, who not only owned 250 shares in the Central Search Association from May (he later became a director), but 2,500 shares in Rhodes's United Concessions, which continued to own the mineral rights signed over in the Rudd Concession, which were now leased to the new British South Africa Company.

Rhodes's letters over the course of 1889 and early 1890 reveal a mastermind at work, spinning the most extraordinary of webs. One

---

* They wanted a charter for a British Imperial Central Africa Company.

sticking point was the refusal of the Gold Fields of South Africa company to participate; in a furious letter to Rudd, Rhodes declared that 'I feel that GFSA have behaved disgracefully. I have no intention of working for those fellows for the balance of my life. A more ungrateful crew I have never come across.'[95] But Rhodes's letters to Beit, a fellow director of the BSAC, are even more extraordinary. In the back and forth, Rhodes dictates his way through the vast stream of issues to be resolved to assemble his great jigsaw: the terms of the grant from Lobengula; the financial arrangements between the BSAC, the Exploring and the Central Search companies; the secret agreement brokered with the Cape government to take financial responsibility for the railway he planned to build north; the negotiation of land grants from London for the track; share allocations; debenture finance for the Bechuanaland section; amendments to the charter's grant; the deal with the African Lakes Company; the arming of De Beers volunteers; the movements of the Portuguese; and, crucially, the need to ensure that his company was properly capitalized. Writing to Beit in October 1889, Rhodes declared: 'I hope you will see to the increase to £1,000,000 of Charter Co… it makes us feel safe. I feel perfectly confident as to getting Matabeleland but it will take 2½ years and I think my plan cannot fail.'[96]

From his bastion of monopoly strength in De Beers, Rhodes had transformed the size and scale of his business empire. Aided and abetted by Sir Hercules Robinson, the queen's governor in Cape Town, and Lord Rothschild, the master of the Stock Exchange in London, Rhodes had created a masterplan for a private company to create an entire country, which would soon bear his name, as Rhodesia was born.

*

Little gold would ever be found in Rhodesia. And so a different solution would be needed. And miraculously, Rhodes now acquired the power to produce one. On 17 July 1890, his lifelong support of the Afrikaner Bond's cause was repaid. With a little bribery and the support of an eclectic mix of political groups, Rhodes was elected Prime Minister of the Cape Colony. At the age of thirty-seven, he dominated not only the boardroom of the greatest diamond and exploration businesses in the world, but the Cabinet room of the Cape Colony. His final decade would now be shaped by three great struggles: the fight for power in the Cape; the battle to annex the Boers; and a war to command the BSAC lands that would eventually bear his name.

Rhodes's first skirmishes were fought from the elegance of the Cape Colony's Parliament buildings and planned from the haven of a new home. In the hills above Cape Town, Rhodes bought 'Groote Schuur', the old Dutch East India Company storehouses nestling in a hollow at the foot of Table Mountain. He had them rebuilt in the old Dutch farmhouse style, including a library brimming with translations of every source used in Gibbon's *Decline and Fall of the Roman Empire*, especially commissioned from Hatchard's in London. The buildings were complemented by 1,500 acres of surrounding mountain and valley. 'I want the big and simple,' he told his architect Herbert Baker, 'barbaric if you like'.[97]

Rhodes's government included members of nearly all of Parliament's sects, including Liberals and the Afrikaner Bond, and it was quickly labelled the 'Cabinet of all talents'.[98] His leadership was avowedly activist at home and abroad. He persuaded the Ottoman sultan in Constantinople to lend him angora goats to cross with Cape stock; he lobbied the US Congress on the protectionist McKinley Tariff, which in 1890 raised US import taxes to damaging levels. When *phylloxera* destroyed southern Africa's vineyards, he bought American vines to replant. He annexed Pondoland (Mpondoland) on the Cape's eastern coast in 1894, finally extinguishing its independence; and in May 1891, he even approached the prime ministers of New South Wales and Canada to propose foreign-policy co-operation: 'between us', Rhodes wrote, 'we must invent some tie with our mother country that will prevent separation'.[99]

His strength, though, was rooted in a firm alliance with the Afrikaner Bond, cemented with laws to enshrine white rule. The old Masters and Servants Act (1856) was amended to let magistrates inflict corporal punishment on black residents for minor offences such as insolence. The Franchise and Ballot Act (1892) disenfranchised more than 3,000 black men while simultaneously bestowing the right to vote on 4,500 white men. The Glen Grey Act, Rhodes's 'favourite child', was presented in late 1894, effectively creating a 'native reserve' for black Africans.*[100] When liberals in his Cabinet began growing restless, Rhodes sacked them. When they retaliated in 1894, questioning the ethics of Rhodes's dual command of both the Cape government and the BSAC, an election was triggered, which Rhodes won with two-thirds of the vote.[101]

Rhodes's command of both Cabinet and Company was now vital to his plans, because, with little gold to be found in the BSAC's lands, a new means of extracting profit from the land was needed. The solution lay not in digging, but in settling. Rhodes had moved with lightning speed to drive a telegraph and railway north from the Cape into Lobengula's lands, and he now needed a pioneer force to inhabit the area.† He had happened across a twenty-three-year-old adventurer, Frank Johnson, over breakfast at the Kimberley Club, who told Rhodes, over his eggs and bacon, that he could lead the venture for the lowest price. 'Everyone tells me you are a lunatic,' observed Rhodes, 'but I have an instinct you are right and can do it.'[102]

Within five days of their meeting, Rhodes and Johnson agreed that the latter would lead a squad of 179 pioneers north. In May 1890, as Dr Jameson presented the BSAC's charter to Lobengula, and to the accompaniment of a military band, along with the queen's three tallest Lifeguards, the pioneers set off. Their reward was 7s 6d a day and the promise of fifteen gold claims and a 3,000-acre farm apiece. On 11 September they reached their new settlement, in Mashonaland, named Salisbury in honour of the British prime minister. 'When at last I found that they were through to Fort Salisbury,' said Rhodes, 'I do not think there was a happier man in the country then myself.'[103]

---

* White people would not be allowed to live on the land – the strict separation of the races was supported by the Bond – and those who owned property in the Glen Grey area were excluded from the franchise. This highly regulated area was one of Rhodes's greatest attempts at controlling the black African labour force.
† Even before the Letters Patent granting a Royal Charter of Incorporation was sealed by the Queen on 29 October 1889, Rhodes was trying to hand over a cheque for £30,000 for a new telegraph from Mafeking. William, *Cecil Rhodes*, op. cit., p. 137.

By 1891, however, with profits thin, the BSAC's shares were trading at a discount. But Rhodes had already spotted his next move: a leap from Lobengula's lands north of the Zambezi, into central Africa, to join forces with David Livingstone's Great Lakes Company, which he knew was short of money. In a letter to Rothschild in October 1888, Rhodes had sketched out the potential of a company controlling land from the Cape to the Great Lakes. Livingstone's son-in-law, Rhodes recorded, had 'pointed out to him, we ought to try and join; that is his company should work down through Tanganyika to the Zambezi to join our development from the South'. By 1893, Rhodes had bought the Great Lakes Company's goodwill and stock in trade and persuaded Lord Salisbury to declare a protectorate over the Lake Nyassa district, with a £10,000-a-year police force paid for by Rhodes.

It was now vital to defend Bechuanaland – the great road north – from the competing claims of speculators and agents for the German and Portuguese governments. But, as Rhodes began building defences, relations with Lobengula were breaking down. 'I thought you came to dig for gold,' the bitter king wrote to the British government, 'but it seems you have come… to rob me of my people as well.'[104] As Ndebele attacks on the settlers multiplied, Rhodes saw the potential for an all-out war he could win. When the Ndebele attacked the Shona people near Fort Victoria in July 1893, Dr Jameson, now Company Administrator, had his excuse. After alerting Rhodes to his plans, the Cape prime minister wired back: 'Read Luke xiv.31' – and promptly sold 40,000 BSAC shares at a loss in order to fund personally the necessary *matériel*. 'I was afraid', he told the South Africa Committee three years later, that 'the Doctor might have a bad time, and I did sell my interest in various things to provide money to carry on the war, because I felt that if there was a disaster, I was the only person to carry it through'.[105]

Into battle against Lobengula's *impis*, numbering 3,000 men, were dispatched 700 of the BSAC's 'Volunteers', armed with an astonishing new weapon: the Maxim machine gun.* Operated by a crew of five, the machine-gun fired 500 rounds a minute, fifty times faster than a rifle

---

* Lord Rothschild had spotted the weapon's potential in 1884; he financed Maxim's merger with Nordenfelt Guns.

could reload. At the Shangani river, the Maxim was battle-tested for the first time. 'The Matabele', wrote an eye-witness, 'never got nearer than 100 yards… for the Maxims far exceeded all expectations and mowed them down literally like grass.' It spat bullets, said the Matabele, 'like heaven sometimes spits hail'.[106]

Fifteen hundred of Lobengula's warriors were slain in this First Matabele War; just four of the seven hundred Matabeleland invaders perished. When the smoke cleared, the BSAC's shares rose immediately on the London Stock Exchange. Lobengula burnt his *kraal* and fled, dying two months later along the Shangani river, reputedly of smallpox. In May 1894, Matabeleland was deemed conquered land and assigned to the BSAC to govern as a Crown Colony, with complete freedom to allocate land as it pleased. The railway was pushed up to Salisbury, and the African Transcontinental Telegraph Company began to thread a line the length of the continent. By 1895, the African Lakes Company was yielding excellent profits, and quickly Rhodes added concessions along the Zambezi Valley, ceded by Barotse Chief Lewanika and bought from a local trader: 750,000 square miles – an area larger than Spain, France and the German Empire – was added to Queen Victoria's dominions.

Triumphant in the north, Rhodes now turned his gaze on the Boers of the neighbouring South African Republic. Rhodes's long political battle with President Kruger had proved one frustration after another. Rhodes had pushed a popular plan to build a railway line from the Cape to the Transvaal, but Kruger's ambition was to skip free of any dependence on his neighbours with a line of his own, running east from his landlocked republic to Delagoa Bay, then under Portuguese control. But not only did Kruger block Rhodes's railway plans, he kept import tariffs on Cape goods high. He eschewed all talk of a customs union. And while the newly emerging 'Rhodesia' seemed near empty of gold, the Witwatersrand seam seemed inexhaustible. Frustrated, Rhodes now began a shift from talk, to war. Preparations for the Jameson Raid were begun.

On Monday 30 December, the morning after Jameson's men left Mafeking, the magistrate had telegraphed news of the troops' departure to one of Rhodes's ministers, Will Schreiner, who immediately forwarded it to Groote Schuur. Summoned late that night, Schreiner found Rhodes in his study, telegrams in his hand. 'The moment I saw him,' remembered the minister, 'I saw a man I had never seen before. His appearance was utterly dejected and different. Before I could say a word, he said "Yes, yes, it is true. Old Jameson has upset my apple-cart... Poor old Jameson. Twenty years we have been friends, now he goes in and ruins me."'[107]

In the Raid's aftermath, Rhodes was at first fêted like a hero in the Cape – but damned in London. He resigned as prime minister in January 1896, to spend a fortune clearing up the mess – some £250,000 on a press fund, legal costs, compensation, ransoms to release prisoners from the Transvaal, including commuting the death sentence on his brother Frank to a fine of £25,000. Hastily, inquiries were convened in both the Cape Parliament and the House of Commons, where, in a committee room off Westminster Hall, the former Cape prime minister was cross-examined. Over five days of questioning, refreshed only by sandwiches and a large tankard of stout, he turned the tables on his interrogators. When the committee finally reported in 1897, Chamberlain, the British Colonial Secretary, was exonerated of complicity, but the raid was condemned and Rhodes was severely censured for misuse of office. In the Cape, Rhodes's alliance with the Afrikaner Bond was destroyed and his political base dissolved.

It was not, however, a wholesale disaster. His membership of Her Majesty's Privy Council was not revoked, and neither was the BSAC's royal charter cancelled. 'I found all the busmen smiling at me when I came to London,' said Rhodes, 'so I knew it was all right.'[108] And so he looked to his future with optimism, confiding to a friend: 'I am confident enough to say that I do not feel that my public career has closed... I am determined still to strive for the closer union of South Africa'.[109] He sailed home via Egypt, where he called on Kitchener to secure a consignment of Sudanese donkeys. And it was here he first heard news of the murders of settlers near Bulawayo, where the Ndebele were holding 4,000 residents under siege. Rhodes was in Salisbury by the end of March.

Ever since the battles of 1893, the Ndebele of Rhodesia had suffered; some were forced into labour; others lost their lands. In the spring of 1896, with the BSAC's leaders distracted by the aftermath of the Jameson Raid, the Ndebele rose in violent revolt. In the summer, the Shona joined them, much to the surprise of the white settlers who believed they treated the tribe comparatively well, often to the chagrin of the Ndebele. The rising was serious – and required force well beyond the compass of the BSAC, and so British troops were deployed to hold the line.

As the costs of conflict multiplied, in October both sides sued for peace and Rhodes now swapped the role of warmonger for peace broker. With considerable personal bravery, he walked unarmed into talks with the Ndebele in the Matopos Hills, and secured both truce and treaty. There was a measure of resettlement, communal tenure and charges of betrayal on all sides. Rhodes's own conduct brought praise. But it was the beginning of the end of the BSAC's control of Rhodesia. A Colonial Office report was highly critical of the company's behaviour and Jameson's administration, and Rhodes resigned from the BSAC leadership.[*]

Happily for him, there was better news in the diamond business, where the market was now rallying, generating for De Beers extraordinary annual dividends of 40 per cent.[110] 'The history of the De Beers Company is simply a fairy tale,' wrote Lord Rothschild to Rhodes: 'You have established a practical monopoly of the production of diamonds, you have succeeded in establishing a remarkably steady market for the sale of your productions, and you have succeeded in finding machinery capable of carrying this through.'

Frustrated in Rhodesia, Rhodes sought a new power-base in the Cape. After some persuasion, in 1896 he took the presidency of the South African League, which actively propagandized for British dominance in southern Africa. He created his own cabal in the Parliament, the Progressive Party, which he propped up with money and newspapers, only to fail in the election of 1898 – the dirtiest his contemporaries had ever seen.[111] In society, Rhodes was equally adrift, oddly, if not intimately, connected to a Polish princess, Catherine Radziwill, who set

---

[*] The 1896–97 conflict is now generally known as the First Chimurenga, or the Second Matabele War.

herself up in Cape society as his 'fiancée' and eventually had to be taken to court for forging his signature.[112]

Around him, however, the slow slide to all-out war seemed inevitable. Years of friction between the Boers and the British were coming to a head, as the Boers sought to defend their homeland; and the British sought to shield what Joseph Chamberlain called 'the cornerstone of the whole British colonial system'.[113]

*

To those looking out from London at the end of the nineteenth century, the Cape was regarded as an indispensable – but imperilled – bridge to India, the land which had become the hub around which Victoria's global system now turned, the source of force, the balance of trade and a hoard of funds. It was India that provided the British Empire's reservoir of troops – a mobile force deployable almost anywhere on earth, fielded frequently to overwhelm opponents, from Africa to Asia. As Europe and America raised tariffs to close their markets, cotton exports to India became critically important to Britain; between 1870 and 1913, India rose from third to first place in Britain's export markets (notably cotton), generating enough foreign earnings to off-set the trade deficit with America. Furthermore, much of India's overseas trade was in the hands of British shippers and merchants; a third of the Empire trade outside Britain passed through India's seaports. British capital, too, was ploughed into India: by the 1870s, £100 million had been invested by 50,000 British shareholders in Indian railways, and in the fifty years before the First World War, £286 million was raised on the London Stock Exchange as India rose to become the fourth-largest recipient of British overseas investment. By 1909, Lord Curzon could remark with some justice that India was now 'the determining influence of every considerable movement in British power to the east and south of the Mediterranean'.[114]

British policy-makers were, therefore, allergic to the very idea of any French or Russian advance in the Middle East, which was identified as a threat to British interests in India as early as 1800. Safeguarding 'the passage to India' therefore became the security strategy that underpinned the creation of a vast armoured zone stretching from Gibraltar to the eastern borders of Persia, the strongest official 'interest' in Britain's world system.[115]

Soon, 'Empire' was a security strategy with the force of political shibboleth. And as Britain's empire grew, the very concept of 'Empire' began to offer a political appeal that won votes for British politicians prepared to follow where entrepreneurs had led. In 1868, the statesman Charles Dilke had 'followed Britain around the world', visiting the far-flung corners of the Empire by steamship, inspiring a vision of *Greater Britain*. Disraeli, too, had spotted the political power of an appeal to Empire, securing in 1876 the title 'Empress of India' for Queen Victoria. By 1883, John Robert Seeley, the slightly priggish holder of the Chair of Modern History at Cambridge, produced a best-seller, *The Expansion of England*, famous for its phrase 'We seem… to have conquered and peopled half the world in a fit of absence of mind', and arguing that 'Greater Britain' now required knitting closer together to hold its own against the emerging powers of Germany, Russia and America.

In Joseph Chamberlain, the first 'self-consciously imperialist politician', he found an ally. Deeply influenced by a visit to Canada in 1887, where he found settlers far more inclined to an alliance with the United States than with Britain, Chamberlain became determined to forge a path to 'the uniting together of kindred races with similar objects', an imperial federation that he sought to forge in practice as colonial secretary in Salisbury's government.[116]

Chamberlain epitomized an idea and an ideal soon popularized in novels, verse, painting, advertising and in the music sung on stage and in church. 'Land of Hope and Glory', 'I Vow to Thee My Country', 'The Yeomen of England' were all composed around the turn of the century, echoing the sentiment described by Alfred Austin, the Poet Laureate in 1900: 'Who dies for England, dies for God… Who dies for England, sleeps with God'. [117] In schools, History was not a compulsory subject until 1900, but patriotic texts such as *Deeds That Won the Empire* (Fitchett, 1897) or the adventure stories of G. A. Henty (*With Wolfe in Canada*, 1886, or *With Roberts to Pretoria*, 1902) sold millions. 'The depth and volume of public interest in imperial questions', wrote one Northcliffe employee, is 'one of the greatest forces, almost untapped, at the disposal of the press'.[118]

It was not hard, therefore, to persuade British politicians to take a robust approach to guarantee the nation's 'interests' in southern Africa. Bordering the sea lanes to India, Africa was critically important; and politically, there was little harm in defending imperial interests with the force of arms. As the nineteenth century drew to a close, the lingering 'problem' of southern African began to loom large in London. When the arch-imperialist Lord Milner was appointed Governor of the Cape Colony, it became only a matter of time before British–Boer relations deteriorated. Taking office in 1897, he was known for his view that southern Africa was too small for 'two absolutely conflicting social and political systems'.[119]

Milner began ratcheting up the pressure on the South African Republic to grant the *Uitlanders* – the white, largely British settlers – the right to vote after five years' residence. It was a cause Rhodes helped to popularize through the work of the South African League, and it now became, in effect, a *casus belli*. As a campaign for (as Chamberlain acknowledged) 'Home Rule for the 'Rand', it was a clear threat to the integrity and independence of Kruger's Boer republic. The Boers began stocking up on Mauser rifles, Krupp's artillery and Maxim guns, and over Christmas 1899 Boer forces struck deep into British territory.

For the British, the early months of this South African War (or the Second Anglo-Boer War) were a disaster. Sent in to relieve the Boer siege of Ladysmith, in Natal, General Sir Charles Warren ordered his men to scale Spion Kop on the night of 24 January 1900. When the morning mist lifted, it became clear that his men were sitting ducks. 'The scenes at Spion Kop', wrote the young war correspondent Winston Churchill, 'were among the strangest and most terrible I have ever witnessed… The dead and injured, smashed and broken by shells, littered the summit till it was a bloody reeking shambles.'[120]

The only respite was the relief of the besieged Mafeking, which at least ended in drama not tragedy. The young Robert Baden-Powell had resolutely held the town, and readers in Britain were treated to 217 days of news about his heroic resistance and morale-raising exercises – cricket matches, dancing, and turns on stage (he was a talented mimic) under the bombardment of the Boer guns. When the siege was relieved on 17 May 1900, there were scenes of almost hysterical jubilation across London.

Slowly, over the summer of 1900, the British Army turned the tide, pioneering a new kind of brutality. Earl Roberts, a veteran of the Indian Army, struck into the Orange Free State and the Transvaal, capturing both Bloemfontein and Pretoria. In the guerrilla war that followed, Kitchener, in search of tactical advantage, devised his 'scorched earth' policy, systematically burning Boers' farms and herding surviving women and children into lethal compounds dubbed 'concentration' camps. Nearly 30,000 – one in seven – of the Boer population would die in them, most of them children. But the war divided British public opinion. So often reported in 'jingoistic' terms, it soon provoked a moral fury. Britain's 'methods of barbarism', as the Liberal Party leader Campbell-Bannerman described them, sparked outrage at what David Lloyd George encapsulated as 'a war of extermination... which... will stain the name of this country'. Nevertheless, stained, blood-soaked and a little humbled, the British Empire prevailed, and a new, united nation of South Africa emerged.

*

The man who did more than anyone else to imagine this new country did not, though, live to see it, nor even the formal peace. Cecil Rhodes lived through the Boer siege of Kimberley, but he was now very ill – fat, bloated, and purple-skinned. On 26 March 1902, his doctor stepped outside the idyllic little cottage on the outskirts of Cape Town to tell the world that Rhodes was dead. His last words, said the doctor, were: 'So little done. So much to do.' [121]

Had Rhodes died before the ignominy and outrage of the Jameson Raid, his plaudits might have been more fulsome. Now the verdicts were equivocal. The *Cape Argus* struggled to conclude whether Rhodes was 'a great man or merely a big man'.[122] English newspapers, keen to gain some distance from the war, gave him a send-off without sentiment. They spoke of his service to Empire, his business acumen, his quiet personal life. A few argued against instant judgement.

His body was carried to the Matopos Hills for burial, where Kipling's eulogy was read out:

Dreamer devout, by vision led
Beyond our guess or reach,
The travail of his spirit bred
Cities in place of speech.
So huge the all-mastering though that drove
So brief the term allowed –
Nations not words he linked to prove
His faith before the crowd.[123]

Rhodes's final will left relatively little for his family, but more than £3 million for the Rhodes Trust to fund an Oxford education for fifty-two single men, to be chosen each year from the nations of the British Empire, along with the United States – which Rhodes believed would one day return to the imperial fold.[124] Money was left for German students, too, along with funds for his favourite political parties, imperial campaigners and for the Royal Institute of International Affairs at Chatham House.[125]

On 31 May 1902, the Treaty of Vereeniging drew the South African war to its conclusion. Forty-five thousand men had lost their lives, and £250 million had been spent. The two Boer republics were swept into the British Empire. It was a British victory, but in the outrage at the blood, treasure and honour lost in the course of the fighting, voters in Britain sacked the Conservative government and swept the Liberal Party back into power in January 1906, after a two-decade absence, with a 243 majority.

The British paid huge compensation for damages. Under the new constitutional arrangements, Boers' voting rights were confirmed – but the rights of non-whites were not assured. Within a decade, Afrikaners, who now made up the majority of voting South Africans, elected their commandant-general in the war, Louis Botha, premier of a new, self-governing British dominion, the Union of South Africa, which in 1910 brought together the Cape, Natal, the Transvaal and the Orange Free State.

In 1860, when Rhodes had been a young boy, the British Empire enfolded some 9.5 million square miles of land. By 1909, it had grown by a third to cover a quarter of the world's land surface, home to 444 million people;[*] it was an empire enveloping, in the words of the *St James Gazette*, 'one continent, a hundred peninsulas, five hundred promontories, a thousand lakes, two thousand rivers, ten thousand islands'.[126] It was acquired, not in 'a fit of absence of mind', but by deliberate, determined political and commercial entrepreneurs. And few were more important than Cecil Rhodes.

---

[*] Yet in 1898, the costs of defence, including the thirty-three barracks and coaling stations dotted around the world, was but £40 million – just 2.5 per cent of net national product. See Ferguson, *Empire*, op. cit., p. 245.

10

WILLIAM LEVER

Global tycoon

On Saturday, 16th November 1912, Sir William Lever stepped aboard the SS *Leopoldville* bound for the 'dark heart of Africa'. Newly knighted, and accompanied by his devoted wife Elizabeth, a phalanx of his closest advisers and one Dr Horn (special emissary of the King of the Belgians), the sixty-one-year-old tycoon was setting sail to see one of the greatest ventures of Britain's greatest global business, deep in the Belgian Congo.

As he boarded ship, he left behind in London swirling rumours of his latest benevolence: his offer to the prime minister to buy the fabulous Stafford House, in St James's, for the nation.* In Liverpool, his architects were finalizing plans for what would become the Lady Lever Gallery, designed to adorn Port Sunlight – his Merseyside company village. In the courts, his lawyers were squaring up to the chemical magnate Sir John Brunner, for the corporate battle of the early century. In Boston, the best minds in advertising were at work in his American headquarters. In Japan and South Africa, his builders were readying new factories; in Sweden, Norway, South Africa and Australia his deal-makers were preparing to snap up his rivals, while in the Pacific islands thousands toiled away on his vast plantations, hundreds of thousands of acres wide. In France, Germany, Belgium, Switzerland, Holland, Austria, Canada, South Africa, Australia, New Zealand and the United States, thousands made and sold his most famous product to millions of customers, with the boast that 'Sunlight Soap... is used from Lands End to

---

* He did buy it – and renamed it Lancaster House, after the county in which he was born.

John O'Groats… in American log cabins… in Canadian homesteads…
by the South African miner… in the Australian bush.'[1] Now William
Lever was about to take on the challenge of his life, a task that was 'little
less than the reorganisation of a principality' in one of the most notorious spots on earth.[2]

By the turn of the twentieth century, the Congo Free State – the vast,
personal fiefdom of the Belgian King Leopold – was dripping in blood,
and the world knew it. The 'infamous, infamous, shameful system' of its
vast, slave plantations was blown open in Joseph Conrad's novella *Heart
of Darkness* (1899) and in the eye-witness report (1904) by British
consul Roger Casement. The outcry forced the king to yield control of
his dominions to his elected government in 1908, and the following
year its ministers, desperate to wipe the stain off the country's soul,
called in William Lever.

'Lever is… a commercial genius,' wrote Belgian Colonial Minister
Renkin, 'enormously, fabulously rich, probably of good heart but also
hard, who sees humanity as a vast engine of production without soul or
desires.'[3] Within a year, the Belgian Parliament had ratified an
extraordinary £1million plan, signed on 14 April 1911, to let Lever
build a huge Congo palm oil industry spread across 2 million acres –
half the size of Wales. The five sites, each 40 miles wide, were separated
by impenetrable jungle.

At first sceptical, Lever now had a convert's enthusiasm. 'The inrush
of a herd of wild elephants would be trifling to the inrush there will be
to the Congo,' he predicted, 'if we prove a success.' Lever set to work; he
was empowered to create canals, railways, telegraphs, telephone systems,
harbours and fifty mills – and a monorail for moving to the mills the
jungle's palm fruit, which grew in reddish golden bunches atop 40-foot
trees. 'Not a building was erected unless the plans had been passed by
him,' wrote his son; 'it is no exaggeration to say that the organisation…
from the shipping base at the port of Matadi and the administrative
headquarters at Kinshasa to the farthest area of Elizabetha, over a thousand miles from the Congo mouth – was his personal creation.'

Just before Christmas 1912, Lever and his party disembarked from
their ship at Matadi, just below the Congo river's rapids, to meet a
special train bound for the capital Leopoldville (Kinshasa). There the

party met the steamer *Lusanga* and sailed up-river among the hippos, elephants, missionary stations and native villages to inspect his creation for the first time.

Before he left Liverpool, Lever had been honest about the task he faced. 'Words cannot tell the value to myself and, I hope, to our business, of this journey, I feel more confidence in our great undertaking than ever, although the difficulties are greater than I judged.'[4] Deep in the Congo he was not disappointed. On New Year's Day 1913, he committed his thoughts to his diary: 'the palm valleys and hill-sides', he wrote, were quite simply 'the grandest sight I have seen in any part of the world.'[5] 'Leverville' would bear his name for nearly another sixty years.*

*

William Lever was born in Bolton, on Monday, 15 September 1851, during a beautiful run of sunny weather in the month before the Great Exhibition closed, and as the last of the English harvest was gathered in. His birthplace, once a humble Saxon hamlet on the Lancashire moors, was settled in the fifteenth century by Flemish weavers migrating to Manchester. Among them was the Lever tribe, which took its name from the Flemish *Leur* and dated its definite Lancashire origins to one Adam de Lever of Great Lever (*fl.* 1420).[6]

In the nineteenth century, Lever's hometown was, wrote Friedrich Engels, 'badly and irregularly built with foul courts, lanes and back alleys', its main street (Deansgate) 'even in the finest weather a dark and unattractive hole'. Sixty thousand people were crammed into a hotspot of Victorian enterprise, energy and filth.[7] Through the 'ruinous and miserable' old town ran a dirty brook like a string of puddles, where houses without furniture crowded in and Irish immigrants huddled in cellars that bred typhus. Here the cotton baron Richard Arkwright made his start in life, as a barber. Samuel Crompton, pioneer of the spinning jenny, had lived just up their road,† and by Lever's teenage

---

* Leverville reverted to the former site's name of Lusanga in the years following the Congo's independence from Belgium.

† He had lived at Hall-in-the-Wood, an old timbered seat of the Starkies in the neighbourhood.

years, 70 cotton mills, print works, and bleach and dye works employed 18,000 people, while another 5,500 laboured away in 33 iron-foundries, engine-works and coal mines.

In a small oasis of middle-class comfort in the middle of town was Wood Street, a short, neat Georgian terrace, where the young William Lever grew up among his family of shop-keepers. Like so many Victorian entrepreneurs, the Levers were Non-conformists, and like so many Non-conformists they worked all the hours God sent. William's father, James (born 1809) had started life as a Manchester grocer's apprentice* and under his master's influence joined the Congregationalist Church, where he met his wife, Eliza Hesketh, the daughter of a cotton-mill manager.

Their son, William, was by all accounts a precocious boy. An early reader, he took great delight in arranging books – in height order – on the family bookshelf, and from the age of six was sent a few streets away to the local private school, where he proved better in the swimming pool than in the classroom or on the sports field. The moors of Rivington Pike above the town were his wandering grounds, while the local library kept him well supplied with books. *David Copperfield* was a lifelong favourite, along with the Psalms; but his life's inspiration was not a Victorian school but a Victorian sage – Samuel Smiles and his 'bible of Victorian liberalism', *Self Help*. 'It is impossible for me to say how much I owe to the fact that in my early youth I obtained a copy of Smiles' *Self Help*', he later wrote, and over the course of his life he gave thousands of copies away to schoolchildren.[8] Published in 1859, the book sold 20,000 copies in its first year, and a quarter of a million by the time of Smiles' death in 1904. Its impact on William was immediate. From the day he read it, said his son, Lever 'cultivated the habit of reckoning out almost each hour of the day and spending it to advantage, making his life a voyage westward with those extra minutes gained each day which are non-existent to him who stands still'.[9]

The young Lever was lucky in friendship, love and work. At school, he met both his lifelong companion Jonathan Simpson and his future

---

* James's father, also called James, was a successful counterpane-maker and quartermaster of the local militia.

wife Elizabeth Ellen Hulme, the daughter of a wholesale draper down the street and while his mother had ambitions for him to become a doctor, his father had other plans.

Long before William was born, James Lever had had a lucky break. A Manchester friend had married a local widow who owned a grocery business and who needed help running the shop. When the couple retired, in 1864, James Lever had taken over the business, shut the shop, and opened a wholesalers – packaging potted meat, mustard, soap, starch, milk, butter and eggs for the stores of prospering Bolton. He needed help, and so, in 1867, aged sixteen, William Lever began his apprenticeship to his father. 'I was never asked if I wanted to go into the grocery business,' William said later in life, 'and it was perhaps a good thing that I was not. My father told me, one day, that I had better get ready to come into the family grocery business, and as the holidays were nearly over, I thought I might as well begin next morning, and I did.'[10]

William's day began at 7am, taking down shutters, sweeping up, and preparing orders, slicing and wrapping bars of soap for the salesmen to deliver. But he was not an apprentice for long. Within five years, he had reorganized the company's accounts, before persuading his father to let him out on the road as a salesman in a one-horse gig, a life that came with one crucial perk: the chance to court the girl he loved.

Elizabeth Hulme's family had moved 35 miles away to Southport, and William's freedom to travel was a freedom to visit. They were engaged at the end of 1872, and, delighted, William's father promptly made his son a partner, on £800 a year. On 15 April 1874, William and Elizabeth were married at St George's Road Congregationalist Church by Reverend W. Hope Davison, the man who had baptized them both.[11]

William Lever's advance now accelerated. The following year, his father semi-retired, and William moved in as general manager, just as a boom-time for English grocers dawned.[12] Soon, Lever was proving his entrepreneurial credentials, searching abroad in Brittany and Ireland for the best supplies, until one day in 1877, Lever decided that it was time to strike out of town for new business. Finishing his rounds at 3.30pm, he ventured south to Ince and, five stores later, had acquired a handful of new orders. It was the beginning of the family's spread across

England's north-west. 'If I had not had an insatiable thirst for expansion and for the trial of novel methods,' Lever later wrote, 'if I had felt at 3.30 that merely because the usual day's work was completed I could return home and do nothing more for the remainder of the day, the present business could never have been built up.'[13]

Before long, Lever's Wigan business needed a warehouse of its own, and when Omerod & Co., a failing local wholesaler, came up for sale, Lever snapped it up. With new advertising and bigger imports, Lever & Co. was, by the early 1880s, one of the largest wholesale grocers between Manchester and Liverpool. Now aged thirty-three, William Lever boasted a good income, a thriving partnership and a happy family. It was, he thought, time to quit the trade that made his first fortune – and to start something rather new.

*

In the summer of 1884, William Lever spent his first holiday in years cruising around the Scottish islands, together with Elizabeth and their friend Simpson. Out on deck he thought about his future. For years, he had watched, first hand, the boom in the soap trade. Back in 1875, he had even registered a trademark, 'Lever's Pure Honey Soap'. It was, he concluded, now time to go 'all in' and so returning home, Lever prepared to leap with a genius that would transform an industry, centuries-old, with science and sales techniques on an industrial scale.

The art of soap-making was very old. For centuries, people had made their own soap, but by the thirteenth century the first soap *industry* had taken shape in Marseilles. By the seventeenth century, the major cities of England were served by soap businesses that stretched back generations, making good soap from olive oil and tallow boiled together for hours, mixed with potash and slacked with lime. Britain's soap-makers sucked up oil supplies brought in by the Muscovy, Greenland and Levant companies, and by King Charles I's day the industry was big enough for a monopoly – the London Society of Soap-Boilers – and prominent enough to be roundly attacked in the Long Parliament: 'like the frogs of Egypt,' it was complained, they were to be found 'in the washbowl and powdering tub'.[14]

It was said to be the Duke of Wellington who popularized the idea of a daily bath. Certainly, the country was filthy enough to need the habit. In 1790, Britain produced some 10 million tonnes of coal; by 1900, it was 242 million tonnes. Over the long nineteenth century, as the cities grew and industry flourished, the nation's air became filled with soot, smoke and fumes. Dirt was everywhere, and bathing became commonplace by the 1860s for anyone who could afford the coal to heat the water and the staff to fill the tub. Soap demand boomed. In 1801, Britain made just over 24,000 tonnes of soap a year – about 3.5 pounds a head – but over the course of the century, consumption per head grew nearly five-fold to 17 pounds per head. As the population tripled, soap output increased fifteen-fold, reaching 353,000 tonnes a year by 1907.

Soap-making businesses proliferated. In 1851, there were 103 firms exhibiting their wares at the Great Exhibition, and by the 1880s hundreds of companies were producing anything up to 26,000 tonnes a year. The north was dominated by family partnerships, such as William Gossage & Sons, Joseph Crosfield's of Warrington and Joseph Watson in Leeds. The west was dominated by Christopher Thomas's, which had started in 1743 and boasted a close relationship with Nobel's for the supply of glycerine. London was ruled by great firms such as John Knight, founded in 1817, which bought up London's tallow supplies; and Pears, founded by a Soho barber, Andrew Pears, in 1789.

By Lever's day, science, salt and steamships had allowed the industry to produce what had become a global product. Chemists were the key to change. In 1793, the Frenchman Nicolas Leblanc had discovered a process whereby sodium carbonate (caustic soda, or soda ash) could be created from salt. In the early nineteenth century, another Frenchman, Michel Eugène Chevreul, investigated the chemistry of animal fats, identifying the alcohol glycerin and fatty acids. Chevreul's discoveries inspired, among other things, a technique called 'saponification', which allowed soap-makers to blend oil or fat – typically tallow (rendered beef fat) and cooking grease – with water and lye (an alkali created by filtering water through wood ashes).

Britain's soap-makers were now in a fortunate position, for the once rare ingredients they now needed could be delivered to the ports by Britain's global network of steamships. For a reasonable price, mutton tallow could be shipped from Australia, beef tallow from the Americas, palm oil from West Africa, copra oil from the coconuts of the South Sea Islands, and cottonseed oil from the southern United States. The great port of Liverpool, a few miles from Lever's Bolton, was not only the centre of this new trade, but also bang in the middle of the Cheshire salt flats. There were few better places for a soap business. William Lever's genius was to bring everything together – to build a business that exploited Britain's international networks, sourcing the ingredients to put into branded packets in a recipe repeated in local businesses in every major market on the planet. And it was all built on the profits from the fast-rising tide of late-Victorian consumerism.

*

Over the second half of the nineteenth century, the combination of a population increasing by a million people every decade, rising wages and falling prices, transformed the spending power of Britain's consumers, creating the world's first mass consumer society. Between 1870 and 1900, the great surge in national trade helped to push up the average income per head by 50 per cent,* and this in turn helped power growth in household consumption after 1886. Free trade blessed the country with a comparatively cheap cost of living. The average Briton was now some 30–40 per cent richer than his or her French or German neighbour. By the First World War, the nation still produced a third of the world's goods and boasted the global British services industry, headquartered in London.

In this new market, the firms making and selling consumer products flourished. Daily they brought to the increasing numbers of consumers employed in steady jobs an ever-growing range of products –starch, polish, tea, cocoa, chocolate, jam, biscuits, syrups, sauces, potted meats, newspapers, cigarettes, pharmaceuticals and drugs, ready-made

---

* This had risen from the equivalent of £29.90 per head in 1870 to £42.50 per head in 1900.

clothing and footwear, and, of course, soap. The products were cus-tomer-ready – bottled, canned, packeted and branded, using skills now decades old. Bryan Donkin's Crosse & Blackwell had opened the country's first food-canning business in 1812, and John Horniman had begun selling packaged tea in 1826. By 1848, Thomas Beecham was putting pills into branded boxes. The Wills family gave their tobacco brand-names such as 'Best Bird's Eye' and 'Bishop Blaze' (in 1847), while John Player perfected its pre-packaged cigarettes after 1877. Bryant and May's introduced standard, pre-packaged safety matches in 1870s, and in the years after the American Civil War British entrepreneurs began to import the new techniques of the great American firms – such as Quaker Oats, William Kellog, Henry Heinz, Joseph Campbell, Anheuser-Busch and Coca-Cola.

Consumers could buy these new goods on the new British high street, transformed by the new cornerstones of British retail. In the 1850s, W. H. Smith & Sons, J. Menzies and Singer's sewing-machine retail chain all emerged, soon joined by John Hepworth's, Boots and the new 'chain stores' or 'multiples', which numbered around 1,500 in the 1880s, burgeoning to 11,645 by 1900. By the First World War, 168 firms boasted more than 25 branches each,[15] but among them were giants: the butchers Eastman's; James Nelson's, which ran over 1,000 stores; and Home & Colonial Tea, the Maypole Diary Co., Lipton Ltd and the Boots Pure Drug Company, which each held more than 500 stores. The great-est of them all was the Co-operative Wholesale Society. With 1.7 million citizens as members, in 1,439 organizations, it was, by the turn of the century, probably the biggest company in the world. Between them, the Co-operative societies, the department stores and the multiples (twice as productive as their German rivals) controlled some 20 per cent of total retail sales.

Key to the success of many of these new consumer products was the new art of advertising. By the 1860s, the pill-seller Thomas Holloway was already spending £40,000 a year on advertisements, and advertising was key to Thomas Lipton's success in building a national chain of grocery stores, from his humble start in 1871. Lipton's was not simply a master of window dressing, but also of highly imaginative stunts: ele-phants hired out to drag huge cheeses through the streets, or the fattest

pigs from the market paraded in public, their stencilled flanks announc-
ing their forthcoming demise and sale as chops.

By the 1880s, the new consumer kingpins – in medicines, in chocolate, in soap – had transformed the world of marketing. It oozed
everywhere. Picture advertisements in magazines began to appear,
along with colour posters, from the 1890s, by which time, Beecham's
was spending an extraordinary £110,000 a year on promotions. For
many, it was a world of horror. 'We live in an age of advertisement,'
lamented Lord Randolph Churchill, 'the age of Holloway's pills, of
Colman's mustard, and of Horniman's pure tea'.[16] 'Advertisements are
turning England into a sordid and disorderly spectacle from sea to sea,'
complained a letter-writer to *The Times* in 1892.[17] But in this new world,
William Lever realized that – like his competitors at Pears – real money
could be made by adding to the fruits of the foreign shores and the
science of chemistry the magic ingredient of advertising.

For a while, soap-makers had been among the leaders of this new
movement. Thomas Barrett, who married into the Pears family, was
perhaps the first to realize that a good brand, a catchphrase and a celebrity endorsement could move thousands of pounds of sales. 'Good
morning, have you used Pears soap?' was a famous early slogan. Lillie
Langtry, the celebrity actress (and for a while mistress of the Prince of
Wales), was employed to declare that 'for years I have used your soap
and no other', in a campaign backed by a huge £120,000 annual spend.

William Lever intuitively understood that a good advertisement
was the key to a good return. And so he turned to the best trademark
and patent agent in Liverpool, W. P. Thompson, for advice on a brand
that would break through. Thompson wrote down half a dozen ideas
on half a sheet of notepaper, but, said Lever; 'really at first blush, none
of those names appealed to me. I had big ideas of some sort of name
– I did not know what.'[18] For days, Lever doodled away, until suddenly
the inspiration hit him. 'When that occurred to me I had to go straight
off to Liverpool and ask Thompson to register it at once: I was all in a
tremble to have it registered, for fear somebody else had go it.'[19] It
turned out his brand-name – 'Sunlight soap' – was unregistered in
every major market.

With a brand in hand, Lever and his brother James – who joined him, in 1884 – now needed a recipe, a factory and a sales force. With typical energy, Lever had all three in the space of months. At first, he had planned to buy unbranded soap, stamp it and enjoy the mark-up. His brother had found an oil-based soap that seemed to offer a perfect combination of sweetness and lather. 'I liked this soap very much,' remembered William; 'I made a speciality of it, and called it "Sunlight Self-Washer", for I claimed that it could wash of it itself.'[20] But when Lever's supplier promptly threatened to jack up prices, Lever realized that serious money would require him to become both maker and marketeer.

The brothers' father was decidedly unsure about his sons' move into manufacture: 'A cobbler', he said, 'should stick to his last.'[21] But with characteristic confidence, William persuaded not only his father, but also friends and financiers, to donate or lend the sum of £27,000 – £2.4 million in today's money – to buy the rights to a new recipe and to lease a Warrington soap-works, Winser & Co., to make it. The Lever soap subsidiary was founded. In August 1885, with two inherited experts in tow, Lever spent months perfecting a blend of copra oil, tallow, cotton oil and resin to produce a pure soap that finally rolled off the production line in January 1886, still called 'Sunlight Self-Washer'.

Just like the Cadbury brothers twenty years before him, Lever understood the marketing appeal of 'purity', and while his recipe was special, his marketing was revolutionary. Lever had noticed the way that his soap, stacked in parchment-covered blocks in grocers' windows, failed to offer much of an image. So, instead of selling long bars to grocers for them to slice up, Lever decided that Sunlight Soap should be cut at source, wrapped in parchment and boxed in brightly coloured cardboard emblazoned with the Sunlight logo. Serious money was now spent on advertising, around Bolton and beyond. A £50 contract was taken out with local railway companies to emblazon stations with posters proclaiming 'Sunlight Self-Washer Soap: See how this becomes the House.'[22] As he later boasted, 'I was the first to advertise extensively a tablet soap... The result was I lifted Sunlight Soap into a class by itself where it has remained ever since.'[23] He bustled with mercurial energy, driven by a focus on sales. Agents were sent out to shop-keepers and direct to the doorsteps of customers. Lever was full of tips, about everything from persuading children to handle the goods, to closing gates, to the importance of not stamping mud into customers' homes.

But Lever knew that bigger sales needed bigger marketing. His philosophy was simple. As he explained to his sales staff, 'Advertising is as near bringing the manufacturing conditions of repetition to the selling side of the business as possible'.[24] Crucially, he had begun to bring in American techniques and adapt them for the British market. He was, for example, among the first in Britain to take up the idea of issuing booklets devoted to getting the best from soap. Thus, *Sunlight Soap and How to Use It* appeared in 1886, full of advice on cleaning everything from clothes to carpets. That was, however, but one trick in a veritable magic set designed to attract attention. Donations to good causes voted on by customers followed; when the Royal National Lifeboat Institution won, Lever donated a boat named *Sunlight Number One*, and pictures of it were splashed across the *Illustrated London News*.

Lever stole shamelessly from his competitors, and with great effect. One such inspiration was Thomas Barrett's 'Bubbles' campaign of 1886. Barrett had bought John Everett Millais's painting, *A Child's World*, of a golden-locked boy, inscribed the words 'Pears' soap' on reproductions, and created a hugely popular image. Lever borrowed the idea and three years later, in 1889, acquired William Powell Frith's painting of a little girl, *The New Frock*, because 'mothers always like to look at a nice little girl'. Snapping it up for 150 guineas, Lever plastered it all over billboards with the caption 'So Clean'. The artist was furious. 'Lively… was my surprise', Frith fumed to the *Pall Mall Gazette*, 'when I found a large representation of my picture with the new title of "so clean" forming the part of an advertiser for a firm of soap manufacturers.' The ensuing row guaranteed huge coverage in the *Gazette*, and its editor, W. T. Stead, declared the paper 'wholly in favour of this high-class method of pictorial advertisement'.[25]

Within just a year of opening his factory in 1886, demand for Lever's product was outpacing its ability to make it. And so, in 1887, together with their father, William and his brother James decided to float the old family firm. The Lever Wholesale Grocery Company Ltd was listed with a capital of £60,000, raised so that Lever Brothers could expand production from 20 tonnes a week in early 1886 to 450 tonnes a week by December 1887. By the end of 1888, soap production was up more than five-fold.*

Now short of cash for an even bigger factory, Lever encountered a problem. His bankers were reluctant to advance a loan, not least because Warrington was home to a bigger beast than Lever – the country's second-biggest soap-maker, Joseph Crosfield. Lever told his father that he wanted out of the family firm. To his great surprise, the seventy-seven-year-old James Lever not only agreed with his son, but went one further. He too would sell. And so, while the old business was floated off to W. H. S. Taylor, and cash in hand, William Lever set off to find a new base. It would be called Port Sunlight.

*

On Saturday, 3 March 1888, to the cheers of crowds, William Lever and a heavily pregnant Mrs Lever, together with 150 companions, stepped off the smartly dressed steam-barge the *Warrington* into a field at Bromborough Pool soaked by the ebbing Mersey. It was time to cut the first sod of the 62-acre site for the Sunlight works.[26]

The architect, William Owen, was asked to say a few words. Apologizing for this latest Lancastrian invasion of Cheshire, he assured the crowds of the 'right hand of fellowship', and he handed a handsome silver spade to Mrs Lever to plunge into the ground. 'I wish you all success,' she declared to loud cheers, 'success to the new works, success to the firm and success to all interested in the sale and manufacture of "Sunlight Soap",' whereupon the party repaired to its steamer and then to the Bear's Paw Restaurant in Liverpool. That evening, among the many who offered toasts, the old works manager, Mr Winser, spoke with pride of how the assembled company had, in a few short years, built one of the biggest businesses in Britain. Port Sunlight would soon help Lever Brothers become one of the biggest businesses in the world.

---

* It was up from 450 tonnes of soap a week to 14,000 tonnes a week by the end of 1888.

William Lever had been influenced by the innovative model village of Agneta Park in Delft, where the great Dutch industrialist J. C. van Marken had set out to build a novel, and more inclusive way of doing business than the grinding, cut-throat norms of much of European capitalism. As Lever explained at the Bear's Paw, 'our idea is that profit sharing should be so managed that those who take profits are those who are working at the works'. Homes, therefore, would be built on site, available at reduced rent – and they would be beautiful. 'It is my hope… to build houses in which our work people will be able… to know more about the science of life than they can in a back slum.'[27] Here was the genesis of Lever's business philosophy that would blossom over the course of his career, to 'socialise and Christianise business relations, and get back again in the office, factory and workshop to that close family brotherhood that existed in the good old days of hand labour'.[28] And so, at Port Sunlight, Lever set out to create from muddy fields not simply a model village but a model society.

The site, at first, was barren. 'Anything more unprepossessing than this site can hardly be imagined,' wrote W. L. George, for it was 'a few feet above high water level and liable at any time to be flooded by high tides'.[29] But Lever was a visionary. On sheets of white foolscap, Lever set out intricate designs bursting with technical notes in red and black ink for his master planner, Owen, and a team of thirty architects to formalize. 'The architects he employed', wrote Lever's son, 'all looked upon him as unique amongst their clients. He did not employ them – he collaborated with them.'

What emerged has been described as a spectacular 'Ersatz version of Merrie England',[30] an ivy-clad, hollyhocked English village of yore, with seven houses per acre, each designed to resemble a half-timbered Lancashire manor house, and fronted with a variety of late-medieval, Jacobean and Queen Anne-style façades, along wide streets christened after the places of Lever's Bolton. The homes were surrounded by green spaces. For Lever, a home required a 'garden in front of it, just as a cup requires a saucer'.[31]

Around his village, Lever built his village society, encompassing all that he could conceive would be useful and good: a primary school; a post office; tennis courts and a bowling green, and football and cricket pitches; a horticultural society; amateur dramatics, a philharmonic society and an English choir; a mutual improvement society, along with clubs for cycling, walking, croquet and quoits; a free library and a museum, replete with the bugle that had sounded the Charge of the Light Brigade; a swimming pool; an auditorium; a parish church – Christ Church; and a pub, which from 1903 was even allowed to sell beer.[32] On their birthdays, the children of Lever's staff received books signed by the Lever family. Twice a season, the works' women were invited to dances. In the summer, there were trips to Anglesey or Blackpool, to see the Diamond Jubilee, and even to Paris and Brussels.

Down the road from Port Sunlight, Lever set up as lord of his new dominions by acquiring Thornton Manor, into which he moved in 1891, with Elizabeth and his eleven-day-old son, William. He gave the place a spectacular overhaul, adding new wings, a new frontage, stables, gardens, a 20-acre lake (replete with canals), a bathing pool, a lagoon and an island, and a somewhat haphazard collection of art. Here, he could enjoy his new eccentricities of sleeping in an open-air bedroom on the roof, sheltered only by a slanting glass panel, until woken every morning at 6.30am for his bath, which was kept a few degrees above freezing. And here he could entertain like a lord, with garden parties for his staff, enlivened with merry-go-rounds, swings, donkey rides, boating on the lake, Punch and Judy shows, and the music of the Port Sunlight Prize Band.

The rules of this new society were Lever's. Every worker was free to apply for a home. At a rent of 7–10 shillings a week for a home with a parlour, they were well within the reach of a male worker on 25 shillings a week; but anyone who lost their job had to move. Lever insisted that his tenants' private lives were none of his business; but only flowers of which he approved could be grown in the front gardens, and the names of any men a girl invited to the dances were vetted by the 'Social Department'.[33]

But Lever never lost sight of business. The genius of Port Sunlight was its profitability. When Lever made his toast in the Bear's Paw restaurant, he explained that not only would the new site be connected by the neighbouring railway to every town in the country, but, as it was up estuary from the Port of Merseyside, Port Sunlight was free of the crippling Mersey dock charges on tonnes of imported ingredients. The result, said Lever, was that 'they would be able to produce soap at a cost below which no one could go'.[34]

By the summer of 1889, Port Sunlight was open for business, the first factory ('Soapery'), a glycerine plant and 300-foot chimney towering over the fields and the homes rising brick by brick from the mud. At the centre of it all, Lever controlled everything. He was, wrote the journalist A. G. Gardiner, 'a bit of human granite'. Short, at 5 feet 5 inches, he was thick set with a sturdy upright body and a massive head topped with a cockatoo crest of thick curly hair, generally topped with a hat. 'He is of the Napoleon breed,' wrote Gardiner, 'born to marshal big battalions and win empires, if not in war, then in peace.'[35]

After rising at 6.30am, Lever typically breakfasted at 7.30, practised his gymnastics most days, and set off to work dressed in his grey tweed suit, with a Victorian-era collar and carelessly worn tie. In the office, he was surrounded by stenographers, who took his dictation for an hour each morning, from comments scribbled on the piles of papers read overnight. At 10am he began his meetings, and throughout the day, from a fabulous glass-walled office in the middle of Port Sunlight, came an unending stream of commands, prophecies and exhortations. Managers everywhere were kept up to the mark with minutely detailed letters, until Lever headed home, to retire to bed no later than 10.30pm, and often as early as 9pm.

At Port Sunlight's opening, five times more soap rolled off the production line than the business had made just three years previously, and before long, thousands were coming from all over Europe to marvel at the place, including, on 28 November 1891, a very special visitor.[36]

William Gladstone had been invited to open the first of the new village halls, to be named after him – the mock-Tudor Gladstone Hall, which still stands outside Lever Hall today. Lever explained just how much he owed to the great statesman:

> It was in April 1853 that you removed the duty on soap, and thereby made the manufacture on a large and scientific scale possible. It was in 1861 that you removed the duty from paper, and so gave the country its greatest boon, a free and cheap press...

without a large circulation it would be useless to advertise… and the day is coming when advertising will take its place as a useful and beneficial art.[37]

In reply, Gladstone explained how much the country owed to Lever:

A very powerful writer said we were approaching a period when cash payment was to be the only, is the only, nexus, the only link between man and man… In this hall I have found living proof that cash payment is not the only nexus between man and man… 'Behold how good and how pleasant it is for brethren to dwell together in unity.' This day must inspire great thankfulness for the last, more hopefulness for the future.[38]

They were words that had a profound effect on Lever. 'I could not sleep much that night… I had to walk up and down the park thinking of him. He made an extraordinary impression.'[39] Within three years of Gladstone's speech, William Lever would float his business for the modern equivalent of £150 million. It was a remarkable accomplishment for a business less than a decade old. Yet, Lever's brilliance was not simply to build a business in Britain's booming consumer market, but to build a huge company from a small island by going abroad. The lessons he learned abroad he brought home to build one of the world's first great global brands. The good ideas he found anywhere, became good business everywhere. And he thrived even as the walls of protectionism began to rise, dividing the world's great markets into smaller plots.

*

While free trade had become a British national religion since the days of William Jardine, few of Britain's neighbours saw things in quite the same way. Even Britain's imperial markets, such as Canada, had tariffs as early as 1858, and in the 1870s a slow-down in global growth had coincided with US and German efforts to nation-build after their respective civil war and unification. The result was that tariffs soared, as politicians everywhere sought to build a world of walled gardens.[40]

Post-Civil War America created tariffs six and a half times higher than Britain's, while on the Continent the 1870s saw the beginning of a twenty-year tariff war.

Britain refused to bargain or use its vast power to retaliate. Indeed, Robert Giffen, the head of the Board of Trade, summed up the 'official' Whitehall mind in a letter to the pro-tariff Joseph Chamberlain in 1903: 'Only a free-trade country, or rather a free import country, can be the centre of the world's international commerce, as we are, which brings us an enormous business and gain, whatever special disadvantages it may have in the shape of "dumping" and so on.'

The result of tariffs elsewhere, however, was that while British exports were a remarkably stable part of the nation's economy between 1871 and 1911, contributing between a quarter and a fifth of output, the country increasingly sold 'old' products to old customers. Textiles, coal, iron and steel accounted for 85 per cent of British exports between 1870 and 1879; and whereas back in 1870 less than a quarter of exports headed to imperial markets, by 1914 the figure was more than one-third. By 1900, Britain could boast two-thirds of world exports in 'declining sectors', but under one-fifth of the new, expanding markets.

Faced with a world market divided up by tariff walls, Lever knew that he needed to build foreign foundations – and he set about the task even before Port Sunlight was open. In September 1888, he left for New York to help his brother-in-law set up shop,* eventually travelling 15,000 miles across the United States and Canada, installing an old Warrington hand, A. J. Wolfendale, in New York and an old school friend, Alfred Robinson, in Canada. Once home, he set out immediately for the Continent, where, in 1889, he blazed a trail across Belgium, Germany and France, where he stopped off to inspect his advertisements at the Paris Exhibition.

Tariffs were not the only obstacle to selling abroad, as Lever well understood: 'The most serious obstacle to international trade in manufactured articles is the great difficulty – I might also say the impossibility – while living in one country, of appreciating the tastes and requirements of another.'[41] And so he set about assembling an extraordinary team to

---

* He was setting up an American syndication service for short stories.

stretch the business across Europe. From Rotterdam, A. P. van Geelkerjen sent salespeople in blue uniforms, riding wagons in Sunlight colours, around the Dutch countryside.* Lever's export clerk, Ernest Brauen, was sent to open up business in Brussels, while Brauen's brother opened up in Hamburg. In Switzerland, Lever hired a trained Egyptologist with a background in running charities, the gigantically talented F. H. Lavanchy-Clarke, after he had wandered into the Port Sunlight yard one afternoon: he was sent to start a Swiss business in a blaze of worldwide publicity, holding a washing competition – the 'Fête des Blanchisseuses' – on the shore of Lake Geneva.[42]

Lever understood that to expand fast he needed to keep raising money. And so, on 27 May 1890, Lever brothers – then making £50,000 profit a year – converted to a private limited company with an authorized capital of £300,000.[43] The basis of Lever's financial strategy was crystallized at the time. Having searched for expansion capital, he was approached by company promoters keen to float his firm for £600,000, selling two-thirds of the shares to the public. When he confessed his doubts, Lever was asked: 'What does it matter to you, when once you have got the money?' Disgusted, Lever withdrew and decided henceforth that ordinary shares – and control of the firm – would stay with him and the family. Only company debt – in the form of debentures and preference shares – would be issued.

With new cash, Lever built faster than ever. In 1892, he set off travelling once again, with his wife and four-year-old son, for a tour of New York, the World's Fair in Chicago, the Sandwich Islands (Hawaii), New Zealand and Australia.† The Canadian business was reorganized, and new factory land was negotiated with the Mayor of Toronto. Lever expressed wonder at the modernity of Honolulu, before comprehensively reorganizing business in Australia and New Zealand. *En route*, he dispatched 879 letters to staff and another 600 to family and friends. For conversation, he spent his journey home debating free trade with the future Lord Curzon.

---

* They also took with them free samples and a free pamphlet by P. T. Barnum on *How to Become Rich*.

† They sailed home on the P&O liner *Australia* with Lord Curzon, who had just finished a tour of the Far East.

By 1894, Lever Brothers was finally ready to float. In one of the commercial events of the year, a prospectus was issued on 26 June proposing an initial capital of £1.5 million. The offer was four times over-subscribed, surpassing Lever's wildest expectations. And yet there was little pause for breath; he was once again back to sea, to prise open the market that was proving far and away the toughest to crack: the United States. Between 1894 and 1898, Lever returned there annually, in what he called his 'Battle of the Nile'.[44] 'It is the biggest undertaking I ever had on hand and I fancy it has depressed me... I should hate to face a failure here,' he wrote to his father in 1895, 'and we have to run the risk.'

*

Lever had now proved that great businesses could be built by taking aim at the prize offered by Britain's booming cities, full of ever richer workers, and which offered one of the greatest *consumer* markets on earth. In these markets, Lever's generation proved that for the right idea, it was perfectly possible to raise the requisite finance to grow – by issuing stocks, preference shares and bonds. Britain lacked the investment banks of the United States and Germany, and when British investors were spoilt for choice with a range of tempting foreign investments paying between 6 per cent and 8 per cent a year, new domestic firms needed to offer excellent potential to win investment.[45] The great challenge for Lever's generation, therefore, was how to build big companies from a small island in a world where few nations shared the British passion for free trade and where, at home, it was hard to acquire the three crucial ingredients new industries needed in order to prosper: scale, science and skill. They were assets the United States offered in abundance, for the nation had now surpassed the United Kingdom to become the world's economic Number One.

Appearances could, of course, be deceptive. When Queen Victoria celebrated her Diamond Jubilee on 22 June 1897, a quarter of the world's population got a day off. As the ageing queen processed past the deafening crowds, through streets 'beautifully decorated... with flowers, flags and draperies of every hue', 50,000 soldiers from every corner of the

British Empire marched through London, while at Plymouth there lay at anchor 165 ships bristling with 3,000 guns. It was, said Gladstone, 'the day on which is completed the longest and perhaps the happiest reign ever known'.[46] 'I remember the atmosphere,' wrote future historian Arnold Toynbee, 'it was "Well, here we are on top of the world, and we have arrived at this peak to stay there forever."'

In terms of sheer might and reach, the British Empire was yet to peak.[*] But the British economy was already second-best, overtaken in overall economic size, at least, three decades earlier by the United States. As the American frontier swept westwards, so the pioneers, railways, telegraphs – and modern corporations – spread, all flourishing in the years after the American Civil War. In 1830, there were just thirty-one stocks traded on the New York Exchange. By 1850, hundreds of thousands of shares were traded every week; in one four-week period, a million shares changed hands.[47] As early as 1851, the newly founded *Economist* predicted that 'the superiority of the United States over England is ultimately as certain as the next eclipse,'[48] and by 1859 huge new Wall Street banks had channelled over $1 billion into the railways.[49] They, in turn, unlocked a continental-sized marketplace, in which giant firms began to flourish.

Before 1880, few American businesses were worth more than $1 million. By 1901, the billion-dollar corporation was born, when J. P. Morgan merged Andrew Carnegie's steel business with its rivals to create the $1.4 billion US Steel Corporation. In the merger frenzy between 1897 and 1904, more than 4,000 firms merged into just 257 gigantic combinations, such as Standard Oil and American Tobacco. Forty per cent of American manufacturing was controlled by just 300 companies.[†]

Across this vast marketplace, American manufacturing workers were already more productive than their British counterparts as early as 1820,[50] and over the decades that followed the US productivity lead in services – transport, communications, commerce and the public

---

[*] It did not reach its maximum stretch until 1919.

[†] Half of the biggest companies at the *end* of the twentieth century were formed during the era between 1880 and 1930.

services – streaked further ahead.* American offices soon widely embraced the innovations of telephones, typewriters, duplicators and modern filing, leaving Britain lagging behind. Britain could not match this productivity or market scale, and soon, the average American citizen was the wealthiest in the West; in 1820, the average Briton was a third richer than the average American. By 1902, the Americans had drawn level.

The challenge for British entrepreneurs was that in most new industries, British competition was so fragmented that entrepreneurs lacked the market dominance that could yield returns to match what could be earned by British investors abroad; in the car industry for instance, eighty-one new car firms opened their doors between 1897 and 1913 – and, unlike Germany or America, Britain did not foster great monopolies protected by great tariff walls.

But Lever's success underlined the truth that Britain had no shortage of great entrepreneurs[51] – including innovators in the new automotive, aerospace, chemicals or electrical-engineering industries. However, Britain found it hard to match both foreign scale and foreign skill. The land of great minds seriously struggled to create great institutions to power the nascent knowledge economy. The nation's education system was lamentable, its technical education amateurish. Modern universities were slow to emerge, government was 'hands off' in nurturing industry, and regulation encouraged fragmentation rather than scale.

Men like Charles Babbage, the computer pioneer, were warning as early as the Great Exhibition that the country needed 'a more intelligent and better educated class of foremen, managers and workmen'.[52] Of course, there was progress of sorts. Mechanics institutes, born in the 1820s, numbered 700 by 1851. Eleven universities opened between 1851 and 1902, often modelled on the German design, and a raft of polytechnics emerged from 1880s to sit alongside the rather patchy science being taught in schools, science colleges and technical schools

---

* By 1910, US railroads were more than twice as productive as British railways; US communications sectors were 43 per cent more productive; US distribution workers 19 per cent more productive, and even the finance sector 20 per cent more productive. See Broadberry, *Market Services and the Productivity Race*, op. cit., pp. 30–5.

(which all subsisted without a lot of help from the state). The City & Guilds training organization was founded in 1879, and new laws of 1889 allowed councils to levy rates to build technical colleges, augmented by 'whisky money' in 1898: 160 colleges were built in this way. From the 1890s, the number of engineers multiplied; but technical education remained a second-class education, overwhelmingly part-time and linked to work. Crucially, it was a system dwarfed in scale by Britain's competitors; in 1901–02, there were 3,000 students in British technical collages, compared with 10,700 in German technical universities. In Germany, universities were funded at a completely superior level; by 1900, they enjoyed six times as much investment in science and technology as universities in England; at the same time, some 2,000 graduate scientists were at work in British industry, contrasting with 45,000 in Germany.[53] Over the next fifteen years, nearly a third of Nobel prizes went to Germany, while just 8 per cent went to Britain. The contrast with America was just as stark. Britain simply lacked the research infrastructure of American corporations such as Bell Telephone Labs or General Electric or Eastman Kodak.[54] By 1906, Members of Parliament were forced to conclude that while 'England compared not unfavourably with other countries in the provision made for... lower and intermediate grades of technical education... The principal deficiency... appears to lie in the sphere of the highest technical education'.[55]

*

Lever knew, therefore, that global success required him to 'go west', to the 'El Dorado of commercial prosperity' of the United States.[56] And so, in between hunting in Arkansas and haggling in New York, he bought an old oil mill in Vicksburg in the heart of the American south. With cash from his flotation, he expanded his mills and set up a new Lever Brothers New York office, before setting sail in September 1895, first for South Africa (to met Cecil Rhodes at Rondebosch and explore the country) and then for Australia, where he bought a factory site in Sydney and laid out plans for the first oil mill south of the Equator. In December 1895, Mrs Lever cut the first sod, before they sailed home.

The timing of Lever's global push was significant. The cut-throat competition in Britain's soap market brought, in 1896, the first fall in sales, of 5 per cent. It was Lever's American business that would now provide him with access to a crucial ingredient to fight back: advertising genius. 'I am certain that if there is any body of people who understand the art of salesmanship and the advertising of domestic articles, it is the Americans,' he once observed.[*]

In today's Unilever company archives at Port Sunlight, overlooking the vast factory site, lie the battered buff and green folders containing Lever's business correspondence with his friends. Reading through the letters, written like Edwardian email, it is clear how, from the mid-1890s, Lever was intensely studying everything American. He was an avid consumer of US newspapers, political speeches, magazines, and books on everything from parks and reservoirs to international relations. Lever scrutinized American direct-sales catalogues, such as those produced by Sears Roebuck, which ran a premium and trading-stamp scheme. 'I understand the books published by MOPH [*sic*] of Chicago are worth studying from the point of view of those who are interested in giving prizes for wrappers...' ran one letter to Lever Brothers America in 1907; 'The wrapper prize for soap is becoming a great craze in England this year.'[57]

Most important was the stream of intelligence from the frontline of his American salesmen. By 1895, his friend Wolfendale was already providing a detailed read-out from conferences of the firm's American sales-team, on everything from competitors' tactics, such Babbitt's distribution cards, to door-to-door sales, advertising, to the best ways of rewarding salespeople. Over the years that followed, Lever was able to draw on salesmen's reports from New York to Kansas and New Orleans, covering an incredible wealth of retail detail: sampling, pricing, advertising, rebates, product strategy, to salaries, sales expenses, shipping costs and box-printing machines, as well as scrappage, waste, ingredients and insurance.

---

[*] Indeed his trick of wrapping soap in vegetable parchment was stolen from the United States. As he wrote to his son, 'we get enormous strength on the selling side in England by our knowledge of selling and advertising in overseas countries, especially in the United States'. Lever, *Viscount Leverhulme*, op. cit., p. 57.

To tame the competition in the United States, Lever realized that he would have to buy it, so in 1897 he acquired three-fifths of the Boston-based Curtis Davis Company; two years later, he bought out Benjamin Brooke & Co., makers of Monkey Brand, the most popular soap in America. He swiftly moved production to Port Sunlight, but crucially he retained the services of the American company's advertising guru, Sydney Gross. Sydney's brother, H. B. Gross, initially stayed on to help run the US business, before resigning a few years later, unhappy at Lever's interference (as he saw it); another brother, Anthony Gross, was sent to Port Sunlight to learn the British business first hand. But it was Sydney who would make the decisive impact as he set to work with Lever.

'Most advertisers', remarked Lever, 'are the slaves of habit and the followers of custom. Not so Mr Gross. Originality marked him at every step.'[58] Between the two of them there now formed a relationship that allowed Lever to harness the best of American marketing savvy, and deploy it to pioneer modern marketing in Britain. The two men became neighbours in Hampstead, and over the years they exchanged ideas, doggerel, and books on anything from water-softening to exercises in bed. They remained intimate for the rest of Gross's life, and day to day worked intensively together, as their correspondence from just a single month, from mid-December 1902 to January 1903, illustrates. In page after page, the friends and partners swapped ideas on everything from the theory of advertising to the details of wrappers for a new toilet soap, 'Plantol', prize schemes, distribution plans for 'YZ' disinfectant, and a new advertising booklet – the designs, typeface, pictures and proofs deconstructed in minute detail.[59] The theory and practice of American marketing is woven throughout. In the exchange of letters on 15 December 1902, along with some notes on glycerine sales, ledger books and thoughts on advertisements for the disinfectant soap 'Lifebuoy', Gross was opining on the virtues of prize schemes. In the United States, he noted 'prizes tend to lower the esteem of the goods',[60] to which Lever responded: 'I would mention that all the leading soap firms in America are giving away prizes of some sort or other... from Colgate's to Procter & Gamble'.[61] The same day, Gross was replying with thanks for Lever's praise for his new advertisements: 'I'm glad you think our advertisements tell the tale', for, unlike chocolate, 'soap has to be imported in a picture'.[62] The next day he returned to the subject of prizes and the American trend for 'giving away prizes to such extent' that the firm seemed to be no longer primarily soap-makers; 'I hope that we shall never be in that position,' he averred, adding that Lever Brothers could not afford to have a consumer who 'gets his toilet soap thrown in gratuitously'.

The design of their 'Plantol' wrapper was a subject of intense discussion. On 23 December 1902, Lever was rejecting designs, though by January the wrapper was in better shape. 'I think that both the green and the white make good colours,' noted Gross.[63] In January 1903, Gross sent over an American advertising sample as an inspiration: 'I enclose you our American Lifebuoy pamphlet which appears to me to be about the right size.'[64]

Throughout it all, Lever never missed a trick when it came to spotting market opportunities, as when an outbreak of disease in his hometown looked promising for soap sales. 'My dear Gross,' he wrote on 10 January 1903, 'It appears there is an epidemic of smallpox in Bolton at present. I enclose an advertisement of Wright's Coal Tar Soap. Perhaps it would [be] as well to push Lifebuoy and YZ in our Bolton advertising at present.'[65]

The fruits of the Lever–Gross relationship were remarkable. Lever was quickly able to route American products through his British sales channels. He noted approvingly to Gross in 1901 that, despite the fact that 'the soap business is going through trying times at present owing to the high price of raw materials', British sales of Monkey Brand were up by 40 per cent; 'This is of course to be expected seeing that we have a force of 200 selling agents who are now carrying it into every shop in the UK.'[66] Critically for Lever, Gross helped transform Lever's British products. Faced with falling sales, Lever changed his wrapper schemes, but more importantly pushed ahead with new products such as 'Lifebuoy'[67] and, in 1899, Sunlight Flakes – which, after experiencing poor sales, was repackaged by Gross in boxes decorated with a happy-looking baby and a new, successful brand-name: 'Lux'.

Thereafter, new products proliferated. Along with the 'Y-Z' Disinfectant Powder, there was 'Vim' scouring powder and soaps in a vast variety of shapes, sizes and smells, such as 'Velvet Skin', 'Plantol', 'Coral', 'Capitol', 'Villa' and 'Sealskin'. Lever was segmenting his market for the first time, with different products for different people, each targeted with distinct advertising messages. 'Sunlight Soap', for example, focused on the labour-saving virtues Lever had long extolled: 'There is no labour, no experience necessary with Sunlight Soap… the Scientific Way', for 'It does the washing itself' and all in all was 'A saver of time, health and strength'. Lest consumers prove recidivists, they were warned: 'Housewives remember the soul-wearying labour of wash-day before the advent of Sunlight Soap.' 'Lifebuoy', on the other hand, rooted its appeal on its disinfecting qualities, with advertisements featuring dirty-looking children for whom the product could provide a shortcut to 'Health and Happiness': 'The housewife no longer needs soap for cleaning and costly chemicals for disinfecting.' 'Lux' flakes, by contrast, offered 'a novel and unique washing preparation' – a more luxurious offer, aimed at the caring mother. 'To mother, the washing of the little garments is a tender duty', ran a typical 'Lux' advertisement featuring cherubic toddlers, especially for the mother who worried 'for the sturdy growing youngsters whose health and comfort she holds as a sacred trust'.

The genius of Lever's business now became clear, for his multinational reach lent Lever the ability to export his marketing *savoir faire* not simply around Britain, but around the world. For, as protectionism grew worldwide, Lever now had to shift from simply using local sales agencies to actually manufacturing in the markets where he sold. As Lever explained it: 'The question of erecting works in another country is dependent upon the tariff or duty… When the duty exceeds the cost of separate managers and separate plant, then it will be an economy to erect works in the country so that our customers can be more cheaply supplied from them.'[68] Lever's factories began to open around the globe. In October 1898, Lever's Swiss agent Lavanchy-Clarke had his small daughter, Christine, start the machinery at the first Continental Lever factory, the 'Savonneries Helvetia' in Olten. On the Rhine, land was readied for a German factory, opened in 1900, while in 1901 De Lever's Zeep Maatschappij (Lever's Soap Company) was incorporated in Holland. In Brussels, in 1904, Ernest Brauen opened a factory to the applause of 2,000 visiting Port Sunlighters.

Lever's strategy tended to be simple: maximum control for the minimum of money, and so factories tended to be stand-alone ventures, co-financed by local businessmen. Lever would generally retain sufficient voting rights to control policy. In Switzerland, for instance, Lavanchy-Clarke owned 40 per cent, while the balance of preference shares were sold to a consortium of Swiss businessmen. The German business was a consortium with the Stollwerck chocolate family and eleven other shareholders.

Everywhere, Lever was able to deploy and adapt the basic advertising formulas that worked so well in Britain and America. Lever's 1897 English advert for Sunlight Soap, for instance, set out the basic claim that 'Grateful women from all parts of the world have expressed their full appreciation of the splendid labour saving advantages of Sunlight Soap.' And so, Lever's advertisements across Europe, whether for the Dutch 'Sunlight *Zeep*' or the German 'Sunlight *Seife*', carried the same basic imagery of the housewife on washing day in local dress, and the same basic appeal: 'labour light – clothes white'.

Helpfully for Lever, he was now able to compare the performance of his firm in markets around the world. Writing to Wolfendale in 1901, he happily reported the 8 per cent return on cash secured by the Olten and Mannheim plants and the $5 profit on a case of a hundred 12-ounce bars. 'What a beautiful state of affairs it would be if we could get $5 in Canada and the States.'[69]

As his firm prospered, Lever was becoming very, very wealthy. And with his fortune began a serious love affair with grand gestures and great paintings. When Rivington Pike – the dramatic landscape where he courted his wife – came up for sale in 1899, he snapped it up and offered it as a 400-acre park for the people of Bolton. Five years later, he acquired the mansion called The Hill, in Hampstead, and the beginnings of a nationally important collection of paintings, wall-hangings, furniture, sculpture and pottery.* He had begun picking up small *objets d'art* in dealers' shops in Bolton in the 1870s, before going on to collect at scale to fill the rooms of Thornton Manor. Not much of it was adventurous or original, and he relied on dealers rather than a single

---

* The Hill was later renamed Inverforth House.

specialist, but – as one dealer, Duveen, put it – Lever 'passionately loved beauty of form and colour' in art, as much as he did in business.

It was a passion that was about to be acutely tested as new pressures combined to put his business – and his reputation – under severe stress.

*

By 1906, about £1 million – a quarter of Lever's capital – was invested overseas. Britain, however, was still Lever's biggest market, and now profits were under pressure as the new margarine-makers began competing for raw materials.[70]

Around the turn of the century, a German chemist, Wilhelm Normanns had invented the process called 'hydrogenation', creating a hardened fat by adding hydrogen to fluid oils. Because the margarine thus produced sold at two and a half times the price of soap, margarine-makers could now afford to bid up the price of the crucial natural oils that Lever needed for his soap. Broadly speaking, a soap-maker could scoop up £24 per ton for soap containing 63 per cent fatty acid, while a margarine-maker could make £60 per ton for a product with 85 per cent fatty acid. For soap-makers, the costs of raw materials began to soar from a third to a half of all costs. Lever knew he could not raise prices, and so he tried to economize. First, he shaved the weight of a 1-pound soap bar to 15 ounces. But bolder steps were needed, and so Lever proposed a revolution: the first soap trust.

Cartels could be found in business everywhere, and informal organization of the soap trade was already well established, dating back to around 1867.[71] By 1897, the northern makers were informally fixing prices, and at the end of the 1890s Lever moved prices up along with the rest of the trade. In 1899 he convened talks amid the 'ruinous' competition. By 1901, the Chairman of the Soap-Makers Association declared that it was not possible 'to make profits without association and combination'. But five years later, Lever was proposing something completely new.

On 27 July 1906, Lever convened a meeting of the country's soap kings in Liverpool to present his paper on 'combines'. 'I believe by amalgamating,' he told them, 'we shall be in a better position to serve the public well and give better value than ever, and also to better serve the interests of the distributors.'[72] An exchange of shares was proposed to enforce an end to 'frenzied advertising', along with proposals to implement co-ordinated lay-offs of travelling salesman, to bulk-buy raw materials and to carry out centralized research. Quick assent was secured from Gossage's, Crosfield's, Thomas Watson, Christopher Thomas, Ogston & Tennant and John Barrington, together with five smaller firms (while two others agreed to sell out)[73] – and Lever tripled his share capital to £12 million to build the requisite war-chest. The prize was enormous. Lever calculated he could save a massive £700,000 a year including £200,000 on advertising – starting with the cancellation of a £6,000 contract with Lord Northcliffe's *Daily Mail*.

It was a bad place to start. Within five days of the trust's quiet announcement, the *Daily Mail* was on the war-path. In the opening shots of a sustained bombardment, its headline on 18 October screamed: 'Soap Trust Arithmetic: How 15 oz makes a pound.' Interviews and 'investigations' followed with laid-off salesmen and washer-women; there were vox pops with the public and questions in Parliament, and finally a campaign to boycott Lever Brothers. The company's share price collapsed by a third. Sales fell 60 per cent, month on month. On 23 November, the soap cartel's members met in Liverpool and agreed to abandon ship.

When the media bombardment switched to targeting Lever's trading practices and working conditions, he decided to sue. On 15 July 1907, in a blaze of publicity, a huge libel action opened at the Liverpool Assizes. Within days, the *Daily Mail* was offering to settle, eventually agreeing to record damages of £50,000. It was a large sum – but it could not, Lever calculated, replace the £500,000 he estimated he had lost in sales. 'I consider the old highwayman of a hundred years ago was a gentleman compared to the modern newspaper proprietor,' Lever remarked ruefully. Still, the damages won could be put to good use. Lever donated it all to Liverpool University to found the schools of Tropical Medicine, Russian Studies and Civic Design.[74]

A change of strategy was needed. If he could not build a cartel, Lever realized that he would have to build a conglomerate. And so began a gigantic buy-out of his competition, not just in Britain, but all over the world. A French business had already been founded, in 1905, and in 1906 Lever had bought out the owners of 'Comfort', his key competition in Canada; he now proceeded to roll up the country's market in a string of acquisitions between 1907 and 1912.* In 1908, he floated a company in Austria, and in 1910 he opened his French factory, laid the foundations for his Japanese factory (at Tori-Shindon near Kobe), in Germany bought a half-interest in the brand 'Dr Thompson's *Seifenpulver*' (Soap Powder) before going head-to-head with Persil.

In South Africa, Lever built a factory outside Durban and bought another in Johannesburg, and early in 1912 made arrangements for a Cape Town factory. In 1913, he added Norwegian and Swedish businesses, opened his Japanese factory, and began negotiations to buy his Australian competitor Kitchens. Two Marseilles firms were acquired in 1914, along with Dr Schlesinger, the founders of the New Transvaal Chemical Company, while in New York a deal was struck with Procter & Gamble to pool hydrogenation patents in a new Hydrogenation Company. The Dutch factory at Vlaardingen was completed in 1915. Over the next seven years, Lever steadily raised his share capital to £14 million, to buy out one competitor after another.

Lever's ambition abroad was matched by his appetite at home. In arranging the 'combine', he had already acquired Hodgson & Simpson and Vinolia; to them he added (in 1908) R. S. Hudson, which was big in soap-flakes, for £1 million, and eventually launched 'Rinso' – a product inspired by his battles with Persil – and commenced an attack in earnest on Gossage's export trade in bar soap. Between 1910 and 1913 Lever methodically took control of a string of companies.† None were bought outright; but all helped Lever limit competition or increase sales. The result was that by 1914, Lever had doubled production under his control to more than a third of British soap – 125,000 tonnes out of 335,000 tonnes.

---

* These acquisitions were consolidated into Canadian Soaps Ltd.
† These were Barrington & Sons (of Dublin), Tyson's (of Liverpool), Edward Cook & Co. (of Bow), Christopher Thomas & Brothers (of Bristol), Isdale & McCallum, Richard Wheen & Sons, Joseph Watson & Co. and John Knight Ltd.

A British multinational of unparalleled scale was taking shape. But Lever had known that it was not enough simply to control the making and selling of soap. Real control required ownership of the very ingredients themselves. And so, over the first decade of the twentieth century, he set out to build a global supply base, from the salt flats of Cheshire across the Pacific and to Africa. Lever's old adviser, Joseph Meek, the head of Lever Brothers in Australia, expressed the strategy well: 'The large soap maker in ten or twenty years from today who has not behind him a raw material scheme must go under no matter what be his advertising... Mere investments in planting schemes will be of no use; the soap maker must own the raw material scheme and have it as a background to their business.'[75]

Lever had first seen the potential of the Pacific on his world tour of 1892, when he grandly declared in his diary: 'Let us make them into planters, cultivators and manufacturers of such articles as can be made out of the raw materials their lands produce.'[76] A decade later he decided that his oil mills in Sydney should be supplied by an investment in the Pacific Islands Company, which aspired to grow coconuts on the ocean's islands.* When that venture failed, Meek persuaded Lever to shift his sights to the Solomon Islands. With typical boldness, Lever decided, together with the enthusiastic Charles Woodford, the island's chief commissioner, to create an enormous plantation. Woodford happily signed away a 999-year lease on 300,000 acres of the Solomon's Russell Islands. Minuting his boss, Lord Ripon, Woodford declared that 'It's not every day that we find a millionaire tenant in the Solomon Islands, and I think we may assume that the rental he pays is the lesser part of the advantage the protectorate will derive from him.'[77]

The business never quite worked. The coconut trees were blighted, as mynah birds, imported from India, struggled to contain a plague of leaf-eating frogatti beetles. Labour conditions were appalling. Lever's plan to import wholesale a new workforce from India drew a sharp rebuttal from the Colonial Office, which, unsympathetic to Lever's

---

* The company was incorporated as the Pacific Phosphates Company and Lever Pacific Plantations was incorporated in 1902. Lever had to buy a ship, the SS *Upolu*, to sail the produce home.

ambitions, pronounced that it was 'not concerned with the private interests of private individuals'. In the end, Lever's Pacific project barely supplied enough for the soap mills of Australia, let alone any other part of his empire. And so, he turned his gaze on Africa.

Lever had long known about the potential of Nigeria, where a company investigator had reported in 1902 'an inexhaustible supply of palm oil and palm kernels... only awaiting development and the opening up of markets'. But the new Liberal government that swept into office in 1906 would offer him only a twenty-one-year land lease, and so Lever eventually bought the principal firms trading with Nigeria in 1910,* and built crushing mills in Opobo and Apapa. But when the agent of the new Belgian King Albert – Dr Max Horn – arrived in Port Sunlight in 1909, offering him 2 million acres of the Congo, Lever leapt at the chance to create a supply base to match the ambitions of his factory town in Port Sunlight.[78] The first Lever mill in the Belgian colony began operating in 1911.

To this mix of foreign oils, Lever still needed Cheshire alkali, for which he was dependent on Sir John Brunner's supplies of caustic soda, mined and refined from the Cheshire salt flats.† Brunner was the nation's 'Chemical Croesus', founding the firm Brunner Mond (which would evolve into ICI), and he had created a powerful dominance over British alkali supplies. Keen to escape a dependence on others, Lever bought, in 1911, the Lymm estate, complete with 1,700 acres of salt-rich Cheshire countryside.

Brunner quickly hit back, buying out the ordinary capital of Lever's two great competitors at the time – Gossage's and Crosfield's – which owned crucial patents for converting liquid oils into hard fats. Brunner now suggested that in return for a new long alkali contract, the sales of Lever, Crosfield's and Gossage's might be co-ordinated. Throughout 1912, negotiations stalled. Retaliating, Lever acquired a licence to a competing hydrogenation patent – the Testrup patent – forcing a court battle over foreign rights to the technology in February 1913, and in this

---

* The companies were, first, W. B. MacIver & Co., the great Liverpool firm trading with Nigeria, followed by Peter Ratcliffe & Co. and Cavalla River Co.
† 'Lever had never embarked on a more critical contest,' wrote the company historian. See Wilson, *The History of Unilever*, op. cit., p. 130.

first great corporate battle of the young century, the courts found for
Lever. Brunner's patents were cancelled, and on 7 May 1913, at Lever's
home at The Hill in Hampstead, the two titans agreed a profit-share
deal for Gossage's and Crosfield's in return for a perpetual alkali contract – and Lever sold the Lymm estate.

*

On the eve of the First World War, Lever stood at the helm of one of the
greatest businesses in the world. Its capital was £30 million – worth
between £9.5 billion and £15.7 billion in today's money.* It made half
the soap in Britain, and controlled a global supply base with a worldwide chain of plantations, trading companies and foreign businesses,
overseen by hundreds of staff from the fourth floor of the Royal Liver
Building in Liverpool. And yet, Lever insisted, 'I am not a lover of
money as money and never have been. I work at business because business is life. It enables me to do things.'[79] In Port Sunlight, one of those
things he would now pioneer was a very new style of industrial relations. Port Sunlight workers had enjoyed an eight-hour day as early as
1889, for which they earned 2 shillings, along with a social life and
company excursions that ventured ever further afield. Eighteen hundred
staff were whisked off to see the Paris Exhibition in 1900, in a long
convoy of vehicles; 4,000 went to the Isle of Man the following year, and
in 1905, 2,000 staff were entertained at the Liège Exhibition, in Belgium,
conveyed on special trains to Folkestone and chartered steamers across
the Channel.

More important than the day trips were the pensions, introduced in
1905, followed by Lever's long-held ambition of profit-sharing – or 'co-
partnership' – introduced for over 1,000 staff in 1909. There were rules,
of course. Share certificates could be cancelled at any time for 'neglect
of duty, dishonesty, intemperance, immorality, wilful misconduct, flagrant inefficiency, or disloyalty to employers.'[80] But henceforth, more
than half of Lever's personal profits would be redistributed to staff.
Seventeen thousand staff would eventually enjoy participation.

---

* In 1913, the company's authorized capital was £30 million.

These were, however, sad years for Lever. On 24 July 1913, his adored wife Elizabeth died of 'pneumonia', and Lever decided to dedicate to her his greatest adornment to Port Sunlight. Lever had bought the entire art collection of the mine-owner George McCullough, including giant works such as Lord Frederic Leighton's *The Daphnephoria*, and he needed somewhere better than Hulme Hall for displays. In 1913, designs were prepared for the exquisite Beaux-Arts, Portland-stone-clad museum, which Lever now named for his wife as the Lady Lever Gallery. On 25 March 1914, King George V laid the foundation stone by pressing a button on a scale model of Port Sunlight, which activated an on-site winch to lower the slab into position, in the heart of Lever's company town. It was an exquisite addition to a tradition of English corporate philanthropy devoted to the public appreciation of art – though the interruption of war would delay the opening of its doors for nearly a decade.[*]

When war came, Lever Brothers supplied more than its fair share of heroes. Within weeks, 700 Sunlighters had signed up at Gladstone Hall. On Sunday, 6 September 1914, Lever presided over a farewell service to bid 'God speed' and to inspire with reminders of the nation's great qualities of 'courage, purpose and endurance'.[81] Aged sixty-three, Lever was too old to fight. But he signed up as a volunteer with an honorary rank, promised to keep open the soldiers' jobs for their return, and guaranteed to make good the difference between Lever Brothers' pay and the army's pay. He now transformed himself into a 'Whitehall warrior', bringing to the role all his qualities of getting things done. 'Charm, tact, decision, power radiated from the man's every word, look, gesture', wrote one civil servant who worked with him; 'I had never met a man who was so obviously megalomaniac and accustomed to having his own way'.[82]

Lever's factories turned out the stuff of war – shells and glycerine – while Thornton Manor became a hospital. His scientists developed chemical weapons, including the highly toxic 'PS' (Chloropicrin), but on the battlefields, the war was merciless for the 'Port Sunlight Pals'

---

[*] Others included Liverpool's Walker Art Gallery (1877), the City of Manchester Art Gallery (1882) Whitworth Art Gallery Manchester (1890), the National Portrait Gallery and the Tate (1897).

– the 13th Service Battalion of the Cheshire Regiment, which was almost wiped out by the Battle of the Somme in 1916. By 1918 so few were left, the battalion was split and its men dispersed.

If war was brutal, it was brilliant for business. Sunlight Soap became standard issue for soldiers and when the German U-boats cut foreign margarine supplies, Lever was tasked with making a substitute. The result, 'Plate Margarine', was supplied by Lever's Planters Margarine Company, and rolled off the production line from November 1914.[83] It was, by all accounts, almost uneatable. 'Several of the maids', wrote one well-to-do customer, 'had told the housekeeper that they would prefer to leave than eat the margarine.'

There were no borders to success. By March 1915, Lever could report new works or extensions underway in Rotterdam (in neutral Holland), Boston, Sydney, Toronto and Japan, as well as new firms targeted for acquisition in Canada, Australia, New Zealand and South Africa. Most important of all was the beginning of the long take-over of his greatest British rival: 'We have acquired an interest in the Ordinary shares of Mssrs Pears,' Lever announced, 'who are the greatest firm of toilet-soap makers in the United Kingdom.'[84] By 1917, Pears was fully part of the Lever empire.

On 4 September 1917, the prime minister, David Lloyd George, came to stay at Thornton Manor. On his last day he toured the plant. 'I was anxious to see these world-famed works,' he told the thronging crowd; 'They show what can be done by one man of great organising genius who has also got a good heart. These works are a triumph of organisation and kind heartedness.'[85] The nation's Liberal leaders had long sought Lever as a candidate and a credential for their party, and Lever had responded sympathetically. 'His liberalism', said his son, 'was always more than a party label, it was a deeply ingrained habit of thought.'* For his consistent service, Lever was rewarded with the rec-

---

* In February 1892, Lever had become chair of his local party, and, on condition that he would not win, stood for Parliament for Birkenhead that year, when he halved the Tory majority. He stood again in 1893, in a by-election, coming within 106 votes of winning, and then again in 1895. He was finally elected to the Commons, for Ormskirk, in the Liberal landslide of 1906, but stood down shortly thereafter. He stood once again for Ormskirk in 1910, unsuccessfully,

ommendation of a peerage. On 4 June 1917, and remembering his wife, he took the title 1st Baron Leverhulme of Bolton-le-Moors. His coat of arms, enjoined with his wife's, boasted two spotty elephants.

At the age of sixty-six, the 'great organising genius' was master of his industry. He began to contemplate an industrious retirement. In 1918, he accepted the Mayoralty of Bolton, and, insisting on chairing every council meeting, he drew up magisterial plans for the town's redevelopment, published as *Bolton: As It is and As It Might be*. His kind offer of Leverhulme Park was gratefully received – but his blueprints were rejected.

Fate now offered Lever another canvas. The Western Isles of Scotland had long been important to him, and when two islands – Harris and Tweed – came up for sale in 1918, Lever rapidly wrote a cheque, moved into Stornaway Castle, and within months had fashioned ambitious plans to transform the ancient islands into a Scottish Port Sunlight, the 'Venice of the North' – a modern Edwardian fishing economy, backed with £5 million of his own cash. Over the next few years, he entertained royally at his castle home, adding to his portfolio with the acquisition, in 1919, of Cardinal Wolsey's former estate, Moor Park, in Hertfordshire.

When peace arrived, Lever Brothers could boast, in 1919, a capital base that had grown by an enormous 50 per cent, to £60 million.[86] It was muscle that Lever now deployed to continue to roll up as much of the British soap industry as possible. One after another, his competitors – Crosfield's & Gossage's (1919, for £4 million), Price's Patent Candle Co. (October 1919), John Knight's (1920) – were swallowed, leaving Lever with 60 per cent of the UK market. Abroad, the US business was now the third-largest on the American continent. New soap-works were built in Norway, Sweden, Denmark, Italy, Austria, India, China and New Zealand.[87] In South-East Asia, a controlling interest was taken in the Philippine Refining Corporation, and Lever Brothers bought out the Southern Whaling and Sealing Co., complete with 'floating factories' and a whaling station at Prince Olaf harbour on South Georgia.

This corporate appetite was, however, a prelude to a near calamity that ended any notion of Lever's retirement.

---

though reducing the Conservative majority.

*

By 1919, Lever's vast soap empire needed a quarter of a million tonnes of oils and fats every year. So when the Niger Company came on to the market, blessed with 100,000 tonnes of oil seeds, Lever was minded to buy. In January 1920, he was in New York negotiating a major margarine deal when he received a telegram from his board asking his blessing for this 'deal of the century'. 'Congratulations,' Lever telegraphed back, 'Price high but suicidal if we had let opportunity lapse.'[88]

Suicidal it nearly was. At £6 10s a share, the deal was worth £8 million – eight times the size of Lever's entire Congo investment. And when he returned home, Lever discovered he owned a disaster in the making. Accounts had not been checked, and control had been left with the old owners for months. Lever had bought at the top of the market, just as the post-war boom in raw materials ran out of steam.[*] Worse, the Niger Company was carrying a £2 million undiscovered debt that was about to be called in. 'He was never nearer disaster,' wrote the company's historian. Barclays, the firm's bankers for years, declined to loan anything. Henry Bell, a director of Lloyds, bluntly told Lever that 'a good many of us feel that you have gone ahead too quickly in view of a difficult financial situation. The truth is that there is not enough money to go round.'[89]

Lever was forced to float new shares without an underwriter. In order to pay the Niger Company's debts, he had to call in the firm's accountant, D'Arcy Cooper, to negotiate a loan with Barclays, using debenture stock for collateral.

It was the alarm-bell Lever had needed. His firm had become an extraordinary conglomerate, a business that stretched from Plymouth saw mills to South Atlantic whaling stations. Now, at the age of seventy, Lever fell on his company with ruthless force. At 4.30am, the night watchman would wake him, earlier than ever, from his open-air bedroom with a loud electric buzzer – for Lever was increasingly deaf – and he would start work, scribbling in red pencil over his reports before departure for the office at 8.30am.[90] Within a year, Lever knew

---

* In April 1920, the price of palm oil fell from £94 per ton to £24 10s per ton. Lever, *Viscount Leverhulme*, op. cit., p. 225.

he needed help. D'Arcy Cooper was recalled, and the corporate head-quarters was moved from Port Sunlight to the old De Keyser's Hotel on London's Thames Embankment, near Blackfriars Bridge, where today, it remains the home of Unilever.

An accountant, from a family of accountants, Cooper had worked for Lever Brothers for years. He held the shareholders centre-stage, telling the firm's managers that 'we are the trustees for some 200,000 shareholders, and we have no right to spend one penny unless we are absolutely certain we are going to get an adequate return'. A state of emergency was declared. Within a year, £1.25 million was saved as departments were closed for a day a week, land and factories sold, and wages cut. Over five years, 3,000 staff were laid off. And this was not all Lever lost. By 1923, his great experiment in Harris and Lewis had ended in disaster. Homes were sold back to residents, and crofts were handed over free to occupiers. Over £1 million had been sunk in, and while Lever remained deeply absorbed by his company MacFisheries – his attempt to build a 'sea to the slab' national fish retail business – his investment in the islands was lost. The castle and its estate were bequeathed to Stornaway, its grounds renamed Lady Lever Park.

*

Lever was now famous worldwide. Travelling constantly, he was met by great crowds and important leaders, such as the United States' President Coolidge, who honoured him with dinner. The Lady Lever Gallery was finally opened, by Queen Victoria's youngest daughter, Princess Beatrice, in December 1922. It offered a beautiful collection: Old Masters, English watercolours, Pre-Raphaelite art, sculpture, tapestries, Chinese pottery and porcelain, Wedgwood, English furniture – and a Napoleon room of Bonaparte memorabilia. Lever, said his son, had 'arranged the whole collection himself devoting many long and happy hours to the task'. [91]

But little gave him as much pleasure as Leverville. He paid his second visit to the Congo in 1923. There he could survey the 1,000 kilometres of road, the 70 kilometres of railway track, the 10 hospitals, the 700 brick houses and schools, the 19 steamers and the 72 barges all built and running in his name. It would prove his final visit. On his way home, the ship's captain invited him to choose and read a lesson. Lever picked Ecclesiastes 2:4: 'I made me great works: I builded me houses; I planted me vineyards… then I looked on all the works that my hands had wrought, and on the labour that I had laboured to do: and behold, all was vanity and vexation of spirit, and there was no profit under the sun.'

In April 1923, William Lever presided over his final general meetings – of Les Huileries du Congo Belge in Brussels, of the Niger Company in London, and of Lever Brothers in Port Sunlight, where he set out with pride the firm's scale: 187,000 shareholders, 85,000 staff, 18,000 co-partners. He weekended at Rivington, and visited the Sunday school at Blackburn Road Congregational Church, before journeying back to London. *En route* he became feverish. Bronchitis was diagnosed, and soon pneumonia set in. On Thursday, 7 May 1924, at 4.30am – the time he normally rose for work – William Lever died. He lay in state for three days at the Lady Lever Gallery, and was buried next to his wife, beneath the western window of Port Sunlight's Christ Church.

The company Lever had founded was now worth £57 million.[92] Four years after his death, it merged with two great Dutch firms – Jurgens and Van den Bergh's – to form Unilever, while the Niger Company was merged with the African and Eastern Trade Corporation to create the United Africa Company. Unilever, chaired by D'Arcy Cooper, was the largest industrial amalgamation in European history. Owned by 300,000 shareholders, it employed a quarter of a million people; it bought and sold a third of the world's fats and oils, and it traded in more places, with more products, than any other firm on earth. Valued at £132 million, it was the largest and most valuable company in Britain. And by 1928, it could boast that it sold more than 2 million bars of Sunlight Soap every working day.

11

JOHN SPEDAN LEWIS

Pioneer of Partnership

On the evening of Tuesday, 17 September 1940, the men and women of 'Green Watch' at John Lewis's great emporium, the largest store on London's famous Oxford Street, retired to bed shortly before eleven o'clock. Katherine Austin, secretary to the staff manager, was on duty that night, one of four young women charged with the care of 200 'terribly nervy' evacuees from the German bombing, now taking shelter in the basement. Hitler's 'Blitz' on London had commenced just ten days before. Buckingham Palace had already been hit, the East End smashed, and before the end of the month nearly 6,000 Londoners would be dead. Now, it was the West End's turn to take a hammering.

Late on the night of 17 September, a flotilla of 268 Luftwaffe bombers crossed the Channel and set course for London. A little over an hour after Katherine went to bed, the bombs began to land.

Katherine had been 'mothering the evacuees', a job that she 'just loved doing'; as she later explained in the John Lewis *Gazette*:

> We were… wakened about 12 by the first direct hit… I told those sleeping near me to dress and wait, and I ran along to the Control Room. The water was pouring down behind our little switchboard and they were already trying to get an ambulance for the wounded fireman… I followed them to the Returns room, where I had about twelve people sleeping, and just as I got there the second bomb fell somewhere in front of me. I had one moment of sheer panic. I could have sworn that the walls in front were going to collapse and the ceiling would then come down upon us all.[1]

An incendiary bomb had hit the store, setting it ablaze and jetting burning oil down the gutters of Oxford Street. One of the watchmen described the scenes:

> I was on the 7th floor on my way to relieve the other watch when a bomb came crashing into the side of the building near the roof. There were two more explosive bombs and then came a shower of oil bombs... By that time I was pretty stunned, having been knocked clean through a door... our first concern was for the people in the shelters below the building. Flames were spouting from the top storey.[2]

When the fire-fighters arrived, they were hit by a new wave of high-explosive ordnance. Three were killed almost immediately. All night, the crews of thirty fire engines fought the blaze – it would take thirty-six hours to bring it under control.

As dawn broke, Katherine Austin walked to Chadwickham House, the John Lewis assembly point around the corner from Oxford Street, where she found:

> ... tea and biscuits ready for us and a lounge, already converted into an office, with small tables, pens and paper all set out. At seven o'clock we started 'receiving' the staff who had been caught by the men of the Watch acting as scouts round the cordon at JL... I cannot tell you how helpful all those men were, and our grand little first aiders stood up to their first big job marvellously.[3]

Minutes later, the air-raid sirens sounded again. The anti-aircraft guns opened up at fresh waves of attackers, while down the Thames, Royal Air Force fighters were scrambled to counter-attack.

In the aftermath, John Spedan Lewis described the night's terrible events for his colleagues – the John Lewis 'Partners': 'The strong wind was doubly unfortunate,' he wrote; 'In whatever direction it had been blowing it would have increased immensely the effect of the oil-bomb... The wind was westerly and it drove the fire across Holles Street onto our East House. That was not burnt so completely as the West but the damage is very great.'[4] Around £848,000-worth (more than £100 million in today's equivalents) of stock had been destroyed. But Spedan was resolute. That day, every Partner was sent a postcard to say they would be paid in full on Friday, as usual.

A week after the bombing, Phyllis Warner, out shopping, observed that 'the big stores are carrying on gallantly in spite of their troubles… John Lewis's great building was bombed and burned until it is only a blackened shell, but it bears the defiant notice "Re-opening on October 5th".'

Katherine Austin signed off her letter to the *Gazette*: 'Please give my love to Mr Lewis and tell him we will fight like… to pull things together again. That word expresses our feelings best, but if you think he would disapprove, please substitute another.' Sure enough, John Spedan Lewis and the Partners had the business open on time. And together, over the next five decades, they and their successors would not only pioneer a new kind of business but rebuild their unique firm, among a 'nation of shopkeepers', as the giant of Britain's high street.

*

The John Lewis business was not named after John Spedan Lewis, but rather after his father, the founder of the family fortunes, who was born in a handsome three-storey Georgian house in Shepton Mallet, Somerset, in 1840. Here, 20 miles south of Bristol, on the old Roman road to Exeter, in a small market town south of the Mendip Hills, the Lewises had lived among around 5,000 souls for at least four generations.

John Lewis's father ran the bakery on the market square, while his mother, Elizabeth Speed, hailed from an old family of shopkeepers, grocers, brewers, basket-makers and milliners. Between 1841 and 1842, tragedy struck, when both parents died, and John was left to the care of his Aunt Christian. She found the money to send him to Shepton Grammar School. But, before the age of fifteen, he was apprenticed to a Glastonbury draper, Peter Marquand, who already employed two of John Lewis's sisters.

John was not in Glastonbury long. In the space of just four years, he moved to Wells and then Bridgwater, then north to Liverpool, where he was sacked for fighting. Borrowing a gold sovereign from a Frenchman, he bought a ticket to London, where on 6 May 1856, he tracked down some relations in Regent Street, found work, and began to dream big dreams. He described the moment, much later in life: 'When I first went to London I took lodgings in a street near Oxford Street. That street captured my imagination, and I said to myself "I will build my business here."'[5]

The 'reprehensibly audacious' Lewis proved a brilliant salesman. Lodged in a hostel with fifty-four other shop assistants, he was a quick master of the draper's art of silk-buying, until the day that changed his life. As his son Spedan later described it, 'One of his regular customers, a wealthy and shrewd old lady, the wife of the provincial Partner in a very great wholesale business… said one day to my father… that a little shop was vacant just the other side of Oxford Circus, and that he ought to take it and try his luck in business for himself.'[6]

John needed no convincing, and sometime in 1864, having borrowed £600 from his unmarried sisters, he opened for business at 132 Oxford Street, in a narrow-fronted Georgian house that was once a tobacconist's. He cashed up, on his first day, the princely sum of 16s 4d. Soon his shop window was jammed full of silks, laces, threads, ribbons, frills and bows. His reputation won him credit, and his strategy won him sales, as the 'shrewd old lady' discovered on a return visit: 'Ah, that's right,' she said, 'I see what you're doing. That is what my husband did. Buy cheap and sell cheap.'[7]

*

Napoleon was not the first to note that Britain was a nation of *boutiquiers*.* But there were few better eras to be a shopkeeper than the times enjoyed by John Lewis – and his son. Between 1861 and 1901, the nation's population grew by almost half to more than 32 million, and, together with a 40 per cent increase in incomes across the last two

---

* The French emperor was probably paraphrasing the Scottish philosopher Adam Smith, who observed in his *Wealth of Nations* that, 'To found a great empire for the sole purpose of raising up a people of customers may at first sight appear a project fit only for a nation of shopkeepers.'

decades of the century, growth ensured new fortunes for Britain's retailers, such as Boots (founded 1849), J. Sainsbury's (founded 1869) and Marks and Spencer's (founded 1884). Shop-workers doubled in number over the half-century after 1850, and almost doubled again in the next fifty years, as huge new retail chains took shape, boasting hundreds – and for some – thousands of branches.

Most profitable of all were the sales to Britain's booming middle class, which, though not huge, was growing fast. In Victoria's day, around a quarter of Britain earned more than £250 – the key to a middle-class life. Although around 40 per cent of these lucky families lived in London and England's south-east, Britain's booming cities – such as Liverpool, Manchester, Salford, Newcastle, Nottingham and Birmingham* – all boasted sizeable well-to-do constituencies, whose inhabitants typically worked in commercial occupations, accountancy or office work, and who lived in new suburban estates of semi-detached and detached houses.†

Success for a retailer such as John Lewis required staying on top of the new tastes – tastes that some sought to satirize. In *Our Mutual Friend*, Dickens lampooned the 'Veneerings' family: 'bran' new people in a bran'-new house in a bran'-new quarter of London', about whom everything was 'spick and span new'.[8] Here was a caste, wrote G. K. Chesterton, that was 'the first generation that ever asked its children to worship the hearth without the altar'.[9] 'Home, sweet home' was the cult of the new class, whose new style of living could be studied and mastered with the aid of text-books such as Isabella Beeton's *Book of Household Management* (1861), lauded by Arthur Conan Doyle as containing 'more wisdom to the square inch' than in 'any work of man'.[10] It quickly sold 60,000 copies to an 'opulent free-spending middle class' hunting the 'paraphernalia of gentility'.[11]

---

* They were arranged, as F. M. L. Thompson observed, in 'layer upon layer of sub-classes, keenly aware of their subtle grades of distinction'. Francis Michael Longstreth Thompson, *The Rise of Respectable Society: A Social History of Victorian Britain, 1830* (Harvard, 1988), p. 173.

† Examples of this include: Birmingham's Edgbaston; Glasgow's Bearsden; London's Dulwich, Richmond and Edgware; Bristol's Clifton, Cotham and Redland; Nottingham's Wollaton, West Bridgeford and Mapperley Park; and Manchester's Victoria Park, Alderley Edge and Wilmslow.

The middle class home was elaborately furnished; as Ralph Waldo Emerson acutely observed from the outside, an Englishman 'in the middle condition... spares no expense on his house... it is wainscoted, carved, curtained, hung with pictures and filled with good furniture'.[12] The clutter of Victoriana was gradually giving way to a more refined, aesthetic approach, inspired by the philosophy of men like William Morris, who famously urged: 'Have nothing in your houses that you do not know to be useful or believe to be beautiful.'[13] It was all good for business and the new consumers flocked to the great department stores of provincial Britain, 200 of which were trading by 1900, and employing thousands of people.

Over the long boom that began in the mid-nineteenth century, every major town and city boasted a store of its own: Liverpool had Lewis's (not to be confused with John Lewis); Manchester, its Kendal Milne, and Glasgow, its John Anderson. Wolverhampton had Beatties, and Sheffield had Cockaynes. London was of course home to the largest number,[14] and by the 1870s, John Lewis found himself surrounded by the businesses of some of the country's most inventive entrepreneurs: Debenhams, Harrods (employing 6,000 people), Selfridges, Army Navy, Dickens and Jones, Marshall and Snelgrove.[15]

Few of these retail entrepreneurs were as pioneering as William Whiteley, a Yorkshireman who helped invent the modern eponymously-named department store. He employed 4,000 people. Starting with a cluster of shops and a vision of himself as a 'universal provider', he commissioned, in 1887, a brand-new, swaggering steel-framed baroque edifice, faced in finely carved stone and advertised as 'an immense symposium of the arts and industries of the nation and of the world'.[16]

Together, these were the firms that created a new science and culture of shopping, brought to its apotheosis by the American Harry Selfridge, who opened on Oxford Street in 1909 with the slogan 'Why not spend a day at Selfridges?' He hosted 80,000 people on the first day, inside his steel-framed emporium of classical design. In the stairwell hung the aeroplane in which Louis Blériot had recently crossed the Channel. Not only was the customer king, but 'the customer is always right' – said Selfridge. Shopping, he believed, was leisure, as well as news and advertising, both now propagated through the new mass newspapers, such as the new *Daily Mail*, and the wealth of new women's magazines.

*

John Lewis looked and learned. He wanted to expand, and slowly, he set about buying out the shops around him in Oxford Street, finally winning the right from his landlord to knock the stores through in 1895 and re-form the giant space into one integrated department store. But he never departed from a basic idea: stocking a huge variety of goods, ruthlessly controlling costs, and passing on the savings to customers. His first-year sales had totalled £5,000; by the 1880s, sales reached £100,000, and they doubled to £200,000 once the new department store was open.

With prosperity, Lewis finally felt free to marry. He first met Eliza Baker – half-sister and ward of the Bristol draper Mills Baker – on a Scottish cruise ship in 1880. When they met again by chance on an Oxford Street omnibus, four years later, they renewed an acquaintance that flourished rapidly into marriage, and soon the betrothed were parents. John Spedan Lewis was born on 22 September 1885, followed, a year later, by his brother Oswald.

Eliza was an extraordinary woman. Eighteen years younger than John Lewis, she was among the first women to study at what would become Girton College, Cambridge. A capable pianist, she graduated top of the roll for the Pass degree in History and Political Economy in 1877, and began work as a teacher in Bedford College, London, the country's first higher-education college for women. She was, said her son Oswald, 'one of the sweetest and most unselfish women that ever lived'.[17] To Spedan, she was a woman with 'a large, strong mind and very little intellectual appetite', yet she tutored him at home and clearly taught him well. When he did attend school, he was obviously bored and, eventually sent down for being 'scandalously idle and insolent', he was soon packed off to Westminster School.

Home life in the Lewis family's great Victorian pile, set in four acres of Hampstead Heath, with a garden populated by pigs, chickens and rabbits, was by all accounts happy and unreligious. Indeed, John Lewis's only creed, said his wife, was 'the divine right of employers'.[18] There were not many holidays, but Spedan fondly remembered his father setting off to work each morning in a grand motor-car. It clearly made an impression. In 1904, having decided that the University of Oxford was not for him, Spedan concluded that 'in our modern world private enterprise was the still molten core of things'.[19] On his nineteenth birthday he joined his father's business for an apprenticeship that would prove rather less comfortable than his childhood.

*

By the time Spedan started work, his father was a Liberal Party councillor, who had served three months in Brixton Prison for contempt of court after refusing to give way in a row with his landlord. It was a vivid illustration of his intransigence. One of his workers, Albert Sheering, remembered how '[John Lewis] would arrive at the main door… almost to the minute and he made a point of making his first job of the day a trip to the marking-off room to inspect the goods his buyers had bought, and woe to the buyer if he did not approve of their quality and price.'[20]

John Lewis's somewhat determined approach to life, it transpired, had not proved so good for business – as Spedan now discovered. The firm's sales numbers rather flattered the truth; the accounts were a mess; space was used without efficiency, rhyme or reason; the stock was outdated; and the staff were treated terribly. The scales quickly fell from Spedan's eyes. 'With his very great qualities… my father was appalling[ly] difficult to work with. As his leading men – almost all of whom had been with him from their boyhood – rose to the sort of salary that he hated having to pay… they were successively driven out of the business.'[21] Spedan had, at home, 'regarded him as a superman, virtually infallible in matters of business. I had not expected… to find that the business was in fact no more than a second-rate success achieved in a first-rate opportunity.'[22] During these formative years, Spedan acquired the two impressions that would shape his life: an antipathy for his father's rule, matched only by a concern for his workers' welfare.

In 1906, John Lewis 'astounded us all', granting the twenty-one-year-old Spedan – and later, his brother too – a quarter-share of the business and £50,000 in capital.[23] It was not long thereafter that Spedan first began to plan how to give it away. One day in 1907, as he was sitting on the London General horse bus, turning from Haymarket into Trafalgar Square, a thought struck him; as he later recalled, 'I can vividly remember the warm glow that ran through me as for a moment I saw something of the satisfaction of those who renounce – and afterwards do not regret renouncing – great wealth and choose a life of extreme material simplicity.'[24]

It was then a near-disaster that blessed him with the time to develop his designs in detail. On 24 May 1909, Spedan was thrown from his horse in Regent's Park as he rode to Hampstead. After painful bouts of pleurisy and emphysema, two operations and the loss of a lung, he almost died. He retreated to a farm in Harrow, to recuperate and to reflect. He had discovered from the company accounts that the 300 employees of the business were earning, together, an amount close to the £16,000 a year that he, his father and his brother received from the business. 'As a whole the staff were getting just a bare living,' reflected Spedan, 'with very little margin beyond absolute necessities and correspondingly little chance to get much fun out of life'. Spedan realized that 'obviously such a state of affairs could not have existed unless the general conditions at the time had been more or less similar. To me… all this seemed shocking.'[25]

A different kind of business model now began to emerge in his mind. 'It may sound odd but it is a fact that, after I had got as far as conceiving the idea of treating a business as a partnership of all its workers, it was quite a while, a good many months, before I saw how such a business could be self-financing. The notion was so obvious that I am puzzled that it did not occur to me sooner.'[26]

It was not, however, until the eve of the First World War that Spedan finally got a chance to develop his own ideas – to break free from his father and set up shop alone. Not far away from the John Lewis store, in Chelsea, was Peter Jones. A once highly successful department store, which its eponymous owner had sold in 1905, it had subsequently lost its way. Sensing a bargain, Spedan's father walked from Oxford Street to

Chelsea with twenty £1,000 notes and £2,500 in loose change – and bought the business.

Unfortunately, Peter Jones was a basket-case, and John Lewis did not improve it. 'His handling of Peter Jones could hardly have been more inept,'[27] noted Spedan in January 1914; 'It was on the edge of complete collapse. It was not merely a derelict. It was a desperate derelict, in the last stages of decay.'[28] His father's failure was Spedan's opportunity, as the young man – a 'tall, bony figure with a rather dictatorial manner', who was handsome, impeccably mannered but with a famously quick temper – began to experiment with a different way of trading.[29]

Spedan threw himself into turning around Peter Jones. But the family rows were growing worse, and Spedan could stand his father no more. 'Roughly once a year,' wrote Spedan, 'my father broke with me.'[30] Although Peter Jones was making losses – £8,000 on £100,000 of sales posted in January 1914 – Spedan was confident that fortunes were turning. Throughout 1915, he wanted to invest more. But his father thought differently. So, Spedan offered an ultimatum. He would exchange his interest in the John Lewis Oxford Street store in return for his father's shares in Peter Jones. 'That was an exchange of a quarter-partnership in one of the soundest businesses in England and the prospect of being my father's sole heir, for a controlling interest in about as forlorn a derelict as could easily have been found in the whole of the drapery trade.'[31] His father accepted Spedan was now the master of his own destiny and it was a power he now planned to share.

*

Spedan was convinced that the route to a better-performing business was a better deal with staff. As he put it later, 'It was soon clear to me that my father's success had been due to his trying constantly to give very good value to people... but it also became clear to me that the business would have grown further... if he had done the same for those who wished to exchange their work for his money.'[32] Six years of collaboration with his father had simply convinced Spedan that 'the relation of employers to employees should be that of lawyers or stockbrokers to their clients'.[33]

Spedan immediately set about improving conditions at Peter Jones, overhauling the living accommodation for staff at the top of the shop, modernizing the dining rooms, improving the catering, and introducing tea-breaks. He also raised pay – indeed, the pay-bill doubled between 1913 and 1916, from £7,200 to £14,500. But Spedan was now working to the plan that had begun to take shape in his mind in 1910: a new kind of partnership based on the principles of sharing 'Knowledge, Gain and Power'.

A 'Committee of Communication' was introduced quickly, in 1915, to elect staff representatives who met with Spedan regularly. The in-house *Gazette* was launched. It first appeared on Saturday, 16 March 1918, with the headline 'To my fellow employees of Peter Jones Ltd', and with it went licence for staff to write anonymous letters, lubricating a genuine two-way dialogue.[34] As Spedan put it, 'a Partnership must be very reluctant that any particular thing must be kept secret'.[35]

Profit-sharing was, at first, a thornier task. Peter Jones was a listed company, and therefore Spedan needed to convince its shareholders to back his scheme. In the war years, there was not much profit to share. At the end of 1916, sales were just £167,000, and debts totalled £45,000. One of the few departments making any money was, in fact, a pub, the Star and Garter, which had been bought in 1911, complete with 40 gallons of 1875 Martell brandy in its cellar. Spedan was forced to admit to the company AGM in 1915 that 'pro tem' the pub business would continue; 'I regret to say we are thriving exceedingly by being publicans.'[36]

The first euphoria of peace, however, brought a chance. Sales had boomed during 1918, hitting £253,000, and Spedan seized his moment. Once he could foresee a profit distribution, he pressed ahead with the formation of the staff council, which first met in the Peter Jones restaurant on 31 October 1919. Composed of eighteen members, with the firm's directors able to attend but not to vote, it met without Spedan after its first session. Spedan then proposed a radical reorganization of the firm's capital structure, issuing each employee of Peter Jones a proportion of 7,000 new preference shares – or 'share promises' – representing 15 per cent of pay.*

Spedan convinced the shareholders to back him; but it took some of the staff – known as 'Partners' from 1920 – a little time to get used to things. One unmarried mother on the staff wondered: 'Are these things really money?' When told 'Of course they are really money, as I keep on telling you silly girls', her reply, reportedly, was 'But I have got thirty of them! Fancy me worth thirty pounds!' – and she burst into tears.[37] For fear of Spedan's father's reaction, these new 'share promises' were not actually issued as securities, sellable on the Stock Exchange. But in due course, staff would be able to swap their share promises for sellable shares, and enjoy a cumulative yearly dividend of 7.7 per cent, which was paid punctually on 1 June and 1 December.[38]

*

The initial economic euphoria of peace did not, unfortunately, last for long. Between 1918 and 1921, a quarter of GDP was lost – four times more than would vanish in the 'Great Depression' of 1930–32 – and the horror was only exacerbated by the deadly misery of Europe's 'Spanish Flu'. Spedan's sales were hit hard.

Before the First World War, nearly half of British manufacturing sales had been earned from foreign markets, and British lending totalled 42 per cent of global investment, earning a nice stream of foreign dividends. But during the war years, foreign markets were lost to both the United States and Japan. Investment income fell too, as the nation liquidated (between 1913 and 1924) 10 per cent of Britain's

---

* Although devised in its essentials by October 1910, Spedan proposed the capital reorganization to the Annual General Meeting of shareholders in 1919. The bones of it were this: the old 'ordinary share capital' was written down to a quarter of its value, and Spedan was to draw a salary or any dividends on his holding (80 per cent of ordinary shares). Over the decade that followed, share promises for staff varied between 15 per cent (1924) and just over 23 per cent (1928). See Cox, *Spedan's Partnership*, op. cit., p. 78.

foreign assets – worth some £2.4 billion.* As countries around the world increased import tariffs,[39] British export values collapsed by almost half, from their pre-war peak of £35 billion to £20 billion in 1921.† Thereafter there was a slow recovery, but the decision in 1924 to return Britain to the Gold Standard, at its pre-war value against the dollar, locked in British export prices, which had appreciated by an estimated 10 per cent against US prices since 1913, creating fresh challenges for exporters.[40]

To support the new exchange rate, higher interest rates were needed, a contractionary monetary policy, in which rates were lifted from 5 per cent to 7 per cent. And to add to the pain, the government had greeted the end of war with plans to rapidly curtail spending. Government expenditure was slashed by 75 per cent between 1918 and 1921. Lost markets, foreign tariffs, high interest rates and rapid cuts to public spending made for a disastrous policy mix. Over the 1920s, unemployment was rarely below 1.5 million; it rose above 2 million in 1920, and above 3 million in 1930, fuelling the turbulence of inter-war politics and protest.

Finding sales abroad ever tougher, British firms asked for protections of their own; indeed, when the Federation of British Industry had surveyed 352 firms and 56 trades in 1917, it found that almost all of them (96 per cent) wanted some form of trade barrier. And so, a century and a half of British free-trade philosophy, campaigned for by men like William Jardine, drew to a close. The McKenna Act of 1915 had already introduced tariff controls on a third of luxury goods entering the country, including cars; the 1919 Key Industries Act extended tariff protection to defence-related firms, and the 1921 Safeguarding of Industry Act widened protection still further.

Perhaps unsurprisingly, in 1921 and 1922 Peter Jones posted losses. Nearby, the queues from the labour exchange tailed down Chelsea's King's Road. Describing the business as it stood in 1920, Spedan noted:

---

* In the three years prior to the First World War, UK capital exports were worth 8 per cent of GDP, and while capital exports rebounded in 1920, overall the decline was inexorable, and ground to a halt in 1929.

† Export volume data expressed as a composite chained volume measure in 2006 prices. See Bank of England, Three Centuries of Economic Data, Data Annex to 'The UK recession in context – what do three centuries of data tell us?'.

All my notions of management had been formed in a business in which there was constantly a superfluity of ready money. Half the transactions at John Lewis were for cash, half on credit, and most of the customers paid within a month. At Peter Jones, 80% of trade was on credit, and they were most recalcitrant in settling accounts. Things went terribly wrong.[41]

A vicious strike hit the Army & Navy department stores, before spreading to affect John Lewis – where staff had had no pay increase since the start of the war – and adding to business tension, John Lewis sacked 400 staff for protesting for the right to join a union. By 1922, Spedan's brother Oswald was arguing: 'Isn't it better to admit you've tried, tried all you know, and failed? Other men have failed before, and not even had the consolation that what they tried to do was well worth doing.'[42] But Spedan held his ground, and with his marriage to Oxford graduate Beatrice Hunter in 1923, and their first child in 1924, came a vital rapprochement with his father. The elder Lewis now brought Spedan back into the Oxford Street business with a formal one-third of it. And as the recession subsided, Spedan began to spread his new style of business.

*

Nestling in the Berkshire countryside, on a brook that feeds the Thames, is a beautiful converted farmhouse, which is now the home of the John Lewis archives. Safely tucked away in the archive's strongrooms – alongside the firm's extraordinary back-catalogue of textiles, proofing prints for textiles on the *Titanic* and samples of Queen Victoria's bonnets – is the epic collection of Spedan's 40,000 numbered memos, typed on paper and neatly filed in cardboard boxes. And they tell the tale of how, upon his return to the business in 1924, Spedan evolved a strategy to marry together the best aspects of his father's business philosophy and that of his own.

Despite his many criticisms of his father's practices, Spedan owed to him the sales approach that had served the business well: 'he had an extremely high standard of probity. He never allowed any sort of deceit or trickery at the expense of any of his customers.'[43] This was the foundation for the firm's famous dictum, 'never knowingly undersold'. As Spedan had put it in the staff *Gazette* in 1920, 'What the public want beyond everything else is value'; to his mind, a business offering 'very much better value than the other' would 'absorb to itself the whole of the business [that] is worth having'.[44] In 1921, Spedan had underlined the idea that 'profit or no profit, we must never be under-sold'.[45] This was the principle he coupled with an appetite for reinvestment and the insight that good people were the key to good business, as he set about planning the future.

As early as 1924, Spedan was prompting the firm's deputy chairman for thoughts on the best way to make new investments, 'now that we are in a position to lay out a few thousands of pounds', and a new approach to investing in people soon followed.[46] Looking back, Paul May (the firm's deputy chairman) reflected that 'When Spedan went into the retail trade, it was considered a very low-class job. A gentleman could just be a wholesaler, but certainly not a retailer... Spedan saw that trained minds could be applied with benefit in retailing as much as in any other activity.'[47]

Spedan first had to weed out the under-performing. From his first days at Peter Jones, he had worked hard at the task; indeed, by 1919, only 3 per cent of the staff he had inherited in 1914 were still with the business. From the early 1920s, Spedan then set about deliberately recruiting the best and brightest he could find. He approached the University of Oxford and asked for details of their top women graduates. They included his future wife, Beatrice, who went on to become a director of the partnership, along with future deputy chairman, Paul May, who came with a First Class Degree in Classics. In May's memory of the hiring experience, Spedan was 'like a rather awesome headmaster, and in those days of course, headmasters were people you were very frightened of'.[48] By 1928, Peter Jones had seventy of the new 'learners' on a staff of 400, working mainly on the shop-floor.

In 1925, better sales meant that Spedan could announce the first partnership bonus for five years. The business, and his almost unique business model, had weathered the storm.

*

On 8 June 1928, Spedan's father died peacefully at Spedan Towers, at the age of ninety-three. He was, said the newspapers, 'a man of great independence of character'. 'A romance of business life', they moured, 'has just ended'.[49] Spedan and his brother had already agreed that on their father's death, Oswald would take out cash, and Spedan would take the business forward. Spedan now seized the chance, not to personally profit but to propel the partnership even wider. It was not long before fresh opportunities arrived.

John Lewis had acquired the great neighbouring T. J. Harries store in 1928, and now Spedan proposed – as the John Lewis archives attest – 'to spend at once money upon the premises… I should be quite willing to use for this purpose £50,000 at least of the spare capital that we have available'.[50] It was the beginning of wholesale modernization of Harries, a firm where little had changed in fifty years, and where male shop assistants still dressed in black frock coats and striped trousers.

As Stanley Carter, a sixteen-year-old shop-worker at the time later explained: 'In 1929, it was all Edwardian in behaviour and dress… Spedan dominated and had an all-pervasive influence over that critically important decade.' Sir Bernard Miller, Spedan's successor as chairman, later described the mood: '1927 to 1939 was for me a time of youthful zest and energy spilling over in all directions; nothing was too zany to look into and everything was possible.'[51] There were changes aplenty. The business was to stay named after Spedan's father, but salaries were updated; stunning new plans were prepared to rebuild Peter Jones;* the Odney Club, on the Thames, was acquired as a place for staff recreation; and perhaps most important of all, Spedan was able to complete the Partnership he had envisaged so many years before.

On Saturday 20 April 1929, the company *Gazette* set out the news that 'On Thursday, the 18th instant, there was taken one of the two final steps in the process of bringing the Partnership into legal existence.'[52] Spedan announced the signing of a Settlement Deed – an Irrevocable Settlement in Trust – 'by which I transferred to three trustees for the

---

* These plans, however, would be delayed by the Wall Street Crash in 1929.

Partnership the whole of my holding'. The £76,632 of issued share-promises were swapped with an issue of shares (saleable on the Stock Exchange) in the firm's new holding company,[53] each with a fixed dividend of 7.5 per cent. The plan first conceived in October 1910, and refined by spring 1920, was now put fully into effect. John Lewis employees were incorporated into a new partnership – a 'cooperative society of producers' – but the shares could actually be traded on the Stock Exchange.

The basic structure was simple.[*] Spedan would sell his interest – which his financial advisers calculated was worth around £1 million – to the Partners, who would pay him back gradually out of future profits, at a rate of around £25,000 a year; in essence, Spedan would live on £1 million of non-interest-paying loan stock, repaid steadily to him by the business over thirty years, generating an income worth (in today's money) more than £2.5 million a year.

He would remain chairman with wide powers, constrained only to a degree by the staff council, which nominated three trustees annually, who together held 60 out of 100 voting shares. In *theory*, these could be wielded in concert to remove Spedan from office, as he held the remaining 40 voting shares. His own rights were set out in the Partnership constitution – all 268 pages of it – which also explained how profits would be distributed to all.

Crucially, the firm's capital structure meant that an increasing share of the firm's profit was retained for reinvestment rather than paid out to shareholders. In this period, British companies generally paid out more than 60 per cent of profits, compared with an average of 50 per cent in US firms; between 1922 and 1939, for instance, car manufacturer Herbert Austin paid out nearly 70 per cent of profits on share

---

[*] He set it out in a memo, dictated in 1932: 'I would form a group of companies to which I would sell my interests for a redeemable non-interest bearing security and for a non-redeemable security of small total value which should leave me with a voting-control, when, in the course of years, the redeemable security should have been paid off'. JSL to EMB, Confidential Memo, 27.1.32, paragraphs 1–5. In practice, the firm underpaid between 1928 and 1932, generating £56,000 compared to forecasts of £120,000, due to investment needs at the Harries business and the Depression. See paragraph 17 of the memo.

dividends and long-term bonds.[54] But John Lewis was very different; indeed, an analysis of the firm's accounts over the course of the 1930s reveals dividend payouts of between 31 per cent and 41 per cent.[55] It was an approach that fostered a very different business atmosphere, as Stanley Carter remembered: 'There was a very strong feeling that the Partnership was different. It was largely a loyalty to Spedan himself. When I met people from other stores, what struck me was a lack of loyalty or belonging.'[56]

*

The world did not wait long to give the fully-fledged Partnership a test. The Wall Street Crash arrived in 1929, and its impact over the next two years – while not as bad as the post-war recession – was serious for the John Lewis Partnership. Profits fell precipitously, and pay was cut. Although share bonuses were maintained, by 1931 the business was close to bust.

As world trade collapsed in the months after the Crash, competitive devaluations and protectionism broke out around the world. In Britain, the new National Government brought forward, in February 1932, the Import Duties Act and a tariff of between 10 per cent and 30 per cent on manufactures. It was, said Austin Chamberlain, the completion of the work his father, Joseph, had begun. Although Britain's 'Great Depression' of 1930–32 was far milder than America's, and British banks did not collapse, unemployment reached nearly 3.4 million and began to fall only when Britain left the Gold Standard in 1931.[*]

Leaving the Gold Standard allowed the government to inaugurate a new era of cheap money. Interest rates fell to 2 per cent, where they stayed for the decade, triggering a bounce-back in consumption and investment, which drove three-quarters of the recovery and fuelled the housing boom in the 1930s. Helped by a twenty-fold increase in hire purchase between 1918 and 1938, and by a huge effort to build 4

---

[*] UK GDP fell 5.8 per cent compared with the 29.4 per cent fall in the United States, where 5,000 banks went to the wall. See Floud, Humphries and Johnson (eds), *Cambridge Economic History*, op. cit., p. 240.

million homes between 1919 and 1939 (1 million of them by local councils), Britain's middle class bought durable goods like never before, driving up spending from £167 million in 1910–14 to £395 million by 1935.[57] As more and more homes acquired electricity – rising from one-third of homes in 1931 to two-thirds by 1939 – their occupiers acquired the new electrical goods. By 1939, 31 per cent of homes were owner-occupied.

The effect was a rebalancing of the British economy – away from trade, and decisively towards a domestically driven services economy. Back in the late nineteenth century, trade accounted for 60 per cent of British GDP (peaking in 1880s at 70 per cent). By 1933, it was just a third of the economy. Whereas in 1913 fewer than half of those employed (44 per cent) worked in the service sector, by 1937 services accounted for almost 60 per cent of jobs. And while unemployment stayed high for much of the period, acute poverty fell. At the end of the nineteenth century, perhaps 30 per cent of people were living in 'total poverty'.[58] By 1938, only 3.6 per cent of households were below the very lowest level of sufficiency, as 'average' incomes rose and family sizes fell.*

This was the era of change so poignantly described by the writer Laurie Lee, as he looked back on his Oxfordshire childhood, remembering the end of 'waiting on weather and growth', the arrival of the car (and the charabanc and motorbikes), register office marriages, the death of the older generation and the advent of radio. 'I belonged to that generation,' wrote Lee, 'which saw, by chance, the end of a thousand years' life.'[59] A new England was taking shape, as J. B. Priestley set out in his wonderful 1930s memoir *English Journey*. Alongside the 'Old England' of the parson and squire, and 'industrial England', wrote Priestley, there was now a new country:

> ... the England of arterial and by-pass roads, of filling stations and factories that look like exhibition buildings, or giant cinemas and dance-halls and cafes, bungalows with tiny garages, cocktail

---

* Indeed, for those at the 50th income percentile, income rose from 22 shillings a week in 1906 to 56 shillings in 1938.

bars, Woolworths, motor-coaches, wireless, hiking, factory girls looking like actresses, greyhound racing and dirt-tracks, swimming pools and everything given away for cigarette coupons.[60]

Britain's new middle-class homes needed cookers, fridges, water heaters, irons, wash-boilers, vacuum cleaners, radios, telephones – and cars. In 1924, there were around 580,000 cars on British roads, and only one in sixty-five people might own a radio; towards the end of the 1930s, 2 million cars were on the roads, and one in fifteen homes owned a radio. The British car industry had grown quickly before the First World War; eighty-one new companies registered between 1897 and 1913, among them pioneers like William Morris and the future Lord Nuffield. He had begun to innovate low-cost standardized vehicles like the Morris-Oxford and then the Cowley, introduced in 1913 and 1915 respectively; which went on to capture more than 40 per cent of the British car market in the 1920s.* At the end of the decade came the famous Morris Minor, costing £125, to compete with the new US mass producers like Ford.

There were big opportunities for new workers in new firms and industries. They profited from the new alliance forced on industry, science and government by the First World War. In 1895, the prime minister, Lord Salisbury, declared that he 'detested the new plutocracy of industrial and financial wealth'.[61] The first months of war revealed the folly of such attitudes.[62] As the war's Official History later noted, 'British manufacturers were behind other countries in research, plant and method. Many of the iron and steel firms were working on a small scale, old systems and uneconomic plant.' Lacking strong domestic manufacturers of everything from – machine tools, to fuses, coal-tar, ball bearings, magnetos, aero-engines, industrial gauges, and optical glass – Britain's war effort was dependent on its imperial suppliers; indeed, half the shells fired in the Battle of Somme were Canadian.

The war years forced Britain into the new age of industrial science,

---

* Between 1921 and 1925, sales grew at the extraordinary annual compound rate of 78 per cent, and, at 81 per cent annually, profits grew even faster.

fusing together a novel alliance of business, government and academia.*
This duly laid the foundation for the industrial policy of the 1920s and
1930s, creating the conditions for the success of ICI (the British Dyestuff
Corporation), a doubling of electrical engineering capacity, and the
modern British aeronautical industry. By 1935, the electrical engineering industry was selling £107 million-worth of goods, the wireless firms
another £6 million, while telephone company sales were £5.5 million;
by 1938, the UK was producing 341,000 cars – many more than the
199,800 made in France or the 276,000 made in Germany.†

*

For entrepreneurs like Spedan Lewis, in a world divided by new barriers
to trade, the home market looked an awful lot better than venturing
abroad – and there were few home markets better than retail. Key to
success were the low interest rates fuelling Britain's housing boom,
which fostered the rising demand of the rising middle class for the
kinds of things that John Lewis sold, especially to women, who now
enjoyed a veritable industry of titles to choose from, such as *Woman's
Weekly* (1911), *Vogue* (1916), *Homes and Gardens* (1919), *Woman and
Home* (1926), *Woman's Journal* (1927), *Harper's Bazaar* (1929), *Woman's
Own* (1932) and, most successful of all, *Woman*, first published in 1937.
To cater for the surge in demand for beauty and fashion products,
department stores made sure they were comfortable places for women
to be – warm, safe and jam-packed with goods, from fabric and trim-
mings to ready-made dresses, coats, hats, shoes, fabrics, furniture,

* The government's Department of Science and Industrial Research was
founded in 1916. University College, London, pioneered the process for fixing
nitrogen, the key to TNT. Manchester University pioneered the mass production
of acetone. Bristol and Oxford Universities perfected both the gas mask and the
mass production of mustard gas, while St Andrews mastered the production of
the anaesthetic novocaine in large quantities. Queen Mary's College, London,
invented the hydrophone, the key to winning the battle with the U-boats.
† Although the car industry accounted for just 6 per cent of employment, and
therefore could contribute only so much. Nick Crafts, 'Economic Growth During
the Long Twentieth Century' in Floud, Humphries and Johnson (eds), *Cambridge
Economic History*, op. cit., p. 43.

china, glass and napery, as well as the new and labour-saving electrical inventions.

As the recovery gathered pace, John Lewis's sales doubled in real terms between 1933 and 1937, as Spedan now seized the opportunity to diversify outside London.[63] He acquired two businesses with four branches in Nottingham and Weston-Super-Mare: Jessop's, run by Zebedee Jessop, and Lance & Lance. Both, in Spedan's words, were 'businesses under performing through lack of investment in staff and systems, or long established family enterprises that had lost their way'.[64] He did not stop there. In 1934, Tyrrell & Green in Southampton, and Knight & Lee of Southsea were both swept up into the Lewis empire, and with each new acquisition adaptation to the John Lewis model was swift, as one Jessop's worker remembered: 'Pay went up, the hostel was closed, the smoke filled dining room replaced. Out went primitive loos… In came Partnership methods and disciplines, brought in by brisk women who struck fear into those not up to the mark.'[65]

With the arrival of better times, Spedan resumed the rebuild of Peter Jones in Chelsea. He hired the architect William Crabtree, fresh out of university, to produce a German-inspired design.[*] With its steel and glass façade and sweeping curves, it opened on the King's Road in 1937 and was voted best building 'of our time' by an *Architects Journal* panel, beating the iconic Battersea Power Station. By 1935, the Partnership boasted six department stores, 10,000 Partners and record first-quarter profits of £182,310 – up by more than 10 per cent on the previous year.[66]

Spedan now opted for a trial retirement from day-to-day operations, retreating to his estate near the village of Leckford, Hampshire, which he had acquired in 1929; his aim now was to focus on driving the 'experimental expansion' of the group. Work had dominated everything, and domestic life was neither easy or normal. Misfortune had struck the family – Spedan's son John died of meningitis in 1932, and his wife miscarried and was unable to conceive again. But Spedan remained obsessive in his work habits, surrounded by secretaries, even at dinner, ready to take down his incessant dictation.

---

[*] The German retailer Schocken's store in Chemnitz, which had impressed Spedan and his colleague Michael Watkins; it was designed by Erich Mendelsohn.

The fruits of his efforts, however, had now earned him some fame, not lease Spedan's unique business model. Its partnership structure was lauded in Liberal propaganda in 1929, and with its new success, magazines such as *Business* were keen to highlight the virtues of a firm where 'Here Labour Hires Capital – and Shares the Profits'; 'there is no doubt,' ran one interview with Spedan, 'that the system has developed in all ranks of the organization a really important degree of a quite new spirit, the exact opposite of that curse of British industry – "ca'canny" – the practice of deliberately holding down output at work'.[67] Spedan's achievement was to create a model of 'industrial democracy' that not only worked, but avoided much of the conflict that bedevilled the British workplace throughout the 1930s, where in too many industries (such as the car industry) management and unions had contrived to create a production system that often paid on the basis of piece-work. It made for a low-cost approach but low-productivity approach, in which profits were kept high, wages and investment were kept low, and control over the shop-floor was 'outsourced'. It was a poor competitor with the United States, whose citizens enjoyed wealth per head 20 per cent greater than Britain's throughout the post-war years, underpinned by far superior productivity where firms invested more in science and the government invested more still. As early as 1913, research and development as a share of the economy was five times bigger in America than Britain, and US enrolment rates in primary to tertiary education were more than 40 per cent higher. Spedan's Partnership model offered something different, as he noted in 1935:

It seems to me that we can reckon that the general efficiency of our personnel… will not be importantly inferior to that of our competitors and that our system and policy will give us over them viewed as a whole a really important advantage. If all this is true, then there should be ahead of us a good many years of quite satisfactory growth.[68]

In 1936, John Lewis Oxford Street neighbour, D. H. Evans, came up for sale. Spedan moved immediately to buy it for £850,000, doubling the store's floor space and creating a John Lewis emporium that now covered two blocks, becoming the largest store in London. An immensely creative period ensued, when Spedan was perhaps at his happiest.* 'He was really more interested in building up the structure than in operating it once he'd got it,' remembered Bernard Miller; 'His eyes really sparkled when he said: "we've got to devise a new structure for buying" or "let's reorganise the central administration of this, that or the other".'[69] Quickly, more acquisitions followed, as the business snapped up factories making hats, leather, furniture, beds, and even chocolate. Central buying was introduced into the stores. 'He was one of the first,' remembers Miller, 'certainly in the department store field to see that if you are going to be a group, it is absolute nonsense if you don't have central buying. You must take advantage of your buying power.'[70]

In 1937, Spedan was again arguing for more investment – £150,000 more in long- or short-term borrowing to be raised to finance growth – and had now spotted his chance to enter the grocery business. William Waite and his partner Rose had opened their first branch of Waitrose in Acton, west London, in 1904, and had slowly grown a reputation for honest dealing that spread into wholesaling and catering. They landed a large contract in the first years of the First World War to supply the army's big training base in Catterick Bridge, Yorkshire. Now, at the age of fifty-six, Waite was looking for an exit. A chance meeting with John Lewis's Michael Watkins led to take-over talks. It was not a large acquisition – indeed, Waitrose's turnover represented just 4 per cent of the Partnership's – but its values were very much in line with those endorsed by Spedan, for Waite had wanted to 'lift the food trade to a higher plane'.[71] In the 1930s, amid acute pressure on working-class living standards, Waite was among those endorsing shop-workers' demands for better pay and conditions, striking a landmark agreement in May 1937 with the shop assistants' union.

---

* He minuted in October 1937: 'We must try very hard indeed to contrive to combine a rate of expansion, that contents us, with an avoidance of money-raising operations in any particular year that are of really serious importance in relation to the general mass of our business and to its ability to squeeze out of itself cash that at a pinch it can manage without.' Chairman to Director of Estimates, Memo No. 23073 (27 October 1937), paragraph 10.

Waitrose's entry to the fold was duly announced in the John Lewis *Gazette* on 16 October 1937: 'The business has a very high reputation, not only for the quality of its goods, but also for the way in which it has been built up and carried on.'[72]

Spedan's breakneck expansion was, however, now creating huge pressure on profits. Bonus levels in 1934 were 9 per cent but fell to 8 per cent in 1936 and then to zero in 1938, provoking sharp internal criticism. The years 1938–40 proved to be the toughest trading years since the early 1920s. The business had grown enormously in twenty years; by 1939, John Lewis boasted 6,000 partners and a turnover of £3 million. But now the business, like the country, would face its toughest test: the challenge of total war.

*

Spedan had helped ensure that the firm's preparations for the impending conflict were well advanced by the time hostilities commenced. As Bernard Miller remembered, 'From about the beginning of 1937, we put a lot of effort into air raid precautions, getting everything organised as far as we could. We had complete copies of our sales ledger sent down to Clearings, one of John Lewis's storage depots in Chelsea, so that when John Lewis was in fact bombed and we lost all our records, we had duplicate sets.'[73] Store basements were readied for refugees. Profits were set aside to subsidize service pay. Steel plate was installed on the roof in Oxford Street. When war commenced, many of the former military men employed by the business were recalled, while others were poached for war service. One of them, Hugh Alexander, joined the secret codebreaking effort, taking over Bletchley Park's Hut 8 from Alan Turing, while Michael Watkins was asked to organize the nation's clothing: he conceived the Utility range, which also included furniture.

Spedan had returned to take the role of Director of Selling in 1939, and with war declared he now took personal charge. He laid off 300 Partners, confirmed that the business would make up the gap between John Lewis's pay and service pay, and asked Partners to consider deferring some of their salary. Sales halved in the first two weeks of war, and yet, as the months wore on, opportunities began to present themselves,

creating what Spedan christened the 'third great expansion' – the acquisition for £30,000, on 3 February 1940, of Selfridge's provincial chain of
shops, Suburban & Provincial Stores.* With a combined turnover of £3.3
million, the acquisition meant that John Lewis's branch trading was
now bigger than that of Oxford Street. The branches, crucially, would
help the group diversify sales beyond the capital after the main store
was bombed in September that year. Just as vital, as Spedan assured his
Partners, was that 'this new expansion....will carry its own expenses'.[74]

'I hope you will like the Partnership,' Spedan wrote to the new
employees:

> Developments along these lines are, so it seems to me, the natural
> next step beyond the family in the evolution of human society.
> The Family has had its day. We are entering the Age of
> Corporations. In business of all kinds savings and investing is
> becoming a function of the Many Small instead of the Few Great.
> Management is ceasing to be combined with ownership.[75]

Spedan knew that the purchase of Suburban & Provincial would
require fresh thinking about how the Partnership would work in the
years to come. Writing about its impact, he said: 'all this will mean a
considerable development of the Partnership's organisation and character... It will make it far easier for Partners to think of the Partnership as
something really large and solid and permanent and really new instead
of thinking of it as an ordinary individual business.' Moreover, he added
that 'This growth of the scale of the Partnership's business will increase
the need for decentralisation. That is to say of giving power to officials
who are in the position of the man on the spot.'[76]

Spedan's first focus was on creating a non-contributory pension
scheme, which was then a rarity outside of the armed forces and the
Civil Service.† But much of 1942 and 1943 were spent overhauling the

---

* These were laid out in *The Gazette of the John Lewis Partnership* (3 February
1940), p. 3. The other key steps Spedan saw as the acquisition of T. J. Harries and
Co. in 1928, and the 1937 acquisition of D. H. Evans.
† The details were spelt out in a long article at the end of July 1941, and very
quickly agreed by Partnership council in 1941.

Partnership's constitution and rules. The 'Principles of the Constitution' in the *Gazette* of 17 April 1943 were a hymn to Spedan's view of business life:

> 1. To confine membership to people able and willing to fulfil the aims of the Constitution and to agree well enough together; 2. To further their true happiness; 3. To serve the general community well... 6. to aim at democracy and to that end to foster among all its Members upon its affairs well informed opinion and freedom of speech.

The new rules included innovations such as lifelong tenure and a forty-hour week. In Spedan's view, 'National education and other developments have been creating such a need for some modification of capitalism that would retain enough of its merits and diminish sufficiently its defects.'[77] The key, concluded Spedan, was that staff needed 'the intellectual and psychological satisfactions and the material benefits of ownership'.[78]

Many of Spedan's team would not live to enjoy the new approach. By 1945, many had been killed or exhausted by their war service. Maurice Trouton, the firm's director of planning, was killed in his home by a V1 rocket in 1944; others had been greatly frayed, including Michael Watkins. And yet Spedan was now determined not to take back control, but rather to give it away.

He set it all out in his extraordinary manifesto, the book *Partnership for All*, published in 1948. Here, Spedan put down the accumulated wisdom of his 'thirty-four year old experiment in industrial democracy', which began in October 1910 – an attempt to 'organise and conduct a business that all the advantages whatsoever of owning it shall be shared as fairly as possible by all working in it'.[79] The book encompassed the principles he had refined over the war years, and provided a model of doing business for new times, learning lessons along the way from other great businesses, such as Ford. Here were Spedan's thoughts on everything from the classless society, to who should be promoted; on pay, tenure and amenities; on trade unions and trading policy, the council and the central board; on the chairmanship, secondary management and executive responsibilities; and even on journalism.

Two years earlier, in *Partnership on the Scale of Modern Industry* (1946), Spedan had described various benefits of Partnership, from its financial mechanics (the pay-sheet, a fixed rate of interest on capital it did not own, and 'due reserves') to the financing of clubs, to the idea of partnership offering hope to those in need. The 'remainder of the profit' could be 'distributed yearly to all the Partners in the proportion of their individual shares of the pay-sheet', and these shares, 'the bottom of the Partnership's financial pyramid', formed 'a constantly accumulating margin of security', enabling 'the Partnership to borrow other capital freely'.[80] In this way, 'the true profit… shall go not to those who save and lend, but to those who work, and… the managers shall divide it reasonably with the managed'.[81] As Bernard Miller put it, 'the first settlement established that the profit belonged to the workers. The second settlement established that the property of the business belonged to the workers. An important step forward.'[82]

Spedan's post-war model included important changes to the firm's governance. The Partnership council was to elect five people to the central board of twelve, to work alongside generalists such as a 'general inspector' and take an across-the-board view of business issues. On 29 April 1950, the *Gazette* ran details of the Final Settlement. Spedan undertook to hand over his controlling interest, in return for a promise to run the business on lines he had set down. But it would take a huge collective effort to ensure the new business was a business of which the Partners could be proud. John Lewis was to find the immediate years of post-war austerity very cold.

*

The exigencies of rebuilding Britain were initially tough for British retailers. The government's focus on boosting exports and foreign earnings meant tightly controlling domestic consumption. Rationing remained, and controls on crucial raw materials such as the steel needed to rebuild the bombed Oxford Street store were tight. As Bernard Miller remembered, 'From 1945 to 1951 we recognised that factories and housing reconstruction would take priority... We applied [for steel] in July 1951 but were refused.'[83]

The new Attlee Labour government was focused, laser-like, on rebuilding international trade. The international economic arrangements agreed in the Bretton Woods settlement of 1944, steered in part by the Treasury's man John Maynard Keynes, offered a stable framework for trade to resume.[*] In December 1945, the Cabinet agreed a vast export push[†] to be pursued 'with the same energy as in time of war, whatever measure of industrial and marketing reorganisation and reconstruction may be necessary'.[84] As the United States and Europe began to recover, Britain's exports boomed – and the economy with it. Production picked up so fast that by 1952 the economy was 14 per cent bigger than its nadir in 1947. Three-quarters of the growth was driven by exports, mostly to America and Europe; indeed, by 1959, exports to the United States had quadrupled, while those to Europe had risen by more than 50 per cent.[‡]

Not all was rosy. Post-war Britain's economic prospects were still undercut by the impoverished state of technical education and skills, highlighted in a number of government reports, which projected a shortfall of 24,000 scientists.[§] More technical colleges were proposed, and indeed in 1953, London's Imperial College was earmarked to double in size over the next ten years, as a centre of technology and engineering excellence. Between 1938 and 1955, the number of science and technology graduates had doubled, yet still Sir David Eccles, President of the

---

[*] Bretton Woods ushered in fixed exchange rates and the institutions of the International Monetary Fund and the forerunner of the World Bank.

[†] Exports were to be expanded by between 50 and 75 per cent.

[‡] There remained, though, a deficit to the dollar area. By 1953, exports to the United States covered only 85 per cent of the value of imports (though better than around 50 per cent in 1948–49). Restocking from America would not have been possible without a boom in our exports to the States. Cairncross, *Years of Recovery*, op. cit., p. 44.

[§] The 1945 Percy Committee on Higher Technological Education and the Barlow Committee both drew an explicit connection between the future of British science and the future of British prosperity. They noted that US universities served a population three times bigger than the UK's, but with ten times more money. Sir Alan Barlow, 'British Report on Man-Power', 27 May 1946.

Board of Trade in the 1950s, noted it was 'nothing like enough'.
Nonetheless, between the 1950s and early 1970s – and for the first time
in decades – British labour productivity actually outstripped performance in the United States and as wages rose, the consumer economy
began to surge.

After rationing ended in 1954, hire purchase began to boom once
more. Commercial television was launched in 1955, and with it a new
arena for advertising, beamed into people's homes. By July 1957, Prime
Minister Harold Macmillan could declare, in Bedford, that one could go
around the country and 'see a state of prosperity such as we have never
had in my lifetime… indeed let us be frank about it – most of our people
have never had it so good.' But not at John Lewis.

*

By the early 1950s, it was clear that the John Lewis Partnership was
under-performing against its competition. Its sales fell 8 per cent in the
second half of 1951; first-half profits, forecast at £600,000, came in at
just £250,000 and to make matters worse, the firm's tax bill was up
twenty-fold on pre-war levels. The year 1952 was worse; first-half sales
were down 18 per cent. Between 1946 and 1958, although John Lewis's
profits rose from £0.4m to £1.2m, profits at Marks & Spencer's soared
from £3 million to £17 million, and by 1959 Woolworth's was boasting
profits of £30 million.

In the eighteen years up to 1955, John Lewis had paid a staff bonus
just five times. When pay cuts were then proposed, staff fought back,
suggesting cuts to the extensive array of amenities that had multiplied,
including the firm's country club (open to all Partners) at Odney, the
sailing club, subsidized fishing on the River Test, a holiday camp at
Leckford, and the subsidies Spedan had offered to save the Glyndebourne
Opera. 'Cut amenities first, pay second', as one writer to the *Gazette*
summed it up.

In the midst of the Korean War, major mistakes compounded the
problem. In the booming inflationary years, the firm had 'built up
rather high stocks when prices were still rising', remembers Miller, who,
with others, pleaded to mark them down.[85] But 'Spedan wouldn't have

it. He said we were throwing money away... He proved to be wrong.' The business lost a small fortune. Waitrose too was challeneged, although some in the partnership saw it as 'satisfactorily profitable', Miller minuted Spedan in February 1952 to say he was 'in favour of getting rid of it... Let's do it quickly while the going is good.'

From 1953 on, trading slowly improved. By 1954, a bonus was set at 4 per cent, followed by 8 per cent in the two subsequent years. Waitrose too, turned a corner. The firm began modernizing the format of the old, outdated shops, which were small, and where customers were served by assistants, food was sold in tins, and bulky provisions (like sugar, flour and butter) arrived in bulk and were packed on the premises. In 1951, the manager of Waitrose's Southend branch had pioneered the self-service format he had seen in the United States and Sweden, becoming one of the first adopters of the new style in Britain. Slowly, branches everywhere were converted; and the first new custom-built 'superstore', built in 1955 in Streatham, south London, with more than 2,500 square feet, with a follow-up store in Epsom, the following year. Over the next fifty years, the staff bonus would now drop just once below 8 per cent.

But just as the John Lewis Partnership was recovering, Spedan's personal life was dealt a devastating blow: the death of his beloved wife Beatrice, from cancer, in 1953. 'I was stunned by the loss,' he wrote, 'so utterly unexpected and in so terrible a way... I said more than once I could be well content to spend any years that might remain to me on a desert island with no company but hers.'[86]

It was time for Spedan to retire. On 22 September 1955, at a huge event at Central Hall, Westminster, the John Lewis Partnership came together to mark the retirement of its founder, and the installation of his successor, Bernard Miller. The question of who should succeed him had taxed Spedan greatly for some years. He had harboured hopes that his son Edward would take on the role. Edward had started work in the hardware department on the bomb site of the Oxford Street branch, but had made it clear in 1950 that he did not want to take on the leadership. 'It was', said Spedan, 'the bitter renunciation of a lifelong hope.'[87] Michael Watkins was the second preferred choice, but he had died in late November 1950. Bernard Miller, deputy chairman since 1951, was now the obvious successor. And so, he stepped into Spedan's shoes at Central Hall, the month before demolition began of John Lewis's derelict old store on Oxford Street to make way for the long-awaited rebuild.

Spedan's peace with his firm, however, did not last long. In 1959, anonymous letters, in Spedan's style, began appearing in the *Gazette*. His contention, in essence, was that Partnership was not expanding fast enough. At the Partners' dinner in 1959, he offered a long melancholy speech. In June 1960, he forced a debate in the Partners' council on an odd motion to give over a quarter of the pages in the *Gazette* to his words and to be consulted more often. At the 1961 dinner, he declared: 'I intended to get into mischief tonight and I think I have'; a year later, he announced: 'You are playing the fool with my life's work and breaking my heart.'[88]

Bernard Miller admitted it was tough. 'He gave me a much freer hand when I was deputy chairman than when I became chairman. I think by that time he had lost his judgement. I used to go down and spend weekends with him... There weren't many things on which we differed but I think it built up in his mind as a sort of festering sore.'[89]

In the event, John Spedan Lewis's retirement lasted less than a decade. On 21 February 1963, the great apostle of Partnership passed away – and a new era at the firm began to gather pace, inspired by Spedan's principles. Now uninstructed, the firm's leaders put into effect as Paul May explained:

> [Spedan] was a genius... with his standards I think he made failure an impossibility – unless his need to experiment had led to too wide a dispersion of trading and too little cohesion. He retired before this could happen, but I believe that for this reason the Partnership only began to work as he intended it should work, both as a social and as a trading organisation, after he retired.[90]

The great Oxford Street store had been reopened in 1960, and, led by the ferocious drive of Stanley Carter, in the five years to 1965 its sales doubled, from £6.1 million to £11.9 million, while profits multiplied five-fold to £1.2 million.[91] By the time Miller retired in 1972, he could survey a Partnership which had profited from the sale of two department stores and lots of its factories, and which had begun to significantly expand Waitrose from three to forty-three stores. Sales were now three times higher and profits up six-fold. Bonus payment had averaged 13–15 per cent, hitting 18 per cent in Miller's last year. Staff holidays had increased too, and pay was up in real terms by 50 per cent. In the year of Spedan's retirement, the firm's margins were a little under 5 per cent. In Miller's last year, they had leapt to nearly 9 per cent, returning £15 million in profit on £172 million of sales. The number of Partners had almost doubled as well, from 12,000 to 20,000.

*

When Spedan died, the *Gazette* he founded ran his words as something of an epitaph: 'The partnership is not only something to live by, it is something to live for.'[92] He was once asked what had motivated him to create so much – and give so much away. His answer was very simple: 'It does not occur to them that there may be people who will devote themselves to the invention of a new system of business for its own sake exactly as a man may devote himself to scientific research or to writing a book or to painting a picture.'[93]

By March 2014, the country's official retail figures explained just what this 'new system of business' was capable of. John Lewis and Waitrose recorded an extraordinary £9 billion in sales – up from £5 billion in 2003, and outstripping Mark & Spencer's performance of £8.9 billion for the first time.[94] The firm's 91,000 Partners shared a bonus pool of more than £200 million, at a rate set the same for everyone, from the chairman to Saturday shelf-stackers, of 15 per cent of pay, or about eight weeks' salary.

The John Lewis Partnership had become the biggest business on the British high street.

CONCLUSION

Lessons for new world-beaters

What do eight centuries of enterprise teach us about what it takes to be a world-beating entrepreneur? Down the ages, striking patterns seem to repeat in the stories presented here. Do they provide lessons?

Today's economy looks very different to the days of John Spedan Lewis, who left us more than five decades ago. Britain still makes a good living in the world – a world slowly recovering from the worst financial crisis since the 1920s, but now transformed by trade and technology, where there are clear signs that a new generation of entrepreneurs, more ambitious than ever before, is busy inventing the future. But rarely is it the entrepreneurs' privilege to have it easy. Thus, they are defined so often by their triumph against the odds.

The markets into which today's entrepreneurs now sell are the largest in history. When John Maynard Keynes sat in the Bretton Woods Conference at the end of 1944, he surveyed the emerging shape of a new post-war world order of business, trade and finance; and declared: 'We have had to perform at one and the same time…the tasks appropriate to the economist, to the financier, to the politician, to the journalist, to the propagandist, to the lawyer, to the statesman – even, I think, to the prophet and to the soothsayer.'* But perhaps even Keynes would have been dazzled by the sheer scale of today's global marketplace. By the time I left secondary school, Deng Xiaoping had led China in its first steps towards 'opening up'. By the time I got to university, the Berlin Wall was torn down. By my second year, Manmohan Singh had begun

---

* Quoted in BBC News, 'How Bretton Woods Changed the World', http://news.bbc.co.uk/1/hi/7725157.stm

to dismantle India's mountain of enterprise-inhibiting bureaucracy – its 'licence Raj'. By the time I graduated in 1992, President Clinton had secured, by just one vote, the first balanced budget in Congress and set the stage for the North American Free Trade Association and the admission of China to the World Trade Organization. Across a decade, decisions on four continents created a global marketplace, linking 6 billion of the world's 7 billion people. It was quite a *fin de siècle*.

Slowly, a multi-polar world – what China's Premier Wen once called the 'larger trend' – has begun to replace the world of American hyperpower. As the editor of *Newsweek* playfully summarized in 'The Post-American World', 'The world's tallest building is in Taipei, and will soon be in Dubai. Its largest publicly traded company is in Beijing. Its biggest refinery is being constructed in India. Its largest passenger airplane is built in Europe. The largest investment fund on the planet is in Abu Dhabi; the biggest movie industry is Bollywood, not Hollywood.'*

This bigger, global market has brought new opportunities – and new challenges, not least the rise of global giants. Since the year 2000, some 2,500 mergers of $1 billion, worth in total some $7.4 trillion, have created a global super-league of corporate behemoths dominating global trade and monopolizing markets in traded goods and services.† Two great firms, for example, control almost the whole market for large commercial aircraft; ten firms control nearly 80 per cent of the world's car business; indeed, the top five firms, boasting sales of between $108 billion and $221 billion, sell half of the world's cars. Three firms control nearly 80 per cent of the world's mobile telecommunications infrastructure. Ten firms control 70 per cent of world pharmaceuticals. Four firms (Anheuser-Busch, SAB Miller, Heineken and Carlsberg) control 60 per cent of the beer market and 75 per cent of the cigarette market. And in their supply chains, there is a similar concentration: three firms dominate aero engines, two firms dominate automotive braking systems, another two firms have cornered the computer chip market, while three firms dominate

---

* Fareed Zakaria, *The Post-American World* (Norton, 2008).

† See Peter Nolan, *Is China Buying the World* (Polity, 2013).

industrial gases, and three firms control the world's market for 200 billion cans of soft drinks.

These companies have all created vast defences against any challenge from newcomers, by outspending on branding and research and development. In fact, the world's top ten companies now spend $2–3 billion a year on branding, and in 2008, the UK's Department for Business found that the world's top 1,400 firms controlled about *half* of the world's R&D spending. Today, the top 1,000 businesses spend over £400 billion a year on research and development.* To make matters even tougher, British entrepreneurs who try to build businesses in new-technology sectors now face competitors in countries such as China, which benefited from an extraordinary $2.15 trillion of public investment in R&D over the course of its 2010–15 Five-Year Plan. Indeed, the OECD estimates that by 2019, China will be spending more on science than the United States.† Many of the world's leading science and technology businesses – and clusters – are no longer Western, but Chinese.‡

*

In Britain, therefore, entrepreneurs face a richer but tougher environment. Since John Spedan Lewis's death in 1963, the British economy has tripled in size, and three decades of globalization have profoundly shifted the country towards specialization in services. In the first decade of the twenty-first century, the UK grew faster than either continental Europe or Japan for the first time in a hundred years, as productivity, wages and wealth per head rose faster than in any of the other G7 nations. A big, new 'leading edge' of the economy has emerged – innovative, fast-growing, and dominated by high-value services, science-based industries and advanced manufacturing, which accounts for perhaps a third of UK economic output (£350 billion), a

---

* www.strategyand.pwc.com/innovation1000

† www.oecd.org/newsroom/china-headed-to-overtake-eu-us-in-science-technology-spending.htm

‡ Kirsten Bound, Tom Saunders, James Wilsdon and Jonathan Adams, *China's Absorptive State* (NESTA, October 2013).

third of businesses (650,000) and a fifth of employment (4.2 million).[*]

But many people, however, not least the average consumer, the years since 2008 have been tough. When the global financial crash hit Europe's shores, problems spread like wildfire through our financial system, eventually costing a million British jobs and £400 billion of UK net wealth – most of it household wealth.[†] And just as challenging for some has been the stubbornly slow growth in living standards. For alongside the new 'knowledge economy', manufacturing has shrunk to a more productive but smaller base, while the low-value part of the economy has grown quickly. Back in 1978, one in four workers was employed in manufacturing; by 2015, it was fewer than one in ten (a little over 3 million people)[‡] while in the non-traded and low-skilled sectors, job numbers have grown rapidly, in retail, logistics and care. Crucially, across the British economy, there is a new, profound disconnection between the way wealth is created and shared. From around 2004, average wages began to fall behind productivity increases.[§] The problem was not unique to the UK; indeed in the United States, *Time* magazine christened the phenomenon 'the death of the American Dream', as a gigantic growth in American productivity produced barely any improvement in the real income of the average American family while technology has begun to automate huge numbers of what were once reasonably skilled, reasonably paid, jobs, creating what economists now call the 'hour-glass': high-skilled jobs, and low-skilled jobs, and very little in between.[¶]

*

---

[*] Liam Byrne, *Robbins Rebooted: How We Earn Our Way in the Second Machine Age* (Social Market Foundation, 2014); www.smf.co.uk/publications/robbins-rebooted-how-we-earn-our-way-in-the-second-machine-age/

[†] Office of National Statistics, *Economic Review* (August 2010), p. 12.

[‡] www.ons.gov.uk/ons/dcp171766_381512.pdf

[§] Commission on Living Standards, *Gaining from Growth* (The Resolution Foundation, 2012).

[¶] The American literature is wide; see Paul Krugman, *The Conscience of a Liberal* (Norton, 2007); Robert Reich, *Supercapitalism* (Knopf, 2007); Jared Bernstein, *Crunch* (Berrett-Koehler, 2008); and more recently, Dambisa Moyo, *Winner Takes All* (Allen Lane, 2012).

Entrepreneurs succeed, however, because they find ways around the obstacles, and over the last four decades, a revolution in enterprise has helped transform Britain. In the early 1970s, the UK boasted some 820,000 firms; today, the figure is closer to 5 million.[*] Britain is sailing into the future with an entrepreneurial appetite that is stronger than at perhaps any time in its history. The number of people working for themselves has grown by around 30 per cent since 2000, and 15 per cent of the workforce are self-employed, the highest level in living memory. Indeed, self-employment accounted for 90 per cent of the jobs created between the downturn in 2008 and 2014.[†] On current trends, the number of self-employed (4.6 million at the time of writing) will outstrip the number of public-service workers before 2020.

And yet, the country could do even better. Britain's thirst for enterprise still lags behind many of our competitors, and in new industries Britain has struggled to build new world-beaters. Fewer than one in ten Britons think they will start a business in the next three years (8.5 per cent), which is about the same level of Germany, but only half the level of either France or the United States.[‡]

So, how can Britain do better? And what can history teach us?

I thought I would find out by sharing the five main lessons that loom out of the history books with some of Britain's greatest entrepreneurs of today, to ask what entrepreneurs of the future can learn from those they follow.

1. Money makes money

As much as I hate to admit it, a real 'rags to riches' story is the exception and not the rule in the history of great British enterprise – and that truth has long been understood. As early as the 1690s, Sir Thomas Pitt could declare that 'There can be no working without good tools';

---

[*] Benedict Dellot, 'Salvation in a Start-up' (RSA, 2014), p. 18; www.thersa.org/globalassets/pdfs/blogs/salvation-in-a-start-up-report-180714.pdf

[†] Ibid.

[‡] Global Entrepreneurship Monitor, *UK Monitoring Report 2014*, p. 11.

indeed, it was a well-known phrase.* Pitt reckoned that £1,000 (between £2 million and £4 million today) was the minimum needed to make a start in the East India business. He was as fond of the advice 'money begets money' as Nathan Rothschild was of his edict that 'money makes money'.

All but three of the entrepreneurs in this tale started life with at least a modest prosperity. Indeed, they offer a fascinating pattern of entrepreneurs transforming a decent inheritance into something spectacular. Robert Rich, Earl of Warwick, for instance – the backer of England's great Atlantic colonies – was one of the country's richest men, heir to £15,000 a year and the nation's largest privateering fleet, and intimately connected to England's Puritan elite. Nathan Rothschild was blessed with a father who was head of one of the fifteen richest Jewish families in Frankfurt, and he took a fortune with him when he moved to London. William Lever inherited a role in his father's prospering grocery business and found little problem raising £2.4 million in 'friends and family' financing to start his soap business, while John Spedan Lewis was reared in his father's hugely successful Oxford Street retail business. Matthew Boulton inherited a family business, and more importantly fortunes, from his two wives. Even George Hudson, the 'Railway Napoleon' who may have started out the poorest among these men, got his start in life with a £30,000 inheritance from his Uncle Matthew. The Cadbury brothers, who inherited a business that was failing, still had a royal warrant and £5,000 inherited from their mother to try and set things right.

Only three subjects in this book – Thomas Pitt, William Jardine and Cecil Rhodes – began their careers with next to nothing. Yet, even this lucky trio, all younger sons, were not born in penury. All three had brains in their head, a decent, but not elite, education and some helpful connections. Curiously, all three set off between the ages of eighteen and twenty to make their fortunes abroad. Pitt got his initial break through the East India Company, already well-established as a road to riches, and Jardine followed suit, backed by an Edinburgh University medical education financed by his brother. And while Cecil Rhodes

---

* Mentz, op. cit., p. 80.

started with little, his rich aunt stumped up for his curative passage to South Africa – and once there he was able to build on what his brother had already staked out as a cotton planter and diamond digger.

Has anything changed? Of any lesson from history, this is perhaps the one that has changed most – but only relatively recently.

Lady Martha Lane Fox co-founded Europe's largest travel and leisure website, lastminute.com, with Brent Hoberman in 1998, which they took public in 2000; today, she is Chancellor of the Open University. We first met when I was looking for advice on starting my own technology business back in 2000, and so I asked her whether she thought *anyone* could make it irrespective of means and background. 'I think there is a limit in the digital world,' she told me:

> It is quite depressing when I think about it; but if you look at the people founding or running globally significant technology firms, it is overwhelmingly white, middle-class men. I tend to reject the idea that all great entrepreneurs are university drop-outs. Very often people need the wherewithal to survive two or three significant failures. Now, it has become easier to go global – but look at the technology landscape today; it's a new industry but a lot of people who are successful in the second wave [of innovation] are the people who were successful in the first wave.

The lesson is starkest when we look at the barriers to women. 'This [technology industry] is a completely new industry,' adds Lane Fox, 'and not a single woman has founded or is even running one of the top globally significant businesses.'

There are other barriers too, not least in the sheer scale of the incumbent businesses with which new entrepreneurs must compete. Sir Robin Saxby is one of Britain's leading technology entrepreneurs, and as Chairman, President and Chief Executive of ARM Holdings created one of the few British tech companies worth more than $1 billion. In the process, he created the intellectual property for an incredible 60 billion micro-chips, powering more than 95 per cent of the world's smartphones. He agreed that it is – obviously – now possible for quick fortunes to be made, but the real lesson is that 'the route to success is very long'.

Saxby began his first experiments with electrical engineering as a teenager, beginning his own television repair business – despite the warnings from his teachers that he would electrocute himself – ably assisted by his mum and dad. He told me that he learned everything he knows about business by the age of fifteen.

He went on to become a brilliant example of an entrepreneur who has made it in an industry where huge amounts of capital are needed to compete – and survive. 'There is [always] a bit of a gamble,' he told me:

> You can have a great strategic vision – but the sales don't come as fast and before you know it you've got a cash funding crisis. It takes longer for the business to come through than the technology. And in the meantime, you've got to keep the business going. You have to have enough cash to keep the business going until the sales come through. The time to success is longer than you think. To start a business you do need seed capital. And today you need more seed capital than in the past.

Despite these caveats, I found that the new consensus was – on balance – that it *is* easier to start today with nothing and make it than ever before in business history. Sir Richard Branson is Britain's most famous, and probably most successful, entrepreneur. Reputedly now worth more than £3 billion, he began his entrepreneurial career at the age of sixteen, and today his Virgin Group comprises some 400 companies. I asked his advice on whether a real rags-to-riches story was more probable today than in the past. He told me that the advent of new technology was a game-changer:

> Modern technology has completely opened up what it means to be an entrepreneur. In the past people usually had to have personal connections or personal wealth to get their idea off the ground.
>
> [When I started] I… had to get inventive. I hustled advertising via payphone before we launched *Student* magazine, and stood outside Royal Albert Hall taking prepaid record orders for Virgin Records. Today's thinkers and entrepreneurs have the world at

their fingertips, and can rely simply on the strength of their idea to raise them the capital they need to get started. Crowd-funding platforms and start-up loans have made life easier for entrepreneurs, and at the same time gifted the world with an abundance of great ideas, products and services.

It is an analysis endorsed by Sir Ronald Cohen. Sir Ronald and I have known each other since we worked on social investment policy. As founder of Europe's biggest private equity firm, Apax Partners, which he built up over thirty-three years to manage more than $40 billion, Sir Ronald has seen the way technology has transformed – perhaps even democratized – access to capital:

> It's much easier now [to get started], because access to capital is much easier. Look at the US success stories. There you've got some very young guys who've been able to mobilize tens of millions of dollars before floating [on stock markets]. Just think: the phenomenon of the thirty-year-old billionaire just didn't exist in the past. Opportunities have been created by technology – and technology is much more easily comprehended by young people. Plus, there's a huge acceleration of time now due to the ease of entry into new markets, which has made it easier; you don't need to make big investments.

Sir Martin Sorrell underlined the point for me. He joined Saatchi & Saatchi in 1975, and as Chief Executive of WPP transformed a shell company, over the course of thirty years, into the world's leading communications company worth some £20.5 billion, with sales of £11.5 billion. He was not someone who started with a fortune: 'Well, it wasn't true for me. And if you look at entrepreneurs today, from Alan Sugar to Richard Desmond, you can see how things are changing. I think actually what's more important today is a decent education. In the old days there was a lot more friction in the system – friction that stopped or slowed down the sharing of ideas.'

Duncan Bannatyne is famous for his role as a business angel on the BBC's *Dragons' Den*. The founder of an empire spanning health clubs, hotels, media and television, stage schools, property and transport, he is also the author of seven books, and he was even more emphatic about the change that has occurred: 'Every successful entrepreneur I know started with nothing; I don't know any entrepreneurs who started with a fortune.'

2. Be in the right place at the right time

My second lesson of history is that the greatest entrepreneurs seem to have a knack for being in the right place at the right time. Now, it is true that I have written here about entrepreneurs who illustrated key changes – or 'discontinuities' – over the broad sweep of the last eight centuries. But I was struck that few found themselves in the great markets purely by accident. For most, it was calculated design. And their extraordinary success underlines the importance of thinking carefully about how to place oneself in opportunity's way.

Robert Rich, Matthew Boulton, Nathan Rothschild, George Cadbury and John Spedan Lewis were all *born* into families that started them off in the right place on the race-track – but they proceeded to race with a style and success of their own; Rich was blessed with a privateering fleet but invested heavily in new colonial ventures. Boulton was born in booming Birmingham, but invested in steam engines to pump the coal mines fuelling the nascent Industrial Revolution. Rothschild was wealthy, but moved to Manchester, the 'shock city', which was the epicentre of industrial change. Both Cadbury and Spedan Lewis took huge gambles to build businesses that profited from roaring new consumer markets. Thomas Pitt and William Jardine, by contrast, chose a path – albeit a well-known one – to foreign markets during some quite extraordinary times. Hudson, Rhodes and Lever, on the other hand, deliberately moved into industries that they gambled were about to blossom.

Curiously, none were 'inventors'; none 'created' their industries. Most were working in trades that were old. Rather, each transformed the industries they found with a vision and determination that was quite exceptional. Today's great British entrepreneurs seem to share a view that while luck is important, strategy and planning are the crucial ingredients.

Richard Branson was very clear:

In my opinion, there's no such thing as an accidental entrepreneur – it's not simply about being in the right place at the right time. To be an entrepreneur means to be interested in the world around you, and constantly looking for ways to improve what's currently on offer. It's deliberate, it's conscious, and it's hard work. It's about finding a gap in a market, and then working to fill that gap with something of substance and purpose. Pole position comes when you understand your market, and provide something that people actually want and need.

It's a sentiment that Ronald Cohen seconded:

Sometimes opportunity knocks on your door – but Bill Gates, Steve Jobs and Mark Zuckerberg all could see an opportunity and found their niche in it. They all left university because they were so scared that someone else would do it before them. Now, the availability of capital is one of the things that's changed this. Today, it's a struggle to keep smart young people in school.

Robin Saxby's career is a good illustration. 'I understood what works and what doesn't,' he told me, 'I deliberately picked the new industry that was clearly going to boom. I hunted to find [the right] job in a growth market – you'll have more fun. You might be lucky. But think of Gates or the founders of Intel – they didn't happen by accident. In technology it's not luck – you have to search for and grab the opportunity. Luck is good planning.'

That said, few think you can discount the role of a little accident and a lot of attitude; as Martha Lane Fox put it, 'I'd reject the idea that luck doesn't play a huge part of the story – of course it does – everyone underestimates luck.' But the right state of mind is the key, as Martin Sorrell describes:

My father used to say that you live life in circles. If you're active in your circle, you'll collide with the other circles around you. He said to me, 'Look, find an industry that you like, and build a reputation in it.' Much of my thinking came from my Dad and [in time] people thought I knew what I was doing – and wanted to do things with me.

It's a point that Richard Branson is keen to underline:

One of the most important lessons that we can take away from the history of entrepreneurship is that those passionate enough to make a difference are the ones that do [so]. Passion keeps entrepreneurs awake and working during the midnight hours, positive during the moments of stress, and determined throughout the challenges. The world's greatest innovations have been driven by passionate people. Passionate people spur change that moves the world forward, and inspire others to believe they can make a difference too.

3. Know when to fold 'em, know when to hold 'em – and know when to go 'all in'

It was Nathan Rothschild who once said: 'It requires a great deal of boldness and a great deal of caution to make a great fortune, and when you have got it requires ten times as much wit to keep it.'* Rothschild alludes to a fascinating pattern that emerges from our journey with these entrepreneurs: once their first modest fortune was made, there was typically a spectacularly ambitious move in pursuit of a 'grand plan' for the future. Like great poker players, great entrepreneurs, having acquired a decent set of cards, know when to go 'all in' – though often the moves can take years, pursued methodically in the manner of a chess grand-master destroying a lesser player.

---

* Quoted, Jules Ayers, 'Introduction', *A Century of Finance, 1804–1904: The London House of Rothschild* (Neely, 1905).

Every entrepreneur here had a yen for risky behaviour – indeed, each one took risks to make first fortunes, sometimes self-sacrificing, sometimes sacrificing others. As a young man, Robert Rich was sailing privateering ships against the East India Company in the Red Sea, and was sued for his efforts by the corporate titans of Stuart England. Thomas Pitt started working life as an 'interloper', earning orders from his masters for his immediate arrest. Matthew Boulton constantly overstretched his lines of credit, while William Jardine faced shipwreck and imprisonment in French warships. Early in life, Nathan Rothschild acquired a reputation for sharp practice and built a London fortune as an expert European embargo-buster. George Hudson was an early master of accounting fraud, paying out high dividends from shareholders' funds. The Cadburys gambled their own last pennies on saving their father's business, while, by contrast, Cecil Rhodes was deeply implicated in the sabotage of his competitor's mine pumps, and the older he got, the bigger the gambles he made, personally, and indeed with the fates of nations. William Lever left a highly successful grocery business for the uncertainty of a new soap business, started from scratch, and John Spedan Lewis swapped his shares in his father's highly successful department store for full control of the failing Peter Jones.

In short, entrepreneurs believe 'nothing ventured, nothing gained'. But what separates the great from the also rans is the ability to think and move 'big'. So, Rich sank a fortune into the Providence Island Company, as did Boulton into Soho House and the Albion Mill, and Cadbury into Bournville. Having spent his life trying to destroy the East India Company in India, Thomas Pitt then threw in his all to save it. Jardine cannily invested heavily in new ships to mine China's opium trade, ahead of the expiration of the East India Company's monopoly, while Nathan Rothschild invested a fortune in the EIC's gold sale of 1814, gambling on his ability to resell it and carve out his position as Wellington's banker. Hudson's sobriquet of the 'Railway Napoleon' said everything about his spectacular roll-up of the railway companies, while Rhodes's single-minded, massive amalgamation of the De Beers mine-owners reflected his conviction that the key to dominating diamonds was control of a vast block of land on a scale that allowed the creation of underground tunnels. William Lever's vision stretched well beyond Port Sunlight, to European, American, indeed global, expansion, while Spedan Lewis backed his vision of a very different kind of retail empire with a huge expansion drive throughout the 1930s.

Richard Branson very much recognized the approach:

> I can't stress how important it is for entrepreneurs to find their market, before going all in and throwing everything behind an idea or business. Find your market, fill a gap, and then make bold moves. This is the story of Virgin's success. We've never been one hundred per cent sure that any of our businesses were going to be successful. We've just always stood by our motto: 'Screw it, let's do it.' The fact is, you'll never know what could happen if you don't give it a go. Opportunity favours the bold, as long as you are making calculated risks, not blind leaps of faith.

'That's definitely part of the character of great entrepreneurs,' added Ronald Cohen. They 'need to spend some time mastering their proof of concept. Then there's often some big infrastructure to put in place – so they'll often spend a lot of time experimenting and then bet big.'

Martha Lane Fox told me that the advent of the internet has allowed much more rapid scaling-up than in the past, at very little marginal cost. 'No one really appreciates how quickly the landscape changes,' she told me, 'and there are these pivot moments – like the way Facebook now dominates mobile, or the way Google is changing. It's a much more profound thing in the world of the internet.' But many successful entrepreneurs clearly start with the ambition to go global the moment the time is right. Martin Sorrell told me how, when that time arrived, WPP embarked on an extraordinary expansion – eighteen deals in eighteen months:

> Harvard [Business School] taught me to do things at scale. If you start in the UK, you have no choice. That's why so many successful entrepreneurs go to the US; if you start in America, you've got some 300 million people to sell to... It's why China is so

important today. If you want scale, you've got to try and build a multinational enterprise.

For Sorrell, rapid expansion would entail a significant loss of control. But, 'the decision for me was would I prefer 16 per cent of WPP, or 8 per cent of a leveraged company thirteen times our size.' Robin Saxby says the same kind of ambition was crucial to building ARM – an ambition he learned travelling on two long-haul flights a month for Motorola, where he spent much of his early career:

> You need to have a global vision. Ninety-nine per cent of ARM's revenue is outside the UK. When I founded ARM I said we need to have global partners. I set out to have global partners from Day One. The number fourteen employee was in California. If you needed to be global back in 1990, it's even more true today… All the start-ups I'm involved in are global. The world needs to be even more joined up. If you've never travelled, how can you possibly know what to do? Not enough people have travelled.

4. True grit and great trust

It was allegedly Cecil Rhodes's great friend Jameson Starr who inspired Rudyard Kipling to compose his poem 'If', replete with the advice to '… meet with Triumph and Disaster / And treat those two imposters just the same'. It was advice by which Rhodes, and most great entrepreneurs, have tended to live. Their combination of doggedness, determination and mastery of detail – for decades on end – marks them out as truly exceptional people. By and large, their success was a life's work.

All the entrepreneurs here began their working lives early; and most ploughed the same furrow for decades on end. Each had an extraordinary ability to bounce back from adversity, and not always with an instant recovery; more often, they built a return to success marked out in years. Robert Rich poured thousands into (the eventual lost cause) of the Providence Island Company and his legal battle against Charles I's taxes was years long; at his lowest ebb, he and his friends were ready to emigrate. But he stayed the course, helped lead Parliament's battle with the Crown, and lived to see Cromwell's 'Western Design' enshrine Britain's Atlantic colonies, his life's work, as the cornerstone of an English empire. Thomas Pitt well understood 'both turns of fortune', but when he lost his own fortune against the French and Dutch in 1690, the thirty-three-year-old adventurer threw himself back into interloping, achieving his riches in trade and diamonds.

Matthew Boulton was nearly bankrupt in the years after 1778, when his troubles came aplenty; but he and his partner, James Watt, ground out success among the rough tin-mine captains of Cornwall, and saw profitability return. Jardine fought a concerted campaign to mobilize Britain into all-out war with China to protect his opium trade threatened with annihilation by the emperor, and the irrepressible George Hudson demonstrated some extraordinary survival skills in his long cat-and-mouse game with courts and rivals after his accounting scandals were exposed. The Cadbury brothers were christened the 'Cheeryble Brothers' on account of their cheery demeanours, as they fought and succeeded in saving their father's business, denying themselves proper meals and (in George's case) forgoing marriage in the process. Cecil Rhodes hustled for anything and everything during the first great diamond depression, while William Lever spent nearly a decade fighting his own 'Battle of the Nile' to triumph in America, winning along the way the American expertise that helped him revolutionize a global brands business. And John Spedan Lewis never gave up on his vision, persisting with his retail expansion and Partnership model through even the toughest years, when profitability crashed. Each, in their own way, lived out Churchill's advice to 'never, never, never give up'.

Yet, this 'true grit' was matched with attention to gritty detail. In researching the entrepreneurs here, I found the most striking feature was the wealth of day-to-day detail in their letters and conversations. Spedan Lewis composed 40,000 memos over the course of his career, on issues varying from the grandly ambitious to the most minute. The intricacy of Cecil Rhodes's plate-spinning – as he sought to align plans for winning concessions, managing share issues, raising capital, and organizing railway lines – is stunning in its complexity.

The letters of William Jardine – like those of Nathan Rothschild – are full of private intelligence on prices, market sentiments and the competition. Hudson's petitions betray an extraordinarily detailed grasp of methodical political organization. As for William Lever and his creation of Leverville, 'Not a building was erected unless the plans had been passed by him… and very often these plans were largely his own; not a piece of plant or machinery nor a craft on the river from the largest stern-wheeler to the smallest launch or barge, was ordered until he had carefully examined and passed the specifications.'* And old Cadbury's workers fondly recalled that 'vision of Mr George, with a row of small tins on a counter in front of him, the tins filled with roasted "beans" just brought in from the factory, and Mr George with unerring skill, testing them and pronouncing judgement'.[†]

These entrepreneurs combined overarching strategic vision with an ability to sweat the small stuff, day in and day out for decades. And they combined true grit with great trust, invested in the small and intimate groups of friends and partners around them. Over the centuries, we see that great success is not a solo sport; it is always a team effort. Robert Rich was surrounded by Puritan collaborators. Pitt was one of an informal partnership of interlopers, and Boulton benefited from immersion in Birmingham's Lunar Society and critical collaborations with Wedgwood and Watt. Jardine found his greatest partner in James Matheson, but could also not have managed without Thomas Weeding in London and Jamsetsee Jeejeebhoy in India. Nathan Rothschild had not only his brothers, strategically placed across Europe, but his father and father-in-law – and such a closeness to senior ministers and European royalty that it inspired rumours of plots and conspiracies. George Hudson had henchmen, such as David Waddington, to help him cook the books, and Rhodes was at the centre of the 'Apostles' on the diamond fields. William Lever created an extraordinary partnership with the US marketing genius Sydney Gross, while John Spedan Lewis set out to create a highly educated, highly trained upper-middle-class management team at John Lewis,

---

* Lever's son, quoted in McQueen, op. cit., p. 213.
† Ibid.

which spent lots of time together at the company's extensive network of clubs and country houses.

Little seems to have changed. Some of Britain's most successful entrepreneurs told me that the same qualities of true grit, gritty detail and a group that works well together are critical today. In Duncan Bannatyne's view, nothing, of course, trumps hard work: 'In my opinion… [success] is about working hard and dedicating yourself to business and what you believe in.' And in today's complex science- and technology-based businesses, you need a combination of skills at the top, in which detail is essential. As Ronald Cohen explained:

The big entrepreneur today is often the CTO (the Chief Technology Officer) – look at Apple or Microsoft for instance. You then have a senior executive brought in to actually run the operation. [But] If you don't pay attention to the detail, you don't get past stage one – and lots of people get stuck at this stage. But what really makes a difference is the obsessive drive of successful entrepreneurs.

Robin Saxby agreed. 'The devil is in the detail. If one transistor is wrong it won't work. If you don't do detail you'll trip up and fail. You don't do everything yourself, but you do look over your shoulder at the weakest link. You have to have a degree of paranoia.'

Successful entrepreneurs tend to have a degree of obsessive focus about both detail and the ability to inspire a team. Martha Lane Fox described her experience:

… our success was that we just went and did it but with a level of obsession. That absolute relentless focus on product is what separates globally successful businesses from the rest. We were worried about every single pixel all the time. Absolutely obsessive about design and what it [our website] looked like. And it's then all about execution. But you have to do it in tandem with creating and inspiring a team – when you're not able to point to what the future is going to look like.

That ability to keep a team going through adversity is something Richard Branson wanted to stress:

> Success comes to leaders who lead from the front, and by example. Who stick it out through the tough times, and have the courage to admit their flaws and mistakes. And to those who listen to their staff and trust them, and know what is going on within all areas of their business. Only when you do all this yourself, can you expect it in return. I'd add another point by quoting Mark Twain, who said: 'Great people are those who make others feel that they, too, can become great.'

There is no getting away from the detail. As Martin Sorrell puts it, 'Once you lose a liking for detail, it's very, very difficult. I saw it first-hand… once you think you could run [a business] by remote control that's when the trouble starts.'

5. Change the world

Perhaps most impressive of all, every character in this story illustrates the sheer potential of entrepreneurs to help change the world. They all thought – and worked – on a grand scale. All worked not only in private business but in public life.

Robert Rich spent a lifetime fighting for England's interests against Spain, and his work as a colonist laid the foundations for Cromwell's establishment of empire. He lobbied for a navy big enough to take on the Dutch, and was instrumental in protecting the new wealth of traders from the depredations of the king. Jardine was instrumental in persuading the country's leaders to deploy firepower in pursuit of free trade against the empire of the east, while Rhodes became the leading empire-builder of his day, with dreams of an Africa 'painted red' by any means. Nathan Rothschild not only transformed the City of London, creating the European bond-market much admired by his obituarists, but, as Wellington acknowledged, he saved the Bank of England at its moment of crisis in 1825. Both Matthew Boulton and George Hudson, in their different ways, changed the country by pioneering the spread of new technology. Both thought big. As Boulton put it, 'I sell here, sir, what all the world desires to have – POWER.'* And as the Sunderland press once said of Hudson, 'The magic of his touch has revolutionised the world.'

In the modern era, Cadbury, Lever and Lewis each set out to create a different kind of company and to reshape the society they served. Their motivations varied. Cadbury was inspired by religion, Lewis by his dedication to the principles of Partnership, while Lever was simply an improver of life: 'I am not a lover of money as money,' he once said, 'I work at business because business is life. It enables me to do things.'†

Together, they helped pioneer a different kind of capitalism. Cadbury was fighting a conscious battle to push back against the evils of the Victorian marketplace; he felt passionately that in order to raise a man's ideals, one had to improve his circumstances. Hence, the creation of Bournville and Cadbury Brothers' sick fund, pension scheme, education services and recreation services. But his passion to change the country went further; hence his acquisitions of the *Daily News* to campaign against the Anglo-Boer War, for social reform, and for the emerging Labour Party. Lever had similar ambitions in Port Sunlight, and he was an early advocate of partnership and profit-sharing, principles that Lewis took to new lengths, creating in the John Lewis Partnership, as he put it, 'something to live for'. That was the level of his ambition.

Many combined service on a grand scale with a day-to-day engagement with public life. Many were Members of Parliament or local councillors, however briefly. Of those that were not, Nathan Rothschild, as a Jew, was specifically prohibited from holding such offices in his era – though he spent most of his career in public finance. Matthew Boulton was a city-builder with few parallels, who led the creation of much of Birmingham's civic infrastructure, and John Spedan Lewis's ideas about industrial organization were already lauded by political parties as early as 1929.

Now, not all entrepreneurs want to change the world, as Duncan

---

* Uglow, op. cit., p. 257.
† Wilson, op. cit., p. 187.

Bannatyne reminded me: 'Some entrepreneurs just want to put food on the table or give their kids a good education; this instinct is important because it helps you work hard for what you want in life.' But the point Ronald Cohen makes is that 'businesses grow to the vision of their founders. The best of the best will do things that change the world. It's the legacy they leave. Think about Henry Ford, or Thomas Watson [founder of IBM]. What characterizes the truly great entrepreneurs is their higher level objectives. They want to do something which is fundamentally meaningful. It's profit with purpose.' Martha Lane Fox agrees:

> I think that is right... there are differences between business with a product and something beyond that. It's more likely to encourage employees and customers to engage with you. Every business must have a social purpose these days, like the early days of Marks & Spencer's. Arguably, it's why a lot of technology companies face challenges today because they've become too opaque. It's not clear if they're shooting for higher purposes or making more gains.

Final words

Over decades to come, power in world markets will profoundly shift, while new technology will create new worlds of possibility, inaugurating what some call the 'second machine age': an era in which our ability to combine technology – processing power, cheap sensors, robotics, networks, social media and big data – will revolutionize the things we can truck, trade and barter, creating new products and services, from driverless cars to the better diagnosis of disease.* There will be profound implications for work and jobs. Some estimates suggest that as many as 47 per cent of jobs in today's economy will become automated.

The possibilities of this new world will be pushed forward by a new generation of inventors and innovators, entrepreneurs and

---

* Erik Brynjolfsson and Andrew McAfee, *The Second Machine Age* (Norton, 2014).

world-beaters. So this book is a call for a change in the way we honour our entrepreneurs – and use our history to inspire a more entrepreneurial future. Entrepreneurs see new ways of doing things. They create jobs. They create wealth. They take inventions and innovate in ways that improve our lives. Entrepreneurs make history by inventing the future. By creating new possibilities, they expand the boundaries of our freedom.

It seems that many of the qualities that define a real history-making leader hold true down the centuries. I hope the story of Britain's entrepreneurial titans can restore them to the centre of the stage on which the national story is told. And I hope that new clarity about the past inspires more people to pursue a life of enterprise. In public life. In private life. Or both. For when historians of the future come to write a book like this, I want them to be spoilt for choice. I wonder who they will chose to feature? I wonder if it will be you.

Endnotes

Preface

1   David S. Landes, Joel Mokyr & William J. Baumol (eds), *The Invention of Enterprise: Entrepreneurship from Ancient Mesopotamia to Modern Times* (Princeton University Press, 2011), p. ix.
2   See, for instance, David S. Landes, *Unbound Prometheus* (Cambridge University Press, 1969); Donald N. McCloskey, 'Did Victorian Britain Fail?', *Economic History Review*, Vol. 23, No. 1 (December 1970), pp. 446–59; or W. D. Rubinstein, *Capitalism, Culture and Decline in Britain, 1750–1990* (Routledge, 1993).

1. The Nation's Foundations

1   Wladyslaw Duczko, *Viking Rus: Studies on the Presence of Scandinavians in Eastern Europe* (Brill, 2004), p. 20.
2   Fernand Braudel, *Civilization and Capitalism, 15th–18th Century, Vol. I: The Perspective of the World* (University of California Press, 1992), p. 93.
3   May McKisack, *The Fourteenth Century, 1307–1399* (Oxford University Press, 1959), ch. 12.
4   E. B. Fryde, *William de la Pole: Merchant and King's Banker* (Hambledon Press, 1988), p. 1.
5   R. Horrox, *The De La Poles of Hull* (East Yorkshire Local History Society, 1983), p. 6.
6   K. J. Allison (ed.), *A History of the County of York East Riding, Vol. I* (Victoria County History, 1969).
7   M. M. Postan, *Medieval Trade and Finance* (Cambridge University Press, 1973) p. 168.
8   Ibid., p. 96.
9   Horrox, *The De La Poles of Hull*, op. cit., p. 6.
10 Janet Nelson, 'Carolingian Contacts', in Michelle Brown and Carol Farr (eds), *Mercia: An Anglo-Saxon Kingdom in Europe* (Bloomsbury, 2005), p. 142.
11 Postan, *Medieval Trade and Finance*, op. cit., p. 7.
12 Eileen Power, *The Wool Trade in English Medieval History: Being the Ford Lectures* (Oxford University Press, 1941), p. 13.

13 Eileen Power, *Medieval People* (Pelican, 1923), p. 143.

14 McKisack, *The Fourteenth Century*, op. cit., p. 346.

15 Power, *Medieval People*, op. cit.

16 See Edwin S. Hunt, *The Medieval Super-Companies: A Study of the Peruzzi Company of Florence* (Cambridge University Press, 2002), for a detailed discussion.

17 Ibid., ch. 2.

18 Fryde, *William de la Pole*, op. cit., p. 63.

19 Ibid., p. 76.

20 Horrox, *The De La Poles of Hull*, op. cit., p. 17.

21 Ibid., p. 133.

22 Dorothy Hughes, *A Study of Social and Constitutional Tendencies in the Early Years of Edward III* (General Books LLC, 2010).

23 Fryde, *William de la Pole*, op. cit., p. 184.

24 Ibid., p. 216.

25 Geoffrey Chaucer, *The Canterbury Tales*, trans. Nevill Coghill (Penguin, 2003).

26 Anne F. Sutton, *The Mercery of London: Trade, Goods and People, 1130–1578* (Ashgate, 2005), p. 130.

27 Gerald Harriss, *Shaping the Nation 1360–1461* (Clarendon, 2005), pp. 258–81.

28 www.historyofparliamentonline.org/volume/1386-1421/member/whittington-richard-1423

29 John Burgon, *The Life and Times of Sir Thomas Gresham* (Robert Jennings, 1839), p. 47.

30 E. G. Ravenstein, *A Journal of the First Voyage of Vasco da Gama, 1497–1499* (Cambridge University Press, 2010), p. 60.

31 Lodovico Guicciardini, *Descrittione di tutti i Paesi Bassi*, cited in Richard Ehrenberg, *Capital and Finance in the Age of the Renaissance: A Study of Fuggers and Their Connections* (Nabu Press, 2011).

32 Stephen H. Goddard, *The Master of Frankfurt and His Shop* (AWLSK, 1984), p. 15.

33 Professor Guido Marnef in 'Gresham and Antwerp', a lecture to Gresham College, Thursday, 19 June 2008.

34 Lodovico Guicciardini, *Descrittione di tutti i Paesi Bassi*, in Ehrenberg, *Capital and Finance*, op. cit., p. 243.

35 Professor Guido Marnef in 'Gresham and Antwerp', a lecture to Gresham College, Thursday, 19 June 2008.

36 Burgon, *The Life and Times of Sir Thomas Gresham*, op. cit., p. 93.

37 See Robert Brenner, *Merchants and Revolution: Commercial Change, Political Conflict, and London's Overseas Traders 1550–1653* (Verso, 2003), p. 56, for a longer discussion.

38 Burgon, *The Life and Times of Sir Thomas Gresham*, op. cit., p. 118.

39 Ibid., p. 114.

40 Ibid., p. 123.

41 Ibid., p. 134.

42 Ibid., p. 159.

43 Alison Weir, *The Life of Elizabeth I* (Random House, 2013), p. 350.

44 S. Alford, *Burghley: William Cecil at the Court of Elizabeth* (Yale, 2011), p. 89.

45 Burgon, *The Life and Times of Sir Thomas Gresham*, op. cit., p. 217.

46 Ibid., p. 221.

47 Ibid., p. 215.

48 Ibid., p. 484.

49 Ibid., p. 486.

50 Brenner, *Merchants and Revolution*, op. cit., p. 56.

51 Burgon, *The Life and Times of Sir Thomas Gresham*, op. cit., p. 263.

52 Ibid., p. 273.

53 Ibid., p. 204.

54 Ibid., p. 260.

55 Ibid., p. 336.

56 Ibid., p. 139.

57 Ibid., p. 195.

58 Johan Frederik Bense, *The Anglo-Dutch Relations from the Earliest Times to the Death of William III* (Springer, 2013), p. 150.

59 Christopher Hibbert, Ben Weinreb, John Keay and Julia Keay, *The London Encyclopaedia* (Pan Macmillan, 2008), p. 717.

60 Burgon, *The Life and Times of Sir Thomas Gresham*, op. cit., p. 87.

61 Ibid., p. 351.

62 Ibid., p. 242.

63 Stephen Broadberry, *British Economic Growth 1270–1870* (Cambridge University Press, 2015), p. ??

64 John A. F. Thomson, *The Transformation of Medieval England* (Longman, 1983), p. 102.

65 Brenner, *Merchants and Revolution*, op. cit., p. 58.

2. Robert Rich

1 W. Frank Craven, *The Life of Robert Rich, second Earl of Warwick, to 1642* (PhD thesis, Cornell University, 1928), p. 219.

2 www.british-history.ac.uk/report.aspx?compid=34840

3 Granville Penn, *Memorials of the Professional Life and Times of Sir William Penn, Vol. I* (James Duncan, 1833), p. 42.

4 Ibid.

5 John Sargeaunt, *A History of Felsted School: With Some Account of the Founder and His Descendants* (E. Durrant & Company, 1889), p. 2.

6 Walter Bourchier Devereux, *Lives and Letters of the Devereux, Earls of Essex* (John Murray, 1853), p. 152.

7 William Drogo Montagu Manchester, *Court and Society from Elizabeth to Anne, Vol. 1* (Spotiswoode & Co., 1864), p. 295.

8   Quoted in Charlotte Fell-Smith, *Mary Rich, Countess of Warwick (1625–1678): Her Family and Friends* (Longmans, Green, and Co., 1901).

9   Quoted in George Smeeton, *Smeeton's Historical and Biographical Tracts, Vol. II* (George Smeeton, 1820).

10 Quoted in Fell-Smith, *Mary Rich*, op. cit., p. 107.

11 Francis Bremer, *John Winthrop: America's Forgotten Founding Father* (Oxford University Press, 2003), p. 4.

12 Edward Hyde, Earl of Clarendon, *Characters of Eminent Men in the Reigns of Charles I and II* (R. Faulder, 1793), p. 107.

13 Arthur Percival Newton, *Colonising Activities of English Puritans* (Oxford University Press, 1914), p. 16.

14 Kenneth Andrews, *Trade, Plunder and Settlement* (Cambridge University Press, 1984), p. 1.

15 Stephen Broadberry, *British Economic Growth 1270–1870* (Cambridge University Press, 2015), p. 205. These figures are expressed in real GDP, in 1700 prices – in the 1300s, GDP was £28.65 million.

16 Broadberry, *British Economic Growth 1270–1870*, op. cit., p. 199.

17 This number is expressed in real terms; see Broadberry, *British Economic Growth*, op. cit., table 5.05, p. 204.

18 Robert Brenner, *Merchants and Revolution: Commercial Change, Political Conflict and London's Overseas Traders 1550–1653* (Verso, 2003), p. 72.

19 Quoted in Paul Johnson, *A History of the American People* (HarperCollins, 2009), p. 17.

20 Michael Jarvis, *In the Eye of All Trade: Bermuda, Bermudians and the Maritime Atlantic World 1680–1783* (University of North Carolina Press, 2010), p. 13.

21 Jarvis, *In the Eye of All Trade*, op. cit., p. 15.

22 Ibid., p. 17.

23 Niall Ferguson, *Empire: How Britain Made the Modern World* (Penguin, 2004), p. 16.

24 Virginia Bernhard, *Slaves and Slaveholders in Bermuda 1616–1782* (University of Missouri Press, 1984), p. 33.

25 Jarvis, *In the Eye of All Trade*, op. cit., p. 27.

26 V. Ives, *The Rich Papers: Letters from Bermuda, 1615–46* (Toronto University Press, 1984), p. 15.

27 Bernhard, *Slaves and Slaveholders*, op. cit., p. 7.

28 Lefroy, *Memorials*, 1:228, quoted in Bernhard, *Slaves and Slaveholders*, op. cit., p. 10.

29 Lewis Hughes to Sir Robert Rich, 19 May 1617, quoted in Ives, *The Rich Papers*, op. cit., p. 13.

30 Ibid.

31 Quoted in Kenneth R. Andrews, *Trade, Plunder and Settlement: Maritime Enterprise and the Genesis of the British Empire* (Cambridge University Press, 1984), p. 245.

32 Quoted in N. A. M. Rodger, *The Safeguard of the Sea: A Naval History of Britain, Vol. 1: 660–1649* (Penguin, 2004), p. 244.

33 Ibid., p. 294.

34 Rodger, *The Safeguard of the Sea*, op. cit., p. 281.

35 W. Frank Craven, 'The Earl of Warwick: A Speculator in Piracy', *Hispanic American Historican Review*, 10 (1930), p. 30.

36 Ibid., p. 31.

37 Ferguson, *Empire*, op. cit., p. 66.

38 Robert Cushman, 8 May 1619, quoted in E. Neill, *The Virginia Company of London* (Joel Munsell, 1869).

39 Craven, 'The Earl of Warwick', op. cit., p. 89.

40 Brenner, *Merchants and Revolution*, op. cit., p. 99.

41 Quoted in Ives, *The Rich Papers*, op. cit., p. 147.

42 Robert Cushman, 8 May 1619. Quoted in Neill, *The Virginia Company*, op. cit., p. 143.

43 Craven, 'The Earl of Warwick', op. cit., p. 37.

44 Ibid., p. 101.

45 Quoted in Craven, 'The Earl of Warwick', op. cit., p. 56.

46 Chamberlain to Sir Dudley Carleton, 26 July 1623, quoted in Neill, *The Virginia Company*, op. cit., p. 413. His analogy is to the notorious factional divisions of northern Italy in the thirteenth and fourteenth centuries.

47 See William Bradford, *History of the Plymouth Plantation* (Boston, privately printed, 1856).

48 Quoted in Bradford, *History of the Plymouth Plantation*, op. cit., p. 101.

49 The Charter for New England can be found at http://avalon.law.yale.edu/17th_century/mass01.asp

50 See, for instance, Francis Bremer, *John Winthrop* (Oxford University Press, 2003); S.E. Morison, *Builders of the Bay Colony* (Oxford University Press, 1930).

51 Brenner, *Merchants and Revolution*, op. cit., p. 254.

52 Adamson, *The Noble Revolt* (Phoenix, 2007), p. 32.

53 Morison, *Builders of the Bay*, op. cit., p. 32.

54 Newton, *Colonising Activities*, op. cit., pp. 33–4.

55 Cited in Newton, *Colonising Activities*, op. cit., p. 104.

56 Ibid., p. 290.

57 See Jarvis, *In the Eye of All Trade*, op. cit., Table 1, p. 28; this was now four times the level of Bermudan exports.

58 Bremer, *John Winthrop*, op. cit., p. 256.

59 Craven, 'The Earl of Warwick', op. cit., p. 192.

60 Ibid., p. 191.

61 Ibid., p. 54.

62 Newton, *Colonising Activities*, op, cit., p. 57.

63 Quotes in Newton, *Colonising Activities*, op. cit., p. 241.

64 Quoted in Craven, 'The Earl of Warwick', op. cit., p. 54.

65 Ibid., p. 196.

66 Robert Barclay, former tutor to the Earl of Argyll, who was the most powerful of the Covenanter nobility. See Adamson, *The Noble Revolt*, op. cit., p. 23.

67 Adamson, *The Noble Revolt*, op. cit., p. 12.

68 Ibid., p. 17.

69 Ibid., p. 18.

70 Ibid., p. 54.

71 Ibid., p. 78.

72 Ibid., p. 57.

73 Ibid., p. 74.

74 Ibid., p. 82.

75 Ibid., p. 26.

76 Ibid., p. 116.

77 Ibid., p. 324.

78 Richard Cust, *Charles I* (Routledge, 2014), p. 296.

79 Craven, 'The Earl of Warwick', op. cit., p. 209.

80 Clarendon, *Characters of Eminent Men*, op. cit., p. 381.

81 Craven, 'The Earl of Warwick', op. cit., p. 163.

82 See Antonia Fraser, *Cromwell: Our Chief of Men* (Grove/Atlantic, 2007), p. 283.

83 Brenner, *Merchants and Revolution*, op. cit., p. 577.

84 Ibid., pp. 583–4.

85 Ibid., p. 631.

86 Ibid., p. 629.

87 Newton, *Colonising Activities*, op. cit., p. 319.

88 Brenner, *Merchants and Revolution*, p. 630.

89 S. A. G. Taylor, *The Western Design: An Account of Cromwell's Expedition to the Caribbean* (Kingston, Jamaica, 1965; reprint ed. London, 1969), p. 2.

90 See Arthur R. Hiscox, *Oliver Cromwell's Western Design: A Study in the Survival of Elizabethan Strategy* (Kent State University, 1973).

91 Karen Kupperman, *Providence Island 1630–1641: The Other Puritan Colony* (Cambridge University Press, 1993), p. 348.

92 Ibid., p. 347.

93 Cromwell, to Major General Richard Fortescue, quoted in Kupperman, *Providence Island*, op. cit., p. 351.

94 Quoted in Taylor, *The Western Design*, op. cit., p. 4.

95 Ibid., p. 9.

96 Newton, *Colonising Activities*, op. cit., pp. 322–3.

97 Taylor, *The Western Design*, op. cit., p. 55.

98 Fraser, *Cromwell*, op. cit., p. 641.

99 Figures derived from C. Knick Harvey, 'Trade, Discovery, Mercantilism and Technology' in Roderick Floud and Paul Johnson (eds), *Cambridge Economic History of Modern Britain, Vol. 1* (Cambridge University Press, 2004).

3. Sir Thomas 'Diamond' Pitt

1   Søren Mentz, *The English Gentleman Merchant at Work: Madras and the City of London 1660–1740* (Museum Tusculanum Press, 2005), p. 110.

2   Jean-Baptiste Tavernier, *Tavernier's Travels in India* (Bangabasi Office, 1905).

3   Cornelius N. Dalton, *The Life of Thomas Pitt* (Cambridge at the University Press, 1915), p. 522.

4   John Towill Rutt (ed.), 'Cromwell's death and funeral order' in *Diary of Thomas Burton esq, Vol. 2: April 1657–February 1658* (1828), pp. 516–30.

5   N. H. Keeble, *The Restoration: England in the 1660s* (Wiley-Blackwell, 2002), p. 42.

6   Robert Brenner, *Merchants and Revolution: Commercial Change, Political Conflict and London's Overseas Traders, 1550–1653* (Verso, 2003), p. 4.

7   Mentz, *The English Gentleman Merchant*, op. cit., p. 232. In later life, Pitt was a patron to over forty people between 1699 and 1709.

8   Dalton, *Thomas Pitt*, op. cit., p. 8.

9   K. N. Chaudhuri, *The Trading World of Asia and the English East India Company 1660–1760* (Cambridge University Press, 1978), p. 419.

10 Dalton, *Thomas Pitt*, op. cit., p. 9.

11 Ibid., p. 10.

12 Davies Gilbert, *The Parochial History of Cornwall, Vol. 2. Founded on the Manuscript Histories of Mr. Hals and Mr. Tonkin; With Additions and Various* (J. B. Nichols and Son, 1838).

13 Dalton, *Thomas Pitt*, op. cit., p. 19.

14 Ibid., p. 20.

15 Ibid., p. 21.

16 Mary Rose (ed.), *The Lancashire Cotton Industry: A History Since 1700* (Lancashire County Books, 1996).

17 Niall Ferguson, *Empire: How Britain Made the Modern World* (Penguin, 2004), p. 12.

18 George White in 'An Account of the Trade to the East Indies' (1691).

19 Mentz, *The English Gentleman Merchant*, p. 149.

20 Chaudhuri, *The Trading World of Asia*, op. cit.

21 Dalton, *Thomas Pitt*, op. cit., p. 25.

22 Ibid., p. 27.

23 Ibid., pp. 29–30.

24 Ibid., p. 36.

25 'Budgerows' is the name of boats used on the Ganges; 'Rashpots', or Rajputs, were the cavalry; and 'Peons' were foot soldiers.

26 Ibid., p. 33.

27 Ibid., p. 45.

28 Brenner, *Merchants and Revolution*, op. cit., p. 376.

29 John Carswell, *The South Sea Bubble* (Alan Sutton, 1993).

30 George-James Welbore Agar Ellis, *The Ellis Correspondence. Letters Written During the Years 1686, Vol. 2* (Henry Colburn, 1829), p. 103.

31 John Keay, *The Honourable Company: A History of the East India Company* (HarperCollins, 1993), p. 174.

32 Dalton, *Thomas Pitt*, op. cit., p. 52.

33 Ibid., p. 64.

34 Keay, *The Honourable Company*, p. 175.

35 Asa Briggs, *A Social History of England* (Penguin Books, 1991), p. 151.

36 Briggs, *A Social History of Britain*, op. cit., p. 152.

37 Carswell, *South Sea Bubble*, op. cit., p. 7.

38 Brenner, *Merchants and Revolution*, op. cit., p. 712.

39 P. Earle, *The World of Defoe* (Weidenfeld & Nicolson, 1976), p. 34.

40 John Strype, *A Survey of the Cities of London and Westminster*, 1720, quoted in White, *A Great and Monstrous Thing*, op. cit., p. 177.

41 White, *A Great and Monstrous Thing*, op. cit., p. 167.

42 Earle, *The World of Defoe*, op. cit., p. 81.

43 Briggs, *A Social History of England*, op. cit., p. 152.

44 White, *A Great and Monstrous Thing*, op. cit., p. 187.

45 Dalton, *Thomas Pitt*, op. cit., p. 67.

46 Keay, *The Honourable Company*, op. cit., p. 177.

47 K. N. Chaudhuri and Jonathan Israel, *The English and Dutch East India Companies and the Glorious Revolution of 1688–9* in Jonathan Israel (ed.), *The Anglo-Dutch Moment: Essays on the Glorious Revolution and Its World Impact* (Cambridge University Press, 1991) p. 416.

48 Keay, *The Honourable Company*, op. cit., p. 178.

49 Ibid., p. 176.

50 Chaudhuri and Israel in Israel, *The Anglo-Dutch Moment*, op. cit., p. 420.

51 J. S. Bromley, *Corsairs and Navies, 1600–1760* (Hambledon, 1987), p. 214.

52 The French lost control once again after the Battle of La Hogue in 1691.

53 Dalton, *Thomas Pitt*, op. cit., p. 74.

54 Chaudhuri, *The Trading World of Asia*, op. cit., p. 430.

55 Ibid., pp. 430–31.

56 Dalton, *Thomas Pitt*, op. cit., p. 81.

57 Ibid., p. 96.

58 Ibid., p. 100.

59 Mentz, *The English Gentleman Merchant*, op. cit., p. 78.

60 Masulipatam is today's Machilipatnam, on the Bay of Bengal coast.

61 Ibid., p. 198.

62 Sarah Levitt, 'Clothing', in Rose, *Lancashire Cotton Industry*, op. cit., p. 129.

63 'Cast Account of the Humble Thomas Pitt Esq with Madam Jane Pitt', August 1700.

64 Mentz, *The English Gentleman*, op. cit., p. 141.

65 Ibid., p. 91.

66 Ibid., p. 124.

67 P. G. M. Dickson and J. Sperling, 'War Finance 1689–1714', in J. S. Bromley (ed.), *The New Cambridge Modern History, Vol. VI* (Cambridge University Press, 1970), p. 285.

68 Paul Kennedy, *The Rise and Fall of Great Powers: Economic Change and Military Conflict from 1500–2000* (Vintage, 1989).

69 Quoted in John Brewer, *The Sinews of Power: War, Money, and the English State, 1688–1783* (Unwin Hyman, 1989), p. 91.

70 Sir Robert Southwell to Samuel Pepys. Quoted Sir John Clapham, *The Bank of England: A History* (Cambridge University Press, 1944), p. 14.

71 Clapham, *The Bank of England*, op. cit., p. 16.

72 Chaudhuri and Israel in Israel, *The Anglo-Dutch Moment*, op, cit., p. 407.

73 Anne Murphy, 'The Financial Revolution and Its Consequences', in Roderick Floud, Jane Humphries and Paul Johnson (eds), *The Cambridge Economic History of Modern Britain, Vol. 1, 1700–1870* (Cambridge University Press, 2014). The old East India Company had bid a loan of £700,000 at 4 per cent interest.

74 Chaudhuri, *The Trading World of Asia*, op. cit., p. 434.

75 Dalton, *Thomas Pitt*, p. 155.

76 Ibid., p. 153.

77 Ibid., p. 183.

78 Ibid., p. 167.

79 Ibid., p. 173.

80 Ibid., p. 191.

81 Ibid.

82 Ibid., p. 197.

83 Ibid., p. 225.

84 Ibid., p. 229.

85 Ibid., p. 313. Pitt et al. to directors 20 December 1707.

86 Ibid., p. 323.

87 Ibid., p. 332.

88 Ibid., p. 291.

89 Ibid., p. 294.

90 Ibid.

91 Ibid., p. 333.

92 Ibid., p. 337.

93 Mentz, *The English Merchant Gentleman*, op, cit., p. 200.

94 Dalton, *Thomas Pitt*, op. cit., p. 360.

95 Ibid., p. 431.

96 Ibid., p. 409.

97 Ibid., p. 456.

98 Ibid., p. 483.

99 Carswell, *The South Sea Bubble*, op. cit., pp. 87–9.

100 Dalton, *Thomas Pitt*, op, cit., p. 552.

4. Matthew Boulton

1   *Newcastle Courant* (19 August 1786).
2   Ibid.
3   *The Scots Magazine* (1 June 1787).
4   www.bl.uk/collection-items/broadside-albion-mills-on-fire
5   *Stamford Mercury* (4 March 1791).
6   John Rule, 'Manufacturing and Commerce' in H. T. Dickenson (ed.), *A Companion to Eighteenth-Century Britain* (Blackwell, 2006), p. 129.
7   Rule, 'Manufacturing and Commerce', op. cit, p. 134.
8   William Hutton, *The History of Birmingham* (James Guest, 1836), pp. 161–2.
9   Ibid., p. 165.
10 Arthur Raistrick, *Dynasty of Iron Founders* (Longmans, 1953), p. 18.
11 Ibid., p. 38.
12 Ibid., p. 20.
13 T. S. Ashton, *An Economic History of England: The 18th Century* (Methuen, 1955), p. 120.
14 J. H. Plumb, *England in the Eighteenth Century* (Penguin, 1990), p. 23.
15 W. B. Stephens (ed.), *A History of the County of Warwick: The City of Birmingham, Vol. VII* (Victorian County History, 1964).
16 Jenny Uglow, *The Lunar Men: The Friends Who Made the Future 1730–1810* (Faber & Faber, 2003), p. 19.
17 W. Smith in Stephens (ed.), *A History of the County of Warwick*, op. cit., p. 38.
18 Hutton, *History of Birmingham*, op. cit., pp. 161–2.
19 Samuel Smiles, *Lives of Boulton and Watt* (John Murray, 1865), p. 164.
20 Asa Briggs, *Victorian Cities* (University of California Press, 1963), p. 241.
21 Ibid.
22 Smiles, *Boulton and Watt*, op. cit., p. 164.
23 Stephens (ed.), *A History of the County of Warwick*, op. cit., p. 209. 'If Hutton's analysis of wealth and income in 1783 is any guide, there were by then 209 people in a town of 50,000 inhabitants who were worth more than £5,000 and of these 103 "began the world with nothing but their own prudence".'
24 Uglow, *The Lunar Men*, op. cit., p. 57.
25 Sylvia Crawley in Sheila Mason (ed.), *Matthew Boulton: Selling What All the World Desires* (Birmingham City Council in association with Yale University Press, 2009), p. 122.
26 Smiles, *Boulton and Watt*, op. cit., p. 165.
27 Uglow, *The Lunar Men*, op. cit., p. 65.
28 Ibid., p. 60.
29 Mason (ed.), *Matthew Boulton*, op. cit., p. 3.
30 Val Loggie, 'Picturing Soho' in Mason (ed.), *Matthew Boulton*, op. cit., p. 23.
31 Ibid.

32　Smiles, *Lives of Boulton and Watt*, op. cit., p. 169.

33　Loggie, 'Picturing Soho', op. cit., p. 23.

34　Smiles, *Lives of Boulton and Watt*, op. cit., p. 170.

35　Uglow, *The Lunar Men*, op. cit., p. 69.

36　Mason (ed.), *Matthew Boulton*, op. cit., p. 3.

37　Loggie, 'Picturing Soho', op. cit., p. 23.

38　Smiles, *Lives of Boulton and Watt*, op. cit., p. 176.

39　Ibid., p. 175.

40　Uglow, *The Lunar Men*, op. cit., p. 7.

41　John Gribbin, *The Fellowship: The Story of a Revolution* (Penguin, 2005), p. 271.

42　Roy Porter, *Enlightenment: Britain and the Creation of the Modern World* (Allen Lane, 2001), p. 36.

43　Ibid., p. 6.

44　Gribbin, *The Fellowship*, op. cit., p. 192.

45　Ibid., p. 267.

46　Mason (ed.), *Matthew Boulton*, op. cit., p. 135.

47　Uglow, *The Lunar Men*, op. cit., p. 53.

48　G. M. Trevelyan, *English Social History: A Survey of Six Centuries, Chaucer to Queen Victoria* (Longmans, 1978), p. 261.

49　Uglow, *The Lunar Men*, op. cit., p. 132.

50　Nicholas Goodison in Mason (ed.), *Matthew Boulton*, op. cit., p. 55.

51　Peter Borsay, 'Urban Life and Culture', in Dickenson, *Eighteenth-Century Britain*, op. cit., pp. 196–7. Quoted in Earle, *The World of Defoe*, op. cit., p. 44.

52　Earle, *The World of Defoe*, op. cit., p. 166. These patterns of consumption and behaviour would persist, in London at least, until the First World War.

53　Earle, *The World of Defoe*, op. cit., p. 118.

54　Smiles, *Boulton and Watt*, op. cit., p. 177.

55　Uglow, *The Lunar Men*, op. cit., p. 195.

56　Ibid., p. 198.

57　Smiles, *Boulton and Watt*, op. cit., p. 177.

58　Ibid., p. 180.

59　Ibid.

60　Ibid.

61　Laura Cox in Mason (ed.), *Matthew Boulton*, op. cit., p. 161.

62　Uglow, *The Lunar Men*, op. cit., p. 119. He was referring to the Birmingham Navigation Trust.

63　Sally Baggott in Mason (ed.), *Matthew Boulton*, op. cit., p. 47.

64　Ibid.

65　Patrick Dillon, *The Last Revolution* (Jonathan Cape, 2006), p. 382.

66　Uglow, *The Lunar Men*, op. cit., p. 101.

67　Ibid., p. 103.

68　Smiles, *Boulton and Watt*, op. cit., p. 185.

69　Smiles, *Boulton and Watt*, op. cit., p. 186.

70 Uglow, *The Lunar Men*, op. cit., p. 133.

71 R. S. Fitton & Alfred Wadsworth, *The Strutts and the Arkwrights, 1758–1830* (Manchester University Press, 1963), ch. 5.

72 Rule, 'Manufacturing and Commerce', op. cit, p. 133.

73 *Shrewsbury Chronicle* (20 January 1781).

74 Rule, 'Manufacturing and Commerce', op. cit., p. 130. Between 1701 and 1710, the great Newcastle coalfields were producing 183,000 tonnes per year, rising to 758,000 tonnes by 1791. Ashton, *An Economic History of England*, op. cit., p. 124.

75 Uglow, *The Lunar Men*, op. cit., p. 248.

76 Ibid., p. 255.

77 Ibid., p. 257.

78 Letter dated 24 February 1776. Smiles, *Boulton and Watt*, op. cit., p. 216.

79 Jennifer Tann, *The Selected Paper of Boulton & Watt: The Engine Partnership 1775–1825, Vol. I* (MIT, 1981), p. 5.

80 Letter dated 24 February 1776. Smiles, *Boulton and Watt*, op. cit., p. 233.

81 Uglow, *The Lunar Men*, op. cit., p. 286.

82 Uglow, *The Lunar Men*, op. cit., p. 291.

83 Smiles, *Boulton and Watt*, op. cit. p. 262.

84 Uglow, *The Lunar Men*, op. cit., p. 294.

85 Ibid., p. 363.

86 Letter dated 17 April 1786. Smiles, *Boulton and Watt*, op. cit., p. 357.

87 Uglow, *The Lunar Men*, op. cit., p. 268.

88 Ibid., p. 368.

89 Ibid., p. 369.

90 Sue Tungate, 'Matthew Bolton's Mints: Copper to Customer', in Mason (ed.), *Matthew Boulton*, op. cit., p. 87.

91 David Symons, 'Bringing to Perfection the Art of Coining', in Mason (ed.), *Matthew Boulton*, op. cit., p. 89.

92 Tungate, 'Matthew Bolton's Mints', op. cit., p. 81.

93 Ibid., p. 83.

94 Uglow, *The Lunar Men*, op. cit., p. 627.

95 Richard Hills, *James Watt: His Time in Scotland* (Landmark Publishing, 1993), p. 112.

96 Letter from Erasmus Darwin to Matthew Boulton, 1783/03/04, Derby Mar. 48.

97 Gilbert Hamilton to James Watt, 20 October 1784, MS 3219/4/19/31.

98 Richard Hills, *Power in the Industrial Revolution* (Manchester University Press, 1970), p. 154.

99 W. H. Chaloner, 'Robert Owen, Peter Drinkwater and the Early Factory System in Manchester 1788–1800' in *Bulletin of the John Rylands Library*, 1954.

100 Ibid., p. 86.

101 Michael M. Edwards, *The Growth of the British Cotton Trade, 1780–1815* (Manchester University Press, 1967), pp. 205–10.

102 James Watt junior to James Watt. A. E. Musson & E. Robinson, *Science and Technology in the Industrial Revolution* (Manchester University Press, 1969), p. 423.

103 Peter Drinkwater to Boulton and Watt, 3 April 1789.

104 James Watt junior to James Watt, 4 April 1789, MS 3219/4/12/25.

105 Ibid.

106 The designs lie in the Boulton and Watt archives; Peter Drinkwater, Pump engine, Picture A3. 31 April–May 1789.

107 Benj Lees to Boulton & Watt, 17 January 1791. Tann, *The Selected Papers of Boulton & Watt*, op. cit., p. 305.

108 Edwards, *The Growth of the British Cotton Trade*, op. cit., p. 204; Hills, *Power in the Industrial Revolution*, op. cit., p. 159.

109 Tann, *The Selected Papers of Boulton & Watt*, op. cit., p. 6.

110 Uglow, *The Lunar Men*, op. cit., p. 467.

111 Smiles, *Boulton and Watt*, op. cit., p. 359.

112 Tann, *The Selected Papers of Boulton & Watt*, op. cit., p. 9.

113 Uglow, *The Lunar Men*, op. cit., p. 468.

114 Ibid., p. 469.

115 Ibid., p. 470.

116 David Symons, 'Bringing to Perfection the Art of Coining', op. cit., p. 98.

117 Tungate, 'Matthew Boulton's Mints', op. cit.

118 Mason (ed.), *Matthew Boulton*, op. cit., p. 228.

119 Ibid., p. 230.

5. Nathan Rothschild

1 Quoted in Asa Briggs, *The Age of Improvement, 1783–1867* (Pearson, 2000), p. 139.

2 Quoted in Christopher Kelly, *A Full and Circumstantial Account of the Memorable Battle of Waterloo* (Rider and Weed, 1817), p. 261.

3 R. H. Gronow, *The Reminiscences and Recollections of Captain Gronow* (Smith Elder and Co., 1864), p. 99.

4 Ibid.

5 See Robert Liberles, 'The World of Dietz's Stammbuch: Frankfurt Jewry: 1349–1870' in Isobel Mordy (ed.), *The Jewish Community of Frankfurt: A Genealogical Study by Alexander Dietz* (Vanderher, 1988).

6 Ibid., p. v.

7 Ibid.

8 Heinrich Heine quoted in ibid.

9 Mary Rose (ed.), *The Lancashire Cotton Industry: A History Since 1700* (Lancashire County Books, 1996).

10 Ibid., p. 156.

11 Ibid., p. 157.

12 Thomas Ridgway in 1799, quoted in R. S. Fitton, *The Arkwrights, Spinners of Fortune* (Manchester University Press, 1989), ch. 1.

13 Fitton, *The Arkwrights*, op. cit.

14 Ibid.

15 Kristine Bruland, 'Industrialisation and Technological Change', in Roderick Floud, Jane Humphries and Paul Johnson (eds), *The Cambridge Economic History of Modern Britain, Vol. 1* (Cambridge University Press, 2004).

16 Sir Peter Hall, *Cities in Civilization* (Pantheon, 1998), p. 313.

17 Michael Edwards, *Growth of the British Cotton Trade 1780–1815* (Manchester University Press, 1967), p. 52, and table b/2 on p. 244.

18 See, for example, Margrit Schulte Beerbuhl, 'Crossing the Channel', in The Rothschild Archive: Review of the Year April 2007–March 2008, pp. 41–2.

19 Asa Briggs, *A Social History of England* (Penguin Books, 1991), ch. 3.

20 Henry Smithers, *Liverpool: Its Commerce, Statistics and Institutions* (Thos Kaye, 1825), p. 119.

21 Ibid.

22 Quoted in Hall, *Cities in Civilization*, op. cit., p. 315. Shalloon is a type of woven wool.

23 John Rule, 'Manufacturing and Commerce' in H. T. Dickenson (ed.), *A Companion to Eighteenth Century Britain* (Blackwell, 2006), p. 130.

24 Pat Hudson, 'Industrial Organization and Structure' in Floud, *The Cambridge Economic History of Modern Britain*, op. cit., p. 37. Only 10 per cent employed more than 100. By 1860 only 30 per cent of workers were engaged in production techniques transformed since 1780.

25 Briggs, *A Social History of England*, op. cit., p. 89.

26 Tristram Hunt, *Building Jerusalem: The Rise and Fall of the Victorian City* (Phoenix, 2005), p. 25.

27 Prussian John Georg May, quoted in ibid., p. 21.

28 Hall, *Cities and Civilizations*, op. cit., p. 344.

29 Hunt, *Building Jerusalem*, op. cit., p. 22.

30 Briggs, *A Social History of England*, op. cit., p. 94.

31 Asa Briggs, *Victorian Cities: Manchester, Leeds, Birmingham, Middlesbrough, Melbourne, London* (University of California Press, 1963), p. 106.

32 Niall Ferguson, *The House of Rothschild: Money's Prophets 1798–1848* (Penguin, 1999), p. 52.

33 Ibid., p. 50.

34 Quoted in Herbert Kaplan, *Nathan Mayer Rothschild and the Creation of a Dynasty: The Critical Years 1806–1816* (Stanford University Press, 2006), p. 5.

35 Ferguson, *The House of Rothschild*, op. cit., p. 52.

36 A. Hertz to N. M. Rothschild, 15 October 1804, Rothschild Archive File Ref: T4/2.

37 A. Hertz to N. M. Rothschild, 11 December 1805, Rothschild Archive File Ref: T4/12.

38 Kaplan, *Nathan Mayer Rothschild*, op. cit., p. 6.

39 Ferguson, *The House of Rothschild*, op. cit., p. 56.

40 Kaplan, *Nathan Mayer Rothschild*, op. cit., p. 25.

41 Ibid., p. 25.

42 Quoted in ibid.

43 Ferguson, *The House of Rothschild*, op. cit., p. 66.

44 Quoted in a letter by the MP Thomas Fowell Buxton, sent on 14 February 1834, quoted in Kaplan, *Nathan Mayer Rothschild*, op. cit., p. 36.

45 See Kaplan, *Nathan Mayer Rothschild*, op. cit., for the best discussion.

46 Ibid., p. 55.

47 Ibid., p. 58.

48 Ibid., p. 60.

49 Mayer & Bruxner to N. M. Rothschild, 16 May 1813, Rothschild Archive File Ref: T4/43.

50 Linda Colley, *Britons: Forging the Nation, 1707–1837* (Yale, 1992), p. 159.

51 See, for instance, Ferguson, *The Ascent of Money*, op. cit., ch. 2.

52 See P. G. M. Dickson and J. Sperling, 'War Finance 1689–1714' in J. S. Bromley (ed.), *The New Cambridge Modern History, Vol. VI* (Cambridge University Press, 1970).

53 Quoted in George Heuberger, *The Rothschilds: A European Family*, (Thorbecke, Boydell, Brewer, 1994), p. 210.

54 Ibid., p. 211.

55 Ibid., p. 200.

56 Quoted in Malcolm Balen, *A Very English Deceit* (Fourth Estate, 2002), p. 5.

57 Philip Ziegler, *The Sixth Great Power: A History of One of the Greatest of All Banking Families, the House of Barings, 1762–1929* (Alfred Knopf, 1988), p. 51.

58 Ibid., p. 58.

59 Quoted in Kaplan, *Nathan Mayer Rothschild*, op. cit., p. 81.

60 Ferguson, *The House of Rothschild*, op. cit., p. 87.

61 Ibid., p. 83.

62 Kaplan, *Nathan Mayer Rothschild*, op. cit., p. 89.

63 Ferguson, *The House of Rothschild*, op. cit., p. 97.

64 N. M. Rothschild to J. M. Rothschild 15 July 1814, Rothschild Archive File Ref: T82/7/4/7.

65 N. M. Rothschild to J. M. Rothschild 9 August 1814, Rothschild Archive File Ref: T82/7/4/15.

66 N. M. Rothschild to J. M. Rothschild 7 October 1814, Rothschild Archive File Ref: T82/7/4/40.

67 Ziegler, *The Sixth Great Power*, op. cit., p. 85.

68 See Heuberger, *The Rothschilds*, op. cit., p. 57.

69 Wilhelm von Humboldt to Count Hardenberg, January 1818, quoted in Heuberger, *The Rothschilds*, op. cit., p. 58.

70 James Rothschild to Nathan Rothschild, 30 March 1818, quoted in ibid.

71 Ferguson, *The House of Rothschild*, op. cit., p. 126.

72 Ibid., p. 138.

73 See Larry Neal, 'The Financial Crisis of 1825', in Federal Reserve Bank of St Louis Review, May/June 1998, p. 56.

74 Quoted in ibid., p. 64.

75 Ferguson, *The House of Rothschild*, op. cit., p. 135.

76 Ibid., p. 137.

77 Ibid.

78 Ibid., p. 162.

79 Ibid., p. 157.

80 *London Standard* (13 June 1828).

81 *The Western Times* (18 October 1828).

82 Ferguson, *The House of Rothschild*, op. cit., p. 146.

83 *Devizes and Wiltshire Gazette* (28 February 1828).

84 Ferguson, *The House of Rothschild*, op. cit., p. 235.

85 Ibid., p. 268.

86 Ibid., p. 215.

87 Ibid., p. 217.

88 Ibid.

89 Lionel de Rothschild to his parents, 27 July 1830, Rothschild Archive File Ref: T17/174.

90 Lionel de Rothschild to his parents, 1 August 1830, Rothschild Archive File Ref: T17/170.

91 Lionel de Rothschild to his parents, 16 August 1830, Rothschild Archive File Ref: T17/180.

92 Lionel de Rothschild to his parents, 19 January 1831, Rothschild Archive File Ref: T17/128.

93 Ferguson, *The House of Rothschild*, op. cit., p. 228.

94 Ibid., p. 230.

95 *Woolmer's Exeter and Plymouth Gazette* (6 September 1834).

96 Ferguson, *The House of Rothschild*, op. cit., p. 292.

97 Ibid., p. 299.

98 *The Times* (4 August 1836).

99 Ferguson, *The House of Rothschild*, op. cit., p. 305.

6. William Jardine

1 http://hansard.millbanksystems.com/commons/1841/jan/26/her-majestys-speech-the-address

2 Edward Belcher, *Narrative of a Voyage Round the World: Performed in Her Majesty's Ship Sulphur, During the Years 1836–1842, Including Details of the Naval Operations* (Henry Colburn, 1843), pp. 147–8.

3 James Matheson to William Jardine, 30 January 1841, quoted in Alain Le Pichon, *China Trade and Empire: Jardine, Matheson & Co. and the Origins of British Rule in Hong Kong 1827–1843* (Oxford University Press, 2006), p. 468.

4 Daniel Defoe, 'Letter XI: South-Eastern Scotland' in *A Tour Through the Whole Island of Great Britain* (S. Birt, T. Osborne, 1748).

5 For a wonderful description of nineteenth-century Macao, see Maurice Collis, *Foreign Mud: Being an Account of the Opium Imbroglio at Canton in the 1830's and the Anglo-Chinese War that Followed* (Faber and Faber, 1946).

6 Robert Blake, *Jardine Matheson: Traders of the Far East* (Weidenfeld & Nicolson, 1999), p. 21.

7 William C. Hunter, *The 'Fan Kwae' at Canton Before Treaty Days 1825–1844* (William C. Hunter, 1882).

8 Thomas Macaulay, 'Lord Clive' in *Critical and Historical Essays* (Methuen & Co., 1903), p. 394.

9 A. J. Arbuthnot, *Lord Clive: The Foundation of British Rule in India* (T. Fisher Unwin, 1897), p. 2.

10 M. Bence-Jones, *Clive of India* (Constable & Co. Ltd, 1974), p. 90.

11 Niall Ferguson, *Empire: How Britain Made the Modern World* (Penguin, 2004), p. 12.

12 Ibid., p. 15.

13 Linda Colley, *Britons: Forging the Nation 1707–1837*, (Yale University Press, 1992), p. 125.

14 Ibid., p. 132.

15 See Thomas Dormandy, *Opium: Reality's Dark Dream* (Yale, 2012).

16 Blake, *Jardine Matheson*, op. cit., p. 28.

17 Julia Lovell, *The Opium War: Drugs, Dreams and the Making of China* (Picador, 2011), p. 21.

18 Ibid., p. 22.

19 Blake, *Jardine Matheson*, op. cit., p. 29.

20 Lovell, *The Opium War*, op. cit., p. 33.

21 Dormandy, *Opium*, op. cit., p. 64.

22 Ibid., p. 64.

23 Blake, *Jardine Matheson*, op. cit., p. 27.

24 See Michael Greenberg, *British Trade and the Opening of China 1800–42* (Cambridge Studies in Economic History, 1951).

25 John Keay, *The Honourable Company: A History of the East India Company* (HarperCollins, 1993), p. 431.

26 Asa Briggs, *The Age of Improvement, 1783–1867* (Routledge, 1999), p. 219.

27 Quoted in Greenberg, *British Trade*, op. cit., p. 176.

28 Ibid., p. 176.

29 *Manchester Mercury*, 29 April 1829.

30 Greenberg, *British Trade*, op. cit., p. 177.

31 James Matheson to W. R. Paton, 17 January 1831, quoted in Le Pichon, *China Trade and Empire*, op. cit., p. 111.

32   Henry Kissinger, *On China* (Penguin, 2012), p. 33.

33   J. L. Cranmer-Byng (ed.), *An Embassy to China: Journal of Lord Macartney* (Longmans, 1962), p. 12.

34   Quoted in Kissinger, *On China*, op. cit., p. 37.

35   See Cranmer-Byng, *An Embassy to China*, op. cit., p. 7.

36   Ibid., p. 150.

37   Greenberg, *British Trade*, op. cit., p. 175.

38   Ibid., p. 30.

39   *Morning Post* (12 July 1833).

40   Horatio Hardy to Jardine Matheson, 26 June 1833, quoted in Le Pichon, *China Trade and Empire*, op. cit., p. 193.

41   Jardine to Thomas Weeding, 20 April 1834, quoted in Le Pichon, *China Trade and Empire*, op. cit., p. 208.

42   Greenberg, *British Trade*, op. cit., p. 189.

43   Blake, *Jardine Matheson*, op. cit., p. 53.

44   Quoted in ibid., p. 53.

45   M. Keswick, *The Thistle and the Jade: A Celebration of 150 Years of Jardine, Matheson & Co.* (Octopus, 1982), p. 23.

46   Blake, *Jardine Matheson*, op. cit., p. 64.

47   Ibid., p. 69.

48   Ibid., p. 71.

49   Lovell, *The Opium War*, op. cit., p. 49.

50   Ibid., p. 60.

51   Lovell, *The Opium War*, op. cit., p. 63.

52   Ibid., p. 64.

53   Jardine to Matheson, 25–27 September, 1839 quoted in Le Pichon, *China Trade and Empire*, op. cit., p. 387.

54   Lovell, *The Opium War*, op. cit., p. 79.

55   There are four letters: MS JM B1/8/P12, MS JM B1/10/P38 and P41, and MS JM B6/8/717, a reference for which I thank John Wells of the Manuscripts and Archive department at Cambridge University.

56   MS JM B1/8/P12.

57   Lovell, *The Opium War*, op. cit., p. 95.

58   William Jardine to James Matheson, 25–27 September 1839, quoted in Le Pichon, *China Trade and Empire*, op. cit., p. 387.

59   Ibid., p. 388.

60   Ibid., p. 387.

61   Extract from Mr Jardine's Letter of 5 October 1839, Jardine Matheson Archives.

62   Quoted in Le Pichon, *China Trade and Empire*, op. cit., p. 388, footnote 97.

63   William Crawford to Robert Wigram Crawford in Bombay, 14 October 1839, quoted in Le Pichon, *China Trade and Empire*, op. cit., p. 393.

64   William Jardine to James Matheson, 3 December 1939, quoted in Le Pichon, *China Trade and Empire*, op. cit., p. 407.

65 Keswick, *The Thistle and the Jade*, op. cit., p. 24.

66 See Lovell, *The Opium War*, op. cit., p. 120.

67 Quoted in Le Pichon, *China Trade and Empire*, op. cit., p. 34.

68 Keswick, *The Thistle and the Jade*, op. cit., p. 78.

69 Lovell, *The Opium War*, op. cit., p. 154.

70 Ibid., p. 170.

71 Keswick, *The Thistle and the Jade*, op. cit., p. 25.

72 Ibid., p. 74.

73 HC Deb, 17 March 1842, Vol. 61, cc759-97759.

74 Palmerston to John Abel Smith 28 November 1842. Quoted in Le Pichon, *China Trade and Empire*, op. cit., p. 44.

75 William Jardine to Jamsetjee Jeejeebhoy on 2 December 1842, quoted in Le Pichon, *China Trade and Empire*, op. cit., p. 520.

76 John Abel Smith to Jamsetjee Jeejeebhoy on 6 January 1843, quoted in Le Pichon, *China Trade and Empire*, op. cit., p. 522.

77 James Mattheson to Jamsetjee Jeejeebhoy, 3 March 1843, quoted in Le Pichon, *China Trade and Empire*, op. cit., pp. 523–4.

78 *Aberdeen Journal* (10 May 1842).

79 Keswick, *The Thistle and the Jade*, op. cit., p. 35.

80 *Aberdeen Journal* (10 May 1842).

7. George Hudson

1 *Leeds Mercury* (1 June 1839).

2 *Yorkshire Gazette* (1 June 1839).

3 Ibid.

4 Ibid.

5 Ibid.

6 Ibid.

7 *Leeds Mercury* (1 June 1839).

8 *Railway Intelligence* (5 June 1839).

9 A. J. Arnold and S. McCartney, *George Hudson: The Rise and Fall of the Railway King* (Cambridge University Press, 2004), p. 1.

10 Robert Beaumont, *The Railway King: A Biography of George Hudson* (Headline, 2002), p. 8.

11 Brian Bailey, *George Hudson: The Rise and Fall of the Railway King* (Sutton Publishing, 1995), p. 3.

12 Cordelia Stamp, *George Hudson and Whitby* (Caedmon of Whitby, 2005), p. 1.

13 Beaumont, *The Railway King*, op. cit., p. 9.

14 N. Gash after Waterloo, quoted in Linda Colley, *Britons: Forging the Nation, 1707–1837* (Yale, 1992), p. 146.

15 Asa Briggs, *A Social History of England* (Book Club Associates, 1983), p. 204.

16 Bailey, *George Hudson*, op. cit., p. 4.

17 Arnold and McCartney, *George Hudson*, op. cit., p. 2.

18 Beaumont, *The Railway King*, op. cit., p. 15.

19 Bailey, *George Hudson*, op. cit., pp. 149–50.

20 David Morier Evans, *Facts, Failures and Frauds* (Groombridge & Sons, 1859), p. 19.

21 Arnold and McCartney, *George Hudson*, op. cit., p. 3.

22 A. J. Peacock, *George Hudson: The Railway King Vol. 1* (Viking Press, 1988), p. 9.

23 Quoted in Stamp, *George Hudson and Whitby*, op. cit.

24 Ibid.

25 Quoted in *Victoria County History*, 1833, reports to Municipal Corporation Commissioners.

26 See *Yorkshire County History Vol. ??*, p. 438.

27 Quoted in R. G. Wilson, *Gentlemen Merchants: The Merchant Community in Leeds 1700–1830* (Manchester, 1971), p. 238.

28 J. James, *History of the Worsted Manufacture in England from the Earliest Times* (1857), pp. 238–9.

29 See Geoffrey Tweedale, *Steel City: Entrepreneurship, Strategy, and Technology in Sheffield 1743–1993* (Oxford University Press, 1995), pp. 29–40.

30 Pat Hudson, 'Industrial Organisation and Structure' in Roderick Floud and Paul Johnson (eds), *The Cambridge Economic History of Modern Britain: Vol. 1. Industrialisation, 1700–1860* (Cambride University Press, 2004), p. 32.

31 Ibid., pp. 51–2.

32 Quoted in Peacock, *George Hudson*, op. cit., p. 17.

33 Arnold and McCartney, *George Hudson*, p. 10.

34 Quoted in Peacock, *George Hudson*, op. cit., p. 14.

35 Beaumont, *The Railway King*, op. cit., p. 21.

36 Another 265 residents did recover from the disease.

37 *The Yorkshire Gazette* (28 July 1832).

38 Quoted in Peacock, *George Hudson*, op. cit., p. 24.

39 Bailey, *George Hudson*, op. cit., p. 8.

40 Beaumont, *The Railway King*, op. cit., p. 23.

41 Steven Brindle, *Brunel: The Man Who Built the World* (Weidenfeld & Nicolson, 2005), p. 76.

42 Christian Wolmar, *Fire and Steam* (Atlantic, 2007), p. 24.

43 Overwhelmingly, coal was needed for the iron trade, which accounted for a quarter of the increase between 1775 and 1830, but by 1830, nearly half of the nation's 30 million tonnes was going to heat homes.

44 Martin Daunton, *Progress and Poverty: An Economic and Social History of Britain, 1700–1850* (OUP, 1995), p. 219.

45 Roger Burt, 'The Extractive Industries' in Floud and Johnson (eds), *Cambridge Economic History*, op. cit., p. 422.

46   Wolmar, *Fire and Steam*, op. cit.

47   *Leeds Intelligencer* (6 October 1825).

48   Wolmar, *Fire and Steam*, op. cit., p. 21.

49   Ibid., p. 3.

50   *Liverpool Mercury* (10 September 1830).

51   Bailey, *George Hudson*, op. cit., p. 8.

52   Quoted in Peacock, *George Hudson*, op. cit., p. 40.

53   Ibid., p. 41.

54   Beaumont, *The Railway King*, op. cit., p. 26.

55   Bailey, *George Hudson,* op. cit., p. 16.

56   Beaumont, *The Railway King*, op. cit., p. 34.

57   Ibid., p. 32.

58   *Yorkshire Gazette* (January 1836).

59   Bailey, *George Hudson,* op. cit., p. 16.

60   *Yorkshire Gazette* (11 November 1837).

61   Quoted in Peacock, *George Hudson*, op. cit., ch. 7.

62   Ibid., p. 72.

63   *Leeds Intelligencer* (1 June 1839).

64   Wolmar, *Fire and Steam*, op. cit., p. 63.

65   Arnold and McCartney, *George Hudson*, op. cit., p. 39.

66   *York Herald* (4 July 1840).

67   Bailey, *George Hudson*, op. cit., p. 23.

68   Beaumont, *The Railway King*, op. cit., p. 47.

69   Arnold and McCartney, *George Hudson*, op. cit., p. 41.

70   *Leeds Intelligencer* (14 November 1840).

71   Quoted in Peacock, *George Hudson*, op. cit., ch. 9.

72   Arnold and McCartney, *George Hudson*, op. cit., p. 43.

73   Ibid., p. 44.

74   Ibid.

75   Bailey, *George Hudson,* op. cit., p. 26.

76   Arnold and McCartney, *George Hudson*, op. cit., p. 60.

77   Ibid.

78   Beaumont, *The Railway King*, op. cit., p. 59.

79   Arnold and McCartney, *George Hudson*, op. cit., p. 83.

80   Quoted in Peacock, *George Hudson*, op. cit., p. 97.

81   Ibid., p. 105.

82   Cited in Arnold and McCartney, *George Hudson*, op. cit., p. 92.

83   Ibid.

84   Beaumont, *George Hudson*, op. cit., p. 66.

85   Ibid., p. 70.

86   Beaumont, *George Hudson*, op. cit., p. 64.

87   Bailey, *George Hudson,* op. cit., p. 38.

88   Arnold and McCartney, *George Hudson*, p. 132.

89   Arnold and McCartney, *George Hudson*, p. 66.

90 Beaumont, *George Hudson*, op. cit., p. 73.

91 Arnold and McCartney, *George Hudson*, op. cit., p. 70.

92 Beaumont, *The Railway King*, op. cit., p. 75.

93 Quoted in Arnold and McCartney, *George Hudson*, op. cit., p. 140.

94 *Newcastle Journal* (26 July 1845) quoted in Arnold and McCartney, *George Hudson*, op. cit., p. 140.

95 Bailey, *George Hudson,* op. cit., p. 54.

96 Beaumont, *The Railway King,* op. cit., p. 82.

97 Peacock, *George Hudson*, op. cit., p. 7.

98 Arnold and McCartney, *George Hudson*, op. cit., p. 171.

99 Bailey, *George Hudson,* op. cit., p. 66.

100 Beaumont, *The Railway King*, op. cit., p. 76.

101 Quoted in Arnold and McCartney, *George Hudson*, op. cit., p. 112.

102 Ibid.

103 Quoted in Arnold and McCartney, *George Hudson*, op. cit., p. 113.

104 Bailey, *George Hudson,* op. cit., p. 84.

105 Arnold and McCartney, op. cit., p. 120.

106 Beaumont, *The Railway King*, op. cit., p. 106.

107 *Newcastle Journal* (7 August 1847).

108 Bailey, *George Hudson*, op. cit., p. 67.

109 Beaumont, *The Railway King*, op. cit., p. 103.

110 Arnold and McCartney, *George Hudson*, op. cit., p. 109.

111 Bailey, *George Hudson,* op. cit., p. 90.

112 Beaumont, *The Railway King*, op. cit., p. 110.

113 Ibid., p. 113.

114 Bailey, *George Hudson*, op. cit., p. 93.

115 David Morier, *Facts, Failures and Frauds*, op. cit., p. 46.

116 Quoted in *The Examiner* (3 March 1849).

117 Quoted in Morier, *Facts, Failures and Frauds*, op. cit., p. 53.

118 Beaumont, *The Railway King*, op. cit., p. 119.

119 Quoted in Morier, *Facts, Failures and Frauds*, op. cit.

120 Ibid.

121 Graham Dalling, *Enfield's Railway King*, Edmonton Historical Society, Occasional Paper New Series, No. 38.

122 Ibid.

123 Beaumont, *The Railway King*, op. cit., p. 126. See HC Deb 17 May 1849, Vol. 105 c581.

124 http://hansard.millbanksystems.com/commons/1849/may/17/eastern-counties-railway#S3V0105P0_18490517_HOC_5

125 Arnold and McCartney, *George Hudson*, op. cit., p. 206.

126 Ibid., p. 132.

127 Arnold and McCartney, *George Hudson*, op. cit., p. 204.

128 Bailey, *George Hudson*, op. cit., p. 123.

129 Ibid., p. 130.

130 Ibid., p. 159.

131 Ibid., p. 165.

132 Quoted in Morier, *Facts, Failures and Frauds*, op. cit., p. 71.

133 Ibid. p. 171.

134 Bailey, *George Hudson,* op. cit., p. 140.

135 *York Herald* (24 June 1865).

136 Arnold and McCartney, *George Hudson*, op. cit., p. 231.

137 Beaumont, *The Railway King*, p. 192.

138 Bailey, *George Hudson,* op. cit., p. 144.

139 Figure from Arnold and McCartney, *George Hudson*, p. 233.

140 Bailey, *George Hudson,* op. cit., p. 147.

141 Beaumont, *The Railway King*, op. cit., p. 198.

142 Arnold and McCartney, *George Hudson*, op. cit., p. 235.

143 Beaumont, *The Railway King*, op. cit., p. 203.

144 *Sheffield Independent* (22 December 1871).

145 Beaumont, *The Railway King*, op. cit., p. 209.

146 T. A. B. Corley, 'Britain's Overseas Investments in 1914 Revisited', *Business History*, 36 (Jan. 1994), p. 80.

8. George Cadbury

1   *Bournville Works Magazine*, No. 6, Vol. XVII.

2   *Dundee Courier* (24 May 1919).

3   *Birmingham Daily Post* (19 October 1918).

4   Gillian Wagner, *The Chocolate Conscience* (Chatto & Windus, 1987), p. 39.

5   Deborah Cadbury, *Chocolate Wars: From Cadbury to Kraft: 200 years of Sweet Success and Bitter Rivalry* (Harper Press, 2010), p. 4.

6   I. A. Williams, 'Cadbury, George (1839–1922)' (*Oxford Dictionary of National Biography*, 2004), p. 3.

7   Carl Chinn, *The Cadbury Story: A Short History* (Brewin Books, 1998), p. 4.

8   Wagner, *The Chocolate Conscience*, op. cit., p. 9.

9   Ibid., p. 10.

10 Ibid., p. 13.

11 Ibid., p. 31.

12 Williams, *George Cadbury*, op. cit., p. 14.

13 Cadbury, *Chocolate Wars*, op. cit.

14 Williams, *George Cadbury*, op. cit., p. 18.

15 Ibid., p. 28.

16 See A. G. Gardiner, *The Life of George Cadbury* (Cassell and Company, 1923), p. 188.

17 Ibid., p. 14.

18 Ibid., p. 15.

19   Ibid., p. 190.

20   Charles Dellheim, 'The Creation of a Company Culture: Cadburys, 1861–1931', in *The American Historical Review*, Vol. 92, No. 1 (Feb 1987), p. 16.

21   Ibid.

22   Wagner, *The Chocolate Conscience*, op, cit., p. 33.

23   J. Crosfield, *A History of the Cadbury Family* (1985), p. 436.

24   See *Birmingham Daily Post* (14 March 1860).

25   Dellheim, 'The Creation of a Company Culture', op. cit., p. 17.

26   From a speech delivered on 1/15/1846, quoted in Aaron Friedberg, *Weary Titan* (Princeton, 1988), p. 29.

27   Stephen Broadberry, *Market Services and the Productivity Race, 1850–2000* (Cambridge University Press, 2009), p. 83.

28   Quoted in Friedberg, *Weary Titan*, op. cit., p. 27.

29   Dellheim, 'The Creation of a Company Culture', op. cit., p. 17.

30   Gardiner, *The Life of George Cadbury*, op, cit., p. 24.

31   Ibid., p. 24.

32   Cadbury, *Chocolate War*, op. cit., p. 56.

33   *Birmingham Daily Post* (24 November 1864).

34   *Birmingham Daily Post* (22 December 1865).

35   Cadbury, *Chocolate Wars*, op. cit., p. 31.

36   Gardiner, *The Life of George Cadbury*, op. cit., p. 25.

37   Ibid., p. 26.

38   Dellheim, 'The Creation of a Company Culture', op. cit., p. 17.

39   Gardiner, *The Life of George Cadbury*, op. cit., p. 27.

40   David Jeremy, *Capitalists and Christians: Business Leaders and the Churches in Britain 1900–1960* (Clarendon Press, 1970), p. 145.

41   Dellheim, 'The Creation of a Company Culture', op. cit., p. 16.

42   Ibid., p. 16.

43   Ian C. Bradley, *Enlightened Entrepreneurs: Business Ethics in Victorian Britain* (Oxford, 2007), p. 135.

44   Gardiner, *The Life of George Cadbury*, op. cit., p. 46.

45   Dellheim, 'The Creation of a Company Culture', op. cit., p. 17.

46   Wagner, *The Chocolate Conscience*, op. cit., p. 34.

47   Dellheim, 'The Creation of a Company Culture', op. cit., p. 17.

48   *Birmingham Daily Post* (20 December 1866).

49   *Birmingham Daily Post* (9 October 1867).

50   *Medical Mirror* (1 February 1868), quoted in *Birmingham Daily Post* (10 March 1868).

51   *Birmingham Daily Post* (6 May 1868).

52   Chinn, *The Cadbury Story*, op. cit., p. 18.

53   Ibid., p. 75.

54   Ibid., p. 18.

55   Wagner, *The Chocolate Conscience*, op. cit., p. 37.

56   Gardiner, *The Life of George Cadbury*, op. cit., p. 63.

57 *Birmingham Daily Post*, (17 July 1878).

58 Gardiner, *The Life of George Cadbury*, op. cit., p. 69.

59 Chinn, *The Cadbury Story*, op. cit., p. 19.

60 Ibid., p. 23.

61 Ibid., p. 20

62 Wagner, *The Chocolate Conscience*, op, cit., p. 57.

63 Ibid.

64 Gardiner, *The Life of George Cadbury*, op. cit., p. 37.

65 *Personal Reminiscences of Bridge Street and Bournville 1870–1929 by 63 men and women living at the time of the Bournville Jubilee 1929*, in the Cadbury archives.

66 Ibid., p. 132.

67 Ibid., p. 33.

68 Dellheim, 'The Creation of a Company Culture', op. cit., p. 19.

69 Patrick Joyce, 'Work' in F. M. L. Thompson (ed.), *The Cambridge Social History of Britain 1750–1950, Vol. 2*, (Cambridge University Press, 1990), p. 32.

70 D. Powell, *Nationhood and Identity: The British State since 1800* (I.B. Tauris, 2002), p. 387.

71 Quoted in Jack Simmons, 'The Power of the Railway' in H. J. Dyos and M. Wolff, *The Victorian City: Image and Realities* (Routledge, 1999), p. 301.

72 Best, *Mid-Victorian Britain*, op. cit., p. 21.

73 Quoted in J. H. and M. M. Clapham, 'Life in the new towns' in G. M. Young (ed.), *Early Victorian England 1830–1865* (Oxford University Press, 1934).

74 Dr John Simon, December 1850, Second Sanitary Report to the City of London, quoted in Best, *Mid-Victorian Britain*, op. cit., p. 60.

75 Thomas Carlyle, *Past and Present* (1843).

76 Quoted in Asa Briggs, 'The Human Aggregate', in H. J. Dyos and Michael Wolff (eds), *Victorian City, Images and Reality*, (London: Routledge and Kegan Paul, 1973), p. 89.

77 See Taylor, 'Ideas in the Air' in H. J. Dyos and Michael Wolff (eds), *Victorian City*, Images and Reality, p. 432.

78 *Illustrated London News*, 1851, quoted in B. Lewis, *So Clean: Lord Leverhulme, Soap and Civilization* (Manchester University Press, 2008), p. 98.

79 Chinn, *The Cadbury Story*, op. cit., p. 23.

80 William Gladstone to George Cadbury, 28 June, 1892. Cadbury replied: 'So far I have felt I can be of most service to my fellow men in connection with religious work, and by taking part in social questions.'

81 Gardiner, *The Life of George Cadbury*, op. cit., p. 143.

82 Crosfield, *Cadbury Family*, op. cit., p. 437.

83 Wagner, *The Chocolate Conscience*, op. cit., p. 58.

84 *Leicester Chronicle* (25 March 1899).

85 Chinn, *The Cadbury Story*, op. cit., p. 37.

86 Williams, *George Cadbury*, op. cit., p. 230.

87 Jeremy, *Capitalists and Christians*, op. cit., p. 144.

88 Ibid., p. 143.

89 Ibid., p. 144.

90 Bradley, *Enlightened Entrepreneurs*, op. cit., p. 139.

91 See Mark Hampton, 'The Press, Patriotism, and Public Discussion: C. P. Scott, the "Manchester Guardian", and the Boer War, 1899-1902', *The Historical Journal*, Vol. 44, No. 1 (March, 2001), p. 185.

92 Gardiner, *The Life of George Cadbury*, op. cit., p. 219.

93 Gardiner, *The Life of George Cadbury*, op. cit., p. 83.

94 Ibid., p. 77.

95 R. Fitzgerald, *Rowntree and the Marketing Revolution*, 1862–1969 (Cambridge University Press, 2007), p. 67.

96 Ibid.

97 *Bournville Works Magazine* (April 1955).

98 George Cadbury jnr at the Representatives Conference, 2 July 1937.

99 Ibid.

100 Chinn, *The Cadbury Story*, op. cit., p. 45.

101 Dellheim, 'The Creation of a Company Culture', op. cit., p. 19.

102 Fitzgerald, Rowntree, op. cit., p. 107.

103 Chinn, *The Cadbury Story*, op. cit., p. 37.

104 Williams, 'George Cadbury', op. cit., p. 136.

105 Dellheim, 'The Creation of a Company Culture', op. cit., p. 36.

106 Jeremy, *Capitalists and Christians*, op. cit., p. 145.

107 Gardiner, *The Life of George Cadbury*, op, cit., p. 244.

108 Ibid.

109 Dellheim, 'The Creation of a Company Culture', op. cit., p. 36.

110 Williams, 'George Cadbury', op. cit, p. 205.

111 Jeremy, *Capitalists and Christians*, op. cit., p. 147.

112 Gardiner, *The Life of George Cadbury*, op. cit., p. 247.

113 Jeremy, *Capitalists and Christians*, op. cit., p. 151.

114 Dellheim, 'The Creation of a Company Culture', op. cit., p. 26.

115 Williams, 'George Cadbury', op. cit., p. 96.

116 Ibid.

117 *Birmingham Daily Post* (19 October 1918).

118 *Yorkshire Evening Post*, 'Big Cocoa Combine' (23 May 1919).

119 Gardiner, *The Life of George Cadbury*, op. cit., p. 291.

120 Bradley, *Enlightened Entrepreneurs*, op. cit., p. 142.

121 Dellheim, 'The Creation of a Company Culture', op. cit., p. 40.

122 Bradley, *Enlightened Entrepreneurs*, op. cit., p. 143.

9. Cecil Rhodes

1   See Chris Ash, *The If Man: Dr Leander Starr Jameson, the Inspiration for Kipling's Masterpiece* (Helicon and Company, 2012).

2   Basil Williams, *Cecil Rhodes* (Constable and Company, 1921), p. 245.

3   Ibid., p. 266.

4   *The Graphic* (1 February 1896).

5   Antony Thomas, *Rhodes: The Race for Africa* (London, 1997), p. 33.

6   James Leasor, *Rhodes & Barnato: The Premier and the Prancer* (London, 1997), p. 23.

7   Ibid.

8   Thomas, *Rhodes*, op. cit., p. 37.

9   Robert I. Rotberg, *The Founder: Cecil Rhodes and the Pursuit of Power* (Oxford University Press, 1988), p. 26.

10 Thomas, *Rhodes*, op. cit., p. 37.

11 Leasor, *Rhodes & Barnato*, op. cit., p. 24.

12 Thomas, *Rhodes*, op. cit., p. 42.

13 Williams, *Cecil Rhodes*, op. cit., p. 10.

14 Leasor, *Rhodes & Barnato*, op. cit., p. 26.

15 Thomas, *Rhodes*, op. cit., p. 55.

16 Thomas, *Rhodes*, 57.

17 Cecil Rhodes to Mrs Rhodes, 18 October 1870, Folios 236-266. I am grateful to Lucy McCann at the University of Oxford for sourcing the correspondence for me.

18 Williams, *Cecil Rhodes*, op. cit., p. 13.

19 Thomas, *Rhodes*, op. cit., p. 69.

20 G. R. Searle, *A New England? Peace and War, 1886–1918* (Clarendon Press, 2005), p. 24.

21 P. J. Cain, 'Economics and Empire: the Metropolitan Context' in Andrew Porter (ed.), *The Oxford History of the British Empire: Vol. III: The Nineteenth Century* (Oxford University Press, 2001), p. 42.

22 Searle, *A New England?*, op. cit., p. 25.

23 Cain, 'Economics and Empire', op. cit., p. 35.

24 See Shula Marks, 'Southern Africa 1867–1886', in Roland Oliver (ed.), *The Cambridge History of Africa, Vol. 6, 1870–1905* (Cambridge University Press, 1985), p. 359.

25 Ibid., p. 367.

26 Williams, *Cecil Rhodes*, op. cit., p. 27.

27 Cecil Rhodes to Mrs Rhodes, Thursday 18 October 1870, quoted in ibid.

28 Rotberg, *The Founder*, op. cit., p. 63.

29 Williams, *Cecil Rhodes*, op. cit., p. 33.

30 Ibid.

31 Ibid., p. 29.

32   Leasor, *Rhodes & Barnato*, op. cit., p. 45.

33   Ibid., p. 49.

34   Ibid., p. 76.

35   Thomas, *Rhodes*, op. cit., p. 91.

36   Ibid.

37   Rotberg, *The Founder*, op. cit., p. 80.

38   Williams, *Cecil Rhodes*, op. cit., p. 38.

39   Leasor, *Rhodes & Barnato*, op. cit., p. 84.

40   J. Oldfield, 'Britain and the Slave Trade' in H. T. Dickenson, *A Companion to 18th Century Britain* (Oxford, 2002), p. 489.

41   See Niall Ferguson, *Empire* (Penguin, 2004), p. 235.

42   Ibid.

43   Quoted in Martin Meredith, *Diamonds, Gold and War: The Making of South Africa* (Simon & Schuster, 2007); see also Francis Statham, *Blacks, Boers and British* (Macmillan, 1881), p. 239; and Freda Harcourt, 'Disraeli's Imperialism', *The Historical Journal*, 1980, Vol. 23, issue 1.

44   Rotberg, *The Founder*, op. cit., p. 93.

45   Thomas, *Rhodes*, op. cit., p. 113.

46   *Essex Standard* (8 March 1878).

47   *Chelmsford Chronicle* (8 March 1878).

48   Rotberg, *The Founder*, op. cit., p. 108.

49   Leasor, *Rhodes & Barnato*, op. cit., p. 120.

50   Ibid., p. 135.

51   Ibid.

52   Thomas, *Rhodes*, op. cit., p. 117.

53   R. D. Fage and Roland Oliver, *Cambridge History of Africa, Vol. 6* (CUP, 1985), p. 369.

54   Rotberg, *The Founder*, op. cit., p. 109. By the end of 1885, the 3,600 claims on the four Kimberley mines had been amalgamated to just 10 on the De Beers site, 19 on Kimberley and 67 on the remaining two 'pipes'.

55   Thomas, *Rhodes*, op. cit., p. 124.

56   Williams, *Cecil Rhodes*, op. cit., p. 55.

57   Rotberg, *The Founder*, op. cit., p. 131.

58   D. M. Schreuder, *The Scramble for Southern Africa, 1877–1895* (CUP, 2009), pp. 142–3.

59   Ibid., pp. 145–59.

60   Williams, *Cecil Rhodes*, op. cit., p. 63.

61   Ibid., p. 97.

62   Ibid., p. 89.

63   Rotberg, *The Founder*, op. cit., p. 173.

64   Colin Newbury, *The Diamond Ring* (Clarendon Press, 1989), p. 669.

65   Leasor, *Rhodes & Barnato*, op. cit., p. 118.

66   Directors' Annual Report, De Beers Mining Company, 1883.

67   Directors' Annual Report, De Beers Mining Company, 1885.

68 Rotberg, *The Founder*, op. cit., p. 201.

69 Williams, *Cecil Rhodes*, op. cit., p. 43.

70 Directors' Annual Report, De Beers Mining Company, 1886.

71 Quoted in *The Times* (12 April 1888).

72 Niall Ferguson, *The House of Rothschild Vol. 2. The World's Banker: 1849–1998* (Penguin, 2002), p. 356.

73 Quoted in *The Times* (12 April 1888).

74 Peter Matthias, *The First Industrial Nation: The Economic History of Britain 1700–1914* (Routledge, 2001), p. 286.

75 See P. J. Cain and A. G. Hopkins, *British Imperialism: 1688–2000* (Routledge, 2006), p. 168 and p. 180.

76 Cain and Hopkins, *British Imperialism*, op. cit., pp. 169–70.

77 Ibid.

78 T. A. B. Corley, 'Britain's Overseas Investments in 1914 Revisited', *Business History*, Vol. 36, Jan 1994, p. 78.

79 Matthias, *The First Industrial Nation*, op. cit., p. 298.

80 Corley, 'Britain's Overseas Investments in 1914 Revisited', op. cit., p. 80.

81 Ferguson, *Empire*, op. cit., p. 243.

82 Williams, *Cecil Rhodes*, op. cit., p. 101.

83 Directors' Annual Report, De Beers Mining Company, 1888.

84 Ibid.

85 Thomas, *Rhodes*, op. cit., p. 180.

86 Fage and Oliver, *Cambridge History of Africa*, op. cit., pp. 432–4.

87 *Morning Post* (17 February 1887).

88 Fage and Oliver, *Cambridge History of Africa*, op. cit., p. 435.

89 Schreuder, *The Scramble for Southern Africa*, op. cit., p. 189.

90 Ibid., p. 172.

91 Ibid., p. 207.

92 Ibid., p. 221.

93 Ferguson, *House of Rothschild*, op. cit., p. 359.

94 Ibid., p. 246.

95 Cecil Rhodes to Charles Rudd, 4 March 1889, f. 12–112. Rhodes Archive, Bodleian Library.

96 Cecil Rhodes to Alfred Beit, 29 October 1889, f. 12–112. Rhodes Archive, Bodleian Library.

97 Williams, *Cecil Rhodes*, op. cit., p. 221.

98 Thomas, *Rhodes*, op. cit., p. 263.

99 Williams, *Cecil Rhodes*, op. cit., p. 199.

100 Thomas, *Rhodes*, op. cit., p. 270.

101 Ibid., p. 269.

102 Williams, *Cecil Rhodes*, op. cit., p. 145.

103 Ibid., p. 151.

104 Ibid., p. 173.

105 Ibid., p. 175.

106 Ferguson, *Empire*, op. cit., p. 226.

107 Williams, *Cecil Rhodes*, op. cit., p. 271.

108 Ibid., p. 285.

109 Ibid., p. 278.

110 Ferguson, *House of Rothschild*, op. cit., p. 358.

111 Thomas, *Rhodes*, op. cit., pp. 330–1.

112 Rotberg, *The Founder*, op. cit., p. 654.

113 Ferguson, *Empire*, op. cit., p. 270.

114 R. J. Moore, 'Imperial India: 1858–1914' in A. Porter (ed.) *Oxford History of the British Empire, Vol. III* (OUP, 1999), p. 443.

115 John Darwin, *The Empire Project: The Rise and Fall of the British World-System, 1830–1970* (Cambridge University Press, 2009), p. 622.

116 Ferguson, *Empire*, op. cit., pp. 247–8.

117 See Searle, *A New England?*, op. cit., p. 7.

118 Ferguson, *Empire*, op. cit., p. 256.

119 Ibid., p. 272.

120 Ibid., p. 273.

121 *Manchester Evening News* (27 March 1902).

122 Thomas, *Rhodes*, op. cit., p. 347.

123 *Gloucester Citizen* (9 April 1902).

124 Rotberg, *The Founder*, op. cit., p. 672.

125 Thomas, *Rhodes*, op. cit., p. 333.

126 Ferguson, *Empire*, op. cit., p. 242.

10. William Lever

1 Brian Lewis, *So Clean: Lord Leverhulme, Soap and Civilisation* (Manchester University Press, 2008), p. 78.

2 Charles Wilson, *History of Unilever, Vol. 1* (Cassell & Co., 1997), p. 168.

3 Lewis, *So Clean*, op. cit., p. 168.

4 Wilson, *History of Unilever*, op. cit., p. 176.

5 William Hulme Lever, 2nd Viscount Leverhulme, *Viscount Leverhulme* (Houghton Mifflin, 1927), p. 171.

6 Lever, *Viscount Leverhulme*, op. cit., p. 12.

7 See Wilson, *History of Unilever*, op. cit., p. 21.

8 Lewis, *So Clean*, op. cit., p. 23.

9 Adam Macqueen, *The King of Sunlight: How William Lever Cleaned Up the World* (Corgi, 2005), p. 13.

10 Ibid., p. 15.

11 Lever, *Leverhulme*, op. cit., p. 31.

12 Wilson, *History of Unilever*, p. 25.

13 Macqueen, *The King of Sunlight*, op. cit., p. 25.

14 Wilson, *History of Unilever*, op. cit., p. 4.
15 Stephen Broadberry, *Market Services and the Productivity Race, 1850–2000* (Cambridge University Press, 2006), p. 177.
16 Lewis, *So Clean*, op. cit., p. 64.
17 Ibid.
18 Wilson, *History of Unilever*, op. cit., p. 27.
19 Ibid.
20 Ibid. p. 28.
21 Lever, *Viscount Leverhulme*, op. cit., p. 39.
22 Wilson, *History of Unilever*, op. cit., p. 28.
23 Lewis, *So Clean*, op. cit. p. 62.
24 Wilson, *History of Unilever*, op. cit., p. 44.
25 Macqueen, *The King of Sunlight*, op. cit., p. 49.
26 *Liverpool Mercury* (Monday 5 March 1888).
27 Adam Macqueen, *The King of Sunlight*, op. cit., p. 58.
28 A comment Lever made to a conference in 1900, quoted in Lewis, *So Clean*, op. cit., p. 99.
29 Wilson, *History of Unilever*, op. cit., p. 34.
30 Vicky Long, *The Rise and Fall of the Healthy Factory* (Palgrave Macmillan, 2011).
31 Lever to a conference in 1907. Quoted in Lewis, *So Clean*, op. cit., p. 114.
32 MacQueen, *The King of Sunlight*, op. cit., pp. 71–2.
33 Ibid., p. 76.
34 *Liverpool Mercury* (5 March 1888). Lever calculated he could save 8s 7d a ton on trans-shipping tallow.
35 A. G. Gardiner, editor of *Daily News* in 1914, quoted in Lewis, *So Clean*, op. cit., p. 2.
36 Quoted in Wilson, *History of Unilever*, op. cit., p. 149.
37 Lewis, *So Clean*, op. cit., p. 64.
38 MacQueen, *The King of Sunlight*, op. cit., p. 81.
39 Ibid.
40 See A. Friedberg, *The Weary Titan: Britain and the Experience of Relative Decline* (Princeton, 1988).
41 MacQueen, *The King of Sunlight*, p. 84.
42 Ibid., p. 85.
43 Lever, *Leverhulme*, op. cit., p. 51.
44 Ibid., p. 66.
45 See Edelstein, 'Foreign Investment, Accumulation and Empire, 1860–1914' in Floyd and Johnson (eds), *Cambridge Economic History*, op. cit., p. 198.
46 *The Daily News* (23 June 1897).
47 Alfred Dupont Chandler, *Scale and Scope: The Dynamics of Industrial Capitalism* (Harvard, 1990), p. 92.
48 Quoted in Sidney Pollard, *Britain's Prime and Britain's Decline: The British Economy, 1870–1914* (Edward Arnold, 1989), p. 262.

49 Chandler, *Scale and Scope*, op. cit., p. 90.

50 See R. Millward, 'Industry and Infrastructure', in Jean-Pierre Dormois and Michael Dintenfass, *British Industrial Decline* (Routledge, 1999), p. 49.

51 For more on this debate see, for instance, Peter J. Cain and Anthony J. Hopkins, 'Gentlemanly capitalism and British expansion overseas II: new imperialism, 1850–1945', *Economic History Review*, Vol. 40, no. 1 (1987); W. D. Rubinstein, 'Gentlemanly capitalism and British imperialism, 1820–1914', *Past and Present*, August 1991; H. Bergoff and R. Moller, 'Tired pioneers and dynamic newcomers?', *Economic History Review*, Vol. 47, no. 2 (1994), and M. W. Kirby, 'Institutional rigidities and economic decline', *Economic History Review*, Vol. 45, no. 4 (1992).

52 Pollard, *Britain's Prime*, op. cit., p. 117.

53 Ibid., p. 120.

54 David Edgerton, *Science, Techology and the British Industrial 'Decline', 1870–1970* (CUP, 1996), p. 59.

55 Pollard, *Britain's Prime*, op. cit., p. 182.

56 Lewis, *So Clean*, op. cit., p. 63.

57 Unilever Archives, LBC/ 140, William Lever to Lever Bros America, 7 September 1907.

58 MacQueen, *The King of Sunlight*, op. cit., p. 89.

59 'People will not read anything that they haven't got to read if it strains their eyes,' noted Gross. Sydney Gross to William Lever, 31 December 1902. Unilever Archives, LBC/40–41 S.Gross, Lever Brothers Ltd (file 1 and 2).

60 Sydney Gross to William Lever, 15 December 1902. Unilever Archives, LBC/40–41 S.Gross, Lever Brothers Ltd (file 1 and 2).

61 William Lever to Sydney Gross 17 December 1902. Unilever Archives, LBC/40–41 S.Gross, Lever Brothers Ltd (file 1 and 2).

62 Ibid.

63 Sydney Gross to William Lever, 6 January 1903. Unilever Archives, LBC/40–41 S.Gross, Lever Brothers Ltd (file 1 and 2).

64 Sydney Gross to William Lever, 27 January 1903. Unilever Archives, LBC/40–41 S.Gross, Lever Brothers Ltd (file 1 and 2).

65 William Lever to Sydney Gross, 10 January 1903. Unilever Archives, LBC/40–41 S.Gross, Lever Brothers Ltd (file 1 and 2).

66 William Lever to Sydney Gross, 3 December 1900. Unilever Archives, LBC/40–41 S.Gross, Lever Brothers Ltd (file 1 and 2).

67 First introduced in 1894, Lifebuoy accounted for 10 per cent of sales by 1898.

68 Wilson, *History of Unilever*, op. cit., p. 99.

69 William Lever to A. J. Wolfendale, 27 February 1901. Unilever Archives, LBC/ 60, A. J. Wolfendale Esq, (file 1).

70 See Lewis, *So Clean*, op. cit., p. 11.

71 Wilson, *The History of Unilever*, op. cit., p. 66.

72 Macqueen, *The King of Sunlight*, op. cit., p. 134.

73   These were Hodgson & Simpson and Vinolia.

74   Macqueen, *The King of Sunlight*, op. cit., p. 142.

75   Joseph Meek to Lever, 4 October 1910. Quoted in Macqueen, *The King of Sunlight*, op. cit., p. 192.

76   Ibid., p. 194.

77   Ibid.

78   See Wilson, *The History of Unilever*, p. 165.

79   Wilson, *The History of Unilever*, op. cit., p. 187.

80   Macqueen, *The King of Sunlight*, op. cit., p. 129.

81   Lever, *Viscount Leverhulme*, op. cit., p. 186.

82   Quoted in Wilson, *The History of Unilever*, op. cit., p. 16.

83   Macqueen, *The King of Sunlight*, op. cit., p. 243.

84   Lever, *Viscount Leverhulme*, op. cit., p. 191.

85   Ibid., p. 194.

86   Wilson, *The History of Unilever*, op. cit., p. 245.

87   Lever, *Viscount Leverhulme*, op. cit., p. 223.

88   Macqueen, *The King of Sunlight*, op. cit., p. 279.

89   Lewis, *So Clean*, op. cit., p. 201.

90   Lever, *Viscount Leverhulme*, op. cit., p. 269.

91   Lewis, *So Clean*, op. cit., p. 43.

92   Lever, *Viscount Leverhulme*, op. cit., p. 222.

11. John Spedan Lewis

1   Letter to Mrs Lewis, *The Gazette of the John Lewis Partnership*, 19 October 1940, p. 696.

2   *Yorkshire Evening Post* (18 September 1940).

3   Peter Cox, *Spedan's Partnership: The Story of John Lewis and Waitrose* (Labatie Books, 2010), pp. 126–7.

4   John Spedan Lewis in a letter to Partners, 19 September 1940. Quoted in Cox, *Spedan's Partnership*, op. cit., p. 123.

5   'John Lewis Dies', *Yorkshire Evening Post* (9 June 1928).

6   John Spedan Lewis, 'Historical', *The Gazette of the John Lewis Partnership*, 8 January 1944, p. 546.

7   Ibid.

8   See Briggs, *Victorian Things* (Sutton, 2003), p. 19.

9   Ibid., p. 214.

10   Ibid., p. 215.

11   Jack Walton, 'Towns and Consumerism, in Martin Daunton (ed.), *The Cambridge Urban History of Britain, Vol. 3* (Cambridge University Press, 2000), p. 725.

12   Richard Trainor, 'The Middle Class' in Daunton (ed.), *Cambridge Urban History*, op. cit., p. 693.

13   Jonathan Glancey, *A Very British Revolution: 150 Years of John Lewis* (Laurence King, 2014), p. 30.

14   Richard Trainor in Daunton (ed.), *Cambridge Urban History*, op. cit., p. 680.

15   John Benson, *The Rise of Consumer Society in Britain, 1880–1980* (Longman, 1994), ch. 2.

16   Glancey, *A Very British Revolution*, op. cit., p. 19. Whiteley was later shot dead in his department store office by an illegitimate son.

17   Cox, *Spedan's Partnership*, op. cit., p. 11.

18   Ibid., p. 20.

19   John Spedan Lewis, 'Historical', *The Gazette of the John Lewis Partnership* (8 January 1944), p. 547.

20   Cox, *Spedan's Partnership*, op. cit., p. 16.

21   John Spedan Lewis, 'Historical', *The Gazette of the John Lewis Partnership* (8 January 1944), p. 547.

22   Cox, *Spedan's Partnership*, op. cit., p. 18.

23   Ibid.

24   Glancey, *A Very British Revolution*, op. cit., ch. 2.

25   Cox, *Spedan's Partnership*, op. cit., p. 32.

26   Ibid., p. 34.

27   John Spedan Lewis, 'Historical', *The Gazette of the John Lewis Partnership* (15 January 1944), p. 558.

28   Cox, *Spedan's Partnership*, op. cit., p. 31.

29   Glancey, *A Very British Revolution*, op. cit., p. 49.

30   John Spedan Lewis, 'Historical', *The Gazette of the John Lewis Partnership* (15 January 1944), p. 557.

31   Cox, *Spedan's Partnership*, op. cit., p. 42.

32   Interview with John Spedan Lewis, BBC West of England, 1957, quoted in Hugh Macpherson, *John Spedan Lewis 1885–1963* (John Lewis Partnership, 1985), p. 9.

33   MacPherson, *John Spedan Lewis*, op. cit., p. 10.

34   *The Gazette* (16 March 1918).

35   Cox, *Spedan's Partnership*, op. cit., p. 53.

36   Ibid., p. 49.

37   A story relayed by Spedan in his book *Partnership for All* (Kerr-Cross, 1948) p. 45.

38   Cox, *Spedan's Partnership*, op. cit., p. 59.

39   See Matthias Morys, 'Cycles and Depressions', in Roderick Floud, Jane Humphries and Paul Johnson (eds), *The Cambridge Economic History of Modern Britain, Vol. 2* (Cambridge University Press, 2014).

40   See Matthias Morys, 'Cycles and Depressions' in Floud, Humphries and Johnson (eds), *Cambridge Economic History*, op. cit.

41   Cox, *Spedan's Partnership*, op. cit., p. 65.

42   Ibid., p. 70.

43   Ibid., p. 11.

44   Ibid., p. 14.

45   Ibid.

46   Chairman to Deputy Chairman, Memorandum No. 5995, 2 October 1924.

47   Quoted in MacPherson, *John Spedan Lewis*, op. cit., p. 66.

48   Ibid., p. 59.

49   'John Lewis Dies', *Yorkshire Evening Post* (9 June 1928).

50   Chairman to Financial Advisor, Memorandum No. 11131, 5 October 1928.

51   Cox, *Spedan's Partnership*, op. cit., p. 77.

52   Legal Establishments of the Partnership, *The Gazette of the John Lewis Partnership* (20 April 1929).

53   See John Spedan Lewis, *Partnership for All*, op. cit., p. 46 for a full description.

54   See Roy Church, *Herbert Austin: The British Motor Car Industry to 1941* (Europa Publications, 1979).

55   I am indebted to the John Lewis archive team for supplying me with Profit & Loss statements and Balance Sheets for the period.

56   Cox, *Spedan's Partnership*, op. cit., p. 83.

57   Sue Bowden, 'The New Consumerism', in Paul Johnson (ed.), *Twentieth-Century Britain: Economic, Social and Cultural Change* (Longman, 1994), p. 243.

58   This was underlined by studies between 1880 and 1901 by Booth (in London) and Rowntree (in York).

59   Laurie Lee, *Cider with Rosie* (Vintage, 2002), p. 216.

60   J. B. Priestley, *English Journey* (Penguin, 1977), p. 375.

61   Quoted in Sidney Pollard, Britain's Prime and Britain's Decline: The British Economy, 1870–1914 (Edward Arnold, 1989), pp. 217–30.

62   Corelli Barnett, 'The Audit of the Great War on British Technology' in Michael Dintenfass and Jean-Pierre Dormois (eds), *The British Industrial Decline* (Routledge Explorations in Economic History, 1998), p. 106.

63   Cox, *Spedan's Partnership*, op. cit., p. 107.

64   Ibid., p. 84.

65   Ibid., p. 85.

66   *Financial Times* (12 June 1934).

67   'Here Labour Hires Capital', *Business* (6 July 1934).

68   Chairman to Director of Estimates, Memo No. 20206 (10 January 1935).

69   Interview with Bernard Miller, quoted in Macpherson, *John Spedan Lewis*, op. cit., p. 30.

70   Ibid., p. 69.

71   William Waite quoted in Cox, *Spedan's Partnership*, op. cit., p. 97.

72   Ibid., p. 103.

73   Macpherson, *John Spedan Lewis*, op. cit., p. 38.

74   Ibid.

75   Cox, *Spedan's Partnership*, op. cit., p. 118.

76   *The Gazette of the John Lewis Partnership* (3 February 1940), p. 4.

77   *The Gazette of the John Lewis Partnership* (11 September 1943), p. 349.

78   Ibid., p. 350.

79   Ibid., p. v.

80   John Spedan Lewis, *Partnership on the Scale of Modern Industry*, 1946. John Lewis Archives.

81   Ibid.

82   Cox, *Spedan's Partnership*, op. cit., p. 143.

83   Ibid., p. 145.

84   Figures from Bank of England and Alec Cairncross, *Years of Recovery: British Economic Policy 1945–51* (Methuen, 1985), p. 65.

85   Macpherson, *John Spedan Lewis*, op. cit., p. 28.

86   Cox, *Spedan's Partnership*, op. cit., p. 149.

87   Ibid., p. 144.

88   Ibid., p. 151.

89   Macpherson, *John Spedan Lewis*, op. cit., p. 42.

90   Interview with Paul May, quoted in Macpherson, *John Spedan Lewis*, op. cit., p. 63.

91   Cox, *Spedan's Partnership*, op. cit., p. 160.

92   Ibid., p. 152.

93   MacPherson, *John Spedan Lewis*, op. cit., p. 11.

94   Zoe Wood, 'John Lewis overtakes Marks & Spencer as darling of the high street', *Guardian* (6 March 2014).

ACKNOWLEDGEMENTS

This book has been a long time coming.

I owe my first inspiration to some remarkable teachers at the Harvard Business School, principally Professor Richard Tedlow, who first opened my eyes to the study of economic history through historical biography. The genre in America is wide and in Britain narrow. And so back in 2000 I began to ponder how best to tell a story of British capitalism through the lives of its great architects.

My agent Georgina Capel and my friend Tristram Hunt were early encouragers of the project, and without the enthusiastic help of Richard Milbank and the team at Head of Zeus, especially my extraordinary editor, Mark Hawkins Dady, the book would still be merely a long-cherished pipe-dream.

Professor Sir Roderick Floud, co-editor of *The Cambridge Economic History of Modern Britain*, offered me not only moral support but inspired my final chapter on John Spedan Lewis and heroically read my manuscript in full. The book is immeasurably better for his expert eyes and advice. A huge number of people helped with individual chapters, and their friendly assistance, always going the extra mile to unearth interesting angles and archives, has been the greatest pleasure in writing this. We are truly blessed in Britain with some incredible library and business archives tended and nurtured by amazing guardians. *The* most inspiring experience writing this book has been working with the archivists and historians managing our great companies' records. On every occasion, I found them to truly represent the best of the values, and yes, the soul of their firm's or institution's founders. The leaders and boards of these organizations should take note!

Dr Valerie Shrimplin, Academic Registrar at Gresham College, provided me with detailed feedback on my introductory chapter. Sir Henry Keswick, Lord Sassoon and Philip Hawkins were of great assistance in identifying sources for my chapter on William Jardine, and I owe particular thanks to John Wells, Under Librarian at Cambridge University's Department of Manuscripts and University Archives, who helped me identify the precise records and correspondence I needed for my research into Jardine, and who undertook a detailed read-through of that chapter. My thanks go to the trustees of the Jardine Matheson archives. Fiona Tait and the team at the Library of Birmingham provided invaluable assistance in helping me sieve through the gigantic Boulton & Watt archives in the city. I owe a huge debt to Simon Linnett, Executive Vice-Chairman of N. M. Rothschild & Sons, not only for his enthusiastic interest in the project but for his invaluable role in connecting me to assistance, especially Melanie Aspey, Director of the Rothschild Archive, who provided me with enormous help, and to the National Railway Museum. I record my thanks to the Rothschild Archive's Trustees.

Tim Proctor at the National Railway Museum in York was immensely kind in assisting me through the records and archives relating to George Hudson, including the extraordinary Victorian petitions, which throw real light on the way Hudson used everything he learned as a political organizer to marshal support for his railway projects. I very much share the hope that this will provide a rich seam of further research.

Back in Birmingham, I was blessed to be able to draw on the wonderful assistance of Sarah Foden, Information Manager and Archivist for the incredible Cadbury Archives based at Bournville, now part of Mondelez Europe. In Oxford, Lucy McCann, Senior Archivist at the Bodleian Library, steered me with expert skill and precision through the Rhodes archives and provided invaluable pointers to literature, annual reports and letters that helped me shape my analysis of Rhodes as primarily a business innovator. In Port Sunlight, Claire Tunstall, the Head of Art, Archives and Records Management at Unilever, was invaluable in pinpointing the sources I needed for my chapter on Lever, and very kindly read through my drafts.

I want to record special thanks to Sir Charlie Mayfield and Andy Street, respectively Chairman and Managing Director of the John Lewis Partnership, for their enthusiastic interest, advice on sources for the chapter on John Spedan Lewis, and for reading through drafts. Huge thanks go to the wonderful team at the John Lewis Partnership Heritage Centre, including Judy Faraday, Manager of Heritage Services, and Owen Munday, Archivist Assistant, for the generosity of their assistance, for ploughing through Spedan's 40,000 memos, the Partnership's records and copies of the staff *Gazette*, and for their help and support assembling financial information on the John Lewis Partnership in the 1930s.

I had always hoped to be able to draw out the lessons of history to help us understand the critical importance of entrepreneurs today. I owe huge debts to Baroness Martha Lane Fox, Sir Richard Branson, Sir Robin Saxby, Sir Ronald Cohen, Sir Martin Sorrell and Duncan Bannatyne for being so generous with their time and reflections on what we can learn from 800 years of business history!

Over the years, great research assistants have helped with particular studies, and I want to pay tribute to the work of Katie Longo and my team, especially James Pignon, Chris Adamson and Sarish Jabeen, who provided invaluable administrative support.

My final and biggest debts are to Sarah and to Alex, John and Lizzie for their patient persistence and tolerance with the absences and immersion in writing this, and indeed the endless visits to bits of Britain's industrial heritage.

Ultimately, this book is for them.

Liam Byrne
Kings Heath, Birmingham

LIST OF ILLUSTRATIONS

Robert Rich, 2nd earl of Warwick by Anthony van Dyck, *c.* 1632–35 (Wikimedia Commons)

Thomas Pitt by Sir Godfrey Kneller (Wikimedia Commons)

Matthew Boulton by Carl Frederik von Breda, 1809 (Universal History Archive / UIG / Getty Images)

Nathan Rothschild from 'Dighton's City Characters', 1817 (London Metropolitan Archives, City of London / Bridgeman Images)

William Jardine in 1832 (Pictures from History / Bridgeman Images)

George Hudson after Francis Grant, 1848 (Rischgitz / Getty Images)

George Cadbury, 1917 (Wikimedia Commons)

Cecil Rhodes, *c.* 1900 (Wikimedia Commons)

William Lever, 1925 (© Illustrated London News Ltd / Mary Evans)

John Spedan Lewis, 1960 (© WENN Ltd / Alamy Stock Photo)

INDEX